JOHN LENNON

THE LIFE

JOHN LENNON

THE LIFE

PHILIP NORMAN

ecco

An Imprint of HarperCollinsPublishers

HarperCollins books may be purchased for educational, business, or sales promotional use. For information, please write: Special Markets Department, HarperCollins Publishers, 10 East 53rd Street, New York, NY 10022.

Grateful acknowledgment is made for permission to reproduce the illustrations: Page 1, top: © Redferns (M. Haywood Archives); bottom: © Pauline Lennon. Page 2, top: © Leila Harvey; bottom: © Getty Images (Popperfoto). Page 3: © Charles Roberts. Page 4, top: © Helen Anderson; bottom: © Ann Mason. Page 5, top: © John O'Connor; bottom: © Bill Harry. Page 6, top: © Redferns (Jurgen Vollmer); bottom: © Camera Press (Wolf-Hinrich Groeneveld). Page 7: © Redferns (Astrid Kirchherr/K&K Ulf Kruger OHG). Page 8: © Michael Ward. Page 9: © Rex Features. Page 10, top: © Bettmann/Corbis; bottom: © Getty Images (Michael Ochs Archives). Page 11: © Tony Bramwell/LFI. Page 12, top: © Getty Images (Popperfoto); bottom: © Bettmann/Corbis. Page 13, top: © Camera Press (Ron Reid); bottom: © Getty Images (Popperfoto). Page 14, top: © Getty Images (Popperfoto); bottom: © Redferns (Steve Morley). Page 15: © Bob Gruen. Page 16: © Bettmann/Corbis.

FIRST EDITION

Designed by Jessica Shatan Heslin/Studio Shatan, Inc.

Library of Congress Cataloging-in-Publication Data is available upon request.

ISBN: 978-0-06-075401-3

08   09   10   11   12   OV/RRD   10   9   8   7   6   5   4   3   2   1

To Jessica

CONTENTS

PART IV

ZEN VAUDEVILLE

PART V

PIZZA AND FAIRY TALES

PART I

THE

COUNTRY

BOY

1

WAR BABY

I was never really wanted.

John Lennon was born with a gift for music and comedy that would carry him further from his roots than he ever dreamed possible. As a young man, he was lured away from the British Isles by the seemingly boundless glamour and opportunity to be found across the Atlantic. He achieved that rare feat for a British performer of taking American music to the Americans and playing it as convincingly as any homegrown practitioner, or even more so. For several years, his group toured the country, delighting audiences in city after city with their garish suits, funny hair, and contagiously happy grins.

This, of course, was not Beatle John Lennon but his namesake paternal grandfather, more commonly known as Jack, born in 1855. Lennon is an Irish surname—from O'Leannain or O'Lonain—and Jack habitually gave his birthplace as Dublin, though there is evidence that his family had already crossed the Irish Sea to become part of Liverpool's extensive Hibernian community some time pre-

3

viously. He began his working life as a clerk, but in the 1880s followed a common impulse among his compatriots and emigrated to New York. Whereas the city turned other immigrant Irishmen into laborers or police officers, Jack wound up as a member of Andrew Roberton's Colored Operatic Kentucky Minstrels.

However brief or casual his involvement, this made him part of the first transatlantic popular music industry. American minstrel troupes, in which white men blackened their faces, put on outsize collars and stripey pantaloons, and sang sentimental choruses about the Swanee River, "coons," and "darkies," were hugely popular in the late nineteenth century, both as performers and creators of hit songs. When Roberton's Colored Operatic Kentucky Minstrels toured Ireland in 1897, the *Limerick Chronicle* called them "the world's acknowledged masters of refined minstrelsy," while the *Dublin Chronicle* thought them the best it had ever seen. A contemporary handbook records that the troupe was about thirty-strong, that it featured some genuinely black artistes among the cosmetic ones, and that it made a specialty of parading through the streets of every town where it was to appear.

For this John Lennon, unlike the grandson he would never see, music did not bring worldwide fame but was merely an exotic interlude, most details of which were never known to his descendants. Around the turn of the century, he came off the road for good, returned to Liverpool, and resumed his old life as a clerk, this time with the Booth shipping line. With him came his daughter, Mary, only child of a first marriage that had not survived his temporary immersion in burnt-cork makeup, banjo music, and applause.

When Mary left him to work in domestic service, a solitary old age seemed in prospect for Jack. His remedy was to marry his housekeeper, a young Liverpool Irishwoman with the happily coincidental name of Mary Maguire. Although twenty years his junior, and illiterate, Mary—better known as Polly—proved an ideal Victorian wife, practical, hardworking, and selfless. Their home was a tiny terrace house in Copperfield Street, Toxteth, a part of the city nicknamed "Dickens Land," so numerous were the streets named after Dickens characters. Rather like Mr. Micawber in *David Copperfield*, Jack sometimes talked about returning to his former life as a minstrel and earning fortunes enough for his young wife, as he put it, to be "farting against silk." But from here on, his music making would be confined to local pubs and his own family circle.

Jack's marriage to Polly gave him a second family of eight children. Two died in infancy, a fact that the superstitious Polly attributed to their Catholic baptism. The next six therefore received Protestant christenings, and all survived: five boys, George, Herbert, Sydney, Alfred, and Charles, and a girl, Edith. Polly did a heroic job of feeding them all on Jack's modest wage. But their diet of mainly bread, margarine, strong tea, and lobscouse—a meat-and-biscuit stew from which Liverpudlians acquired the nickname Scouses—was chronically lacking in essential nutrients. This had its worst effect on the fourth boy, Alfred, born in 1912, who as a toddler developed rickets that stunted the growth of his legs. The only remedy known to pediatrics in those days was to encase both of them in iron braces, hoping the ponderous extra weight would promote growth and strength. Despite years burdened by the braces, Alf's legs remained puny and foreshortened, and he failed to grow any taller than five feet four inches. He was, even so, a good-looking lad, with luxuriant dark hair, merry eyes, and the distinctive Lennon family nose, a thin, plunging beak with sharply defined clefts over the nostrils.

Jack's musical talents were passed on to his children in varying measure. George, Herbert, Sydney, Charles, and Edith all had passable singing voices, and the boys played mouth organ, the only instrument young people in their circumstances could afford. Alf, however, showed ability of an altogether higher order, allied to what his brother Charlie (born in 1918) called "that show-off spirit." He could sing all the music-hall and light operatic songs that made up the World War I hit parade; he could recite ballads, tell jokes, and do impressions. His specialty was Charlie Chaplin, the anarchic little tramp whose film comedies had created the unprecedented phenomenon of an entertainer famous all over the world. At family gatherings, Alf would sit on his father's knee in his Tiny Tim leg irons, and the two would sing "Ave Maria" together, with sentimental tears streaming down their faces.

Jack died from liver disease, probably caused by alcoholism, in 1921. Unable to survive on the state widow's allowance of five shillings per child per week, Polly had no choice but to take in washing. It meant backbreaking, hand-scalding work from four a.m. to dusk, scrubbing other people's soiled linen on a washboard, then squeezing out the sodden coils through a heavy iron mangle. Even so, as her granddaughter Joyce Lennon remembers, the cramped little house remained always spotless with "floors you could eat your dinner from," the kitchen range cleaned with graphite religiously every Monday morning, the front step scoured almost white, then edged in red with a chip of sandstone. Polly ruled her five sons like Mrs. Joe in *Great Expectations*, not hesitating to chastise them with a leather strap even when they were nearly grown men. Like many Liverpudlians of the most down-to-earth kind, she had her mystical side, believing herself a psychic, able to read the future in spread-out playing cards or the pattern of tea leaves in an empty cup.

As hard as Polly worked, the task of supporting her six-strong brood proved beyond her. Fortunately, a means was found to take Alf and Edith off her hands without breaking up the family or damaging her fierce self-respect. Both were offered live-in places at Liverpool's Bluecoat Hospital (i.e., charity school) in Church Road, Wavertree, a stone's throw from a then-obscure thoroughfare called Penny Lane. Founded in 1714, the Bluecoat still attired its male pupils in an eighteenth-century costume of gold-buttoned blue tailcoat, breeches, stockings, and cravat. The educational standard was high, the regime not unkindly, and any child granted admittance was considered fortunate. Alf and Edith, even so, found it traumatic to leave their cozy, soapy home in Copperfield Street and the mother they worshipped. Of the two, cheery Alf adjusted better to institution life: he did well at lessons, became mascot of the soccer team, and entertained his dormitory mates with the same song and dance and Charlie Chaplin skits he used to do for his family and neighbors.

From earliest childhood, his one wish had been to follow his father into show business. It very nearly came true one night when he was fourteen, and his brother Sydney took him to the Empire Theatre in Lime Street to see a troupe of singing, dancing juveniles called Will

Murray's Gang. After the show, Alf talked his way backstage and performed an impromptu audition for Will Murray, the Gang's adult ringmaster, who there and then offered him a job. When his brothers Herbert and George, now in loco parentis, refused to entertain the idea, Alf ran away from the Bluecoat Hospital and joined up with the Gang en route to Glasgow for their next appearance. But a Bluecoat teacher came after him, led him back in disgrace, and subjected him to ritual humiliation in front of his assembled schoolmates.

A year later, the Bluecoat sent him out into the world, equipped with a good education, plus two suits with long trousers to confirm his entry into manhood. He spent a few unhappy weeks as an office boy before realizing that a far preferable career—one, indeed, almost comparable with going on the stage—lay right under his nose. For this was the golden age of transatlantic liner travel, when Liverpool vied with Southampton as Britain's busiest passenger port. Huge, multifunneled ships daily nosed up the River Mersey to be met by emblazoned boat-trains from London, packed with rich people, their furs, and cabin trunks. In Ranelagh Place, the splendiferous Adelphi Hotel had just been built to provide a painless transition from shore to ship, with its *Titanic*-size palm court, its bedrooms like staterooms, its below-waterline swimming pools, hairdressers, and masseurs.

So Alf went off to sea as a bellboy on the SS *Montrose*. It was, as he soon discovered, a life he seemed born to lead. His friendly, cheery nature made him popular with passengers and his superior officers and kept him on the right side of the homosexual mafia who ran the ships' catering departments. "Lennie"—his onboard nickname—rapidly won promotion to restaurant waiter on the cruise vessels plying between Liverpool and the Mediterranean. In off-duty hours, he would entertain his fellow workers with songs and impressions in their cramped, fetid communal cabins or in the crew bar, known on every ship as the Pig and Whistle. His specialty (one his father Jack would have especially appreciated) was blackening his face with shoe polish and "doing" Al Jolson, the minstrel offcut whose schmaltzy anthems to "Mammy" and "Dixie" sold records by the million in the twenties and early thirties.

He could think himself always in a kind of spotlight, whether serving rich food to "nobs" in his gleaming white mess jacket and gloves, or crooning Jolson's "Sonny Boy," down on one knee, with clasped hands, to the beery delight of his shipmates, or returning home to Copperfield Street laden with the contraband ship's delicacies that are every steward's God-given perk. Between voyages, too, in some dockside saloon-bar or other, he could always find an audience eager to be regaled with stories about the exotic places and peoples he had seen and the racy shipboard life of a single young waiter.

Despite all his lurid sailor's yarns, there had only ever seemed to be one woman for Alf Lennon. Sometime in 1928, not long after leaving the Bluecoat Hospital, he was strolling through Sefton Park resplendent in one of his two new suits, topped off by an outsize bowler hat, and smoking a cheap Wild Woodbine cigarette fixed dandyishly into a holder. Seated alone on a bench beside the ornamental lake was a girl with fluffy auburn hair and the facial bone structure of a young Marlene Dietrich. When Alf moved in to chat her up, he was met with gales of derisive laughter. Realizing that his top-heavy bowler was the cause, he whipped it off his head and sent it skimming into the lake. So began his long, troubled relationship with Julia Stanley.

In Julia—variously known as Juliet, Judy, or Ju—destiny had paired Alf with a character whose craving for glamour and urge to entertain were almost the equal of his. Julia, too, had a better than average singing voice and, unlike Alf, was a practiced instrumentalist. Her grandfather, yet another stagestruck Liverpool clerk, had taught her to play the banjo; she also could give a passable account of herself on piano accordion and ukulele.

Julia's musical talent, personality, and enchanting prettiness made her an obvious candidate for the professional stage. But the hard slog entailed by a career on the boards was not for her. When she left school, age fifteen, it was merely for an dull office job in a printing firm. She quickly gave this up to become an usherette at Liverpool's plushest cinema, the Trocadero in Camden Street. Like Alf's role at sea, it was a life of glamour by proxy, working amid deep pile carpets and soft lights, clad in a trim Ruritanian uniform with cross-buttoning tunic and pillbox hat.

Her looks won her many admirers, and even the manager of the Trocadero, a magnificent personage who wore evening dress all day, also made periodic attempts to woo his prettiest usherette by leaving gifts of stockings or chocolates in her locker. For such a siren, Alf Lennon with his Chico Marx hat and little legs seemed not much of a catch. But their happy-go-lucky natures and zany sense of humor were exactly in tune. They also shared a passion for dancing—which in those days meant the "strict tempo" ballroom variety. Waltzing or quickstepping in each other's arms, they would imagine themselves the most famous dancing couple of the cinema screen, with redheaded Julia becoming Ginger Rogers while Alf metamorphosed into Fred, as in Astaire.

To outward appearances, Alf and Julia might seem to have been from roughly similar backgrounds. Both belonged to large families—she having as many sisters as he had brothers—and both were offspring of men in shipping. Like every other stratum of British life, however, the seafaring world in those days was governed by rigid class distinction. And it happened that Julia's father, George Stanley, known to his family as Pop, stood several notches above Alf in the rigidly defined mercantile hierarchy. He had trained as a sailmaker in the not-so-distant days when many ships putting into Liverpool still relied on canvas as a supplement to steam. After many years at sea with the White Star Line, he had joined the London, Liverpool and Glasgow Tug Salvage Company, helping to retrieve the wrecks that storms or human error frequently caused in the treacherous deeps between the Mersey estuary and the distant North Wales shore.

Pop Stanley therefore mingled on equal terms with ships' captains and pilots, the bluebloods of the sea. His other four daughters. though lively and strong-willed, all comported themselves in a manner befitting this social eminence, keeping company with young men destined to be navigators or marine engineers. Only Julia had ever dragged down the family by going out with "a mere steward" like Alf Lennon. In his displeasure, Pop found strongest support in his oldest daughter, Mary, known as Mimi. "Why she picked [Alf] I'll never know," Mimi would still lament at the very end of her life. "I couldn't believe she ended up with a seaman. He was a good-for-nothing . . . the type to have one in every port. Fly-by-night is what I called him."

Alf himself, unfortunately, possessed the same sharp wit and withering bluntness that would be among his future son's strongest characteristics. Mingling as he did with actual blue bloods every day of his nautical life, he found the Stanleys' attitude ludicrous, and made no bones about saying so. Whenever Julia tried to introduce him into her tight-knit family circle, there would invariably be some upset—if not with Pop then with Mimi—that ended with his leaving the house or being ordered out of it. Had the pair been left alone, Julia probably would have tired of Alf and found someone her family considered worthier of her. But, true to her nature, the more he was snubbed and criticized, the greater became her determination to hang on to him.

So their courtship meandered on through the thirties, kept fresh when it might otherwise have staled by Alf's periodic long absences at sea. He grew reasonably friendly with Julia's sisters Elizabeth, Anne, and Harriet, and liked her mother Annie (née Millward), a woman so sweet-natured and kind that she would sometimes buy shoes for children she saw running barefoot in the street. But Pop (whom even Mimi described as "a bully") always remained bris- tlingly hostile. Like most young courting couples of that time, with nowhere to meet but pubs, family front parlors, and park benches, Alf and Julia reached their early twenties without having experienced any physical intimacy beyond kissing and petting. In spite of Mimi's dark suspicions about "one in every port," Alf always swore he re- mained faithful to Julia on his travels, and wrote to her at every op- portunity. The Stanleys accused Alf of being work shy—"swallowing the anchor" in nautical slang. However, he seems to have remained employed more successfully than a great many others in Liverpool during that era of grinding economic depression. His official Board of Trade seaman's employment record gives the standard of his work and personal conduct for voyage after voyage as a consistent VG. At one point, Julia's family made a highly disingenuous move to "help" him by finding him a place aboard a whaling ship, which would have had the blessed result of taking him away for about two years. When

Alf refused to consider the idea, Pop Stanley ordered him out of the house once again.

Alf and Julia finally married in December 1938, when he was twenty-six and she twenty-four. A few weeks earlier, Britain's prime minister, Neville Chamberlain, had returned from Munich waving the piece of paper that "guaranteed" peace with Hitler's Germany in return for abandoning Czechoslovakia to invasion and genocide. The mood of national euphoria, while it lasted, produced a sharp surge in the marriage rate as many young people felt their future to be more secure. But Alf and Julia took their belated plunge with no more thoughts of the future than they ever had. According to Alf, she dared him to do it one night at the pub, and he was never one to refuse a dare.

Neither of their families was told in advance what they had decided. On December 3, Julia left home as if it were just another working day and at noon rendezvoused with Alf at the register office in Bolton Street, behind the Adelphi Hotel. The only witnesses to the ceremony were Alf's brother Sydney, whom he'd let into the secret at the last moment, and one of Julia's usherette colleagues. Afterward, Sydney stood the new Mr. and Mrs. Lennon drinks and a meal of roast chicken at a pub over the road called the Big House; they spent the evening at the cinema, watching a Mickey Rooney film (which happened to be about an orphanage), then separated to spend their wedding night at their respective homes. Mimi was never to forget the heart-sinking moment when Julia walked in, threw her wedding certificate onto the table, and said, "There, I've done it! I've married him."

Pop Stanley's initial reaction was also one of explosive horror and disgust. But, under the gentler influence of his wife, Annie, he accepted that there was nothing that could be done—indeed, that as a conscientious father he must try his best to give the newlyweds a proper start in life. Swallowing his feelings, Pop volunteered to leave the family flat in Berkeley Street and rent more spacious accommodation so that Julia and Alf could move in with Annie and him. The chosen property was number 9 Newcastle Road, a bay-windowed terrace house a few minutes' walk from Penny Lane and Alf's alma mater, the Bluecoat Hospital.

The four coexisted in relative harmony throughout 1939, as war with Germany drew nearer and Britain succumbed to a fever of gas-mask issuing, child evacuation, and air-raid precautions. For Pop Stanley in particular, it was an eventful time. In June, a brand-new Royal Navy submarine, the *Thetis*, sank during her trials in Liverpool Bay. Pop joined the massive operation to recover the vessel, whose stern was initially visible rising vertically from the water. The crew considered themselves in no great peril, tapping out cheerful Morse messages to their rescuers on the steel hull as cables were passed underneath to drag it to the surface. But at the crucial moment, the cables snapped and the submarine disappeared for good, taking seventy-one men with her.

Alf had gone to sea again, on the SS *Duchess of York*, but returned home in time for the first Christmas of World War II. His only child with Julia was conceived at 9 Newcastle Road one day in January 1940. Finding themselves, unusually, alone in the house for a couple of hours, they made love on the kitchen floor. They had not been trying for a baby, and Julia's immediate pregnancy was equally dismaying to them both. "Ninety percent of people [of my generation] were born out of a bottle of whisky on a Saturday night, and there was no intention to have children," the baby would one day observe bitterly. "I was never really wanted."

Julia's pregnancy coincided with the bleakest months in Europe's history, as Hitler's mechanized armies swept across Belgium and France, the battered remains of the British Expeditionary Force were evacuated from Dunkirk, and RAF fighters whirled like fiery gnats around the Luftwaffe's incoming swarms of heavy bombers. Alone and braced for invasion, the country often seemed to have nothing to sustain it but the voice of its new prime minister, Winston Churchill, whose bulldog-like mien and gift for blood-igniting oratory made the most desperate moments seem somehow glorious.

In August, Alf sailed away again on the SS *Empress of Canada*. With London under nightly bombing and Britain seemingly defenseless, the RAF made a surprise hit-and-run raid on Berlin—an event that the Luftwaffe's commander, Hermann Goering, had boasted could never happen. A furious Hitler promised to retaliate by razing all

Britain's other major cities. As a key port for the nation's vital Atlantic food convoys, Liverpool prepared for the worst.

Julia's sister, Mimi, would often relate how the baby's arrival on October 9 was marked by an especially ferocious German night attack. According to Mimi, when news came that Julia had been delivered of a seven-and-a-half-pound boy, the air-raid sirens were wailing, and all public transport, as usual, had ground to a standstill. Such was her excitement that she ran the two miles from her parents' home to the Oxford Street maternity hospital, oblivious of bombers and their parachute-borne land mines. The worst that Hitler could do seemed trivial by comparison with this marvelous event.

The week in question was certainly a bad one for Liverpool. The records of its Watch Committee show that on the night of October 7–8, high-explosive bombs fell on Stanley Road and Great Mersey Street in the city center and Lichfield Road and Grantley Road, Wavertree, causing damage to houses and demolishing the Welsh Chapel. The next night came two separate raids, hitting Everton Valley, Knotty Ash, Mossley Hill, and Mill Street in the first, and the Anfield area in the second. On the night of October 11–12, two more raids dropped tons of high explosive on the City and North Docks first, then on Alexandra and Langton Dock, causing serious damage to the Harbourmaster's House, sheds, railway tracks, Admiralty stores, and four ships.

But on the night of October 9–10, the Luftwaffe unaccountably stayed away. As Mimi hurried toward Oxford Street, she would undoubtedly have seen the results of previous bombing, in rubble, shattered glass, and white-helmeted A.R.P. wardens. On later visits to Julia, the situation could have been as she remembered that first night, with a land mine falling next to the hospital and the new baby being wrapped in a rough blanket and put under his mother's bed for safety. Uppermost in Mimi's thoughts on October 9 was concern for her sister, mingled with delight that a boy had entered the overwhelmingly female Stanley family. Possibly it was the strength of her own emotion when she first held her nephew in her arms that helped give the scene its apocalyptic quality in her memory.

E. M. Forster once wrote that "there is a battle fought over every baby." The battle over this particular Liverpool baby was to be fiercer than most—revealing not that he "wasn't wanted," as he came to believe, but that too many people wanted him too much. Nor would it become clear for some little time who had won him.

About his name, at least, there was no conflict. Julia decided to call him John, which pleased Alf as a tribute to his paternal grandfather, the sometime Kentucky minstrel, but was also classically English middle-class, suggesting every quality the Stanleys most admired—plain, upright, steady, predictable, uncomplicated. And, with fierce wartime patriotism in common, neither side of the family could object to his mother's giving him the middle name Winston, after Prime Minister Winston Churchill.

Alf's long absences from home would later brand him in his son's eyes as feckless, selfish, and unloving, but it should be remembered that as a merchant sailor he was doing one of the most vital and dangerous jobs in Britain's war effort. Thousands of other Liverpool men were in his situation, facing the same dangers from German U-boats—drowning in icy seas or turning into oil-soaked human torches—while, back at home, children they barely knew were raised by committees of women. Undoubtedly, for all its hazards, the sea provided an escape from dull routine and responsibility, where Alf could turn into "Lennie" and live out his fantasies as an entertainer (now adding a skit on Adolf Hitler's storm troopers to his repertoire of Jolson and Eddie Cantor). Another deterrent to seeking a safer shore job was that he was climbing the ladder of his profession. In September 1942, he gained promotion to saloon steward, the shipboard equivalent of headwaiter.

At the time, it appears, the most hostile of his in-laws no longer found anything to criticize about his nautical station, especially as he always returned home laden with booty from the ships' pantries, meat and butter and fresh fruit otherwise impossible to obtain under wartime rationing, which he would share out liberally among them. While at sea, he would send programs of ships' concerts featuring himself for Julia to show to John, who for years afterward would associate his father's name with a mysterious number called "Begin the Beguine."

Alf was at sea as saloon steward on the SS *Moreton Bay* from September 26, 1942, to February 2, 1943. Though air attacks on Liverpool had diminished since the horrendous "May blitz" of 1941, the city center was still considered a danger area. To make a safer as well as cleaner environment for John, Mimi persuaded Julia to move from 9 Newcastle Road out to suburban Woolton, where she herself had recently settled with her husband, George Smith. For several months, mother and son occupied a small house named the Cottage in Allerton Road, a short walk from Mimi's home. It was here that John formed the first definite impressions of Julia as she sang him to sleep at night. "She used to do this little tune . . . from the Disney movie," he would remember. " 'Want to know a secret? Promise not to tell. You are standing by a wishing-well . . .' "

The move was to put the first serious stress on a marriage that had never exactly been founded on maturity or trust. After being paid off by the *Moreton Bay*, Alf drew a stretch of shore leave long enough for him to register for fire-watching duties at Liverpool docks. Expecting Woolton to be a quiet retreat for Julia, he discovered that, on the contrary, she had acquired the habit of visiting local pubs, getting tipsy, and flirting with unattached men while Mimi or a neighbor named Dolly Hipshaw looked after John. One day, Alf answered the door to a noisy group of Julia's new friends, who plainly had no idea she was even married. A furious argument followed, in which Julia poured a cup of hot tea over Alf's head. He lashed out and caught her across the face, making her nose bleed.

John's maternal grandmother, the sweet-natured Annie Stanley, had died earlier in 1943, before she could imprint any but the vaguest picture of herself on his mind. Reluctant to stay on alone at 9 Newcastle Road, Pop Stanley decided to turn the house over to Julia and Alf while he moved in with relatives. For a time, at least, the rent was paid by Alf's older brother, Sydney. The anonymous little bay-fronted house, duplicated a thousand times in neighboring streets, became for John "the first place I remember . . . red brick . . . front room never used, always curtains drawn . . . picture of a horse and carriage on the wall. There were only three bedrooms upstairs, one on the front of the street, one in the back and one teeny little room in the middle . . ." He was already sharply observant, as Alf had realized the previous Christmas, when every department store in central Liverpool advertised its own Santa Claus grotto. "How many Father Christmases are there?" John asked.

In July 1943, Alf traveled to New York to work on Liberty Ships, the prefabricated merchantmen that America was mass-producing to replenish Britain's battered Atlantic convoys. He would be absent for sixteen months on a bizarre journey that took him halfway around the world, showed him the inside of two prisons, saw an ominous amendment on his employment card from VG to D (Declined comment) and put the collapse of his marriage into overdrive. No "lost weekend" his son would experience in future years even came close to this.

Alf later portrayed himself as the innocent victim of circumstance, bad advice from superiors, and his own trusting nature—and, to be sure, the hysteria and malign happenstance of the war itself seems to have been as much blameworthy as any misdeed or mistake of his. In New York, he was kept waiting so long to be assigned a berth that he found a temporary job at Macy's department store, acquired a Social Security card, and drank and sang his way through most of the better-known Broadway bars. Finally ordered to report to a Liberty Ship in Baltimore, he discovered he had been demoted to assistant steward. His only hope of keeping his proper "rate," so a colleague advised, was to stay with the vessel until her first port of call, New York, then jump ship and take his problem to the British consul. Alf naïvely adopted this strategy and was promptly arrested for desertion and locked up for two weeks on Ellis Island.

On his release, he was ordered to accept a berth as assistant steward on a ship named the *Sammex*, bound for the Far East. When the *Sammex* docked in Bône, Algeria, Alf was arrested for the "theft by finding" of a bottle of whiskey and, by his own account, chose to take the rap rather than betray the friend who actually had committed the offense. He spent nine days in a horrific military prison, where he was forced to scrub latrines and threatened with death if he ever spoke about the conditions he had witnessed. Turned loose into the city's dangerous casbah district, he met a mysterious Dutchman, known only as Hans, who not only saved him from being robbed and possibly murdered but also helped him rough up the British official he held partly responsible for his incarceration.

Finally, in October 1944, exhausted and half starved, with only a couple of dollars and his U.S. Social Security card in his pocket, he managed to scrounge passage back to Britain as a D.B.S. (Distressed British Seaman) on the troopship *Monarch of Bermuda*. In Liverpool, meanwhile, the shipping company had ceased paying his wages to Julia, who had no idea whether he was alive or dead. When he reached home, she informed him she was pregnant by another man. She had not been deliberately unfaithful, she said, but had been raped. She even gave Alf the name of the man she held responsible, a soldier stationed out on the Wirral Peninsula. Today, the police would instantly be called in; back then, the proper course was for Alf to confront the alleged rapist and demand what he had to say for himself.

Fortunately, Alf's brother Charlie, by now serving with the Royal Artillery, was on hand to lend moral support. Charlie would later recall the episode in terms rather like a deposition to a court-martial: "[Alf] told me he had come home and found [Julia] six weeks gone, but not showing. She claimed she'd been raped by a soldier. She gave a name. We went over to the Wirral where the soldier was stationed. . . . Alfred wasn't a violent man. Hasty-tempered but not violent. He said to him 'I believe you've been having affairs with my wife and she accuses you of raping her.' No such thing, says the soldier. It wasn't rape—it was consent."

The upshot was that soft-hearted Alf took a shine to the soldier, a young Welshman named Taffy Williams, listening sympathetically to his protestation that he loved Julia and wanted to marry her and bring up the baby on his family's farm (though John seemed to feature nowhere in this plan). Alf decided he had no option but to step aside—a decision that possibly did not come too hard after Julia's recent behavior. He persuaded Williams to accompany him back to 9 Newcastle Road, where, over a conciliatory pot of tea, he told Julia he was willing to let her go. No more inaccurate reading of the situation could have been possible. "I don't want you, you fool," she told her erstwhile lover disdainfully, recommending him to finish his tea and then "get lost."

To Alf's credit, he expressed himself willing to take Julia back and bring up the baby as his own. But Pop Stanley, fearing the inevitable public disgrace, insisted it must be put up for adoption. On June 19, 1945, five weeks after the war's end, a girl was born to Julia at Elmswood, a Salvation Army maternity home in North Mossley Hill Road. Victoria Elizabeth, as Julia had named her, was adopted by a Norwegian couple named Pederson, who renamed her Ingrid Maria and took her off to Norway, out of her real mother's life forever.

This period of crisis and upheaval in the Stanley family saw four-year-old John, for the one and only time, handed over to the care of his Lennon relatives. During Julia's pregnancy and confinement, he was sent to live with Alf's brother Sydney, a man whose respectability and drive to better himself even Mimi had come to acknowledge. Sydney, his wife, Madge, and their eight-year-old daughter, Joyce, welcomed John to their home in Maghull, a village between Liverpool and Southport. He was left with Sydney and Madge for something like eight months. The life they provided for him was stable and loving and, as time passed, they assumed that they'd be allowed to adopt him officially. So confident were they of this outcome that they put his name down to start at the local primary school the following autumn. Then Alf turned up one night without warning and announced he was taking John away. Despite Sydney's protests about the lateness of the hour, he insisted they had to leave immediately. All the family were distraught at losing John, Madge in particular. Soon afterward she adopted a six-week-old baby boy to fill the void he had left.

If Alf had hoped his display of magnanimity over Victoria Elizabeth would save his marriage, he was to be disappointed. In 1946, he returned from another cruise to find Julia openly involved with a sleek-haired hotel waiter named John—aka Bobby—Dykins. This time, however, the cuckolded husband wasn't prepared to take it lying down. A furious night altercation took place at 9 Newcastle Road between Alf, Julia, her new man friend, and Pop Stanley after Julia announced she was setting up home with Dykins and taking John with her. Awoken by the angry voices, John came to the stair head in time to see his mother screaming hysterically as Alf manhandled Dykins

out the front door. When Alf himself awoke the next morning, John
had been spirited away by Pop Stanley, and Julia was moving out her
furniture, helped by a female neighbor. Alf pitched in to help them,
telling Julia with the ostentatious self-pity of a country-and-western
ballad to leave him only "a broken chair" to sit on.

The sea, his old comforter, beckoned as alluringly as ever, and
in April 1946, he found a berth as night steward aboard the Cunard
company's flagship, the *Queen Mary*, plying between Southampton
and New York. The ship was within an hour of sailing when he received a telephone call from his sister-in-law, Mimi Smith, urging
him to return to Liverpool immediately.

It was not an easy call for Mimi to make, and it doubtless caused
even the unvengeful Alf a measure of quiet satisfaction. For the Stanley family's hostility toward Julia's new man friend Bobby Dykins
was more virulent than anything he himself had ever suffered at
their hands. According to Mimi, Julia and John had moved back
into 9 Newcastle Road, and Dykins was also now in residence there,
confronting John with the daily spectacle of his mother—in the
accepted phrase—"living in sin." Of most immediate concern was
that John seemed not to like his "new daddy" and had turned up
on Mimi's doorstep in Woolton, having walked the two miles from
Newcastle Road on his own. Despite all her hostility to Alf, she had
been forced to concede that he missed and needed his real father. Alf
then spoke to John, who asked him excitedly when he was coming
home. He replied that he couldn't "break Articles" by deserting his
ship, but promised to come as soon as the *Queen Mary* returned to
Southampton, two weeks later.

He duly made his way back up north, arriving at Mimi's late one
night after John was in bed and asleep. The homecoming mariner
was not offered a meal, only a cup of tea, which Mimi served to him
accompanied by a further angry recital of Julia's misconduct with
Bobby Dykins. She also presented Alf with a bill for various necessi-
ties which she said she'd had to buy for John since his arrival. Fortunately, thanks to profitable black-market dealings in nylon stockings
and other contraband, Alf had plenty of cash with him. He gave
Mimi £20, and in that moment—so he would afterward claim—

decided he had no alternative but to abduct his son the following day. As he would later write, "I finally made up my mind that I would take [John] to Blackpool with me, making some excuse that I was taking him shopping or to see his granny."

Alf stayed overnight at Mimi's and the next morning was awoken by an exuberant John bouncing up and down on his chest. His suggestion that the two of them should go out together for the day was greeted with wild excitement. Mimi offered no opposition, believing the purpose of the outing was to buy some new clothes for John. Father and son then caught a tram into Liverpool, where Alf took his older brother Sydney into his confidence, swearing him to secrecy. Sydney reiterated his own willingness to adopt John, though Alf later claimed never to have seriously considered this option.

Blackpool was Alf's chosen destination not only as a northwestern seaside resort of fabled child appeal but also as the hometown of his shipmate and fellow black marketeer Billy Hall. For something like three weeks, he hid out there with John, staying with Billy's parents and spending his abundant spare cash on every carnival ride and sticky treat the little boy could desire. The kindly Halls also found themselves added to the waiting list of John's would-be guardians. Alf's initial idea was that, when his money ran out and he returned to sea, John should stay on with the Halls in Blackpool. When it transpired that they were about to sell their home and emigrate to New Zealand, a more complex scheme took shape. Mr. and Mrs. Hall would take John with them, posing as his grandparents; a little later, Alf, Billy Hall, and Billy's brother would obtain their own passage to New Zealand free of charge by signing on to some Australasian-bound liner, then jumping ship when it reached Wellington.

The plan had no chance to mature any further. Julia had by now picked up Alf's trail and, one sunny June day, turned up at the Halls' house, accompanied by Bobby Dykins, to take John back. Initially her demand was not backed up by any real force. When Alf outlined the New Zealand scheme, she agreed it could be the start of a wonderful new life for John and indicated her willingness to let him go, merely asking to see him one last time. When John was brought into the room, his first reaction, after their days of fun and intimacy, was to climb into Alf's lap. But when Julia admitted defeat and turned to leave, he jumped down and ran after her, burying his face in her skirt, sobbing and begging her not to go. To break the impasse, Alf pleaded with her to give their marriage another chance, but Julia would have none of it.

Alf then told John he must choose between going with Mummy or staying with Daddy. If you want to tear a small child in two, there is no better way. John went to Alf and took his hand; then, as Julia turned away again, he panicked and ran after her, shouting to her to wait and to his father to come, too. But, paralyzed once more by fatalistic self-pity, Alf remained rooted in his chair. Julia and John left the house and disappeared into the holiday crowds.

That evening, good-hearted Mr. and Mrs. Hall sought to cheer Alf up by taking him to a pub called the Cherry Tree and persuading him to do his Al Jolson routine for its assembled customers. His all-too-appropriate song choice was Jolson's "Little Pal," a eulogy to some angelic Sonny boy tucked in a soft, safe nursery as his faithful dad watches adoringly over him. Instead of "Little Pal" in each verse, Alf sang "Little John." It made tears stream down his cheeks, although—ever the pro—he sang the song to its end, amid a storm of clapping and whistling. Unlike the little pal he had given up, Alf Lennon would never find crowds oppressive nor applause wearisome.

2

THE NORTHERN CONFEDERACY

Shall I call you Pater, too?

Britain emerged from the Second World War looking far more like a defeated nation than a victorious one. Crippled financially as well as bombed to ruins, the country remained in a state of crisis and privation long after the lights had begun to go on again all over the rest of Europe—even in Germany. Meat, butter, and sugar continued to be doled out in miserly amounts dictated by coupons from dun-colored ration books. Clothes were drab, shapeless, and as devoid of individuality as the uniforms they had replaced. Every day seemed to bring some fresh shortage or restriction or appeal by the grim-faced new socialist government for self-sacrifice or thrift. In the pervading climate of shabbiness, inconvenience, chilblains, and snot-green smog, the young and the old were almost indistinguishable. Youth had been permanently canceled, it seemed, along with any kind of frivolity, spontaneity, or joy.

Yet despite the icebound grip of this so-called Austerity era, British life went on in much the same way it always had. The class system still operated as feudally as ever, the Royal Family was still sacred, the aristocracy still revered. Authority received unquestioning trust and respect, whether manifested in politicians, doctors, lawyers, the clergy, the armed forces, or the police. Newspapers voluntarily suppressed anything that might upset the status quo. While rapidly dismantling their colonial Empire, Britons continued to regard themselves as masters of the world, despising all foreigners, treating as natural inferiors all races with skins darker than theirs, and using terms like *nigger* and *wog* (not to mention *Jewboy* and *yid*) without a qualm. Endemic class snobbery came from beneath as much as from above. Most people on even the lowest social rungs aspired to speak a little "better" than they really could, taking as their model the clipped enunciation of royalty, prime ministers, Shakespearian actors, and announcers on the BBC.

Like all great cities of the north, Liverpool lay in ruins for so long that grass grew over the bomb sites and wildflowers sprang up around the disued shelters and the giant letters SWS (for Static Water Supply). An Ealing Studios film called *The Magnet*, shot on location there and released in 1950, shows how, five years after Victory in Europe, whole districts around the docks still consisted of nothing but craters and rubble heaps, the latter now used by children as unofficial playgrounds.

Seaports by their very nature tend to be individualistic places where life is lived in tougher, freer, more eccentric ways than in the nonmercantile hinterland. Even in the pungent company of Britain's ports, Liverpool has always stood alone. Its particular character dates back to the eighteenth and early nineteenth centuries, when Liverpool merchants were the mavericks of the shipping world, earning fortunes on the infamous Triangle route that transported black slaves from Africa to the Americas, then brought home the proceeds as cotton, sugar, and tobacco. In the American Civil War, while the rest of the country maintained uneasy neutrality, Liverpool sided firmly with the slave-owning South, gave it space to open an embassy (which has never been officially closed), and built its most famous warship, the *Alabama*. Indeed, the final episode of the conflict did not take place in America at all, but in this faraway safe haven for rebels and secessionists. As defeat for the Stars and Bars became inevitable, another Confederate warship, the *Shenandoah*, appeared in the River Mersey. Rather than turn her over to the victorious Yankees, her captain had crossed the Atlantic to surrender to Liverpool's lord mayor.

Such was the attitude Liverpool would maintain into the twentieth century—its back turned to the rest of Britain, its gaze fixed admiringly, yearningly, above all knowingly, on America. America came and went each day in transatlantic liners like the *Queen Mary* and *Mauretania*, and in the savoir faire of Liverpudlian crews whose easy familiarity with fabled cities far away earned them the nickname Cunard Yanks. Even the skyline that greeted ships as they came up the Mersey had a touch of New York's. It was composed of a wide riverfront piazza called the Pier Head and an acropolis of three giant gray stone buildings known as the Three Graces, respectively the headquarters of the Docks and Harbour Board, the Cunard organization, and the Royal Liver (pronounced "ly-ver") Insurance Company. The last named was embellished fore and aft by a pair of matching green domes, on each of which a stone "Liver Bird" flapped its wings defiantly at the encircling gulls.

For all this incurable New World bias, Liverpool was also the quintessential northern city, epitomizing Victorian civic pride with its central cluster of Athenian-style public buildings dominated by St. George's Hall (called by John Betjeman "the finest secular hall in England") and equestrian statues of the Queen-Empress and Albert the Prince Consort. Apart from the bomb sites, everything still looked very much as in Atkinson Grimshaw's famous waterfront scene of the 1890s—the stately trams known as Green Goddesses, the pinnacled hotels, theaters, and variety halls, the gilt-encrusted chemists' shops with giant globes of blue liquid in their windows, the grocers displaying enamel signs for Bovril or Mazawattee Tea.

To people down south, it was a vaguely sleazy and menacing place, whose Lime Street was famously a beat for the folk-ballad prostitute Maggie May, and whose polyglot mix of Welsh, Irish, Chinese, and

West Indians hinted at the nameless perils and vices of some cold-water Barbary Coast. Almost equal ill fame sprang from its reputation as a hotbed of extreme left-wing politics and trade-union militancy, not only on the docks but in the factories and car plants that made up Merseyside's industrial sprawl. For many years, its most prominent personality was Bessie Braddock, Labour Member of Parliament for Liverpool's Exchange district, a battleship of a woman whose abrasive rhetoric seemed to convey all the grimness of her home city as much as it did her government's zeal to make everyone as uncomfortable and miserable as possible.

However, there was another, very different Liverpool, far removed from the world of wharves and warehouses and teeming, brawling dockside pubs. The shipping industry also employed a vast white-collar class of executives, managers, and clerical workers, as keen in their social aspirations as any other section of Britain's bourgeoisie. Outside the city's grimy hub and across the Mersey in Cheshire lay neat, decorous suburbs where the Scouse accent was barely detectable—self-contained middle-class communities, kept in pristine order by benign local authorities and well supplied with high-class shops, leafy parks, golf courses, and first-rate schools.

The Magnet, the Ealing film mentioned earlier, recounts the adventures of a well-spoken small boy from such a suburb who gets mixed up with some riotous street kids in tough downtown Liverpool. With hindsight, it seems prophetic.

The oft-repeated tale of how Mimi Smith came to assume sole responsibility for bringing up her six-year-old nephew, John Lennon, could not be simpler or more heart-warming. Mimi was of the type that English people of earlier generations called a "good sort" or a "brick," a modern-day Betsey Trotwood whose exterior brusqueness camouflaged a heart of purest gold. When John's real father and mother proved deficient, she took it on herself to fill the role of both together, making it her single-minded mission to give him, in her own words, "what every child has a right to—a safe and happy home life."

That was the version of events John himself always firmly believed.

"My parents couldn't cope with me," he was to tell countless interviewers in those words or similar ones, "so I was sent to live with an
auntie . . ." Nothing can detract from Mimi's care and self-sacrifice
in the years that followed. But the background circumstances were
rather more complicated than either of them remembered, or cared
to remember.

Born in 1906, Mimi was one of those people, very like Betsey
Trotwood and other sinewy Dickens females, who seemed never to
have known youthful passion or indiscretion. She was a person of exceptional intelligence, highly articulate and an omnivorous reader,
who should have gone on from school to college, and might have
done equally well as a lawyer, doctor, or teacher. Instead, she had
always been expected to act as an extra parent to her four younger
sisters and to regard the values of home and family as paramount.
In young womanhood, the brisk and practical side of her seemed to
promise more than the intellectual one. When she was nineteen,
she enrolled as a student nurse at Woolton Convalescent Hospital,
staying on there after she qualified and eventually reaching the rank
of ward sister. During the early thirties, she became engaged to a
young doctor from Warrington whom she had met on the wards,
but before wedding plans could be made, her fiancé died from a virus
passed on to him by one of his own patients.

Not that her early life was without its exotic moments. At the convalescent hospital, her charges included some former employees of
a wealthy industrialist named Lynton Vickers, who remained conscientiously concerned for their welfare and came regularly to visit
them. Between the caring plutocrat and the angular young ward
sister there developed a mutual respect and affection. At Vickers's
invitation, Mimi took a sabbatical from nursing to become his secretary, living in at his Gothic mansion in Bettwys-y-Coed, in north
Wales.

Such diversions came to an end with her marriage to George
Smith, at the mature age of thirty-three in 1939. The Smith family
were dairy farmers in Woolton, a place which at that time, with its
open fields and leafy lanes, resembled a country village more than
a big-city suburb. George first got to know Mimi because the con-

valescent hospital where she worked was part of his morning milk round. The dairyman's thoughts soon turned to marriage, but Mimi proved more cautious, declaring herself unwilling to be "tied to a gas stove or a sink" and regarding George as no more than a reliable standby "whenever I was hungry or stuck in town." Even for that buttoned-up time and place, theirs was a relationship singularly lacking in romance. When Mimi finally did agree to get engaged, it was sealed with a businesslike handshake rather than a kiss. "George was different from me . . . chalk and cheese, really," she would remember. "I was always filibustering about, but he was a quiet man. Set in his ways a bit, but a kind man." She recalled, too, how George's mild nature made him easily controllable, without resort to "filibustering." "I used to give him a look and he'd know all right if he'd upset me. Just give him The Look and he'd know."

Possibly in reaction to their domineering father, all the Stanley sisters but Julia had ended up with quiet, unassertive men whose sole function in the family was to be breadwinners and who took little or no part either in its management or its complex internal politics. Elizabeth, the second eldest, known as Mater, had first married a marine surveyor named Charles Molyneux Parkes; after Parkes's death in 1944, she had married a Scottish dentist, Robert ("Bert") Sutherland. Anne, the third in seniority, known as Nanny, had married a Ministry of Labour official named Sydney Cadwallader. Harriet, known as Harrie, the second-youngest of the five sisters and most adventurous of the quartet, had first married an Egyptian engineering student named Ali Hafez and emigrated with him to Cairo. Just prior to the war, Hafez had died of septicemia after a routine tooth extraction, and Harrie had returned to Liverpool with their daughter, Liela. Having given up British nationality, Harrie was classed as a foreign alien and obliged to report regularly to the authorities. A judiciously swift remarriage to Norman Birch of the Royal Army Service Corps restored her UK passport to her.

Mimi, Mater, Nanny, and Harrie were recognizably a clan. Though none was as strikingly pretty as Julia, all four had a rangy, suntanned elegance—not the Marlene Dietrich type so much as the Katharine Hepburn. All dressed immaculately, never setting foot out of doors without hats, gloves, and matching shoes and handbags; all were immensely house-proud, capable, talkative, humorous, and forceful. Later in John's life, he would talk of writing a story on the lines of John Galsworthy's Forsyte Saga about the "strong, intelligent, beautiful women [who] dominated the situation in the family. I was always with the women. I heard them talk about the men and talk about life. They always knew what was going on. The men never ever knew." Their husbands were categorized, even openly referred to, as outsiders—a tag that would also be given the marriage partner of every child in the family.

But of the four, only Mimi had remained childless. Her explanation was that she'd had to be a mother to the others during their girlhood, and didn't want to go through it all again. She was, in fact, thought not to care very much for small children, preferring them when they grew older and could join in intelligent conversation about things she cared for, such as reading and music.

From gentle George Smith, Mimi received social standing as a farmer's wife in a salubrious part-rural area, and a home that more than met her exacting standards. This was a house named Mendips, at 251 Menlove Avenue, Woolton, where the couple took up residence in 1942. Even to someone less attuned to nuances of class, the dwelling proclaimed its superiority in diverse ways: the fact that it was semi-detached rather than terraced; that, instead of plain brick, it was coated in knobby gray pebble dash; that it stood on an avenue, so much more exclusive-sounding than a mere street or road; above all that, far from being just a number on the postman's round, it also had a name, grandiosely identifying it with a range of hills in far-off Somerset.

On the inside, Mendips was designed to suggest an Elizabethan manor house. Its entrance hall had a half-timbered finish, the lower beams serving as display shelves for Mimi's prized collection of Royal Worcester and Coalport china. The baronial-looking staircase ascended past a large stained-glass window inset with a Tudor rose motif. The remaining windows had stained-glass borders decorated with Art Nouveau flowers. In addition to the ground-floor living room and dining room, there was the country-manor touch of a morning room, a space rather more modest than its title suggests, immediately adjacent to the kitchen. When the house had been built in 1933, its first owners would have employed a uniformed housemaid rather than just an occasional cleaning lady. Above the morning-room door still hung a board with a row of five panels, indicating where electric bells once summoned the maid to the dining room, drawing room, front door, front bedroom, or back bedroom. Yes, the future self-proclaimed working-class hero grew up in a house equipped with servants' bells.

Mimi always described her acquisition of John solely in terms of family duty—the habit ingrained since childhood of straightening out her younger sister's muddles. "Julia had met someone else, with whom she had a chance of happiness," she would say. "And no man wants another man's child. . . ." In fact, the relationship between Julia and her headwaiter, Bobby Dykins, had never excluded John in any way. Far from discriminating against "another man's child," Dykins was prepared to bring John up as if he were his own. He was serious enough about this to have persuaded Julia to move out of 9 Newcastle Road with John and into a small rented flat in Gateacre, where the hoped-for family unit might evolve with less pressure from her relatives.

But for Mimi, Julia's "living in sin" so publicly with Dykins threatened to make her sister the object of scandalized gossip such as even Alf Lennon had never visited on the super-respectable Stanley family. Julia might be old enough to lead her own life, but little John should not have to live in such an atmosphere of moral laxity.

Mimi had other motives, too, compounded not only of her unassailable moral certitude but also her reluctance or inability to have a baby by the usual channels, and the almost mystical affinity she had felt with John since first seeing him newly born in his mother's arms. "She decided she wanted him," her niece Liela Harvey says. "And who could blame her, because he was the cutest little fellow you ever saw."

Mimi therefore enlisted her father in a campaign against Julia and Dykins that today might almost be defined as harassment. One day, she and Pop Stanley both turned up unannounced at the Gateacre flat, declaring it an unfit place for John to live and demanding to remove him. But Julia, supported by Dykins, refused to give him up. Mimi then sought the intervention of a Liverpool Corporation child-welfare officer, who visited the flat and expressed concern that John was sharing Julia and Dykins's bedroom. Even by the puritanical ethos of 1940s welfare services, this was not sufficient reason to separate him from his mother. Such a decision could only be Julia's.

Despite the Stanleys' disparaging nickname of Spiv (war slang for a small-time shyster), Dykins was generally a kindly and civilized man. However, when he took a drink too many, the suave, decorous headwaiter turned into an all-too-typical Liverpool male who could "lose his rag" in an instant, bellowing abuse at Julia, sometimes hitting her. And, as ever in times of emergency, her oldest sister was her first port of call. One day while John was with Mimi at Mendips, his mother came in, as he later remembered, "wearing a black coat and with her face bleeding." He was told she had had an accident, but clearly suspected something more sinister. "I went out into the garden," he recalled. "I loved her, but I didn't want to get involved. I suppose I was a moral coward. I wanted to hide all feelings."

The upshot was a furious argument between the sisters, as Mimi herself later recounted, which yet again dragged up Julia's wartime affair with the Welsh soldier, and baby Victoria Elizabeth. "[Julia] was looking for sympathy but as far as I was concerned she'd made her bed and had to lie on it, and I told her 'You're not fit to be a mother.' She reacted like I'd slapped her in the face. I just said I think I should have John . . . [it] just seemed to make sense. George was very fond of him. In many ways our house was a lot quieter than the places he'd been living in and we could give him some stability. He'd had a bit of a bumpy ride up till then."

In Mimi's version, Julia was by now ready to agree willingly, even thankfully. But John's cousin Liela, who was also in the room, saw a very different end to the long tug-of-love. "I remember Mimi standing in front of John and telling Julia, 'You're not having him.'"

Once she had won him, Mimi devoted herself completely to John's care. What little social life she and George used to enjoy she willingly sacrificed; in later life it would be her proud boast that "for 10 years [after John was in bed] I never crossed the threshold of that house at night." She was careful always to leave a light on outside his room, until a voice sternly called after her, "Mimi . . . don't waste light!"

Mimi gave John's life an order and structure he had never known with easygoing Julia—meals served as regularly as clockwork, bed at the same fixed (early) hour each night, baths and shampoos a regular ritual in the house's single bathroom with its black-and-white checked linoleum and freestanding, claw-footed tub. Before meals—usually served in the morning room but sometimes in the rather somber rear dining room—he would be called on to say grace. He was not allowed to come to the table without first washing his hands, or to leave it without asking, "Can I get down?"

Above all, Mimi was determined that he should speak like a nice middle-class boy from the suburbs, not a coarse, raucous "wacker." Under her tutelage, there was soon not the slightest taint of inner-city Liverpool in John's voice. "I had high hopes for [him] and I knew you didn't get anywhere if you spoke like a ruffian. I remember once he came home from town on the bus and he'd heard these Liverpudlians talking to each other—Scouse, you know—and he was shocked, he couldn't understand what they were talking about. . . . I told him he should avoid people like that. . . . He was a country boy . . . he would never meet [them] except if anyone came to the house to mend something. It was a world away really."

Yet Mimi's care, for all its scrupulousness, was not maternal. She remained at heart a hospital nurse who ran her home, and its occupants, with the brisk efficiency of her old ward. Once, John asked her why he still called Julia "Mummy" and her "Mimi" even now that Julia was the less dominant figure in his life. "Well, you couldn't have two mummies, could you?" Mimi answered with impermeable grown-up logic. Back then, it was quite rare for a child to receive dispensation to call an adult—other than perhaps a nursemaid or other domestic servant—by their first name. With Mimi and John it did not denote intimacy, but a certain measure of distance between them.

With his burly, jovial Uncle George, by contrast, John developed what was probably the most uncomplicatedly loving relationship of his whole life. George, quite simply, treated him like the son he may well have yearned to have with Mimi. In the early war years, when the dairy farm was still active, he would take John around Woolton with him on the milk cart, showing him off to customers as proudly as if he were his own. John loved to go with him to the milking parlor or to the field where Daisy the cart horse spent her leisure hours. When he came home at night, he would open his arms, and John would fly into them, as Mimi remembered, "like two trains colliding in the doorway." They were always kissing each other, a ritual John called "giving squeakers."

George's career as a cow-keeper (his description on his business card) had ended with his call-up for military service at the late age of thirty-eight. During his absence with the army in France, his brother Frank had run down the dairy business, and its fields had been swallowed by a factory making Bear Brand nylon stockings. For a time, George tried an alternative career as a bookmaker, working out of Mendips in contravention of current gaming laws, which allowed bets to be placed only with licensed operatives at racecourses. He soon abandoned the venture, persuaded jointly by the risk of police prosecution and Mimi's distaste for the kind of people it brought traipsing through her home. After that, the only work he could find was as night watchman at the Bear Brand factory; the most minor of employees on property his family had once owned.

This meant that he was around the house all through the day, to play with his small nephew and soften or undermine his wife's strict regimen. Although John already loved the cinema, Mimi had a fierce mistrust of "picturedromes," possibly a result of Julia's former employment in one. John was therefore limited to seemly entertainments such as the periodic Disney screen epics, *Bambi* or *Snow White*, and the Christmas pantomime at the Liverpool Empire. Sweets were still issued by ration-book "points," as they would be until 1953: John's daily allotment was a single piece of health-giving barley sugar each evening at bedtime.

But George would defy the wifely Look that otherwise ruled him by taking John to Woolton's little cinema or smuggling sweets or

chocolate upstairs to him after lights-out. Mimi felt almost envious—
though it was beyond her to admit as much—when she saw the two
of them flying paper airplanes in the back garden or hugging each
other and laughing. Even John's tendency to tell fibs never clouded
the sunshine of their relationship. "Tell you what," George would
say to Mimi with a chuckle. "He's never going to be a vicar."

As Julia had before him, John soon identified Mimi's weak spot:
her sense of humor. In summertime, while she sat in the back garden
in a deck chair, he would stealthily open an upstairs window and
flick water onto her head in artfully small, irregular amounts, so
that she'd keep thinking she felt raindrops but would never be quite
sure. Despite her combustible temper, she did not smack him when
he misbehaved; instead, they had shouting matches more suited to
combative siblings than aunt and nephew. Afterward, exhausted as
well as exasperated, Mimi would flop down in the easy chair beside
the morning-room window. John would creep around the side path,
then suddenly rear up and make monster noises at her through the
glass. "However cross I was, I'd find myself roaring with laughter,"
Mimi recalled. "He could always get me going, the same way Julia
could."

His education, too, assumed an even keel that gave Mimi every
hope for his future. In November 1945, just after his fifth birthday,
his father had enrolled him at Mosspits Lane Infants School in Woolton. But he remained there only five months, leaving at the end of
the spring term in 1946. It would later be claimed that the upheavals
in his family life had caused some serious behavioral problems and
that he was expelled from Mosspits Lane for bullying other children.
However, the school's logbook makes no mention of any expulsion,
giving the only reason for his premature departure as "left district."

When Mimi took charge a year later, she sent him to Dovedale
Primary School, near the Penny Lane traffic roundabout. After a few
initial bus journeys there together, John insisted on going by himself. "He thought I was making a show of him [making him look
foolish]," Mimi remembered. "Imagine that! So what I used to do
was let him get out of the house and then follow him to make sure
he didn't get into any mischief." Dovedale proved the perfect choice.

After only six months, he was reading and writing with complete confidence. "That boy's as sharp as a needle," Mr. Bolt, the head teacher, told Mimi. "He can do anything as long as he chooses to do it." Uncle George had helped by sitting John on his knee each night and picking out words in the *Liverpool Echo*—thus fostering what would become a lifelong addiction to newsprint.

He had always loved to draw and paint, begging to be bought pencils, paint boxes, and paper rather than toys, spending hours wrapped up in worlds of his own creation. At Dovedale he won several prizes for art, including a book entitled *How to Draw Horses*, which he was to treasure for years afterward. His choice of subjects could sometimes startle teachers accustomed to normal infant renditions of pussycats or "My Mummy." The notable example was a painting he once did of Jesus Christ—a longhaired and bearded figure like a psychic vision of himself twenty years into the future. But mostly his work tended to be caricatures of his classmates and teachers, crazily distorted yet instantly recognizable, which made their models, child and adult alike, howl with laughter. Though good at running and swimming, he was less successful at team sports like soccer and cricket, owing to a disinclination—and, it soon proved, genuine inability—to keep his eye on the ball. He had inherited his mother's extreme nearsightedness, and by age seven was pronounced to be in need of glasses. Under the new socialist National Health Service, these were now available free of charge. But John so hated the standard issue, with their round wire frames and pink nosepieces, that Mimi agreed to buy him whatever kind he liked. He was taken to a private optician and allowed to choose an expensive pair with more comfortable plastic frames. He could not abide wearing even these, however, and left them off whenever he could.

As a result, his view of the world was largely created by sheer myopia—the weird new forms that everyday people and things can take on for the nearsighted and the wild surrealism that can flow from printed words misread. In addition, he possessed the very Liverpudlian traits of a fascination with language and an irresistible compulsion to play around with it. If his weak eyes did not misrepresent some word accidentally, his quick mind did so deliberately, missing no chance of a pun, a spoonerism, or double entendre; he was an instinctive cartoonist in speech as well as on paper. When he suffered a bout of chicken pox—his childhood's one serious ailment—he called it "chicken pots." Away on holiday, with pocket money in short supply, he sent Mimi a postcard saying, "Funs is low."

Small boys in glasses tend to have a weak and vulnerable air. But with John, the opposite was the case. Also at Dovedale, although not in the same class, was a boy named Jimmy Tarbuck, like himself destined one day to write Liverpool's name across the sky. "If ever there was a scrap in the school yard, John was likely to be involved," Tarbuck says. "And I'll always remember the way he looked at you. His glasses had really thick lenses, the kind we called bottle-bottoms. At school, we used to have this thing, if you were out for trouble with another kid you'd say 'Are you lookin' at me?' But John's lenses were so thick, you could never tell if he was looking at you or not."

Julia and Bobby Dykins, meanwhile, had settled on the Springwood council estate in Allerton, just a couple of miles from Menlove Avenue. Whatever his faults in Mimi's eyes, Dykins was at least a hardworking man, and a provident one. He now had the prestigious job of headwaiter in the Adelphi Hotel's sumptuous French restaurant. And, notwithstanding her misadventures with two children thus far, he had persuaded Julia to become a mother again. They were to have two daughters together, Julia, born in 1947, and Jacqueline Gertrude, born in 1949, although Alf Lennon's continued failure to begin divorce proceedings would prevent them from ever becoming man and wife.

Mimi had initially discouraged Julia from seeing too much of John, fearing that she might upset the wholesome new habits instilled at Mendips. But as time passed, the frost gradually thawed. Dykins was never allowed to join the meek males on the family's bottom rung, but his daughters were fully accepted by Mimi—and the other sisters—and John was allowed to spend unrestricted time with Julia.

It would have been difficult to do otherwise, since the sisters operated as a team, not merely supporting and confiding absolutely in each other, but helping run one another's domestic affairs and look after one another's families. As well as Mendips, therefore, John had the run of three alternative homes, all equally welcoming, happy, and secure. His Aunt Harrie lived only a short walk away at the Cottage, the old Smith dairy farmhouse where Julia and Alf Lennon had briefly settled during the war. His Aunt Mater lived "across the water" at Rock Ferry, Cheshire, in a rambling house with a large garden. When Mater married Bert Sutherland and moved with him to his native Scotland, the house was taken over by her sister, Nanny.

The cousins with whom John played during these regular family get-togethers ranged from his Aunt Nanny's and Harrie's toddler sons, Michael and David, to Stanley, the only child of Mater's marriage to Charles Parkes, who was seven years John's senior. Stanley had been responsible for the sisters' eccentric pet names, first mispronouncing Mary as "Mimi," calling Anne "Nanny" when she'd looked after him during the war, and dubbing his own mother "Mater," in tune with her fastidious elegance, when he went away to boarding school and began learning Latin. John extended the habit by calling his Uncle George "Pater." Alf Lennon's most abiding memory from their ill-omened flight to Blackpool was of a small boy who spoke "like a gentleman" and gravely inquired, "Shall I call you Pater, too?"

He was especially fond of his cousin Liela, the daughter of Aunt Harrie's Egyptian first marriage, a stunningly pretty girl with a smile that can still light up a forty-year-old sepia snapshot. Liela was only three and a half years John's senior, so she became his most regular playmate and accomplice inside the family. Liela remembers a sunny-natured, affectionate small boy who had no inhibitions about hugging and kissing her. "Think of all those songs about love that John wrote before he was even twenty-one," she says. "How could he have done that if he hadn't had a lot of love in his own life?"

He seemed to remember little of the war that had been waged over him, or of being passed around competing would-be parents like a parcel. Mimi volunteered little information, replying to his questions in only the briefest anodyne fashion. "[She] told me my parents had fallen out of love," he would recall. "She never said anything directly against my mother and father. I soon forgot my father. It was like he was dead." But Alf was very much alive and, to begin with at least, still a very real threat to Mimi's guardianship. She had not officially adopted John, nor would she ever do so; Alf remained married to Julia and in a position of moral ascendancy as far as the law was concerned. At any moment, he could have walked through the front door and demanded that his son be returned to him.

This danger was soon neutralized, in large part thanks to the hapless Alf himself. After parting from John in Blackpool, he had drowned his sorrows at sea again, signing aboard the Royal Mail steamer *Andes* on her maiden voyage to Argentina. Buenos Aires had produced another of those apocalyptic misadventures that only seemed to happen to him. Picked up with some other British mariners in a routine police sweep, he found himself held in solitary confinement for two days. The explanation was that his captors had misread the page in his passport where his signature, "A.Lennon" was immediately preceded by the name of his next of kin, given simply as "John." He was therefore assumed to be "John Alennon." A notorious murderer in Argentina at the time also bore that name, and the police had mistaken Alf for him. On regaining his freedom and returning to Britain, he resumed service, on the *Dominion Monarch*, but in posts of declining importance, first as Assistant Boots (shoe cleaner), then as Silverman (custodian of restaurant silverware).

By his own later account, he still cherished hopes of winning John back and carrying out their Blackpool scheme of emigrating to New Zealand. When the *Dominion Monarch* returned to Tilbury in December 1949, he resolved to catch a train from London to Liverpool and have it out with Julia again. On his way to Euston Station, however, he was diverted by some shipmates into a Soho pub crawl. This ended in the early hours of the following morning with a riotously drunken Alf smashing the display window of a West End department store and attempting to waltz with the manikin inside. Hauled before an unsympathetic magistrate, he was sentenced to six months in Wormwood Scrubs.

Alf's plight could not better have suited the purposes of his unofficial judges in Liverpool. According to his brother Charlie, Mimi wrote to him while he was in prison, threatening to tell John his father was a "jailbird" if ever he tried to contact him again. The possession of a criminal record also effectively ended Alf's career at sea.

Defeated and dejected, he took a menial job as a dishwasher in a hotel kitchen and seemed to give up all thought of ever contacting John again.

Not only his father but the whole Lennon side of his family was now firmly airbrushed from John's consciousness. For the rest of his life, he would have no idea what decent, brave, and loyal people also bore his surname. His grandmother, the redoubtable Polly, had refused to leave her house throughout the war, even though Toxteth was in one of the worst-blitzed quarters of Liverpool. John had been wont to visit Copperfield Street only with his father or during his stay with his Uncle Sydney and Aunt Madge. After the parting from Alf, his visits there ceased. When Polly died in 1949, of stomach cancer, she had not seen him for something like three years. "That side of John's family was never mentioned," his cousin Liela remembers. "As children, we didn't even know it existed."

Even when no aunts and cousins happened to be visiting, Mendips was always a lively and crowded place. To supplement George's small income, Mimi took in a succession of boarders—"paying guests," as they were known in the fifties—whom she provided with meals as well as bed-sitter accommodation in the bay-windowed front bedroom. These lodgers, exclusively male, were usually students at Liverpool University and tended to become part of the family, helping out in the garden, keeping George company at his local pub, and joining in John's games. The household also included three animals: a large black-and-white cat named Samuel Pepys, which always sat on George's lap, a Persian cross named Titch, and an adoring mongrel bitch named Sally.

John adored cats as much as did Mimi and George. One snowy night when he was no more than seven or eight, he returned home carrying a bedraggled brown-and-white Persian kitten, which he said he had been unable to dissuade from following him. He begged to be allowed to keep the kitten, but Mimi said that, since it was obviously valuable, they must first advertise for its owner in the *Liverpool Echo*. No owner came forward, so the kitten stayed and was given the name Tim. "We had Tim for twenty years," Mimi recalled. "Wherever he was in the world, John was always wanting to know what Tim was up to."

As well as its country cottages and Art Deco villas, Woolton had many curious old houses, nestling in woodland or behind forbidding stone walls, carved from Liverpool's native sandstone and embellished with the turrets and gargoyles of fairy-tale castles. The most familiar to John, being only a short walk from Mendips, was a gloomy Gothic mansion bearing the anomalous name of Strawberry Field. No strawberries grew in its extensive grounds, and few were ever tasted in its interior, now a refuge for orphan girls run by the Salvation Army. The inmates attended various schools in the locality but wore their own distinctive uniform of blue-and-white striped dresses and summertime straw hats trimmed with red.

On walks with Mimi or Uncle George, John would always linger outside Strawberry Field, peering through its heavy iron gates and up at its windows as if he felt some affinity with the less fortunate children who lived there. He never missed the chance to visit the home each summer when it held a fund-raising garden fete with homemade cake stalls and games offering prizes of plaster Scottie dogs, peppermint rock candy, or lone goldfish suspended dejectedly in water-filled jam jars.

"I'd give him sixpence to spend on the stalls," Mimi remembered. "He'd hear the Salvation Army band and he'd pull me along, saying, 'Hurry up, Mimi! We're going to be late!'"

3

THE OUTLAWS

I'd say I had a happy childhood . . .
I was always having a laugh.

Thanks in largest part to his minstrel grandfather and his would-be minstrel father, but also to numerous others on both sides of his family, John could be fairly said to have had music in his bones. Yet in his early years the odds seemed weighted against his becoming a musician at all, let alone the one he finally did.

In early-fifties Britain, music was something most people got along without. The technology for listening to it in the home consisted of gramophones with manually cranked turntables, and thick wax 78 rpm (revolutions per minute) discs the size of car hubcaps, which came in plain brown paper covers and broke when dropped. Rare was the household whose record collections numbered more than about a dozen of these sepia-wrapped, dust-attracting monsters.

Back then, one did not hear music playing incessantly in shops, office buildings, airports, station concourses, doctors' waiting rooms, and elevators, as a background to news bulletins or from the earpieces of telephones. Portable radios were hulking battery-powered objects designed to look like small suitcases. Tape recorders for private use were almost unknown. Sound came in mono only and did not travel. In public places like parks or beaches, the only noise would be human hubbub. Most residential areas passed their days and nights in the same unbroken silence.

Television was still a fabulously expensive novelty, enjoyed in only a few thousand homes and served by a solitary BBC channel offering a scanty program in the afternoon and early evening. Radio, likewise the BBC's monopoly and better known as the wireless, broadcast music largely as a public duty, to keep the factories running and the food lines quiet. So afraid was the corporation's Light Programme of overexciting its listeners that records with the faintest sexual frisson were banned from the airwaves, and continuity announcers forbidden to use such inflammatory terms as *hot jazz*. Professional musicians were a tiny faction who had mastered their complex craft only after years of study, possessed little personality outside their playing, and in general projected an aura that was at once middle-aged, irritable, and foreign.

For Mimi Smith, nothing more clearly defined the Alf Lennon world from which she had rescued John than people enjoying raucous-accented singsongs in their front parlors or—worse still—in the pubs wrapped around a thousand and one inner-Liverpool street corners. The only music Mimi cared for was the classical kind, as played by the Liverpool Philharmonic Orchestra, Manchester's revered Halle, and BBC radio's cathedral-solemn Third Programme (whose announcers wore dinner jackets even though visible to none but their own studio staff). Between classical and popular music in this era there was no possible meeting point. Pop lovers regarded classical as impossibly difficult and highfalutin; classics lovers regarded pop as just so much horrible noise.

In John's family as now constituted, there was only one person of any musical ability. His mother Julia, though otherwise not noted for consistency, still kept up the banjo- and piano accordion–playing she had learned as a girl. She was a natural entertainer, liable at the slightest encouragement to break into impromptu performance.

"Judy [the children's name for her] played the banjo and accordion really well," her niece Liela remembers. "She had a lovely singing voice that I can only compare to Vera Lynn's. And she was a wonderfully witty and entertaining person to be with. She could keep going for hours at a time, singing, telling jokes, doing impersonations, and you'd never get tired of it."

From John's earliest childhood, his response to music was instant and visceral. In 1946, just before his sixth birthday, the BBC Light Programme started the nightly fifteen-minute adventures of Dick Barton, Special Agent, an Austerity forerunner to James Bond, introduced by a melodramatic theme tune called "The Devil's Gallop." Mimi remembered how deathly white John's face always went each evening at 6:45 as its frantic strains echoed through the house.

Under the Stanley sisters' mutual support system, he would spend a long holiday in Scotland each summer with his Aunt Mater and Uncle Bert. The high point of his stay was the Edinburgh Tattoo, an extravagant military band display with the city's medieval castle as its dramatic backdrop. Among the redcoated phalanxes playing "Annie Laurie" or "Scotland the Brave," there would sometimes be an American Air Force band in the Glenn Miller mold that—as John later recalled—"swung like shit." He never forgot his emotion during the Tattoo's closing ritual, when all the lights went out and a lone set of bagpipes wheezed and wailed its valediction for another year.

Mendips, of course, boasted nothing so newfangled and showy as a television set. The only wireless stood on the morning-room sideboard: an imposing artifact with a lacquered wood cabinet, gold knobs, and a dial that could theoretically find European stations like Limoges and Hilversum. Kindly Uncle George wired it to an extension speaker in John's room so he could listen while lying in bed. But that was mainly to the comedy shows that came after his 7:30 lights-out—*Take It from Here*, *Variety Bandbox*, *Much-Binding in the Marsh*, or *Stand Easy*. His favorite was *Life with the Lyons*, a sitcom about an American family in London, featuring the thirties' screen stars Bebe Daniels and Ben Lyon with their real-life children, Barbara and Richard.

Aged seven or eight, he took up the mouth organ, just as both his parents, not to mention several of his uncles, had done at roughly similar ages. The epiphany occurred when a medical student who was boarding at Mendips casually took one of the little silver oblongs from his pocket and blew a few notes on it, to John's huge fascination. The student offered to buy him a mouth organ of his own, provided he learned to play a tune on this one by the next morning. John disappeared with it and in no time had learned to play two.

The mouth organ revealed that he had a natural musical ear just like his mother's, his father's, and most of those unknown Lennon uncles. He soon outgrew his first cheap little instrument, graduating to a chromatic model—with a sliding bar for changing key— and buying a teach-yourself manual, *The Right Way to Play Chromatic Harmonica*, by Captain James Reilly. With Captain Reilly's help, he mastered dozens of tunes, from old English airs like "Greensleeves" to film music like the theme from *Moulin Rouge*. Traveling by Ribble Company bus from Liverpool up to Mater's in Edinburgh, he sometimes would hardly stop playing for the whole six-hour ride. On one of these journeys, the driver offered to give him a mouth organ that had been left behind by a previous passenger if he would come to the Edinburgh bus depot next day to collect it. John kept the appointment, chaperoned by his cousin Stanley, and duly received a magnificent top-of-the-line chromatic Hohner. "I believe it was the same mouth organ he played on his records," Stanley says.

He quickly progressed to tinkering on any piano he encountered, at school or in friends' houses, discovering the same instant facility in his fingers as on his lips. But Mimi, so indulgent in every other way, refused his plea to have his own piano at Mendips. "I wouldn't have it," she remembered. " 'We're not going down that road, John,' I told him. 'None of that common sing-song stuff in here.' "

In the house overlooking Mendips's back garden lived Ivan Vaughan, a Dovedale Primary classmate whom John had instantly dubbed Ivy. The two would communicate with whistles or on scraps of paper stuffed into tin cans and swung back and forth by the rope that hung from John's tree house. A few doors along from Ivan in Vale Road lived Nigel Walley, a cheerful, enthusiastic boy John had met while briefly attending Mosspits Lane school. Nigel, too, became his eager follower, receiving the nickname Walloggs.

The favorite meeting place for local children was a dirt field known as the Tip, in prewar years the site of an artificial lake. It was here that John first encountered a fellow seven-year-old whose rubicund face was topped by a mat of curly hair so sandy pale as to be almost albino. His name was Pete Shotton.

Pete had previously regarded Ivan and Nigel as his gang, and felt some hostility to the kid from Menlove Avenue who seemed to be taking them over. Discovering that John's middle name was Winston, he began taunting him as "Winnie, Winnie, Winnie!" The resultant scuffle ended with Pete on the ground on his back and John kneeling on his shoulders, pinning down his arms. There John was willing to let matters rest so long as Pete promised never again to call him Winnie. Pete gave his promise and was released—but, once at a safe distance, broke out again with "Winnie, Winnie, Winnie!" John was at first so angry that he couldn't speak. Then, at the sheer effrontery of it, his face broke into a grin. He had found his first soul mate.

In those days, children roamed freely out of doors for hours on end without their families needing to feel the least anxiety. And Woolton and its environs offered many inviting places for John and his friends to explore. Across from the Tip was a rugged open space called Foster's Field, with thickets of blackberry bushes and a pond where they caught tadpoles, newts, and frogs and paddled a home-made raft. There were meadows that frothed creamily with cow parsley in summer, and tracts of dense woodland haunted by cuckoos and corncrakes. Calderstones Park and Reynolds Park lay within easy walking distance, as did the grounds of Strawberry Field and of a vanished stately home named Allerton Towers. On the opposite side of Menlove Avenue from Mendips stretched the greens and bunkers of Allerton Golf Course.

Their games were fueled by make-believe, demanding vigorous activity rather than the modern child's sedentary trance. The favorite of all was cowboys and Indians, with the participants shooting each other and falling down "dead" with no conception of pain, and Native Americans cast as villains in obedience to Hollywood mythology. But John's version was different. "He always wanted to be the Indian," Mimi recalled. "That was typical John, to support the underdog. And because he was leader of his little group, the Indians always won." Rather than white Western icons like Buffalo Bill or Wild Bill Hickok, his hero was Sioux Chief Sitting Bull. Mimi would stain his face with gravy browning and daub it with lipstick for war paint. From their local butcher's shop she begged cock-pheasant feathers to make him a chief's headdress. "He loved it, . . . he never took it off. I can see him in it now, dancing around Pete Shotton, tied to a tree in our garden."

The center of Woolton village, socially as well as spiritually, was its Anglican church, St. Peter's, a sandstone edifice with a square Norman-style clock tower. John attended Sunday school in its church hall, as did Pete, Ivy, and Walloggs, plus a boy named Rod Davis from King's Drive and a precociously pretty little girl named Barbara Baker. On leaving home after Sunday lunch, they would each be given a few pennies to put into the collection plate or the cottage-shaped money box for Dr. Barnardo's homes. At John's instigation, they spent the money on chewing gum instead, masticating it showily through their couple of hours' Bible study.

His pure treble singing voice quickly won him a place in the church choir, to which Nigel Walley also belonged. At first, he seemed to enjoy the ritual of dressing up in a white surplice and turning out for services twice every Sunday as well as Saturday weddings, which meant a half crown (12.5p) payment for each chorister. He was also mysteriously drawn to St. Peter's little churchyard (or the bone orchard, as he called it) where mossy, weather-beaten tombstones traced Woolton families back two centuries and more. He would read and reread the etched inscriptions with their familiar local names, their forgotten tragedies between the lines, and their comforting euphemisms for death:

Also ELEANOR RIGBY

THE BELOVED WIFE OF THOMAS WOODS

AND GRANDDAUGHTER OF THE ABOVE

DIED 10TH OCTOBER 1939, AGED 44 YEARS

ASLEEP

Mimi would later remember how comforted John seemed by the notion in Eleanor Rigby's epitaph that "it wasn't gone forever . . . just asleep."

The rector of St. Peter's was a middle-aged Welsh bachelor named Morris Pryce-Jones, known to his younger parishioners as Pricey. Far from the grim stereotype of his native land, Pricey was a kindly and tolerant man, prepared for boys to be boys up to a point. But he was utterly unprepared for boys to be anything like John Lennon. One Sunday during a particularly arduous sermon, John's fellow chorister David Ashton began surreptitiously reading a *Boy Scouts' Pocket Diary*, which included the maxim "A Boy Scout is Thrifty." John produced a pen and altered it to "A Boy Scout is Fifty," sending everyone around them "into tucks"—the Liverpool term for laughter so uncontrollable that it puckers up the entire body as if by some invisible drawstring. Both boys were docked their next wedding payment.

One Sunday school teacher, "Ma" Davies, had an altercation with John during a lesson about Jesus's encounter with the Scribes and Pharisees. So incensed was he by the story that he announced Christ's persecutors "must have been Fascists." Ma Davies told him that Fascists were far worse than Scribes or Pharisees, but John refused to be convinced. The teacher might have given him some credit for such strong emotions on behalf of the Redeemer; instead, she excoriated him for "making trouble" and ordered both him and David Ashton, who had supported him, to report to Pricey for punishment.

Deciding that a mere telling-off would have no effect, the rector decided to take the rare step of caning them. Unfortunately, the nearest to a cane he could find was an umbrella belonging to a female chorister named Bertha Radley, a relative of the Eleanor Rigby memorialized in the churchyard. Her umbrella was an ornate one, covered in crocodile skin, with a handle shaped like a crocodile's head. "John got it first, one on each hand," Ashton remembers. "Then when Pricey hit me, the handle broke off. I remember to this day Bertha saying 'Oh, my poor crocodile!'"

The choicest of this rich crop of misbehavior and insubordination occurred, suitably enough, at Harvest Festival time. Woolton still remained agricultural enough for harvesting to have real significance, and St. Peter's always rose to the occasion, decorating its altar lavishly with grain sheaves and offerings of vegetables and fruit from local greenhouses and garden plots. When Pricey emerged from the vestry to lead the singing of harvest hymns like "We Plough the Fields and Scatter," he found the altar fruit depleted as if by a flock of predatory crows. A glance along the giggling choir stalls was sufficient to identify the pilferer. John was expelled from the choir, and he and Pete Shotton were banned from the church altogether.

Mimi urged him to beg reinstatement, but in vain. "I told him 'It's all part of your education, John.' But he just shouted back 'kayshued-shun, kayshuedshun!' He was always inventing daft words. And he used to make me laugh by taking off the choirmaster—he'd pull a funny face and conduct the cats."

His bedroom, situated directly above the front porch, was a tiny, elongated space, almost filled by single bed with a blue-green canopy, pushed against the right-hand wall. A diminutive clothes cupboard and a table and chair by the window were its only other furniture. John would always classify himself as "a homebody," and this was where he spent as many contented boyhood hours by himself as he did in the open air with his friends. At such times, the house would fall so utterly silent that Mimi presumed he was out. Then she'd push open his bedroom door and find him on his bed with a book, in a position of seeming perverse discomfort. He would lie flat with his body twisted around and his legs resting up the wall. All his life, he could never fully savor print without first folding himself into that awkward hairpin shape.

He had caught Mimi's love of reading—though with John it was always to be more like an insatiable physical hunger. Years later, his aunt would mimic the half-truculent way he used to scoop a volume from a shelf and turn away, his eyes already devouring the print like twin piranhas. Children's literature in the early fifties offered a limited choice compared with what would come later—A. A. Milne's *Winnie-the-Pooh*, Kenneth Grahame's *The Wind in the Willows*, Arthur Ransome's *Swallows and Amazons*, Hugh Lofting's adventures of Doctor Dolittle. The genre was dominated by Enid Blyton, with her prolific adventures of the Famous Five and the Secret Seven and her chronicles of the girls' boarding schools Mallory Towers and St. Clare's. Lying on his red quilt, with his feet higher than his head, John read them all.

The two outstanding favorites of his youngest years were Lewis Carroll's *Alice's Adventures in Wonderland* and *Through the Looking-Glass*. He loved the pure anarchy that lay behind their prim Victorian facade, the incessant punning and spoonerizing, the lunatic logic, always spelled out in flawless syntax and perfect scansion; the songs whose hypnotically simple refrains ("Will you, won't you, will you, won't you, will you join the dance? . . .") needed no setting to music. In Carroll's fabulous bestiary, if he had known it, lay several future incarnations of himself—the hyperactive Mad Hatter, the sleepy Dormouse, the Caterpillar puffing smugly on its hookah, the derisively grinning Cheshire Cat, Alice herself, as she experiments with life-transforming pills and potions, the Walrus, on that nightmare beach where the sun never goes down, sweet-talking a school of baby oysters into becoming hors d'oeuvres. Most influential of all was the mock-epic poem entitled "Jabberwocky"—to the boy with his legs up the wall, nothing less than a tutorial in how nonsense can be made infinitely more descriptive than sense:

> 'Twas brillig, and the slithy toves
> Did gyre and gimble in the wabe:
> All mimsy were the borogoves,
> And the mome raths outgrabe. . . .

Through the Looking-Glass ends with a little known coda, which runs:

> A boat beneath a sunny sky
> Lingering onward dreamily
> In an evening of July . . .
>
> Still she haunts me, phantomwise,
> Alice moving under skies
> Never seen by waking eyes.

Twenty-five years in the future, there would be a song about that same phantom girl, that same "boat on the river," and "marmalade skies" recalling the Orange Marmalade jar Alice sees during her fall into the White Rabbit's burrow.

At the opposite end of the scale, he devoured the weekly boys' comics that existed in huge quantity in the early fifties, from the *Rover*, *Wizard*, and *Hotspur*, which contained serial stories (usually about wartime Nazis going "Himmel!" and "Donner und Blitzen!") to the all-cartoon periodicals the *Beano*, the *Dandy*, *Radio Fun*, *Film Fun*, and *Knockout*. Along with sweets and picturedromes, Mimi had forbidden him comics, except perhaps the high-minded *Eagle* (edited by a clergyman), but his Uncle George would defy the Look by smuggling *Beano*s or *Dandy*s up to him—and in any case they were freely available at the homes of his friends.

He would write his own adventure stories, like the ones in *Wizard* and *Hotspur*, but with himself as their hero, and invent his own cartoon strips like the ones in the *Beano* and *Knockout*. At the age of seven, he handwrote and drew a whole magazine entitled "Speed and Sport Illustrated" by J. W. Lennon, with portraits of soccer players in action, cartoon strips, and the beginning of an adventure serial. "If you liked this," the first installment ended, "Come again next week. It'll be even better." But of all the diverse high and low cultural sources that fed his imagination—and shaped his character forever—none could compare with William Brown.

William was the creation of Richmal Crompton Lamburn (1890–1969), a Lancashire classics teacher who switched to writing under the name Richmal Crompton after being stricken by polio. Her eleven-year-old hero had originally been intended for an adult readership, but children quickly latched on to him, ensuring his continuance through thirty-seven story collections. William was the archetypal naughty small boy in the innocent decades before vandalism, mugging, joyriding, and alcopops changed the agenda. Incorrigibly noisy and untidy, his pockets bulging with catapults, marbles, and live frogs, he is the bane of his conventional parents, his uptight older brother and sister, and every schoolteacher, clergyman, and nervous elderly spinster in his orbit. He has three companions, Ginger, Douglas, and Henry, with whom, in a gang known

as the Outlaws, he roams the countryside, trespassing, birdsnest-
ing, playing Red Indians, waging guerrilla war against his sworn
enemy, Hubert Lane, and dodging his besotted follower, a prototype
groupie named Violet Elizabeth Bott. The Outlaws form an unbreak-
able blood-brotherhood against repressive and pompous adults: they
have their own private language, secret signs, and sacred rituals, and
their own cavernous hideout-cum-auditorium, the Old Barn.

William is a many-sided character: a leader whose authority over
his followers is absolute; a daydreamer who imagines exotic careers
as a big-game hunter, secret agent, or circus clown; a virtuoso of
scorn and sarcasm and an inventive liar; an exhibitionist, given to
singing at the top of his voice, playing mouth organs and trumpets
at top volume, dressing up in exotic clothes, and wearing elaborate
false beards and mustaches; a hustler, forever trying to raise money
for new water pistols or cricket bats; a tender-hearted animal lover;
a tireless novelty seeker and observer of new trends and fashions; an
indefatigable writer of lurid stories, dramas, and poems in his own
individual spelling; and organizer of plays, shows, and exhibitions in
his bedroom or the Old Barn. His greatest joy is to escape from his
own genteel environment and run around with "vulgar" working-
class children, swapping his nice clothes for their scruffy ones and
trying to imitate the fascinating crudeness of their speech. His spirits
are never lower than when he is discovered among these unsuitable
companions and restored to the outraged bosom of his family.

Having gobbled up the few red clothbound William books on
Mimi's bookshelf, John began to collect them, following their hero
through the twenties, thirties, and Second World War to the threshold of the space age. He loved the caustic prose style, which made no
concession to young readers, freely using words such as *inamorata*
and *rhododendron*, yet always sided with William against a largely risible grown-up community of choleric retired colonels, ditzy vicars'
wives, dimwitted policemen, and sandal-wearing vegetarians. William's world, moreover, was uncannily like the one that John himself inhabited—same "village" surrounded by countryside, same
genteel home with servants' bells. He identified totally with William's rebelliousness, his audacity, his humor, his flights of fantasy,

his need always to be the kingpin yet always to have companions, his share-and-share-alike generosity, his proneness to hilarious misspellings and mispronunciations, even his preference for Red Indians over cowboys and addiction to playing the mouth organ. And it was William who inspired him to create his first gang of four, united against the world.

The Outlaws have an unchanging hierarchy, with William at the top, supported by his "boon companion," Ginger, and Henry and Douglas forming a less essential second division. In John's Vale Road following, Ivy Vaughan and Nigel "Walloggs" Walley corresponded to Henry and Douglas, while albino-blond Pete Shotton, his prime accomplice and audience, was a natural Ginger.

With John as their leader, they devoted after-school hours, weekends, and holidays to reincarnating William and the Outlaws in Woolton. Many of their escapades were dastardly only in their own eyes—walking on grass in defiance of KEEP OFF THE GRASS signs, entering and exiting wherever NO ENTRY or NO EXIT was proclaimed, drinking from taps marked NOT DRINKING WATER, and—in the words of their Sunday school classmate Rod Davis—"running into Marks and Spencer's and shouting 'Woolworths!'" At other times, they flouted authority and risked life and limb in ways that would have caused apoplexy in their respective homes. One of their favorite games was to hang on behind the trams that clanked up and down Menlove Avenue. Another was to climb a tree over a busy main road and play a version of Chicken with the double-decker buses passing beneath. When a bus approached, one of them would poke a leg into its path and dangle it there until the last possible moment before impact. Whoever kept his nerve for longest was the winner. If anyone's shoe actually touched the bus roof, that counted as bonus points.

Lennon's gang, as people soon took to calling them, became the curse of a district otherwise blessedly free from persecution or disturbance. They trespassed on Allerton Golf Course, annoying the grave businessmen at play there and conducting riotous games of their own. They crept in through the back entrances of cinemas without paying and disrupted performances until ejected by furious usherettes. Their "scrumping" of apples from other people's gardens became so pestilential that one enraged grower appeared with a shotgun and fired both barrels at John's fleeing form.

Like William, he became a Boy Scout, joining the 3rd Allerton troop, but also like William, he had little time for the Scout code of duty and respectfulness. David Ashton, his companion in the troop's "Badgers" section, recalls the alternative marching chorus he encouraged the others to sing as they tramped along in their shorts, bush hats, and neckerchiefs: "We are the Third! The mad Third! We come from ALLeerTON and we are MAD! MAD!"

A frequent background for William's and the Outlaws' adventures are summer fetes and garden parties. Their Woolton disciples, too, were invariably to be found when some local church or institution set out its innocent fund-raising paraphernalia of raffia stalls, lucky dips, and kiddies' fancy-dress parades. They would sneak into the tents where home-made cakes and pies or lovingly nurtured raspberries awaited the judges' inspection, and make off with whatever they fancied. Once stuffed to the gills, they would entertain themselves by mocking the well-meaning people who were attempting to raise money for good causes, and the families innocently enjoying themselves. Nigel Walley has a mirthful recollection of one garden fete "run by the nuns" where they spotted a group of monks seated together on a bench. "Somehow John got hold of this robe and dressed himself up as a monk. He was sitting with the other monks, talking to them in all these funny words while we were rolling about under the tent, in tucks."

The portrayal, however, contained one major departure from character. Whereas William, for all his lawlessness, never stoops to intentional larceny, John—egged on, as always, by Pete—became a habitual and dedicated shoplifter. Confectioners in those days would often trustingly display sweets and chocolate on their counters in open boxes or arranged in glass dishes with paper doilies. "We'd go into this certain place that was run by a little old lady," Nigel Walley remembers. "John'd point to things he said he wanted on the top shelf, and all the time he'd be filling his pockets from the counter. He did the same at a shop that sold Dinky Toys in Woolton, opposite the Baths. He'd put a tractor or a little car in his pocket while the bloke was looking the other way. We went back to that same shop later, but this time John hadn't got his glasses on. He couldn't understand why his fingers couldn't get at the Dinky cars. He couldn't see that the bloke had covered them with a sheet of glass."

Mimi was generous with pocket money, giving John a weekly allowance of five shillings (the same amount received by William's pampered arch-foe, Hubert Lane), on condition that he did certain household jobs, such as mowing the lawn. Like William, he shared whatever he had with his "boon companions." He found it impossible to hang on to money, just as he would all his life; nor was he willing to earn a bonus by legitimate means. The one time he ever received physical chastisement from Mimi was when she found he'd stolen some cash from her handbag. "I was always taking a little, for soft things like Dinkies," he would recall. "This day I must have taken too much."

In contrast with his kind heart and impulsive generosity, he could show a lack of sensitivity and compassion that even roistering Liverpool boys sometimes felt to be going too far. This was not an era of verbal tact toward the physically and mentally handicapped, but John seemed to find all forms of affliction hilarious. His drawings teemed with hideously misshapen, obese, or skeletal figures, endowed with too few or too many limbs and covered with warts or sores. A blind person tapping along with a white stick, or a child-on-crutches collection box would reduce him to giggles—a device with which many people try to disguise fear or repugnance. He often entertained his followers with what they called his "cripple act" when he would shamble and cavort like Quasimodo, grinning with the blank-eyed oblivion of a simpleton and holding one hand crookedly like a claw.

Even then, when nothing in his daily life even hinted at it, he seems to have had premonitions of his strange destiny, almost as if his grandmother Polly's reputed psychic powers were reaching out to him, too. So vivid and exciting were his dreams that he looked forward to going to sleep in his red-quilted bed almost as much as to a theatrical performance or movie. As he later remembered, he always dreamed in brilliant color and weird shapes that gave his subsequent first encounters with painters like Salvador Dalí and Hieronymus Bosch the shock of déjà vu.

The most prophetic of his dreams recurred time and again. In one, he was circling in an airplane above Liverpool, looking down at the Mersey, the docks, and the twin Liver Birds on their towers, climbing higher and higher with each circuit until the city disappeared from view. In another, he was engulfed by seas of half crowns, the big old predecimal silver coins with milled edges that used to be worth 12.5p but had purchasing power equal to £5 today. In yet another, he recalled "finding lots of money in old houses—as much of the stuff as I could carry. I used to put it in my pockets and in my hands and in sacks, and I could still never carry as much as I wanted."

In 1951, two new Liverpool University students arrived at Mendips to share the bay-windowed room next to John's. One of them was a nineteen-year-old biochemistry student from Leeds named Michael Fishwick, the other a medical student named John Ellison. Fishwick was to become Mimi's favorite paying guest—though as yet neither of them dreamed what that would ultimately entail—and, from his privileged insider's position, was to share in both the great tragedies of John's childhood.

The boarders paid £3 5s—which, as Fishwick remembers, was "slightly above the odds"—for their accommodation and (very good) meals on the gateleg table in the morning room, which Mimi always served in a sitting apart from George and John. He recalls John as a friendly, "malleable" boy, whose behavior at home gave little hint of the tearaway he was outside, and who spent most of his time reading or drawing pictures of "wart-infested trolls" or caricatures of the new lodgers. Both students at this point seemed to be equally in Mimi's favor for their good manners, their upmarket love of rugby football, and their willingness to help out with the gardening, sometimes aided by a reluctant John. The pair would take him out for the day, their usual destination Hoylake on the Cheshire Wirral, where the shipping consisted of graceful white-sailed yachts rather than the Mersey's dredgers and tugs.

Even the family circumstances that singled him out from other boys seemed in those days more a bonus than a deprivation. With Mimi taking care of him, his mother close at hand, his three other aunts in ever-dependable backup, John lived in an atmosphere of feminine admiration and solicitude, petted and lionized even more than the youngest of his cousins. He had somehow realized that Mimi's title to him was only of the most tenuous, unofficial kind; as time passed, he became adept at exploiting her constant fear of losing him. If aunt and nephew had a particularly explosive argument, over the state of John's room, for instance, he would stomp off to Julia's in Allerton for the night, sometimes the whole weekend, throwing dark hints over his shoulder that he might never come back again.

The little council "semi" at 1 Blomfield Road where Julia lived with Bobby Dykins could not have been more a contrast to Mendips. For Julia shared none of her eldest sister's devotion to tidiness, routine, and domestic protocol. At Julia's one did not have to wipe one's feet or hang up one's coat in the proper place; meals kept no fixed schedule, but might appear on the table at any time. "That's not to say she wasn't a good housekeeper," her niece, Liela, remembers. "There was always a stew or a casserole on the stove. And if anyone came to the door when we were about to sit down, an extra place would automatically be laid."

John seemed to feel no jealousy of the two half sisters, Julia and Jackie, who enjoyed his mother's attention seven days a week; they in turn regarded him as a big brother, nicknamed him Stinker, bounced up and down on him in the morning as he lay in bed, and loved the tales of monsters and Mersey mermaids he told them, and the dancing skeletons he would cut out of paper. "Julia always made it clear how much she adored him," Liela says. "She had photographs of him all over the house." Just the same, he would have been conscious at every minute that she was no longer really his.

Julia was one of the first in John's circle to have television, another powerful reason to visit her. In those times, anyone so blessed was under obligation to invite friends and neighbors to "look in," as the phrase went, filling their living rooms with extra seats, extinguishing lights and drawing blinds to create a cinemalike darkness. Early television variety shows sometimes featured elderly survivors of the music hall and even the minstrel eras—Hetty King, singing "All the Nice Girls Love a Sailor"; Leslie Hutchinson, aka Hutch, who had first popularized Alf Lennon's beloved "Begin the Beguine"; and Robb Wilton, the Liverpool-born "confidential comic" whose quavery monologues always began "The day war broke out . . ." Julia's favorite was George Formby, a chipper Lancastrian with an outsize grin who strummed a banjolele while singing songs of innocent double entendre about Chinese laundries and window washers. "Judy adored Formby, and John caught it from her," Liela says. "I remember one day when he was on TV, and the money in the electric meter suddenly ran out, Judy almost went mad."

At Julia's, the wireless was always on, tuned to the Light Programme and blaring out the dance music that Mimi could not abide. She also had a gramophone and came home almost every week with a brand-new 78 rpm single in its dull brown wrapper. Thanks to her, John knew everything that was happening on Britain's early pop music chart—called the Top 12 before it became the Top 20—in particular, whenever the effortless dominance of American performers like Guy Mitchell and Nat King Cole was briefly broken by some homegrown upstart like Ruby Murray or Dickie Valentine.

In the very early fifties, the blood of a British boy was most likely to be stirred by Frankie Laine, who sang suboperatic arias with cowboy themes, like "Ghost Riders in the Sky" and "Gunfight at OK Corral." John relished the over-the-top showmanship of Laine and also of Johnnie Ray, who wore a hearing aid and ostentatiously burst into tears during his big hit, "Cry." Surprisingly, though, the hardcase Woolton Outlaw also liked sentimental ballads, even when sung by the "old groaner," Bing Crosby. One Crosby song included a play on words that instantly stuck to the flypaper of his mind: "Please . . . lend your little ears to my pleas . . . Please hold me tight in your arms . . ."

During John's visits, Julia was always the bright, carefree, funloving person he looked on more as an elder sister than a mother. But after he had gone, her daughter Julia remembers, she would sit down in the suddenly quiet living room, open up the gramophone, and put on the record that, for obvious reasons, was her favorite one

of all: "My Son John," by the British tenor David Whitfield. During
the climactic closing verse, with its eerily accurate prophecies—"My
son John . . . who will fly someday . . . have a wife someday . . . and a
son someday . . ." her eyes would fill with tears, as though, somehow
or other, she guessed she would never see it.

4

SHORTSIGHTED JOHN WIMPLE LENNON

I thought, "I'm a genius or I'm mad. Which is it?"

These were days when the Eleven Plus examination regulated every British child's progress through the state educational system like traffic lights, sending the brightest to grammar schools and the less bright to either secondary modern or technical schools. Throughout John's latter years at Dovedale Primary, as he would recall, the idea had been ceaselessly drummed into him that "if you don't pass the Eleven Plus you're finished in life . . . So that was the only exam I ever passed, because I was terrified."

For boys who brought such distinction on themselves and their families, the traditional reward was a brand-new bicycle. Uncle George, in no doubt that John would sail through, had picked out a bike for him long before the joyous news reached Mendips. It was an emerald green Raleigh Lenton—almost his own surname—fitted with luxurious extras like a Sturmey-Archer three-speed gear, a dynamo-operated front lamp, and a matching green leather saddle-bag. True to the spirit of their extended family, John's cousin Liela could not be allowed to feel left out, so Mimi and George bought her a new bicycle at the same time.

John's achievement gave him the pick of several excellent grammar schools in central and suburban Liverpool. Mimi's choice was Quarry Bank High School on Harthill Road, an easy bicycle ride from Mendips via the path across Calderstones Park. He started there at the beginning of the 1952 autumn term, shortly before his twelfth birthday.

Quarry Bank's designation as a "high school" implied no affinity with the mixed-gender informality of American high schools but rather was a subtle hint of elevation above other boys' grammar schools in the vicinity. Founded in 1922, it took its name from the local sandstone quarries that had begotten so many major Liverpool buildings, including the Anglican cathedral. The school itself was housed in an ornately neo-Gothic sandstone mansion, built in 1867 by a wealthy merchant named John Bland. Although part of the state system, and charging no fees, it modeled itself on a high-echelon school like Harrow or Winchester, with black-gowned masters, a house system, and a general air of tradition and antiquity.

Tuition might be gratis, but each pupil's family was expected to supply the compulsory uniform of black blazer and cap and black-and-gold striped tie. The blazer was an especially natty affair, with its breast-pocket badge of a gold stag's head above the Latin motto *Ex Hoc Metallo Virtutem*—"from this rough metal [comes forth] manhood." The cuffs were decorated like those of a junior naval officer, with a raised black stripe surmounted by a ring of gold stags' heads. The blazers were costly enough when bought from the school's official outfitter, Wareings in Smithdown Road. Mimi, however, preferred to have John's made to measure by his Uncle George's tailor for the whopping sum of £12 apiece, nearly as much as George had paid for the new bike. No real parents could have been more dotingly insistent that he had the best of everything.

The start of a new academic epoch scattered the Woolton Outlaws in widely different directions. Academically gifted and hard-working Ivy Vaughan had won a place at Liverpool Institute, the most renowned of the inner city's grammar schools. Nigel Walley was bound for the Bluecoat School, near Penny Lane, the former Bluecoat Hospital where Alf Lennon had been a pupil thirty years earlier. But happily for John, his arch crony Pete Shotton also had got into Quarry Bank. "We went through it like Siamese twins," Pete would remember. "We started together in our first year at the top and gradually sank together into the sub-basement."

John himself later maintained that he arrived at grammar school determined to do well and be a credit to Mimi and Uncle George. All such good resolutions melted away at his first sight of his new class-mates, tearing and whooping around Quarry Bank's playground. "I thought 'Christ, I'll have to fight my way through this lot, having just made it at Dovedale. There were some real heavies there. The first fight I got in, I lost. I lost my nerve when I really got hurt. If there was a bit of blood, then you packed it in. After that, if I thought someone could punch harder than me, I said, 'OK, we'll have wres-tling instead.' . . . I was aggressive because I wanted to be popular. I wanted to be the leader. It seemed more attractive than just being one of the toffees. I wanted everyone to do what I told them to do, to laugh at my jokes and let me be the boss."

Quarry Bank's founding head, R. F. Bailey, had been an outstand-ing educator with a special talent for spotting the potential in off-beat or eccentric boys. He had retired five years before John's arrival, handing over the reins to an austere ex-serviceman and Methodist lay preacher named Ernest R. Taylor. Quarry Bank pupils of "Ernie" Taylor's era remember him as an unapproachable figure, striding along corridors lost in aloof, headmasterly thought, his black gown billowing out behind him.

As at most boys' school of that era, corporal punishment was rou-tinely administered. Pete Shotton never forgot the first time John and he were called to the head's study to be caned. While they waited outside together, John reduced the nervous Pete to tucks by speculating that the head's cane might be produced like some royal regalia from a case studded with jewels and lined with velvet. They were called in separately to receive their punishment, John going first. A few moments later, the door opened and he emerged on his hands and knees, groaning melodramatically. What Pete didn't realize was that a small lobby lay between the head's study and the corridor, so Ernie was quite unaware of this performance. "I was laughing so much when I went in that I got [the cane] even harder than John had."

The five houses in which the boys were grouped supposedly fostered loyalty and brotherhood as well as giving a competitive edge to sporting activities. Each house was named after one of the adjacent suburbs and consisted only of pupils from that neighborhood, so perpetuating the rivalries and social snobberies that existed between them. Woolton house, which claimed John and Pete, lay about midway in this social microcosm, not quite so select as Childwall or Allerton, but a decided cut above Wavertree and Aigburth.

Also among Quarry Bank's 1952 intake was Rod Davis, their former classmate at St. Peter's Sunday school. All three were put into the "A" stream of boys considered most intelligent and promising of the batch. From there, while Rod went from strength to strength, John and Pete were quickly downgraded to the "B" and thence with minimum delay to the "C" stream, stopping at that point only because there was nowhere lower to go. "I never really understood how that happened," Rod Davis says. "It was always obvious that John was just as bright or a good bit brighter than anyone else around. But right from the beginning it was obvious he'd made up his mind not to subscribe to the system in any way."

A strong contributory factor was his extreme nearsightedness, coupled with his obstinate refusal to wear the glasses he so detested. Rather than risk being taunted as a "four-eyes" or a "drip," he preferred to walk around in a state of such mole-like myopia that he could read the number on a bus stop only by shinning halfway up the pole. Davis, it so happened, had even weaker sight but made sure he missed nothing on the blackboard by reading it through opera glasses. John, however, was content to skulk with Pete Shotton at the back of the room, letting sentences, dates, mathematical equations, and chemical formulae all swim together into the same untranslatable blur.

Pete's analogy with Siamese twins may have been more telling than he knew, for John, the one-off, the super-original, never liked acting alone. As he would prove time and again in the future, to flourish at his most individualistic he needed a partner—a kindred spirit perfectly tuned to his special wavelength, acting simultaneously as a stimulus and an audience. Wherever some school rule was most flagrantly broken, the resultant hue and cry would be after "Lennon and Shotton," which John turned into "Shennon and Lotton" to symbolize their inseparability and unanimity of purpose, or purposelessness. Like two chain-gang escapees handcuffed together, neither of them could do anything without the other helplessly following suit.

Over the following terms, Quarry Bank's punishment book thronged with the diverse crimes of Shennon and Lotton: "Failing to report to school office" . . . "Insolence" . . . "Throwing backboard duster [eraser] out of window" . . . "Cutting class and going AWOL [Absent Without Leave]" . . . "Gambling on school field during house [cricket] match . . ." Sometimes their offenses went off the scale even of Quarry Bank's draconian punishments, leaving Ernie Taylor no choice but to call in their respective families. Back home at Mendips, Mimi grew to dread the peal of the telephone during school hours. "A voice would say, 'Hello, Mrs. Smith, it's the [head's] secretary at Quarry Bank here . . .' 'O Lord,' I'd think. 'What's he done now?'"

The duo were more or less permanently in detention, either writing out hundreds of lines beginning "I must not . . ." or engaged in military-style fatigues around the school grounds. It was during such a work detail that they learned the untruth of the axiom "Crime does not pay." While emptying rubbish into a trash can, Pete came upon three bulky brown envelopes addressed to the headmaster. Inside were used dinner tickets, the vouchers purchased by boys at a shilling apiece to exchange for their school lunch (a meal still commonly known as dinner throughout northern England). Used tickets being indistinguishable from unused ones, Shennon and Lotton could resell the whole cache at sixpence each, a bargain that left the purchaser half his daily lunch allowance to spend as he pleased. "We had fifteen hundred dinner tickets up in John's bedroom," Pete remembered. "They were worth £75, which was like almost £1,000 today. We were rich. We even gave up shoplifting while that was going on."

Any teacher showing less than drill-sergeant ruthlessness could expect no mercy from Shennon and Lotton. One afternoon when they returned to Ernie's study to be carpeted yet again, they found the head absent and his mild little deputy, Ian Gallaway, facing them over the magisterial desk. As Mr. Gallaway bent forward to peer at the punishment book, John began gently tickling the few wisps of hair on the deputy head's cranium. Thinking a fly had landed there, he brushed absentmindedly at it without looking up. "John was laughing so much that he actually pissed himself," Pete Shotton remembered. "Then Gallaway said, 'What's that puddle on the floor?' John said, 'I think the roof must be leaking, Sir.'"

The curious thing about this stubborn ne'er-do-well was that, away from the classroom and its hated compulsion, he was a bookworm whose taste in literature far outpaced Quarry Bank's English syllabus and who, left to his own devices, spent hours in the posture of the most conscientious student, reading, writing, or drawing.

Quarry Bank's head of English, Lancelot ("Porky") Burrows, was never one of his classroom targets and, indeed, regarded him as a stimulus to other pupils rather than a distraction. Porky dealt with John by appealing to his sense of the absurd, for example instituting a punishment known as whistling detention: if John persisted in whistling when told not to, he would be kept in after school and forced to whistle for ten or so fatiguing minutes. Porky also artfully fostered his interest in poetry via his talent for art. An English exercise book from his junior year at Quarry Bank—neatly covered in brown paper and titled MY ANTHOLOGY—demonstrates what pains he would take if his enthusiasm were aroused. Quotations from classic poems like Longfellow's *Song of Hiawatha* and Tennyson's "Morte d'Arthur" are framed by watercolor cartoons showing a remarkable maturity of line and grasp of perspective as well as their unmistakable scatty humor. Porky kept the book to show future generations of juniors the standard they should aim for.

Two comic artists, one British, one American, were to have a profound influence on John's style. He loved the intricate, scratchy technique of Ronald Searle, whose sadistic St. Trinian's schoolgirls were modeled on Searle's guards as a Japanese prisoner of war in Burma. And, thanks to Aunt Mimi, he became a devotee of James Thurber, both the writings for *The New Yorker* and the cartoons, whose surreally wavering lines were a product of Thurber's own near-blindness. John later said he began consciously "Thurberising" his drawings from about the age of fifteen.

He kept a special exercise book for caricatures of his teachers and classmates, organized with a meticulous care that would have astonished Quarry Bank staff other than Porky Burrows. Pete Shotton ("A Simple Hairy Peters") popped up repeatedly, with his pale curls and rosy face, shaking a baby's rattle or peeping from a garbage can. There was even a portrait of the artist himself, wearing his hated National Health glasses and self-deprecatingly captioned "Simply A Simple Pimple Shortsighted John Wimple Lennon." In this case, "Wimple" did not mean a medieval veil but was the name of a character in one of John's favorite radio programs, *Life with the Lyons*.

The book was passed around among John's cronies each time a new character was added to it. Harry Gooseman was once even allowed to take it home overnight to show to his family. John liked to regard it as a campaign of subversion that would bring authority's direst wrath on his head if it were ever discovered. In fact, Quarry Bank's teachers were no less sorely in need of some comic relief than the boys, and they tended to laugh just as loudly if they chanced to see his lampoons of them. One summer term, during preparations for the school's fund-raising garden fete, he even found his subversion co-opted to official ends. Half facetiously he proposed decorating squares of card with caricatures of his teachers, then pinning them up for people to throw darts at—but to his amazement, the idea was accepted. The game attracted a large crowd and Shennon and Lotton were later commended for raising more money than any other stall, despite having kept back £16 of the take for themselves.

Even the po-faced early fifties had not quite extinguished a time-honored British trait, handed on from Lewis Carroll and Edward Lear to W. S. Gilbert and P. G. Wodehouse—that of using all one's intelligence to be unbelievably silly. Until John reached his teens, he was like a prospector, panning through the drab shale of logic and common sense that constituted his daily life at Quarry Bank and Mendips for those few stray, gleaming nuggets of absurdity. The school library introduced him to Stephen Leacock, Canadian author of "nonsense novels" like *Q: A Psychic Pstory of the Psupernatural* and *Sorrows of a Supersoul, or the Memoirs of Marie Mushenough (Translated out of the Original Russian by Machinery)*. Early children's television programs featured occasional appearances by "Professor" Stanley Unwin, a pious-looking man who told fairy stories in innuendo-laced gibberish, such as "Goldiloppers and the Three Bearlodes." English lessons at Quarry Bank provided an unexpected seam in the Middle English of Geoffrey Chaucer's *Canterbury Tales* ("When that Aprille with his shoures soote . . .") so often like Stanley Unwin speaking from the fourteenth century.

All this was mere marginalia, however, in comparison with *The Goon Show*, which had begun its first series on BBC radio in 1951 but hit full stride in 1953, the year of Queen Elizabeth II's coronation. Scripted almost single-handedly by a sometime jazz musician named Spike Milligan, it superficially harked back to the Second World War (*Goons* had been Allied prisoners' nickname for their German guards) and to a Conan Doyle-esque world of spies, intrigue, and derring-do. But in content, it was mold-breakingly anarchic, a mélange of demented voices and lunatic situations such as had never before been offered to a British audience, least of all on the sanctified airwaves of the BBC.

Together with a little-known variety comedian named Peter Sellers, Milligan created a gallery of characters who often seemed to have only the most nodding acquaintance with the human race—the decrepit Colonel Bloodnok, the quavery duo of Henry Crun and Minnie Bannister, the moronic Eccles, the supersmooth Grytpype-Thynne, the whining hermaphrodite Bluebottle. Embedded in the madness like hooks in blubber were jibes against previously inviolable national institutions such as the army, the church, the Foreign Office, and even the BBC itself (which the corporation, amazingly, never noticed).

The Goons' most besotted fans were middle-class preadolescent schoolboys, those overserious war babies who had hitherto believed the oppressive sanity of life to be everlasting. For John, between 1953 and 1955, they were the brightest spot in his whole existence. Nothing could unstick him from the wireless on evenings when the cut-glass voice of announcer Wallace Greenslade presaged another Milligan free-form fantasy such as "Her" (a parody of H. Rider Haggard's *She*) or "The Sinking of Westminster Pier," featuring Minnie and Henry as oyster-sexers, with frantic musical interludes by Dutch harmonica player Max Geldray. John could do the voices and catchphrases of every character, from Minnie's senile gurgle to Bluebottle's scandalized shrieks of "I do not like dis game," "Dirty, rotten swine!," and "You deaded me!"

As the terms passed, "Cutting class and going AWOL" became an ever more frequent charge against Shennon and Lotton in Quarry Bank's punishment book. The bicycles that had been a reward for scholastic excellence allowed them to escape far from the school precincts and any likelihood of detection. By their third year, they had discovered smoking, a habit then practiced almost universally by adults and attended by no health warnings. The usual routine was to filch a packet of Wild Woodbines or Players Weights from some unsuspecting tobacconist, then repair to Reynolds or Calderstones Park, rest their bikes on the grass, and smoke all ten "ciggies" at one go, while John blew salvoes on his mouth organ or shouted in Bloodnok or Bluebottle voices at passers-by or the ducks on the lake.

He was not irrevocably twinned with Pete Shotton. Sometimes on weekends or in the school holidays, he would forsake Pete and his Raleigh Lenton and go for a long bus ride by himself, past the Penny Lane roundabout and through the descending suburbs into central Liverpool. His usual destination was the Kardomah coffeehouse in Whitechapel, where he had a favorite stool at the ledge along the street window. He would sit there for so many hours, sketching in his book and on the steamed-up window or, as he put it, "just watching the world go by," that Mimi nicknamed him the Kardomah Kid.

To Mimi, his drawings and poems were no more than time-wasting distractions from schoolwork. Often he would come home and find she had conducted a guerrilla raid on his bedroom and thrown every piece of paper she could find into the kitchen wastebin. There would a furious argument in which even his usual ally, Uncle George, dared not take his side. "I used to say [to Mimi] 'You've thrown my fuckin' poetry out and you'll regret it when I'm famous,'" John remembered. "I never forgave her for not treating me like a fuckin' genius."

Prior to John's fifteenth year, the British had regarded the process of growing up as perfectly straightforward. The system was that children went on being children until puberty was well advanced; then, virtually overnight, they turned into grown-ups, wearing the same kind of clothes as their parents, aspiring to the same values, and seeking the same amusements. The effect of rioting hormones on immature and impressionable minds had yet to be studied in any depth by scientists or sociologists. The continuance of wartime's mass conscription claimed all able-bodied males at age eighteen and put them through two years of military discipline that, in most cases, left a permanent mark. Only university students, then accounting for just 2 percent of young people, were permitted an interlude of free will and indulgence—even some public unruliness—before assuming the burdens of adulthood.

American films made John and his friends enviously familiar with a society that, on the contrary, recognized the years between thirteen and twenty as a distinct season of life and catered to it with superabundant lavishness. A blissful interlude it seemed, with its open-to-all college campuses, its high schools so very different from Quarry Bank, its giant-lettered boys' jerseys, its girls' ponytails, its hamburgers, Coca-Cola, cheerleaders, and hops. Long before it had any personal relevance for him, John had picked up on the fundamental cultural difference: "America had teenagers. . . . Everywhere else just had people."

American young people as Hollywood projected them—which, of course, meant young white people—had always been gee-whiz happy and healthy-minded and, if possible, even more respectful and conformist than their British counterparts. But since the war, ominous cracks had begun to appear in this cornerstone of the American Dream. Nineteen fifty-one saw publication of J. D. Salinger's *Catcher in the Rye*, a novel written in the voice of a seventeen-year-old boy,

Holden Caulfield, alternately mocking and reviling the Utopia into which he had been born. In 1953 came *The Wild One*, a film about the terrorizing of a small town by a group of leather-clad teenage motor-cyclists (collectively known as the Beetles). "What are you rebelling against?" a woman character demands of the young Marlon Brando as the pack's leader. "Whaddaya got?" he replies.

All these vague, discontented mutters and hormonal stirrings first took definite shape in James Dean, a young stage actor from the Midwest, schooled with Brando in the Method technique and then picked up by Hollywood. Gaunt and melancholic, Dean was the first star with specific appeal to teenagers of the new troubled and troublesome variety. He wore their to-hell-with-it uniform of T-shirts and shabby jeans, suffered their same agonies of uncertainty and hypersensitivity, spoke in their same surly or shy mumble. Their feeling of alienation from a seemingly bountiful and indulgent world was perfectly expressed in *Rebel Without a Cause*, the 1955 film that was both Dean's apotheosis and farewell. That same year, he died in an auto accident in his Porsche sports car, thereby achieving im-mortality.

In Britain also, the postwar years had seen rising concern over what was still patronizingly termed "the younger generation." Juve-nile crime increasingly dominated newspaper headlines, from the Craig-Bentley murder case (in which a London policeman's sixteen-year-old killer was judged too young to face otherwise automatic capital punishment) to the rise of so-called coshboys (young men who carried blackjacks almost like a fashion accessory) as a threat to formerly safe urban streets.

But the first generalized outbreak of deviancy among the younger generation occurred in no place more sinister than tailors' fitting rooms. During 1955, a proportion of British youths rejected the tweed jackets and baggy gray flannels prescribed for them almost by statute, and took to going about in knee-length coats with black velvet collars, frilled shirts, leopardskin waistcoats, bootlace ties, ankle-hugging "drainpipe" trousers, fluorescent orange or lime green socks, and chukka boots raised on two inches of spongy rubber. The style being reminiscent of Edwardian dress, its adherents were dubbed Teddy

Boys, though dandified Wild West heroes like Wyatt Earp or Wild Bill Hickok also represented a strong influence. Their most radical departure from convention was their hair—no longer planed into an army-style short back and sides and flattened with Brylcreem, but blow-dried into a flossy forelock, backswept over long sideburns, and interleaved at the rear into a D.A., or duck's arse.

Teddy Boys were exclusively working-class young men who by rights should have been welcomed as symbols of growing national affluence. Since no men's outfitters stocked such outlandish garments, they had to be expensively tailor-made, often to the client's own design. Unfortunately, some (though by no means all) of these style pioneers were also apt to get into street brawls, using weapons like coshes, brass knuckles, and bicycle chains. As a result, for a decade to come, unusual suits and long hair would be synonymous in the British mind with proletarian criminality and riot.

In Woolton, John and his circle were too young—albeit by just a whisker—to be swept up in James Dean mania or join the first blow wave of Teddy Boys. For John, the latter were no more than comic curiosities to be recorded in his sketchbook (like a Scotsman with a "drainpipe kilt"). Liverpool "Teds" took their reputation as hard men with special seriousness, none more so than John's old Dovedale Primary schoolfellow Jimmy Tarbuck, now very big and tough and disinclined to any humor where his wardrobe was concerned. "We were all dead scared of Tarbuck," Len Garry remembers. He'd only got to say 'Are you looking at me?' and we'd run . . . John the fastest of all."

Woolton did not offer much encouragement to would-be Teddy Boys. The village's two barber's shops, Ashcroft's and Dicky Jones's, both treated their teenage clientele merely as so many sheep to be sheared. John and his friends preferred to have their hair cut at Bioletti, in the little parade of shops off the Penny Lane roundabout. The proprietor and sole operator was an elderly Italian who had also cut John's father's hair—though John had no idea of this— when Alf Lennon was at the Bluecoat Hospital, thirty years earlier. Signor Bioletti's hands were famously shaky, but his trembling scissors would make at least a stab at more modish styles. And in his shop window—as a song would one day commemorate—were head shots of satisfied customers triumphantly coiffured like James Dean, Tony Curtis, or Jeff Chandler.

One sunny evening during that June of 1955, Mendips's most regular boarder, Michael Fishwick, was finishing supper in the morning room, and Uncle George was due to take his place at the table before starting night-watchman duty at the Bear Brand factory. Suddenly, as Fishwick recalls, there was "a terrible bang on the stairs." On his way down, George had collapsed from what the biochemistry student recognized as massive internal bleeding. He was rushed to Smithdown Road Hospital but died soon after admission; the cause was given as a hemorrhage of the liver.

John was away in Scotland with Aunt Mater and Uncle Bert, and knew nothing of what had happened until his return home a couple of days later. As Mimi would remember, "He came bouncing in, his usual excitable self, and asked where George was. When I told him he was dead [John] just went very quiet. He didn't cry or anything like that. He just went up to his room. If there was any crying to do, he would do it on his own. He wouldn't want anyone else to see him like that."

The family member thought best suited to keep John company at such a devastating moment was his Aunt Harrie's daughter, Liela. She remembers arriving at Mendips to find Mimi "sitting outside on the coal-bunker, looking lost." Alone in his bedroom with this trusted childhood ally, John could at last give vent to his emotions, which he did not do by crying but by cackling with uncontrollable laughter. "We both had hysterics," he later remembered (though Liela has no recollection of joining in). "We laughed and laughed. I felt very guilty afterwards."

George's death had a devastating effect on Mimi, made worse, perhaps, by recollecting how little overt affection she had shown him in return for his generosity, good nature, and ever-dependable kindness. "Our world was never the same," she would remember. "John took it on the chin . . . but never the same. The place seemed empty, but we muddled on. I mean, you don't give up, do you?"

George had never been much of a businessman and—so the family always maintained—had been denied his fair share of the Smith dairy farm when his brother Frank sold it for development in the latter war years. Mimi thus found herself left with little in the way of capital to continue educating and providing for John and maintaining the comfortable home to which he was accustomed. She did not discuss these financial anxieties with him, and he never dreamed that at least once a year she discreetly visited a pledge shop in Smithdown Road and pawned her diamond engagement ring.

In the northern England of that era, a woman widowed in her early fifties was expected to regard her life as over. Although Mimi was only just over forty, the thought of remarriage—or any other relationship with a man—never crossed her mind. From here on, so she thought, her only raison d'être would be the care and protection of John.

Her main support were the four sisters whose lives and families remained as closely meshed as ever. And ironically, the one she turned to most frequently for consolation was Julia, the "baby sister" whose unreliability she had so often deplored. Though Mimi still could not bring herself to accept Bobby Dykins, she formed a closer bond with Julia than had existed since their childhood; henceforth a day seldom passed when Julia did not drop in at Mendips for a cup of tea and a chat.

Coping singlehandedly with fourteen-year-old John was a task that required all Mimi's old hospital-bred toughness as well as her bottomless reserves of diligence and self-sacrifice. He was always to remain in awe of her flights of temper, when she would pick up anything at hand and fling it at him, regardless of consequences. Rather than provoke her ire over neglected homework or unsuitable friends, he often preferred to tiptoe noiselessly out of the house on stocking feet; for the rest of his life, he would retain this habit of padding around as noiselessly as a cat. But more often than not, just as he reached the back door and liberty, a stern voice from above would call, "Is that you, John?"

The lack of a man about the house was accentuated by John's inability to perform even the simplest domestic tasks. When his two small cousins, Michael and David, arrived for a visit, Mimi would give them the many overdue little jobs that were beyond him. "I remember often changing the light-bulb in John's bedroom," Michael Cadwallader says. "He'd never even learned to do that."

Mimi's straitened finances increased her reliance on her student boarders. Fortunately, Michael Fishwick was now preparing for a biochemistry PhD and so needed accommodation for most of the year rather than just a regular student's three college terms. He was allotted the back bedroom Mimi had formerly shared with George, while she moved into the larger bay-windowed one adjoining John's. Considering Fishwick an old friend, as well as a link with George, she took to confiding in him as she seldom had in anyone outside the immediate family. When she visited a solicitor to probate George's will, she asked Fishwick to accompany her, and also recounted the circumstances that had brought John into her care. Once she even showed him a letter from John's father, Alf, sent from prison, which all these years later still "made steam come out of her ears."

The loss of George's kindly, understanding masculine influence could not have come at an unluckier time, with John poised on the edge of adolescence and clamoring for information, advice, and reassurance. Sex education did not feature on Quarry Bank's syllabus, and Mimi could not be interrogated on such matters in other than the most general and theoretical terms. Like most of his generation, John had to piece together the facts of life from dirty jokes and diagrams on the walls of public urinals.

It was still almost universally believed that masturbation called down the same heavenly wrath as the Old Testament's Onan suffered for "letting his seed fall on the ground." Boys who wanked, tossed off, beat their meat, pulled their wire, or gave themselves a hand-shandy did so at the supposed risk of going blind, growing hair on their palms, or being permanently shut away in psychiatric institutions. As a Boy Scout, John had been bombarded with such warnings via Baden-Powell's *Scouting for Boys* manual, with its puzzling metaphors about rutting stags and its advocacy of fresh air and exercise to stave off any inclination to "beastliness."

He became a dedicated wanker, undeterred by any fear of heavenly retribution and, as always, in company with his arch-crony,

Pete Shotton. It was a further symbol of their closeness, without any suggestion of the homoerotic; they wanked together as an act of Shennon-Lotton rebellion and defiance and mutual showing off. John proved to have a particular aptitude and near-inexhaustible stamina. Once, he accepted Pete's challenge to do it ten times in a single day, the prize being unlimited access to the Shotton family's television set. He failed to reach this target, but only by one go.

The wider circle of Lennon followers would also sociably wank all together, stimulating themselves and their neighbors by shouting out the names of sex goddesses like Sophia Loren or Gina Lollobrigida. Sometimes at the critical moment, John would call out "Winston Churchill" or "Frank Sinatra," and the onanists would collapse into giggles.

As if there were not enough going on in 1955 already, Britain's wankers were presented with a riveting alternative to "tit" magazines like *Spick and Span*. Twenty-one-year-old Brigitte Bardot, already well known to French cinemagoers, made her first English-language film, *Doctor at Sea*, and changed every preconception of sexuality on the big screen. Whereas conventional Hollywood sirens like Ava Gardner or Lana Turner were remote, untouchable, and curiously ageless, Bardot seemed hardly more than a schoolgirl with her startled-doe eyes and dimpled chin, as dewily innocent as she was knowingly voluptuous. Her very nickname, "the sex kitten," was almost enough to bring her overheated young British admirers to spontaneous orgasm. John became obsessed by her, cutting her picture from a magazine and pasting it to the ceiling above his bed.

He was by now intensely aware of the strong sexual atmosphere between his mother and "Twitchy" Dykins at 1 Blomfield Road. Once, as he would always remember, he accidentally walked into their bedroom while Julia was fellating Dykins, half-covered by a sheet. As his hormones began to run riot, he also became increasingly conscious of Julia's physical allure, the more so as she had always treated him in a jokey, flirtatious manner, more like a sportive young aunt. One afternoon when he was playing truant from Quarry Bank as usual, he lay on her bed next to her as she took an afternoon rest. He never forgot what she was wearing: "a black Angora short sleeved round-necked sweater, not too fluffy, maybe it was that other stuff, Cashmere, soft wool anyway, and, I believe, that tight dark green and yellow mottled skirt." As they lay there, he accidentally touched Julia's breast, "and I was wondering if I should do anything else. It was a strange moment because at the time I had the hots, as they say, for a rather lower-class female who lived on the opposite side of the road. I always think I should have done it. Presumably she would have allowed it."

Early that summer, Ivy Vaughan asked one of his classmates at Liverpool Institute, a lanky, humorous boy named Len Garry, to come and meet John and the Woolton gang. Len agreed but did not rush to take up the invitation: he had several more-pressing social commitments, among them cinemagoing with another Institute classmate, Paul McCartney.

Finally Len made the trip from his Wavertree home on the bicycle he'd been given for passing his Eleven Plus. He met Ivy walking along Vale Road toward Menlove Avenue in a little group that also included John. He recalls: "John had a piece of paper in his hand that he was showing to the others. When Ivan introduced us, he didn't say much, just gave me a look. I got the feeling I was being weighed up."

The newcomer quickly proved himself made of the right stuff. He was an aficionado of William books and the Goons, he knew the words to Johnnie Ray and Frankie Laine songs, and, as a bonus, could reproduce the hideously drawn-out jungle cry of Tarzan the Ape Man as portrayed in films by Johnny Weissmuller. It wasn't long before John felt sufficiently at ease with Len to show him the piece of paper that the others had been passing around and chortling over. This was not just a drawing but a miniature newspaper singlehandedly written and illustrated by John. Entitled "The Daily Howl," it consisted of gossip-style paragraphs, single cartoons, and comic strips, hand-lettered, ruled, and colored with all their creator's usual extracurricular care. There were running jokes about celebrities like Fred Emney, Stanley Unwin, and the bald TV magician David Nixon; about John's own middle name of Winston; and, inevitably, about black people and "cripples," some phrases being phoneticized

("Thik ik unk," for instance, meaning "This is a") to signify a speech impediment. Despite all the work that went into each edition, their author kept "Daily Howls" coming at the rate of several per week.

Len Garry joined the group of bike riders that John led like a squadron of cavalry around the quiet Woolton lanes, looking for girls to chat up. Almost invariably, this feminine quarry would also be out with bikes and also dressed in school uniforms but, by the game's unwritten rules, walking and pushing rather than riding. Between cavalry and giggling infantry, sooner or later, the right signal would be sent and answered, and the varicolored school blazers and bikes would come together.

John was not good-looking in any conventional sense, with his slanted eyes and plunging beak of a nose. Yet he invariably proved the most successful, both in the chatting-up ritual and the encounters that followed. When the riders compared notes later, it would be John who described feeling right inside a heavily engineered brassiere, or sniffed ostentatiously at the lingering aroma of what Liverpudlians call finger pie. Part of every almost adolescent boy's experience is to see small girls he has hitherto ignored or taken for granted suddenly grow into desirable young women. For John this happened spectacularly with Barbara Baker, whom he had known since they were toddlers together, seated on the floor at Mrs. Clark's Sunday school. For years, he had regarded Barbara with the contempt that William Brown always showed to little girls, but at the age of fifteen, she suddenly metamorphosed into a curvaceous strawberry blonde who deliberately modeled her hair and clothes on cinema sex sirens—and even had the mystic initials BB. In Reynolds Park one day, she and a girlfriend found themselves being followed in a meaning way by John and Len Garry. On this occasion, it was Len who first made the running. "Len asked me to join him on a walk a few nights later, and I said 'Yes,'" she remembers. "But I could see John watching me."

She soon dropped Len and became John's first "steady" girlfriend, as the sedate fifties phrase had it. In many ways, theirs was a relationship straight out of Enid Blyton: they would go for bike rides together or ice-skating at the Silver Blades rink in central Liverpool.

Barbara got to know John's mother and Aunt Mimi, and was often taken home to tea at Mendips, joining Michael Fishwick, and any aunts and cousins who were visiting, around the lavishly spread gateleg table. She remembers John as a romantic, naturally chivalrous boy, who bombarded her with love notes and drawings, was definitely not a Teddy Boy, and, thanks to Mimi's hard verbal schooling, still did not speak with a Scouse accent.

As a rule, the courtship rituals went on without adult interference. A line was crossed one day, however, when a group including John, Barbara, and David Ashton went for a petting session into the field owned by St. Peter's Church—i.e., virtually hallowed ground. Because John and Ashton were still members of the 3rd Allerton Scout Troop, both were summoned to explain their sacrilege before an official Scouts board of inquiry. "My Dad had been a scoutmaster, so the court was held at my house," Ashton remembers. "As I was coming home beforehand, I met John. 'Don't you fuckin' tell what you know,' he said, and then hit me over the eye. I had a black eye for days afterwards."

Len Garry shared John's fondness for music—the "pop" aimed squarely at their parents' generation—but for neither was it anything resembling a passion. As they cycled around, they would sing out loud, trying to outdo each other in the number of current hit songs they knew and in their skill as impersonators. "I was always better at ballads," Len says. "But John was better at the uptempo stuff. A song he particularly liked was Mitchell Torok's 'Caribbean.' I remember how, even when he was riding against the wind, standing up on his pedals, he always got the timing just right."

They had little initial interest, therefore, in the Bill Haley phenomenon, which reached the first of several climaxes during that summer. Michigan-born Haley had been an obscure country-and-western singer until 1951, when he recorded a song called "Rock the Joint," exchanging his usual cowboy yodel for the style and intonation of black rhythm and blues. America's racial situation being what it was, the disk could be marketed only if no biographical details about Haley were given. His country music public would have been appalled by the idea of a white man singing a "negro tune," while no black listener would have taken the performance seriously.

Three years later, by now fronting a group named the Comets, Haley recorded "Rock Around the Clock," an exuberant piece of horological nonsense that was already a year old, with one unsuccessful version by black vocalist Sunny Dae on the market. Haley's reinterpretation caused equally little stir until added to the soundtrack of *The Blackboard Jungle*, a film on the timely subject of delinquency in a New York high school. This change in context produced a devastating effect throughout America; wherever Haley's voice rang out with "One, two, three o'clock, four o'clock RAHK . . ." the gritty drama on the screen was totally eclipsed by mayhem among the audience. Boys and girls alike went literally berserk, shrieking like banshees, tearing at the fabric of their seats, lurching out to dance in the aisles or engage in mass brawls that required dozens of police to contain them.

The separate terms *rock* and *roll* had always existed in black music as synonyms for rhythm-enhanced sex. Who exactly first joined them together to define the keening saxophone and hand-thwacked double-bass beat of Haley and his Comets can never be known for certain. The most likely contender was a Cleveland disc jockey named Alan Freed, who billed his show on station WJW as *The Moondog Rock 'n' Roll Party*.

Britain's press, to begin with, treated rock 'n' roll as merely another bizarre American novelty, like pie-eating contests, pole-squatting, or wedding ceremonies at the bottom of swimming pools. The mood changed as it became clear that Teddy Boys—and their scarcely less bizarre and repugnant Teddy Girls—were Haley's most fanatical converts, and seemingly intent on destroying just as many cinemas as had their American cousins. Screenings of *The Blackboard Jungle* were canceled wholesale, "Rock Around the Clock" was banished both from radio and television, and dance halls banned the jitterbuggy dance that went with it. The result was as might have been expected. Haley's record shot to number one in the Top 20 in May 1955, remaining on the chart for twenty-two weeks. The following October, it made number one again, and stayed on the chart a further seventeen weeks.

With hindsight, "Rock Around the Clock" looks like a kind of Phoney War—a warm-up for the cultural blitzkrieg soon to follow. Most of the excitement it generated was damped down by the sight

of Bill Haley himself, a man already pushing thirty, with a cheru-
bic smile and query-shaped kiss curl on his too-high forehead, who
looked little different from the parents who so condemned him.

To capitalize on sales of the "Rock Around the Clock" recording, a film of the same name was rushed out, featuring Haley and
the Comets with other emergent rock-'n'-roll celebrities like Freddie
Bell and the Bellboys, the Platters, and "Moondog" Alan Freed. John
went to see it expecting a life-changing experience but came away
disappointed. "I was very surprised." he would recall. "Nobody was
screaming and nobody was dancing in the aisles like I'd read. I was
all set to tear up the seats, too, but nobody joined in."

As if to prove the fad had done no serious harm, John's school
report for the 1955 summer term was considerably less of a disaster
than usual. *English*: "He is capable of good work and has done quite
well . . . a good knowledge of the books." *History*: "He has tried hard
and worked well." *Art*: "Very satisfactory." *Handwork*: "Satisfactory
progress." *Physical training*: "(height 5, 6 and a half, weight 9 st, 4 lbs
[130 pounds]) F[airly] satisfactory." *Geography*: "Undoubtedly trying
harder." *General science*: "An encouraging result. His work has been
satisfactory but his behaviour in class is not always so." The only
wholly negative entries were for French ("disappointing" through
fondness for "obtaining a cheap laugh in class") and Religious Knowledge ("His work has been of a low standard").

"The best report he has had for a long time," noted a surprised
Ernie Taylor in the space reserved for headmaster's comment. "I
hope this means that he has turned over a new leaf."

5

THE GALLOTONE
CHAMPION

Please God, give me a guitar.

He first heard about Elvis Presley from a Quarry Bank classmate named Don Beatty, one of the participants in the Great Dinner Tickets Swindle. Don had a copy of the *New Musical Express*—at that time rather a rarity in the far northwest—and pointed out a reference to America's newest rock-'n'-roll sensation and his just-released new record, "Heartbreak Hotel."

John reacted guardedly at first, remembering what a letdown *Rock Around the Clock* had been. "The music papers were saying Presley was fantastic, and at first I expected someone like Perry Como or Sinatra. 'Heartbreak Hotel' sounded a corny title, and his name seemed strange in those days. But then when I heard it, it was the end for me . . . I remember rushing home with the record and saying 'He sounds like Frankie Laine and Johnnie Ray *and* Tennessee Ernie Ford.'"

When Presley erupted into popular music and mythology that spring of 1956, he was by no means the first entertainer to cause mass hysteria. During the 1920s, the silent screen idol Rudolf Valentino and the prototype crooner Rudy Vallee had each driven female audiences to frenzy—Vallee earning the nickname of "the guy with the cock in his voice," Valentino attracting a screaming crowd of ten thousand even to his funeral. Two decades later, the young Frank Sinatra inspired a whole new species of female worshipper, the "bobby-soxer," whose demented reactions at concerts ultimately competed in newsworthiness with the singer himself. Nor was such incontinence purely emotional: after Sinatra's legendary opening at the New York Paramount Theater in 1947, it was found that many bobby-soxers, unable to contain themselves, had urinated where they sat.

All this was taken to uncharted new levels, however, by a twenty-one-year-old former truck driver from Memphis, Tennessee, with dyed black hair and the face of a supercilious baby. For Presley did more than touch the trigger of feminine mass fantasy; he also gave release to the tension that had built up in young men with no more global conflict to burn off their testosterone. Here, rolled into one person, was a Valentino with a voice, a Sinatra with still greater power over young girls' bladders, a James Dean in close-up more mesmeric than even Hollywood could contrive—in short, a rock-'n'-roll hero who looked every bit as gloriously disruptive as he sounded. The Phoney War of plaid jackets, soppy smiles, and kiss curls was over: all-out bombardment had finally begun.

For the vast majority of Britons, Presley could not have been more incomprehensible if freshly beamed down from Mars. Bill Haley at least had a name that was recognizably human (one he happened to share with the current editor of *The Times*). But "Elvis Presley" was the strangest configuration of syllables yet to have crossed the Atlantic—more so than Joe DiMaggio, Efrem Zimbalist Jr., or even Liberace, which some newspapers felt obliged to render phonetically ("Lee-ber-arch-ee"). Commentators were also intrigued by the fact that Presley performed his gyrations while simultaneously playing—or appearing to play—a guitar slung around his neck. Americans were familiar with the guitar as a normal accessory for singers of both country and blues; in Britain it was perhaps the most anonymous of all musical instruments, glimpsed fleetingly in the back rows of dance bands or as shadowy silhouettes behind Spanish flamenco dancers.

When John first heard "Heartbreak Hotel," the whole edifice of rumor and ridicule that the media that created around Presley instantly melted away. All he needed to know was in the song's opening fanfare—that anguished, echoey cry of "Well, since my baby left me . . ." answered by double stabs of high treble electric guitar. It was, in fact, not rock 'n' roll or even a ballad, but a blues shout in a traditional pattern that Robert Johnson or Blind Lemon Jefferson would instantly have recognized. But while blues songs deal with adult themes, "Heartbreak Hotel" reached directly to the primary adolescent emotion, melodramatic self-pity. For the first time, any spotty youth dumped by his girlfriend, for whatever good reason, could now aspire to this metaphorical refuge for "broken-hearted lovers," "down at the end of Lonely Street."

Far from the mindless nonsense Presley's critics accused him of peddling, the lyrics were neat and skillful enough to be dissected in a Quarry Bank literature test, the hotel metaphor sustained by a bellhop whose "tears keep flowing" and a "desk clerk dressed in black." The arrangement had the visceral simplicity of blues played live in the wee, small hours, switching between foot-stomping bass, jangly whorehouse piano, and jagged guitar half-chords suggesting the bottleneck style of Delta bluesmen. Those riffs are still potent today after ten thousand hearings; to an adolescent in 1956 who'd never heard a guitar played as an offensive weapon, they were stupefying. No sound ever had been, or ever would be, more perfectly tuned to hormones going berserk.

That May, a second Presley single, "Blue Suede Shoes," joined "Heartbreak Hotel" in the UK Top 20; in August came a third, "I Want You, I Need You, I Love You," and in September a fourth, "Hound Dog." Each drew John still further into this intoxicating new world where guitars rang like carillons of victory bells, pianos pounded like jackhammers, and drums spat like machine guns. Each announced more joyously than the last that life need not be the gray, humdrum vista he and his fellow war babies had always known. As he himself put it: "Rock 'n' roll was real. Everything else was unreal."

Film clips of Presley's American TV appearances now also began to filter through, revealing him to be almost ludicrously good-looking, albeit in a baleful, smoldering style more usually associated with female glamour icons. Here, indeed, was history's one and only male pinup for straight males. In common with his other British converts, John obsessively read and reread every newspaper story about Presley, cut out and saved every magazine picture of him, pored over every detail of his hair, clothes, and sublimely sullen face for what it might reveal of his private character and lifestyle. At Mendips he chattered so endlessly about his new hero that an exasperated Mimi finally brought down the guillotine. "It was nothing but Elvis Presley, Elvis Presley, Elvis Presley," she recalled. "In the end I said 'Elvis Presley's all very well, John, but I don't want him for breakfast, dinner and tea.'"

Like thousands of other boys who had never previously cared a button for their wardrobe or grooming, he began to model his hair, his dress, his whole being, on Presley's. Like many Quarry Bank boys, he did what he could to Elvis-ize his school uniform, fastening only the bottom of his three blazer buttons to create a drape effect and stretching his gold-and-black school tie into the nearest possible semblance of a Slim Jim. The great problem was the trousers, which men and boys alike still wore in the baggy cut that had prevailed since the 1920s. Scarcely any men's outfitters yet stocked ready-made "drainpipes," so one's only recourse was to take a conventional pair to an alterations tailor, sartorial equivalent of the back-street abortionist, and have their cuffs tapered from twenty-four to sixteen or (in cases of ultimate daring) fourteen inches.

No fiercer controversy raged in British families of the mid-1950s than this. No matter that the British Empire had been largely built by men in narrow trousers, nor that every palace, stately home, and museum in the land thronged with portraits of narrow-trousered kings, dukes, prime ministers, and generals. The style was now identified with lawless, low-class Teddy Boys and, by the more knowing, with homosexuals—although, paradoxically, it was deemed quite respectable in fawn cavalry twill, if worn by off-duty Guards officers together with riding jackets and tweed caps.

At Mendips, Mimi was predictably horrified and outraged by her nephew's attempted metamorphosis into a "common" Teddy Boy. She might be unable to stop John ruining the hang of his tailor-made blazer and leaving his top shirt button permanently agape above his mutilated school tie. She might not have prevented Signor Bioletti at Penny Lane from restyling his nice, wavy hair, as she put it, "like an overgrown lavatory brush." But with trousers she dug her heels in: John was absolutely forbidden either to buy "drainies" or have any of his existing pairs tapered. His response was to smuggle some to a compliant tailor and wear the finished product only outside Mimi's field of vision. He would deposit them at Nigel Walley's or Pete Shotton's and change into them there, or leave Mendips wearing them underneath an ordinary pair of trousers, peeling off this outer layer once safely out of Mimi's sight.

One grown-up, at least, could be relied on not to shudder at rock 'n' roll or pour scorn on its lip-curling godhead. John's mother Julia adored Presley's records, thought he was dishy to look at, and relished all the ways he was upsetting the generation whose values had always so oppressed her. It was Julia who, daring Mimi's wrath, bought John his first real rock-'n'-roll clothes—a colored (as opposed to plain gray or white) shirt, a pair of black drainpipe jeans, a "shortie" raincoat with padded shoulders. When a kitten was given to John's two small half sisters, Julia and Jackie, their mother named it Elvis.

With every passing week of 1956, the heavenly noises from across the Atlantic multiplied and diversified. From New Orleans came Antoine "Fats" Domino, a singer-pianist with the body of a whale and the face of a kindly Burmese cat, who had already been around and playing much this same stuff since 1949. From St. Louis came Charles "Chuck" Berry, a loose-limbed youth with a lounge-lizard mustache, who not only wrote and performed his witty anthems in the former Whites Only realm of expensive cars and high schools, but also simultaneously played cherry-red lead guitar, jackknifing his skinny knees or loping across the stage in profile like a duck.

From Macon, Georgia, came a former dishwasher named Richard Penniman, aka Little Richard, a shock-haired imp endowed with the dual gift of being able to roar like an erupting volcano and ululate like an entire Bedouin tribe in mourning.

If black rock-'n'-rollers, like Presley himself, teetered on the edge of comedy, Richard's exultant gibberish ("Tutti-frutti O-rooty . . . Awopbopaloobopawopbamboom!") was a deep-South descendant of Lewis Carroll's "Jabberwocky." "The most exciting thing . . . was when he screamed just before the solo," John later recalled. "It used to make your hair stand on end. When I heard it, it was so great, I couldn't speak. You know how it is when you are torn. Elvis was bigger than religion in my life . . . I didn't want to leave Elvis. We all looked at each other, but I didn't want to say anything against Elvis, even in my mind."

As with almost every other new American idea, gauche and unconvincing British replicas quickly followed. In the wake of Presley's onslaught, a young Londoner named Larry Parnes launched the United Kingdom's first native rock-'n'-roller—a cockney merchant seaman named Tommy Hicks, now renamed Tommy Steele. Provided with the requisite exploding hair and Presley-style guitar, Steele drew crowds of screaming girls wherever he appeared and had several Top 10 hits. But his whole marketing exemplified the notion of rock 'n' roll as a passing fad or soon-to-be-unmasked confidence trick. One of Larry Parnes's first acts was to move him into cabaret by booking him into London's Café de Paris in the footsteps of Marlene Dietrich and Noël Coward. In little more than a year, his career as a teenage idol would be metaphorically wound up by a film entitled *The Tommy Steele Story*.

Even Steele's patent harmlessness could not mitigate adult Britain's hatred and terror of rock 'n' roll and the resolve to stamp it out, if not by frontal attack and ridicule, then by attrition. The BBC carried no news items about even its most famous performers and mentioned its very name only with lip-curled distaste. Apart from records, its main public outlets were jukeboxes in the newfangled espresso coffee bars, which explained why such places were always packed with teenagers and also why adults viewed them rather like speakeasies in Prohibition America. At traveling fairs, rock 'n' roll would blare out over carousels and bumper cars, so strengthening its perceived links with the grubby, the dishonest, and the violent.

The steadiest source of supply was Radio Luxembourg, out in mysterious mainland Europe, which operated a daily English-language music service playing all the latest rock-'n'-roll hits with American-style disc jockeys, advertisements, and station IDs. But Luxembourg did not come on the air until 8:00 p.m., and reception on British wirelesses was always erratic. Like all teenagers up and down the land, John listened in late at night with a portable radio at low volume under the bedclothes so that Mimi would not hear it.

With rock fizzing in his veins around the clock, even things he had once regarded as treats now seemed irksomely unreal. During the school summer holidays of 1956, he paid his usual long visit to his Aunt Mater, Uncle Bert, and cousin Stanley in Edinburgh, accompanied by Aunt Nanny, her nine-year-old son, Michael, and Harrie's nine-year-old son, David. (Husbands seldom featured in these inter-sister excursions.) Part of the time was spent at Uncle Bert's croft in Durness, Sutherland, near Cape Wrath, the furthermost northwesterly tip of Scotland. This was a working farm, set in vast, unspoiled tracts of sheep-dotted moorland and peat bogs. The family party roughed it in a primitive farmhouse, lit by oil lamps and candles, and noisy with the screeches of Mater's pet parrot, Harry Parry.

As well as running the croft, Uncle Bert was carrying out extensive improvements, and John and young Michael and David found themselves allotted a punishing schedule of heavy manual work. "We were scything hay, building dry stone walls, carting wheelbarrow-loads of sand," Michael Cadwallader remembers. "John soon got fed up with that, and wasn't thrilled by the company of two nine-year-old boys. He obviously couldn't wait to leave."

Rock 'n' roll had no fiercer enemy in Britain than followers of traditional jazz, who either did not know or preferred to forget that the two were actually first cousins. Jazz had always overlapped with blues and country, the twin streams that produced Elvis Presley. The more enlightened traditional jazz bandleaders, like Humphrey Lyttelton, acknowledged this by incorporating both into their repertoire, even occasionally bringing over American bluesmen like Big Bill Broonzy to make guest appearances at their concerts. However, in music, as everywhere else, the British class system held firm. Rock-'n'-rollers were firmly bracketed at the most unsavory end of the lower working class, while jazzers were middle-class student types who wore striped college scarves and drank half pints of cider.

The most archivally minded trad bandleader of pre-rock-'n'-roll times was the trombonist Chris Barber. Since well before Presley hit Britain, Barber's shows had featured his foxy-faced banjo player, Tony, aka "Lonnie," Donegan, on guitar with a small rhythm section, performing in an otherwise forgotten American folk style known as skiffle. The word (like jazz itself) was onomatopoeic, harking back to the bleak Depression era of the thirties, when poor whites, unable to afford conventional instruments, would beat out a shuffly rhythm on makeshift ones like kitchen washboards, empty boxes, and trash-can lids.

In January 1956, Donegan and a three-strong skiffle group scored a surprise hit with "Rock Island Line," a train song associated with the thirties' blues giant Huddie ("Leadbelly") Ledbetter. Undoubtedly helped by the word *rock* in its title (though the reference was purely geological) it reached number eight in Britain, was accepted for U.S. release on the London label, and by April stood at tenth place in the American charts. For any British-made record to catch on in America was rare enough; for one to do so by reinterpreting such a uniquely American idiom was unprecedented.

British skiffle was essentially boys' music, a gift out of the blue to boys like John who had been just too young for rock 'n' roll's first uprising and felt excluded from the tough Teddy Boy culture that now monopolized it. Skiffle was rock 'n' roll in a milder, more socially acceptable form, also intoxicatingly American but without the taint of sexuality or violence. In its Anglicized version, it drew on every ethnic source—blues, country, folk, and jazz—though its young British performers seldom knew one genre from another, let alone understood what social conditions had inspired the songs or what pain or anger or sense of social injustice had gone into their creation. All that mattered was the frantic, pattering beat and those magic references to railroads, penitentiaries, and chain gangs.

Elvis Presley had made the guitar an unreachable symbol of glamour and sexual allure to young British males; now Lonnie Donegan made it a reachable one. For skiffle followed the traditional twelve-bar blues pattern of four chords, in their simplest versions requiring only one or two fingers. Anyone could play them, pretty much instantaneously.

Skiffle became the British pop sensation of 1956–57, relegating even Presley and rock 'n' roll to the sidelines. Lonnie Donegan and his skiffle group began a run of Top 10 hits that would not be surpassed until the next decade, with genuine or ersatz folk titles such as "Lost John," "Bring a Little Water, Sylvie," "Don't You Rock Me, Daddy-O," and "Cumberland Gap." Record companies began a frantic hunt for alternative skiffle stars, concentrating their efforts on London's Soho district, specifically the 2 I's coffee bar in Old Compton Street, where Tommy Steele had made some early live appearances. A fledgling record producer, the Parlophone label's George Martin, advanced his career just a little by finding his way to the 2 I's and signing up a skiffle quintet named the Vipers.

Most important, skiffle electrified ordinary youths, far away from London, who had never considered themselves musical and once would rather have committed hara-kiri than get up and sing in public. All over the country, youthful skiffle groups were formed with names hopefully evoking the great American open road—the Ramblers, the Nomads, the Streamliners, the Cottonpickers. Kitchens were stripped of washboards and brooms; guitars that had gathered dust for years in music-shop windows disappeared overnight. In an echo of not-so-distant Austerity years, the newspapers were soon reporting a national guitar shortage.

A few would-be boy skifflers did not start as absolute beginners, thanks to fathers, older brothers, or uncles who were pro or semi-pro musicians. But only a very few can have owed their head start to their mothers, as John did. For Julia could play the banjo, an instrument even more unexpectedly catapulted into fashion than the guitar. Well before skiffle arrived, she had begun teaching John to pick out single-string versions of "Little White Lies" or "Girl of My Dreams" on the sound principle that if he could play an instrument, he'd always be popular. But now the banjo was forgotten. "I used to read the ads for guitars," he would recall, "and just ache for one. Like everyone else, I used God for this one thing I wanted: 'Please God, give me a guitar.'"

His Aunt Mimi has gone down in history as the person who bought John his first guitar, launching him on his roundabout path to immortality. Many times would she later recount how, weary of his endless pleas and nagging, she took him by bus down into central Liverpool and paid out £17 she could ill afford at Hessy's music store in Whitechapel. Mimi certainly did buy John a guitar, and at some financial sacrifice, but that was a step or two further along the path. The first one he owned, and used until long after his skills had outgrown it, was given to him by Julia.

Whether that was the first guitar he played is another matter. John himself was to recall initially borrowing one from another boy and experimenting rather inconclusively with it before he got his own. This may well have been in the interval between being promised his heart's desire by his mother and actually holding the wondrous object in his hands. After several weeks' unsuccessful search around Liverpool, Julia finally obtained one by mail order on the installment plan. No record of the vendor has survived; the likeliest one seems to have been a mail-order firm named Headquarters and General Supplies of Coldharbour Lane, London SE5. At around the moment John got lucky, H & G announced their acquisition of "1,000 only" Gallotone Champion guitars, a mass-produced make imported from South Africa. The cost was £10 19s 6d (£10.95) each, or 10 shillings (50p) deposit and eighteen two-weekly payments of 18s 11d (90p). The guitar was an acoustic Spanish flamenco-style model but with steel rather than gut strings, strummed not with the fingers but with a tortoiseshell plectrum. Inside the sound hole was a label saying GUARANTEED NOT TO SPLIT.

He was not the only Quarry Bank pupil able to flaunt such a status symbol in that autumn term of 1956. A fellow member of Woolton house, a studious, scientifically minded boy named Eric Griffiths, had also got hold of a Spanish-style guitar similar to John's in size, shape, and cheapness. Although the two boys had never been especially friendly, they agreed to go for guitar lessons together with a tutor in Hunts Cross. However, the tutor wanted them to learn to read music, which neither could be bothered to do. The easy shortcut suggested by Julia was that she should tune their six-string guitars like a four-string banjo—that is, using only the guitar's four thinnest treble strings and ignoring the two thick bass ones. Then she herself could teach them all the chords they needed for the music they wanted to play.

From here on, there was no stopping John. Whenever Pete Shotton or Nigel Walley visited Mendips, they would find him seated on the end of his bed, struggling to stretch his left hand into a C or G chord shape, pressing down hard and rippling the pick again and again until the sound rang clear and true, oblivious of the painful grooves that the steel strings cut into his fingertips. "He'd sit there strumming," Nigel remembers, "singing any words that came into his head. In a couple of minutes, he'd have a tune going."

Mimi tried to protest about the neglect of his schoolwork, especially with GCE (General Certificate of Education) exams now only a few months away, but to no avail; as Liverpudlians say, never more aptly than here, he was "lost." From the kitchen or living room, Mimi would shout an admonition destined to be given back to her one day, chidingly, engraved on a mock-ceremonial plaque: "The guitar's all very well, John, but you'll never make a living at it."

According to Eric Griffiths, neither John nor he had thought of starting their own skiffle group until another Quarry Bank boy, George Lee, suggested it one day during break. Alas for the donor of this stupendously bright idea, he himself was not to join or have anything whatsoever to do with the group that resulted. More than a year was to pass before its personnel included anyone named George.

John, as usual, refused to consider any enterprise that did not include his fellow Outlaw Pete Shotton. This being skiffle, Pete's lack of even the smallest particle of musical talent was not an issue. He took on the role of washboard player, for which the sole qualification was possession of a washboard—not as straightforward as it might appear, since skifflemania had also created a national washboard shortage. The group was initially called the Blackjacks, but within about a week Pete Shotton suggested something more in tune with the skiffling ethos of hoboes and chain gangs. Quarry Bank's school song had a line in which the pupils apostrophized themselves as "Quarry men, old before our birth . . ." Quarries were where chain gangs worked, and John and Pete indubitably regarded themselves as convicts at hard labor. So their skiffle group became the Quarrymen.

Two more recruits quickly emerged from their immediate circle of friends in Woolton house. (George Lee belonged to a rival house, Aigburth, which may perhaps account for his exclusion.) One was the studious Rod Davis, playing the banjo his parents had recently bought him on a trip to Wales. The other was a boy known to John—and featured in his cartoon gallery—as Bill "Smell Type" Smith, plunking the one-string skiffle "bass" composed of a broomstick and an empty tea chest. To make the tea chest less starkly utilitarian, Rod's mother covered it in brown wallpaper, on which musical notes and a large treble clef were then outlined in white.

Most skiffle groups featured no percussion other than strummed guitars and the rattle of the washboard player's thimble-capped fingers. If drummers did feature in the lineup, they tended to play only a single snare drum on a stand. The Quarrymen, however, started out with the luxury of a drummer in possession of his own complete kit (something that would seldom come along quite so easily again). He was not a Quarry Bank pupil but an acquaintance of Rod and Eric named Colin Hanton, who had already left school to become an apprentice upholsterer at the Guy Rogers furniture factory in Speke. At eighteen, he was two years older than the others, though his diminutive build and innocent face made him look younger—so much so that he had to carry his birth certificate around with him to prove to pub landlords that he was of the legal drinking age.

Strictly speaking, he was not quite in the other Quarrymens' social bracket; nor had he any performing experience beyond playing along with jazz records at home; nor was he nearly as much interested in percussion as he was in downing pints of black velvet (Guinness stout mixed with cider) at every possible opportunity. Such considerations were easily waived in view of the almost brand-new drums that came with him. And, working man or not, he seemed happy enough to throw in his lot with a gaggle of schoolboys, even getting a printer friend to stencil QUARRY MEN (splitting the name for space reasons) on the side of his bass drum.

From the beginning, as Hanton remembers, John naturally took on the role of leader. "He was the only singer in the group, so he was the one who said what we played and in what order. And, if we wanted to sound any good, we had to learn to play the songs he knew."

Prophetically, there was soon upheaval in the Quarrymen's lineup. Although Bill Smith had seemed keen enough to play tea-chest bass, he proved so bad about turning up for rehearsals that the others unanimously voted him out. A resentful Smell-Type retaliated by holding the tea chest hostage at his house: when all requests for its return were ignored, John led a night expedition to retrieve it from the Smiths' garage. After this, the role of bass player was divided between Nigel Walley, Ivan Vaughan, and Ivan's Liverpool Institute friend, Len Garry.

The Quarrymen's repertoire at first consisted mainly of Lonnie Donegan songs: "Cumberland Gap," "Lost John," "Gamblin' Man," "Wabash Cannonball." As well as "Rock Island Line," Leadbelly's blues oeuvre supplied another couple of easily accessible four-chorders, the upbeat "Cotton Fields" and the doleful "Midnight Special." Rod Davis, a passionate folk-music fan, introduced Burl Ives numbers like "Worried Man Blues," while John would do the occasional country number, like Hank Williams's "Honky Tonk Blues." He had, in fact, been a fan of Williams—the prototype singer-songwriter—well before Presley came along, and been conscious of the strong country-music following among Merseyside's Irish population since he was a small boy. The first guitar he ever remembered seeing had been played "by a guy in a cowboy suit . . . with stars and a cowboy hat and a big Dobro [self-amplifying metal guitar] . . . There had been cowboys before there was rock 'n' roll."

The folk input even included a few traditional British ballads, most notably "Maggie May," the requiem for an archetypal Liverpool "tottie," or tart, from the well-worn hookers' beat between Lime Street and Canning Place. John had always vaguely known the words, and was given a refresher course by his mother, playing his guitar in the living room at Mendips, watched also by Mimi and her regular boarder, Michael Fishwick. Julia knew the whole bawdy lyric that most skifflers dared not sing, and she articulated every word ("No more she'll rob the sailor, or be fucked by many a whaler . . .") with Vera Lynn clarity and sweetness. Fortunately, most of it went completely over her straitlaced sister's head.

Otherwise, in these days when tape recorders were rare and fabulously expensive, learning the words of a song could be a laborious business. Every pop record that was released was still also published as sheet music with a one-color cover picture of the vocalist, the words spelled out in the style of operatic libretti ("You ai-n't nu-thin' but a ho-und dog . . .") and anachronistic directions such as "Allegro" or "bright, lively rhythm." But for a schoolboy like John, buying the record itself at six shillings per copy was costly enough. The only way to learn it was to play it over and over again, each time scribbling down another phrase, or part of one, and gaining another clue as to which chord changed into which. Since Mimi refused to have a record player at Mendips, John had to take his records to Julia's and learn them from hers.

As always if he really wanted to do something, he never gave up. When he finally sold his copy of "Rock Island Line" to Rod Davis, he'd thrown it back onto the gramophone so many times and so roughly that the hole in its center had been worn out of shape by the turntable stem. The first time Rod tried to play it, it wobbled so crazily that the song was barely recognizable.

The Quarrymen's first gig was at St. Barnabas Church Hall—popularly known as "Barney's," close to the Penny Lane roundabout where John used to get off the bus for Dovedale Primary. No advertisements appeared in the local press, so we can only roughly date his debut in front of a live audience as September or October of 1956. Nothing else is known of the event except that his mother turned up loyally to cheer him on, accompanied by his steady girl-friend, Barbara Baker.

The next significant booking was an anomalously upmarket one at the Lee Park Golf Club in Gateacre. Lee Park was that common fifties institution, a "Jewish-only" club, catering to those whose religion excluded them from playing on other courses in the area. Nigel Walley had recently begun working there as an apprentice golf pro, and he talked the secretary into booking the Quarrymen as an extra attraction at a Saturday-night club dance. They played in the round, while a formally dressed and largely adult crowd sat and watched. There was no fee, but a cold supper was provided and a collection taken for them afterwards.

From the very first, John dominated the stage as if born to it, pounding his cheap little mail-order guitar, singing in the high, slightly acid voice that, unusually, he made no attempt to American-ize. To be heard above five frantically skiffling companions, usually without a microphone, the only option was all-out attack. On such public show, it was more unthinkable than ever for him to wear his hated glasses, even though without them he could barely see the edge of the stage. As a result, he adopted a slightly hunched, splay-legged stance, his face thrust forward and eyes narrowed to slits in a way that onlookers took to be aggressive and challenging but often was no more than effort to get his surroundings in focus. Though he never indulged in overt displays of egotism, his companions were left in no doubt as who was boss. "John used to go at his guitar so hard that he'd often break a string," Rod Davis remembers. "When that happened, he'd hand his guitar to me, take my banjo and carry on playing while I changed the guitar-string for him."

Perform it though he did with his whole heart and soul, skiffle was never enough for John. What he really wanted to be playing was rock 'n' roll, not the historically meaningful tracts and protests of Leadbelly and Woody Guthrie but the magic, molten gibberish of Elvis Presley and Little Richard. And time was pressing. Every day brought a fresh hail of adult calumnies against rock 'n' rollers and seemingly authoritative predictions that they would all soon have passed into richly deserved extinction. As evidence, the finger was pointed at Presley himself and how he already seemed to be hedging his bets by recording fewer rock-'n'-roll rabble-rousers and more ballads. December 1956 found "the King" starring in his first Hollywood movie, *Love Me Tender*, and topping the charts with a theme song that was less ballad than hymn.

So John, at the very earliest stage, began mixing rock 'n' roll into the Quarrymen's skiffle repertoire in small, surreptitious doses, like nips of vodka added to orange juice. He was, anyway, in the habit of making up his own words to current hit songs when he hadn't been able to decipher their real ones. So he'd play rock-'n'-roll songs as skiffle, slipping in a folksy reference here and there to mollify the purists. The example always cited by his former companions was "Come Go with Me," a 1957 million seller for the Del-Vikings in the doo-wop, or part-singing, style created by a cappella vocal groups on urban street corners. John's Quarrymen version—perhaps the seeds of a future song lyric's invitation to "let me take you down"—ran:

Come come come come
and go with me
down down down down to
the Penitentiary

One immediate effect of his new passion was a slight improvement of his profile at Quarry Bank High School. In October 1956, the remote and humorless Ernie Taylor had retired from the headmastership and been replaced by William Ernest Pobjoy, at only thirty-five one of the youngest school principals in the northwest. Mr. Pobjoy had been warned in advance about the malign influence of Shennon and Lotton, by now sometimes too extreme even to feature in the official punishment log. "I was told there was a certain member of staff that Lennon had actually thumped," the former head remembers now. "The poor man was so humiliated that he'd begged for the matter not to be reported."

Despite his youth and far lighter touch, "Popeye" Pobjoy was no pushover. Soon after his arrival, he found it necessary to give John three strokes with the cane—an experience that helped convince him to phase out corporal punishment from the school altogether. Early in 1957, while Popeye was temporarily absent, Shennon and Lotton were each suspended for a week by the deputy head, Ian Gallaway.

But in general John's guitar made him more a member of the school community than he'd ever wished or expected to be. Now when he went to the headmaster's study, it might not necessarily be for the cane but to ask in all politeness if the Quarrymen could play at the next sixth-form dance. In a turret of the old Gothic schoolhouse was a little-used classroom where—with Popeye's tacit permission— John, Pete, and Eric Griffiths would hold practice sessions during break or at the end of afternoon school.

Rehearsal space for the whole eight-man group (if you count all three alternating bass players) was less easy to find. At Mendips, John's bedroom was too small, and Mimi's house-proud eye too vigilant, for them ever to feel quite comfortable there. They might convene at Eric's or Colin's house or, if the weather were fine, in the back garden of Rod Davis's. Next door lived the grandparents of the future Olympic runner Paula Radcliffe; as John tried out the latest Donegan or Presley number, the Radcliffes would jokily throw pennies to him over the garden fence.

But most times the Quarrymen would pick up a packet of Wild Woodbines and a newspaper parcel of fish and chips, and go over to their unofficial den mother's house in Blomfield Road. However many they were, they could depend on the same warm welcome from Julia; she would make them endless cups of tea, share their ciggies, be a sounding board for their latest numbers and a sympathetic listener to their latest adventures and misadventures. The practice session itself would usually be held in the bathroom, whose uncarpeted floor and tiled surfaces maximized the volume and echo of acoustic skiffle instruments; to get the very best effect, John, Eric, and Rod would stand together in the bath. No matter if Julia happened to be bathing John's two half sisters when the musicians arrived: the little girls would be evicted, the water would be drained, and the two guitarists and banjo player would take off their shoes and clamber into the vacated tub.

Only skiffle groups composed of affluent working men could afford their own private transport. Rod Davis's father had an Austin Hereford car in which he'd occasionally chauffeur the Quarrymen to their gigs. Most of the time they had to travel on Liverpool Corporation's ever-plentiful and reliable green double-decker buses, somehow packing the tea chest and Colin Hanton's drums into the luggage compartment under the stairs. On these journeys a weather eye always had to be kept open for two local heavies named Rod and Willo, who, for unexplained reasons, had vowed to get them, and of whom even John made no secret of being terrified. One night when the Quarrymen got off their bus in Woolton village, Rod and Willo were waiting in ambush. The skifflers all managed to escape, but at the cost of abandoning their tea-chest bass, which stayed in the road where they dropped it for several days afterwards, being sideswiped this way and that by passing traffic.

After John, the group's most extrovert member—and the only other one with any noticeable singing ability—was Len Garry. By far the best of their three original alternating bass players, Len soon took over the role from Ivan Vaughan and Nigel Walley. Bookish Ivan returned to his school studies with some relief, while "Walloggs" became the group's manager. He approached the role with great seriousness, writing earnest letters in longhand to local dance promoters and persuading even the Woolton newsagents who had suffered most from John's shoplifting to display advertisements for the Quarrymen free of charge in their front windows. He also gave out business cards, expressed with old-fashioned formality and claiming an impressive command of musical styles:

Country—Western—Rock 'n' roll—Skiffle

THE QUARRY MEN [sic]

Open for engagements

Their fee varied between £3 and £5, according to length of performance, divided among six of them, since their manager also took an equal share.

John's insistence on putting rock 'n' roll first onstage, if not in print, was to cause Nigel many headaches with promoters of skiffle-only venues, as well as some little embarrassment in his day job as an apprentice golf pro. In the Lee Park clubhouse, he had become friendly with a doctor named Sytner, whose son, Alan, was about to open a jazz club in central Liverpool. Its premises were the cellar of an old warehouse in Mathew Street, and—in a conscious echo of jazz joints on the Parisian Left Bank—it was to be named the Cavern. Alan Sytner agreed to book the Quarrymen (advertising them as "Quarry Men") for a skiffle session in company with other local groups, including the Deltones, the Dark Town Skiffle Group, and the Demon Five.

But the Cavern in this first incarnation proved hostile territory, peopled by traditional jazz fans of the most earnest and intolerant kind. Skiffle they could tolerate, for its blues and folk ancestry, but rock 'n' roll had much the same effect on them as a string of garlic on a vampire. John nonetheless launched into his Presley and Fats Domino numbers, oblivious of the nauseated silence that greeted each one. "I tried to argue with him," Rod Davis remembers, "not because I was a purist myself, but because it was so obviously a suicidal thing to do with that particular audience." John carried on regardless, so "lost" that when a note was passed up to him, he took it to be a song request. But it was from the Cavern's management, and contained a single terse instruction: "Cut out the bloody rock."

Just as it had for his father, Alf, two decades earlier, the Empire Theatre in Lime Street represented John's ultimate ambition as a performer. True to its time-honored place on the music-hall Number One Circuit, the Empire now presented all the country's top skiffle and rock-'n'-roll stars, usually at the head of a traditional variety bill whose jugglers and comedians had to struggle to make themselves heard over anticipatory teenage screams.

Alf Lennon had never gotten further than backstage at the Empire. But his son received an early chance to tread its hallowed boards when a Carroll Levis Discoveries show came through town in June 1957. Levis was an oleaginous Canadian, known in glamour-hungry and credulous postwar Britain as "Mister Star-maker." During the fifties, he used to tour provincial theaters, holding talent contests for every kind of would-be entertainer, from singers and comedians to parakeet trainers and players of musical saws.

When the Quarrymen turned up at the Empire for the contest's Sunday heats (minus Rod Davis, whose religious parents would not let him take part), they found several other skiffle groups also hungry to be discovered by Mister Star-maker. Their main competition, they decided, was a group from Speke, the Sunnysiders, who included a midget named Nicky Cuff on tea-chest bass. The Sunnysiders' act was partly comic, with Cuff (in everyday life, a workmate of Colin Hanton's) running onstage dressed in a top hat and tails and explaining that he'd lost his way to the Adelphi Hotel. His other gimmick was being able to stand on his tea chest while belaboring its single string.

The Quarrymen did better, however, getting through to the Wednesday-night finals while the Sunnysiders' comic dimension actually lost them points. But on the Wednesday, when winners were judged on audience applause, John's outfit found themselves up against a group from Wales who had arrived with a busload of supporters to cheer them on. Rod Davis remembers how these Welsh skifflers used extrovert showmanship, flinging themselves around, even lying flat on the stage, "while we just stood still, like purists." Nonetheless, the applause-measuring "Clapometer" initially showed a dead heat between the two groups. But on a retry, the Welsh group were announced to be just ahead. So Mister Star-maker—not for the only time, it would turn out—missed the greatest discovery of his life.

Rock 'n' roll continued to defy every forecast of its imminent self-destruction, boosted by an unexpected endorsement from Hollywood. Late 1956 had seen the release of a film comedy called *The Girl Can't Help It*, originally intended as a vehicle for the huge-bosomed screen goddess Jayne Mansfield, with jibes at teenagers and their music by way of a subplot. Instead, the satire on rock somehow turned into a celebration of it—to this day, still the most potent ever captured on celluloid.

When *The Girl Can't Help It* finally reached Liverpool early in the summer of 1957, it showed John America's new rock-'n'-roll stars as living beings for the very first time—minus Elvis, admittedly, but featuring cameo performances by others he worshipped almost as much, plus a few he'd barely heard of, all in voluptuous Eastman-color and megascreen CinemaScope. Here was Little Richard shrieking the title song in voice-over as Jayne Mansfield's mighty cleavage sashayed along a street, making men's glasses shatter in their frames and milk spurt out of bottles as though in premature ejaculation. Here was Eddie Cochran, a hunky young Elvis clone, singing "Twenty Flight Rock" while aiming his gorgeous vermilion guitar to left and right like a tommy gun. Here was another white newcomer, Gene Vincent, a bony ex-sailor with an eerily high and sibilant voice, keening a second classic piece of rock-'n'-roll Jabberwocky, entitled "Be-Bop-a-Lula." Here, even more fascinatingly to John, were Vincent's backing group, the Bluecaps: not merely tacked-on session men but fellow spirits who shared their leader's aura of dissipation and menace, and counterpointed his vocal with almost animalistic whoops and yaps and cackles.

The messages from jukeboxes and Radio Lux were not all uproar and anarchy. Early June brought the first chart appearance of the Everly Brothers, Don and Phil, two former child country stars whose almost feminine close harmony created some initial confusion with Britain's own Beverley Sisters. The Everlys' number-six hit, "Bye Bye Love," so appealed to John's softer, melodic side—never mind the notion of having someone so close as a brother to sing with—that he began looking around for a partner to form an Everly-style duet. Since his usual blood brother, Pete Shotton, couldn't sing a note, he had a few tentative vocalizing sessions with Len Garry. But the closer-than-Everly brotherhood he was destined to form only a few weeks from now would not be called Lennon and Garry.

On June 22, Liverpool celebrated the 750th anniversary of the charter it had been granted by King John. The occasion was marked by street parties throughout the city, each street competing with its neighbors in lavishness of decoration, food, and outdoor entertainment. Like several others, Rosebery Street catered to the younger element by having a skiffle group, in this case John and the Quarrymen. Rosebery Street was deep in the heart of Liverpool 8, a quarter where grammar-school boys from Woolton normally would not care to stray. But it was also the home of Charles Roberts, Colin Hanton's printer friend, who had stenciled QUARRY MEN on his bass drum, so a quid pro quo was felt to be in order.

The Quarrymen played on the back of a coal truck, giving one performance in the afternoon and another in the early evening. At the second, their audience included a hugely proud Julia, who made the long bus journey from Bloomfield Road, bringing John's half sisters, Julia and Jackie. The two little girls sat on the truck's tailboard while Julia watched from the Roberts family's living room.

Many cameras were in use that day, and one of them chanced to take the first-ever picture of John in performance. There he is on the coal-dusty stage, wearing the checked shirt Julia had bought him at Garston's open-air market, singing raptly into a stand microphone whose cord extends perilously off the truck and through the open ground-floor window of the house behind, to the nearest accessible electrical outlet. His fellow Quarrymen are grouped slightly behind him, all but for little Colin Hanton, in a garish two-tone jumper, who sits some way to the left—"half-cut," as he now admits, on pints of black velvet. The backdrop of grimy Victorian brickwork and celebration flags makes it more like a scene from the late-nineteenth century than the mid-twentieth.

During their second show, as dusk was falling and fairy lights twinkled on overhead, Colin's rather isolated position on the truck turned out to be providential. Just behind it stood a group of tough boys from neighboring Hatherley Street whom he overheard plotting to "get Lennon" after the show. When their last number ended, the Quarrymen did not wait for applause but bundled their instruments off the stage and sought sanctuary in Charlie Roberts's house, where his mother regaled them with a high tea. The Hatherley Street roughs were not easily deterred, banging on the windows and calling on John to come out. The problem was solved by the arrival of a single policeman, in those days a magisterial presence, who warned off the troublemakers, then gave the Quarrymen safe escort to their bus stop.

Summer's ritual festivities promised more busy times ahead. On July 6, the Quarrymen were booked to appear at the annual garden fete of their own parish church, St. Peter's, Woolton. John had lately astonished Pricey, the rector, by submitting himself for formal confirmation into the Church of England—not through any deep religious awakening, as he would later admit, but for the sake of the cash gifts that confirmation candidates traditionally receive from their families. Whether or not Pricey realized this, John was once again persona grata at St. Peter's, and his group was not only to perform at the fete itself, but also aboard one of the motorized carnival floats that paraded through Woolton village beforehand. Shades of his grandfather Jack, in days when Andrew Roberton's Colored Operatic Kentucky Minstrels always came to town in triumph, plinking and plunking on the back of a decorated wagon!

6

BUDDIES

It went through my head that I'd have to
keep him in line if I let him join.

Paul McCartney had known John well by sight for
some time before their carefully arranged official introduction. To Paul, judging solely by appearances, "John was the local Ted. You saw him
rather than met him . . . This Ted would get on
the bus and I wouldn't look at him too hard in case
he hit me."

The two might have been expected to strike up a natural acquain-
tanceship, living as near to each other as they did, with close friends
in common and a mutual, consuming passion for rock 'n' roll. The
main obstacle was an eighteen-month age difference between them.
John, at sixteen and three quarters, was considered to be on the edge
of manhood, while Paul, having only just turned fifteen, was still
in the outer reaches of boyhood. The discrepancy would never be
an issue once they knew each other, and would grow less noticeable with each passing year; but in their first brief encounters on the

Allerton-Woolton bus, it had prevented them from exchanging even so much as a nod.

The fact that Paul went to school with two cronies of John's, Ivan Vaughan and Len Garry, brought no fast-track introduction either. Ivan, it so happened, had long since marked Paul down as being of potential value to the Quarrymen, but guessed how John might react if a new recruit were too pointedly shoved under his nose. So Ivy bided his time until the right moment came, which it did not do until Saturday, July 6, 1957, when the Quarrymen were to play at St. Peter's Church fete in Woolton. Having presold Paul to John as "a great fellow," Ivy then oh so casually invited Paul, who oh so casually agreed, to cycle over from Allerton, watch the Quarrymen in performance, and say hello to their leader afterwards.

The baby-faced fifteen-year-old whom John was to meet on this innocent summer's afternoon—the more-than-collaborator, more-than-partner, more-than-brother destined to share his life and live in his mind and voice for almost the whole of the next decade—would always seem like his polar opposite in every possible way. Yet in their origins and family backgrounds they were remarkably similar.

As John's late grandfather George Stanley had done, Paul's father, Jim McCartney, held a position of the utmost respectability in Liverpool's mercantile world. Jim was a salesman for Hannay & Co., a firm of cotton brokers he had faithfully served for almost three decades, except for a necessary interlude in a war munitions factory. Despite the industry's steep postwar decline, working "in cotton" remained as much a badge of prestige among Liverpool's upper working class as having assisted salvage operations on the *Thetis*. With his brown chalkstripe suits, polished brogues, and stiff-collared shirts, Jim McCartney was a type of man now—sadly—almost vanished from British commerce: diligent, loyal, principled, and seemingly devoid of greed, ruthlessness, or ego.

Like John, Paul had grown up in an atmosphere of social aspiration. His mother, Mary, was a trained nurse (like John's Aunt Mary) who subsequently became a domiciliary midwife employed by the local authority to tend to the large numbers of women who still chose to give birth at home. This meant that, although Paul and his younger brother, Michael, were raised on the succession of council estates where their mother was based, they always had a sense of being slightly apart and special. Mary McCartney was a woman of natural refinement who encouraged her sons to try to speak more "nicely" than the estate children they played with.

Like John, Paul came from Irish forebears, with all the lyricism and charm that implies, and had music and the instinct to perform in his genes. As a young man in the 1920s, Jim McCartney had led a small amateur dance band, to whose syncopated rhythms, it is more than likely, John's parents, Alf and Julia, had Charlestoned or Black-Bottomed in their good times as a couple. Though Jim's bandleading days were long past, he still played the upright piano he had bought on the installment plan from North End Music Stores (NEMS) in Walton Road. Paul had inherited his father's instinctive musical ear and an ability to sing in harmony, which Jim encouraged with the same community-spirited maxim John had so often heard from Julia: if he could do a song or play something, he'd always be popular at parties.

Like John, Paul had shown himself to be clever and artistic at an early age, had passed the Eleven Plus and won a place at a renowned city grammar school, Liverpool Institute in Mount Street. Like John, he wore a black uniform blazer with a Latin motto, in this case *Non nobis solum sed toti mundo nati* ("We are born not for ourselves only, but for all the world"); like John, he excelled in English, was a fan of Richmal Crompton's William books, and showed a talent for cartooning and caricature.

Paul's life had already been blighted by a tragedy that, all too soon, was to repeat itself in John's. In October 1956, Mary McCartney died from breast cancer. After an initial period of emotional collapse, fifty-three-year-old Jim rallied heroically, teaching himself to cook and keep house for his two sons while continuing to travel for Hannay's. The three lived a bachelor existence in the last council house Mary's job had provided, number 20 Forthlin Road, Allerton, a short bus ride away from Menlove Avenue. Without Mary's extra income, money was tight, but a circle of good-hearted aunts helped care for Paul and Michael just as a corresponding one always had for John. Although never educated to any advanced degree, Jim was as much a proponent of reading and linguistic fluency as was Aunt Mimi: a recent spelling test at Liverpool Institute had shown Paul to be the only boy in his class able to spell *phlegm*.

But Paul, while being as much an individualist as John, possessed none of John's reckless rebelliousness. He had a profound and most un-Liverpudlian dislike of all overt aggression and confrontation, preferring to bend others to his will by charm, diplomacy, and the sometimes deceptive innocence of his oversize brown eyes.

Well before rock 'n' roll hit Britain, Paul had been able to pick out tunes on the family piano and, with Jim's encouragement, had begun learning the trumpet, hitherto the most glamorous instrument on the bandstand. As soon as he heard Elvis and saw Lonnie Donegan, he took his trumpet back to Rushworth and Draper's department store and swapped it for a £15 Zenith guitar with cello-style f-shaped sound holes. Being left-handed, he found he had to play his instrument in reverse, strumming with his left hand and shaping chords on the fretboard with his right.

Although by now a more than proficient guitarist with an obviously usable voice, he had not been snapped up by any skiffle group—nor, apparently, sought to be. Like John, he had been captivated by the Everly Brothers' close harmony, and vaguely planned to form an Everly-style duo with a friend named Ian James (as John had with Len Garry), but nothing came of it. On the daily bus trip to school, he'd become friendly with another Institute boy, George Harrison, who shared his fascination with guitars and rock 'n' roll. Though George was nine months his junior, they found common ground in drawing pictures of curvaceous guitar bodies and comparing new chords, and had become close enough to go on a hitchhiking vacation together.

The hot Saturday of July 6 did not seem an auspicious one for John. In the morning, Mendips's mock-Tudor hallway echoed to another blazing argument when he came downstairs in his chosen outfit of drape jacket, open-necked checked shirt, and ankle-hugging black jeans. "Mimi . . . said to me I'd done it at last, I was a real Teddy boy," he would recall. "I seemed to disgust everyone, not just Mimi."

The afternoon unfolded with the slow-motion predictability of every village pageant John had ever read about in a William story. The procession of decorated carnival floats made its way down Allerton Road, Kings Drive, and Hunts Cross Avenue, at its head the brass band of the Cheshire Yeomanry ("By permission of Lt. Col. C.G.V. Churton, M.C., M.B.E"), at its rear a flatbed coal-merchant's truck bearing the Quarrymen. Despite the grinding slowness of the parade, it was difficult to play with any effectiveness on such an unsteady perch, and John quickly gave up, took off his guitar, and sat on the tailboard with his legs dangling. A little way on, he spotted his mother and two half sisters in the crowd. Julia the younger and Jackie walked behind the truck, trying to make him laugh, but he still regarded himself in serious performance mode and refused to respond.

At the fete itself, his group had been allotted two brief spots, at 4:15 and 5:45, separated by a display of dog-handling from the City of Liverpool Police. By John's own account, that afternoon was the first time he ever attempted Gene Vincent's "Be-Bop-a-Lula" live onstage. One can shut one's eyes and almost hear the crazy words that, for once, he didn't have to invent ("We-e-ll she's the woman in the red blue jeans . . .") rising and falling against the competitive clamor of craft and homemade cake-stalls, games of hoop-la, quoits, and shilling-in-the-bucket, children's cries, indifferent adult conversation, and birdsong. Paul McCartney, quietly checking him out from the sidelines, remembers him also doing his reworded version of "Come Go with Me."

A famous photograph of him in midperformance was taken by his Quarry Bank schoolfriend Geoff Rhind from directly in front of the low open-air stage. Jacketless and tousled, visibly wilting in the heat, he has the narrow-eyed, challenging look that always went with leaving off his glasses. Behind him is a screen of ragged hedgerow; to his right stand a knot of expectant-looking younger boys, rather like the village children who always collected around William, hoping he would liven things up. At one point, so the story goes, he looked down into his audience and met the horrified gaze of his Aunt Mimi. According to Mimi, she had been unaware that John was performing that afternoon until a loud clash and a familiar raspy voice penetrated the refreshment tent, where she was savoring a quiet cup of tea. She would describe how when John saw her, he turned the words he was singing into a mock-fearful running commentary: "Oh-oh, Mimi's here! Mimi's coming down the path. . . ." However, his cousin Michael Cadwallader, then aged ten, remembers being at the fete in a large family group that, besides Julia and John's two half sisters, included two more aunts, Nanny and Harrie, and his ten-year-old cousin, David. "I got the sense that we'd been rounded up to go," Michael says. "And Mimi was the only one who could have been behind that."

The Quarrymen were also booked to play at the Grand Dance, which was to round off the day's merrymaking—that is to say, they'd been given another brief youth-pleasing spot in an evening of conventional quicksteps and foxtrots by the George Edwards Band. It was while they were setting up their gear in the too-familiar surroundings of St. Peter's Church Hall that Ivan Vaughan brought in the schoolfriend he wanted John to meet.

Even at this early time, it seems, Paul knew how to make an entrance of maximum effect. The pop ballad hit of the summer was "A White Sport Coat (And a Pink Carnation)," written by the American country star Marty Robbins but covered in the United Kingdom by a briefly burning Elvis clone named Terry Dene. And here was Ivy's much talked-about schoolfriend, resplendent in just such a white sport coat (or sports jacket, as the British call it)—a wide-shouldered, long-lapeled confection, dusted all over with silver flecks, reaching almost to his knees and set off by the narrowest pair of black drainies yet to have been smuggled past a vigilant father.

Introductions were made a little stiffly; this was, after all, a very youthful interloper and a particularly tight-knit group. Paul broke the ice by picking up one of the Quarrymen's guitars—whether John's or Eric Griffiths's no one now remembers—and levitating straight into "Twenty Flight Rock," as played by Eddie Cochran in *The Girl Can't Help It*, which he'd learned from the record a few days earlier. The song was a tricky one to sing and strum simultaneously, not just for a left-handed guitarist on a right-handed guitar but also because, thanks to Julia, the instrument was tuned like a banjo, its two bass strings slack and useless. Even so, the combined effect of the backswept hair, the baby face, the high yet robust voice, and the white sport coat was irresistible.

Years later, in a foreword to John's first published book, Paul would affectionately recall what a grown-up and dissipated character the Quarrymen's leader seemed on that day. "At Woolton church fete I met him. I was a fat schoolboy and as he leaned an arm on my shoulder, I realised he was drunk . . ." Hallowed myth has always stated that, in reaction to his strife with Mimi, and possibly against the oppressive sanctity of the occasion, John had laid hands on a supply of beer and, by late afternoon, was seriously under the influence. Four of the Quarrymen—Davis, Hanton, Garry, and Griffiths—have disputed the story. "Except for Colin Hanton, we none of us had any money to get tanked up on beer," Rod Davis says. "John might have managed to sneak a half-pint of bitter, but that would have been it."

Paul himself is now inclined to revise the degree of John's intoxication, which he says did not become apparent until after "Twenty Flight Rock" was over. "I also knocked around on the backstage piano and that would have been 'A Whole Lot of Shakin' by Jerry Lee [Lewis]. That's when I remember John leaning over, contributing a deft right hand in the upper octaves and surprising me with his beery breath. It's not that I was shocked, it's just that I remember this particular detail."

More desultory conversation followed while church helpers completed preparations for the Grand Dance or emptied dregs from tea urns in the adjacent kitchen, unaware of an encounter that was to rank alongside Gilbert's first with Sullivan or Rodgers's with Hart. Paul made himself still more impressive by tuning John's and Eric's guitars as guitars, giving them their full six-string span for the very first time. He remembers they did all go out to a pub in Woolton village later that evening, when he and John—and all the others except pint-size Colin Hanton—had to lie about their ages before being served. The visitor felt himself even more in dangerous adult company when talk arose of an impending raid by Teds from Garston and a mass punch-up in the center of the village. "I was wondering what I'd got myself into. I'd only come over for the afternoon and now I was in Mafia-land."

As John remembered, he asked Paul to join the Quarrymen when they first met in St. Peter's Church Hall, though Paul did not take it as official until Pete Shotton formally repeated the invitation a couple of weeks later. John realized at the time it was a major step, though how major he could not have dreamed. "I thought, half to myself, 'He's as good as me.' I'd been kingpin up to then. Now I thought 'If I take him on, what will happen?' . . . The decision was whether to keep me strong or make the group stronger . . . It went through my head that I'd have to keep him in line if I let him join. But he was good, so he was worth having. He also looked like Elvis. I dug him."

Eleven days after the Woolton fete, John reached the end of his final term at Quarry Bank High School. He had sat the GCE Ordinary-level examination in seven subjects and failed every one—though by a margin narrow enough to indicate that he could have passed with a minimum of extra effort. Even in art, his outstanding subject, he could not be bothered to meet the unexacting O-level standard. "All they were interested in was neatness," he would recall. "I was never neat. I used to mix all the colors together. We had one question [in the exam-paper] which said do a picture of 'travel.' I drew a picture of a hunchback with warts all over him."

Without O-levels, there was no question of entering Quarry Bank's sixth form for the two-year A-level (Advanced) GCE course on which university and college entrance depended. Since John was not prepared to sit his O's again, any more than the school was to let him, he had no choice but to leave.

Had he been born a few months earlier than he was, the period after school-leaving would have been amply occupied. Since 1939, all young British males had been subject to compulsory military service, a two-year term that, in the mid-fifties, might find them facing Soviet Russia in the West German nuclear front line, fighting terrorists in Malaya, Kenya, or Cyprus, or merely drilling pointlessly on some home base like Catterick or Aldershot. But in 1957, National

Service was abolished, saving John in the nick of time from "square-bashing" and sergeant majors. The only time he would ever don a khaki uniform or pick up a gun would be when acting in a film.

He himself had given no thought to his career, other than inwardly vowing never to become the doctor or pharmacist or veterinarian that Aunt Mimi hoped he would. "I was always thinking I was going to be a famous artist and possibly I'd have to marry a very rich old lady, or man, to look after me while I did my art . . . I didn't really know what I wanted to be, apart from ending up as an eccentric millionaire. I had to be a millionaire. If I couldn't do it without being crooked, then I'd have to be crooked. I was quite prepared to do that—nobody obviously was going to give me money for my paintings—but I was too much of a coward."

With seafaring men on both sides of his family, it was natural for his thoughts to turn to the docks that still flourished along the Mersey, and the exotic worlds to which they led. One day, he brought home a slightly older boy who had followed Alf Lennon's calling of ship's steward and—so it seemed to John—led a life of dazzling glamour and affluence. "His hair [was] in a Tony Curtis, they called it, all smoothed down with grease at the sides," Mimi remembered. "'Mimi,' John whispered to me in the kitchen, 'this boy's got pots of money. He goes away to sea.' I said, 'Well, he's no captain and he's no engineer—what is he?' 'He waits at table, John said. 'Ha!' I said. 'A fine ambition!'"

Shortly afterward she stumbled on a pact between John and Nigel Walley to enroll together in the training course that would have turned them into junior stewards. We just thought we'd like to see the world while we were still young," Walley remembers now. However, when John tried to sign up for the course, he was told that at his age he needed consent of a parent or guardian. "I was rung up by this place at the Pier Head—some sort of seamen's employment office," Mimi remembered. "'We've got a young boy named John Lennon here,' they said. 'He's asking to sign up. . . .' 'Don't you even dream of it,' I told them."

The main enticement of going to sea for young men those days was the unlimited sex it promised. But that, at least, formed no part of John's motivation. Alone of his circle, he was known to have lost his virginity with his curvaceous strawberry-blonde steady, Barbara Baker, and since then had racked up a mounting score with several of the Quarrymen's more brazen camp followers. "Going all the way," it used to be called, though the term is hardly accurate. In those days, the predominant form of contraception was the sheath, not yet known as the condom but as the French letter or rubber Johnny, and sold only by pharmacists and barbers amid fandangos of furtiveness and embarrassment that few teenage boys were willing to brave. With the girls who would let him, John therefore used the risky method of coitus interruptus. In Liverpool it was known as "getting off at Edge Hill," that being the last station on the northbound railway line where one could alight before the climactic downhill run into the Lime Street terminus.

Since neither he nor Barbara had a place of their own, there was nowhere to do it but al fresco in the woods or on the grounds of some neighborhood stately home, or even in a churchyard whose monuments at least provided a relief from damp grass. Years later, he would ungallantly remember "a night, or should I say a day . . . when I was fucking my girlfriend on a gravestone and my arse got covered in greenfly [aphids]. Where are you now, Barbara? That was a good lesson in karma and/or gardening. . . ."

In 1957, Barbara became pregnant. Despite their long physical relationship and his dangerous habit of getting off at Edge Hill, John was not responsible. Tired of sharing him with the Quarrymen's embryo groupies, she had chucked him some time before and taken up with one of his friends just to spite him. To avoid the inevitable stigma on her family, she was sent away from Liverpool to have the baby, which was then immediately put out for adoption. John, she says, was almost as mortified as if he'd been the father. "He was beside himself. . . . He came round to our house and he went crazy . . . kicking a panel of the fence in and shouting. . . . He was saying 'It should have been mine! It should have been mine!' He said he would marry me. It was typical of John, that. He came to see me and said it would be the best thing if we got married. He would stand by me." When Barbara returned home, they began going out again, but things were never the same, and the relationship faded away.

As his final term at Quarry Bank drew to a close, John was the

only one among his cronies still to have no idea what came next. Rod
Davis was to go into the sixth form to do A-level French, Spanish,
history, and Latin—and ultimately become head boy. Eric Griffiths
was to train as a ship's navigation officer. Even John's closest partner
in crime, Pete Shotton, had astonished his teachers—not to mention
his erstwhile fellow shoplifter and dinner-ticket racketeer—by winning a cadetship at the Police Training College in Mather Avenue.

Since John seemed incapable of formulating any ideas, his future
had to be discussed over his head by Mimi and the Quarry Bank
principal, Mr. Pobjoy. "Pobjoy asked me what I was going to do with
him." Mimi recalled. "I said, 'What are *you* going to do with him.
You've had him for five years.'" The only faint ray of hope his headmaster could see was his unquestioned talent for drawing. If his aunt
consented, Mr. Pobjoy would put John's name forward to the Liverpool College of Art, with a special letter pleading for his failed O-
level in that subject not to count against him. To Mimi, "It was better
than nothing; at least he was going to college. Then I found out I
would have to go on supporting him for the first year, so I thought if
I am paying for his education, then he's going to go there and learn
something."

Mr. Pobjoy made it a condition of recommending John to the art
college that his behavior must be impeccable for the rest of that final
term. Not until Quarry Bank actually let out and his teachers all corroborated his good conduct would the letter to the college be sent.
John duly sat out his remaining classes with an expression of choirboy innocence and took pains to avoid overt trouble. However, there
was one final act of subversion on his conscience that could have
ruined everything.

Summer term's most sacred ritual was the school photograph,
a black-and-white portrait of all two hundred–odd pupils and staff
assembled on the lawn outside the main building. Such wide-angle
shots required a tripod-mounted camera with a special panoramic
lens that took several seconds to make its exposure, panning from
one end of the group to the other. According to school folklore, it
was possible for a boy on one side to be snapped by the lens, then
run to the opposite side and be snapped again as it completed its arc,

so appearing in the picture twice. When Quarry Bank mustered in eight ascending black-blazered rows for the 1957 photograph, John decided to put this theory to the test.

Rather than conduct the experiment in person, he nominated his classmate Harry "Goosey" Gooseman. "John had heard it was possible, but rather than do it himself, he got me all fired up and raring to go," Gooseman remembers. "Anyway, you can see what happened when you look at the photograph. . . . When the camera began its slow move, I ducked down and ran along behind the line and popped up in another place. Sadly for me, . . . I moved too soon, and so you see this empty space where I should have been standing, right behind John. And then when I tried to race the camera and to get onto a chair or bench further along, there was no way in for me, so you can just see a bit of my head peeping through. Some of the lads didn't know what was happening, but John did. You have only to look at his face . . . and the smirks of his gang. I remember him laughing out loud when we were finally presented with the photograph, and he saw the empty space behind him where I should have been."

Fortunately, Mr. Pobjoy never noticed the gap at one end of the school group or the blur of an intruding head at the other. On the last day of term, July 17, the letter went to Liverpool College of Art, recommending John for entry. The head also supplied a personal reference that generously accentuated the positive: "He has been a trouble spot for many years in discipline, but has somewhat mended his ways. Requires the sanction of 'losing a job' to keep him on the rails. But I believe he is not beyond redemption and he could really turn out a fairly responsible adult who might go far."

It was not such a tremendous coup that had been accomplished on John's behalf. Under the easygoing educational system of late-fifties Britain, virtually anyone showing the faintest glimmer of creative ability could get a place at art college and be assured a generous local authority grant to support them. From this large intake, it was accepted that only a tiny minority would turn into actual artists. Some would become teachers, and a few would gravitate into the undeveloped sphere of design and graphics still mundanely known as commercial art. For the rest, studying art was merely an exotic interlude when they could put on airs and acquire calligraphic handwriting before yielding to the banalities of a business career or marriage.

Becoming an art student introduced John to a part of inner Liverpool that was almost unknown to him. Around the college's gray Victorian facade in Hope Street lay a raffish area of coffee bars, bric-a-brac shops, and student lodgings catacombed among elegant Georgian streets and curving terraces originally built for the city's shipping aristocracy. On St. James's Mount towered the sandstone bulk of Giles Gilbert Scott's Anglican cathedral, begun in 1904—and destined not to be fully inaugurated until 1978. Close at hand lay Britain's oldest West Indian and Chinese communities, the former bubbly with calypso and steel-band music, the latter so well assimilated that some pubs announced closing time in Cantonese as well as English. The mix of period grandeur and bohemian informality reached its apogee in the Philharmonic Dining Rooms—adjacent to the Liverpool Philharmonic Orchestra's recital hall—which boasted wood paneling to rival any first-class saloon on the great transatlantic ships, and men's urinal stalls carved from rose-colored marble.

John was to study for a National Diploma in Art and Design, a course intended to occupy him full-time for the next four years. During the first two, he would take a range of subjects, including graphics, art history, architecture, ceramics, lettering, even basic woodworking. A college exam would then decide if he had reached a sufficient standard to continue in some specialist field like painting or sculpture. Since he did not qualify for a grant until age eighteen, he remained dependent on Mimi, who, as well as providing free board and lodging at Mendips, gave him a weekly allowance of 30 shillings for his bus fares and meals.

For his first day as an art student, he wore his best gray-blue Teddy boy suit, set off by a Slim Jim tie and Elvis-inspired blue suede shoes with fancily stitched uppers. He was a defiant daub of rock-'n'-roll proletarianism set down among middle-class-aspiring jazzers of the very same type who'd stopped the Quarrymen's show at the Cavern club. An observant girl named Ann Mason, who also started the Intermediate course that day, remembers how painfully he stood out among the Shetland knits and duffle coats, and his dogged air of determination not to care.

He had little idea of what studying art would entail, beyond an ardent hope, fostered by the comembers of his wankers' circle, that sketching nude women came into it somewhere. In fact, his daily timetable as an Intermediate student proved dispiritingly similar to life at the school from which he thought he had escaped. As at Quarry Bank, an attendance roll was called each morning, then came lessons in classrooms or the steep-tiered lecture theater, when oldish men in tweed suits, with a war-veteran air, spouted facts about Renaissance painters and pediments that he hadn't the smallest interest in studying. Before being allowed to draw a real person from life, he had to do hours of tedious groundwork in human anatomy, consisting largely of copying outsize plaster ears or arms or parts of the articulated human skeleton that the college numbered among its teaching aids.

Among the earliest kindred spirits he discovered was Helen Anderson, a beautiful sixteen-year-old from Fazakerley who had previously attended the college's junior art school. A precociously talented painter, Helen had been featured in the national press a few months earlier when Lonnie Donegan, the King of Skiffle himself, commissioned her to do his portrait and invited her to stay with him and his family during the sittings. John had read about this at the time, and, as soon as he arrived at college, made a point of seeking her out and demanding to hear the story firsthand. "He explained that Lonnie was a bit of a hero to him," Helen remembers. "He wanted to hear everything that had happened. And I had to tell him again and again."

Mimi's hope was that, if nothing else, art college might lessen the influence of Donegan and Elvis over John, and stimulate him to pursuits more elevated than traveling around by bus with a wallpaper-covered tea chest. There certainly was reason enough for the Quarrymen to have disintegrated that summer. Rod Davis, their banjo player, had unrancorously drifted away, feeling of no further use amid the increasingly rock-'n'-roll repertoire—which meant none of their personnel now had any connection with Quarry Bank High

School. However, John was determined to keep the group going, however awkwardly it sat with his new student persona, and for the present did not bestir himself to think up an alternative name.

On October 18, four months after having been invited to become a Quarryman, Paul McCartney finally took his place in the lineup. Though he had attended a few practice sessions back in August (and also joined the regular wanking school convened at Nigel Walley's house), his stage debut had been postponed by a spell at Boy Scout camp and a visit with his father and brother to Butlins Holiday Camp in Filey, Yorkshire.

His first appearance with the Quarrymen was at the New Club-moor Hall, a Conservative club in the Liverpool suburb of Norris Green. The booker was one Charles McBain, aka Charlie Mac, a local impresario best known for presenting strict-tempo ballroom danc-ing, whose press advertisements used the motto "Always Gay." Paul had been awarded his own instrumental spot using his f-hole Zenith on Arthur Smith's "Guitar Boogie." But at the crucial moment, as he recalls, he was attacked by "nerves leading to sticky fingers. [It] was one of the first gigs I'd ever played, and the sheer terror of it got to me." Charlie Mac adjudicated the overall performance much as he would have done a samba competition, scribbling "Good and bad" on one of Nigel Walley's business cards.

Despite that equivocal judgment, the Quarrymen began to make regular appearances at McBain's various "Rhythm Nights," chiefly at Wilson Hall opposite the Garston bus depot. Though a step up in prestige from church fetes and youth clubs, the prospect was a daunting one. Garston was famously the haunt of Liverpool's tough-est Teds outside the docks—velveteen-collared psychopaths who waged gang warfare with weapons that, in some cases, would not have shamed the Spanish Inquisition. A Garston Ted bent on a night's pleasure first wrapped around his wrist a thick leather belt studded with industrial-size washers, its buckle filed to razor sharp-ness to increase its efficacy as a flail. Some sewed razor blades into their jacket revers as a surprise for anyone who tried grabbing them by the lapels.

The only sure way not to fall foul of these awesome beings—

pulling the thorn from the lion's paw as it were—was to give them the rock 'n' roll they loved. In this endeavor John now had an accomplice who was not only gifted at imitating Eddie Cochran and Jerry Lee Lewis but could also passably simulate the dementia of rock's ultimate chaos maker, Little Richard. One night at Wilson Hall while the Quarrymen were in midset, a massive Ted clambered up onstage and went eyeball-to-eyeball with Paul in classic Liverpool "look, pal . . ." mode. But it was merely to request him, quite politely in Garston terms, to sing "Long Tall Sally."

Paul's presence had an immediate effect within the Quarrymen, changing what was still essentially a group of mates having a laugh into something altogether less easygoing and more focused. And the mates were not always best pleased by the improvements he suggested. One of these was that as manager Nigel Walley should no longer receive an equal share of the collective earnings because he didn't actually appear onstage. "Walloggs," however, successfully resisted the idea, pointing to an upswing in the standard of recent gigs, which had included a performance for the social club at Stanley Abattoir. Another of Paul's concerns was that Colin Hanton's drumming was not of a high enough standard. In addition to playing guitar, piano, and trumpet, Paul was a competent drummer and, as Len Garry remembers, was always beating on tabletops and chairs with his hands or sticks or even pieces of cutlery, as if to demonstrate how much better he would be at the job. But John defended Colin, thinking mainly of what a grievous loss his drum kit would be.

The new McCartney-inspired professionalism was quickly in evidence. When the Quarrymen returned to New Clubmoor Hall to play a further gig for Charlie Mac on November 23, 1957, they had swapped their former casual mélange of plaid shirts and striped knitwear for matching black jeans, white shirts, and Western-style bootlace ties. A historic snapshot taken that night shows John and Paul sharing prominence at the front, each with his own stand microphone. While their sidemen are in shirtsleeves, they wear drape-cut jackets, which, Eric Griffiths remembers, were of a creamy or oatmeal shade. Even in that quaint, pseudo-cowboy guise, they are so obviously the only two who matter.

A crucial factor in John's early relationship with Paul was the con-current reduction of Pete Shotton's presence in his life. With the Quarrymen fully weaned to rock 'n' roll, Pete's skiffle washboard was now an embarrassing anachronism. But he knew John thought too much of him to drop him from the group, however much of a passenger he became. Finally, one night at a drunken party in Smith-down Road, the situation was resolved without grief or embarrass-ment to either side. John picked up the washboard and smashed it over Pete's head, dislodging the central metal portion and leaving the wooden frame hanging around his neck like a collar. Pete, as he remembers, sank to the floor, weeping tears of laughter mixed with relief. "I was finished with playing but I didn't want to say so, nor did John. This way let me out and it let John out." Paul thus stepped neatly into Pete's shoes as the partner, private audience, and sounding-board John could not do without.

A major geographical coincidence also played its part in fostering their friendship. The art college to which John dispiritedly journeyed each day was literally next door to Paul's school, the Liverpool In-stitute. The two seats of learning occupied the same L-shaped build-ing whose neoclassical facade extended from Hope Street around the corner into Mount Street. Their respective populations worked in sight and earshot of one another and mingled in the cobbled streets outside during breaks and lunch periods. John was thus free to meet up with Paul privately all through the day as well as on Quarrymen business during the evening.

But rock 'n' roll and guitars were only part of what drew them together so immediately and powerfully in those last months of 1957. The affinity was intellectual as much as musical; they were top-of-the-form English literature students as much as would-be Elvises. Paul had read many, if not quite all, of the books that John had; he could quote Chaucer and Shakespeare and was a keen habitué of Liverpool's Everyman Theatre. To his surprise, he discovered that the self-styled beer-swilling desperado who claimed to have hated all schoolwork secretly devoted hours to composing stories, poems, and playlets, all via the disciplining medium of a typewriter. For all Paul's neat, methodical ways, he shared John's addiction to non-sense across its full historical spectrum, Lewis Carroll to the Goons.

Phrases from Lennon works-in-progress, such as "a cup of teeth" or "the early owls of the Morecambe," produced another instant meeting of minds; the Lennon-McCartney collaboration in its earliest form consisted of sitting around and thinking up further puns for John to type.

Paul was always conscious that John came from a social drawer above his, however much John tried to disown it. "We [the McCartneys] were in a posh area, but the council house bit of the posh area. John was actually in one of the almost posh houses in the posh area . . . in fact, he once told me the family used to own Woolton, the whole village." It was also impressive that, whereas Paul and his brother had "aunties," John had more formal and patrician-sounding "aunts," with oddball nicknames like Mater and Harrie rather than plain, cozy Millie or Jin. For Paul, this whole Richmal Crompton, tennis-club atmosphere was summed up in the name Mimi, which he'd previously associated with 1920s flappers brandishing long cigarette holders.

Despite his pleasing appearance, politeness, and charm, his reception at Mendips was initially not very cordial. Mimi by this point clearly could not conceive of John bringing home anyone but "scruffs" whose aim could only be to lead him even further astray. Paul later said he found her treatment of him "very patronising . . . she was the kind of woman who would put you down with a glint in her eye, with a smile—but she'd put you down all the same." Mimi, for her part, felt suspicious of the way Paul invariably chose to sit on a kitchen stool at teatime as if, she said, "he always wants to look down on you."

At a significantly early stage, John and he began holding guitar-practice sessions away from the other Quarrymen. They tried playing seated side by side on John's bed, but there was so little room to maneuver that the heads of their guitars kept clashing together. Most times they would end up in the covered front porch, to which Mimi often banished John—and where the brickwork gave their tinny guitars an extra resonance. Sharing new chords was complicated by Paul's left-handedness, which meant that each saw the shape in an inverted form on his companion's fretboard, then had to change it around on his own. "We could read each other's chords backwards," Paul remembers, "but it also meant that if either of us needed to borrow the other's guitar in an emergency we were forced into having to play 'upside-down' and this became one of the little skills that each of us developed. The truth is that neither of us would let the other re-string his guitar."

The McCartneys' house in Forthlin Road was only a few minutes' walk from the Springwood estate where John had his secondary and utterly different home. Paul was soon introduced to Julia and told of the arrangement whereby John lived with his aunt even though the mother whom he clearly adored, and who clearly adored him, was only a couple of miles away. Julia was captivated by Paul's angelic charm and full of sympathy for the loss he'd suffered a few months before. "Poor boy," she would say to John, with what now seems heartbreaking irony. "He's lost his mother. We must have him round for a meal." Paul in turn thought Julia "gorgeous" and was impressed that she could play banjo, an accomplishment which even his highly musical father did not possess. Julia was always suggesting new numbers for the two of them to learn—mostly standards like "Ramona" and "Those Wedding Bells Are Breaking Up That Old Gang of Mine," which were to have as much influence on great songs still unwritten as would Elvis or Little Richard.

Despite the aching lack of a mother in Paul's life, the modest council house where he lived with his cotton salesman father and younger brother seemed to John an enviably uncomplicated place. The result was that he and his guitar spent increasing amounts of time at 20 Forthlin Road, where the parental welcome was at first not a great deal warmer than Paul's at Mendips. Jim McCartney was too much of a realist to try to ban John from the house, but he gave Paul a warning that was to prove not ill-founded: "He'll get you into trouble, son."

In his 1997 authorized biography by Barry Miles, *Many Years from Now*, Paul would describe how the two seeming opposites beheld a mirror image in much more than the chord-shapes on their respective fretboards:

> John, because of his upbringing and his unstable family life, had to
> be hard, witty, always ready for the cover-up, ready for the riposte,
> ready for the sharp little witticism. Whereas, with my rather com-

fortable upbringing, a lot of family, lots of people, very northern, "Cup of tea, love?" my surface grew to be easygoing. . . . But we wouldn't have put up with each other had we each only had that surface. I often used to boss him around, and he must have appreciated the hard side in me or it wouldn't have worked; conversely, I very much appreciated the soft side in him.

John had a lot to guard against and it formed his personality; he was a very guarded person. I think that was the balance between us: John was caustic and witty out of necessity and, underneath, quite a warm character when you got to know him. I was the opposite, easygoing, friendly, no necessity to be caustic or biting or acerbic but I could be tough if I needed to be . . . The partnership, the mix was incredible. We both had submerged qualities that we each saw and knew. [We would] never have stood each other for all that time if we'd just been one-dimensional.

The practice sessions at Paul's generally took place on weekday afternoons when both participants would "sag off" from their respective studies at college and school. At first the sessions were simply to practice the songs they had learned, or were still struggling to learn, from records or the wireless. John in those days had a liking for purely instrumental numbers and, so Paul remembers, did "a mean version" of the Harry Lime Theme, making his Gallotone Champion sound as much like a Viennese zither as it ever possibly could.

Bouts of playing would be punctuated by listening to the radio or to records, pun making, sex talk, and horseplay. The McCartneys had just acquired a telephone—no small thing for a council house in 1957—which Paul and John would use to make anonymous nuisance calls in funny voices to selected victims like John's former headmaster, Mr. Pobjoy. Once they tried writing a play together about "a Christ figure named Pilchard" who was to remain enigmatically offstage throughout in the manner of Samuel Beckett's Godot. "We couldn't figure out how playwrights did it," Paul remembered. "Did they work it all out and work through the chapters, or did they just write a stream of consciousness like we were doing?" Unable to resolve this dilemma, they gave up after page two.

The idea of writing original songs to perform, rather than merely recycling other people's, was firmly rooted in Paul's mind well before he met John. He had begun trying it virtually from the moment he acquired a guitar, combining melodic gifts inherited from his father with a talent for mimicking and pastiching the American-accented hits of the moment. His first completed song, "I Lost My Little Girl," had been written in late 1956, partly as a diversion from the trauma of his mother's death, partly as an expression of it. Around the time he joined the Quarrymen, he had something like a dozen other compositions under his belt, mostly picked out on the family upright piano, including a first draft of what would eventually become "When I'm Sixty-four" (which he thought "might come in handy for a musical comedy or something").

For a fifteen-year-old Liverpool schoolboy—indeed, for any ordinary mortal—this was breathtaking presumptuousness. In Britain's first rock-'n'-roll era, as for a century before it, songwriting was considered an art verging on the magical. It could be practiced only in London (naturally) by a tiny coterie of music-business insiders, middle-aged men with names like Paddy or Bunny, who alone understood the sacred alchemy of rhyming *arms* with *charms* and *moon* with *June*.

The writing first appeared on the wall for Paddy and Bunny in November 1957, when "That'll Be the Day" by the Crickets topped the UK singles chart. It was the most uproariously guitar-driven rock-'n'-roll song yet, with its jangly, wind-chime treble intro and solo and its underlay of thudding bass. The Crickets' leader, twenty-one-year-old Buddy Holly, was a multifaceted innovator: the first white rock-'n'-roller to write his own songs, the first to sing and play lead guitar, the first to subsume himself into a four-person group whose name was a whimsical collective noun. Holly's vocal style was as unique as Presley's and, if possible, even more acrobatic, veering between manic yells, lovelorn sighs, and a hiccuping stutter that could fracture even a word like *well* into as many as eight syllables.

For British boys struggling to make the leap from skiffle to rock, Holly was less a god than a godsend. Most of the previous American rock-'n'-roll hits, including almost all of Elvis's, had been far beyond their power to reproduce with their piping little voices and tinny instruments. But the songs that Holly wrote and recorded were built on instantly recognizable chords, E's and D's and B7's, their familiar changes and sequences rearranged to create a drama and stylishness they'd never seemed remotely capable of before. Equally imitable were the vocal backings, the blurry *Ooo*'s, *Aah*'s, and *Ba-ba-ba*'s that were presumed (mistakenly) to come from Holly's three fellow Crickets. With these elementary tools, every fading-from-fashion skiffle group could instantly refashion itself as a top-of-the-range rock combo.

Holly's most radical departure from established rock-'n'-roll style was an outsize pair of black horn-rimmed glasses. Coincidentally, this was a time when the new beatnik culture, simultaneously emanating from New York and Paris, and the first screen appearances by Anthony Perkins, had led many young men to cultivate just such an earnest, intellectual air. Holly's glasses, allied to his neat appearance and polymathic talent, made him appear like some star student, sitting exams in each sphere of rock and passing every one with honors.

With Buddy on the charts, John no longer needed to feel his poor sight automatically cast him down among the nerds, drips, weeds, and swots. After years of fruitlessly begging him to wear his glasses, Mimi now found herself being pestered to buy him a new pair, with frames far more conspicuous than the ones he had. Mimi, of course, had no idea who Buddy Holly was or why he should have superseded Elvis as John's mental menu for breakfast, dinner, and tea. She bought him the black horn-rims because she could refuse him nothing, in the hope that he'd now spend less of his time walking around half blind.

She might as well have saved her money. Even Buddy Holly–style frames could not overcome John's phobia about being seen in glasses. He put them on only when absolutely necessary, for close work at college or his practice sessions with Paul at Forthlin Road. To be allowed to see him wearing them was a mark of intimacy, granted to almost no females and only a select circle of males. Among the latter was Paul's brother Michael, a keen amateur photographer whose lens sometimes caught the horn-rimmed John studying his guitar fretboard with a librarian's earnestness. But by the time Mike clicked his shutter again, the horn-rims would have vanished.

That winter of 1957–58 brought a stream of further Buddy Holly songs—"Oh Boy," "Think It Over," "Maybe Baby"—each intriguingly different from the last yet still as easy to take apart and reassemble as children's building blocks. For John and Paul in their facing armchairs, it was the most natural step from playing songs Buddy had written to making up ones he might easily have done. Paul would later describe how they'd sit there, strumming Buddyish chord-sequences, exchanging Buddyish hiccups—"Uh-ho! Ah-hey! Ah-hey-hey!"—until inspiration came.

PART II

TO THE
TOPPERMOST
OF THE
POPPERMOST

7

MY MUMMY'S DEAD

It was the worst thing that ever happened to me.

By his second term at Liverpool College of Art, John was known as the most problematic student in any age group or any course: a troublemaker and subversive who resisted doing serious work himself and tried his utmost to distract his fellow students from theirs. Most of his instructors quickly decided he was unteachable, demanded little or no work from him, and avoided any confrontation over his behavior. His sculpture tutor, Philip Hartas, for one, was frankly intimidated by "a fellow who seemed to have been born without brakes."

The sullen sartorial outsider of registration day had metamorphosed into something vaguely resembling an art student, though he would never completely discard his would-be tough Teddy Boy persona. "I became a bit artier . . . but I still dressed like a Ted, with tight drainies," he recalled. "One week I'd go in with my college scarf . . . the next week I'd go for the leather jacket and jeans."

The young people with whom he now spent his days were a

great deal less shockable than his old classmates at Quarry Bank. The word *fuck* and its derivatives—still absolutely taboo in polite society and all printed matter—were used throughout college with a casualness that even the doggedly foul-mouthed Woolton Outlaw at first found surprising. Many students had flats of their own, and so could have sex whenever they pleased, in privacy and comfort rather than hastily and furtively in the cold outdoors. Almost everyone, male and female, drank heavily and chain-smoked; some even took illegal drugs, mostly acquired through the neighboring West Indian community—though John, at this stage, did not even dream such things existed.

On the outside, he might have been all swagger and defiance, but inside he was consumed with self-doubt, believing that he had got into college only by a fluke and possessed no aptitude for the work he was expected to do. "I should have been an illustrator or in the painting school," he complained years later. "But I found myself in Lettering. They might as well have put me in sky-diving for the use I was at lettering." (Once again, he sold himself short: the private sketchbooks containing his cartoons, nonsense poems, and stories were always lettered immaculately.)

"I think he felt frustrated, though he would never admit it," recalled one of his first tutors, Arthur Ballard. "There he was, surrounded by people who had some talent with art, and I think he felt in a bit over his head. He would act in a daft manner to distract people and probably take away the fact that he wasn't as good an artist as they were. He would act the fool, but underneath all that I could see he actually was a thinker."

John liked Arthur Ballard, a friendly, red-whiskered bear of a man who had once been the army's middleweight boxing champion. But in Ballard's classes, he initially shone no brighter than in any others. Every Friday the members of his twelve-person Intermediate group were expected to display a painting or drawing in progress for assessment by Ballard and general discussion and criticism. John's offerings were always far below the standard of the others'; on many occasions, he seemed too embarrassed show anything at all.

In an attempt to stimulate John's enthusiasm, Ballard would sometimes take him to a club called the Basement in Mount Pleasant, run as a sideline by the painter Yankel Feather. "Ballard used to come in with this very serious-looking young lad, and talk to him for hours at a time," Feather remembers. "Even in those days, I used to think he looked sort of half-Japanese. I remember the look he always used to give me, as if he wanted to tangle with me and see what I was made of.

"At the back of this old wine-cellar we used to have a grand piano with half its keys missing. John would get on that sometimes, and do Chuck Berry's "Roll Over Beethoven." One time when he was bashing away, I told him 'If you don't stop that fucking noise, I'll throw you out!' In the vestibule of the club, I'd hung this big semi-abstract painting that I'd done; and as John walked past it on this day, he got a key or something out of his pocket and ripped the canvas along its whole length. 'Cheerio, boss,' was all he said."

Ballard was beginning to despair of conjuring any worthwhile work from John when, in an empty lecture room one day, he happened on a notebook full of caricatures of college professors and students, poems, and satirical commentaries, which he thought "the wittiest thing I'd ever seen in my life." The book contained no clue as to its author; Ballard had to do some detective work before discovering it was John's. He didn't let on that he'd found it until the next time his class were pinning up their work for discussion. "I brought out [his] notebook and we discussed the work in it," Ballard remembered. "John had never expected anyone to look at it, let alone find it funny and brilliant. 'When I talk about interpretation, boy, this is the kind of thing I mean as well,' I told him. "This is the kind of thing I want you to be doing."

Yet he had abilities that went far beyond cartooning, even if he chose to reveal them only in flashes, and almost never on demand. He certainly was not the poor relation in his set when they were sent out of college to sketch from life in the cathedral precincts or the Williamson Square livestock market. The accepted method was to work in small dabs and stabs, with painstaking shading and cross-hatching. John, however, could capture a face or object in a single bold, unwavering line, much as one of his earliest artist heroes,

Henri Matisse, was wont to do. He was also capable of impressing his painting tutor, an energetic Welshman named Charlie Burton. "I thought he had the potential to be very good," Burton says. "But he didn't really have the right temperament for a painter, which means spending a lot of time on your own. John always had to have a crowd around him—and he had to be in control of them. One day, I told his group what I wanted them to do, and went out of the room for a few minutes. When I came back, John had them all rolling around in fits of laughter. Then he gave them a look as if to say 'What a load of absolute idiots you lot are.' Chilled them to the bone, he did."

Just as he and his fellow Woolton wankers had fantasized, his course did include life drawing of a nude female, to which Intermediate students eventually graduated from Grecian busts and the college skeleton. Not only that; June Furlong, the model who usually sat for John's group, was a gorgeous twenty-seven-year-old with the kind of voluptuous severity as a rule seen in shadowy "art" photographs. A forthright Scouser despite her exotic looks, she had modeled at most of London's premier art schools and was on friendly terms with many famous painters, among them Francis Bacon, Lucian Freud, and Frank Auerbach.

June ran the life class more strictly than any tutor, quelling the smallest hint of unrest among its male members with a ferocious eye, creating the severely practical atmosphere of—in her own phrase— "a clinic." She had received advance warning of John's fractiousness, and prepared herself for the worst when she saw him perched with dangling legs on the wooden shelf above the sink where students washed their brushes and palettes. (The shelf's being just too high to sit on with comfort made it irresistible to John.)

"But I never had the slightest bit of trouble with him," June remembers. "And never had a bad word from him. When he came in for a class, he'd pull his chair right up close to me and we'd talk, talk, talk for the whole time—about art, about the colleges where I'd worked in London and all the artists I'd met. And there was something about him you couldn't help but take notice of, even though no one seemed to think his work was much good. I remember thinking 'You, mate . . . you'll either end up at the bottom or you're going to the very top.'"

Clinical though June made the ambience, fascinating though her anecdotes about Augustus John and the Slade Art School, she was still the sexiest woman John had encountered outside Brigitte Bardot films or the pages of *Razzle* magazine. He once made an attempt to proposition her, as hundreds must have done before him, but was rebuffed without serious damage to his amour propre. "I said to him 'How much money have you got, John? I'm not sitting over a half of bitter at Ye Cracke, you know. I go to the Adelphi.'"

He needed an accomplice at college no less than at school, and Russell Jeffrey Mohammed soon stepped into the role of Ginger to his William, Lotton to his Shennon. Jeff Mohammed lived in Didsbury, Manchester, but boasted a complex pedigree—a father who was an Indian silk merchant and an Italian mother born within the sacred precincts of Vatican City in Rome. Aged twenty-seven, ten years older than John, he epitomized the college's open-door policy; before deciding to study art, he had experimented with a variety of jobs and done National Service as a military policeman in Malaya.

Jeff was tall and handsome, with the bearing of an Indian rajah and a voice that still bore traces of the public school to which his polyglot parents had sent him. He played jazz clarinet and was a passionate trad enthusiast who treated the latter encroachments of modern jazz as a personal insult. When the great Humphrey Lyttelton temporarily forsook the Dixieland style to make records with a more modern feel, Jeff waited until Lyttelton played a gig in Manchester, then confronted him, denounced him as a traitor, and ended by punching him in the nose.

By the time he met John, his eccentricities were already a byword among his fellow students. When he received his grant money, he would change it all into half-crown coins, turn the light off in his bedroom, then fling them far and wide, so that in later weeks when he became hard up, there was always hope of finding a stray half-crown under his bed or on top of his wardrobe. One of his favorite tricks was to select a pub or workmen's "caff" where every face was uncompromisingly white and fling open its door with a ringingly authoritative cry of "Right! All foreigners out of here!"

Despite their age difference, the pairing of John and Jeff Mohammed had something inevitable about it. They belonged to different workgroups and so spent most of each day apart, but wherever their paths crossed, John's manic laughter instantly redoubled. Although Jeff's greater worldliness and experience were part of the attraction for him, they always treated each other as equals. They had the same fondness for books, poetry, and language, the same interest in mildly occult things like Ouija boards and palmistry, the same unerring eye for human oddity, the same inexhaustible compulsion to make fun. Even their mutually inimical musical tastes, trad versus rock, caused no serious disagreement. Jeff never managed to turn John on to Satchmo Armstrong or Kid Ory, just as he himself remained impervious to the magic of Elvis and Buddy Holly. However, he possessed a large collection of jazz record albums, in those days almost the only kind to feature contemporary design and typography on their covers. John grudgingly conceded there was something in the look, if not the sound.

The two were most commonly to be found at Ye Cracke, an eccentric little mock-Tudor pub in Rice Street, just a couple of blocks from college, where both students and teaching staff would democratically forgather. Its art-college clientele favored the larger rear bar whose walls displayed two outsize etchings—one of Marshal Blucher greeting the Duke of Wellington at the Battle of Waterloo, the other of Horatio Nelson's death at Trafalgar. John's and Jeff's favorite roost was a bench below the Nelson scene, between side panels of British sailors watching their admiral's last moments. The horrified look on every face in the composition led John to retitle it Who Farted?

This being northern England, the beer came in pints, in straight glasses rather than tankards, wherein to leave the slightest drop cast doubt on the drinker's very manhood. Army life had made Jeff a seasoned drinker whose affability never faltered as the score of pints mounted. But John, then and always, needed little more than the proverbial "sniff of the barmaid's apron" to put him under the influence. And a drunk John, then and always, turned into an addle-brained kamikaze, ready to insult anyone and assault anyone. "I always got a little violent on drink," he would admit. "[Jeff] was like a bodyguard for me. So whenever I got into some controversy, he'd ease me out of it."

Occasionally they made up a threesome with Jeff's girlfriend, Ann Mason, whose sharp eye had noted every wrong detail of John's Registration Day outfit and who—like other females on their course—regarded him with an uneasy mixture of distaste and awe. Ann says that while Jeff's pranks always had an underlying kindliness, John seemed to recognize no boundaries of conscience or compassion in his urge to flout authority and do down the softies and drips. On the annual Panto Day, for instance, when the college joined with Liverpool University to raise money for charity, he would simply pocket the contents of the collection tin he had taken through the streets. He also continued his boyhood habit of shoplifting, even though the risks in central Liverpool were far greater than in rural Woolton. One of his habitual targets was an art-materials shop run by a pair of old ladies, both too nearsighted to realize how many of their brushes, pencils, and sketchbooks he was filching.

One day, when John and Ann sat near each other in a lecture, she began idly sketching him. Later, in one of the painting rooms, she developed her sketch into the first full-length portrait she had ever done—and the only one she ever would. John sat for her for a couple of hours with surprising forbearance, though, as she recalls, "I had to pretend I wasn't painting him and he pretended he wasn't posing." The portrait shows him seated on a turned-round wooden chair with his arms folded tightly over its back and his knees thrust out on either side; he is wearing a dark jacket and olive suede shoes (bought on a grant-spending spree with Jeff) and his usually hidden Buddy Holly glasses. The effect is of barely contained energy: a figure coiled to spring, or maybe run for cover.

John may have learned next to nothing from his college teachers. But that does not mean he learned nothing at college. His friendship with Stuart Sutcliffe amounted to a one-man degree course, even if largely conducted in student flats and smoky bar-parlors. And here, no scholarship boy with a virtuous cargo of GCE passes could have been more attentive, receptive, or enthralled.

Stu was the same age as John but had arrived at college from Prescot Grammar School a year earlier. He was far and away the

most talented student in the place, gifted with a seemingly effortless mastery of every medium he touched, drawing, painting, or
sculpture. He was also phenomenally energetic, filling canvases and
sketchbooks with work of a maturity that dazzled his instructors,
then hurtling on to the next thing almost before they had time to
articulate their praise. Small and feminine featured, with luxuriant
backswept hair, he was often likened to the short-lived screen idol
James Dean—a comparison that would prove all too sadly appropriate. In fact, the dark glasses he often wore denoted a more obscure
role-model, Zbigniew Cybulski, protégé of the Polish film director
Andrzej Wajda and sometimes called "the James Dean of Poland."

Stu functioned on an altogether more grown-up level than John.
Though his Scottish middle-class parents lived in Liverpool, he had
a flat in Percy Street, which he shared with his close friend Rod
Murray. Recognizing him to be in a class of his own, the college let
him do much of his work there also. His main tutor, the tolerant
Arthur Ballard, would drop by regularly to see him, bringing half
a bottle of whiskey for refreshment, but seldom made any effort to
control the roaring flood of his creativity.

John met Stu through Bill Harry, another fellow student destined to
play a significant role in his later life. Bill, in fact, was the archetypal
working-class hero, having fought his way to college from an impoverished childhood in Parliament Street, near the docks, where wartime
bomb rubble remained still uncleared and terrifying mobs with names
like the Chain Gang and the Peanut Gang ruled the neighborhood. A
compulsive reader, writer, cartoonist, organizer, and entrepreneur, he
found few kindred spirits apart from Stu and Rod Murray in a student
body he considered largely time-wasting "dilettanti."

Bill discovered that John shared his own interest in writing and,
at Ye Cracke one lunchtime, asked to read some of his work. Dif-
fidently murmuring something about "a poem," John pulled two
bedraggled sheets of paper from his jeans pocket and handed them
over. Bill expected the standard teenage knock-off of Byron or the
American Beats; instead, he found himself reading a Goonish pastiche of *The Archers*, BBC radio's agricultural drama, that made him
guffaw out loud.

John, as it happened, already knew about Stu Sutcliffe, and was more than happy for Bill Harry to introduce them formally at Ye Cracke, under the distracted gaze of the dying Lord Nelson. "If John ever thought anything or anyone was really good," Rod Murray remembers, "he turned into a completely different person. Much quieter, more thoughtful . . . ready to talk seriously about serious things. And he thought Stu was *really* good."

The admiration was by no means all on one side. Along with other diverse subject matter, Stu also enjoyed cartooning, as did Bill Harry. To John's amazement, both of them heaped praise on his drawings for technique as well as wit, comparing him with Saul Steinberg, whose whimsical, perspectiveless covers for *The New Yorker* magazine they had found in the college library. Suddenly, John was being taken seriously by the most talented artist on his horizon.

Stu's sister Pauline—in later life a respected therapist—thinks it hard to overrate the redemptive effect of this. "John had a desperate quest for a certain kind of nurturing. Stuart's nurturing was unconditional. . . . He loved him. And John recognized that Stuart believed in him . . . that he believed he wasn't just a mad, destructive anarchist, but was somebody of worth. Stuart freed John's own creative spirit."

John in effect led a double life at college, reflecting the two utterly different sides of his personality. For every drunken foray with Jeff Mohammed there would be a long, serious talk with Stu Sutcliffe, together with Bill Harry and Rod Murray or tête-à-tête. In common with only a few visual artists, Stu could verbalize his aims and intentions, and possessed intellectual curiosity outside his own field. At the time he met John, his personal reading list included Turgenev, Benvenuto Cellini, Herbert Read, Osbert Sitwell, and James Joyce. He was also heavily into Søren Kierkegaard, the nineteenth-century Danish philosopher who first said that in an irrational world, truth can only be subjective and individual. "We'd sit around for hours, asking, 'Who are we? Why are we here? What are we for?'" Bill remembers. It was from Stu that John first heard about Dadaism, the principle—to be so spectacularly demonstrated by his future second wife—that no subject matter is too shocking or absurd to deserve the name of art. "Without Stu Sutcliffe," Arthur Ballard said, "John wouldn't have known Dada from a donkey."

For John, the most surprising and winning aspect of this pint-size powerhouse was that he had nothing to do with the college's dominant trad jazz crowd but, on the contrary, had adored rock 'n' roll from its beginning. And already its unhinged sounds and tawdry glitter were firing his imagination as potently as anything from the Renaissance or the French Impressionists. Among his early paintings was an abstract entitled "Elvis Presley," clearly influenced by Picasso's *Guitar Player*, executed in garish jukebox colors and spotted with names of Presley songs, "Blue Moon [of Kentucky]," "Hound Dog," and "Heartbreak Hotel."

Another prescient belief shared by Stu, Bill, Rod, and now John, was that the city to which they belonged was unique in Britain—in the whole world—and deserved to be celebrated in art and culture just as American Beat poets like Lawrence Ferlinghetti and Gregory Corso had enshrined San Francisco. As regular attendees of poetry readings at Liverpool University, they disliked the way that almost all young contemporary British poets seemed to have fallen under the Beats' spell. They agreed to form a four-man society called the Dissenters (an echo of William Brown's many secret societies) to uphold Liverpool's own native idiom against these outside invaders: Stu and Rod would do it through art, Bill through writing, and John through music.

Now more than a year old, the Quarrymen still idled along under their obsolete name, mixing the death rattles of skiffle with already dated rock-'n'-roll classics and the latest easy-to-follow blueprint helpfully lobbed across the Atlantic by Buddy Holly.

The first months of 1958 brought further personnel changes. Once Paul was sure of his own position, he had begun enthusing to John about the guitar-mad Liverpool Institute boy with whom he used to travel to school by bus each day when the McCartneys still lived in Speke. The crucial defining mark of a rock combo was a lead guitarist playing instrumental breaks aside from the collective strum. Paul suggested that his schoolmate George Harrison might suit this role.

In contrast with the class ambiguities surrounding John (and, to a lesser degree, Paul), there was never any doubt about George's place in the social scale. His father, Harry, was a Liverpool Corporation bus driver, hardworking, respectable, and entirely comfortable with his station. Born in February 1943, George had spent infant years in the Liverpool from which Mimi had so thankfully rescued John, where homes stood claustrophobically side-to-side and back-to-back, linked by cobbled lanes known as jiggers; where the toilet was an outdoor shed, and the only way to have a bath was in a zinc tub before the kitchen fire.

George was an unlikely convert to rock 'n' roll—a serious, taciturn boy who hated many of the enforced intimacies of his working-class background and had an almost phobic abhorrence of "nosey neighbours." With this earnest nature went an acute sense of style and a refusal to conform that, in its quiet way, was almost the equal of John's. While other boy skifflers were content merely to strum in A or E, George applied himself to mastering the single-string solos that more experienced players automatically assumed to be far out of reach. He also owned a spectacular guitar: a cello-style Hofner President with what the catalog termed a "brunette sunburst finish" and a cutaway shoulder, for reaching the high notes at the base of the fretboard.

Paul's selling of George to John was a more protracted affair than Paul's own by Ivan Vaughan had been. For some time he was merely another Quarrymen follower, one of a not overlarge constituency, whose pale, unsmiling face could often be seen near the stage-front at Wilson Hall before all chance of serious musical appreciation was terminated by belt-lashing Teds. Formal introductions were finally made—so drummer Colin Hanton remembers—at an illegal club called the Morgue in the basement of an old house in Oakhill Park. By way of audition, George played "Raunchy," a bass-string instrumental that was currently a hit for Sun Records' producer Bill Justis. On the evidence of that and other bass-note workouts like "Guitar Boogie Shuffle," not to mention his splendiferous Hofner President, there seemed every reason for the Quarrymen to haul him on board before some other group did.

The objection was that George was still not quite fifteen and, despite his carefully poised coiffure and ultrasharp clothes, looked barely old enough to be out alone at night. The nine-month age difference between Paul and him was just about tolerable, as was the eighteen-month one between Paul and John. But John was George's senior by almost two and a half years. To the worldly art student, the intense little Ted with his big cutaway guitar and protruding ears was inevitably "just a kid."

John's answer was to accept George as a guitarist but not as an equal and still less, to begin with, as a friend. "[George] was just too young. I didn't want to know him at first. He came round [to Mendips] once and asked me to go to the pictures with him, but I pretended I was too busy." Nor was it from John alone that snubs and belittlement had to be endured. On the occasion of George's first visit to Mendips, Aunt Mimi also happened to be there. Mimi had considered Paul McCartney a sufficiently unwelcome visitant from the Scouse-accented netherworld. Unassuming little George, with his bus-driving dad, his Speke council house, his Saturday job as a butcher's errand boy—above all, his unusually deep, adenoidal Liverpudlian voice—could hardly have dismayed her more if he'd marched into the front hall and begun laying about its Royal Worcester and Coalport china with a hatchet. "He's a real wacker, isn't he?" she commented witheringly after he'd gone. "You always seem to like the low-class types, don't you, John?"

George swallowed all such slights—though he did not forget them—and by March 1958, having by now turned fifteen, was a full-fledged Quarryman. That month Paul wrote to a man named Mike Robbins, the husband of his cousin Bett, who was entertainments manager at Butlins Holiday Camp, in Filey. With true McCartney hubris but, alas, unsuccessfully, he offered the Quarrymen as resident performers during the next summer vacation.

George brought the number of guitarists in the Quarrymen to four, a not unusual complement for strum-happy skiffle groups but too many for the cooler, more calculated image of rock 'n' roll. Balance could be restored only by dropping Eric Griffiths, the last of John's original sidemen from Quarry Bank school. He was not an especially accomplished player and had never enjoyed the friendship with John that would have protected his back.

The group had also, coincidentally, lost Len Garry, the only other one who might perhaps have accompanied John, Paul, and George to their eventual destiny. In July 1958, Len collapsed at home and was rushed to Sefton General Hospital in a coma. He was found to be suffering from meningitis, an illness triggered, among other things, by breathing fetid air in subterranean dives like the Cavern. Once off the danger list, he was moved to the convalescent hospital at Fazak-erley, where he remained until January 1959.

Eric Griffiths said later that John offered him a chance to stay on in the Quarrymen if he would replace Len on bass, but using one of the new electric bass guitars rather than an outmoded tea chest. When he replied that such a technological marvel was far beyond his means, the plot against him moved swiftly. His best friend in the group, Colin Hanton, was visited by Nigel Walley, informed of the collective will, and persuaded not to walk out in sympathy—for Colin's drum kit, if not Colin's drumming, remained a vital collective asset. The next time a group rehearsal was scheduled, Griffiths was simply not told about it. Colin then delivered formal notification that he was out.

Ironically, the change of image that was meant to improve the Quarrymen's fortunes seemed to have a quite opposite effect. After the departure of Garry and Griffiths, the supply of paid gigs dwin-dled almost to nothing. For the next year, as graver matters over-shadowed John's life, his group would teeter constantly on the edge of extinction yet somehow never quite topple over it.

During this extended drought, most of the occasions when he shared a stage with his two young Liverpool Institute sidekicks had nothing to do with performing. Although the Institute and the art college occupied the same building complex, they did not interact in any way, and all interior connecting corridors had been sealed since their hiving-off from the old Mechanics Institute in the 1890s. However, there was an exterior side passage from the Institute to a section of the college yard close to a door that led to its cafeteria. Sev-eral times a week on their lunch break, Paul and George would do their best to obliterate their school uniform by buttoning their black raincoats to the neck over their ties. Then they would slip along the passage into the college precincts to meet up with John in the cafeteria.

It was strictly against the rules of both college and school: had the two intruders been recognized by anyone in authority, they would have been ejected and reported to their headmaster. As Paul remembers, the thrill of danger always suffused this lunchtime habitat of John's, where egg and chips was served instead of dreary school meat and veg, where fascinating females engaged in racy banter with arty young men, and where everyone could smoke as they pleased. "You'd see Paul and George sneak in," Ann Mason remembers. "Then John would join them, looking quite nervous. The cafeteria had a stage, which we used for our college plays and shows. They usually sat up there together, because it was near the door, I suppose in case Paul and George needed to make a quick exit."

John and Paul meanwhile continued writing songs together, seated in their facing chairs in the McCartney living room. After something like six months of these mostly illicit afternoon sessions, they had around twenty compositions they thought worth preserving—though for what, they still had no idea. Paul kept them in a school exercise book, their lyrics and chord sequences set out in his neat hand, each page headed "A Lennon-McCartney Original" or "Another Lennon-McCartney Original."

In every songwriting partnership they had ever heard of, one partner produced the melody, the other the lyrics. John and Paul made no such division of labor; both did words and music. Each song on which they collaborated was not only an expression of their mirror-image affinity but also an exercise in one-upmanship. From opposite sides of the fireplace, they would bat new ideas and chord changes back and forth like a table tennis match, each half-hoping the rally would continue forever and half that his opponent might miss and the ball go bouncing out of control among the coal scuttle and the fire tongs.

To begin with, they used the traditional Tin Pan Alley lexicon of *moon, June, true,* and *you,* from which rock 'n' roll, for all its seeming iconoclasm, had not significantly departed. "There's no blue moon that I can see / There's never been in history," ran one lyric destined to go nowhere. Now and then, the composers would subconsciously reveal their common grounding in English literature. A casual Ping-Pong exchange around G major, for instance, produced the phrase "love, love me do," a locution straight from the Lewis Carroll era ("Alice, Stop daydreaming, do! . . .") Tape recorders at this date were still cumbersome reel-to-reel machines, costing far more than the pair could hope to scrape up between them. Consequently, they had no idea how their voices sounded together, nor any means of preserving rough versions of songs that might deserve to be polished later. Instead, a simple rule of thumb was adopted: if they came up with a new number on one day and could both still remember it on the day after, it worked.

So the titles kept accumulating in Paul's exercise book, some predictable and derivative, others already giving off an unmistakable tang of originality and humor: "Keep Looking That Way," "Years Roll By," "Thinking of Linking," "Looking Glass," "Winston's Walk." In relation to their present life as musicians, the exercise was completely pointless. The audiences for whom the Quarrymen played, when they did manage to play, wanted nothing but skiffle chestnuts or American rock-'n'-roll covers. Those Lennon-McCartney Originals seemed destined not even to enjoy the limited exposure of John's "Daily Howl."

The old skiffle scene was growing more sophisticated in every way. Whereas once groups would audition for gigs in person, many of them now preferred to put songs on tape to circulate among promoters and club managements. Since the Quarrymen had no tape recorder, nor access to one, there was only one way so to advertise themselves. In the Kensington area of Liverpool was small studio where, for not too high a price, amateur performers could have their efforts enshrined on an actual gramophone record. Somewhat as a last resort in their hunt for work, the Quarrymen found the requisite cash among them and booked an appointment.

The studio was owned by an elderly man named Percy Phillips, who operated it single-handedly in a back room of his Victorian terrace house. Here, one afternoon in mid-1958, John, Paul, George, and drummer Colin Hanton assembled, plus a schoolfriend of Paul's named Duff Lowe, who was blessed with the gift of playing Jerry Lee Lewis–style arpeggios on the piano.

Even at this important moment, Lennon-McCartney Originals were left in the background. For their A-side, they chose "That'll Be the Day," Buddy Holly's breakthrough hit with the Crickets, released in September of the previous year. They had been trying for months to work out Holly's back-somersaulting guitar intro and, thanks mainly to John, had just succeeded in getting it note-perfect. The B-side was "In Spite of All the Danger," a country-and-western pastiche—and a rather good one—written by Paul with help from George, which explained Duff Lowe's presence on piano. John took the lead vocal on both tracks, with Paul and George singing backup harmonies.

The experience of "making a record," about which they had been boasting to their friends and families, proved rather lacking in glamour. They were allowed only a single take for each song, then had to sit and wait while Mr. Phillips cut the disk on a machine somewhat like an industrial lathe. The price was £5, but for an extra £1, he told them, he could first transfer their recording to tape and help them edit it before putting it on wax. "We'd only just managed to raise the five quid between us," Colin Hanton remembers. "John said there was no way we were paying another £1."

Their money bought them just the one shellac disk in the new, shrunken 45 rpm size, with a yellow label saying "Kensington" and the song titles and composer credits handwritten by Percy Phillips. Nigel Walley duly hawked it around the clubs and dance halls, but without notable success. Merseyside as yet had no local radio that might have picked it up, nor discotheques that might have introduced it to live audiences. The most effective plugger turned out to be Colin's printer friend, Charles Roberts, who worked for the Littlewoods mail-order organization. Roberts managed to get John's rendition of "That'll Be the Day" played over the public-address system to Littlewoods' largely female employees.

The disk became the common property of its makers, each enjoying custody of it in turn, one week at a time. John had it for a week, then passed it to Paul, who had it for a week, then passed it to

George, who had it for a week, then passed it to Colin, who had it for a week, then passed it to Duff Lowe, who had it for the next two decades, until it was worth a fortune.

All these new people and preoccupations in his life had helped blind and deafen John to an unbelievable thing going on under his very nose. Aunt Mimi was having a clandestine affair with her boarder, the biochemistry student Michael Fishwick. Yes, Mimi, that brisk suburban Betsey Trotwood, who seemed so scornful of normal feminine susceptibilities—scornful of the entire male species—had a lover half her age and only eight years older than the nephew in her care.

She had taken to Fishwick from the moment he arrived at Mendips as a nineteen-year-old undergraduate in 1951. It was not just that the Yorkshire teenager was studious and serious beyond his years and able to provide the intellectual stimulation Mimi had craved in her mundane marriage to George Smith. Something about him recalled the only real love of her life, the young doctor from Warrington who had died from a virus in 1932 before they could marry. She would later give Fishwick the gold cuff links she had bought her doomed fiancé as an engagement present and secretly had cherished ever since.

After George's death, Mimi had leaned heavily on Michael Fishwick, making him almost a surrogate head of the household and increasingly turning to him for advice in coping with John. A few months later—to their mutual astonishment—friendship turned into something more. He was twenty-four and she was fifty, though she said she was forty-six. The affair was consummated, revealing the exact nature of poor Uncle George's fabled "kindness." Mimi was still a virgin.

Their relationship, Fishwick now recalls, was punctuated by his absence during university vacations and was carried on almost entirely at Mendips. Occasionally they would go together to an art exhibition—like the big Van Gogh show in Liverpool—or stroll around one of the National Trust stately homes in the neighborhood, always taking care to do nothing that might set Woolton's tongues wagging and front-room curtains twitching. Once, when Mimi was with John at her sister Mater's in Edinburgh, she left him there and returned home so that she and Fishwick could have the house to themselves for a few days.

John never once suspected what was going on, often beyond a flimsy plaster wall in the bedroom next to his. Nor did Mimi confide in her three sisters, despite their unspoken vow to share everything. Julia, the one with the most highly tuned sexual antenna, had recently noticed a change in her—an indefinable blooming—and told the others she might have a "fancy man," but never guessed his identity.

In July 1958, Fishwick returned to Mendips for another extended stay. Three months earlier, he had been drafted into one of the last batches of young Britons compelled to do National Service. He was now an RAF officer trainee on the Isle of Man but applied for leave to return to Liverpool, as he said, to check over the PhD thesis he was having typed at the university.

Mimi was deeply worried about John's lack of progress at art college, and more than that: when taking his coat to be dry-cleaned, she had found a packet of Durex "rubber Johnnies" in one of the pockets, a precaution doubtless inspired by what had happened to Barbara Baker. Fishwick was the only person to whom she showed the packet, opening a tightly clenched hand to reveal it and asking, "What do I do about this?" His advice was not to make too big a thing of it—which she evidently took, for on this occasion, at least, he recalls, there was no fiery argument between aunt and nephew, no door-slamming exit by John to seek sanctuary at Julia's.

Sunday, July 15, brought Merseyside warm, sunny weather that showed the woods, golf greens, and trim hedges of Woolton at their lushest. John, on vacation from college, was around the house in the morning but, as Fishwick remembers, "drifted off later with some friends." Mimi's only visitor was Julia, who dropped in that afternoon for a cup of tea and a chat as she invariably did. It wasn't until late evening—past nine thirty—that she left to catch her bus back to Allerton. The longest day of the year had been only three weeks earlier. Dusk was only just starting to fall.

Julia's bus stop was in Menlove Avenue, about two hundred yards from Mendips's front gate, on the other side of the busy two-lane road, with no pedestrian crossing anywhere near—though a 30 mph speed limit was in force. Usually Mimi walked to the stop with her, but this evening she said she wouldn't if Julia didn't mind. "That's all right, don't worry," was the cheerful reply. "I'll see you tomorrow." Just then, Nigel Walley turned up at the front gate, looking for John. But John had not returned home all afternoon—and, in fact, was now over at Blomfield Road, waiting for his mother's return. Julia explained this to Walloggs, adding in her flirtatious way, "Never mind. You can walk me to the bus-stop."

Mimi watched from the front door as they strolled off together, Nigel chuckling at some remark of Julia's. They parted at the junction with Vale Road; Nigel turned right toward his home while Julia crossed Menlove Avenue's southbound lane to the median strip. This marked the route of the old tramway, where John and his Outlaws used to play their urchin games, and was now grassed-over and planted with a hedge. Julia stepped through the hedge and was halfway across the northbound lane when a bulky Standard Vanguard sedan, registration number LKF 630, loomed out of the twilight. Nigel heard a screech of brakes and a thud, and turned to see Julia's body thrown high into the air.

The noise was loud enough to reach Mimi and Michael Fishwick in the kitchen at Mendips. "We looked at each other and didn't say a word," Fishwick remembers. "We both just ran like hell." They found Julia lying in the road, with a stunned Nigel Walley kneeling beside her. Nigel would always be haunted by the memory of how strangely peaceful she looked, with a stray lock of her auburn hair fluttering in the summer breeze. The impact seemed to have left no mark, though Fishwick could see blood seeping through the reddish curls; she was still just barely alive. "[But] when I ran across the road and saw her," Mimi remembered, "I knew there was no hope."

An ambulance arrived within minutes to take Julia to Sefton General Hospital. Mimi got into the ambulance, still wearing the slippers in which she'd rushed out of doors. Fishwick joined her at the hospital later, bringing her some shoes and her handbag. Her immediate concern was that he should telephone other family members with the news, so that one of them could break it to John. "She didn't want John to find out just from a policeman turning up at the door."

Unfortunately, that was exactly how it happened: a Liverpool bobby in a Praetorian-crested helmet, knocking on the front door of 1 Blomfield Road and asking John in embarrassed officialese if he was Julia's son. At this unspeakable moment, the only person with him was the member of his extended family he least cared about: Bobby "Twitchy" Dykins. "Twitchy took it worse than me," John would recall. "Then he said 'Who's going to look after the kids?' And I hated him. Bloody selfishness. We got a taxi over to Sefton General, where she was lying dead . . . I talked hysterically to the taxi-driver all the way, ranted on and on, the way you do. The taxi-driver just grunted now and again. I refused to go in and see her. But Twitchy did. He broke down.

"It was the worst thing that ever happened to me. We'd caught up so much, me and Julia, in just a few years. We could communicate. We got on. She was great. I thought 'Fuck it, fuck it, fuck it. That's really fucked everything. I've no responsibilities to anyone now.'"

Michael Fishwick met Mimi at the hospital, then took her to Blomfield Road, where John's aunts Nanny and Harrie and their husbands had now arrived. Mimi collapsed into her sisters' arms while Fishwick was given a large whiskey by one of the ever-subordinate menfolk. When John finally left the house, it was not to return home but to seek out his old girlfriend, Barbara Baker, and tell her the news. As Barbara would recall, the two of them went into Reynolds Park and "stood there with our arms around each other, crying our eyes out." Late that night, Mimi's next-door neighbor, a Mrs. Bushnell, saw John playing his guitar in his usual place out in Mendips's front porch—the only real form of comfort or healing he could find.

Julia's death was recorded by a brief announcement in the *Liverpool Echo*, which allowed Bobby Dykins to claim her as the spouse she'd never officially become:

Dykins—July 15th—Julia, died as result of car accident, beloved wife of John Dykins, and dearly beloved mother of John Winston

Lennon, Julia and Jacqueline Dykins, 1 Blomfield Road, Liverpool 19.

Julia's funeral took place at Allerton Cemetery on the following
Friday, July 20. There was a bitter argument between Twitchy and
her sisters when it emerged that he had intended her to be buried
in a pauper's grave, subsidized by the city corporation. Instead, the
four women clubbed together to pay the funerary expenses. Among
the mourners were John's cousin Liela, his childhood playmate and
secret teenage crush. Now a medical student at Edinburgh University, she had been summoned by telegram from the Butlins Holiday
Camp where she had a vacation job as a chalet maid. Liela remembered John lying with his head in her lap for most of that day, too
numbed to speak or even move.

The car that struck Julia had been driven by an off-duty policeman, twenty-four-year-old Eric Clague of 43 Ramillies Road, Liverpool 18. The matter therefore became the subject of an internal
police inquiry by a team that included John's friend Pete Shotton,
currently on attachment to the CID (Criminal Investigation Department) from training college. The officer was only a learner driver
and so should not have been out in a car by himself. Since the police
of those days were rigorous in prosecuting their own, an accusation
of causing death by dangerous driving seemed likely. But no criminal
charge of any kind resulted. The whole matter was dealt with by the
inquest, four weeks later—though, unusually, this was conducted
before a jury, and its proceedings were closed to the press.

Clague attested that he had not been driving carelessly and had
been doing no more than 28 mph in the 30 mph zone. Nigel Walley,
the only eyewitness, testified that Clague's car seemed to have been
traveling at abnormal speed and to have swerved out of control
on the steep camber of the road as Julia suddenly stepped through
the hedge. Though himself the son of a police superintendent, he
sensed that the court regarded him as too young to be taken seriously. "The Coroner seemed to be bending over backwards to help
this man who'd killed Julia," Mimi remembered. "It emerged that
he was driving too fast, but you could see it was a bit of a men's club

really." When the young policeman was exonerated of blame, Mimi exploded in fury and threatened him with a walking stick. "I got so mad . . . That swine . . . If I could have got my hands on him, I would have killed him."

The findings were reported in a further brief *Echo* news item:

DASHED INTO CAR

Misadventure Verdict on Liverpool Woman

A verdict of misadventure was returned by the jury at the Liverpool inquest today into Mrs Julia Lennon, aged 44, of 1 Blomfield Road, Liverpool, who died after being struck by a motor car while she was crossing Menlove Avenue on July 15.

A witness, the Coroner (Mr J.A. Blackwood) told the jury, had said that Mrs Lennon had not appeared to look either way before she walked into the roadway. Then she saw the approaching car, made a dash to avoid it, but dashed into the car.

Julia's death left Bobby Dykins a broken man, ridden with guilt over his past drunken misuse of her and vowing tearfully never to touch alcohol again. Even after all these years, her sisters had never brought themselves to like or accept Dykins; their opinion of him now sank to rock bottom when—echoing his first panic-stricken cry to John—he announced he couldn't cope with raising his two young daughters by Julia. The sisters' mutual support group then swung into action to look after eleven-year-old Julia and nine-year-old Jackie, much as it had for John twelve years earlier. Since Mimi had more than enough on her plate this time around, it was decided that the girls should live with their Aunt Mater and Uncle Bert in Edinburgh.

In an attempt to soften the blow, Julia and Jackie were told that their mother was merely ill in hospital, and then packed off to Edinburgh on a supposed holiday with Mater and Bert. Within a short time, however, Mater decided she had bitten off more than she could chew, and Julia and Jackie were brought back to Woolton to live with Harrie at the Cottage, having still not been told that Julia was dead.

The deception somehow struggled on for weeks more, until Harrie's husband, Norman, could bear it no longer and blurted out, "Your Mummy's in Heaven."

Unable to stay on at 1 Blomfield Road without Julia, Dykins moved to a smaller house on the outskirts of Woolton, eventually acquiring a new woman friend and a dog. But he maintained contact with his daughters and kept Harrie well supplied with money for their keep. He also continued to feel a stepfatherly obligation toward John, giving him a key to the new house and encouraging him to use it whenever he pleased. When Dykins subsequently became relief manager at the Bear's Paw restaurant, he got John a vacation job there and ensured that a lion's share of the tips always went his way.

However deficient the *Echo*'s inquest report, it at least gave Julia her proper surname. For her marriage to Alf Lennon had never been officially dissolved, any more than Mimi's custody of John had been officially ratified. Her death in such shocking circumstances might have been expected to reconnect John with the long-absent father who nonetheless was still his legal guardian. But the family could not have got in touch with Alf even if it had wanted to.

Since leaving the merchant navy, Alf had, in his own romantic parlance, become "a gentleman of the road," the once-immaculate saloon steward now a semivagrant whose only employment was occasional menial jobs in hotel and restaurant kitchens. He was washing dishes at a restaurant called the Barn in Solihull, Warwickshire, when his brother Sydney sent him the *Liverpool Echo* cutting about Julia's death. He did not return to Liverpool until just after the following Christmas, having spent the preceding weeks in a London Salvation Army hostel recovering from a broken leg. It was at the hostel that a Liverpool solicitor finally contacted him and told him that, as Julia's legal next of kin, he was heir to the whole of her small estate. Alf duly returned north and presented himself at the solicitor's office, but only to give up his right to Julia's few possessions in favor of John. He made no attempt to see or communicate with John, however, and after a few days disappeared on his travels again. His reasoning was that, thanks to Mimi's years of propaganda, John would regard him as nothing but "a jailbird."

For Mimi herself, the blow went beyond losing her sister and seeing John lose his mother. Now that John was approaching manhood, she had realized she must prepare for a time when he would longer need her. For the first time in her dutiful, self-sacrificing life, she could think of herself—and bring her relationship with Michael Fishwick into the open. Fishwick had been offered a three-year research post in New Zealand, where, as it happened, several of Mimi's mother's family had emigrated. Not long after George's death, an uncle out there had died and left her a property worth £10,000. Mimi's plan, confided to no one, had been to follow Fishwick and live with him in the house she had inherited. "If it hadn't been for Julia's death," Fishwick says, "she'd have been gone by the end of fifty-eight."

Now there was nothing in the world that could have made her leave John. "I worried myself sick about [him] then," she remembered. "What he would turn out to be . . . what would happen if it was me next."

Despite Mimi's suspicions, police constable Eric Clague did not get off scot-free. He underwent a period of suspension from duty and, soon afterward, resigned from Liverpool Constabulary to begin a new career as a postman. By a horrible coincidence, one of the delivery routes he was later assigned included Forthlin Road, Allerton. Many times as John sat in the McCartneys' living room, he would have heard their afternoon mail drop onto the front doormat, little suspecting that "Mister Postman" was his mother's killer.

8

JEALOUS GUY

I was in a blind rage for two years.
I was either drunk or fighting.

Late-fifties Britain had none of the aids to coping with personal tragedy that we so depend on today. There were no family bereavement counselors to help John come to terms with his loss; no therapists, support groups, helplines, agony aunts, confessional television shows, or radio call-ins yet existed to tell him that the most private emotions are better made public and that broken hearts heal quicker if worn on one's sleeve.

In 1958, Britons throughout the whole social scale still observed the Victorian empire builders' convention of the stiff upper lip. Tears were the prerogative of females only and, for the most part, shed in decent seclusion; males were expected to show no emotion whatever. The closest members of a stricken family rarely expressed their feelings to one another, let alone to strangers. Such reticence had always been strongest in the north, strongest of all in those northern parts where privet hedge grew and hallways were half-timbered. Thus the shock and pain and outrage of Julia's death would stay bottled up in John until their release like a howling genie more than a decade into the future.

Among Julia's four sisters, there certainly was no weeping or wailing, only the most modest, muted signs of heartbreak. On the day after the tragedy, she had been due to go and see her sister Nanny at Rock Ferry. In anticipation of the visit, Nanny already had deck chairs set out in the back garden. She took a photograph of the unused chairs which she kept always beside her until her own death in 1997.

Mimi herself was never seen to cry, although Nanny's son, Michael Cadwallader, often saw silent tears well in her eyes. John would put his arms around her and say "Don't worry, Mimi . . . I love you." But such moments were never shared with outsiders. Three days after Julia's death, Michael Fishwick had had to report back to his RAF station, missing the funeral and not returning until the end of the year. Close though he was to Mimi, she never mentioned the events of July 15 to him, nor did she and John ever discuss them in his presence. In her traumatized state, the secret affair could hardly continue and, by unspoken agreement, she and Fishwick returned to being just friends. His visits became more infrequent until finally he met a young woman his own age and married her in 1960, ensuring that henceforward there would be only one man in Mimi's life.

The boys who had known John since toddlerhood were all equally at a loss about what to say to him. Pete Shotton, to whose house a distraught Nigel Walley had run immediately after the accident, could manage only a muttered "Sorry about your mum, John," when they met in Woolton the next day. As the last person to speak to Julia, Nigel himself would always harbor a lingering sense of guilt. He felt John blamed him for not saying the extra couple of words that might have stopped her crossing the road when she did.

It was, in fact, a new and still largely untried friend who most empathized with John's situation. For barely a year had passed since Paul McCartney had lost his own mother to breast cancer. "We had these personal tragedies in common, which did create a bond of friendship and understanding between us," he says. "We were able to talk about it to some degree [and] share thoughts that until then had remained private. . . . These shared confidences formed a strong basis for our continuing friendship and insight into each other's' characters. . . ." They could even summon up a weak smile at their common predicament after bumping into an acquaintance of Paul's mother Mary who also knew Julia, but had no idea that either had died. Having first blunderingly inquired of Paul how his mother was, the acquaintance turned to John and asked him the same question.

Most of his fellow art students did not learn what had happened until the college reconvened for its autumn term, two months after Julia's death. "Hey, John," a tactless girl shouted to him on registration day, "I hear your mother got killed by a car." Onlookers thought it must be some kind of sick joke until he nodded and muttered, "Yeah, that's right." The only person not mortified by the faux pas seemed to be John himself. "He didn't choke on it," a witness of the incident remembers. "He didn't register anything. It was like someone had said 'You had your hair cut yesterday.'"

The only person let under his guard was Arthur Ballard, the prizefighter-turned-professor in whom he seemed to find some of the reassuringness of his beloved Uncle George. Ballard was always to remember climbing the main college staircase and finding a red-eyed John sprawled miserably on the big window ledge halfway up. "I think he cried on Arthur's shoulder," June Furlong, the life model, says.

Unable to express, let alone share, his feelings, he turned to Liverpool's well-tried method of anesthetizing them. Most afternoons, he would stagger back to college from Ye Cracke with Jeff Mohammed, helplessly drunk and bent on ever more mindless disruption and devilment. One day, Arthur Ballard found him trying to urinate into the elevator shaft. The verbal cruelty he had always used on even his best friends seemed to grow still sharper and more unpredictable as he sensed their pity and confusion. "He tried it on with me," Bill Harry says. "But I came from a tough background; I told him to fuck off, and never had any trouble with him again. Stu Sutcliffe was different, though. John admired his work, but he could be terrible to him on a personal level. He'd make fun of Stu for being small . . . go on and on about it. And Stu never seemed to answer back."

The truth was that Stu possessed a maturity and wisdom beyond his eighteen years. He recognized that the price of John's friendship were these occasional venomous outbursts, and decided that it was a price worth paying. "John came to rely on that," says Stu's sister Pauline. "He knew Stuart could be pushed, but that he'd never be pushed away."

Almost everyone Stu met ended up being drawn or painted by him, and John was a subject he seemed to find more fascinating than most. A pencil sketch, made not long after they first met, shows John hunkered down with what looked like a skiffler's washboard—faceless yet still unmistakable. In a Sutcliffe oil painting of the student crowd at Ye Cracke, he dominates the foreground, seated on a barstool in a tan sweater and blue (suede?) shoes, clutching his pint glass, and staring off into the distance, lost in his own acrid thoughts.

The experience of knowing John also inspired Stu temporarily to forsake paint and charcoal for prose. In late 1958, he began writing a novel whose central character was named John and was very obviously drawn from life: "capricious, incalculable and self-centred, yet at the same time . . . a loyal friend." The novel seems never to have had a title, and it petered out after a few hundred words in Stu's meticulous italic handwriting. The surviving fragments read less like fiction than a case study of its hero and the "terrible change" that comes over him nine months after the narrator meets him. (It was about nine months after Stu first encountered the real-life John that Julia was killed.)

Even Aunt Mimi, never one given to idle praise, would later call Stu the best and truest friend John ever had.

The first steady girlfriend he had found at college was Thelma Pickles, a stunningly attractive Intermediate student whom he met through Helen Anderson. Thelma was as much of an individualist as he, and their relationship, while it lasted, was often stormy. "He could be very unbearable at times," she would remember. "He was never violent . . . but he would say things to hurt you. I think it was a defence thing, because he could be vulnerable at times [like] when you talked about his mother. He would become almost dreamy and very quiet. It was his weak spot. . . ." She also had a tongue every bit as sharp as John's, and did not hesitate to use it if ever he tried to vent his anger and anguish on her. "Don't blame me," she once lashed back at him, "just because your mother's dead!"

Of all possible successors to Thelma, Cynthia Powell seemed the least likely. A year older than John, she was a mildly pretty, bespectacled girl of the hardworking and conformist type he termed "spaniels." At college she had impinged on his notice only as an object of ridicule, thanks to her school head-prefecty Christian name and the fact that she came from Hoylake, on the Cheshire Wirral, a supposed bastion of suburban gentility and decorum. "No dirty jokes please, it's Cynthia," he would admonish his cronies sarcastically when she approached, seldom failing to make her blush to the roots of her mousy, permed hair.

She was not in John's workgroup but in Geoff Mohammed's and thus shared a classroom with him only in a few general activities such as Lettering. For this detested but unavoidable weekly penance, he would slouch in late, his guitar slung troubadour-style on his back, and, somehow, always take the seat immediately behind her. He never had any of the proper equipment, so would have to borrow her meticulously kept pencils and brushes, usually going off with them afterwards and not bothering to return them.

Cynthia's future at this point seemed as neatly laid out as the materials on her desk. She had a steady boyfriend named Barry, whom she planned to marry before pursuing her chosen career of art teacher. She was not in the market for any new beau, least of all one whose ways were so turbulently and distastefully unlike the ways of Hoylake. Yet John had a powerful, half-fearful fascination for her. On a couple of occasions, she watched him perch on a desk and play his guitar, and was stirred by the very different look this brought to the usually hard, mocking face. "It softened. . . . All the aggression lifted," she would recall. "At last there was something I had seen in John that I could understand."

Her feelings clicked into focus one day in the college lecture theater when she was seated a few places away from John, and saw the attractive Helen Anderson suddenly start to stroke his hair. There was nothing between Helen and him; she was simply bewailing his greasy Teddy Boy locks and urging him to have them shampooed and cut shorter. Nonetheless, Cynthia felt a sudden, irrational surge of jealousy.

From that moment, rather than avoiding John's eye, she set out to catch it. She grew her hair down to her shoulders in the fashionable bohemian manner and exchanged her mumsy woolens and tweed skirt for the white duffle jacket and black velvet slacks favored by college sirens like Thelma Pickles. She also gave up wearing the glasses, which, as she thought, most condemned her as a swot and spaniel to John. Since she was extremely nearsighted and could not afford contact lenses, then still an expensive novelty, this aspect of her makeover brought its problems. In the morning, her bus regularly carried her far beyond the art college stop when she failed to recognize it in time.

One day she and John were in a group of students who began a game of testing one another's vision. To her amazement, Cynthia discovered that he was as myopic as she was, and equally self-conscious about wearing glasses. He in turn discovered that, only a year earlier, Cynthia's father had died of lung cancer, leaving her as devastated as he now was himself. Better than all the clear-sighted people around, this shy, prim Hoylake girl knew just what he was feeling.

The end of the 1958 winter term was celebrated by a midday get-together in one of the lecture rooms. A gramophone was playing, and, egged on by Jeff Mohammed, John asked Cynthia to dance. Thrown into confusion by this unexpected move, she blurted out that she was engaged to a fellow in Hoylake. "I didn't ask you to fuckin' marry me, did I?" John snapped back. After the party came a drinking session at Ye Cracke, which John persuaded the usually abstemious Cynthia to join. They ended up spending the rest of the afternoon alone together at Stu Sutcliffe and Rod Murray's flat in Percy Street.

Among their fellow students—the female ones at least—there was no doubt as to who had the better bargain. "Cynthia was a catch for John," Ann Mason says. "She could have had anyone she wanted. She had lovely eyes and the most beautiful pale skin. And she was the sweetest, nicest person you could ever meet."

She was different indeed from the strong-willed, caustic females who had hitherto dominated John's life. She was soft, gentle, and tranquil (although secretly prone to bouts of paralyzing nerves). She also possessed the notions of male superiority shared by many young women in the late fifties, which could have won them unconditional employment in a geisha house. She deferred to John in everything, never questioning or arguing, always complying with what she later called his "rampant" demand for sex. Normally, he might quickly have tired of such a companion, but in the desolation of Julia's death, Cynthia answered his deepest unspoken needs. "I think [she] offered him a kind of mother thing," the former Thelma Pickles says. "She was so warm and gentle. She was the kind of person anyone would have been proud to have as a mother."

The two began dating in a manner reflecting their suburban backgrounds as much as their bohemian student life. Since both of them still lived at home, they had nowhere to be together in private, unless Stu and Rod Murray both tactfully absented themselves from the Percy Street flat. Their trysts therefore consisted mainly of cinemagoing or sitting for hour after hour in a coffee bar, holding hands over their foam-flecked glass cups. At John's insistence, Cynthia stayed in town until the latest possible moment each night, catching the last train from Lime Street to Hoylake amid homegoing drunks and hooligans "[for] the longest 20 minutes of my life," then walking unaccompanied through the dark streets to her home.

Everything he asked, she gave unstintingly. Her eight-shilling (40p) daily subsistence allowance kept him in coffees, fish-and-chips, Capstan Full-Strength cigarettes, and replacement guitar strings. She did his college work for him when he could not be bothered to finish—or begin—it and neglected her own whenever he demanded attention. To please him, she changed her whole appearance into one hopefully resembling his ultimate fantasy woman, Brigitte Bardot, dyeing her hair blonde and wearing tight skirts and fishnet stockings with garter belts. Waiting for John in such attire at their usual rendezvous, outside Lewis's department store, she would dread being mistaken for a totty, or Liverpool tart.

On bus journeys, he would choose a seat behind some balding

elderly passenger and softly tickle the fluff on the man's cranium, withdrawing his hand and assuming an expression of blank innocence each time his victim turned around. Then the laughter would fade in Cynthia's throat as he sighted some human infirmity more pitiable than baldness—a blind beggar or mentally handicapped child—and instantly went into his own pitiless-seeming overparody, crooking his back, freezing his face into an idiot stare, inverting his hands into claws. "John had a great need to shock and disgust people, and certainly shocked me on these occasions," she would remember. "Of course when his mates were around, he was the star turn."

The real terror of illness and suffering that underlay this apparent callousness showed itself one afternoon when the two were alone together in Stu Sutcliffe's bedroom-studio at Percy Street and Cynthia suddenly collapsed with excruciating stomach pains. John's idea of tender loving care was to rush her to Lime Street and put her on a train to travel back to Hoylake on her own. When a grumbling appendix was diagnosed, he could not bring himself to visit her in the hospital without bringing George Harrison along for support. Having pined for days to spend time alone with him, Cynthia produced a rare show of temperament by bursting into tears. Love was still new enough for John to bundle the bewildered George out of the ward and spend the rest of his visit assiduously making amends to her.

As "going out with" moved into its next phrase, "going steady," the time came for John to introduce Cynthia to Mimi. Woolton and Hoylake being spiritually so close, and Cyn being of so obviously superior a class to other art-school girls, he expected only wholehearted approval. And certainly, the welcome at Mendips seemed warm—expressed in the usual Mimi fashion of an enormous egg-and-chips high tea with mounds of bread and butter, served on the morning room's gateleg table. Unfortunately, the hand that hospitably poured the tea had also marked Cyn's card in terms that nothing she could say or do hereafter would alter. In her, Mimi saw a rival for John's affections who, even at this early stage, was unscrupulously dedicated to taking him away forever.

Cynthia's widowed mother, Lilian, was the opposite of Mimi: a small, hyperactive woman who cleaned their Hoylake home only at long intervals and spent much of her time buying secondhand furniture and knickknacks at local auction sales. With her two sons now grown up and living away from home, she focused her whole attention on Cyn, much as Mimi did on John, and had definite ideas about which young men were and were not good enough for her. When Cyn first brought John home to tea, she dreaded the sharp maternal comparisons that were likely to be made with his predecessor, the so-eligible, so-Hoylake Barry. However, John was polite and respectful, as he could be when he liked, and the occasion went better than Cyn had dared to hope.

Under the rules of going steady, the next step was for Lilian and Mimi to meet. Mimi accepted an invitation to tea at the Powell home, turning up in her usual immaculate coat, hat, and gloves, and, for a time, all went well. Then, in her abrupt fashion, she began complaining to Lilian that Cyn was distracting John from his college work. Lilian naturally defended Cyn, and in no time a furious argument was raging between the two women. John, who had a horror of domestic confrontation—no doubt implanted by all he had seen as a small boy—simply jumped up and bolted from the house. Cyn found him cowering at the end of the street, so she later said, "in tears."

This whiff of adversity took the relationship to a level for which Cyn had been totally unprepared. John became obsessed with her, sometimes filling an entire letter with declarations of his love, bewailing their midnight farewells at Lime Street station until she agreed to throw away her last Hoylake scruples and spend whole nights with him in town. Fortuitously, Stu Sutcliffe and Rod Murray's landlady at 9 Percy Street had rented the whole ground floor to a new tenant who in turn sublet its large back room to Rod. This made Rod and Stu's first-floor studio-cum-bedsit more regularly available as a refuge for John and Cynthia. She would tell her mother she was staying with her college friend, Phyllis McKenzie; he would tell Mimi he was sleeping over with one of the Quarrymen after a late gig.

Although Cynthia showed John nothing but devotion, he became increasingly possessive and insecure. She had only to smile at another boy in the most casual, friendly way to throw him into anguished fantasies that it might be some kind of secret code for an affair in progress or about to begin. At one college hop, he punched a fellow student who'd merely asked her to dance. As they sat together, he would hold on tightly to her hand, as if afraid she might fly away at any moment. Cynthia later said that he often showed symptoms of a nervous breakdown—a diagnosis with which John himself later concurred. "I demanded absolute trust[worthiness] from her because I wasn't trustworthy myself. I was neurotic, taking out all my frustrations on her."

In these days, it was still considered quite normal for men of every stamp—and northern Englishmen above all—to keep "their" women in line by physical chastisement if and when they saw fit. "As a teenager all I saw were films where men beat up women," John would recall. "That was tough, that was the thing to do, slap them in the face, treat them rough, Humphrey Bogart and all that jazz. . . ." Cynthia's autobiography, *A Twist of Lennon*, published in 1977, made no mention of having suffered physical abuse from him. Some twenty years later in a BBC documentary, she recounted how, one night when she was not seeing John, she and Phyllis McKenzie had gone to an out-of-town club and afterwards been given a lift home by two boys they had met. Next day at college, she mentioned the innocent episode to John. Phyllis then described finding her in tears after he'd "slapped her face."

Cynthia's second autobiography, published in 2005, had a harsher story to relate. One evening at a party, John "went mad" after someone told him she was dancing with Stu Sutcliffe. They stopped as soon as they saw the look on his face, and Cyn hastened to mollify him. The next day, however, he followed her down to the ladies' toilets in the college basement. When she came out, he hit her across the face so hard that her head struck a heating pipe on the wall, then walked off without a word. As a result, she chucked him, and they stayed apart for three months until John persuaded her to take him back. Even according to this score-settling account, he was never again physically violent to her.

Summer of 1959 brought the multipart examination that Intermediate students had to pass before moving on to their chosen specialty. Despite his dismal past performance in almost all the areas covered by the exam, John managed to scrape through. Well-wishers and not-so-well-wishers alike rallied round to help him make up the deficiencies of the past five terms. Stu Sutcliffe gave him a crash course in basic painting skills, devoting night after night to the task in an empty lecture room, while Cynthia waited patiently at an adjacent desk.

As well as taking the examination, he was required to submit course work in the form of paintings or drawings. "The trouble was, he hadn't done anything like enough," Ann Mason remembers. One day, while I was going through my stuff with Arthur Ballard, I saw John standing there, looking a bit despondent. So I offered him some of my drawings to put in for the exam. I wondered if I'd get one of his tongue-lashings, but he just said 'Oh, yeah . . . great!'" Both Cynthia and Thelma Pickles would also later recall making similar contributions to his portfolio.

The college had just inaugurated a Department of Commercial Design, for which the polymathic Bill Harry was already bound. To Ballard, it seemed the obvious place to develop John's talent for cartooning and satire. Because of his reputation as a troublemaker, however, the department head, Roy Sharpe, refused to accept him. A fuming Ballard retorted that Sharpe would be better off "teaching in a Sunday school."

The college's only alternative was to put John into the Painting School alongside Stu Sutcliffe, tacitly hoping that over the next two years Stu's talent, energy, and dedication might prove to be contagious.

In March 1958, Elvis Presley had been drafted into the U.S. Army, the glorious inky billows of his hair planed to the scalp, his blue suede shoes traded for heavy-duty boots, the inimitable name rendered down to a mere serial number, the insolent flaunt of his crotch replaced by a stiff-backed salute.

"The King" was the greatest but by no means only loss to rock-'n'-roll's barely erected pantheon. In February 1959, Buddy Holly was killed when his chartered plane crashed on a tour of the snow-bound American Midwest, so leaving thousands of British boys—John among them—bereft of a friend whose speaking voice they had never heard, wondering where their next lesson in how to play rock music would come from. Yet just before his death, Holly, too, had apparently decided to move on from rock 'n' roll; his final recordings were thoughtful ballads, with his backing group, the Crickets, replaced by a string orchestra.

On every hand, deities that once had flashed and thundered invulnerably from the heavens now seemed to be plummeting to earth. During a 1957 Australian tour, Little Richard had seen Russia's Sputnik space satellite flash through the night sky and interpreted it as a personal summons to him from God. Symbolically throwing a costly diamond ring into Sydney Harbor, he had given up singing "Good Golly Miss Molly" and begun training for the ministry. Jerry Lee Lewis had been hounded out of Britain when it emerged that he was bigamously married to his thirteen-year-old cousin, Myra Gayle. Chuck Berry had been arrested on immorality charges connected with a teenage waitress, for which he would eventually receive two years imprisonment.

Across the Atlantic, however, rock was suffering no such vertiginous decline. Performers like Bill Haley, Gene Vincent, Eddie Cochran, and the Everly Brothers, who had become yesterday's men in their homeland, continued to release records and play concerts in Britain—and across Europe—and be welcomed there as rapturously as ever. Britain also by now had its own fledgling rock-'n'-roll scene, which gained in strength and confidence as its American exemplar lost heart.

One British city, above all, devotedly kept the rock-'n'-roll flame alive. In Liverpool, dozens of scrubby skiffle groups of yesteryear had metamorphosed into rock combos whose names combined unalloyed Yank-worship with native humor and wordplay: Karl Terry and the Cruisers, Derry and the Seniors (a play on America's Danny and the Juniors), Cass and the Cassanovas, Rory Storm and the Hurricanes, Kingsize Taylor and the Dominoes, Gerry and the Pacemakers, the Silhouettes, the Four Jays, the Bluegenes. Several of the groups were far more than mere Buddy Holly copyists, featuring pianos and saxes like the "rockin' bands" behind Little Richard and Larry ("Bony Moronie") Williams.

At the bottom of the heap, so far down that few people even knew they existed, were John Lennon and the Quarrymen. Indeed, despite all the shaping-up that had gone on since Paul's arrival, there was serious doubt if they would last very far into 1959. January 1 found them back onstage at Wilson Hall, playing for the overdue Christmas party of the Garston bus depot's social club. The booking had came through George Harrison's bus-driver father, who in his spare time acted as the club's entertainments secretary and compere. Harry Harrison had also persuaded the manager of a nearby cinema, The Pavilion, to drop by and catch their act with a view to giving them further work in the future.

"To start with, everything went really well," drummer Colin Hanton remembers. "We were even given our own dressing-room to rehearse and tune up in. The act went over great—all the bus-drivers and clippies [conductors] really dug us. When they tried to draw the stage curtains after our first set, something went wrong with the mechanism, and the curtains wouldn't pull. John made a joke about it to the audience, which got a big laugh, and we played an extra number while the problem was sorted out. When we came offstage, feeling really pleased with ourselves, we were told 'There's a pint for each of you lads at the bar.' We ended up having more than just a pint, so for our second set we were pissed out of our minds, all except George—and we were terrible."

The aftereffects of beer and failure inevitably led to a row on the bus journey home. As an older workingman, Colin had no taste for sick humor and took exception when Paul began joking around in John's "spastic talk"—"thik ik unk," and so on. After a heated exchange, he jumped up, rang the bell one stop too early, piled his drums off the bus, and never showed up for another performance.

John was thus left alone with his two schoolboy sidemen Paul and George—a matchless combination one of these days but back in British rock-'n'-roll's Ice Age an unmitigated catastrophe. For without a drummer, however indifferent, three acoustic guitarists, however resourceful, could not hope to be taken seriously as a live group. Without the underpinning beat of bass pedal, snare, and tom-tom, their songs did not qualify as rock, merely a form of jumped-up skiffle or folk that in the average riotous Liverpool hall would have to fight even to be heard. They put a brave face on it, and approached several promoters for work as a nonpercussive trio, but from each one came the same brusque query: "What about your rhythm?" John's hopefully reassuring reply of "The rhythm's in the guitars" was the cue for slammed doors all over town.

One that remained slightly ajar led to a place he had previously thought an impregnable bastion of anti-rock-'n'-roll prejudice. Stu Sutcliffe and Bill Harry both sat on the entertainments committee of the art college's union society, the students' social body, and managed to talk down the trad jazz zealots sufficiently to get the Quarrymen occasional bookings for college dances. At Stu's and Bill's prompting, the committee also voted funds to buy an amplifier, officially for the use of all visiting entertainers but in practice so that John, Paul, and George could give the rhythm in their guitars some extra bite.

The college provided only occasional gigs, for negligible payment, and John, at least, took them with not much more seriousness than public rehearsals. One day, Helen Anderson had to give him a bright yellow cable-stitch sweater she was wearing when he hadn't bothered to put together a stage outfit for that evening's show. In exchange, he gave her his Quarry Bank exercise book, with its carefully indexed cartoons of "Shortsighted John Wimple Lennon," "Smell-type Smith," and the rest.

Times became so slow for the Quarrymen that George Harrison took to sitting in with other small-scale groups, in particular one called the Les Stewart Quartet, who appeared regularly at the Lowlands coffee bar. George's defection looked to become permanent when the Stewart Quartet were offered a residency at a club named the Casbah, which was about to open in the Liverpool suburb of West Derby. It belonged to an attractive, dark-eyed woman named Mona Best, whose husband, Johnny, had for many years been Liverpool's main boxing promoter. At the outset it was not intended as a serious business venture, simply a meeting place for Mrs. Best's sons

Rory and Peter and their friends in the basement of their rambling Victorian home in Hayman's Green. But on the eve of opening night, August 28, the quartet broke up in acrimony, and Mrs. Best asked George if he knew any musicians who could take their place. He volunteered himself, John, and Paul.

The Casbah's opening saw John graduate at last from the vermilion Gallotone Champion guitar ("Guaranteed not to split") that his mother had bought two years previously. In August, he persuaded Mimi to stake him to a Hofner Club 40 semisolid model (i.e., playable both acoustically and electrically) with a fawn-colored cutaway body, a black scratchplate and an impressive cluster of tone- and volume-control knobs. The trip they made to collect it from Hessy's in Whitechapel would be enshrined in Mimi's memory as buying him his first guitar for the—to her—hefty sum of £17. In fact, that was merely a down payment: the Club 40's retail price was £28 7s, which installment-plan charges (supposedly to be met by John) increased to £30 9s.

John, Paul, and George played at the Casbah for seven successive Saturday nights, still billed as the Quarrymen and augmented by a fourth guitarist named Ken Brown, a member of the disbanded Les Stewart Quartet. The club proved an instant hit, attracting such crowds that Mrs. Best had to hire a doorman to back up her own formidable presence behind the snack and soft drinks bar. West Derby's weekly paper did a story headlined "Kasbah [sic] Has New Meaning for Local Teenagers," accompanied by the first-ever press picture of John in performance with the new Club 40, supporting its cutaway body on one white-trousered knee and clearly glorying in his power to reach the topmost notes on the fretboard.

Among the Saturday-night regulars was Dorothy (Dot) Rhone, a petite sixteen-year-old from Childwall, whom John took to calling Bubbles, even though her hair didn't have so much as a ringlet. Dot was drawn to his "rugged" looks the moment she set eyes on him but, learning that he already had a steady girlfriend, agreed to go out with Paul McCartney instead. Despite her extraordinary cuteness, she was even milder than Cynthia Powell and submitted without protest to the same rules from Paul that John imposed on Cyn—

total adoration, fidelity, availability, and revising her appearance and wardrobe to look as much as possible like Brigitte Bardot. "Paul was always supposed to be the charming one, but John was more compassionate," she remembers. "When Paul and I had a row, he'd often tell Paul to be nicer to me."

In Mona Best's happy combination of club and Enid Blytonish secret den, the Quarrymen seemed to have found an ideal home. Mrs. Best made them part of her family circle, frequently inviting them upstairs for cups of tea or meals in the rambling house, which was crammed with exotic mementos of her Indian upbringing. They grew particularly friendly with her younger son, Peter, a strikingly handsome eighteen-year-old whose reserved manner and crisply styled hair earned him frequent comparison with the film star Jeff Chandler.

Then, on the Saturday night of October 10, everything suddenly turned sour. Ken Brown, the new fourth Quarryman, reported for duty with a bad cold. In her matriarchal fashion, Mrs. Best decided he wasn't well enough to play and sent him upstairs to sit in the warm with her elderly mother. At the evening's end, however, she still gave him his quarter share of the Quarrymen's £3 fee. John, Paul, and George protested that, as Brown hadn't performed, he shouldn't be paid; when Mrs. Best stood firm, the three of them walked out in a huff.

However John might blag about the rhythm being "in the guitars," it was clear that if his group was to go on playing anywhere outside the art college's basement, they had to find a drummer to replace Colin Hanton. But the task seemed a hopeless one. All the good players around were already comfortably ensconced in prestigious groups like Cass and the Cassanovas or Rory Storm and the Hurricanes, where their personalities as well as percussive showmanship often proved as great a draw as the singers. The Cassanovas had upholsterer John Hutchinson, aka Johnny Hutch, a famous tough guy, known to hit equally hard whether the skin in question covered drum or human jaw. The Hurricanes had Ritchie Starkey, a sad-eyed boy from the tougher-than-tough Dingle area whose love of flashy finger ornamentation had led him to adopt the stage name Ringo Starr.

Musical nobodies John, Paul, and George might be, yet they still had the chutzpah to enter their names against the cream of Liverpool's drummer-enhanced groups when heats for another Carroll Levis "Nationwide Search for a Star" competition was held at the Liverpool Empire. To camouflage the drummer problem, they appeared as a vocal trio with John in the center, minus guitar, resting one hand on Paul's shoulder and one on George's. It was an effective and rather daring idea, since Paul's and George's left- and right-handed guitar necks pointed neatly in opposite directions, and physical contact between young males, onstage or off, was still taboo.

The need to pull out something special for Carroll Levis also finally extinguished that tired old skiffle handle, the Quarrymen. For days beforehand, John and Paul racked their brains for a new name with an American lilt that hadn't already been taken by some other group, national or local. Their final choice was a nod to a currently successful U.S. instrumental act, Johnny and the Hurricanes, and also to rock 'n' roll's founding father, Alan "Moondog" Freed. When they took the stage for their first heat at the Empire, it was as Johnny and the Moondogs.

They performed two Buddy Holly songs, "Think It Over" and "Rave On," with enough panache to reach the area semifinals at the Hippodrome theater in Manchester on Sunday, November 15. As with John's previous Carroll Levis experience, the winners were decided in an end-of-show finale, when the applause for each contestant was measured on Levis's Clapometer. Unluckily, however, this climax came at a much later hour in Manchester than it had in Liverpool. Too poor to afford an overnight hotel stay, Johnny and the Moondogs had to leave before the finale to catch their last bus and train home. All three of them felt bitterly disappointed and cheated, though only John actively expressed his resentment of the competitors who were able to stay. "That night," Paul remembers, "someone [in a rival group] was relieved of his guitar."

With no drummer in prospect, an easier and slightly cheaper way of strengthening the beat was to add one of the electric bass guitars now in general use around Merseyside bandstands. The electric bass with its fretted neck being relatively easy to play, John did not have to break in another outsider, but could simply invite one of his art college friends to make up a fourth with Paul, George, and him. During another late-night jam session at 9 Percy Street, he threw the bass player's job open to both Stu Sutcliffe and Rod Murray—whichever was first to get hold of the requisite instrument. Rod set to work to build his own, using equipment in the college woodworking depart-ment to cut out its body and neck. He was just pondering how to electrify and string it when he found he'd been beaten to the post.

Every two years, the Littlewoods football-pool magnate John Moores sponsored an exhibition at Liverpool's illustrious Walker Art Gallery to which local painters and sculptors were invited to submit works. For the John Moores show of November 1959, Stu intended to offer one of his outsize abstracts, consisting of two eight-by-four-foot panels. With Rod Murray's help, he took the first of the finished canvases to the exhibits' assembly point, then got sidetracked by John and the others at Ye Cracke, and somehow never got around to delivering the second panel. Unaware that they were looking at only half the intended picture, the judges included it among only a handful of local entries to hang at the Walker. So enamored of Stu's technique was the great John Moores that he bought the single panel for an impressive £65.

The windfall allowed Stu to splash out on an impressive Hofner President bass guitar and step into the vacancy in John's group. John reassured him that he'd soon pick up bass playing, since it didn't involve learning "chords and stuff," just simple, repetitive patterns over four strings rather than six. A friendly bassist with a rival group, Dave May of the Silhouettes, agreed to coach him in the rudiments.

His college tutors, and several of his friends, felt that Stu was making a disastrous wrong turn. No one could have been a stron-ger supporter of John's music than Bill Harry—as he would one day prove in spades. Yet he felt mystified, and rather let down, that some-one at such exalted level in the visual medium should wish to start at the very bottom of rock 'n' roll. "The image was what appealed to Stuart more than the music," Harry says. "He loved the romance of it. And the fact that John wanted him in the group. He just couldn't say no to John."

9

UNDER THE JACARANDA

I was never—repeat NEVER—known as Johnny Silver.

Just before Christmas, Mrs. Plant, the long-suffering owner of 9 Percy Street, had paid her property a surprise visit and been horrified by what she found. A cache of antique furniture awaiting renovation in the basement had been chopped up and used as firewood to warm the ex-Quarrymen's practice sessions and John's illicit nights with Cynthia. The Adam fireplace in Stu Sutcliffe's studio had been torn out to create a contemporary open-hearth effect, and had since disappeared. ("We left bits of it all over town," Rod Murray admits. "Like getting rid of a dead body. . . .") So outraged was Mrs. Plant by this wholesale vandalism that she gave every tenant in the building an eviction notice.

By early January, Rod and Stu had found new accommodations at 3 Hillary Mansions, Gambier Terrace, a handsome Georgian-style block overlooking the unfinished Anglican cathedral. To share the spacious first-floor flat they enlisted three other college friends, Margaret Morris (known as Diz), Margaret Duxbury (known as Ducky), and John.

Aunt Mimi was informed of his decision to leave Mendips with typical bluntness. "He told me, 'Mimi, all the others have flats on their own . . . and anyway, I don't like your cooking,'" she recalled. "He'd had it soft with me around to do all the cooking and washing for him. I knew even before he went that he couldn't cope on his own. He didn't even know how to light a gas-cooker, let alone cook a tin of beans. He told me he could live off 'Chink food.' I said to myself, 'We'll see, John Lennon, we'll see.'"

The flat consisted of three oversize bed-sitting-rooms, a kitchen, and a bathroom with a Geyser water heater, lit by a flame that responded with a threatening *Woomph!* if anyone tried to light it. As signatory of the lease, Rod chose the best quarters, at the front, with the cathedral view and fancy iron balustrade; John and Stu took the barnlike room at the rear.

For John, the Gambier Terrace flat served two equally important purposes. It provided a place for him, Paul, and George to rehearse with their new bass player, his new flatmate. And it allowed him to spend unrestricted nights with Cynthia, albeit in conditions even more rough-and-ready than at Percy Street. The room he shared with Stu was also a communal art studio for the other tenants, and so permanently littered with shabby easels, half-squeezed paint tubes, empty bottles, misappropriated traffic signs, old fish-and-chips wrappings, and cigarette butts. "The floor was filthy," Cynthia recalled. "Everything was covered with muck." On mornings when the Geyser failed and they had to wash in cold water, they would arrive at college "looking like a couple of chimney sweeps."

But, as Mimi had predicted, it wasn't long before John's appetite for self-reliance waned and he began to miss the home comforts he had always taken for granted. "For about three weeks I didn't hear from him. Then one night he arrived back on the doorstep looking very sorry for himself. I said to him, 'I'm cooking dinner, do you want some?' but he was too proud to admit that he was hungry or that he couldn't stand living away. He went away again that night, but about a week later he turned up again. This time I was cooking a steak pie, and I didn't bother asking whether he wanted any or not. That got him mad. He could smell the food and yet he was too stubborn, too proud, typical John really, to let on that he was hungry or that he'd made a mistake.

"In the end the smell got too much for him and he burst in on me, saying, 'I'll have you know, woman, I'm starving!' He wolfed his food down and then he decided it was getting late and that he wanted to stay in his room for the night. It was his way of coming back without admitting he was wrong to leave." From then on, he made regular trips home to get his washing done and fill up on Mimi's cooking. But even the most succulent of her steak pies couldn't lure him back permanently from Gambier Terrace, Rod, Diz, Ducky, and Stu.

The idea had been that Stu would master the bass within a week or so, then take his place as an equal among John's onstage brother-hood. Unfortunately, it was not as simple as that. Stu's small hands, so quick and sure while painting, drawing, or sculpting, showed none of the same deftness with his shiny new Hofner President. Even the most basic underlay patterns of rock 'n' roll were laborious for him to learn and troublesome to execute. He was angered and frustrated by his slow progress and would have given up altogether had not John sat with him for hours in their huge back room at Gambier Terrace, demonstrating the patterns time and again on the bass strings of his own Club 40. Just as Stu had made John believe in himself as an artist, so he was now determined Stu should believe in himself as a musician, whatever the evidence might be to the contrary.

He therefore insisted that Stu should join Paul, George, and him onstage when still all too obviously the rawest of beginners. The principal object was to show off the Hofner President: as George later recalled, "Having a bass player who couldn't play was better than not having a bass player at all." To hide his embarrassment, Stu would turn on his James Dean persona, wearing dark glasses and standing with his back half-turned to the audience as if lost in some mystic communion with his fretboard, rather than just lost.

Apart from getting Stu up to standard, the most urgent task was finding a name for the new lineup. Johnny and the Moondogs had been no more than a hasty improvisation for Carroll Levis and was now too much redolent of lost chances and premature homeward trains. Rather than the modish formula of such-and-such and the so-and-so's, Stu suggested they should revert to another plain collective noun, ideally one with the chirpy unpretentiousness of Buddy Holly's Crickets. Pursuing this entomological theme, they came up with the Beetles, unaware that it had been Holly's own original choice. (Contrary to myth, it had nothing to do the Beetles motorcycle gang in Marlon Brando's *The Wild One*, which none of John's circle had seen.) To avoid an off-putting image of crawly black bugs, John changed it to Beatals—not a pun on "beat" music at this stage, but on beating all competition.

Stu also acted as their manager, insofar as there was anything to manage, and during March drafted a weightily worded and not overly truthful appeal for bookings to an unnamed promoter or club manager. "As it is your policy to present entertainment to the habitues of your establishment, I would like to draw your attention to the Quar [crossed out] 'Beatals.' This is a promising group of young musicians who play music for all tastes, preferably rock and roll. . . ." But their gigs remained mostly stuck at the piffling level of student dances and socials, where they were usually known as "the college band." Stu's painting tutor, Austin Davis, had them to play at a party he gave at his Huskisson Street flat early in 1959. The event went on for about two days and was so riotous that Davis's wife, the future novelist and Dame of the British Empire Beryl Bainbridge, had to remove their two young children from the premises. (Later, it would even be cited among the grounds for the couple's divorce.)

Outside pub hours, John and Stu were generally to be found at a little coffee bar in Slater Street, on the fringes of Chinatown, called the Jacaranda. At night, its basement became a club, attracting crowds from all the surrounding black and Asian quarters, with dancing to a West Indian steel band and liberal consumption of spiked soft drinks and the substance still known, if at all, as Indian hemp. "The Jac" was also a haunt of heavyweight local groups—Rory Storm and the Hurricanes, Kingsize Taylor and the Dominoes, Cass and Cassanovas, and others—who would meet there after their night's gigs around town.

To John, these were almost godlike figures, with their carefully blow-waved hair, matching Italian suits, flashy guitars, and so-

enviable drummers. Each group pumped out its American rock-
'n'-roll repertoire with Liverpudlian eccentricity and flamboyance.
Ted "Kingsize" Taylor, a brawny apprentice butcher, kiss curled and
plaid jacketed, combined the personae of Solomon Burke and the
Big Bopper. "Cass," aka Brian Casser, and his three sidemen wore
shawl-collared tuxedos with Chicago gangster–style black shirts and
white ties, and hung up their own special banner on the stage behind
them. Most extrovert by far was blond, suntanned Rory Storm, aka
Alan Caldwell, a mountaineer manqué who during his set would
clamber up one side of the stage proscenium, not stopping until he
clung precariously forty or more feet above his audience. Even so,
he was not selfish with the limelight, granting his drummer Ringo
Starr a special solo spot billed as Starr Time.

The star groups' foot soldiers often proved more approachable
than their commanders. At the Jacaranda, John struck up a friendship with the Cassanovas' bass guitarist, nineteen-year-old John
Gustafson, aka Johnny Gus. Generous about sharing bass-playing
tips, Gustafson also became a willing accomplice to John's love of
exhibitionistic sick humor. "When we walked round town," he remembers, "we'd pretend to be two old cripples, helping each other
across the road." One day he went back to the Gambier Terrace flat
with John and Stu to hear John play the latest Lennon-McCartney
composition, "The One After 909."

Johnny Gus's friendliness was counterpointed by the Cassanovas'
hard-man drummer, Johnny Hutch, who intimidated even members of his own group, and made no secret of regarding musicians
who were also art students and grammar-school boys as "a bunch
of posers." "John was always terrified of Johnny Hutch," Gustafson
says. It didn't stop him from going down to the Jacaranda's basement when Cass and the Cassanovas were setting up, and asking
to sit in with them on a couple of numbers. "He played "Ramrod,"
the Duane Eddy instrumental," Gustafson remembers. "And Ray
Charles's "Hallelujah, I Love Her So," doing the guitar breaks as well
as the vocal. We had to admire his nerve."

The Jacaranda's owner, Allan Williams, was one of the more colorful figures to be found around Liverpool 8. A stocky Welshman,

with curly hair and a piratical black beard, he had worked as a door-to-door salesman and artificial jewelry manufacturer before starting his coffee bar, with his Chinese wife, Beryl, on capital of just £100. At twenty-nine, Williams had no particular interest in teenage music, preferring the Welsh hymns and thirties ballads for whose dramatic tenor rendition he was famous in pubs from Canning Square to Upper Parliament Street. But, like many another small provincial entrepreneur, he was attracted by its increasingly powerful scent of easy money.

John was familiar to Allan Williams as leader of the "right crowd of layabouts" from art college who sat around the Jac, nursing the same frothy coffee or fivepenny (2p) portion of toast and jam for hour after hour of conversation about Kierkegaard or Chuck Berry. To begin with, however, his entrepreneurial eye focused on Stu Sutcliffe's art rather than John's music. Among Stu's recent projects were a series of vivid abstract murals, designed and painted in partnership with Rod Murray, one of which now adorned the front window of Ye Cracke, another the interior of a Territorial Army hall in Norris Green. Williams commissioned the pair to do the same for the Jac's street window and the walls of its basement club. For the latter, they created a garish voodoo-inspired design, then roped in John and another sometime flatmate, Rod Jones, to help them paint it.

Britain in 1960 had only one nationally known pop manager. This was Larry Parnes, a young Londoner, originally in the dress business, who had helped launch the nation's first teenage idol, Tommy Steele. Since striking gold with Steele, Parnes had gone about the country seeking out handsome young men and turning them into rock singers under American-flavored pseudonyms that blended the cute with the suggestive: Marty Wilde, Vince Eager, Duffy Power, Dickie Pride. From among this so-called Larry Parnes Stable, the most successful was Billy Fury, who, as Ron Wycherly, had previously worked as a deckhand on a Liverpool tugboat—though, of course, that unglamorous fact was always played down by his publicists.

As well as manufacturing homegrown teen idols, Parnes was also the principal importer of American rock-'n'-roll stars to their ever-faithful British constituency. That first spring of the brand-new decade, he brought over Gene Vincent and Eddie Cochran to costar with indigenous acts in a touring spectacular billed as the Fast-Moving Anglo-American Beat Show. Vincent in the flesh proved a disconcerting figure, weasely and emaciated, though still aged only twenty-five, with one leg in braces following a near-fatal motorcycle accident. Cochran looked much the same glossy young hunk who'd inspired Paul McCartney to sing "Twenty Flight Rock" but was secretly prey to the darkest fears and neuroses. He had been hit hard by the death of his close friend Buddy Holly a year earlier, and now believed himself fated to meet a similarly premature end.

The Fast Moving Anglo-American Beat Show came to the Liverpool Empire for a week in mid-March, playing to rapturous capacity audiences that included John, Cynthia, Paul McCartney—and Allan Williams. Paul would always remember the demented female shriek that went up as the curtains opened to reveal Eddie Cochran with his back turned, nonchalantly running a comb through his hair. John, however, was furious when the screaming drowned out Cochran's virtuoso playing of his wafer-thin red guitar.

After the show, Williams sought out Larry Parnes and suggested how Liverpool's evidently fathomless adoration of Gene Vincent and Eddie Cochran might be exploited still further. Williams's grandiose idea was a joint promotion between Parnes and himself that would combine the American stars and other Parnes acts with the best of Merseyside's own rock-'n'-roll talent. Parnes took the bait, agreeing to bring Vincent and Cochran back for a second appearance, supported by other nationally known groups like the Viscounts and Nero and the Gladiators, while Williams supplied local crowd-pullers like Rory Storm and the Hurricanes and Cass and the Cassanovas. The spectacular would be for one night only at the city's boxing stadium, behind the Exchange railway station, on May 3.

Thanks to the combined rival attractions of Cynthia and Stu, Paul McCartney had recently felt himself taking "a bit of a back seat" with John. But the Easter vacation of 1960 brought a major rebonding between them. Packing up a few clothes and their guitars, the pair hitchhiked two hundred miles south to stay with Paul's relatives Mike and Bett Robbins, who were now running a pub, the Fox and Hounds, in Caversham, Berkshire. They spent a week helping out at the pub, sharing a bed in an upstairs room as innocently as children.

Their reward for unstinted bottle stacking and glass washing was to be allowed to perform for the Fox and Hounds' customers over the weekend prior to their return home. Mike Robbins watched them rehearse and offered hints on presentation—for instance, that they shouldn't tear straight into "Be-Bop-a-Lula," as they planned, but build up to it with an instrumental number, Les Paul and Mary Ford's "The World Is Waiting for the Sunrise." They gave their show seated on barstools in the pub lounge, billing themselves with a touch of Goonery as the Nerk Twins.

Eddie Cochran and Gene Vincent had by now reached the West Country, playing to yet another sold-out house at Bristol Hippodrome on the Saturday night of April 16. Before returning to Liverpool in three weeks, both had arranged to make a brief trip home to America. En route to catch a flight from Heathrow Airport right after the Bristol show, their rental car went out of control and smashed into a concrete lamppost. Cochran, Vincent, and Cochran's girlfriend, the songwriter Sharon Sheeley, all suffered serious multiple injuries and were rushed to a hospital in nearby Bath. Cochran died two days later, fulfilling his own prophecy that he'd "be seeing Buddy soon."

On hearing what had befallen the two headliners of his copromotion with Larry Parnes, Allan Williams understandably thought the show would have to be canceled. Parnes, however, insisted that it should go ahead as planned on May 3 and that the hospitalized Gene Vincent would be fit enough to take part. In compensation for Cochran's absence, Parnes provided extra acts from his London roster while Williams rounded up further local groups, among them Gerry and the Pacemakers, Bob Evans and His Five Shillings, and the Connaughts.

The Beatals did not even try to get on the show, knowing they were automatically disqualified by their lack of a drummer. They could only watch from the audience as Rory Storm and the Hurricanes, Cass and the Cassanovas, and Gerry and the Pacemakers in turn pulled out all the stops to impress Larry Parnes. A photograph of the packed ringside crowd picked up John standing near the front, his face half-hidden among a thicket of hysterical girls. From a distance of thirty-odd feet, you can still see the envy and longing in his eyes.

Despite its organizational shortcomings, the event gave Allan Williams instant huge prestige as Larry Parnes's ambassador on Merseyside. Even John was sufficiently awed to forget his usual fierce independence where his music was concerned and beg help of this seeming miracle-worker. A few days after the concert, he buttonholed Williams at the Jacaranda's kitchen door with a muttered plea to "do something" for the Beatals.

From the local talent on show at the boxing stadium, Parnes had singled out only one potential addition to his stable. John Gustafson, the darkly handsome bass player with Cass and the Cassanovas, was invited to accompany Parnes back to London afterward and be groomed for stardom in his inimitable fashion.

To the rest, the opportunity Parnes offered was not to become pampered thoroughbreds so much as all-purpose workhorses. He was currently in urgent need of musicians to back his solo vocalists on the extensive tours through Britain that were their most lucrative market. Billy Fury himself, the stable's premier attraction, was about to begin a string of nationwide appearances, but as yet had no group to accompany him. Hiring local sidemen to play on shows in the north and Scotland was an attractively cheaper option for Parnes than paying to transport them all the way up from London.

He therefore detailed Allan Williams to assemble the best performers at the boxing stadium along with other deserving candidates for a mass audition–cum–talent contest. The winners would get the job of touring with Billy Fury, while the runners-up would be assigned to lesser Parnes protégés like Duffy Power and Dickie Pride. Parnes would conduct the audition in person, returning in a week and bringing Fury with him to assist in the selection process. Under pressure from John, Williams agreed to overlook the Beatals' minor league status and let them take part. There was one essential precondition, however. A star from the Larry Parnes stable could not conceivably take the stage backed by musicians whose rhythm was "in the guitars." They had less than a week to solve the problem that had defeated them for more than a year and find themselves a drummer.

A bout of frantic asking around the groups at the Jacaranda turned up only one even remote possibility. From Brian Casser, the singer with Cass and the Cassanovas, they heard of someone named Tommy Moore, who occasionally sat in on drums at the Cassanovas' own ad hoc club above the Temple Restaurant in Dale Street. Moore proved to be a forklift driver at Garston's bottle factory, diminutive in size, nervous in manner, and at age thirty-six, in their eyes, practically an old-age pensioner. On the overwhelming credit side, he possessed his own full drum kit, could whack out a serviceable rock-'n'-roll beat, and, best of all, did not collapse with laughter at the idea of joining up with them. After the briefest audition in John and Stu's room at Gambier Terrace, Tommy Moore was in.

The second pressing need was for yet another new name. "The Beatals" had never really worked, either visually or aurally, and had led to much teasing from the acts who nightly beat them all over Liverpool. After further brainstorming by John and Stu, it was decided to become the Silver Beetles: not so much crawly live insects now as ornamental scarabs in some 1920s detective story. From rival musicians, the response was yet again an array of downturned thumbs. Style-conscious Brian Casser in particular urged them to follow the accepted formula—for instance, putting the silver and John's name together for a Treasure Island effect, Long John and Silvermen, or Pieces of Silver, or Johnny Silver and the Pieces of Eight. But the scarabs had made their decision, and would not budge from it.

The audition took place on May 10 at the Wyvern Social Club, a run-down premises in Seel Street that Allan Williams planned to convert into an upscale nightclub named the Blue Angel. Here the Silver Beetles found all the usual crushing competition with their right-on names: Rory Storm and the Hurricanes (featuring Ringo Starr's "Starr Time"), Derry and the Seniors, Cass and the Cassanovas. Slim chance though the Silver Beetles stood of being chosen to back Billy Fury, there was at least the thrill of meeting the star himself as he sat at a table with Larry Parnes, rather like adjudicators in a school music festival. He was in every way the antithesis of his name: a shy, polite Wavertree lad, permanently coated in orange makeup, who cared less for girls than for his pet tortoise and already suffered from the heart trouble that would eventually kill him at forty-one. To create the necessary camouflage of his Liverpool origins, he spoke with a vaguely American accent but otherwise was refreshingly unpretentious, treating the Silver Beetles like potential sidemen as plausible as any others and signing an autograph when John nervously approached him on the others' behalf.

These pleasant preliminaries quickly turned into nightmare. The Silver Beetles' new drummer, Tommy Moore, was supposed to rendezvous with them at the Wyvern after collecting some stray equipment from the Cassanovas' club room in Dale Street. When their turn came to play, Tommy still had not arrived. To fill in for him, Allan Williams deputed Johnny Hutch from Cass and the Cassanovas, the intimidating tough guy who always so loudly dismissed John and his group as "a bunch of posers" and "not worth a carrot." "Johnny hated having to sit in with them," John Gustafson remembers. "He only did it because Allan told him to."

A local freelance photographer was on hand to capture them apparently blowing their big moment in agonizing detail. For once, they were wearing uniforms of a sort—dark shirts, matching jeans with patch pockets oddly outlined in white, and cheap two-tone Italian shoes that Parnes, in the half-light, mistook for "tennis shoes." John and Paul had decided that the way to catch the great man's eye, and distract his attention from the flawed lineup, was to leap and jump around like Elvis at his most hyperactive. In painful contrast to these joined-at-the-hip ravers, self-conscious George barely moved at all, while Stu, as usual, was too ashamed of his poor bass playing even to face his front. Behind this mismatched ménage sat their temporary drummer, Johnny Hutch, in ordinary street clothes, making his feelings clear with every passionless roll and perfunctory cymbal smash.

The audition, as expected, proved to be a carve-up among Merseyside's heavy hitters. The plum job of backing Billy Fury went to Cass and the Cassanovas, while Derry and the Seniors were hired for Fury's stablemate, Duffy Power. But, despite the Silver Beetles' lack of luster, something about them appealed to Larry Parnes. It so happened that Parnes also needed backing musicians for another of his artists, Johnny Gentle, who was booked for a Scottish tour from May 20 to 28. The Silver Beetles, to their astonishment, were offered the job at a fee of £18 each.

Though its dates fell smack in the middle of college and school term time, there was no question of anyone turning it down. George had by now left Liverpool Institute to become an apprentice electrician and, like Tommy Moore, could take the time as holiday. Paul, theoretically cramming for his GCE A-levels, persuaded his father that a spell of traveling around Scotland would give his brain a rest. Stu and John simply cut college classes for a week, a decision that horrified Stu's teachers—and his mother Millie—because he was just about to take his finals. John did not tell Mimi about the tour, knowing too well what a storm of protest it would unleash. A week was about the maximum time he could disappear off her radar screen without making her wonder what he was up to.

There was a general feeling that, as employees of Parnes, however junior and temporary, they should adopt stage names after his own well-tried principle. So Paul became Paul Ramon, thinking it had a sultry, tango-dancing feel; George became Carl Harrison in homage to Carl Perkins, the writer of "Blue Suede Shoes"; and Stu became Stu de Stael after the Russian abstract painter Nicolas de Stael. In later years, John would deny with some annoyance that he did follow Cass's advice after all and identify himself with the peg-legged sea cook of *Treasure Island*. "I was never—repeat NEVER—known as Johnny Silver," he wrote to music journalist Roy Carr more than a decade later, "I always preferred my own name. . . . There was one occasion when a guy [Cass?] introduced me as Long John and the Silvermen . . . in the days of old when they didn't like the word Beatle!! I'm actually serious about this . . . it gets on my TIT!" But according to Paul, "He was Long John throughout that Scottish tour . . . and he was quite happy to be Long John."

Johnny Gentle was, in fact, yet another fellow Liverpudlian, a former merchant seaman named John Askew who had first found his voice by singing to fellow crewmen and passengers (although, of course, no one wanted to know about any of that). Aged twenty-four, he was the usual mix of brawny good looks and big hair from the Parnes cookie cutter. But despite extensive promotion as a gentler alternative to Fury and Power, he had not yet made any impact on the UK record charts.

He did not meet his new backing group until they came off the train at Alloa, a small town on the River Forth. There was time for only half an hour's rehearsal before they went onstage together at the Town Hall in nearby Marshill. This first show was so bad that Parnes's Scottish copromoter, a sometime poultry farmer named Duncan McKinnon, almost sent the Silver Beetles back to Liverpool on the next train. But Gentle liked them and managed to convince McKinnon they would improve with practice.

Any illusions about the glamour of rock-'n'-roll touring melted away quicker than a Scotch mist. The six remaining gigs were not in big cities like Glasgow or Edinburgh but remote towns scattered up the northeast coast and deep into the Highlands: Inverness, Fraserburgh, Keith, Forres, Nairn, and Peterhead. The venues were ballrooms, municipal buildings, or agricultural halls, with Gentle heading a bill otherwise composed of local singers and groups. He and his five sidemen traveled together with their equipment in one small van, driven by a McKinnon employee named Gerry Scott. "We were playing to nobody in little halls," George remembered, "until the pubs cleared out, when about five Scottish Teds would come in and look at us."

While Gentle, as the star, was accommodated in hotels, the sidemen had to make do with shared rooms in grim Highland boardinghouses and bed-and-breakfasts, where Calvinist texts decorated the walls and light and heat were measured out by coin meter. Thanks to their rock-bottom allowance from Parnes, they could afford to eat only in the cheapest workmen's caffs and fish-and-chip shops. John's cold comfort holidays at his Uncle Bert's croft in Durness, away to the west, seemed luxurious by comparison.

As things turned out, few Scottish teenagers even realized they were watching "Long John" Lennon, Paul Ramon, Carl Harrison, and Stu de Stael—or even the Silver Beetles, for that matter. Press advertisements and posters billed them simply as "Johnny Gentle and his group." There had apparently been some loss of nerve over the new name: a gig at Lathom Hall on May 14 saw them truncated to the Silver Beats, and, according to Johnny Gentle, they had reverted to calling themselves the Beatals by the time they reached Alloa.

Fortunately for them, the star was a through-and-through Scouser whose life in the Parnes stable had not made the least swollen-headed. So John, Paul, and George put themselves out for Johnny, conscientiously learning his Ricky Nelson ballad repertoire, goosing it up with livelier Presley numbers like "Wear My Ring Around Your Neck." He in turn did what he could to make them more like a conventional, uniformed backing group. "They'd come without any proper stage clothes," he remembers. "George had a black shirt and I had one, too, that I didn't wear. So I let them have that, and we scraped up enough money between us to buy another one so that at least their three front men would look roughly the same."

On their van journeys through the Highlands, John took the lead in quizzing Gentle about life as a teen idol and the quickest route to achieving it. "He was inquisitive about everything . . . what was Billy like . . . what was Marty like . . . should he and the others go to London and try to get discovered . . . where would they stay? He was going places, and he knew it even then. At one place after we played, he and the others got pushed aside by some girls crowding round to get my autograph. John shouted out 'That'll be us some day, Johnny.' "

The long intervals of discomfort and boredom that had to be endured gave extra edge to John's sarcastic tongue and his impulse to pillory human weakness or frailty wherever they revealed themselves. Tommy Moore, the group's too-elderly drummer, was a frequent target of Lennonesque practical jokes—often cruel, usually pointless, sometimes perpetrated for an audience no larger than himself. As Tommy lay in bed at night, John would softly open the door of his room, lasso his bedpost with a towel, then pull the bed by slow degrees toward the door. However tireless the baiting of Tommy, he got off lightly in comparison with Stu Sutcliffe. It was as if standing onstage with the Hofner president like a sunburst millstone around his neck robbed Stu of everything that had made John respect, or even like, him. The others took their cue from John, mocking Stu's musicianship and appearance, making sure he always got the van's most uncomfortable seat, the metal ledge over the rear wheel. "We were terrible," John would later admit. "We'd tell him he couldn't sit with us or eat with us. We'd tell him to go away, and he did."

Inverness found the star and his group for once in the same over-night accommodation, with the bonus of a pretty view across water. Here it emerged that Billy Fury was not the only Parnes singer in the arcane business of writing his own material. Gentle, too, had already composed several Buddy Holly–ish songs, and he took advantage of this respite to work on a half-finished ballad called "I've Just Fallen." John, who was listening in, mentioned that he did "a bit of songwriting" and suggested that Gentle's middle eight—the gear change after the opening couple of verses—didn't quite work. He had a spare middle eight, he said, that Gentle was welcome to put into the song.

> We know that we'll get by
> Just wait and see.
> Just like the song tells us
> The best things in life are free.

Although never to make the charts, "I've Just Fallen" had a respectable enough career ahead of it. A year afterward, the producer John Barry picked it up as an album track for Britain's then most successful pop star, Adam Faith. In 1962, Gentle himself recorded it as a B-side under the new name of Darren Young. That simple minor-key middle eight—for which he received neither credit nor payment—thus represents the first John Lennon words and music ever to be professionally recorded. Ironically, both versions appeared on Parlophone, the label that soon would spout out his hits like a geyser.

En route from Inverness to Fraserburgh, Gerry Scott, the van driver, was feeling hung-over, so he asked Johnny Gentle to take a

spell behind the wheel. At a confusing road fork, Gentle turned the
wrong way and hit an approaching car head-on. The impact hurled
a sleeping John from the back of the van into the front and sent the
piled-up stage equipment cannoning into Tommy Moore with such
force that two of his front teeth were loosened. The first arrivals at
the crash scene were a pair of teenage girls from a nearby house;
recognizing Gentle, they took the opportunity to collect autographs
from him and his five dazed companions.

Fortunately no police were involved, but Tommy Moore had to
be driven to a hospital suffering from concussion. Despite his traumatized state, there was no question of Tommy being excused his
so-crucial role onstage. While he was still being treated in the emergency room, John turned up accompanied by the show's promoter
and virtually frog-marched him off to duty. He had only a confused
memory of playing that night, full of painkilling drugs and with a
bandage around his head.

Things went rapidly downhill from there. The sidemen had by
now spent all their small subsistence allowance from Larry Parnes,
but had seen no sign of the second installment Parnes was meant to
send them via Allan Williams. For the tour's last couple of days, they
were reduced to semivagrancy, skipping out of cafés without paying
and sleeping in the van. Good-natured Johnny Gentle, who suffered
no such hardships, offered to telephone Parnes on their behalf to
chase up the missing payment. When Gentle seemed not to be pitch-
ing it strongly enough, John grabbed the receiver. "He didn't hold
back. It was like 'We're fuckin' skint up here. We haven't got a pot
to piss in. We need money, Larry!'" Gentle remembers. "Anyway, it
seemed to work because Williams did send them up a few pounds
more." Stu's mother also made a contribution to help pay for their
train tickets home.

If the Scottish tour did little for the Silver Beetles' finances (Tommy's girlfriend was horrified to think how much more he could
have made in a comparable period at Garston bottle works), at least
it put them on a significantly improved footing back in Liverpool.
Johnny Gentle sang their praises to Larry Parnes, saying he would

happily tour with them again and urging Parnes to put them under permanent contract. But Parnes had enough on his plate with solo singers like Dickie Pride, the so-called "Sheik of Shake," who was prone to drink, drugs, and stealing cars. He preferred not to risk multiplying such headaches by five.

In any case, the Silver Beetles had by now acquired a manager-cum-agent in Allan Williams—albeit one who would always regard the office more as a burden than a privilege. Williams began handling their Merseyside bookings under the same loose arrangement he had with their one-time gods Rory Storm and the Hurricanes and Derry and the Seniors. In between, they were granted a second-string residency in the Jacaranda basement, appearing every Monday, when the West Indian steel band had the night off.

Early in June, an arts festival at the university brought the celebrated young poet Royston Ellis on what he intended to be only a short visit to Liverpool. Nineteen-year-old Ellis was a beat poet in the literal sense, having conceived the unprecedented notion of fusing highbrow spoken verse together with lowbrow—or, rather, no-brow—live rock 'n' roll. Other than John Betjeman, he was the only British poet regularly seen on prime-time television, when he would read his work backed by, among others, Cliff Richard's Shadows and the future Led Zeppelin guitarist Jimmy Page.

After his Liverpool University gig, Ellis gravitated to the Jacaranda, there falling into conversation with "a dishy-looking boy" whose name turned out to be George Harrison. Later that evening, George took him to Gambier Terrace to meet John and Stu. They all hit it off so well that Ellis was invited to miss his train from Lime Street and stay over on one of the mattresses on the floor. During his stay, he showed his new friends a useful aid to staying awake in their all-night lives as musicians and artists. Ordinary nasal inhalers, sold over the counter at every drugstore, contained wicks impregnated with Benzedrine. One had only to break the plastic tube and chew the wick inside to get the same effect as any expensive pep pill. "I also told them that statistically one person in every four was homosexual," he remembers. "John's eyes widened at that."

Since Ellis had plenty of money and was an enthusiastic cook, the cuisine at Gambier Terrace during his stay improved dramatically. His most ambitious culinary effort, a chicken pie with mushrooms, unfortunately got left for too long in the decrepit gas stove and burst into flames, almost setting fire to the whole kitchen. John, he recalls, was fascinated by the idea of combining rock music and poetry, and awed that someone of his young years should already have published a poetry collection. Ellis replied that his real ambition was to turn out prose for the lucrative mass market; as he put it, he wanted to be "a paperback writer."

To wind up his visit, he gave a poetry reading at the Jacaranda, backed by John, Paul, George, Stu, and Tommy. The event was such a success that Ellis urged them to forget their college, work, and school commitments and just go for it in London, the way he himself had done from Pinner, Middlesex, three years earlier. His valediction, so he claims, was to end their wavering between Silver Beetles and Beatals, and nail the pun properly at last. It should be "Beatles," he told John, as a double play on beat poetry and beat music.

There has probably never been a title whose authorship was more fiercely disputed. But Ellis's stay at Gambier Terrace and this final, irrevocable name change undoubtedly did coincide. Early June brought two regular bookings over the water in Cheshire for the same promoter, Les Dodd: one at the Grosvenor Ballroom in Liscard, Wallasey, the other at Neston Institute on the Wirral. For the Grosvenor gig, the Wallasey newspaper advertised the Silver Beetles, "jive and rock specialists"; a local press story on their Neston debut a few days afterward called them the Beatles. This second mention still listed the pseudonymous Paul Ramon, Carl Harrison, and Stu de Stael, but the name of "their leader" was given as plain John Lennon once more.

The Scottish tour had left Tommy feeling more battered than his drums, not to mention grievously out of pocket; he was also tired of the sarcasm and backbiting that John ceaselessly orchestrated against Stu, and—as a conscientious workingman—appalled by John's beatnik philosophy. "Lennon once told me he'd commit suicide rather than get a conventional job. " 'Death before work'—those were his very words. His girlfriend, Cynthia, was sitting in the front seat of the van at that time." On June 11, Tommy failed to rendez-vous with his colleagues at the Jacaranda for that night's appearance at the Grosvenor Ballroom. Yielding to pressure from his girlfriend, he had decided to return to his more lucrative job on the forklift at Garston bottle works, so becoming the only person ever to resign from the Beatles.

The gap was temporarily filled by a picture framer named Norman Chapman, an accomplished spare-time percussionist whom they hap-pened to overhear late one night practicing alone in an office building close to the Jacaranda. Chapman proved amenable to joining them and fitted in well enough, but he had time to play only three gigs at the Grosvenor—including an impromptu reunion performance with Johnny Gentle—before being spirited away as one of the very last victims of National Service. The Beatles were beatless yet again.

With no outside promoter willing to book them, almost the only work to be had through that hot Mersey midsummer was in Allan Williams's own ever-growing entertainments empire. Williams's newest venture was a strip club in Kimberley Street, just off Upper Parliament Street, grandiosely styled the New Cabaret Artists Club and run in partnership with a West Indian calypso musician known as Lord Woodbine. Here during their virtually gig-free July, the Beatles made a one-shot afternoon appearance as backing group to a stripper named Janice, with Paul McCartney taking the drummer's seat. In terms of eroticism, it barely packed the charge of John's col-lege life-drawing class, particularly since Janice expected her musi-cians to play appropriate mood pieces like "The Gipsy Fire Dance" from sheet music.

Around the middle of the month, Allan Williams was drinking at Ye Cracke when he fell into conversation with a couple of out-of-town journalists. They said they were from the *Empire News*, the dullest of Britain's downmarket Sunday papers, and were research-ing a feature article on how college students managed on their state grants. Seeing a chance to get himself into the article, Williams held forth at length on the poverty of Liverpool art students (omitting to mention his own opportunistic employment of them as decora-tors and strip-club musicians). He then took the journalists to John and Stu's Gambier Terrace flat, introduced them to its occupants, and hung around while interviews were conducted and photographs taken.

Williams had been misled, however. The hacks were not from the *Empire News*, but from its huge-circulation and scandal-hungry stablemate, the *People*. Nor was the article about student grants, but about the growing influence of America's beatnik movement among British youth. In America, beatniks had been considered at worst faintly comic, with their folk music, horn-rimmed glasses, and earnest reading of Camus and Sartre. In Britain—or, at least, to Britain's gutter press—they had taken over from Teddy Boys and Teddy Girls as symbols of juvenile delinquency.

THIS IS THE BEATNIK HORROR screamed a double-page spread in the *People* on Sunday, July 24. A purportedly nationwide survey gave harrowing details of the "unsavoury cult" that was said (without any evidence) to have turned young Americans by the thousand into "drug addicts and peddlers, degenerates who specialise in obscene orgies . . . and outright thugs and hoodlums." As an instance of the "unbelievable squalor that surrounds these well-educated young-sters," the report described a three-room flat in "decaying Gambier Terrace in the heart of Liverpool." The accompanying photograph showed several of the tenants in what was called the living room, but was actually John's and Stu's bedroom. No squalid detail was left unlisted, from its broken armchairs and debris-strewn table to the floor "littered with newspapers, milk bottles, beer and spirits bottles, bits of orange-peel, paint-tubes and lumps of cement and plaster of Paris."

Of the figures shown in the picture, Allan Williams alone was recognizable, by his black beard—his journalist pals taking pains to make clear he was just a visitor who'd dropped in to Beatnik Hell—to "listen to some jazz." The only tenants mentioned by name were Rod Murray and Rod Jones. Mid-July being vacation time, John was probably not even in residence, but back enjoying the home comforts and steak pies of Mendips. This very first time that the media search-light shone into his life, it missed him completely.

Before August 1960, everything that John, Paul, George, and Stu knew about Hamburg between them could have been written comfortably on the back of a one-penny stamp. They knew it vaguely as a northern port in the then Federal Republic of West Germany, whose name often appeared on the sterns of ships tying up in the Mersey. They knew of it even more vaguely as the one city on mainland Europe whose sexual daring surpassed even that of Paris. For years, Liverpool mariners had brought home lurid tales about its red-light district, the Reeperbahn, where female nudity was said to flourish on a scale as yet undreamed of in Britain and the cabarets to feature barely imaginable acts with whips, mud, live snakes, or even donkeys. The tarts of Lime Street seemed like maiden aunts by comparison.

Unlike London's Soho or New York's Forty-second Street, the Reeperbahn had no history of fostering music alongside the sex. But by the late fifties, thanks mainly to West Germany's American military occupiers (who, of course, included Elvis Presley) rock-'n'-roll culture was seeping in even there. To attract the younger customers, a club owner named Bruno Koschmider hit on the idea of presenting live beat groups at his establishment rather than simply relying on a jukebox like his competitors. The requisite live sound being still beyond West German musicians, or Belgian or French ones, Koschmider had no option but to recruit his groups from Britain. Through a convoluted chapter of accidents that would need a chapter of its own to relate, the place from which he ended up recruiting them was Liverpool, and the person who became his main supplier was Allan Williams.

Williams's first export to Herr Koschmider and the Reeperbahn had been the highly professional and versatile Derry and the Seniors. So powerful a draw did they prove at Koschmider's club, the Kaiserkeller, that he sent an enthusiastic request for more of the same. Despite protests from the Seniors, that such a "bum group" would spoil the scene for everyone else, Williams decided to offer the gig to the Beatles.

The engagement was for six weeks, beginning on August 16; it could not be slotted in among other commitments like the Johnny

Gentle tour, but would require all of them to abandon their various respectable courses in life for the precarious existence of full-time musicians. They would be working for an unknown employer in a foreign city hundreds of miles away, among a people who, not many years previously, had tried to bomb their country into extinction. Nonetheless, the response to Williams's offer was an instant, resounding affirmative.

To the many admirers of Stu Sutcliffe's art, the decision seemed little short of insane. He had just been awarded his National Diploma in Art and Design with painting as his specialist subject, and was about to begin a postgraduate teacher-training course. He himself fully realized what was at stake, and had initially refused the Hamburg offer, but then John had said that the Beatles wouldn't go without him, and he couldn't let John down.

His tutor, Arthur Ballard, was appalled by this seemingly pointless sacrifice of a brilliant future, and furious with John—and Allan Williams—for encouraging it. Stu had been such an exceptional student, however, that the college showed willingness to bend the rules for him. He was told he could begin his postgraduate course later in the academic year if he wished.

Paul McCartney and George Harrison were also putting excellent career prospects at risk, as their respective families and teachers unavailingly told them. Paul had just taken his GCE A-levels and, like Stu, planned a teaching career, probably specializing in English. George had an apprenticeship as an electrician at Blacklers, the central Liverpool department store, which in those days virtually guaranteed him employment for life.

Alone of the five, John seemed to have nothing to lose. He had no prospect of gaining any meaningful qualification from art college, and no idea what he wanted to do as a career. The sole obstacle to be reckoned with was his Aunt Mimi. As his guardian, albeit never legally recognized as such, Mimi had the power to veto the whole trip. And, to be sure, her mixture of horror and mystification when first told about it were precisely as John expected. Mimi had no more understanding of rock 'n' roll than when she first sent him out to practice in Mendips's soundproof front porch four years previously;

to her, it was still no more than a hobby that interfered with his studies, involved the most unsavory possible people and places, and could
never conceivably earn him anything like a proper living.

Now, at least, John could reply that it *would* be earning him a
living. The Beatles' collective weekly wage in Hamburg would be
close to £100, which admittedly boiled down to only about £2.50 per
day each, yet still seemed astronomical compared with the pittances
they were paid in Liverpool. Fortunately, Mimi had never even heard
of the Reeperbahn, let alone what was reputed to happen there. Her
objections to "Humbug," as she persisted in calling it, were that John
would be giving up college and that he'd be associating with the
erstwhile bombers of Liverpool. In the end, she decided—probably
rightly—that if she didn't give permission, he'd simply run away, and
then might never come back again.

Like most British teenagers in 1960, John had never been abroad
and did not even possess a passport. To apply for one, he had to produce his birth certificate, a document that had somehow gone missing after the frantic tug-of-love that had followed his birth. It turned
up in the nick of time—but the way to Hamburg wasn't all smooth
sailing yet.

The Beatles' new employer, Herr Koschmider, would obviously
expect them to have a drummer. In the absence of any successor to
Norman Chapman, Paul agreed to take on the role permanently, assembling a scratch kit from odds and ends that previous incumbents
had left behind. The problem was that Koschmider had requested a
group exactly like Derry and the Seniors—i.e., a quintet. That left
only two weeks to find a fifth Beatle. At one point, John even considered asking Royston Ellis to join, in the role of "poet-compere,"
as if he expected the Reeperbahn to be like some earnestly attentive
student union.

On August 6, complaints from surrounding residents about noise,
drunkenness, and violence shut down the Grosvenor Ballroom in
Wallasey, thereby depriving the Beatles of their last regular Merseyside gig. For want of anything better to do that night, they ended up
at the Casbah coffee club in Hayman's Green.

In the ten months since John, Paul, and George had played there as the Quarrymen—and walked out in a huff over a 15 shilling payment—the homely basement club had gone from strength to strength under Mona Best's vigorous management. Even more gallingly, Ken Brown, the former Quarryman and cause of that bitter 15-bob tiff, had formed a new group, the Blackjacks, who now regularly drew bigger weekend crowds than even Rory Storm and the Hurricanes. A major factor in their success was Mrs. Best's moodily handsome son, Peter, playing a sumptuous new drum kit in a pale blue mother-of-pearl finish (with real calfskins), which his adoring mother had bought him.

Pete Best and his blue drums solved both of the Beatles' predeparture problems at a stroke. "We just grabbed him and auditioned him," John remembered. "He could keep one beat going for long enough, so we took him."

10

MACH SCHAU

The Germans liked it as long as it was loud.

What Liverpool had endured at the time of John's birth Hamburg received back with compound interest. On the night of July 24, 1943, an Allied "thousand bomber raid," code name Operation Gomorrah, dropped 2,300 tons of bombs and incendiaries on this most crucial of Hitler's ports and industrial centers, unleashing greater destruction in a few hours than Merseyside had known over weeks during the purgatory of 1940. Four nights later, Gomorrah's cleansers returned, creating a 150 mph firestorm that reduced eight square miles of the city to ashes and claimed 43,000 civilian lives, more than Britain had lost during the entire Blitz.

Now, only fifteen years after the war's end, with its scars still far from healed, young survivors from that bomb-battered British city were taking music to young survivors of that devastated German one. In its small, unwitting way, it was a notable act of reconciliation that was to bind Liverpool and Hamburg together forever afterward and foreshadow the apolitical youth culture soon to dominate the whole Western world. Though John never thought of it as such, he had embarked on his very first peace campaign.

To deliver Bruno Koschmider's new employees as cheaply as possible—and being unable to resist any kind of lark—Allan Williams offered to drive them to Hamburg personally. In the end, a party of nine squeezed into Williams's battered green-and-white Austin van outside the Jacaranda early on August 15, 1960. Besides John, Paul, George, Stu, and new drummer, Pete Best, the Welshman took along his Chinese wife, Beryl, his brother-in-law, Barry Chang, and his West Indian business partner, Lord Woodbine. In London, they picked up an additional passenger, a German waiter named Georg Steiner, who had also been hired by Koschmider. The van was not like a modern minibus with rows of seats, but a bare metal shell: those in its rear had nowhere to sit but on the piled-up stage equipment and baggage.

The two-day journey was fraught with problems that somehow only Liverpudlians could have created and only Liverpudlians had the resilience and humor to endure. At Harwich, whence they were to cross the North Sea to the Hook of Holland, dock workers initially refused to load the grotesquely overloaded vehicle aboard the ferry. According to Williams, it was mainly John who persuaded them to relent, striking up a rapport as easy as if he himself had spent a lifetime on the dockside.

In those days, when foreign package tours were still in their infancy, most Britons setting foot on mainland Europe underwent a profound culture shock. Now every European nation wears the same clothes, drives the same cars, listens to the same music, eats the same fast food. But for nineteen-year-old John, this first-ever trip abroad meant entering a totally alien landscape where not a single person or thing looked or sounded or smelled the same as at home, food and toilet arrangements were hideously unpredictable, and drinking water, bizarrely, came in bottles rather than from the tap. There was as much fear as fascination in that introductory whiff of continental coffee, disinfectant, drains, and tobacco as darkly pungent as licorice.

With customary disregard for detail, Williams had not obtained the work permits his charges needed in order to appear for six weeks in a West German club and be paid in West German currency. If challenged en route, he said, they should pretend to be students on vacation. Fortunately, this was an era of mild frontier controls when, with wartime shortages still lingering, the most serious contraband was not drugs but food. The recurring official challenge, Paul McCartney remembers, was whether they had any illicit coffee. As with the Harwich stevedores, it was usually John's mixture of charm and cheek at checkpoints that got them waved on with friendly smiles.

He was not always such a ray of sunshine. In Holland, Williams insisted on making a patriotic detour to Arnhem, scene of the Allies' disastrous Operation Market Garden airborne landings in 1944. There Barry Chang took what would become a famous snapshot of Paul, George, Pete, Stu, Williams, Beryl, and Lord Woodbine around the casket-shaped memorial with its partially prophetic inscription THEIR NAMES LIVETH FOR EVERMORE. John, however, refused to leave the van. One can picture the scene in the bleary Dutch dawn—the big side door sliding back; the hunched and sleepy figure disinclined to move; the attempts to rouse him answered by a torrent of swear words.

He also took time for some shoplifting, finding the unsuspicious Netherland store owners absurdly easy victims after Woolton and Liverpool 8. The haul he later showed to Pete Best included jewelry, handkerchiefs, guitar strings, and a harmonica. Years later, when every detail of his early life was pored over by millions, that harmonica thoughtlessly pocketed in a Dutch music shop would cause many of his admirers pangs of vicarious guilt. Finally, a group of them resolved to set the matter right. Traveling to the Arnhem area, they found the same shop still in business and, to its owner's bewilderment, solemnly repaid the cost of the stolen instrument.

Though the term had still to be coined, Hamburg's Reeperbahn was one of the world's earliest experiments in sex therapy. The thinking—later to spread like wildfire through Europe, even unto Britain—was that being open about extreme or deviant sexual practices was healthier than being secretive. It was also a way to manage the problems of the harbor area, corralling pleasure-bent sailors all in one place and so saturating them with off-the-radar pornography that they would hopefully be less inclined to rape or other sexual crimes outside its boundaries. The district of St. Pauli, which includes the Reeperbahn, was a perfect location, handily close to the dockside and well away from Hamburg's swiftly rebuilt center and many respectable suburbs. This supposedly untamed carnal frontier was in effect a department of City Hall, governed by a mass of surprisingly straitlaced rules and regulations and watched over by a large and zealous police force.

Dusk was falling on August 16 when Allan Williams's van eventually found its way through Hamburg to St. Pauli, and John, Paul, George, Stu, and Pete received their first sight of their new workplace. After the almost seamless nighttime blackout of Liverpool, the Reeperbahn was an eye-mugging spectacle. Continuous neon signs winked and shimmered in gold, silver, and every suggestive color of the rainbow, their voluptuous German script—*Mehrer, Bar Monika, Mambo Schankey, Gretel and Alphons, Roxy Bar*—making the entertainments on offer seem even more untranslatably wicked. Though it was still early, the whole strip teemed with people—or rather, with men—and had the lurching, anarchic feel of pub-closing time back home. As the arrivals would soon learn, this was a place where times of day meant nothing.

Their new employer, Bruno Koschmider, might have stepped straight from one of John's more fanciful cartoons. Aged about fifty, he was a tiny man with an outsize head and wooden-puppet face, topped off by an elaborate silver coiffure. Thanks to a war-disabled leg, he walked with a limp, thus instantly qualifying for the copious Lennon gallery of "cripples."

A guided tour of Koschmider's Kaiserkeller club, in the Reeperbahn's busiest and most garish sector, did much to compensate for his strange appearance. A teeming barn of a place, it had no obvious affinity with the Great War's "Kaiser Bill," being decorated on a nautical theme with ornamental life belts, brass binnacles, pipe-clayed cording, and booths shaped like rowboats. Only now did the newcomers learn that they were not to appear here, with Derry and the Seniors, as they'd been led to believe. In the nearby Grosse Freiheit (Great Freedom) Koschmider also operated a run-down strip club named the Indra. The Beatles' job would be to make the Indra as big a teenage draw as Derry and his colleagues had the Kaiserkeller.

Worse followed when Koschmider led the way to the living quarters he had contracted to provide for them. A couple of blocks away in Paul Roosen Strasse, he owned a small cinema named the Bambi, which showed a mixture of porn flicks and old Hollywood gangster movies and Westerns. The Beatles' quarters were a filthy, windowless room and two glorified broom closets immediately behind the screen. The only washing facilities were the adjacent cinema toilets. "We were put in this pigsty," John remembered. "We were living in a toilet, like right next to the ladies' toilet. We'd go to bed late and be woken up next day by the sound of the cinema show [and] old German fraus pissing next door."

The working hours laid down by Koschmider were the biggest shock of all. Back in Liverpool, they had never been onstage longer than about twenty minutes. At the Indra club they would be expected to play for four and a half hours each weeknight, in sets of an hour or an hour and a half, with only three thirty-minute breaks in between. On Saturdays and Sundays, the playing time increased to six hours.

The quintet made their debut the following night, August 17, clad in matching lilac jackets that had been tailored for them by Paul McCartney's next-door neighbor. It was far from a rip-roaring success. The thinnest sprinkle of customers watched from red-shaded tables, surprised not to see the club's usual entertainment, a stripper named Conchita. Koschmider's advance publicity, such as it was, had created some uncertainty as to the exact nature and purpose of the new attraction, "Beatle" being easily confused with the German word *peedle*, or little boy's willy. The room reeked of stale beer and wine and was lined in dusty velvet drapes that muffled already feeble amps and made Pete Best feel as if he was "drumming under the bedclothes."

All five "Peedles" were still wiped out by their journey, awed by their new surroundings, and doubtful of their ability to connect with their new public. For the opening numbers, they stood as still and stiff-faced as lilac-tinted zombies. Dismayed by their lack of animation but unable to communicate in English, Koschmider shouted at them, *"Mach schau!"*—"Make a show"—a command usually given to dilatory striptease artistes. "And of course whenever there was any pressure point, I had to get us out of it," John would remember. "The guys said, 'Well okay John, you're the leader.' When nothing was going on, they'd say, 'Uh-oh, no leader, fuck it,' but if anything happened it was like 'You're the leader, you get up and do a show.'

"We were scared by it all at first, being in the middle of the tough clubland. But we felt cocky, being from Liverpool, at least believing the myth about Liverpool producing cocky people. So I put my guitar down and did Gene Vincent all night, banging and lying on the floor and throwing the mike around and pretending I had a bad leg. . . . We did mach schau-ing all the time from then on."

According to myth, it was Hamburg that produced the first serious growth spurt in Lennon and McCartney's songwriting partnership. Actually, the Beatles spent almost their whole time in West Germany as a "covers band," although that underrates the ingenuity they were forced to employ. The repertoire of mainstream rock-'n'-roll hits they first brought with them from Liverpool were exhausted as quickly as their last few English cigarettes. To get through sets an hour and a half long, they had to delve deep into the creative hinterland of all their musical idols—Elvis, Chuck Berry, Little Richard, Fats Domino, Buddy Holly, the Everly Brothers—seeking out little-known B-sides and unregarded album tracks. They had to find other rock-'n'-roll songs by American artists, black and white, singular and plural, that had never crossed the Atlantic, let alone made the British Top 20, and also ransack the milky post–rock-'n'-roll charts for ballads they could play without nausea, like Bobby Vee's "More Than I Can Say." With the continuing popularity of Duane "Twangy Guitar" Eddy, they had to be as much an instrumental as a vocal group, churning out bass-string psychodramas like Eddy's "Rebel-Rouser" or "Shazam." When rock, pop, country, and even skiffle could not fill out the time, they had to reach into the realm of standards and show tunes that Paul overtly loved—and John covertly did—with old wind-up gramophone favorites like "Red Sails in the Sunset," "Besame Mucho," "Somewhere Over the Rainbow," and "Your Feet's Too Big."

Performing nightly in their out-of-the-way, unalluring venue, they were somewhat like old-fashioned fairground barkers, first drawing in the patrons, then working like blazes to keep them there. The best come-on, they found, was a heavy, stomping beat, laid down by Pete Best's blue bass drum, and perhaps not a million miles from the militaristic march tempo that had recently echoed across Europe. "We really had to hammer," John recalled. "We had to try anything that came into our heads. There was nobody to copy from. We played what we liked best, and the Germans liked it as long as it was loud."

The most famous Reeperbahn story, told and retold in Liverpool dockside pubs, was that you could see a woman being mounted by a donkey with a washer around its penis to restrict penetration. Though this new concept of donkey work proved a myth, St. Pauli had much else to shock and amaze. First, it had all the nudity it had been credited with and more—not coyly concealed by turned backs and crossed arms, as at home, but full-frontal, full-rear-al nudity, pulsing with youth and warmth and invitation. For all five teenage Beatles, sooner than they could ever have imagined, bouncing breasts and grinding, weaving G-strung bottoms became merely so much incidental furniture.

In some clubs, they could see men and women have full, unprotected sex in twos, threes, or even fours, in every possible and improbable configuration, often in the taboo combination of white and black. In others, they could see nude women wrestling in a pit of mud, cheered on by plump businessmen tied into communal pinafores to guard against the splashes. In the numerous *Schwülen laden* (queer dives) like Bar Monika or the Roxy Bar, they could watch men give each other blow jobs or meet male transvestites as beautiful and elegant as Parisian models who only in the final stages of intimacy would unveil their gristly secret.

At the same time, Germanic bureaucracy, health regulation, and anomalous concern for the moral welfare of the young were as om-

nipresent as neon tubing. To discourage organized crime, pimps
were allowed to run only two prostitutes each, making their trade
largely a spare-time one carried on by waiters and barmen. In some
streets, club patrons were allowed to see female pubic hair, in others
not. St. Pauli's pièce de résistance, the Herbertstrasse, where whores
sat on display in shop windows, was screened from general view by a
high wooden fence. Most relevant to the Beatles, a curfew came into
force at 10:00 p.m., obliging all under-eighteens to leave the area.
Each note that seventeen-year-old George Harrison played at the
Indra after that time was a breach of the law.

Many places, like Koschmider's Kaiserkeller, were straightforward
bars, vastly bigger than any Liverpool pub, where seafaring men of
all nations and personnel from American and British NATO bases
congregated by the riotous thousand before and after hitting the
nudie joints. Reeperbahn waiters were renowned for toughness and
ruthlessness, Koschmider's most of all. When fights broke out, which
they did almost continuously, a squad of waiters would swoop on
the culprits like a highly-trained SWAT team, pulling lead-weighted
saps from under their white jackets. Koschmider himself went about
armed with the leg of an old German chair in knotty hardwood,
which he kept concealed down one trouser leg. Sometimes, rather
than merely ejecting a troublemaker, the Kaiserkeller waiters would
carry him into their employer's office for a prolonged work-over.
When the victim was pinned down and helpless, Koschmider would
weigh in with his antique chair leg. "I've never seen such killers,"
John remembered.

Even by northern British standards, the German intake of beer
was prodigious, and the Liverpool lads were soon competing with
the best of them. This was not the tepid, woody ale they were used
to, but chilled draft lager served in fluted, gold-rimmed glasses
that, back home, still featured only in upmarket cocktail bars. After
ninety minutes of *mach schau* on the Indra's stage, their thirst for this
frosted gold nectar was almost unlimited. Any customer for whom
they played a request would show appreciation by sending them *ein
bier* each; by the end of an average night, the stage front would be
littered with empty and half-empty glasses.

Playing and drinking at these levels brought on fatigue such as

none of them had ever known before. On the round-the-clock Reeperbahn, it was a common complaint, with its own well-tried remedy.
Friendly Indra staff introduced them to Preludin (phenmetrazine), a
weight-loss tablet available over the counter at any pharmacy, which
made the metabolism work at roughly twice normal speed. A secondary effect was to make the eyes bulge like ping-pong balls, dry
up the saliva, and so redouble the craving for cold beer.

None of the five except George was a virgin when they arrived
in Hamburg. But, as soon became clear, even their best results with
Liverpool girls had taught them next to nothing. Sex was the Reeperbahn's main recreation as well as its currency. And five relatively
innocent Liverpool lads were the freshest and tenderest of meat. As
they built a following at the Indra, they found themselves besieged
by invitations from female customers, barmaids and waitresses, or
dancers and strippers who would drop by the club after a night's
work. It was done in a casual, no-nonsense style that antedated so-
called sexual liberation in the rest of the world by a full decade. A
woman who fancied a bit of boy-Scouser would indicate her choice
by pointing, or sometimes reaching up in midsong to fondle his leg.
Many dispensed with even these slight formalities, going directly to
the Beatles' squalid quarters at the Bambi Kino, finding their way
behind the screen, and waiting in one or other of the ratty beds until
their quarry arrived. As Pete Best later recalled, such encounters
would often happen in pitch darkness, the girl not knowing which
Beatle it was and he never seeing her face—hence the almost dehumanized term "muff-diving" that the Liverpudlians coined for
them.

Living at such close quarters meant fucking at close quarters also.
When George did finally lose his virginity, John, Paul, and Pete were
all in the same room and, as he would recall, "clapped and cheered at
the end." Paul remembered that "I'd walk in on John and see a little
bottom going up and down and a girl underneath. It was perfectly
normal, you'd go 'Oh shit, sorry . . .' and back out of the room." Pete
Best, himself no mean sexual athlete, was amazed at John's capacity,
and that he still had enough libido left over to be a connoisseur of the
Reeperbahn's spectacular "wank mags."

Freed at last from the long leash of Woolton and Mendips and the choke chain of his Aunt Mimi, John went wild. While the other four all recognized the need for some caution and self-control, he knocked back the cold yellow beer and gulped the tiny white Preludin tablets, never bothering to keep count. The lethal, eye-popping, thirst-inflaming mixture of pills and alcohol spurred him to ever wilder onstage antics in the name of *mach schau*. Limping and lurching around in his demented parody of Gene Vincent at the Liverpool boxing stadium was only the beginning. He would jump up onto Paul's shoulders, and cannon sideways into George or Stu, and leap off the stage to land among the dancers on his knees or in a split. At unpredictable moments he would stop singing and taunt his audience as "fuckin' Nazis" and "Hitlerites" or, with appropriate idiot grimaces and claw hands, as "German Spassies" (spastics). Punk rock, twenty-five years into the future, would have nothing on this.

Though not the vicious and racially torn gangland it would later become, St. Pauli in 1960 was still a highly dangerous place. The *Polizei* might be scrupulous about checking papers and issuing medical certificates, but they paid little attention to the grievous bodily harm inflicted nightly throughout its neon wonderland by blackjacks, knives, brass knuckles, and tear-gas pistols. Yet by an unwritten law, so long as they observed a few basic rules, Liverpool's boy rock-'n'-rollers were immune from all harm. Friendly waiters advised them where to go and not go, to whom to be polite, and whose girlfriend never to muff-dive. Horrific fights would break out around them, leaving them unscathed like a scene from some Marx Brothers film. Most extraordinarily, in all the drunken melees through which they passed, not one person ever called them to account for the ruin and death their countrymen had so recently inflicted here. John's "Nazi" taunts were either not understood or taken in a spirit of badinage.

The few hours between playing and sleep they spent mostly out on the street, drifting from bar to café and doorway to doorway with the tide of sex tourists, and touts peddling anything from dirty books to diamonds. A short walk from the Reeperbahn was a music store named Steinway, which stocked an impressive range of imported American guitars and amps, and proved just as accommodating about paying in installment as Hessy's back in Liverpool. Here John found the guitar of his dreams, a double-cutaway Rickenbacker Capri 325 whose shorter-than-usual neck gave it the look of a skirmish weapon as much as a songbox. Although still theoretically paying off Hessy's for his Hofner Club 40, he put himself in hock a second time for a Rickenbacker with a "natural" ivory white finish that was to be his faithful companion throughout all the tempests ahead.

Despite his countless new bedfellows, he suffered bouts of missing Cynthia and sent her regular, edited accounts of his Hamburg life, marking the envelopes S.W.A.L.K. (Sealed With a Loving Kiss) or "Postman, postman, don't be slow / I'm in love with Cyn' so go man go" like any ardent young swain. Back in Liverpool, Cyn and Paul's girlfriend, Dot Rhone, kept rigorously to the code their lords and masters had laid down for them, refusing even the friendliest, no-strings offers of dates from other young men; regularly photograph-ing one another as proof that their regulation Brigitte Bardot look was being kept up to scratch. If Dot was not around to take Cyn's picture, she would squeeze into a Woolworths photo booth, wearing her sexiest outfit, with her hair newly done, and give sultry come-hither looks to an invisible John as the impatient light flashed. John responded with similar passport-size snaps of his most deformed hunchback poses and leering "spassie" grimaces.

Like others before him, Pete Best saw how John's fondness for mimicking deformity turned to horror and revulsion at any sight of the real thing. Once as the two sat in a restaurant, a badly maimed war veteran was helped to a nearby table. Though John had already ordered his meal, he jumped up and bolted.

Given their different personalities and very different levels of musical prowess, the five Hamburg Beatles shook down to-gether remarkably well. At this point, it was hardly an issue that the lineup included John's two closest friends, who had always pulled him in diametrically opposite directions.

Paul McCartney and Stu Sutcliffe were never going to be close, but both were civilized for their young years and thus got along tol-erably enough. What chiefly concerned Paul was Stu's commitment to the group: that he should apply himself fully to his bass playing and not distract John with impractical questions of art and aesthetics. And for a time, both those requirements seemed to be being met.

Stu saw the trip to Hamburg as a clean break from his life at art college, his home city's predictable subject matter, and the "tricks" he believed he had come to rely on in his work there. Despite the garish colors and teeming subject matter around him, he resisted all temptation to paint or draw, let alone to encourage John to do so. With the disillusionment that in youth can be actively pleasurable, he described himself as "a romantic gone sour . . . I have shrivelled like a sucked grape. I must dig deep and plant myself and grow."

As even Paul conceded, Stu was a strong visual asset to the group, a James Dean movie in miniature, with his upswept hair and brooding shades, while the others played Groucho and Harpo. To relieve their Preludin-parched throats, he had to take a share of the vocals, doing not at all badly with slow Presley ballads like "Love Me Tender." And his employer, at least, had no complaints about his playing. A few weeks after the Beatles opened at the Indra, Koschmider removed Stu from their ranks and put him into an ad hoc quartet that was to play in alternation with Derry and the Seniors at the Kaiserkeller. This hybrid group included Howie Casey, the Seniors' much-respected sax player, who found no serious fault with Stu's musicianship either. He thus became the first Beatle to get the gig that they all coveted.

Liverpool had not, in fact, provided the very first young Britons to rock the Reeperbahn. That distinction belonged to Tony Sheridan, who, with his backing band, the Jets, had come over via London's Soho the previous June. Born Anthony Esmond Sheridan McGinnity, Sheridan, like John, was not yet twenty but already boasted an impressive pedigree: he was the first rock-'n'-roller ever to play an electric guitar on British television (in days when they were still considered a fire hazard), and had made regular appearances on *Oh Boy!* and in Larry Parnes's touring revues, backing big American names like Eddie Cochran and Conway Twitty.

Sheridan both sang and played lead guitar—in those days still a highly unusual accomplishment—and had developed a technique that would influence John more than any, perhaps, since Elvis's.

While performing, he planted his legs wide apart and leaned forward, with shoulders slightly hunched and head down, as if facing directly into a hurricane. Like other Reeperbahn ravers, he could not find enough pure rock 'n' roll to last through the long nights, so had to draw heavily on the ostensibly square world of ballads and standards. But when Sheridan played an oldie, it was always in a brand-new, often startling interpretation, with shades of mockery or innuendo its original composer never intended and chord changes no one else would have dared. Musically, as in life, he was a born subversive.

Sheridan had started out as resident act at the Kaiserkeller, watching Koschmider rough up customers and sleeping under threadbare Union Flags in the basement. When the Beatles finally met up with him, he was playing at a strip club named Studio X. "We were all acting tough, shut into our leather jackets and putting on a hard face that said 'Don't mess with me' even though we were all as soft as syrup inside," he recalls. "But John in those days seemed scary. Here was this guy in glasses who'd take his glasses off and stare at you in that blank, vacant way, as if he was willing trouble to happen. I sometimes used to think, 'Is he like this back in Liverpool? And if so, why is he still alive?'

"But as soon as you got to know him, you saw that underneath he was a mass of insecurities. He didn't think he was a good singer—because, remember, his voice wasn't like any of the other guys' who were around at that time. And he didn't rate himself as a guitarist, chugging along on three fingers the way he did. He saw himself as just the motor of the group, the mouth that said 'We're from Liverpool, and none of you bastards is gonna stop us.'"

Sheridan widened John's musical horizon in every direction, encouraging him to stray outside the three-finger chord style Julia had taught him and venture down the new Rickenbacker's stubby fretboard into riskier high-register minors and sevenths. The inveterate jazz-hater was even persuaded that not everything from that genre could be written off as pretentious and "soft." Sheridan's current idol was Ray Charles, a jazz-reared singer-pianist whose genius embraced rock, soul, and even country, and whose instant classic "What'd I

Say" was a godsend to any group in need of time-consuming material. "Almost all of my conversations with John were about music.
He wanted to learn everything he possibly could. But even if he was
asking for help, it came out in a typical sort of sarcastic Lennon quip,
like 'Come on, Sheridan. You're supposed to know all about this
stuff.' "

With his four months' greater experience, Sheridan was an ideal
guide to the Reeperbahn's more exotic diversions, like the *Schwülen
laden*. Stu Sutcliffe later wrote home in amazement that the transvestites were "all harmless and very young" and it was actually possible
to speak to one "without shuddering." Though raised amid the same
homophobia as his companions, John seemed totally unshocked by
St. Pauli's abundant drag scene; indeed, he often seemed actively to
seek it out. "There was one particular club he used to like," Tony
Sheridan remembers, "full of these big guys with hairy hands, deep
voices—and breasts. But they used to make an effort to talk English.
There was something about the place that seemed to make John feel
at home."

Sheridan also brought with him a crucial friend and ally from
within the St. Pauli community. Horst Fascher was a pocket-sized
twenty-four-year-old of fearsome reputation: trained at the Reeperbahn's own boxing academy, he was an ex-featherweight champion with a prison record for accidentally killing a sailor in a street
brawl. He was at the same time a hopeless romantic, besotted by
rock 'n' roll and fascinated by the humor and speech patterns of the
young Englishmen who were spraying it over his home turf. He had
become Sheridan's unofficial protector at the Kaiserkeller and now
called himself his manager, though the role had little to do with
taking bookings or collecting fees. "There were always drunks in
the place who thought they could sing better than the musicians and
would jump on the stage and try to grab the mike. I would always be
there to stop these guys from bothering Tony."

Fascher first met John at Harald's, the little café where the Beatles
would go for chicken soup after their night's work at the Indra. "He
was drinking beer though it was four, five o'clock in the morning.
And his eyes were sticking out like *untertassen* [saucers] from the
Preludin. He still make me laugh more than I ever laugh in my life

before. Tony said to the five of them 'If you get any problems, Horst will sort it out.' "

From then on, the Beatles, too, were under Fascher's protection. "I could see that if I didn't watch out for them, John would get them into big trouble, or himself on his own. He was playing the tough guy with nothing to back it up, which was a dangerous thing to do on the Reeperbahn. But I love the guy from the moment I first meet him. I never hit him, although he often try to make me; he call me a fuckin' Nazi bastard. Words were only over our lips, but in our hearts we know that we needed each other, that we respected each other, that we could depend on each other."

At the Indra club meanwhile, after nearly seven weeks' hard labor, John's dedication to *mach schau* had paid unexpected dividends. Directly above the club lived an elderly war widow who subjected Bruno Koschmider to such a relentless stream of complaints about the noise that St. Pauli's municipal authority stepped in, ordering Koschmider to terminate live music at the Indra and return it to its less disruptive role of strip club. As they had always wanted, the Beatles were moved to the Kaiserkeller in place of the cobbled-together quartet who had been alternating with Derry and the Seniors; Stu Sutcliffe was restored to their ranks and their original three-month contract was extended to December 31.

For this privilege, they were expected to give an even longer nightly show, starting at 7:30 and finishing at 2:30, a total of five and a half hours punctuated by only three half-hour breaks. To fill up the time, John would later recall, "every song had to last about 20 minutes and have 20 solos." Ray Charles's "What'd I Say," with its call-and-response "Hey—he-ey . . . Uh—u-uh" and endlessly repeatable and exciting guitar-piano riff, could be stretched out almost indefinitely. They learned to keep playing no matter what the distraction, over the deafening hubbub of a thousand beer-stoked voices, even during fights that were like scenes from some epic Western, with people smashing chairs over one another's heads and swallow-diving from tables. As John remembered, one sure portent of trouble was a familiar whiff of Senior Service cigarettes, meaning that "the English were in," either sailors or army national servicemen.

In the Kaiserkeller's prime stageside boat-booths could be found a more affluent and subtly threatening clientele. According to John, these were "gangsters . . . the local Mafia. They'd send a crate of champagne on stage, imitation German champagne, and we'd have to drink it. . . . I used to be so pissed I'd be lying on the floor behind the piano while the rest of the group were playing. I'd be onstage, fast asleep. And we always ate onstage, too, because we never had time to eat. . . . George threw some food at me once, onstage. . . . I said I would smash his face in for him. We had a shouting match but that was all. I never did anything. And I once threw a plate of food over George."

On October 5, Derry and the Seniors reached the end of their contract with Bruno Koschmider. Rather than promote the Beatles to headline status at the Kaiserkeller, Koschmider called on Allan Williams for yet another Mersey group, and Williams sent out Rory Storm and the Hurricanes. On arrival, they found they were expected to take over their predecessors' squalid sleeping quarters in the Kaiserkeller's basement. This they declined to do, preferring the comparative luxury of being five in one room at the dockside seamen's mission.

The double attraction of "Rory Storm and his Hurikan und the Beatles Liverpool-England" appeared in split shifts, playing alternating sets of an hour and a half each over an incredible twelve-hour period. In the nightly *mach schau* stakes, John now faced formidable competition, not only from extrovert Rory himself, with his toppling blond cockade, his turquoise suit, and his love of dancing on pianos and shinning up walls, but also from the Hurricanes' lead guitarist, known by the cowboyish tag of Johnny Guitar, and even from their drummer, Ringo Starr, who by comparison with the stolidly pounding, impassive Pete Best seemed a veritable human Catherine wheel.

Although the Kaiserkeller's stage looked solid enough, it stood on a mess of half-rotten timbers supported only by a few flimsy orange crates. After the rival bands discovered this, the sole object of *mach schau* was to see who could first actually stomp his way through this worm-eaten edifice. To John's chagrin, Rory Storm won the contest one Saturday night, leaping onto the piano during Jerry Lee Lewis's

"Whole Lotta Shakin' Goin' On" with such force that it splintered the floor beneath and sank from view with Rory still on top like a cowboy on a bucking bronco.

Before these nights of shared endeavor in Hamburg, the Beatles and Ringo Starr had had little to do with one another. Back home, Ringo had always seemed a rather remote figure, as far above them in local celebrity as he was below all of them, except perhaps George, in class. Although only four months John's senior, he seemed much older, with his Ford Zephyr car and fondness for personal jewelry, especially rings, which he wore four or five on each hand. In those days, it was rare to see a man's fingers, especially a workingman's, so encumbered, hence the initial nickname Rings, which had evolved to Ringo with a little help from John Wayne's Ringo Kid.

His appearance was not prepossessing, the large nose and drooping Bassett hound eyes overdramatized by a Teddy Boy forelock and a scrubby beard. George Harrison had always thought "he looked like a tough guy . . . with that grey streak in his hair and half a grey eyebrow and that big nose," and even John later incredulously recalled having been a little scared of him.

Working together at the Kaiserkeller and looning around the Reeperbahn together after hours dispelled all such preconceptions. Ringo might come from the Dingle, Liverpool's poorest area, and have had next to no formal education, the result of chronic bad health throughout childhood, but he possessed a natural articulateness, perceptiveness, and—one can call it only—sweetness that endeared him instantly to each of the very different Beatles. His droll, deadpan way with words was often the equal of John's, though the two were never competitive, verbally or otherwise. Here, indeed, was one of the very few people around him destined never to feel the lash of the Lennon tongue.

Even at this early stage, Pete Best had begun to show fatal signs of keeping to himself, with the result that Ringo increasingly made up a fourth with John, Paul, and George. On October 15, they cut a demo record together, acting as sidemen to one of Ringo's fellow Hurricanes, Lu Walters, whose deep, bluesy voice was chafing for solo exposure. At a tiny studio named Akustik, behind Hamburg's central railway station, John, Paul, George, and Ringo backed Walters through a set of mainstream ballads, including George Gershwin's "Summertime," from *Porgy and Bess*.

As George said, and John did not demur: "When there were the four of us with Ringo, it always felt rockin'."

One late October evening, a customer walked into the Kaiserkeller who, unusually, was a resident of Hamburg rather than a sailor, a sex tourist, or a drunk spoiling for a fight. He was twenty-one years old and devastatingly good-looking, with large, liquid eyes, chiseled cheekbones, and long hair combed down around his ears and over his forehead as only a few young men on mainland Europe, and none in the English-speaking world, yet dared to do. His name was Klaus Voormann.

Klaus was a graphic designer, just starting out in the world of newspapers, glossy magazines, and advertisement agencies for which Hamburg was secondarily famous. His clothes identified him as a beatnik and, therefore, respectably middle class, though here the movement's look and spirit were markedly different from in Britain, America, or France. Hamburg's beatniks called themselves *exis*—short for existentialists—and were stylistic radicals; boys and girls wore the same hairstyle (unusually long for one, unusually short for the other) and favored a minimalist, black leathery look that still had uncomfortable resonances of Hitler's SS.

Exis as a rule congregated in their own candlelit coffeehouses and bars and were most emphatically never seen amid the tawdry unsubtleties of St. Pauli. Klaus Voormann had found his way there almost by accident, while walking off an argument he'd had with his girlfriend earlier that evening. He stopped in at the Kaiserkeller for *ein bier*; instead, he got the Beatles.

"For me it was like hearing every great rock-'n'-roll tune there had ever been, sung by all the greatest singers," Klaus recalls. "They were like chameleons. John would be Gene Vincent, then he'd be Chuck Berry. Paul would do Elvis, then he'd do Fats Domino, then he'd do Carl Perkins. And in between, the two of them would argue . . . 'I want to do "Be-Bop-A-Lula"' . . . 'No, I want to do it!'"

Whatever John's insecurities about himself, they were hidden from the transfixed German boy at his feet. "He loved singing, he loved the songs, and he loved playing rhythm guitar—he was a great rhythm guitarist. But what I felt most of all was the mind of this guy. All he wanted was to be outside the ordinary. To do something different. To do something outrageous."

Forgetting their earlier squabble, Klaus hurried off to his girlfriend, Astrid Kirchherr, and told her excitedly what he'd found. If he was beautiful, Astrid was a stunner, elfin yet voluptuous, the somber *exi* rig perfectly setting off her creamy skin, huge, black-rimmed eyes, and boyish crop of pale gold hair. At twenty-two, she was clearly destined for great things in Hamburg's media world, having landed a job as assistant to the noted photographer Reinhart Wolf.

Astrid was rather shocked to hear that Klaus had been slumming in St. Pauli and, at first, not at all keen to accompany him back to the Kaiserkeller as he wished. In the end, their whole *exi* circle went together, hoping for safety in numbers. On the stage, the Beatles became aware that a sizable portion of the audience now consisted of black leather.

For all their ferocious cool, the exis were—if the word had only been around then—an uptight lot. Guilt over a war for which they bore no blame caused them to tiptoe through life as timidly as their black-leathern predecessors had arrogantly goose-stepped through it. "These Liverpool people were to us like magic," Klaus Voormann says. "We could only look on them as fantastic creatures because they were open, they were friendly, they were quick, very very quick humor. And we loved it. And we knew how stiff we were, how hard we found it to let go. They had no problem, they talked about anything, they took the mickey out of themselves all the time. And we had to learn that. To laugh about our own hang-ups."

Since Klaus spoke the best English, he was deputed to make formal contact with the magical ones during their brief breaks between performances. He was himself a would-be guitarist and, it so happened, had recently been commissioned to design a record album cover, the Ventures' *Walk, Don't Run*. Hoping this might make a more eloquent self-introduction, he brought it to the Kaiserkeller and showed it to

John, the one among the five he most wanted to meet. "I didn't get that good a reaction," he remembers. "John took only a brief look, then muttered 'You should give it to Stu. He's the arty one around here.'

"John liked to intimidate people. As long as I knew him, he always would intimidate me. He was trying all the time to be the hard rock-'n'-roller. That's why I was particularly proud that I found the courage to go over to him and speak to him. But even though he seemed so tough, I had the feeling that he was looking up to Stuart."

Astrid was mesmerized as Klaus had been, both by the music and the force of John's personality. "I couldn't believe there was a young boy who could put all his heart and soul into what he was singing. That was pretty amazing. He became the music and the lyrics. He had this strong attitude; I got the feeling it will be hard to get through to him or to get a nice answer."

But it was not John who drew her back to the Kaiserkeller time and again "like a drug." It was the English boy as diminutive as herself who stood across the stage from John, wearing dark glasses and half turned away with his heavy bass guitar as if embarrassed by his own playing. To Stu Sutcliffe's astonishment, he began to be showered with compliments in forthright German style from the Beatles' new *exi* following, especially the regular threesome of Astrid, Klaus, and another aspiring photographer, Jurgen Vollmer. "Just recently," Stu wrote to his mother, "I have found the most wonderful friends, the most beautiful looking trio I have ever seen . . . the girl thought that I was the most handsome of the lot. . . . Here was I, feeling the most insipid working member of the group, being told how much superior I looked—this alongside the great Romeo John Lennon. . . ."

Astrid had fallen for Stu in the first moment she set eyes on him. But to begin with, she hid her feelings behind a photographer's professional interest in the group. Flattered by the admiration of so gorgeous a girl, the five Beatles needed no persuasion to do some pictures with her during their few daytime leisure hours. "I picked them up in my car," she remembers. "They were all so sweet, they'd washed their hair and put on their best clothes."

As a location, she took them into Der Dom, the amusement park where Bruno Koschmider first had the idea of bringing live rock 'n' roll to St. Pauli. It was a chill, drizzly autumn day, with few people about, so Astrid was free to pose her slightly mystified subjects clustered at leisure around old-fashioned calliopes or perched on silent traction engines. Speaking so little English, she had to communicate her instructions mainly by gesture, sometimes physically twisting them around, moving their limbs or turning their heads in the required direction. She had expected John to be the most difficult and disruptive of the five. "In private he was always joking, doing faces and things, and was never serious. But when I took the pictures, he was so dead professional it was unbelievable."

The prints that Astrid subsequently produced could not have been more of a surprise. To begin with, they were not the glossy living color in which German Agfa then led the photographic world, but grainy matte black and white, more suggestive of the late-nineteenth century than the mid-twentieth. The subjects, too, had an almost Victorian air, posed on and around the heavy old industrial artifacts, their efforts to look cool and hard and don't-give-a-damn only emphasizing their almost ridiculous youth and innocence and vulnerability. So was created not only a revelatory self-image for this pop group but the template of all pop groups forevermore.

Paul McCartney, Pete Best, even the gawky George Harrison, had always possessed a degree of confidence in their own looks. But John thought himself ugly, hence that preemptive impulse to make himself grotesquely so whenever a camera was pointed at him. Astrid's lens caught his face, for the first time since long-ago childhood, without any of its self-conscious and defensive idiot stares or leers: one could see the fine cheekbones, inherited from his mother; the delicacy of the mouth in repose; the shadows of sadness that still haunted the close-set eyes. "He was as beautiful as any of them," Astrid says. "He just never saw it before. He loved his pictures. I realised what a tremendous respect he had for perfectionism. That was the first time I felt that he respected me."

During the Der Dom shoot, Astrid's feelings for Stu, and his for her, came into the open, and from then on, their relationship made rapid strides. In the absence of paint, Stu communicated his rapture and astonishment in words that glowed almost as much; Astrid, he wrote to a Liverpool friend, was "like a rose that has run its dark leaves over the wall to look at the sun . . . [her] eyes full of fire, and now full of dew. . . ."

Together with her beauty and stylishness, Astrid possessed all the solid instincts of the hausfrau. Rather than try to compete with John and the other Beatles for Stu's attention, she took all five under her wing, inviting them to her comfortable home in the suburb of Altona, letting them have much-needed baths there, cooking them huge meals of steak or eggs with English-style chips, even washing their clothes. Never again would any girlfriend—let alone one from an alien culture—be welcomed into their inner circle in the same unreserved way. John's letters home to Cynthia were so full of admiring references to Astrid that Cyn began to feel pangs of jealousy.

His visits to Astrid's brought out all the sides of John she would never have suspected—the Woolton-bred politeness, the secret homebody, the instant response to any maternal warmth with the faintest echo of Julia's. "The amazing thing was how he loved my mother. They couldn't understand a word of one another; Mummy didn't talk English and John didn't talk German. But as soon as he used to come in, he always said 'Where's Mummy?' He'd rush into the kitchen to see her and he seemed to become a completely different person. That tough rock 'n' roller, the guy who didn't care, just disappeared. That was correct what he did with my Mummy, hugging her and being with her, looking into the pots to see what she was cooking."

Even with the little English that she spoke, Astrid became instantly aware of the strange, seesawing relationship between Stu and John; how John would defer to Stu at one moment and at the next, mock and belittle him seemingly beyond any forgiveness; how Stu at one moment could appear the more dominant of the two, but at the next curl up into unprotesting victimhood. "Stuart was someone John really, really loved. Now I'm thinking that when he treated him badly, it was because he was afraid anyone might see how much he loved him."

Winning such a girl did more than boost Stu's standing with John and the other Beatles; it also kicked his hibernating visual creativity back into life. Spending time as he now did with Astrid's *exi* group of photographers and art students, it wasn't long before he felt a rekindling urge first to draw, then to paint. A sketchbook once more became an indivisible part of his person and, with the teeming Reeperbahn color and grotesquery all around him, his pen or pencil was seldom idle. To a former girlfriend in Liverpool he wrote of his exaltation at "being the artist again." The letter was written from his dark cubbyhole at the Bambi Kino, in the faint beam of a flashlight strapped to his forehead like an old-fashioned coal miner's lamp.

In mid-November, barely a month after their first meeting, Stu and Astrid decided to get engaged. The news met with equal approval from John and the other Beatles (guaranteeing, as it did, hot baths, meals and hand-laundering for the foreseeable future) and from Astrid's mother, who idolized Stu almost as much as did her daughter and also seems to have had prescient fears of his health. Appalled by Astrid's description of his living conditions at the Bambi, Frau Kirchherr insisted that he move into her home forthwith, occupying a spare room at the top of the house that had formerly been Klaus Voormann's.

Klaus himself bore Stu no resentment for displacing him; his relationship with Astrid had been cooling off anyway, and he felt more than compensated by his new friendship with the Beatles, especially with John. He had been tinkering around on a guitar for some time, but now, with John's encouragement, he began to think that a German boy, too, could aspire to play rock 'n' roll. "I learned so much from watching John onstage," he remembers. "And he was the one who taught me how to really play rhythm guitar. He had a special way of strumming only two strings and muffling the others with the flat of his hand."

Astrid had always chosen Klaus's clothes for him, in true *exi* style making them as much like hers as possible. But Stu was not only her same height and build but also had her exact waist and leg measurements: she could dress him in her almost sexless jackets, turtleneck shirts, and pants like some life-size doll. Stu now became as style conscious as Astrid, and even more adventurous than she in the matter of *exi* cross-dressing. In her wardrobe was a black corduroy suit with the unequivocally female feature of a round "shawl" collar. "Stu loved this suit and decided to wear it to the Kaiserkeller one night," she recalls, "When he walked in, John and the others burst out laughing and shouted 'Borrowed mum's suit, have you, Stu?'"

For all of them, however, the *exi* look was a vast improvement on the cheapo Italian one with which they had first arrived in Hamburg. To replace their lilac jackets and cardboard two-tone shoes—which by now had almost decomposed from the accumulated sweat of long nights onstage—they bought fancily tooled cowboy boots that reached halfway up their shins, and had black leather jerkins with matching trousers made to measure by a local tailor.

The lack of Stu's civilizing influence in off-duty hours may partly have accounted for the grubbiest episode in John's Hamburg career. One night, short of money as usual, he and the other three remaining Beatles decided to follow long-established St. Pauli custom and mug a sailor. The chosen victim was a German in a seemingly helpless state of inebriation who plied them with drinks all night onstage at the Kaiserkeller, then took all of them out for a meal, showing frequent, unwise glimpses of a wallet stuffed with cash. The whole group were supposed to lend a hand in parting him from this when they left the restaurant and headed for a suitably unlit and deserted area. At the critical moment, however, Paul and George lost their nerve and melted away, leaving the dirty work to John and Pete.

The sailor proved a less easy mark than expected, putting up a ferocious battle with his fists that felled each of his assailants in turn, then threatening them with a wicked-looking handgun. Actually, it fired nothing more lethal than tear-gas shells, but by the time this became apparent, both would-be muggers were fleeing for their lives back to the sheltering darkness of the Bambi Kino. Many nights afterward did John anxiously scan the Kaiserkeller's promenaders, certain that the victim would return to take revenge supported by his whole ship's company. Amazingly, he never did. But retribution of a different kind was just around the corner.

In late November 1960, the Kaiserkeller suddenly lost its monopoly as the Reeperbahn's live rock-'n'-roll venue A few doors away appeared a rival called the Top Ten Club, converted from an old indoor

circus whose bareback horse riders also used to be bare. The Top
Ten's owner, Peter Eckhorn, a former steward with the Hanseatic
shipping line, was young, go-ahead, and determined to outdo Bruno
in every way possible. His first headline attraction was Tony Sheridan, who had originally found fame at the Kaiserkeller; he also hired
the lethal Horst Fascher as club manager and head of security. Then,
using Fascher as an intermediary, he invited the Beatles to leave Koschmider and come over to him.

Eckhorn offered better pay and living accommodations and, most
important, was a rock-'n'-roll fan rather than just an exploiter. With
no manager on the spot to raise tiresome ethical questions, the five
simply walked out on their Kaiserkeller contract, which still had
until December 31 to run. Rather than try to outbid Eckhorn, Koschmider resorted to fury and veiled threats, fingering the knotty
chair leg concealed inside his trousers and hinting that if they de-
fected to the Top Ten, they had better take care out on the street
after dark. But with Horst Fascher and his killer punch on their side,
Bruno's bludgeon held no terrors.

Crossing such a powerful, well-connected St. Pauli figure was still
not something to be done with impunity. By the strangest coincidence, just after this showdown with Koschmider, the Reeperbahn's
Ausweiskontrolle, or youth-protection squad, received a tip-off that
George Harrison was under eighteen and so had been violating its
nightly 10:00 p.m. curfew for the past three months. George was immediately deported, traveling home to Liverpool by train.

An even riper opportunity for revenge presented itself on the following day, when Paul and Pete Best went to the Bambi Kino to
move their clothes over to the Top Ten Club. In a puerile act of defiance as they left their squalid dormitory for the last time, they set
fire to a condom in the corridor. The condom's thin rubber produced
only a fitful flare, and the corridor was made of stone; nevertheless
Koschmider had them arrested for attempted arson, and they were
thrown into a cell at the Reeperbahn's police headquarters. When
Stu Sutcliffe turned up later, accompanied by Astrid, he too was held
and interrogated. John found himself in the novel position of being
the only one not in trouble.

Though Koschmider dropped the arson charge, Paul and Pete

were also instantly deported for working without permits, returning home together next day by air. John and Stu for some reason
escaped deportation but had to sign official pledges not to take any
further employment of any kind in West Germany. Stu had the security of the Kirchherr house, where he was to spend the imminent
Christmas holiday. But without work, money, or lodgings, John had
no choice but to follow the others home by train. For someone too
myopic to read most English signs, let alone foreign ones, it was a
nightmare ordeal, struggling from country to country and platform
to platform with his suitcase and guitar case, his amplifier strapped
to his back. His great fear was that the amp might be stolen before
he'd even paid for it.

And where was the Hamburg outlaw heading, like an arrow from
a bow? Where else but to the neat bay window and stained-glass
porch of Mendips? Arriving late at night, he had to awaken Aunt
Mimi by throwing pebbles up at her bedroom window. Except for
the amplifier and the cowboy boots, it could have been yet another
scene from *Just William*.

11

THE SINGING RAGE

I wasn't too keen on reaching twenty-one. I
was thinking . . . that I'd missed the boat.

For the next couple of weeks, John lay low in Menlove Avenue, more thankful than he had ever been
for Aunt Mimi's spotless home and good cooking—
even if the latter was spiced by sharp references to
the tramplike condition in which he'd reappeared,
the fortune in German marks he'd failed to bring
with him, and his new boots. Stretched on his familiar narrow bed,
with some almost known-by-heart children's classic balanced on his
chest and his legs resting up the wall, he felt no compulsion even to
contact the other Beatles, let alone decide when or where they would
regroup.

"I didn't know what they were doing," he remembered. "I just withdrew to think whether [playing music] was worth going on with. I was
always a sort of poet or painter and I thought 'Is this it? Nightclubs
and seedy scenes, being deported and weird people in clubs?' You see,
part of me is a monk and part of me is a performing flea."

But there could be no going back to his former Left Bank life in Liverpool 8. He had burned all his bridges at the art college, which in any case held no allure since the expulsion of his partner-in-mischief, Jeff Mohammed, the previous summer. The apartment share in Gambier Terrace was no more, Rod Murray, "Ducky" Duxbury, and company having been evicted following the *People*'s beatnik exposé and mounting complaints from other tenants about noise. While Stu Sutcliffe still remained in Hamburg, John's only link with college was his girlfriend Cynthia—who knocked at Mendips's front door on the day after his return, delighted by his unscheduled reappearance and touchingly convinced that he had been as faithful to her during their three-and-a-half-month separation as she to him. With no one now to steal her pens and brushes in the weekly lettering class, Cyn remained on course to sit her National Diploma and, as she thought, become a children's art teacher.

Mimi had hoped that, if nothing else, "Humbug" would end John's involvement with someone she still regarded, contrary to all appearances, as a duplicitous vamp, scheming to steal him away for ever. Alas, their reunion only threw gasoline on these fires of suspicion. A few days later, John took Cynthia into Liverpool and spent £17—almost every penny he had brought home—on buying her a brown suede coat from C&A Modes. They then returned to Woolton, taking along a cooked chicken for tea. When Mimi saw the coat, she flew into a rage that was spectacular even for her, calling Cyn John's "gangster's moll," flinging the chicken at him, then following it up with a dust brush.

Paul McCartney and George Harrison were also lying low in their rather less sheltered habitats, waiting for some word from the leader but by no means sure that it would come. George initially did not realize that Paul and Pete Best had also been kicked out of West Germany, and for a time thought the Beatles must still be playing at the Top Ten Club with another lead guitarist in his place. As for Paul, his homecoming to 20 Forthlin Road almost unrecognizably emaciated had stirred even the normally placid Jim McCartney to real anger about the educational opportunities that had been sacrificed by following "that Lennon." To appease his father, Paul agreed to find a proper job and took the first available one: that of driver's mate on a dockside delivery van.

To add to the feeling of gloom and anticlimax, those months abroad had seen a radical change in both the sound and look of British pop, which seemed to leave them lagging far behind. In October, Cliff Richard's backing group, the Shadows, had scored a massive hit on their own account with a tango-flavored instrumental number called "Apache." Like Richard, the Shadows seemed part of a movement to make rock's beat less alarming to adults: they wore matching shiny suits, smiled and bowed in unison, and while playing did a little dance in unison, one step forward, one back, one sideways, as disciplined and restrained as a seventeenth-century gavotte. All over the nation, as a result, groups were frantically buying bow ties and demoting their vocalists in favor of lead guitars with quavery tremolo arms. Any still singing rock 'n' roll in black leather risked being laughed off the stage.

Not until mid-December did John rouse himself to get back in touch with Paul, George, and Pete. One homecoming gig, at least, was in the bag. Pete's mother, the forceful Mona Best, still operated the Casbah club in the cellar of her West Derby house. They played there on December 17, announced by by posters proclaiming the "Return of the fabulous Beatles." A chemistry student named Chas Newby, who had been with Pete's former group, the Blackjacks, agreed to fill in on bass until Stu Sutcliffe came home, sometime after Christmas.

In the wider world outside West Derby, hopes of employment lay mainly with Allan Williams, whom they still regarded as their manager even though he had been of no help in the Hamburg crisis. But Williams's previously booming entrepreneurial career had suffered a serious setback. Inspired by the evident huge profitability of the Reeperbahn's music-and-drinking dens, he had decided to open a place on similarly grandiose lines in Liverpool. Trusting to his usual Midas touch, he had taken premises in Soho Street, borrowed the name of the Hamburg club where the Beatles were to have headlined, and hired an accomplished local disc jockey, Bob Wooler, as resident emcee. But somewhere along the line, he seemed to have upset one person to many. Liverpool's Top Ten Club opened its doors on December 1, 1960; six nights later, it mysteriously burned to the ground.

For the Beatles, this Wagnerian catastrophe brought a stroke of luck. Bob Wooler also worked regularly for a dance promoter named Brian Kelly, whose venues included Lathom Hall, Aintree Institute, and Litherland Town Hall. Impressed that the Beatles had played abroad, even though he had not yet heard them play at home, Wooler secured them a £6 booking at Litherland Town Hall on December 27, along with the Del Renas, the Deltones, and the Searchers. On the posters they were billed as "Direct from Hamburg."

The Litherland Town Hall crowd had no clear collective memory of any group called the Beatles, only of indifferent performers variously known as the Silver Beetles, the Beatals, or the Quarrymen; it was thus generally assumed that "Direct from Hamburg" meant they were German. And certainly there was nothing recognizably English about the figures clad all over in storm-trooper black leather, not step-dancing Shadows-style but *mach-schauing* in wild asymmetry as they pounded out the stomping beat the Reeperbahn had hammered into them. The very first blast had a stunning effect on their audience, girls and boys alike abandoning the normal dance-hall pursuits of jiving, chatting each other up, or looking for trouble, and almost stampeding to the stage front—the first-ever recorded outbreak of Beatlemania.

From here on, they would never again have to beg for work. Brian Kelly hastily block-booked them for further shows at Litherland and his two other venues, even stationing a bouncer outside their dressing-room door to stop rival showmen from getting to them. But the task proved impossible. A promoter named Sam Leach, who caught them at Hambleton Hall—an experience he likened to James Stewart's discovery of a "noo sound" as Glenn Miller in the Hollywood biopic—booked them for two city-center clubs, the Cassanova and the Iron Door. It was as if their whole, inglorious pre-Hamburg career had never been. The new fans who mobbed them after each show now realized they were fellow Scouses yet still treated them somehow like foreigners, honored guests immune from the normal

Liverpool heritage of ruthless criticism and put-downs. One night at Aintree Institute, a tiny, flaxen-haired girl named Patricia Inder sought them out backstage to tell them, "You'll be as big as Cliff one day." Whatever John's later attitude to Richard and the Shadows, he was as "made up" (delighted) as all the others.

Mona Best also claimed her share, putting them on both at the Casbah and at dances she also now ran at St. John's Hall in Tuebrook. The Casbah became the Beatles' operations center almost as much as the Jacaranda; Mrs. Best or the methodical Pete organized their schedule, and the club's bouncer, Frank Garner, doubled as their driver.

Lodging with the Bests was a friend of Pete's, a young trainee accountant named Neil Aspinall, who by day worked in the Prudential building in Dale Street. Neil had been at Liverpool Institute with Paul and George and was a friend of Duff Lowe, the Quarrymen's sometime pianist. He owned a red-and-white van he had bought for £8, with two rough wooden seats in its rear. For the consideration of a pound or two, he was only too happy to take over from Frank the bouncer in driving the Beatles to their night's gig. After helping them unload their equipment, he would return to the Bests' house to work at his accountancy correspondence course for a couple of hours until it was time to pick them up. "I noticed this strange thing about them not having a leader," he remembered. "They might not have had a front man, like Rory Storm and the Hurricanes, but when you saw John you always knew exactly who the leader was."

Another new ally, just as important—though nowhere near as long-lasting—was the disc jockey Bob Wooler, who presided at almost every hall where they played. Portly and dignified, Wooler looked older than his thirty years, but his voice resonated with all the gee-whiz enthusiasm his adolescent public could wish. John mocked him for his red face and senatorial manner, but also respected him as a kind of Alan Freed figure, Merseyside's very own Moondog, whose encyclopedic knowledge of pop, standards, and even classical music helped the Beatles keep an edge over their competition. It was Wooler, for instance, who suggested they dramatize their opening by playing a few thunderous bars of the William Tell Overture, then striking up their first number before the stage curtains opened to reveal them.

He received the same respectful attention even when pointing out what other observers, in Hamburg as well as Liverpool, had already noted: that the group member with the most ardent female following was not John, or even Paul, but Pete Best. On Wooler's advice, one night they tried moving Pete's drums from the rear of the stage to the center foreground. The new look was abandoned, however, after screaming girls almost dragged Pete off the stage.

In mid-January, Stu Sutcliffe finally came back from Hamburg, reluctantly leaving his German fiancée, to enroll for his deferred teacher-training course at the art college. John was overjoyed to see him, as his sister Pauline remembers. "[John] came round and they talked for hours. They went out of the door that night like Siamese twins."

The Beatles' newfound wild popularity made Stu seem even more of a misfit in their ranks. Having not touched a bass for something like six weeks, he had forgotten almost all he'd ever learned, and allowed his fingertips to soften so that pressing the heavy strings down on their frets was as painful as when he was a beginner. Beatle converts up and down Merseyside puzzled over this new lineup of four figures basking in the limelight and a fifth, much smaller one with his back turned in embarrassment. George and Paul began to show active resentment at having to carry a passenger with so many searching Liverpool eyes now trained on them. Only John seemed to notice nothing amiss.

Stu had been appalled by the "brutality" of the Reeperbahn, but somehow had always led a charmed life there. Back in Liverpool, where Teddy Boys considered an evening without bloodshed an evening wasted, he was not so fortunate. Only a couple of weeks after he rejoined the Beatles, they were playing Lathom Hall, one of the toughest venues on their circuit. After the performance, while the others were loading equipment into Neil Aspinall's van, a group of Teds cornered Stu backstage and began to wade into him. John and Pete Best came to his rescue, John fighting off the attackers with such reckless fury that he broke the little finger of his right hand. He wore a splint on it for a couple of weeks afterward, but even so it always remained slightly deformed.

Stu's mother, Millie, later recalled going to Stu's bedroom after he came home, and finding blood everywhere. He told her he'd been in a fight and had been kicked in the head, but forbade her to summon medical help—even threatening to walk out of the house if she tried. Next morning, he relented and was examined by the family's doctor, who reassured Millie that he'd sustained no serious harm and that a day in bed should see him right again.

While the Beatles were off on their travels, there had also been a radical change to Liverpool's own musical map. The Cavern club had finally come to its senses.

Gone—or at least going—was that stronghold of trad jazz zealots where John's attempt to play rock 'n' roll with the Quarrymen three years earlier had brought him a stern public warning. Early in 1960, faced with declining receipts, the Cavern's founder, Alan Sytner, had passed the business to his family's accountant, a neat, precise man named Ray McFall. Though himself certainly no rock fan, McFall realized which way the winds of youthful obsession were blowing. That August, while the Beatles were touring Scotland with Johnny Gentle, the Cavern presented its first-ever "beat sessions," featuring Rory Storm and the Hurricanes and Gerry and the Pacemakers.

Anxious at the same time not to cast off his jazz clientele, McFall hit on a way of accommodating both genres so that their respective audiences need not even set eyes on each other. Mathew Street, where the Cavern was located, stood in the very heart of Liverpool's commercial district, barely a minute's walk from teeming thorough-fares like North John Street and Whitechapel. The young female office and shop workers who were the beat groups' main constituency swarmed through the quarter by the hundred each lunchtime, gazing aimlessly into store windows or eating their sandwiches on the steps of Victorian monuments. Ray McFall's brain wave was to put on lunchtime beat sessions at the Cavern, from one to two p.m.

Mona Best, as the Beatles' de facto agent, had recommended them to McFall soon after their return from Hamburg. Early in 1961, when Bob Wooler was hired as the Cavern's resident emcee, he, too, urged his new employer to book them without delay. The difficulty was that the Cavern beat-music nights still took place only on Wednesdays, when Brian Kelly had the Beatles tied up for weeks to come. The only available slot was the weekday lunchtime sessions.

Playing at this time of day was tricky for the great majority of groups, whose members had precious nine-to-five jobs in factories or offices. With John, George, Pete, and Stu it was no problem, but for Paul McCartney it brought a moment of truth that could well have left pop music history the poorer. In his zeal to placate his father, Paul had now found work with the electrical coil–winding firm of Massey and Coggins, where, quickly singled out as potential man-agement material, he had been put into the office on a—for then—very healthy wage of £7 per week. Absenting himself for three hours each day (one to set up, one to play, and one to dismantle) could well put this promising career in jeopardy.

John reacted to Paul's dilemma with little of the understanding and forbearance he showed to Stu. "I was always saying 'Face up to your dad, tell him to fuck off. He can't hit you . . . he's an old man.'" But Paul fretted on about Massey and Coggins and how playing at the Cavern could ruin his prospects there, until at last John's patience snapped. "I told him on the phone 'Either come or you're out.' So he had to make a decision between me and his dad, and in the end he chose me."

By even the lowest modern standards of health and safety, the Cavern could never have existed. The cellar of a warehouse storing fruit and cheeses in transit to or from the docks, its amenities as a place of entertainment were virtually zero. From a narrow door-way in Mathew Street, seventeen stone steps descended to a space measuring no more than about fifty by thirty feet, lined with close-set red Victorian bricks and divided into three arched bays. It had no heating (at least, not the mechanical kind), no air conditioning, no exhaust fans, no limit on the numbers who could be admitted, no smoke alarms, no sprinkler system, and no emergency exit.

The stage, situated at the inner end of the central bay, was barely two feet high, its only lighting a crude wooden batten studded with ordinary 60 watt bulbs directly overhead. Behind the stage was a single communal dressing room–tune-up area, from which Bob

Wooler (aka Mister Big Beat) announced the various acts over the club's PA system and played records from his large personal collection during intermissions. Toilet facilities had to be shared with the customers, though these were so unpleasant that most—particularly females—found it more advisable to "go before they came."

When the Cavern was full, as it almost always was, the heat in its unventilated brick cockpit became stupefying. Former patrons remember how, as one descended the steps, the sweltering exhalation from below gradually coiled up around one's legs like a serpent. Within it were multiple odors—the sour vomit aroma of cheese-rind seeping from the warehouse, cigarette smoke, hair lacquer, body odor, disinfectant, mildew, oxtail soup, and rat droppings. The combined heat and vibration caused a constant shower of tiny flakes from the whitewashed ceiling—known as "Cavern dandruff"—to drizzle gently down onto the dancers beneath. Girls regularly fainted, as did boys; in the crush of bodies, the only way to get them to fresh air was to pass them in supine bundles over everyone else's heads.

The Beatles' first lunchtime appearance at the Cavern took place on Tuesday, February 9, for a collective fee of £5. The result was a smaller-scale, subterranean replay of the hysteria at Litherland Town Hall. There and then, Ray McFall signed them up as the club's resident lunchtime group, working in alternation with Gerry and the Pacemakers.

But if John pictured himself storming the jazzers' sacred citadel in one triumphant bound, he was soon disillusioned. For McFall's policy was to wean the Cavern's customers off Humphrey Lyttelton and Chris Barber and onto Jerry Lee Lewis and Chuck Berry only by gradual degrees. Therefore, even though they were such a hit at lunchtimes, the Beatles could not immediately play there in the evenings. On weekends, the club was still consecrated to trad; on Tuesdays, the only weeknight other than Wednesday that it opened, McFall featured the Bluegenes, who played a mixture of rock and jazz with an old-fashioned stand-up double bass.

The first nighttime spot he could offer was not until six weeks later and then only as an opening act in the Bluegenes' weekly "guest night." As at noontime, the female cohorts from Litherland, Lathom, and Aintree came pouring in; the Bluegenes' clever jazz-rock fusion was thrown into total eclipse. Afterward, two of the group gave McFall a furious tongue-lashing for letting their prestige be undermined in such a way.

With the Cavern's other resident lunchtime group, Gerry and the Pacemakers, there was no such tense standoff. Their singer Gerry Marsden, a happy-go-lucky eighteen-year-old from the Dingle, had known John since they were both schoolboys with skiffle groups (Gerry's for a long time always well in the lead). "John was my mate," he remembers. "We had the same sense of humour. We used to spend hours together reading the Bible backwards, putting in our own made-up words and doing funny voices."

When disaster overtook the Beatles in Hamburg, Gerry and his group had been booked to open Peter Eckhorn's Top Ten Club in their place. The Pacemakers had a very different presentational style, dressing in smart blazers with monogrammed pockets and featuring an electric keyboard, but they played across the same wide musical spectrum as the Beatles, from rock 'n' roll to ballads, and had much the same irrepressible sense of fun. "We made an agreement with John and Paul not to pinch one another's numbers," Gerry says. "We were the deadliest rivals onstage, but the dearest of friends off."

Narrow, cobbled, uneventful Mathew Street thus began to lead an unexpected new life in daylight hours. At noon, Mondays to Fridays, a four-abreast line would begin to form at the Cavern's hatch-like entrance, growing by the minute until it stretched back past the warehouses and delivery trucks and piled-up fruit crates, eighty-odd yards to the junction with Whitechapel. By modern standards, everything was wondrously peaceable and self-disciplined. A single doorman kept order on the outside and was more than adequate for the task; inside, there was no "security" whatever. Admission cost one shilling per person for members, one and sixpence for nonmembers. No alcohol was sold either at lunchtimes or at night, only coffee and soft drinks.

Gerry Marsden was nicknamed the Human Jukebox for the dozens of songs he knew by heart, but even he struggled to match the variety, ambition—and, often, sheer contrariness—of the Beatles' Cavern repertoire. With John's and Paul's powers of mimicry and George's skill in decrypting chords, they could almost instantly reproduce the most complex American number: Larry Williams's "Slow Down," Carl Perkins's "Glad All Over," the lusty call-and-response of Gary U.S. Bonds's "New Orleans," and the weird blues harmonica waltz time of James Ray's "If You Gotta Make a Fool of Somebody." Audaciously, in that macho culture, they would also play songs by black American female groups, like the Marvelettes' "Please Mister Postman" or the Shirelles' "Will You Love Me Tomorrow?"—often not bothering to change the lyrics. There was, for instance, a Shirelles track called "Boys," which hooked them instantly with its frantic background chorus of "Bop shoowop, bop-bop shoowop"; in all the times that "Boys" rang through the Cavern's arches, neither they nor their audience ever seemed to notice that they were singing a hymn of adoration to their own sex.

The veering between tough and tender sometimes bordered on the schizophrenic. At one moment, John could be snarling Barrett Strong's "Money," wringing every ounce of shock value from its belligerent materialism: "The best things in life are free, but you can give 'em to the birds and bees . . . I want money! . . ." Then the stomping rock beat would fade into a cocktail-lounge samba as Paul put his mouth close to the mike, glanced around the subtropical gloom with huge, sad brown eyes, and sang "Till There Was You," as recorded by Peggy Lee, from Broadway's hit show *The Music Man*. The two could exchange moods as ambidextrously as they did their guitars; without a blink, Paul might be belting out "Kansas City" or John crooning the Teddy Bears' ballad "To Know Him Is to Love Him."

As they poured forth this cornucopia of rock 'n' roll, pop, R&B, country, blues, standards, and show tunes, it was still only dimly realized that the pair also wrote songs of their own. Bob Wooler later recalled that, out of around a hundred numbers played regularly by the Beatles at the Cavern, only about five were Lennon-McCartney compositions. As Paul McCartney now explains, "We started doing our own fledgling stuff [mainly] in order to have one or two songs that the other bands couldn't do before we went on." These tended to be ballads—Paul's "Like Dreamers Do," for example—and for a long time were greeted with no more than polite indifference. "The fans weren't highly impressed, because it wasn't what they'd come to hear," Gerry Marsden remembers. To John, in comparison with rock-'n'-roll classics, his and Paul's handiwork seemed "a bit wet . . . but we gradually broke that down and decided to try them."

Paul still nourished the ambition to compose a stage musical, which had led him to write "When I'm Sixty-four" aged little more than sixteen. According to Neil Aspinall, he made a short attempt to steer John away from rock and into Rodgers and Hammerstein territory. "Paul told me that they went to see some show like *Oklahoma* together—but after about ten minutes, John just said 'Fuck it' and walked out. Guys singing to girls and girls to guys . . . that just wasn't his scene."

Every major Liverpool group had devoted, even fanatical, female devotees. But from February 1961, when they began appearing daily at the Cavern, the Beatles' following displayed the characteristics of a fully formed movement. At every show, the first two dozen rows of undersize wooden chairs under the center arch would be packed solid with their beehive hairdos, balloon skirts, and black-daubed eyes, like some restless Sunday school class in Hades. This was a very Liverpool kind of fandom, adoring yet not in the least reverential. Before each show, like all the other Beatles, John would be deluged with phone calls (Aunt Mimi's number was in the book, still under Uncle George's name—GATeacre 1696) asking him to play requests. And after each performance, all five had their pick of a human smorgasbord, even more willing than they had known in Hamburg. "I once got into my van after collecting them, but couldn't get it to start," Neil Aspinall remembered. "Its front wheels were being lifted right up off the road. When I went and opened up the back door, they had eighteen girls in there with them."

But the Beatles at the Cavern were not just a girl thing. Boys who had once furiously resented their inamoratas' interest in a pop musician on record or the cinema screen, let alone in live performance, now succumbed to an equal if less demonstrative fascination. In an era of growing male fashion consciousness, boys were intrigued by the Beatles' allover black leather and cowboy boots, and tried to dress like them as far as Liverpool's menswear shops would allow. Girls might swoon for shy Pete or baby-faced Paul, but the quieter masculine fan worship settled mainly on John, with his turned-up collar, his two-horned Rickenbacker, and the go-to-hell attitude that was so very largely bluff.

The Beatles in these days were as much a comedy turn as a beat group. John sang almost as many songs in joke accents—German or French or "Speedy Gonzales" Mexican—as he did straight, and disrupted even the holiest rock-'n'-roll texts with his "cripple" leers, hunched back, and claw hands. While playing, they puffed on cigarettes, swigged soft drinks from the bottle, cracked private jokes with one another, or carried on conversations with friends in the audience. When, as often happened, the strain on the precarious electrical outlets became too much and their amps died into silence, John and Paul would do a Morecambe and Wise comedy routine or a scene from *The Goon Show* ("Oo, he's fallen in duh watuh! . . .") or sing the TV jingle for Sunblest sliced bread.

Among John's most devoted regular followers was Patricia Inder, the tiny blonde girl who'd made his night at Aintree Institute by saying the Beatles would be "bigger than Cliff one day." A docker's daughter, Patricia lived above the post office in Granby Street and worked in the fabrics department at Blackler's store, where bolts of cloth were still cut with giant shears in the Victorian manner. "Everywhere the Beatles went, I used to go," she recalls. "But it wasn't just about sex; we were all mates in a gang together. After their gig, we'd collect a few loosies [cigarettes sold singly for halfpence each], a bag of chips and a bottle of cheap wine, and go back to someone's place and just sit around talking about music. I loved rock 'n' roll, and being with them was like being around five Eddie Cochrans."

Like most of her friends, she was initially attracted to Paul, whom they called "the Legs," but, to her amazement, gradually realized that John liked her. "He wouldn't make a move on me, though, because when I first met him I was only fifteen, and especially when he found out that I was still a virgin. He took his cue from George, who used to say, 'I don't do virgins.'"

His Aunt Mimi still had no idea how he spent his days, believing him to have reenrolled at college after his return from Hamburg. Eventually Mimi's suspicions were aroused by the knots of girls who had taken to hanging around Mendips's front gate. "Then I heard that John was being seen playing with the Beatles at this cave place."

Furious at having been hoodwinked for so long, she decided to catch him red-handed at the Cavern, and mobilized her sisters Nanny and Harrie to lend moral support. "I was shocked. I'd never seen such a place," she recalled. "It was just like a cellar. The man on the door told me, 'You can't go in there.' I told him, 'Oh yes I can, I'm John's Aunt Mimi.' I had to watch I didn't fall on the steps, they were so steep, and it was dark. I couldn't see at first, and then I could see him up on the stage. I'd never heard such a din. It wasn't music to me—just a din. I watched him cavorting around. I wasn't amused. I was hopping mad. I wanted to pull him offstage by his ear."

John in his turn was stunned to look out into the Cavern's sweltering gloom and behold not one but three aunts with their usual immaculate coats, hats, patent leather handbags, and umbrellas, seated in the front row among the Bulldog Gang and the Woodentops. "He started singing like he did that day at the church fete," Mimi remembered. "'Oh-oh, Mimi's here. . . .' I gave him a piece of my mind after the show. I was mad at him because he ought to have been at the art college studying, not playing at a place like that. I thought he was making a laughingstock of himself."

Before winter was out, the Beatles began to feel stirrings of nostalgia for Hamburg. They remained in friendly contact with the Top Ten Club's young owner, Peter Eckhorn, and had an open invitation to work for him if their problems with the immigration and youth-welfare authorities could be sorted out. Talking to Gerry and the Pacemakers, who had inaugurated the Top Ten in their place, made John in particular yearn to be back among strippers, transvestites, and rainbow neon, drinking chilled lager from liter mugs rather than half pints of inky "mild." Hamburg, moreover, held no possibility of looking into one's audience and finding a trio of censorious aunts. So, at the nod from John, Pete telephoned Eckhorn and found the offer still open.

Considering the dramatic quasi-criminal exit that three of them had made from St. Pauli the previous November, their return was arranged without undue difficulty. George Harrison, having turned eighteen in February, was now perfectly legal on the Reeperbahn after 10:00 p.m. Placatory letters from Mona and Pete Best, Paul McCartney, and Allan Williams convinced the West German Foreign Office that Paul and Pete had not tried to burn down the Bambi Kino, and the deportation order against them was conditionally lifted for one year. John, of course, atypically had nothing to apologize for, so he could reenter the country whenever he chose. A month's engagement with Peter Eckhorn was agreed on, beginning April 1.

The moment should have been a perfect one for Stu Sutcliffe to leave the Beatles without loss of face to himself or to John. Stu was to remain in Liverpool and begin the teacher-training course he had been virtually guaranteed by the art college. Anticipating a lengthy separation from his German fiancée, Astrid Kirchherr, he had brought her over from Hamburg to meet his parents and two sisters, but still had made no definite plans for their marriage. While naturally regretting that he and John now had to pursue separate paths, he was bursting with eagerness to return to his proper métier.

Stu's interview for the course, which he had understood to be a mere formality, took place on February 23. To his astonishment, he was turned down. All his previous exemplary record at college could not persuade any senior staff member to plead his case. Not until some time later did his mother find out the reason for the college's sudden animosity. Questions were finally being asked about the amplifier that the student entertainment committee had bought for John and the Quarrymen to use at their dances, which had disappeared permanently from college circa July 1959. As both a committee member and a sometime Quarryman, Stu was held responsible for its theft.

When appeals to the college authorities proved hopeless, he decided his only option was to return to Hamburg and Astrid, which implicitly meant playing on with the Beatles at the Top Ten Club. He made the journey alone on March 15, moving back into his attic room at Astrid's mother's house and tying up final details of the group's amnesty before their arrival by train two weeks later.

At the Top Ten, the Beatles divided star billing with that other errant art student, Tony Sheridan. Though technically Sheridan's backing group, they were far more than mere sidemen. Sheridan's main interest was playing lead guitar, and he willingly ceded most of the vocals to John or Paul, or John and Paul together. The work schedule was as punishing as at the Kaiserkeller: seven p.m. to two a.m. from Monday to Friday and seven to three on weekends, with a fifteen-minute break every hour. Eckhorn did not pay much more than Bruno Koschmider, about £21 each per week, but he offered infinitely better living conditions. Above the club's streamlined portico was a Hansel-and-Gretel facade of dormer windows with crisscross beams. John, Paul, George, Pete, and Sheridan shared a fourth-floor room equipped with bunk beds and adjacent washing and toilet facilities. After dossing in the dark behind a cinema screen, it seemed like the Waldorf-Astoria.

The once alien nightscape was now full of welcoming supporters. Led by Astrid, Klaus Voormann, and Jurgen Vollmer, the *exis* had deserted the Kaiserkeller and brought their black leather and pale, androgynous faces over to the Top Ten en masse. As its club manager and security chief, Eckhorn had employed Horst Fascher, the former boxing champion who regarded watching John's back almost as a vocation.

Despite the Reeperbahn's sexual banquet, John still hated being apart from Cynthia and continued writing conscientiously to her, as Paul did also to his own steady, the petite Dorothy Rhone. With conditions so much more civilized this time around, it was decided to bring both girlfriends over for a visit during Cyn's Easter college vacation. Having convinced their respective mothers that one would effectively chaperone the other, they set off together by boat and rail on what was Dot's first-ever trip abroad.

German friends rallied round to make the girls' two-week stay as comfortable as possible. Paul and Dot borrowed a houseboat belonging to Rosa, the elderly washroom attendant from the Bambi Kino, while Cynthia was put up at Astrid's mother's home in Altona. She had dreaded having to spend time with Astrid, whom she found intimidatingly beautiful and stylish—and still half suspected of en-

snaring John. But Astrid could not have been friendlier or more hospitable, attending to Cyn's every comfort, lending her clothes and
shoes to spice up her limited wardrobe, each evening driving her
down to the Reeperbahn to watch John play. Still as possessive as
ever, he detailed Horst Fascher to make sure no other men tried to
chat her up while he was onstage. "I had quite two or three fights
just from taking care of Cynthia," Fascher says.

John took almost voyeuristic pleasure in showing the sheltered
Hoylake girl every sleazy nook and cranny of his working environment, not forgetting the whores in the Herbertstrasse's shop windows. To keep awake with their beaux into the small hours every
night, both Cynthia and Dot also had to take uppers, Preludin and
a new variety named Purple Hearts, supplied by the ever-obliging
Rosa. "We thought they were great," Dot remembers. "They didn't
just keep you awake, they made you feel wonderful as well. Usually, the pair of us hardly dared say a word, but when we took those
things, we couldn't stop talking."

Stu meanwhile seemed to find consolation for the blow he had
suffered by putting not only Liverpool but his very nationality far
behind him. Living with Astrid and her mother, he had picked up
German with such remarkable speed that he often seemed more
comfortable with it than with English. Thanks to his superstylish
fiancée, the one-time sloppy-jerseyed art student now dressed at
the height of *exi* chic, in pin-fastened shirt collars, sleeveless leather
waistcoats, and high elastic-sided boots, or in jackets from Astrid's
own wardrobe with the cloth-covered buttons and round collars that
to John and the other Beatles still hilariously connoted something
borrowed from Mum.

Many *exi* boys wore their hair wedged over their foreheads in what
was known on the Continent as the French style (France's concept
of masculinity then being unlike any other). Astrid herself had cut
Klaus Voormann's hair that way when they were girl- and boyfriend,
mainly to hide Klaus's rather prominent ears. Now Stu demanded
that she do the same for him. So one night she unpicked his Teddy-
boy cockade and reshaped it into a shallow busby with bangs that
barely cleared his eyes. The new style brought out all the feminine

delicacy of Stu's features—indeed, made the artless Liverpool boy and the ethereal German girl look uncannily alike.

To any red-blooded British male in 1961, combed-forward hair like that of some Roman senator or medieval troubadour—or Frenchman—was an idea beyond repugnance. In contemporary English-speaking culture, the one and only fringed man was Moe Howard of the Three Stooges, a knockabout comic whose spidery black bangs seemed designed only to encourage additional slaps and blows from his two colleagues. Sure enough, when Stu first took the new haircut to the Top Ten Club, he was mercilessly ribbed by the other Beatles, John especially. Yet, as even John realized, Stu was at the cutting edge while they, with their Elvis forelocks, were not. A couple of days later, George Harrison went to Astrid and asked her to do his hair like Stu's. On seeing the results, he panicked and hastily combed it up into its old stack again. John and Paul kept up unremitting mockery of the style but were both secretly intrigued by it; at one point, John and George even borrowed scissors and set about one another's heads in an abortive attempt to re-create it. Only Pete Best remained perfectly happy (and so a little further alienated) with his crisp, vertical Jeff Chandler.

In fact, neither Stu's disappointment nor his new life as a fashion plate could extinguish his creative drive for long. He still planned to find a teacher-training course somewhere back in Britain and meanwhile began half illicitly to attend drawing classes at Hamburg's large and well-appointed state art college. By a happy chance, the college teaching staff included Edouardo Paolozzi, a thirty-six-year-old Scots-Italian who resembled an orangutan but whose radically surrealist sculpture had won admirers, including Giacometti and Braque. Expatriate professor and student clicked immediately, not least because Paolozzi, too, had fled abroad to escape what he felt to be Britain's stifling provincialism. So impressed was he by Stu's work that he took him into his own hand-picked class, even arranged for him to receive a maintenance grant from the Hamburg city council.

This unexpected boost to his self-esteem reignited the almost demented energy that used to dazzle Liverpool teachers like Arthur Ballard. In his attic room at the Kirchherr house, Stu began to paint again on his old heroic scale, using canvases so large that he could barely reach their tops. This time, however, the work was not inspired pastiche but wholly original—closely detailed abstracts in which the colors of the red-light district he now knew so well, its chaos, vitality, even its noise, seemed to be distilled. And, as always, his passion kicked off a reciprocal motor inside John. "Whenever John came to our house to see Stuart, he would sit down and start to draw," Astrid remembers. "But always cartoons of crippled people . . . or Jesus hanging on the Cross with a pair of slippers underneath. I didn't realise then but I found out later all about the way his own mummy had died. He was very angry with God for taking his mummy away from him."

Inevitably, the greater Stu's absorption in painting, the less interest and energy he had left over for the Beatles. "People started getting mad at him because he wouldn't practise," Astrid says. "As it was, he didn't have enough hours in the day for all the work he wanted to do." According to Astrid, John remained unconcerned by Stu's deficiencies. "He always used to say the same thing if ever anyone criticized Stuart's playing: 'Never mind—he looks good.'" But George and Paul, especially Paul, were becoming openly resentful of Stu's attitude and John's seeming readiness to put friendship above the good of the group as a whole. Paul had always felt himself in competition with Stu for John's attention, even though their respective friendships with John were on entirely different levels. With his omnivorous musical talent, he was already a far better bass player than Stu could ever hope to be—and also at least as good a drummer as Pete Best. Onstage at the Cavern, he had once been heard to shout at Stu and Pete, "You may look like James Dean and you may look like Jeff Chandler, but you're both crap!"

The end result was the only onstage fight the Beatles ever had, ironically between their two least aggressive members. One night at the Top Ten, in the middle of a number with Tony Sheridan, Paul and Stu suddenly both stopped playing and began throwing punches at each other. According to Sheridan, Paul had made a snide remark about Astrid, knowing full well that it would provoke even the passionately nonviolent Stu beyond endurance. But neither was much of a bruiser, and Paul now says it was not a real fight, "more a stand-off . . . We gripped each other fiercely until we were prised apart." On the night in question, Cynthia and Dot were still in town but away from the club, visiting Astrid. Stu took the incident seriously enough to telephone and angrily order Paul's girl out of his girl's house.

A far nastier dustup—offstage this time—took place between Pete Best and the Beatles' ad hoc vocalist, Tony Sheridan, with John in his favorite role of agent provocateur. "John orchestrated the whole thing," Sheridan remembers. "He made Pete his mouthpiece for some niggles against me; my Irish blood was roused, and Pete and I ended up having a slugging match, out in the back corridor of the club, that must have gone on for a couple of hours. John didn't even wait around to see the end of it. I think he felt a bit guilty the next day, though, because both Pete and I were so battered that we could hardly get up on the stage."

Generally speaking, the Beatles' stint at the Top Ten Club was an upbeat time, with their name firmly established back on Merseyside and inklings that their West German stardom might extend beyond the Reeperbahn, possibly even outside Hamburg. Early in April— foreshadowing what was soon to happen in Liverpool—the Top Ten received a visit from a celebrated local entrepreneur who had heard about the wild young English group in residence there, and decided to check them out for himself. Thirty-seven year-old Bert Kaempfert was at that time West Germany's most famous popular musician, both as leader of an orchestra in the easy-listening mode and as composer of international hits like Elvis Presley's "Wooden Heart." He also scouted talent and produced records for the Polydor label, pop music arm of the venerable Deutsche Grammophon company, but a brand as yet barely known outside mainland Europe.

Kaempfert, it transpired, was mainly interested in Tony Sheridan as a potential solo star for the domestic pop market. After several exhaustive live auditions, Sheridan was offered a recording session for Polydor, with the Beatles as his sidemen, all under the supervision of Kaempfert himself. John, at least, had no doubt of their superiority over anything else in the Polydor stable. "When the offer came through, we thought it would be easy," he recalled. "The Germans had such shitty records. Ours were bound to be better."

The session took place, disappointingly, not at Polydor's headquarters but in the assembly hall of a local kindergarten, where Kaempfert set up his equipment on the stage, then created a flimsy form of sound insulation by closing the curtains. The Beatles backed Sheridan through five numbers, of which the best known would be two ancient chestnuts, "My Bonnie Lies Over the Ocean" and "When the Saints Go Marching In," both set to the same Reeperbahn-rousing rock beat. The other three were slightly more original: Hank Snow's "Nobody's Child," Jimmy Reed's "Take Out Some Insurance," and a composition of Sheridan's, "Why (Can't You Love Me Again)?" The occasion marked the transference of bass playing from Stu Sutcliffe to Paul, though Stu still turned up to lend moral support. Despite Kaempfert's eminence, he had little idea of how to produce rock 'n' roll, still less how to highlight the Beatles' instrumental and vocal idiosyncrasies. "It's just Tony . . . singing with us banging in the background," John would later complain of the Sheridan tracks. "It's terrible. It could be anyone."

Kaempfert, though, was sufficiently impressed by the Beatles' playing to let them record two numbers on their own. As possible choices, John and Paul put up four or five of the original songs they were still turning out, largely into a vacuum. A skilled composer himself, Kaempfert recognized the quality of their work, but as a pragmatic producer he knew it to be way off beam for the oompah West German market. More commercially promising was an instrumental John and George had built around an echoey treble guitar riff, much like those that were giving the Shadows almost nonstop hits back in the UK. This was recorded with the ironic title "Cry for a Shadow."

The one Beatles-only vocal track would be John singing "Ain't She Sweet," a twenties jazz song that was always one of Julia's favorite banjo-plunking party pieces. He himself had been doing it onstage for years, initially like Gene Vincent's 1956 version, "very mellow and high-pitched, but the Germans shouted 'Harder, Harder!' . . . They wanted it a bit more like a march." Kaempfert therefore got "hard" John, with the same snarl bunched at the back of his throat that he used for singing Chuck Berry to drunken sailors or besotted Cavernites. Yet his fondness for the hoary old favorite couldn't help showing, as when he remolded a line of the chorus (". . . well, I ask you-oo ver-ee-ee a-confidentially . . ."), suddenly more scat singer than rocker. "Oh me oh my!" also got an extra lift, as if another John Lennon, his blackface minstrel grandfather, were fleetingly resurrected.

Kaempfert had prescience enough to sign the Beatles to a one-year recording agreement, but then made no further effort to develop them. Polydor did not release "Cry for a Shadow" or "Ain't She Sweet," preferring the Tony Sheridan versions of "My Bonnie" and "When the Saints," and denying the Beatles even a secondhand share in the glory. To avoid any risk of confusion with peedles, they were billed on the record as the Beat Brothers. Meanwhile, the first commercial recording of John's voice was cast into the vaults and forgotten.

One of the few art college friends with whom John kept in touch was Bill Harry, the curly-haired graphic-design student who first turned him on to beat poetry, Kierkegaard, and Saul Steinberg. Bill remained at college, though it seemed dull without John and Stu; he also still cherished the ideal they had formulated together as the Dissenters, that Liverpool should become as hallowed a name to Britain's beat generation as San Francisco was to America's. In the summer of 1961, his entrepreneurial nature turned idealism into reality.

A prolific writer, trivia hound, and compiler of statistics, Bill had already edited various samizdat publications for the college and Hessy's music store. His ambition, however, was to start a real newspaper to chronicle the city's boisterous youth culture in a way the staid old *Liverpool Echo* never had. By spring, he had raised the £50 starting capital for a compact-size newsprint weekly, to be run entirely by himself and his girlfriend, Virginia, from one room above a liquor store in Renshaw Street. Its name—mixing together Kerouac, music, and the muddy river that nurtured it—was *Mersey Beat*.

Its main role was to be an information exchange, allowing fans to learn when and where their favorite groups were playing. But Bill also sought articles and columns with a special insight into the beat music scene. Looking around for contributors, he remembered the nonsense stories and poems his fellow Dissenter wrote at college and half bashfully passed around among selected cronies at Ye Cracke. Before the Beatles' departure to Hamburg in April, he asked John to write a brief history of the group for the benefit of their Cavern club following. *Mersey Beat*'s first issue appeared on July 6, four days after their return home. Half the front page was taken up by John's contribution:

BEING A SHORT DIVERSION ON THE DUBIOUS ORIGINS OF THE BEATLES

(translated from the John Lennon)

Once upon a time there were three little boys called John, George and Paul, by name christened. They decided to get together because they were the getting together type. When they were together they wondered what for after all, what for? So all of a sudden they grew guitars and fashioned a noise. Funnily enough, no one was interested, least of all the three little men. So-o-o-o on discovering a fourth even littler man called Stuart Sutcliffe running about them they said, quite "Sonny get a bass guitar and you will be alright" and he did—but he wasn't alright because he couldn't play it. So they sat on him with comfort 'til he could play. Still there was no beat, and a kindly old man said, quote "Thou hast not drums." We had drums, they coffed. So a series of drums came and went and came. Suddenly, in Scotland, touring with Johnny Gentle, the group called the Beatles discovered they had not a very nice sound because they had no amplifiers. They got some.

Many people ask what are Beatles? Why Beatles? Ugh, Beatles, how did the name arrive? So we will tell you. It came in a vision—a man appeared on a flaming pie and said unto them "From this day on you are Beatles with an A." Thank you mister man, they said, thanking him.

John never expected the piece to be used—though even the faint possibility that it might had made him nervous enough to bring in George as a collaborator. Seeing his words in print for the very first time, exactly as he'd written them, thrilled him to the marrow. And, in common with all writers, that first byline awakened a hunger for more. Bill Harry remembers his calling at *Mersey Beat's* office soon afterward with a thick bundle of his accumulated drawings, stories, and poems, some 250 items in all.

Mersey Beat confirmed the Beatles as undisputed kings of the Liverpool group scene. John's friend the editor lost no opportunity to write about them (though Bill was not one to award "puffs" without good reason). John's own contributions proved so popular that Bill Harry gave him a regular space under the pseudonym Beatcomber—a pun on J. B. Morton's whimsical Beachcomber column in the *Daily Express*. A typical example parodied *Mersey Beat's* page-three entertainments guide, with Lennonesque transfigurations of city landmarks like the Pier Head and Bold Street as well as clubs like the Casbah, the Jacaranda, and the Odd Spot, restaurants like La Locanda, and ballrooms like the Grafton and the Locarno. Such was the addictiveness of being in print that he would even pay to insert small humorous ads in the paper's classified section. The August 17 issue had five of these cod announcements, purchased at four old pennies per word and scattered among the serious ones to create a cumulative effect:

> HOT LIPS, missed you Friday, RED NOSE . . .
> RED NOSE, missed you Friday, HOT LIPS . . .
> ACCRINGTON welcomes HOT LIPS and RED NOSE . . .
> Whistling Jock Lennon wishes to contact HOT NOSE . . .
> RED SCUNTHORPE wishes to jock HOT ACCRINGTON

During their stint at the Top Ten Club, the Beatles had decided that, since they'd arranged the gig without Allan Williams, there was no obligation to pay Williams his usual 10 percent commission. Not for the last time, John and Paul shirked doing the dirty deed themselves; instead, Stu Sutcliffe was deputed to write to Williams in what was his last duty as a Beatle. Williams responded with an aggrieved letter vaguely threatening to have them blacklisted by every talent agent in the universe if he were not paid. However, he took no action beyond expelling them from his client roster, thus sealing his destiny as "The Man Who Gave the Beatles Away" (or, as John would later have it, "The Man Who Couldn't Give The Beatles Away").

With Williams out of the picture, their management was shared among several hands, and seemed little the worse for that. Mona Best's Casbah club, and the rambling house above, still provided their main meeting place and operations center, as well as their tireless driver Neil Aspinall. Ray McFall, the Cavern's owner, did as much as Bill Harry and Bob Wooler to keep them at their local pinnacle. It was McFall who first put them onstage with a nationally famous music act, booking them for a Cavern-sponsored Mersey cruise, or "riverboat shuffle," on August 27, aboard the MV (motor vessel) *Royal Iris* as support to Mister Acker Bilk and his Paramount Jazz Band.

The summer also brought a growing involvement with Sam Leach, whose beat promotions at the Iron Door club in Temple Street were Ray McFall's main competition. Also situated in an old warehouse, the Iron Door was larger than the Cavern and a more grown-up, edgy place, serving alcohol as well as coffee and soft drinks. Though in many ways as scatterbrained as Allan Williams, Sam Leach had no doubt of the Beatles' potential, and pursued a somewhat more coherent strategy for realizing it. He tried selling them to London pop agents like Roy Tempest and Tito Burns, but from each he received the traditional haughty southern brush-off: "We've already got 5,000 beat groups in London. Why should we need one from Liverpool?"

With the approach of John's twenty-first birthday in October, he began to have serious doubts that his career as a musician could advance much further. "I wasn't too keen on reaching twenty-one," he remembered. "[A] voice in me was saying 'Look, you're too old.' Even before we'd made a record, I was thinking . . . that I'd missed the boat, that you'd got to be seventeen. A lot of stars in America were kids. . . . I remember one relative saying to me, 'From now on it's all downhill,' and I really got a shock. She told me how my skin would be getting older and all that kind of jazz."

At times he even found himself wondering if he had been wrong to give up studying art and whether he could find any way back into it, preferably with Stu Sutcliffe not too far away, to bolster his self-confidence as of old. He wrote constantly to Stu in Hamburg—long, scrawly letters, devoid of his usual puns and misspellings, using almost plain English to lay bare what he called "a little part of my almost secret self" in all its anger, nihilism, and loneliness. From John's perspective, Stu seemed to have found the perfect life, with his painting, with his studies under Edouardo Paolozzi, with Astrid and her warm-hearted "Mummy" to look after him, and with St. Pauli to play in after dark.

But the idyll was not quite as John enviously imagined it. The intensity with which Stu now worked seemed to have brought disturbing changes in him, both physical and mental. He had become painfully thin and begun to suffer blinding headaches and bouts of nausea against which ordinary domestic remedies had little or no effect. His mood could change abruptly, from the sweetness and mildness that had first captivated Astrid to furious accusations that on their last night's round of the Reeperbahn bars she had flirted with other men. "His jealousy was the hardest thing for me to take," Astrid says, 'because there was never any reason for it."

Astrid and her mother finally persuaded him to see a doctor and undergo tests, and in July he wrote to his own mother with the results. His life in and out of the Beatles these past two years had produced a grim inventory of ailments: gastritis (inflamed stomach lining), a shadow on his lung, a dodgy appendix, and a glandular imbalance that might account for his sudden mood swings. The Hamburg doctor ordered him to cut out smoking and alcohol, prescribed medication and a strict diet, and warned him not to delay having his appendix removed. In late August, he returned to Liverpool, intending to have the operation there, and bringing with him his Hamburg X-rays. The Liverpool specialist who viewed these, however, judged them all "within the limits of normality" and pronounced Stu's symptoms to be "nervous in origin." Furious at being accused of hypochondria, he returned to Hamburg without having the appendectomy.

John's twenty-first birthday presents on October 9 included the munificent sum of £100 in cash from his Aunt Mater and Uncle Bert. Seasoned traveler that he now was, he decided to spend it on a Continental holiday, inviting Paul McCartney to accompany him. The two just disappeared without explanation to George or Pete, despite a customarily packed schedule of Beatles gigs. They had intended to hitchhike to Spain, but instead went by train to Paris and remained there for two weeks, staying at a cheap hotel on the Left Bank. It was meant to be a total break from music, though they did visit a club in Montmartre and one night masochistically attended a concert by the laughable French rock-'n'-roller Johnny Hallyday. In the flea markets, they found an extraordinary innovation—jeans that were not drainies but bell-bottomed like the uniform trousers of British sailors. John and Paul bought a pair each but then, fearing the look "too queer," slimmed them down to normal ankle-hugging dimensions.

The main reason for detouring to Paris was that their Hamburg *exi* friend Jurgen Vollmer had recently moved there to become assistant to the photographer William Klein. Like Klaus Voormann and Stu, Jurgen wore his hair in the combed-forward French style, and, after a few days' immersion in all things French, John and Paul decided they were finally ready to follow suit. It was only a mild version of what would become the Beatle cut, but it still changed John completely, making his face seem rounder, his nose sharper, his mouth more oddly feminine. The wedge of hair just clearing the shortsighted eyes somehow gave them an even sharper glint of subversiveness and mockery.

When John's birthday money was all spent, the transformed truants returned home to find hairstyles the last thing on anyone's mind. The promoters they had let down were all incandescent with fury, and George and Pete Best were both on the point of quitting in disgust. Even John could not demur at the stern lecture they received from Bob Wooler, Ray McFall, and their other unofficial handlers about honoring engagements and behaving professionally.

Fortunately, just at that moment, the irrepressible Sam Leach came up with a scheme that both reunified the Beatles as a band and reasserted their superiority over all local competition. Tired of promoting gigs in small halls and cellars, Leach began scouting for a venue where thousands rather than just dozens of beat fans could gather. He found it at New Brighton, a Wirral seaside resort that had once boasted a 544-foot steel facsimile of Paris's Eiffel Tower. Though the tower had been demolished after the Great War, its immense ballroom continued to function, vaulted in baroque white and gold, with a sprung floor that could accommodate a thousand couples.

On November 10, Leach hired New Brighton Tower Ballroom for what he named Operation Big Beat, a five-and-a-half-hour marathon attended by four thousand people, with the Beatles headlining over Rory Storm and the Hurricanes, Gerry and the Pacemakers, the Remo Four, and Kingsize Taylor and the Dominoes. The Beatles played one spot in the early evening, hurried back across the water for a show at Knotty Ash village hall, then returned to New Brighton for a second set at 11:30. The night ended with a wild car race with Rory Storm through the Mersey Tunnel, during which Rory's car barely escaped a head-on collision.

In later life, John would nostalgically recall those carefree months of going nowhere in particular, the camaraderie between the groups, and the freedom and spontaneity of their music. "We repeated the shows many, many times, but never the same. Sometimes we'd go on with 15 or 20 musicians and play together, and we'd create something that had never been done onstage by a group before." He could only have meant a night at Litherland Town Hall when the Beatles and Gerry and the Pacemakers amalgamated as "the Beatmakers." Gerry Marsden sang and alternated on lead guitar with George Harrison, Pete Best shared the drumming with Gerry's brother Freddy, and John and Paul were just sidemen on piano and rhythm guitar alongside Pacemakers Les Maguire and Les Chadwick.

There spoke the monk rather than the performing flea—half-wishing they had left him alone to pound his piano anonymously in the background. "I'm talking about before we were famous, about the natural things that happened before we were turned into robots that played on stage. We would naturally express ourselves in any way that we deemed suitable. And then a manager came and said 'Do this, do that, do this, do that' and that way we became famous by compromise."

12

SHADOWLANDS

Yeah, man, all right, I'll wear a suit—I'll wear a
bloody balloon if someone's going to pay me.

A recurring theme of Richmal Crompton's William stories is the power that eleven-year-old William's inventiveness and zest for life can exert over the most unlikely seeming adults. Time and again it happens that some high-powered celebrity arrives in the district to attend a formal grown-up function but instead finds his way to the Old Barn, where William and the Outlaws are putting on one of their shows. The truant VIP will pay a few pennies' entrance fee and sit in his posh clothes on an upturned orange-box, more captivated by the performance than any of the village urchins around him. So did John's life parallel William's yet again when Brian Epstein happened on the Cavern.

Brian was then aged twenty-seven and, to outward appearance, the last person likely to be found in old barns or caverns. The elder son of a well-to-do Liverpool Jewish family, he seemed blessed with

all a young man of that era could ask—good looks, charm, and sophistication, allied to a seemingly fulfilling niche in life. He ran his
father's large electrical store, NEMS, in Whitechapel, the heart of the
city's shopping district. In the basement was a record department,
which Brian had developed with such flair that it could justifiably
advertise "The Finest Record Selection in the North."

But behind the suave exterior was a complex, troubled character
who, prior to November 1961, considered his life to have been one
of almost unmitigated failure. He had been expelled from school,
ended his army National Service prematurely and under a cloud,
and given up on an acting course at the Royal Academy of Dramatic
Art (RADA) in London. Only after reluctantly entering the family
retail business (which encompassed furniture and housewares as
well as electrical goods and records) had he shown any positive abilities: clever salesmanship, meticulous administrative efficiency, and
a knack for eye-catching presentation and design.

Most troubling of all—overshadowing his whole unhappy adolescence, undermining his latter success and self-vindication—Brian
Epstein was homosexual. In prejudice-bound Britain of 1961, especially in a city as ferociously macho as Liverpool, there was no worse
burden for a young man to carry. Legislation originally passed in
1886 perpetuated the Victorian view of homosexuality as a "perver-
sion," an offense against every religious doctrine, and a creepingly
infectious social disease. Sexual acts between males, however private and consensual, were crimes punishable by imprisonment. Fear
and loathing of the condition permeated every level of society, apart
from the sheltered worlds of the theatre and haute couture. Anyone
showing the slightest hint of effeminacy in manner or eccentricity in
dress—suede shoes, for instance, or a waistcoat with brass buttons—
could expect instant denunciation and persecution as a "queer," a
"homo," a "nancy-boy," or a "poof."

Brian's upright and devout Jewish parentage meant a still more
pressing need for secrecy and a redoubled burden of guilt and self-
loathing. However, his problems did not end even there. Despite the
endemic homophobia, many gay men were able to find happy and
stable relationships with others like themselves. But it was Brian's

misfortune to be attracted to heterosexual males at the furthest possible remove from his own gentle and refined nature. To find gratification, he had to go curb-crawling in the city's toughest dockside areas or cottaging (cruising) in public lavatories, putting himself in constant danger of police entrapment, blackmail by his pickups, or attack by the "queer-bashing" gangs that haunted such locales.

Brian had known about the Beatles in a subliminal way for several months before officially discovering them. The NEMS shop in Whitechapel lay only about a minute's walk from Mathew Street, and daily thronged with overspill from the Cavern's lunchtime sessions, chattering excitedly about what they were about to see or had just seen. John, Paul, George, and Pete themselves were regular customers, usually seeking out-of-the-way import disks to bolster their repertoire. When *Mersey Beat* began publication in July, Brian had ordered large quantities to sell at NEMS. He even began to contribute a column about new record releases, which often appeared in proximity to some further Beatles update or zany jeu d'esprit by John. At his shop, Brian was no aloof executive figure, but prided himself on serving customers himself and taking a personal interest in their musical taste. From scores of habituées—tiny, blonde Patricia Inder among them—he would have heard plenty about the Cavern and its favorite sons.

But in 1961, a twenty-seven-year-old, especially one of Brian's social standing and sophistication, had no affinity with pop music or teenage culture. His involvement was purely that of a conscientious retailer, ending as soon as NEMS put up its CLOSED sign; in private, he listened almost exclusively to classical music and was an ardent devotee of opera, ballet, and the theatre.

By his own later account, it was not until October 28 that a customer order for the Beatles' pseudonymous Polydor recording with Tony Sheridan (which the deejay Bob Wooler had been dutifully plugging all over town) finally woke him up to their existence. His version was that, having been unable to trace the record through NEMS's usual supply channels, he discovered with surprise that they were a Liverpool group, playing daily and nightly—and now sometimes all night—just a stone's throw away. He paid a visit to their Cavern lunchtime show and, overwhelmed by the blazing talent that met his ears and eyes (something William's Old Barn productions could never be accused of), realized that his destiny was to become their manager.

In fact, Brian had never seen a pop group play live before, so could not have known how different this one was, or could be, from any other. But he happened to be feeling bored with the retail trade and sensed a use for his creative talents beyond just window-dressing his shop. Most compellingly, in four sweating, skylarking black-leather-clad boy musicians he saw his secret vice made available in an utterly blameless and harmless form: rough trade without the bruises.

For someone of his class and background even to contemplate going into pop management was highly unusual. Managers of this era were by definition proletarian gamblers, the natural heirs to door-to-door con men and street-corner three-card monte tricksters. But Brian was already wealthy, sporting the tailor-made suits and driving the luxury cars of which every down-at-heel Mersey hustler dreamed. Thanks to public school education and his RADA training, he spoke in smooth, modulated tones without a trace of Liverpudlian. Though only six years John's senior, he seemed much older; part of the generation sworn to fight against pop, not nurture it. His first exploratory overtures sent a wave of excitement through the Beatles' circle, even cool-headed Paul McCartney talking in hushed whispers of the "millionaire" who was interested in them.

Despite the trouble that Brian took to hide his sexual orientation, most people on the Liverpool music scene were fully aware of it. Not long previously, his cover had almost been blown when a more than usually vicious blackmail attempt by one of his dockland pickups left him no choice but to go to the police. A trap had been laid—of necessity in the NEMS shop itself, after hours—and the blackmailer brought to trial, with Brian giving evidence under the pseudonym Mr. X. Many more people around the city than he ever dreamed knew about this horrible episode. Many who did not still guessed his secret instantly, for all the impeccable straightness of his appearance and manner. As several friends whispered to John or Paul in typically vivid Scouse argot: "You'd have to be galloping past on a wild horse with soap in your eyes not to know he's queer."

On December 3, Brian invited the Beatles to a meeting in his office above the NEMS shop to discuss the terms on which he might take over their management. Unfortunately, they refused to treat the encounter with due reverence, turning up very late accompanied by Bob Wooler (whom John facetiously introduced as "me Dad") and sidestepping all their nervous and increasingly flustered host's attempts at serious business talk. Things were different, however, at a second meeting between just the four of them and Brian on December 10, fortuitously the day after a disastrous foray with Sam Leach down south to Aldershot, where they had ended up playing to just eighteen people. The burning question, put by Paul, was whether being adopted by Brian would mean changing the kind of music they played. On being assured that it would not, John spoke for the others without bothering to take a vote: "Right then, Brian . . . manage us."

Three of the four were under twenty-one, so could not sign any legal papers without their guardians' consent. Before going any further, therefore, Brian had to visit the McCartney, Harrison, and Best homes in turn, setting out his intentions—and allaying some instinctive prejudice against him as a Jew. Only John was of age and able to sign on his own account. But Brian still had to call at Mendips and square things with Aunt Mimi; indeed, he recognized Mimi as by far the most important target in his charm offensive. "There was a knock at the door," she remembered, "and standing there was this smart young man . . . he had a clean white shirt on and a tie, and he said, 'Hello, I am Brian Epstein,' and my first impression was 'You'll do.' He was very direct . . . 'I want to manage John and the group' . . . and I made him a cup of tea and he said he wanted to reassure me that everything would be fine and that he'd look after John.

"I was flabbergasted because [Brian] told me he thought John was really talented and that [the Beatles] were going places . . . and I thought the only place John would be going was the employment exchange. He was very educated, very polite, knew his p's and q's, came from a good family, so I knew he meant well. He said that whatever happened, he'd always take care of John. I think I must have said I would agree or something . . . it turned out they'd already agreed to him being their manager, but John had wanted my approval, I suppose. . . . He always wanted to know what I thought."

Brian's immediate objective was to get the Beatles a recording contract, a task in which he foresaw no great difficulty. As a leading record retailer, he enjoyed cordial relations with all the major London labels; via their sales departments he could get straight through to talent scouts and producers, with NEMS's importance as a client adding weight to his petition. By Christmas he had contacted Polydor and—on the promise of a substantial order from NEMS—persuaded them to release Tony Sheridan's "My Bonnie Lies Over the Ocean" in the United Kingdom in January, its backing now correctly credited to the Beatles, not the Beat Brothers. He also quickly found sympathetic ears at one of NEMS's foremost suppliers, the mighty Decca organization. Decca valued his custom enough not merely to listen when he said he had a group potentially "bigger than Elvis" but to send a producer named Mike Smith all the way to Liverpool to see them at the Cavern. Against all expectations, Smith liked what he heard, and reported positively back to his superiors.

A formal audition took place on New Year's Day 1962—back then not a public holiday—at Decca's studios in Swiss Cottage, North London. It was an occasion destined to top the list of Great Music Industry Blunders forever afterward, but in fairness the Beatles that day could hardly have looked less commercial. The playlist—chosen by Brian to show off their versatility—was a mixture of R&B stompers like "Money" and "Memphis, Tennessee," soft pop like "Take Good Care of My Baby" and "To Know Her Is to Love Her," cocktail-time ballads like "Till There Was You" and "September in the Rain," and crusty old standards like "Besame Mucho" and "The Sheik of Araby." Rather than impressing Decca, this created confusion: were they R&B, pop, country, middle-of-the-road, or old-fashioned music hall? Three Lennon-McCartney compositions, "Like Dreamers Do" and "Love of the Loved" by Paul and "Hello Little Girl" by John, passed almost unnoticed amid the motley. As a final perverse twist out of focus, they did Leiber and Stoller's "Three Cool Cats," a comic variation on "Three Blind Mice" sung by George with ad-libs by John as Speedy Gonzales ("Hey, man, save-a one chick forr *me* . . ."). Fifteen tracks were recorded in a single take each, on two-track mono, without editing or overdubbing, the whole session wrapping in little more than an hour.

Despite some initial positive signs, Decca notified a formal rejection just over three weeks afterward. The official reason—comparable with Hollywood predictions in 1927 that talkies had no future—was: "Four-man guitar groups are on the way out." John, rightly, blamed Brian's choice of material and vowed it would be the last time anyone told the Beatles what to play. "We were good," he insisted later. "At least, we were good for then."

Pending further initiatives in London, Brian set about organizing the Beatles with the same meticulous efficiency that he applied to his NEMS record stock. Where "the Boys" (as he instantly took to calling them) were concerned, expense seemed to be no object. His first act was to pay off the backlog of installment debts on their equipment, including John's long-discarded Hofner Club 40 guitar. Press announcements for Beatles gigs ceased to be wordy small-type "Woolertins" and became display ads with elegant black rules, calling them Polydor Recording Artists and trumpeting their official ascendancy to Liverpool's number one group, as confirmed on January 4 by a readers' poll in *Mersey Beat*.

Before a gig, their driver, Neil Aspinall, would receive lengthy typewritten instructions from Brian about where, for whom, and for how long they were to play, stressing the need to be punctual and professional and give the same unstinted value onstage that he gave over the counter of NEMS. Every Friday, each Beatle received a detailed summary of the past week's earnings and disbursements as if the sums involved were thousands of pounds rather than just tens. The public, don't-give-a-damn John pretended to find all this bureaucracy ridiculous, but the secret, organized side of him was impressed, as he would eventually admit. "We were in a daydream before [Brian] came along. We'd no idea what we were doing. Seeing our marching orders on paper made it all official."

Brian was less assured when it came to dealing with the tough, often uncouth local promoters on whom the Beatles depended for regular work. Recognizing his own inexperience, he sought help from a tall, soft-spoken young man named Joe Flannery, with whom, years before, he had had an atypically happy and stable love affair. Though now managing a rival group, Lee Curtis and the All Stars, fronted by his younger brother, Flannery agreed to help out with the Beatles behind the scenes. It was a decision prompted partly by love of Brian, partly by the good impression John made on him at their first meeting. "One night when my brother's group and the Beatles were both on at the Iron Door, our bass amplifier broke down, so I had to ask the Beatles to lend us theirs. I went upstairs to their dressing-room which was just a big empty space, littered with great lumps of broken masonry. I asked Paul about borrowing the amp, but he told me I'd have to speak to John. 'Sure, man,' John said. 'The show must go on.'"

Flo Jannery, as John dubbed him, became a part of the Beatles' support team, negotiating their fees on Brian's behalf and acting as a supernumerary fixer, adviser, and driver. "I'd often have to pick up John from his auntie's, though she never let me in further than the bottom step of the front stairs. Sometimes he'd come out onto the top landing and beckon me up to his room without her knowing."

One of the Beatles' favorite after-gig recreations was an American-style tenpin bowling alley in Tuebrook. If no lane happened to be free, they would hang out at Flannery's flat in nearby Gardiner Road. On these visits, John would always be drawn to a hand-colored photograph of Flannery's mother, Agnes, as a pretty young woman in the 1920s, with her hair styled in a bulbous golden bob. "He was fascinated by that picture of my mother," Flannery remembers. "He always loved French women, and he used to say she looked just like Leslie Caron." It was Agnes, with her gold bangs, so her son believes, who inspired the true Beatle Cut, as opposed to the prototypes created by Astrid Kirchherr and Jurgen Vollmer. "John came in one time and went straight to the picture of my mother, the way he always did. He said 'I've been thinking it over. *That's* the way we're going to have our hair.'"

In hindsight, a simple explanation would be given for Brian's interest. With his unerring knack of fancying the wrong person, he had fallen in love with John. Paul may have been prettier, Pete Best more Hollywood handsome, George more dewily boyish. But it was

tough-looking Teddy Boy John, with his black leather jacket and
dagger-toed boots, who unwittingly ticked every box in a middle-
class homosexual's fantasy of rough trade. As it happened, even John's
feelings about "queers" and "arse bandits" ran second to his ambition
for the Beatles. Years later, he would admit he had been ready to do
anything that might help persuade Brian sign up the group—and
indicated as much. But, from a mixture of innate decency and crip-
pling shyness, Brian refused to take such advantage of him.

There was also an affinity between the two of them that had
nothing to do with sex and everything with class. Notwithstanding their difference in age, and religion, both had much the same
half-timbered suburban background, John in Woolton, Brian in just
half-a-social-notch-higher Childwall. And, despite their common rejection of formal education, both had cultural interests far beyond
NEMS's record basement or playing rock 'n' roll at the Cavern. At
all events, John was the only Beatle that Brian knew socially: he
would often be invited to the substantial Epstein family home in
Queens Drive, just as Brian continued visiting Mendips even after
Aunt Mimi's support was in the bag. "John and Brian became very
interested in each other," Mimi would remember. "But not in any
sordid way. That makes me sick to hear anything like that. What
people don't realise and only I know is that Brian and John both had
a great love of art. They would talk for hours on end about art and
paintings, and would go to the galleries together. Brian was an intellectual, and I think John found someone he could talk about things
to on the same level."

Despite his youth, Brian was a deeply paternal character who by
rights should have married and raised a family. All those hitherto un-
gratifiable impulses to be provident and protective—and indulgent—
he now poured into managing the Beatles, treating them not as his
clients but as his children. This approach worked most powerfully
on the one who, behind a carapace of toughness and independence,
had longed for such a presence in his life since his Uncle George's
death six years earlier.

However, while being impressed, even awed, by what Brian was
doing and promised still to do for the Beatles, John resolutely refused

to show him any awe or even undue respect as a person. After their first meeting, he took to calling him "Eppy," a habit picked up by the other Beatles and ultimately by staff at NEMS. Brian hated the nickname for undermining his carefully nurtured executive gravitas but, even more, for suggesting the comical femininity of some butch maiden aunt. "The Beatles never talked to Brian about being gay," Joe Flannery says. "They certainly never mocked him about it, to his face. But John had ways of letting him know that they knew: he'd do little gestures, roll his eyes or mimic the way Brian spoke. Worst of all for John was if he pretended he wasn't . . . for instance, if he talked about "one of my girlfriends," which he did actually have. Then John wouldn't care what he said to deflate him. And, with the way Brian felt about John, there was nobody else in the world who could hurt him quite so much."

Brian at this point saw no more future in Lennon and McCartney's songwriting than did the pair themselves. His objective was to turn the Beatles into a nationally successful stage act, which under 1962 rules did not just mean appealing to teenagers but also being unthreatening and showbizzy enough to get onto grown-up television and radio. And, even with his limited grasp of youth culture, he knew there was only one possible example to follow. "Brian took them all to see the Shadows play at the Empire," Bill Harry says. "He told them that if they wanted to make it, that was how they'd got to be."

In other words, everything that had made their name on Merseyside—everything, indeed, that first attracted Brian to them—would now have to go. Instead of fooling around onstage as they did at the Cavern, drinking, smoking, eating, and trading banter with friends or foes in the audience, they must be as formal and restrained and carefully choreographed as the sedate strummers of "Apache" and "Wonderful Land," smiling politely, moving minimally and ending each number with a unified, humble, and grateful bow. And instead of the allover black leather that signified rock 'n' roll in its grubbiest outcast years—and, to many, still recalled Hitler's Gestapo—they would have to wear Shadows-style, showbiz-style matching suits.

John, at first, was appalled even to think of giving up the rebel persona he had worn like a battle honor for all these years, and being smarmed and groomed and goody-goodied as Brian proposed. Rich-mal Crompton's William, forced to don an Eton jacket for a danc-ing lesson, could not have been more outraged. "He came home in a right old mood, banging around," Mimi remembered. And even-tually it came out. Brian had decided they should wear suits—and, worse than that for John, they had to wear ties, too. I don't think [he] had worn a tie since he was at art school. . . . I thought 'Ha ha John Lennon, no more scruffs for you.' . . . I thought it was hilarious."

John made a brief attempt to organize resistance, but when he found no takers, principle yielded to pragmatism. "[Brian told us] 'Look, if you wear a suit, you'll get this much money' and everyone wanted a good, sharp suit . . . we wanted a good suit even to wear off stage. 'Yeah, man, all right, I'll wear a suit—I'll wear a bloody bal-loon if someone's going to pay me.'"

Brian therefore ordered four identical Italianate suits in gray brushed tweed, which—this being Brian—did not come from some multiple outfitter like Burtons or Hepworths but from a bespoke tailor in Birkenhead at £40 apiece. After some out-of-town previews, the new look was formally unveiled at the Cavern in March, the Beatles playing one set in their leathers, then coming back later in suits. To mark the watershed moment, Brian had their portrait done by a wedding photographer for whom a "group" normally consisted of bride, groom, and assorted relatives. John, in his brushed tweed jacket, round-collared shirt, and tie, mostly communicates all the joie de vivre of a police lineup. But, according to Paul, being dressed in a modish outfit that hadn't cost him a penny was less traumatic than he'd expected. "Check the pictures. John's not scowling in all of them."

The story of Brian's efforts to find the Beatles a record deal would later be recounted like some modern Labor of Hercules: how, week after week, he would travel to London and pitch them to label after label, but without scoring so much as an audition; how smug, all-knowing metropolitan executives only just kept from sniggering at the notion of a Liverpool group becoming "bigger than Elvis" and, with affected kindliness, advised him to stick to shopkeeping; how, night after night, he would be met off the train at Lime Street station by four hopeful faces, soon to be downcast once more.

At these glum debriefings, usually held at a station-exit coffee bar named the Punch and Judy, John would, surprisingly, not lambast Brian for his failure but be sympathetic and resolutely upbeat, joking that if all else failed they could try Embassy, a label dealing in inferior cover versions of current chart hits and sold only through Woolworths. When the other three's spirits flagged, he would pep them up with a routine inspired by cornball Hollywood musicals like *The Band Wagon*. "Where are we goin'," fellas?" he'd call out in a cheesy American accent. "To the top, Johnny," they would obediently chorus back. "And where's that?" "To the toppermost of the poppermost, Johnny!"

Brian certainly suffered rejection and belittlement at the hands of London A&R (artists and repertory) men. But it was barely three weeks after Decca's formal turndown that he struck a one-in-a-million lucky break. On February 13, he found his way to George Martin, the head of EMI's Parlophone label. Totally against type, thirty-six-year-old Martin was a gentlemanly figure with a voice more suggestive of the BBC than the Top 20. As two cultured accents met with mutual surprise, the ball started rolling at last. Martin listened to recordings from the Decca audition, decided that, for all the eccentric choice of material, "something" was there, and expressed a willingness to give Decca's rejects a hearing in person.

In addition to being a gentleman, Martin possessed an unusual combination of qualities that made him dream casting for the epic ahead. First, he was a trained classical musician; second, he had a pedigree as a producer of spoken-word comedy records, often in the form of shows before a live audience. At this stage, no firm date was made for his and the Beatles' first encounter. But—to paraphrase lyrics he would one day know well—a splendid time was guaranteed for all.

Brian's hasty study of pop-star management had taught him one golden rule for young male stars and would-be stars. To win the devotion of teenage girls, they must seem to be footloose, fancy-free—and thus theoretically available to each and every one of their fans. Wives were a complete nonstarter, fiancées and regular girlfriends almost as risky—and boyfriends, of course, completely off the chart. Though all four Beatles were sexually active, not to say hyperactive, only two were going steady, John with Cynthia Powell and Paul with Dot Rhone. Cynthia and Dot were now told they could no longer attend Beatles gigs and should be seen as little as possible with their swains in public. Schooled as they were in obedience and loyalty, both accepted the ruling without protest.

For Cyn, now in her final year of teacher training, it was not a good time to be shut out in the cold. The previous summer, her widowed mother, Lilian, had emigrated to Canada to make a new life as a children's nanny. With the Powell family home in Hoylake rented out, it had seemed a neat solution for Cyn to join Mimi Smith's student boarders at Mendips, taking a vacation job at a local Woolworths to help pay her rent. For some time after John's return from Hamburg, they had lived under the same roof, albeit occupying separate bedrooms, with all hanky-panky strictly forbidden.

Cyn did her best to be helpful and unobtrusive, even taking on a share of the housework. But having such a rival for John's attention actually in the house soon began to grate on Mimi's never very resilient nerves. However late he came in from a gig, she had been used to waiting up for him, ready to make him tea and a snack, and hear the night's news. Now, not unnaturally, Cyn would be waiting up for him, too—"hanging around in her night-dress," as Mimi put it disapprovingly to sister Nanny. After a few weeks, the tension became too much, and Cyn left Menlove Avenue to board with her Aunt Tess on the other side of town.

In the absence of a firm audition date from Parlophone Records, West Germany rather than southern Britain still seemed the Beatles' most promising territory. At Christmas, the pleasant and fair-dealing Peter Eckhorn had come over from Hamburg, met Brian, and booked them for a return appearance at his Top Ten Club that following spring. A couple of weeks afterward, Eckhorn's security chief, the giant-killing Horst Fascher, also turned up in Liverpool with a singer-pianist named Roy Young, sometimes known as "Brit-

ain's Little Richard." Fascher, it transpired, had fallen out with Eckhorn, quit the Top Ten and was seeking acts for a brand-new St. Pauli
rock venue, the Star-Club.

"When I come to Liverpool, I'm told the Beatles have a new
manager called Brian Epstein that I have to talk to," he remembers.
"Brian says to me 'I'm sorry, the boys are already booked to play the
Top Ten.' I tell him 'If the Beatles don't come to my club, there will
be no fuckin' Top Ten Club . . . we'll smash the fuckin' place up.'"

For Stu Sutcliffe in Hamburg, the prospect of John's return was a
bright spot in a life that—all unbeknownst to his best friend—had
become increasingly shadowed by pain and anxiety. The headaches
that had plagued Stu for the past year were now so intense that he
could sometimes barely move or even speak while in their skull-
splitting throes; his skin grew drained of color even as his canvases
rioted with it; his weight plummeted, and he suffered spells of diz-
ziness and nausea. His violent mood swings and outbursts of irrational jealous rage against Astrid had soured a relationship that had
once seemed ideal, postponing the wedding that once had seemed so
urgent. His letters home to his family seemed to reflect an increasing mental confusion, the formerly regular italic script now wild and
disjointed, like messages from an unhappy ghost.

Yet the attacks were as sporadic as they were unpredictable. For
days at a time, Stu would be free from pain and seemingly back to
normal: lapping up his master classes with Eduardo Paolozzi at the
state art college, working with near-drunken euphoria in his attic
studio at the Kirchherr house.

On January 22, he wrote optimistically to his mother, Millie, that
he was enjoying his painting, his German college grant had just
been increased, and "my little Astrid is happy and contented." A few
days later, he required treatment in the local hospital's outpatients
department after apparently suffering a kind of fit. The Kirchherrs'
doctor sent him for blood tests, an electrocardiogram, and an X-ray,
which ominously recorded an "increase in skull-pressure." He began
a course of cranial hydrotherapy and massage, which had such immediate beneficial results that he stopped it before it was completed.
Astrid wrote to his mother that he was "very ill" but that, with vari-

ous treatments, including the long-delayed appendectomy, he would be cured "in 7 months."

Early in February, he returned to Liverpool to see his mother, who had herself been seriously ill and recently undergone surgery. Though he looked pale and wraithlike even for him, none of his Beatle ex-colleagues, least of all myopic John, noticed anything untoward. He saw them play at the Cavern, met Brian Epstein, and even discussed taking some future role as designer or art director for the group. "I didn't know anyone as lovely as you existed in Liverpool," Brian wrote to him afterward.

Back in Hamburg, he suffered a further bout of convulsions, followed by more racking headaches. The Kirchherrs' doctor recommended specialist treatment at a neurological clinic, including induced sleep, but no spare beds for such care were available. Stu wrote to his mother that he was "very ill, bed-bound . . . can't walk far without falling over." Three days later, he had another seizure, this time serious enough to make the doctor suspect epilepsy. Unable to sleep, he was tortured by fears of going mad or blind, or both, by remorse for saddling the Kirchherrs with his medical bills, and by recurrent urges to jump to his death from his studio window. With eerie prescience, he even asked Astrid's mother to buy him a white coffin to be buried in. "My head is compressed," he wrote to his sister, Joyce, "and filled with such unbelievable pain. . . ." And John knew nothing about any of it.

The Beatles were due in town on April 11—for the first time arriving grandly by air—to inaugurate the Star-Club two days later. On April 10, in his studio at the Kirchherrs," Stu suffered a seizure lasting more than half an hour. With Astrid out at work, it was left to a distraught Frau Kirchherr to make him as comfortable as possible, then send for the doctor who had been treating him. The doctor arrived to find him in a coma, and arranged his immediate admittance to the neurological unit at Heidberg Hospital. Astrid returned home just in time to go with him in the ambulance. He died during the journey, cradled in her arms. He was twenty-one.

In the traumatic hours that followed, no one thought to break the news to his best friend. When John took off from Manchester next morning with Paul and Pete (George was recovering from measles and would follow with Brian a day later), he still no idea that Stu was dead. He found out from Astrid and Klaus Voormann in the arrivals hall at Hamburg airport. As after Uncle George's death, his first reaction was uncontrollable hysterical laughter. "It was frightening," Astrid remembers. "John was laughing but also kind of crying, saying 'No, no, no!' and lashing out with his hands."

When Brian and George arrived next day, Stu's mother was on the same flight, bound for the ordeal of identifying his body, sorting out his effects, and arranging his transportation home. But the John who greeted her in Hamburg showed no sign of his wild outburst twenty-four hours earlier. Millie Sutcliffe was always to be mystified and hurt by his apparent lack of feeling.

As in all cases of sudden death, an autopsy had to be performed on Stu before his funeral could take place. This found he had died from "cerebral haemorrhage due to bleeding into the right ventricle of the brain." No explanation for the fatal rupture could be found, other than an indentation at the front of the skull, suggesting it had once suffered "trauma"—that is, some powerful impact or blow. In all Stu's peaceable twenty-one, there seemed only one moment when he might have sustained such an injury. That was after the Beatles' Lathom Hall gig in early 1961, when a group of Teds had cornered him backstage, knocked him down, and kicked him in the head.

Almost forty years were to pass before Stu's younger sister, Pauline, published a memoir containing another explanation of the damage to his skull. According to Pauline, he did not suffer it at Lathom Hall, but a few weeks later in Hamburg during the Beatles' residency at the Top Ten Club. One day while he and John were walking together near the club, John had allegedly attacked him without provocation or warning, punching him to the ground, then repeatedly kicking him in the head as he lay there. Paul McCartney was also said to have been present. Since John instantly fled from the scene, it was left to Paul to pick up Stu—who had been left bleeding from the face and one ear—and help him back to the Beatles' quarters at the Top Ten.

Pauline said she had been told of the incident by Stu himself, during what was to be his last trip home to Liverpool. As she understood it, various grievances had been fermenting together in John's mind—Stu's poor musicianship and the trouble it was causing within the group, mingled with jealousy of Stu's new life as a "real" artist, perhaps even some secret hankering after Astrid. Unhinged by the usual Hamburg combination of drink, pills, and sleeplessness, he had suddenly lost control and lashed out.

According to Pauline, her family knew about the attack at the time but, in the misery following Stu's death, were unable even to discuss it among themselves, let alone make it public. That it never emerged in the decades that followed was due to Millie Sutcliffe, specifically her determination to have Stu recognized as a creative force in his own right, not merely a footnote to the Beatles. So strongly did she feel on this point that she swore her two daughters to place an embargo on Stu's letters and memorabilia—and by implication this particular story—for fifteen years after her own death, which came in 1984. The allegation was thus never made in John's own lifetime. Nonetheless, Pauline believes, he always remained haunted by what he had done, fearing it might have been a contributory factor in the fatal hemorrhage.

Other people close to them both at the time are reluctant to believe John could have made such a mindlessly vicious attack, however drunken or crazed. They point out how protective he had always been of Stu, how in the Lathom Hall fracas, he had even broken a finger in battling with Stu's attackers. They deny that Stu's poor musicianship was ever a serious issue with John (he was, in fact, almost out of the Beatles at the time of the alleged assault) or that John ever felt jealousy of his work or any covetousness regarding Astrid. Paul McCartney, the only named witness, has no recollection of it. "It's possible Stu and John had a fight in a drunken moment," he says, "but I don't remember anything that stands out." Astrid herself remains convinced that no such incident ever took place, "because if it had, Stuart would have told me."

Stu's death caused huge shock, not only to his friends but to the teachers and ex-teachers who recognized him as a prodigious talent as well as a beautiful boy. He was buried at Huyton Cemetery on Maundy Thursday, April 19. John did not interrupt his Hamburg engagement to attend and, later, delivered a characteristically terse epitaph: "I looked up to Stu. I depended on him to tell me the truth."

A subsequent letter from Astrid to Millie Sutcliffe, however, showed a glimpse of his real feelings: "Why can't we go for other people to Heaven? John asks me that—he said he would go for Stuart in heaven because Stuart was such a marvellous boy and he is nothing. . . . One day he showed me and Klaus his little room. Every piece of paper from Stuart he have stick on the wall and big photographs by his bed."

The Beatles' new employer, Manfred Weissleder, was among the Reeperbahn's most respected, and feared, denizens. His clubs enjoyed mysterious immunity from racketeers and protection gangs, prompting rumors of friendly links, to put it no higher, with Hamburg's criminal underworld. From his numerous employees he demanded the ring-kissing obeisance of a Mafia don. "If you show Manfred any disrespect, you get fired," the saying went. "But if you do it in front of a woman, you'll be lucky to be left alive."

Weissleder's Star-Club was St. Pauli's biggest and plushiest music venue to date, a two-thousand-capacity space with cinema-style raked seating and bars that seemed to run away to infinity, overhung by forests of trendy tubular lamps. For headlining a five-act bill (also featuring Tony Sheridan, Roy Young, Tex Roburg and the Playboys, and the Bachelors), the Beatles received 500 deutschmarks (£44.50) each per week, plus shares of an under-the-table cash bribe that Fascher had paid Brian Epstein to secure them. Compared with what they were used to, the work hours seemed almost leisurely: four sixty-minute performances on one night, then three on the next, with an hour-long break rather than the customary fifteen minutes between sets. But they were still on call from eight p.m. to four a.m. seven nights a week, and in the entire six weeks would have only one day off.

Best of all, for one Beatle at least, the engagement meant putting Brian's restyling plans temporarily in abeyance. Having delivered them safely and seen the opening show, he had returned to Liverpool to work on more long-term strategic matters, chiefly the still-unscheduled audition date with Parlophone Records and George

Martin. The Beatles could therefore go onstage every night in just shirts and jeans—accompanied by Roy Young as pianist and co-vocalist—without having to make any attempt at Shadow-boxing. The Star-Club's clientele did not want bows and smiles; they wanted the crazy, *mach-schau* young Englanders they had followed from the Indra through the Kaiserkeller to the Top Ten. And this John gave them with a vengeance.

He had always been hardest to hold in Hamburg. But those around him in these days and nights immediately following Stu Sutcliffe's death felt a special intensity—almost a desperation—in the way he swilled beer, swallowed pills, and created mayhem, onstage and off. "It was like 'Stuart's dead and we're still alive,'" Horst Fascher says. "'Let's make all the shit we can, because tomorrow it may all be over.'"

John, Paul, and Pete Best all by now had regular Hamburg girl-friends whose existence their Liverpool girlfriends—like sailors' wives in an earlier era—never suspected. For a long time, John's was one of the Star-Club's barmaids, Bettina Derlien, a devout Beatles enthusiast who would signify approval of a particular number by making the long lamps above the bar jiggle and jog crazily together. "When it got late at night and the inside of the club was nearly empty, Betty would give John a blow-job behind the bar-counter," Fascher says. "Not once . . . many times."

He wrote regularly to Cynthia, with a mixture of passion and pathos, begging her for lyrics to songs like "A Shot of Rhythm and Blues," sometimes adding bits to the same letter over several days to that it ended up more like diary extracts, several hundred words long. As part of Cyn's teacher-training course, she was now receiving practical classroom experience at a kindergarten in one of the tough-est parts of Garston. To save herself the long daily bus ride from her aunt's—and make herself more available to John when he returned home—she had taken a bed-sitting-room in Garmoyle Road, not far from Penny Lane. Her companion in anonymity, Paul's girlfriend, Dot Rhone, was to have shared the room, but John objected that she would spoil their romantic times together ("with the Sunday papers, choccies and a throbber"), so Dot took the adjacent room instead.

Working for the Reeperbahn's acknowledged Godfather theoretically shielded all the Beatles from ordinary dangers and hassles. Every Weissleder employee was issued a gold Star-Club lapel badge denoting a protected species whom hustlers hustled and bouncers bounced at their peril. But not even this talisman was proof against John's incorrigible mischief-making. One morning, during the customary postperformance mooch around the harbor fish market, he persuaded some fellow musicians to join him in buying a live piglet. Their not-over-gentle efforts to control the squealing, terrified creature so outraged German bystanders that the *Polizei* were called and they found themselves under arrest for alleged animal cruelty. As none of them carried any identification, they were put into a cell until Fascher could be called to vouch for them.

The living accommodation provided by Weissleder was a small second-floor flat with a balcony, across the street from the club and immediately adjacent to St. Joseph's Catholic Church. Here, squalor quickly set in on scale unknown even in Gambier Terrace. When George vomited next to his own bed, the mess stayed on the floor for days, decorated with matchsticks and referred to almost affectionately as the Thing. To a nauseated Weissleder, John explained that it was their pet hedgehog.

Most Sunday mornings, an after-show party would be starting at the flat just as the more pious Freiheit residents made their way to early mass at St. Joseph's. With only one small toilet among many partygoers, it was commonplace for males to relieve themselves over the balcony into the street. The most enduring of all John-goes-wild-in-Hamburg legends would be that on one such morning, as a group of nuns were passing beneath, he deliberately urinated on their heads. Investigation reveals that the victims of this unwelcome shower may not actually have been wearing habits but, Horst Fascher attests, "They were still very, very holy people."

Klaus Voormann witnessed a more calculated act of sacrilege by the erstwhile Woolton choirboy. One day when Klaus went up to the Beatles' flat, John was seated on his bed, drawing on an outsize piece of cardboard and muttering to himself. "I see that he's drawing Jesus, hanging on the Cross, with this big prick. All the time, he's talking in a kind of sermon, working himself up. Then he goes onto the balcony, holds up the Cross and starts preaching to the people down in the street. Some of them laugh, some cringe and look away, some get angry and start shouting back at him. This is not just a little joke . . . this is heavy. If the police had seen him, he could have been in real trouble, maybe even gotten deported."

As it happened, John's disruptions were about to be eclipsed by a master. On May 28, the Star-Club's rolling bill was joined for two weeks by the legendary Gene Vincent. Barring Elvis and Buddy Holly, no American rock-'n'-roll pioneer had given John more inspiration since his first shaky "Be-Bop-A-Lula" at the St. Peter's Church fete. Although still not yet thirty, Vincent had been prematurely aged by fame, quick-following decline, and the physical injuries life had showered on him. But he sang with the same eerie lisp (even if it now took three half bottles of Johnnie Walker whiskey per night to induce) and wore the black leather that he'd been first to make the rocker's emblem. "We met Gene backstage," John would remember. "Backstage? It was a toilet. And we were thrilled."

"Don't make any shit tonight, John," Fascher would plead before every show, and on quite a few nights he didn't, seeming content to scream out every Chuck Berry song the Star-Club crowd demanded or croon "To Know Her Is to Love Her" as tenderly as if the only "her" on his mind was patient Cynthia back home in Garmoyle Road. The constant influx of new support bands, notably Gerry and the Pacemakers, kept him on his mettle in finding new songs to cover. There was a second recording date for Polydor (more minstrel-flavored oldies, like "Sweet Georgia Brown" and even "Swanee River") to wind up the one-year contract with Bert Kaempfert. And a telegram from Brian Epstein produced excitement that needed no fueling by beer or pills or gorilla suits. Parlophone's George Martin had finally fixed the Beatles' audition (or "recording session," as Brian put it) for June 6, a week after their return home.

"I haven't seen Astrid since the day we arrived," John wrote to Cynthia, probably to allay any suspicion that he might be moving in on Stu's girl. In fact, Astrid says, she could not have had a more sympathetic or supportive friend. John refused to let her cry alone at home, insisting that she attend the Beatles' Star-Club opening and come back often afterward. Whenever misery threatened to overwhelm her under the tubular lamps, he would be there with a dose of pragmatism as astringent as smelling salts. "He'd always say 'Let's have a bean [Preludin] and talk,'" she remembers. "He convinced me it wasn't possible to just give up, that I had to get through my grief and carry on. He put it very, very harshly, like he was almost telling me off: 'You have got to decide if you want to die or go on living, but make a decision.' He was the one who saved me really."

As the "bean" took effect, John would open up about his own feelings for Stu, that strange, unstable mixture of hero-worship and casual cruelty. As much as grief-stricken, he seemed almost bitter toward Stu for fading out of his life with so little warning. From there, the talk would often turn to another such offender, though on an incalculably greater scale—his mother, Julia. "John used to say that Stuart was the second person to have left him," Astrid remembers. "First his mummy left him, then Stuart. I think it was the root of his anger . . . that people he loved the most always left him.

"Once I just asked him 'Did you really love Stuart from all your heart?' and he said, 'Yes.' I said, 'Why didn't you show it then?' He said, 'Well, it's not done, is it?' John was very conservative."

When George Martin finally met the Beatles at EMI's Abbey Road Studios, he had a private agenda that, had John suspected it, could have strangled one of pop music's greatest collaborations at birth. Although Martin's Parlophone label had some pop output, it was negligible in comparison with EMI's flagship label, Columbia, whose glittering roster was headed by Cliff Richard and the Shadows. Whereas Parlophone's trademark comedy records each required a huge effort to conceive and develop, Columbia's label boss, Norrie Paramour, could just sit back and watch Cliff-and-the-Shadows hits, Cliff-only hits, and Shadows-only hits roll forth like an automated production line. Martin wanted a Cliff and some Shadows of his own, and he hoped the Liverpool boys might fit the bill, or be made to fit it.

The encounter could not have begun more intimidatingly. In

1962, records were still made with much the same formality they had been in 1902. The engineers wore long white coats like doctors or laboratory technicians, symbolizing how far their craft lay beyond the understanding, let alone participation, of ordinary mortals. The producer, or A&R man, was an omnipotent figure who not only chose his artists' material but dictated exactly how it should be sung or played. It was assumed, usually with good reason, that pop stars were musical illiterates who needed all the skill of professional songwriters, arrangers, and session players to enrich their puny sound, and all the arcane wizardry of the engineers to make it releasable.

Martin had originally not meant to audition the Beatles personally but to leave it to his assistant, Ron Richards, who dealt with Parlophone's other few pop acts. Only when Richards alerted him to something possibly out of the ordinary did he come up from the canteen to inspect them. Then, against all the odds, everything began to go right. For, despite appearances, Martin was not really upper class at all. A North London carpenter's son, he had acquired his patrician languor by osmosis, first in the wartime Fleet Air Arm, later at the Guildhall School of Music. Moreover, as a producer of comedy records, he had worked and been on friendly personal terms with the arch-Goons Spike Milligan and Peter Sellers. On that basis alone, John was practically willing to kiss his shoes.

Despite this rapport, Martin kept to his secret agenda. What the Beatles believed to be a general audition was actually a test for John and Paul in turn, to see which might be turned into the stand-alone front man. Martin jointly had in mind a Cliff Richard and a recent Peter Sellers comedy routine as a rock-'n'-roll singer named Clint Thigh. In the event, he found it impossible to choose between John's voice and Paul's, especially when the two melded together. "Paul's was sweeter, but John gave the combination its interest and sharpness. He was the lemon juice against the virgin olive oil."

Where Martin differed from all previous auditioners was in giving as much credence to John's and Paul's own songs as to their interpretation of other peoples'. Of the four tracks recorded on June 6 as demos for a future single, three were Lennon-McCartney compositions—"Love Me Do," "P.S. I Love You," and "Ask Me Why." The first dated back to truant afternoons in the McCartneys' Allerton living room; the remaining two demonstrated just how far the truants had developed since. Both were ballads, virtually identical in tempo, each bearing its originator's unmistakable footprint, yet with words, music, and performance equally unmistakably imprinted by his partner. "P.S. I Love You" was a Paul love-letter song, as sweet and romantic as had ever been committed to Basildon Bond notepaper, but with John's voice chiming on random words almost tonelessly like a warning P.P.S.—I've got my eye on you. "Ask Me Why" showed John determined to match Paul in melodic adventurousness, with two different bridges and a close-harmony chorus and falsetto line straight from black American soul. The irrepressible wordsmith popped up everywhere, as in the punctilious to the rhyming of *believe* and *conceive.*

The audition proved a fateful one for Pete Best. Afterward, Martin took Brian aside and told him Pete wasn't a good enough drummer to play on the Beatles' debut single, whatever it turned out to be. He did not say Pete should be fired, only that he preferred to use a session drummer accustomed to the very different demands of working in a studio. But his words concentrated the minds of the other three on what had become a nagging problem within their ranks. As a personality, Pete had never really fitted into the group. His taciturn manner, his fondness for his own company, his steadfast refusal to take pills, especially his film-star good looks and crisp, short haircut, all created an aloof, uninvolved air that had not mattered so much when they were nobodies but was becoming increasingly noticeable and irksome now they were starting to be somebodies.

Since their very first Hamburg gig, the others had been covetously eyeing Rory Storm's drummer Ringo Starr, the doleful-faced Dingle boy whose humor meshed with theirs as naturally as his sticks found their backbeat. Ringo it so happened, had recently become disaffected with Rory and quit the Hurricanes for brief period, only rejoining for lack of anything better. Back in February on a night when Pete was unwell, he'd sat in with John, Paul, and George yet again, and again proved what a perfect fit he was. After so long seemingly far beyond their reach, he was suddenly there for the asking.

Yet firing Pete Best, even with the excuse that Parlophone de-

manded it, would create all manner of complications. Not only did
Pete have his own huge following among the Beatles' hometown
fans, but his mother Mona had been their unofficial agent and tireless advocate. Moreover, his close friend, Neil Aspinall, was their indispensable driver—and, in a twist worthy of Gilbert and Sullivan,
Neil and Mona Best had been having an affair, which ended with
Mrs. Best becoming pregnant. For John, the dagger thrust into Pete's
back would be hardest of all. "He'd always got on well with Pete up
until then," Bill Harry says. "They used to go out drinking together
a lot in Hamburg. Pete had been the one to stand by John when they
tried mugging that sailor, and was also against dropping the black
leather and going into suits. John respected Pete as the kind of hard
man he himself always wanted to be."

John was already busily engaged in making his own life more complicated. On July 6, the Beatles played on another Cavern-sponsored
"riverboat shuffle" aboard the cruiser *Royal Iris*, once again as support to Mister Acker Bilk and his Paramount Jazz Band. Since the
previous summer's trip down the Mersey together, Bilk had enjoyed
a massive hit with his clarinet solo "Stranger on the Shore," dominating the UK's Top 20 for over six months and becoming the first
British musician in years to make number one in America. So taken
was he with his rock-'n'-roll shipmates this second time afloat that he
presented each of them with a black bowler hat like the one he himself always wore onstage. At the Pier Head later, when Neil Aspinall
counted bowler-hatted Beatles back into the van, John was missing.
He had gone off with Patricia Inder.

Patricia had long been one of the Beatles' inner circle of female
fans, the ones they knew by name, tried hardest to please, and even
consulted about their performance. Since their arrival at the Cavern,
she had seldom missed a show, day or night, conspicuous among the
arch-worshippers in the front row with her tiny stature, waist-length
blonde hair, and huge bush-baby eyes. She had always known John
liked her but that he considered her far too young and innocent for
any serious dalliance; when they'd first met, backstage at Aintree
Institute, she was still only fifteen. "He used to call me 'my little
Brigitte Bardot.' And he wrote 'Hello Little Girl' for me. When the

Beatles first played it at the Cavern, he said, 'This is for someone special and she knows who she is.'"

Patricia was nineteen now, so no one could accuse him of cradle snatching. After the riverboat shuffle, he invited her to a party at a mutual friend's flat, but when they arrived there, the place was empty. "I asked John who was coming to the party. He said 'Just the two of us.'" That first night, she says, John only kissed her, but at their next tryst, a couple of days later, she willingly lost her virginity.

They began regularly spending nights together, Patricia telling her parents she was with her friend Sue, while John told Cynthia he was writing songs at Paul's house. When the evening's gig at the Cavern or elsewhere was over, they would rendezvous at Sue's flat in Princes Road, which fortunately possessed a large spare bedroom. Since Paul was partial to Sue—as well as to several of Patricia's other friends—he, too, would often be having a sleepover there. George Harrison accepted the situation less easily, making Patricia wonder if he might also have had designs on her. "When George found out about John and me, he took it really badly. In fact, he slapped my face."

The routine in Sue's spare room seldom varied. "John always used to light a candle beside the bed. Then he'd put a fresh packet of chewing gum under his pillow. I'd thought he'd be like he was onstage, all tough and don't-care, but he was incredibly thoughtful and gentle and romantic. He was the first fellow I'd ever known who kissed my eyes. He'd sometimes put my face between both his hands and run his fingers over my skin as if he was a blind person. Some lads, when they kissed you, they'd suck you in and spit you out and it was horrible, but John was the best kisser I'd ever met."

To Patricia, as to few others—especially women—he would sometimes reveal the lack of confidence behind his attention-grabbing, wisecracking stage persona. "He'd say 'What do you see in me? I'm ugly . . . I've got a big nose. . . .' I don't think he really believed he had the looks to make it in pop music, because he never used to talk about becoming a star. But he always said he'd end up a millionaire."

He spoke often about his mother, how beautiful and funny she had been and how much he still missed her. Sometimes he would even talk about his father, a subject that still remained taboo inside his family circle and one he seldom discussed with even his closest male friends. Patricia herself still had both parents, but knew that did not automatically make for a happy family. Her mother was a fanatical ballroom dancer and seldom at home; her docker father spent most of his leisure hours drinking with workmates. "I told John I never saw my dad either, because he was in the pub all day. John said, 'But at least you know he's there.'"

Cynthia never suspected a thing, even on those few-and-far-between nights when she was allowed to leave her secret bedsit in Garmoyle Road and come into town to see John at the Cavern. More than once she and Patricia found themselves alone together in the primitive ladies' room, where a rat had once been seen scuttling along the top of the door. "Our eyes would meet in the mirror," Patricia says, "but I never got any vibe that she knew."

With both his official and clandestine girlfriends, John was no more scrupulous about contraception than he had ever been. Patricia feared the worst when her period was two weeks overdue, but it proved a false alarm. Cynthia was not so lucky when, responding at last to the same persistent discouragement, her own monthly "friend" failed to arrive on schedule. An examination by a coldly disapproving woman doctor confirmed that she was pregnant.

For almost every young couple in this situation, especially in northern England, there could be only one possible outcome. The day had yet to dawn when women would question their age-old duty to reproduce life at whatever cost, and demand control over their own bodies. Surgical abortions were performed only in cases of extreme medical necessity, taking no account of how much the child was wanted or would be loved; the only alternative was an illegal and dangerous backstreet world of rusty scalpels, hot baths, and gin. The baby must be born and its father persuaded, or coerced, into saving its mother from social leperhood by "giving it a name."

Characteristically, Cyn blamed no one but herself for what had happened, and was in mortal dread of telling John—especially at this moment when he seemed poised on the edge of stardom and was meant to be shedding emotional encumbrances rather than acquiring them. She expected anger or icy hailstones of contempt; instead, he reacted quite calmly and matter-of-factly, saying without any prompting that they'd better get married, the sooner the better.

Patricia Inder heard the two-part news from Paul McCartney first, then John himself confirmed it. "He told me, 'I love Cynthia, but I'm in love with you.' He said it didn't have to make a difference to us, and that he still wanted to go on seeing me. I said, 'You can't be serious . . . Cynthia's pregnant . . . you're going to marry her.' John said, 'I still want to go on seeing you.'"

Meanwhile, the plot to dump Pete Best and replace him with Ringo Starr was moving to fruition. Ringo himself was currently in Skegness, Lincolnshire, where Rory Storm and the Hurricanes had a summer residency at Butlins Holiday Camp. John and Paul secretly visited him there to sound him out; then Brian Epstein telephoned him with a formal invitation to join that was immediately accepted. A couple of days later, the still unsuspecting Pete was called into the NEMS shop and told by Brian that the others wanted him to go. None of them was present at the meeting, nor did any of them offer any personal regrets to Pete afterward. According to Bill Harry, John thought the matter had been handled in a "despicable" way. He went along with it nonetheless, to the disillusionment of many who had always respected his honesty and openness. Even Patricia Inder reproached him for choosing "the coward's way out."

Ringo's debut took place on August 18 at a deliberately low-key out-of-town gig, the annual dance of the Port Sunlight Horticultural Society. But that merely postponed the backlash from Pete's numerous loyal fans among the Beatles' following. When they first played the Cavern with Ringo, they found Mathew Street full of angry protesters and were heckled onstage by chants of "Pete Best for ever—Ringo never!"; as they came off, George was head-butted and given a black eye. Assailed on one side by a wrathful Mona Best, on the other by tearful customers in his own shop, Brian declared himself "the most hated man in Liverpool" and refused to visit the Cavern without a bodyguard. To compound the plotters' discomfiture, Pete himself behaved with dignity and magnanimity, putting no pressure on his friend Neil Aspinall, as he might easily have done, to resign in sympathy as their driver and roadie.

On August 22, Granada Television sent a film crew up from Manchester to record the Beatles playing at the Cavern for a magazine program called *Know the North*. This first professional film footage of them—the precursor of millions of miles to come—featured two R&B covers, "Kansas City" and "Some Other Guy." Uniformed in leather waistcoats and slim-jim ties, bangs heat-plastered to foreheads, they already looked too good for their brickwork bower. Ringo kept the beat as if he'd always been there, though occasionally with a rather hunted look in his spaniel eyes. Amid the applause for "Some Other Guy," Granada's recording engineer picked up a still-dissident cry of "We want Pete!"

The next day's edition of *Mersey Beat* reported that the Beatles had received a firm date to record their first single for Parlophone and that Pete Best had left the group "amicably." Later that muggy, rain-squally morning, at the Mount Pleasant register office, John married Cynthia.

He had delayed breaking the news to his Aunt Mimi until the last possible moment, knowing only too well what her reaction would be. For Mimi, it was his final renunciation of all her care, protection, and direction—proof that, despite everything she had done, he was the same hapless drifter his father, Alf, had been. As a further gouge at her heart, she recognized Julia, her beloved, exasperating baby sister, even more than Alf throughout the whole affair: Julia blithely wasting her talent and throwing away her future; Julia the ever flippant, unpractical, and improvident; Julia walking into 7 Newcastle Road that day in 1938 and defiantly flinging her marriage certificate onto the table.

Though initially volcanic enough to rattle Mendips's Art Nouveau windows in their frames, Mimi calmed down somewhat as the realization dawned that John was at least "doing the right thing" and there would be no illegitimate baby, like Julia's, to besmirch the family name. Since he was in his usual penniless state, she gave him £10 to buy Cynthia a wedding ring, though adamant that she herself would not be at the ceremony. On the night before, he paid her another visit on his own and roamed distractedly around the house, casting wistful looks at his old bedroom and his favorite reading and drawing niches in the morning room and living room, and muttering that he didn't want to be married and become a father. In the end—so Mimi told the family later—he sat in the kitchen and actually cried.

The marriage threatened to have disastrous consequences for John's career with the Beatles, just as they finally seemed to be going somewhere. Most managers faced with such a threat to their teen appeal would immediately have tried to replace him with the requisite fancy-free bachelor. Brian Epstein, however, had the intelligence to realize that such an option did not exist and that the best must be made of the situation as it stood. Stronger even than Brian's concern for his boys' marketability was his desire to establish himself in their eyes—John's, above all—as an all-powerful smoother of paths, solver of problems, and shield against life's harsher realities. He therefore stepped in to stage-manage the whole wedding, such as it was, attending to all the details that were beyond John to cope with, and adding a touch of style to what would otherwise have been a gloomy occasion.

Neither of the participants' absent fathers, indeed, could have been more supportive or solicitous. It was Brian who obtained the special license needed for a marriage on such short notice; it was Brian who arranged for a chauffeur-driven car to pick up Cynthia and bring her to the register office, a star for the one and only time in her life; it was even Brian, rather than Paul or some art college crony like Jeff Mohammed, who acted as John's best man. His wedding gift also happened to be a handy way of keeping Cyn measurably under wraps while John was away with the Beatles. Since (like Alf and Julia Lennon in 1938) the pair had no idea where they would live, Brian offered them unlimited, rent-free use of a flat he owned at 36 Falkner Street.

Mimi, hurtfully, kept her vow not to attend. Cynthia's mother, Lilian, briefly home from Canada when the news broke, had had to return the previous day, unable to change her boat ticket. Other than Brian, the only witnesses were Paul, George, Cyn's brother Tony, and her sister-in-law Margery. The bride's outfit was a rather well-worn checked jacket and skirt, brightened up with a blouse given to her by Astrid Kirchherr. During the ceremony, a jackhammer began rattling outside the window, almost obliterating the registrar's voice and the responses. Afterward, in torrential rain, the party ran across the road to Reece's restaurant for a chicken lunch at 15 shillings each, paid for by Brian. Since Reece's was not licensed to serve alcohol, the toasts to the newlyweds had to be drunk in water.

As had been the case with Alf and Julia, there were no wedding photographs—and no honeymoon. John spent his wedding night playing with the Beatles at the Riverpark Ballroom in Chester while Cynthia assembled the components of their first home. It was not the best augury for marriage or parenthood.

13

LUCKY STARS

You can hear that I'm just a frantic guy doing his best.

The whole story could very well have ended a couple of months from here. In October 1962, America discovered that Russia was installing nuclear missiles in Cuba that could reach Washington, D.C., and other key U.S. military centers within twenty minutes. The young, untried President John F. Kennedy warned Russia's Nikita Khrushchev that if the missiles were not removed, America would invade Cuba, triggering the nuclear Third World War everyone had so long expected. For twelve tense days until Khrushchev backed down, humankind contemplated a future in which there would have been no Sixties, no Beatles, no John Lennon: no nothing.

Contrarily, rather than scanning the horizon for mushroom clouds, Britons developed a sudden obsession with a part of their own backyard they had scarcely noticed before. Films like *Saturday Night and Sunday Morning*, *Room at the Top*, *The Loneliness of the Long Distance Runner*, and *A Kind of Loving*, all based on bestselling novels, focused on north-country working-class life, seen through the eyes of an angry, alienated but unquenchably defiant young antihero. Millions each week watched the BBC's *Z-Cars*, a police series of a new, grittily naturalistic kind, set in a Merseyside suburb modeled on Kirkby. Billions would ultimately watch Granada TV's *Coronation Street*, a soap opera about ordinary lives in a back-to-back terrace located in Salford, Greater Manchester, but identical to the one in Toxteth where John's Lennon forebears had grown up and where some still lived. Thus, when he himself finally entered the spotlight, pop music's self-styled "working class hero" would find the ground not totally unprepared.

While America responded to the nuclear threat with stiff-backed patriotism, Britons positively gloried in the undermining of national values and morale. In 1961, four Oxbridge graduates, Peter Cook, Dudley Moore, Jonathan Miller, and Alan Bennett, scored a massive West End success with *Beyond the Fringe*, a satirical revue snapping at the sacred hindquarters of parliament, the military, and the church (its live cast recording, produced by George Martin, available on Parlophone). By 1962, the so-called "satire boom" had even reached BBC Television in a prime-time Saturday night show called *That Was the Week That Was*, fronted by an obscure cabaret performer named David Frost. The same year saw publication of *Private Eye*, a scurrilous and smutty-minded satirical magazine destined for a longevity rivaling *Burke's Peerage* or *Country Life*. The satirists spoke in public-school accents yet came from lower-middle- or even working-class families; they wore patrician striped shirts and elastic-sided boots along with the flattop haircuts and shiny suits of parvenu pop stars. It was getting harder by the minute to know who was who.

If George Martin had felt no qualms over the *Beyond the Fringe* team's original material, he still was not convinced that Parlophone's other "fringe" act had it in them to write a hit. For the Beatles' debut single, therefore, he exercised his A&R man's prerogative and chose a song out of the current crop on offer from outside writers. This was "How Do You Do It?" by twenty-year-old Mitch Murray, a playful ballad much like John's and Paul's own experiments in the same genre, but giving off chart potential as pungent as blue cheese. Martin had it put on a demo disk and sent it to Liverpool for the Beatles to rehearse before their recording session on September 4.

In contrast with the friendly atmosphere of their June audition, this got off to the stickiest possible start. After an initial tryout, Ringo's drumming was pronounced to be substandard, a pro session drummer was brought in to take over, and poor Ringo was relegated to bashing a tambourine. Then the Beatles gave "How Do You Do It?" a unanimous thumbs-down, protesting that its Pollyanna tone would make them a laughingstock up in Liverpool and clamoring to do a Lennon-McCartney song instead. Martin rejoined tersely that no Lennon-McCartney song he'd heard so far came close to this, and he was not going to pass up an obvious number one record. They responded with a classic Merseyside industrial "go-slow," taping a version of "How Do You Do It?" in which every note and nuance of John's lead voice made clear their utter apathy. Ramming the point home, John embellished its middle eight with a sarcastic "Ooh la-la" like an aural one-finger salute.

Martin was not the type to yield to such pressure—and anyway the track still had charm and originality enough to merit release. But it happened that one Lennon-McCartney song from the June 6 audition, "Love Me Do," had improved sufficiently meanwhile to become a contender. The fresh element was John playing harmonica in an intro and solo and as a bluesy skein throughout the vocal. This instrument of his Boy Scout boyhood had enjoyed a recent unexpected surge in the charts, first on Frank Ifield's "I Remember You," then—and more groovily—on "Hey Baby" by Bruce Channel, a white Texan with one of the "blackest" sounds around. Back in June, Channel had done a show with the Beatles at New Brighton Tower Ballroom, and his harmonica player, Delbert McClinton, had spent fifteen minutes teaching the "Hey Baby" riff to John.

After intensive polishing at Abbey Road on September 4 and in a further session a week later, the schoolmasterly figure in the control room was satisfied. Martin agreed to shelve "How Do You Do It?" and use "Love Me Do" as the A-side, with "P.S. I Love You" on the B-side.

In the labyrinthine bureaucracy that was EMI, each label head submitted his proposed new releases to a committee of senior executives for formal approval. Almost without exception, the musical mandarins who had to green-light "Love Me Do" were baffled by it. Most as-

sumed that, with performers named the Beatles, it must be another of
Parlophone's trademark comedy records. John's part of the harmony
sounded more mocking than pleading; the beat kept stopping with
a jokey cymbal smash; even the "Hey Baby"–ish harmonica seemed
to be covertly laughing up its sleeve; only Paul McCartney's plaintive
solo "Whoa-oh, love me do" seemed entirely on the level. Compared
with the complex instrumentation and sound effects of current hits,
it had a stripped-down, almost naked feel, to quote the critic Ian Mac-
Donald, "like a bare brick wall in a suburban sitting-room." Amid
the rampant Americana, real and ersatz, it was unmistakably British
and unapologetically northern; a first breath of *Z-Cars* and *Coronation
Street* blowing off the TV screen and onto vinyl.

The single was released on October 5, with all the halfheartedness
a mighty organization could muster. In Liverpool, although *Mersey
Beat* trumpeted it to the skies, there was some disappointment that
the Beatles' first record did not better convey their onstage personality. Apart from a vast window display in Brian Epstein's NEMS store,
promotion was confined to a few microscopic ads in the record-trade
press and some scattered spots on the BBC Light Programme. Like
EMI's top brass, the rather aged and supercilious disc jockeys of the
day presumed that a name like the Beatles could not be serious, so
introduced "Love Me Do" in the spirit of a joke without a punch
line. For the four themselves, the most exciting moment was its first
play on Radio Luxembourg, through Continental static still almost
as thick as when Elvis's first messages had come through to John
under the bedclothes at Mendips six years earlier.

If EMI would not do it, Brian had to find other ways to show that
his boys had reached a whole new level. In July, Gene Vincent had
made his first visit to Liverpool since the chaotic Boxing Stadium
spectacular of 1960. Back then, John had been just a wistful face in
the crowd; now, as old Hamburg buddies, Vincent and the Beatles
played the Cavern together on one of the wildest, most asphyxiating
nights it had ever known. A candid camera caught John under the
arches with Gene and Paul, restored to black leathers for that one
evening only, and giving a final, almost wistful "Don't mess with
me" look before compulsory suits, ties, and smiliness overwhelmed
him.

The release of "Love Me Do" coincided with an even bigger blast from his past. A Southern promoter named Don Arden had brought Little Richard to Britain on a tour coheadlined by America's main black heartthrob of the moment, Sam Cooke. Brian contacted Arden and arranged that his legendary import would give a one-night performance at New Brighton Tower Ballroom on October 12, with the Beatles second on the bill and a string of other local groups in support. For Merseyside at least, there could be no clearer proof of their having joined the immortals.

This was, alas, not quite the same Little Richard who had screamed John's blood awake with "Good Golly Miss Molly." The wild licorice-whip locks had been planed flat, the glittery gold zoot suit replaced by conventional thin-lapeled sharkskin, the former joyously mindless glare on the mustached, mascaraed face exchanged for a disconcerting look of thoughtfulness and piety. Since hearing the Word of God, Richard had been disappointing audiences the world over by regularly refusing to sing any music other than gospel. Holy or not, short-haired and charcoal-grayed or not, meeting this supreme icon of their misspent schooldays was the Beatles' greatest gift from Brian to date. "He used to read from the Bible backstage," John remembered. "Just to hear him talk, we'd sit around and listen. . . ." Initially, they were too shy even to ask Richard to be photographed with them; instead, Paul's camera-buff brother, Mike, took his picture from the wings in midperformance, with Paul and John watching reverently on the opposite side.

The Little Richard show was such a success that Brian brought him back for a second appearance with the Beatles on October 28, this time at the Liverpool Empire, topping a bill that also featured nationally known acts like Craig Douglas, Jet Harris, Kenny Lynch, and Sounds Incorporated. It was the day that the Cuban missile crisis was resolved, Russia stood down her offshore nuclear threat to America, and World War Three did not happen after all. As midevening news bulletins repeated that mankind was saved, John walked onto the hallowed stage he had last trodden with his Quarrymen hoping to be a Carroll Levis Discovery.

Despairing of any significant support from EMI, Brian decided to recruit his own PR team to promote "Love Me Do" and introduce the Beatles to the still largely oblivious national media. His first valuable acquisition was Tony Barrow, a young Liverpudlian who worked in London as a copywriter for Decca Records but also contributed a widely read record column to the *Liverpool Echo* under the pseudonym Disker. Having advised Brian unofficially on PR for some months, Barrow was invited on board in November 1962. "I was introduced to the Beatles in a pub called the Devonshire Arms, near EMI headquarters," he remembers. "And I'll never forget John's opening line: 'If you're not queer and you're not Jewish, what are you doing working for Brian?' It wasn't actually in front of Brian, but he was within earshot."

Since Barrow was still officially employed by Decca, his publicity releases on behalf of "Love Me Do" were issued via a nineteen-year-old PR man named Tony Calder, who worked out of a shared one-room office in Poland Street, Soho. "I liked the record," Calder says. "I told Brian the first thing he had to do was bring the Beatles down to London to meet some journalists. National papers didn't cover pop then; I was talking about music papers, the trade press.

"So the boys came down and I spent a whole day taking them around the various offices, doing half an hour in every place. Paul did all the talking; John hardly uttered a word. Our last appointment was at around six o'clock, with this git of an editor in a white Bri-nylon shirt who thought he was God Almighty. When the Beatles walk into his office, the first thing he says is 'It's all over for guitar groups.'

"John sits there, still not saying anything, and eventually this editor grudgingly says 'OK, I'll put a bit in the paper about you, just something small.' Then as we all get up to go, John manages to catch the overhanging lip of the guy's desk with his thighs and lift it right up, so that everything on the top slides off. It's all one beautiful, smooth moment, he wrecks the guy's desk, reaches over and shakes his hand, then turns to me and says 'Let's fuckin' get out of here.'"

Two months on from that hasty, halfhearted ceremony at Mount Pleasant Register Office, the reality of John's hugely altered station in life had barely even begun to sink in. The recording of "Love Me Do," the Little Richard experience, and the ever-increasing workload imposed by Brian had left little time to consider his new responsibilities as a husband and father-to-be. "I did feel embarrassed, walking around married," he would later admit. "It felt like walking round with odd socks on or your flies open."

As Mrs. John Lennon, apart from the £10 ring on her finger, Cynthia's life had not changed to any significant degree. John was still off playing with the Beatles almost every day and every night, in places farther and farther afield. Cynthia stayed on at Brian's flat in Falkner Street, coped alone with her pregnancy, and accepted her topsy-turvy role: not a secret mistress, as in all the canons of romantic fiction, but a secret wife.

She maintained such an obediently low profile that even most of her friends and former teachers at the nearby art college never realized she was there. A few doors along, at number 58, lived June Furlong, the model who still ruled the college life-drawing classes with a rod of iron. "One day when I got home from work, I was told that a fellow called Lennon had called round to ask me to a party," June remembers. "He left me a few other invitations, to parties or to Ye Cracke, but I was always too busy with my classes, so I never did see the place Brian had lent him." Sighting John in the city center one day, she was surprised at how opulent he now looked. "He was in the Kardomah in Whitechapel, wearing a new and very expensive-looking purple sweater. 'That's a lady's sweater, John,' I told him. He pulled back the neck and showed me the label, to prove that it came from Watson Prickard, the most expensive men's shop in Liverpool."

Little of this new affluence seemed to have rubbed off on Cyn. Her old college friend Ann Mason recalls bumping into her one day in Mount Street and finding a worried, distracted young woman, very different from the serenissima of their Lettering class. "Cynthia told me that she and John owed some money in income tax, and that Brian was sorting it all out. She also said she only had a single £1 note in her purse at that moment, and she was terrified that John would find out about it and take it."

On John's visits home, most of Cyn's time was spent in washing and ironing his stage wardrobe, cooking and caring for him in a never-attainable wish to match his Aunt Mimi, and keeping up the bachelor-boy masquerade to the point of absurdity. Even when he first brought Ringo to meet her, he did not mention that she was his wife or that she was pregnant.

Mostly she was by herself in Brian's elegant pad, lonely and bored by day, and at night often terrified out of her wits. The house's front door stood permanently open, and shady characters were always wandering through the communal hall that Cyn had to cross to go from the living room to her bedroom. If that were not enough, her pregnancy became increasingly troublesome; during one of John's trips away, she began to suffer bleeding and was told by her doctor to stay in bed or run serious risk of a miscarriage. Too weak and nervous to keep crossing the hall to the bathroom, she stayed in her bedroom for three days with "a bucket by the bed and a kettle [as] my only facilities."

A solution clearly had to be found that would not entail John's staying home for a single minute longer than he did already. It emerged in the petite form of Dot Rhone, Paul McCartney's former steady, who had accompanied Cynthia to Hamburg and occupied the next bedsit to hers in Garmoyle Road. Dot had special cause to sympathize with Cyn's predicament: toward the end of her relationship with Paul, she too had fallen pregnant, and the pair had been saved from a similar shotgun wedding only when Dot miscarried at three months.

Directly below Brian's flat was a small basement apartment, currently unoccupied. The obliging Dot agreed to move in there so that in any future medical emergencies, Cyn would not be all alone. Despite worries over her pregnancy, Dot recalls, Cyn's wifely duty to John came before all else. "Once, when she went to her brother Tony's for the weekend, she asked me if I'd look after John. He came in very late, a bit drunk, and we had a long talk. He told me that if some other woman that he really fancied came along, he'd leave Cynthia just like that. Nothing in the world was ever going to stop him doing what he wanted to do. He did make a pass at me, too. I just said, 'John, we've been friends too long for anything like this.'"

While he was traveling with the Beatles, swamped by eager girls and virtually under oath to hide his wedding ring, monogamy could not be expected to have much of a hold. But closer to home, even on his very doorstep, it was no different. Marriage had not ended his affair with Patricia Inder: they still regularly spent nights together when Cyn did not know he was back in Liverpool, or thought him to be burning midnight oil over some new song with Paul. "I wasn't happy about it," Patricia says. "I'd say, 'How can you be doing this, with a wife at home and a baby on the way?' John always said, 'A man needs more than one woman in his life.'" True to his word, he was also simultaneously having an affair with a girl named Ida Holley, who lived near Princes Park, appearing with her quite openly at Liverpool nightspots like Allan Williams's Blue Angel club.

It seemed the worst possible timing that right after the release of "Love Me Do," the Beatles had to return to Hamburg for a two-week stint at the Star-Club, from November 1 to 14. Despite the huge change in their circumstances since January, Brian would not renege on this or the remaining part of the block booking he had made with Horst Fascher. John in particular viewed it as a bore and an imposition, forgetting that without Hamburg he might still be playing for pennies at Aintree Institute. "We hated going back," he would recall. "Brian made us . . . fulfil the contract. If we'd had our way, we'd have copped out on the engagement because we didn't feel we owed them fuck-all."

According to close associates, including Joe Flannery and Peter Brown, Brian ordered ten thousand copies of "Love Me Do," roughly ten times the quantity he could possibly have sold through NEMS, to guarantee its entry into the Top 20. John, however, always insisted the song had succeeded on its own merits, through that magic element, word of mouth, and its chart history tends to support him. A week after its release, *Record Retailer* magazine showed it at only number forty-nine. From there it made a slow and erratic ascent through the thirties and twenties, gaining a few places, dropping a couple, then creeping up again. Far more crucial than any bulk order from Brian had been Tony Calder's insistence that free promotional copies be circulated to the country's two main ballroom chains, Mecca and Top Rank, both of which featured the earliest form of disco. Radio and TV might not have been playing "Love Me Do," but the teenagers were dancing to it.

By the time the Beatles returned home on November 15, the single was indisputably on its way, receiving greater promotional efforts from EMI, getting more radio plays and press mentions, being treated more and more as a pop rather than comedy single, and eventually peaking at number seventeen (albeit only in the chronically unreliable *Record Retailer* chart). Awaiting them were invitations to give performances both on national BBC radio and Radio Luxembourg, and also on three regional television programs with a combined broadcast area representing a good fifth of the whole country.

Mythology has it that Brian toned down and conventionalized the Beatles' appearance. But in truth, the quartet with which he presented Britain's TV viewers in late 1962 looked almost possessed of a sartorial death wish. Their stage suits, now pale rather than dark gray, had the Cardin-style round collars that Stu Sutcliffe had been so derided for in Hamburg. John's, Paul's and George's rather straggly, irregular "French" hairstyles had been barbered into identical, eye-fringing mops, and a fourth one issued ready-made to Ringo Starr. They were, in short, young males who in every essential visual detail resembled rather mature and out-of-date females. It was a moot point which was more foolhardy: the concealment of their foreheads or of their ties.

Equally outlandish was the air of democracy: no Cliff Richard–inspired lead singer, no obvious star, no one to decide on the instant that one liked or hated. Attention tended to settle first on Paul McCartney, at far left, playing the left-handed Hofner violin-shaped bass that was as much a novelty as his hair and suit, and already showing a gift for buttonholing the camera with his big puppy-dog eyes. George at this stage was no more than a bulb of hair and a thin, knobby guitar; Ringo, a background bulb of hair and a clatter. Rather like one of the panoramic cameras used for photographing Quarry Bank School, the eye tended to move in an arc, reaching John last of all, alone on the right.

Despite his transformed appearance, the stance was still that of lead Quarryman: feet planted apart, shoulders slightly hunched, face thrust forward and slightly upward in that old familiar blend of defiance and myopia. It was a pose somehow complemented by the stubby-necked Rickenbacker 325, which, in another splurge of affluence, had been fitted with a new bridge and refinished from "natural" ivory to glossy black. As both singer and harmonica player on "Love Me Do," he strummed no chords, merely slapped the guitar in time with one hand while his lips shaped the so-elementary words in a brittle cupid's bow. Only when he played the harmonica passages did he seem completely involved, his face softening above his crossed-over hands as who knew what tinny-voiced echoes of boyhood were blown back to him.

On November 26, the Beatles returned to EMI's Abbey Road Studios, if not yet conquering heroes then at least as professionals deserving respect from the men in white coats. To take maximum advantage of their minimal fame, George Martin wanted a follow-up single for release early the following year. However, this time there was no question of calling in "professional" songwriters. Among the Lennon-McCartney songs already demoed was a John song, written some weeks earlier in his Aunt Mimi's living room, amid the Coalport china and pedigreed cats. In its original form, it was a dramatic ballad after the style of Roy Orbison, ascending into ever higher regions of pleading and pain. For a title John reached back to the punning Bing Crosby lyric he used to love as a toddler with Julia: "Please lend your little ears to my pleas . . ." The song was called "Please Please Me."

At the November 26 session, this was pulled out of the drawer and, on Martin's advice, given a radically different treatment. The angstridden ballad turned into an exuberant all-out rocker by John and Paul in an Everly-Brotherly duet, punctuated by harmonica wails and throaty bass, its tone no longer lonesome or lovelorn but as jokey as any average Scouser trying to steer his "gerl" into a back alley for a knee-trembler. Indeed, the ascending chorus of "Come on . . . Come on . . . COME ON!" climaxing in a falsetto "Whoa yeah!" had all the mirthful exhilaration of orgasm in a cold wind. After a single take, Martin switched on the studio monitor from his control room and told the four they had their first number one record.

To learn the truth or otherwise of this prediction, they would have to wait until January; meanwhile, all that set the Beatles apart from a hundred other pop acts with half a hit was the tireless dedication and sheer chutzpah of their manager. This was never better shown than when Brian pitched them to Arthur Howes, then Britain's foremost promoter of pop package shows. He devoted hours of research and persuasion to finding out Howes's private telephone number, then rang up one Sunday night, correctly guessing it was the likeliest time to catch the promoter at home. This one cold call persuaded Howes to put them into a show at the Embassy cinema, Peterborough, on December 3, albeit with no payment other than traveling expenses.

For a group long used to knocking audiences dead with their live act, the Peterborough appearance was a severe humiliation. Top of the bill was Frank Ifield, whose number one single "I Remember You" had helped inspire John's harmonica riff on "Love Me Do." The so-called "fabulous Beatles" were bottom, ranking below the Lana Sisters and a xylophone duo named Tommy Wallis and Beryl. Their performance met with stony indifference from their East Midland audience and later was sternly criticized by the local paper, the *Peterborough Standard*, for being "too loud," especially in a number called "Twist and Shout." But Arthur Howes saw something in them and offered them a second national tour, this one headed by American stars Chris Montez and Tommy Roe, scheduled to last through most of March.

As Christmas approached, Brian drew up an elaborate full-page advertisement detailing the Beatles' "Year of Achievement" for *Mersey Beat* readers: their EMI contract and acquisition of a "recording manager," a "press representative," and a fan club; their radio and TV appearances; the far-afield venues they had played and major stars with whom they had appeared; the current UK chart position of "Love Me Do" at number twenty-one; the stop-the-presses news that in the *New Musical Express*'s annual popularity poll, they had come in fifth in the category of British Vocal Groups.

The two weeks between December 18 and 31 found them back in Hamburg, working off the last installment of their commitment to the Star-Club with palpable bad grace despite bigger-than-ever star treatment from Manfred Weissleder. "We could feel that they thought we were history already," Horst Fascher remembers. "Brian had been telling them it might be bad for their image to say they had worked in St. Pauli, and they better keep their noses clean. Paul kept telling John, 'Don't do that,' and John sometimes even listened, which I never saw before."

Midway through the irksome Christmas fortnight came a surprise: Patricia Inder turned up in Hamburg with a companion named Jean, ostensibly to see her friend Johnny Gustafson of the Big Three. "John's face lit up when he saw me," Patricia remembers. "He lifted me on his shoulder and carried me all around the Star-Club. Later on, after the Beatles had finished playing, he came to where I was sitting and threw a coat over both our heads, and we had a good snog. I couldn't understand why I kept getting all these filthy looks from Bettina, the barmaid."

Though full of the plans and possibilities of 1963, he did his best to convince Patricia they should go on seeing each other secretly at her friend Sue's flat, with the candles and fresh packs of chewing gum under the pillow. " 'It doesn't have to end,' he kept saying to me. If I'd been a bit older and wiser, I'd have kept on with him. But I was looking for love, and I knew that, the way he was going, I could only ever have a tiny part of John. It broke my heart, but I told him we had to finish."

On Christmas Day, since the Beatles had nothing else to do, Kingsize Taylor took them along to the special festive lunch provided by the dockside seamen's mission. "There were all the trimmings, turkey and Christmas pudding, and a blessing beforehand," Kingsize remembers. "When Grace was over, John shouted out 'Thank Christ for all this food. . . .' " Two days later, as a belated Christmas gift, "Love Me Do" reached its number seventeen peak in the UK. Elvis Presley was at number one with another of his bland post-army ballads, "Return to Sender"; Cliff Richard was number two with "The Next Time" and the Shadows number three with "Foot-Tapper."

That New Year's Eve, the Beatles bade farewell to their old life with a ragged, drunken performance on the Star-Club stage, captured for posterity by Kingsize Taylor's tape recorder. "We all had a meal first at the Mambo Schankey. As we left, I saw John pick up a knife and fork from the table and shove them into his pocket. When the Beatles come onstage, the first thing he does is pull out the knife and throw it at someone in the audience. Admittedly it was only a table knife."

The most crucial exposure that the Beatles had with "Please Please Me" was an ABC-TV pop show called *Thank Your Lucky Stars*, transmitted at 5:40 p.m. each Saturday. Their appearance, recorded on January 13 and shown six nights later, happened to coincide with the heaviest snowfalls for almost a century. The maximum number of teenage consumers were therefore gathered around the home hearth, eating high teas of eggs, chips, and baked beans on soggy toast drenched in thick brown sauce. Many scarcely even realized this was the same quartet that had recorded the cool, ironic "Love Me Do." For now, along with the crazy hair, bizarre necklines, and mutant violin bass, came energy and exuberance such as no homegrown pop group had ever dared show, on or off television. The call burst out of the black-and-white screen into some four million living rooms with beige-tiled fireplaces and plaster ducks flying up walls: "Come on! . . . Come on! . . . COME ON!" Britain's blue-collar youth needed no second bidding.

Reviews in the music and trade press—a vital factor in both wholesale orders and retail sales—reflected the same excited surprise. The all-important *New Musical Express*, in the person of disc jockey Keith Fordyce, said "Please Please Me" was "a really enjoyable platter, full of vigour and vitality," while the *World's Fair* prophesied, not inaccurately, that the Beatles had "every chance of becoming the big star attraction of 1963." From the day of its release, the single flew off the shelves with no market manipulation needed from NEMS of Liverpool. Nonetheless, the Beatles' own friends and family members were mobilized to push it along by every possible means. One of the most influential radio outlets was the BBC Light Programme's *Two-Way Family Favourites*, a record-request show for military personnel and their families posted overseas. According to John's cousin Michael Cadwallader, even Aunt Mimi was persuaded to send in a request for "Please Please Me" in the guise of a serviceman far from home.

Meanwhile, the Beatles were touring the snowy wastes of mid-land and northern Britain as the humblest and lowest-paid attraction on an Arthur Howes package show headlined by Helen Shapiro. In 1961, while they were far away in Hamburg, Shapiro had become the sensation of British pop—a fourteen-year-old London schoolgirl with a voice low and smoky enough to be mistaken for a man's. At sixteen, she was a cross between a diva and a Jane Austen heroine, following behind the tour bus in her own chauffeured limousine and sheltered from the crudity and loucheness of life on the road by a middle-aged chaperone.

The Beatles had the least prestigious position at the start of the show: an eight-to-ten-minute spot, allowing for perhaps four num-bers, that to St. Pauli's all-night ravers seemed to come and go with barely a blink. If not in dove-gray Cardin mode, they wore charcoal or black suits with high-fastening jackets on which the new deep-cut, button-down shirt collars sat as weightily as neck braces. In con-tinuing rebellion against their new bespoke image, John habitually left his top shirt button undone and his tie crooked; often before they went onstage, in an almost wifely—or motherly—gesture, Paul would stand him still and do up the button for him. After the last song, following Brian's formula, the three guitarists performed a synchronized low bow, steadying their guitar necks with one hand. "John's other hand would always be behind his back, doing some-thing it shouldn't," Neil Aspinall remembered. "Waggling its fingers or making a V-sign."

Aboard the bus, their knockabout humor was one of the few consolations for the long, slushbound journeys between gigs and the perishing cold. Even the precious Infanta Helen took to leaving the heated interior of her limousine and dodging her chaperone to sit beside John as he covered the steamed-up window with cartoon figures or rubbed a clear patch through which to make hideous grimaces at unsuspecting passers-by. Confident that fame was only just around the corner, he and Paul would each borrow a stack of Helen's giveaway photographs and retire to the backseat to practice signing autographs across her smiley, bouffant-crowned face.

On February 8, when the tour reached Carlisle, the Beatles made national headlines for the very first time. After that evening's performance at the ABC cinema, they accompanied their headliner to a dance organized by the town's Young Conservatives and were asked to leave for being inappropriately dressed in black leather jackets. On the scale of pop-star misbehavior, it was pretty trifling, especially compared with John's riper exploits in Hamburg. But Britain's newspaper readers were never to know them as badder boys than this.

On February 22, the *New Musical Express* chart showed "Please Please Me" sharing the number one position with Frank Ifield's "The Wayward Wind"; a week later, it occupied the summit alone. The Beatles had been notified of their triumph a few days in advance, so Bob Wooler could announce it at the Cavern when they played there on February 19 during a brief furlough from the Helen Shapiro tour. Wooler expected cheering and applause; instead, the entire three front rows of hardcore female fans burst into tears. For they knew they had lost their private idols forever.

For any pop act with a hit single, the next step was a 33 rpm, twelve-inch long-player, traditionally representing the poorest possible value for the money. Though available since the early fifties, LPs were still a minuscule part of the record business, selling only tens of thousands while singles sold millions. In the worlds of balladeering and jazz, where they were more classily known as albums, time and expense might be lavished to showcase the differing facets of a Sinatra, a Louis Armstrong, or a Johnny Mathis. With pop performers who got lucky, the LP was simply a means of recycling a chart hit and its B-side, augmented by a haphazard selection of cover versions and standards. The album cover would be a crude color photograph; on the monochrome reverse would be a list of the tracks, some biographical notes, and, if the product were from EMI, a recommendation to use Emitex cleaning solvent for keeping record grooves free of dust and fluff.

In setting up the first Beatles LP—preemptively titled *Please Please Me*—George Martin faced two problems. First, even with a chart-topper to their credit, EMI was unwilling to spend more than a pittance on the endeavor; second, their touring schedule left precious little time for working in the studio. On the plus side, however, was Martin's experience in recording shows and revues with an atmosphere of intimacy and spontaneity. Two singles and their B-sides

("P.S. I Love You" and "Ask Me Why") were already in the can, which meant cutting ten more tracks in short order. Having managed to assemble the Beatles at Abbey Road on November 11, Martin decided to record them as nearly like a live act as possible. He told them to play the best items from their stage act just as if the Cavern audience were watching, and switched his equipment on.

The result was a feat of stamina as impressive as anything Hamburg had ever seen. Although still tired from their long drive south through the snows, and racked by winter coughs and sniffles, they managed to complete the LP in a single all-day session, using no stimulants beyond tea and Zubes throat lozenges. Four of the tracks were John-Paul compositions: "I Saw Her Standing There," "Misery," "Do You Want to Know a Secret?" and "There's A Place." The others were their favorite left-field cover versions of black American pop.

Listening to the album today, one still catches the excitement of Paul McCartney's opening "One-two-three-FAW!"—the prelude to so many unbelievable things ahead. Almost every one of its fourteen tracks now seems fresh and surprising enough to have been issued as a single: from Paul's near-jazzy vocal on "A Taste of Honey," evoking all those modish "kitchen sink" films and plays, to the anomalously cheery teenage angst of "There's a Place" and "Misery," to the unabashed borrowings from black female groups, the Shirelles' "Baby It's You" and "Boys" and the Cookies' "Chains." The effect was the total opposite of usual shortchanging LPs, revealing how vastly more skillful and versatile and experimental and eccentric the Beatles actually were than had been revealed on their two singles to date, and also subtly suggesting the world they inhabited as well as the extraordinary range of styles at their command. Every song, every guitar note, every Scouse-thickened chorus of "Sha-la-la" and "Bop-shoowop" hinted what fun it was to be them.

Paul is, naturally, omnipresent and precociously brilliant, and George is in there too, far more than one appreciated at the time. But John is the dominant presence, as much so in backup as in lead: the chanting harmonica, the voice that keeps its rock-'n'-roll buzz through the most lovelorn ballads, the occasional note of sarcasm but more constant one of utter sincerity, the tough tenderness that now and again speaks directly to "You, girl." And John's is the show-stopping track, the Isley Brothers' "Twist and Shout," screamed out with such desperate abandon at the very end of the eleven-hour session that Martin had serious fears for his vocal cords. "I was always bitterly ashamed of it," he would recall, "because I could sing it better than that. . . . You can hear that I'm just a frantic guy doing his best."

John and Paul's own songs were by now accumulating in something more than a dog-eared school exercise book. Through George Martin, Brian met Dick James, a tubby, avuncular man who had recently turned to music publishing after a moderately successful career as a dance-band vocalist. James secured publishing rights to "Please Please Me" and its B-side, "Ask Me Why," as a quid pro quo for getting the Beatles' their all-important first appearance on *Thank Your Lucky Stars*. To ensure that subsequent John-Paul compositions did not go elsewhere, he came up with a plan that, for hidebound, grasping Tin Pan Alley, was little short of revolutionary. Rather than publishing their future work under the imprimatur of Dick James Music, at the standard minuscule royalty for sheet-music sales and radio plays, he set up a self-contained company, dealing exclusively in Lennon-McCartney songs and splitting the income, 50 percent to James and his business partner, 20 percent each to the composers and 10 percent to Brian. The company was called Northern Songs, a name redolent of newly modish factory chimneys and rain-shiny cobblestones.

Having now each enjoyed the triumph of having both their words and their music on a hit single, John and Paul might easily have evolved into autonomous songwriters, feeding the same group. But the habit persisted of working together, batting words and tunes back and forth, shuttlecock-wise, as they used to in the McCartneys' living room. "We wrote together because we enjoyed it," Paul would remember. "It was the joy of being able to write, to know you could do it. There was also the bit about what 'they' would like. The audience was always in my head, 'They'll dance to this' and such. So most of the songs were oriented just to the dances."

The habit also stuck of giving every song their joint byline, no matter how much one had contributed and how little the other.

The double credit, so they both felt, had an impressive, Broadway musical kind of feel to it, like Rodgers and Hammerstein or Lerner and Loewe. Their earliest efforts, listed in Paul's exercise book, had always been called "Lennon-McCartney Originals." On the *Please Please Me* album, their own songs were credited to "McCartney-Lennon"; thereafter, the formula reverted to "Lennon-McCartney," a brand ultimately ranking with Broadway's finest. To belong to such a fabulous creative entity might seem more than enough for any mortal. But years later, as its surviving member, Paul would reveal what bitterness he had always felt in coming second. "I wanted it to be McCartney-Lennon, but John had the stronger personality and I think he fixed things with Brian before I got there. That was John's way. He was one and a half years older than me, and at that age it meant a little more worldliness.

"I remember going to a meeting and being told, 'We think you should credit the songs to Lennon-McCartney.' I said, 'No, it can't be Lennon first, how about McCartney-Lennon?' They all said, 'Lennon-McCartney sounds better, it has a better ring.' . . . But I had to say 'All right, sod it'—although we agreed that if we ever wanted it could be changed around to make me equal."

At roughly the same time, another decision was taken that in years to come would store up further below-surface resentment, like Philip Larkin's "deepening coastal shelf." "It was an option to include George in the songwriting team," Paul would later admit. "I remember walking up past Woolton church with John one morning and going over the question. Without wanting to be too mean to George, should three of us write or would it be better to keep it simple? We decided we'd just keep the two of us."

As the Beatles' in-house publicist, Tony Barrow initially projected them according to pop-idol conventions of the time. Among his first presentational suggestions to Brian was rebranding them as John Lennon and the Beatles, to conform with the Cliff-Richard-and-the-Shadows stereotype. "Putting Paul's name out there as front man would have been just as OK with me, and I don't think Paul would have had any problem with it. But Brian explained very firmly that the Beatles weren't like that. They were a democracy."

A time-honored format for covering beat groups in music papers were Life Lines, or biographical questionnaires that each member filled in himself. The accepted tone was a mixture of earnestness in the boxes about musical taste and influences, and flippancy in the personal ones. John's Life Lines, as circulated by Tony Barrow, set a new standard in both categories:

Height: 5, 11. Weight: 11, 5 [159 lbs]. Colour of hair: brown. Colour of eyes: brown. Brothers, sisters: no. Age entered show business: 20. Hobbies: writing songs, poems and plays; girls, painting, TV, meeting people. Favourite singers: Shirelles, Miracles, Chuck Jackson, Ben E. King. Favourite actors: Robert Mitchum, Peter Sellers. Favourite actresses: Juliette Greco, Sophia Loren. Favourite foods: curry and jelly. Favourite drinks: whisky and tea. Favourite car: bus. Favourite clothes: sombre, Favourite [big] band: Quincy Jones. Favourite instrumentalist: Sonny Terry. Favourite composer: Luther Dixon. Likes: blondes, leather. Dislikes: stupid people. Tastes in music: R&B, Gospel, Personal ambition: to write musical. Professional ambition: to be rich and famous.

Where collective publicity like interviews or personal appearances were concerned, Barrow usually told Paul McCartney what was required and he rounded up the others. "Paul was a born diplomat, and always had an instinctive understanding of what journalists wanted. I tended to be a bit wary of John at the beginning. In his eyes you were his enemy until you'd proved yourself as his friend. It wasn't until later that I realized it was all bravado—that it came from a lack of self-confidence. John was the one of the Beatles it took me longest to get through to. But once that happened, he became the best friend I had in the group."

Despite having Barrow on the case full-time, Brian was open to anyone else who might have power to secure his boys a single additional column inch. Backstage at *Thank Your Lucky Stars* he had met Andrew Loog Oldham, a nineteen-year-old publicist who would later enjoy almost as spectacular a managerial career as his own. Oldham was already in partnership with Brian's original London PR rep, Tony Calder and, during early and mid 1963, he took over from Calder in the Beatles' media blitz.

With the national popular press still largely indifferent to youth culture, and the "quality" press seemingly not even aware of it, the best route to their target audience was through magazines produced specifically for teenage girls, such as *Jackie* and *Boyfriend*. Oldham therefore lost no time in taking them to *Boyfriend*'s office, just off Regent Street, and turning them loose on the magazine's staff writer, a stunningly attractive blonde-bouffanted nineteen-year-old named Maureen O'Grady. "We did a photo shoot with them in the little studio we had upstairs," she recalls. "Pop stars in those days tended to get a bit above themselves . . . wearing silk suits with camel-hair coats slung around their shoulders. Craig Douglas used to smoke a cigarette in a holder. But the Beatles were just so friendly and down-to-earth. They called me 'Mo' right away, as if I'd known them all my life.

"In one of the first pieces I ever wrote on them, I made a really silly mistake about John. I was so young and naïve that I assumed everyone had a mother and a father just like I did, so I mentioned John's mother without checking as if she was somewhere up there in Liverpool. When I next saw the Beatles, John said, 'There was something wrong in what you printed about me,' and then he took me on one side and explained that his mother was dead. I was very upset, and apologised, but he was perfectly calm and nice about it. Because I admitted my mistake and said sorry, he just forgave me and never mentioned it again."

Boyfriend's good opinion was so vital that Brian arranged for O'Grady and a photographer to go up to Liverpool and catch the Beatles in one of their very last ballroom appearances in the city, then join them afterward at the Blue Angel club. "That was the first time I ever saw how brutal John could be with Brian. I was with them in the dressing room when Brian came in, doing his efficiency number, like 'Now then, what's the running-order tonight?' John really laid into him . . . 'The music's our business, you just do the bookings and take your percentage. . . .' Epstein said nothing, just fiddled with a sheet of paper and drifted away."

More important than any print medium in first bringing the Beatles to national attention was the radio wavelength that had once
brought John *The Goon Show, Dick Barton—Special Agent,* and *Life
with the Lyons.* They had auditioned for the BBC Light Programme
back in February 1962, and passed, albeit with some reservations.
("Paul McCartney—no. John Lennon—yes," the producer jotted at
the time.) On January 26, 1963, they made their first appearance on
Saturday Club, a two-hour live performance show that John and Paul
had each listened to avidly on their Saturday-morning lie-ins since its
launch in the tea-chest-and-washboard era as *Saturday Skiffle Club.*

Sunday mornings brought further atypical swathes of live pop in
Easy Beat, an hour-long show, almost replicating *Saturday Club's* ten
million listeners, sandwiched between morning worship and *The
Archers.* Both programs—like TV's *Thank Your Lucky Stars*—were
emceed by Brian Matthew, a thirty-five-year-old former actor who,
unusually, combined the starchy tones of a classic BBC announcer
with a genuine interest in pop music and musicians. It was Matthew
who had bestowed the Beatles' highest accolade to date, calling them
"musically and visually the most accomplished group to emerge
since The Shadows."

Whether *Saturday Club* or *Easy Beat,* the format was the same. The
Beatles would give a live studio performance, without any technical enhancement, often reaching far back into their Hamburg repertoire for R&B or pop covers they no longer played onstage and
would never record. In between would come Goonish repartee with
an indulgent Brian Matthew that listeners soon began to enjoy as
much as the music.

JOHN (*shouting*): OK, Ring'?

RINGO (*in distance*): All right, John. Can you hear me?

JOHN (*to Matthew*): Can you hear him?

MATTHEW: Not really. I hope not.

JOHN (*in whisper, as if Ringo is geriatric patient*): We've brought you
the flowers.

RINGO: Oh, good.

JOHN: And the grapes.

RINGO: Oh, I like grapes.

PAUL: He likes grapes, you know.

JOHN: Brian's nose is peeling, listeners.

Among the PR duties entrusted to Tony Barrow by Brian, none was more important than preserving the fantasy of John's bachelor-hood. No Fleet Street newspaper of this era cared whether or not a newly successful pop musician was married and about to become a father. But to magazines like *Boyfriend*, it certainly was an issue. "Rumours started to go around that John had a wife hidden away up in Liverpool," Maureen O'Grady remembers. "But when I asked him if it was true, he always denied it. And on the tours and when the Beatles were down in London, he always acted like a totally free agent."

Brian's flat in Falkner Street had provided only a temporary answer to the Cynthia problem. After a couple of late-night scares from oddballs wandering in off the street, with John away and only little Dot Rhone to protect her, Cyn felt too nervous to continue living there. Showing the Stanley family's famous solidarity yet again, John's Aunt Mimi invited him to bring Cyn back to live at Mendips, where she could enjoy a peaceful and secure environment until the baby was born.

To minimize friction this time around, Mimi divided the house into two halves. John and Cynthia had the whole ground floor, enjoying sole use of the kitchen, morning room and drawing room, and sleeping in the former rear dining room. Mimi retreated upstairs, sleeping in the old student lodgers' room and cooking scratch meals on a Baby Belling stove in John's boyhood room above the front porch. The house's single bathroom also had to double as her makeshift scullery.

John's return to Mendips in his new persona of famous pop star caused excitement throughout the extended family circle that had helped to raise him. His cousin Michael Cadwallader remembers his distributing copies of the *Please Please Me* album as proudly as he used to hand round his cartoon strips and handwritten magazines. One early, impressive sign of his new wealth was taking Cynthia off to Paris for a delayed honeymoon: they stayed at the luxurious

George V Hotel—a place destined to recur in Beatles history—went shopping, and met up with Astrid Kirchherr for a boozy evening out that ended with all three of them passed out in bed together.

John was also quick to repay Mimi at least some of what she had spent on him. He paid off the balance of the mortgage on the house and bought a showy three-piece suite for the drawing room and numerous other luxuries and domestic gadgets, whether needed or not. Thanks to the guitar that she used to declare would never earn him a living, Mimi now knew financial security for the first time in her adult life. No more would that diamond engagement ring have to be pledged with the pawnbroker in Smithdown Road.

But the cost of having John at home again was Mimi's cherished peace and privacy. Local Beatles fans quickly divined his new address and took up permanent station in clumps of two and three, like industrial pickets, outside the front gate. In the whole of Mendips's quiet mock-Tudor life, even during the war years, its back door had never needed to be locked. Now, if Mimi left it ajar for even a minute, she would find her kitchen ransacked of plates and crockery by the house's souvenir-hungry besiegers.

Unlike modern first-time mothers, Cynthia attended no prenatal classes and received no preparation of any kind for giving birth and what lay beyond. And John on his fleeting visits home was either too buoyed up with excitement or dead with fatigue to worry about how she was feeling physically or how anxious or bewildered might be her state of mind. Even in pregnancy, he expected her to keep up the image he liked, for the odd moments when he might like to see it. Once while he was away on the road, a failure of communication at the hairdresser's led to Cyn's Bardot-length hair receiving a severe crop. When John came home and saw it, he refused to speak to her for two days.

With the Beatles as a foundation, Brian Epstein now began assembling a roster of Liverpool talent whose success rate would make the Larry Parnes stable of old seem broken-winded. In March, his second signing, Gerry and the Pacemakers, reached number one with "How Do You Do It?"—the sure-fire hit that the Beatles had so ungratefully rejected. In May, a third NEMS acquisition, Billy J.

Kramer and the Dakotas, reached number two with "Do You Want to Know a Secret?"—a ballad showing John and Paul at their cutest, which George had sung through heavy winter catarrh on the *Please Please Me* album.

The Beatles did not object to this diversification of their manager's energies or resent their fellow Merseysiders' success. It was John, in fact, who urged Brian to sign up the Big Three, the city's hardest rock combo, featuring his friend John Gustafson on bass. He was also friendly and encouraging to Priscilla ("Cilla") White, a sometime coat-check attendant at the Cavern, who sang with various bands around town, displaying a vocal power that could almost shatter glass. The Beatles backed Cilla—"Cyril," as John called her—at a first, unsuccessful audition for Brian at the Majestic ballroom in Birkenhead. Nine months later, after hearing her sing jazz rather than R&B, he put her under contract as Cilla Black, so creating one of the best-loved personalities in British show business.

The emergence of so many hitmakers and would-be hitmakers from the same faraway and hitherto obscure city opened Fleet Street's eyes to pop music as a source of news at long last. Stories began appearing with increasing frequency about what was dubbed the Mersey Sound or Liverpop. The accent that so many southbound entertainers over the years had tried to purge from their voices became the last word in new northern chic. All at once, it seemed, the country couldn't get enough Scouse.

Mimi would later recall her astonishment one night at seeing John on television, speaking in the thick, lugubrious "wacker" accent she had managed to keep at bay throughout his boyhood. "I was shocked to hear him. When he came home, I said, 'John, what's all this about, what's happened to your voice?'" His reply was to parody the broadest Toxteth or Dingle dialect—which pronounces *this* as "dis," *them* as "dem," and *there* as "dere"—both as a tease to Mimi and a reassurance that what she'd seen was quite deliberate and calculated. "'It's all dis-dem-dere, Mimi, dis-dem-dere,'" he said. And he'd do a little dance, a kind of Fagin act, rubbing his hands, and laugh and go "'Money, money, money.'"

"Ask anyone who knew him then . . . he didn't really talk like that.

I brought him up properly, not to talk like a ruffian. But John knew enough about the music world to put it all on. The fools believed he was really like that. The fools!"

There are few trickier tasks than finding a follow-up to a hit single, especially one as explosively original as "Please Please Me." The Beatles knew it might have been just a lucky shot they would be unable to repeat, and were all too aware of what must follow. Parlophone would halfheartedly underwrite a couple more attempts, then give up; like hundreds before them and thousands since, they would sink into the painful obscurity of one-hit wonders.

Their follow-up, "From Me to You," therefore repeated its predecessor's winning formula of Lennon harmonica and toppling falsetto, though with a more leisurely John-led harmony—an almost childlike "la-la-la da-da dum-dum-dum"—and a subtler, minor-chorded middle eight. Despite the sharp drop in power and risky foray into subtlety, it reached number one within two weeks of its release on April 11. The Beatles by this time had joined their second Arthur Howes national package tour, this one costarring two imported American heartthrobs, Tommy Roe and Chris Montez. As on the Helen Shapiro show a month earlier, the headliners found it progressively more of a struggle to keep their audiences' attention.

It was only after this second hit that the names of the individual Beatles became generally known. And, in those days, their names had the same novelty value as everything else about them. After the creaky artifice of pop-star pseudonyms—the Billys and Dickies, the Storms and Wildes and Furies—"John Lennon" and "Paul McCartney" had a refreshing candor. "George Harrison" indeed was almost too frank in its evocation of some cloth-capped war veteran playing dominoes in a pub with sawdust on its floor. Only "Ringo Starr" added a traditional touch of Yank-worshipping fantasy.

Now, too, came growing awareness that, as well as being bold enough to perform under their real names, John Lennon and Paul McCartney wrote songs, both for their own group and other artistes with whom they contested the charts. In addition to Billy J. Kramer's hit with "Do You Want to Know a Secret? the *Please Please Me* album inspired two further cover versions. Duffy Power, from the Larry Parnes stable, released a bluesy version of "I Saw Her Standing There," and Kenny Lynch recorded "Misery," which had originally been written for Helen Shapiro. For John, Lynch's soulful treatment was marred by the presence of Bert Weedon, doyen of British session guitarists—even though Weedon's "Play in a Day" tuition book had once been his bible. "I saw the Beatles up in Dick James's office, when he was presenting them with a set of cuff links each for 'Please Please Me,'" Lynch remembers. "John said to me 'What'd you want to have Bert Weedon on the session for? I would have played if you'd asked me.'"

On April 8, at Liverpool's Sefton General Hospital, Cynthia Lennon gave birth to an eight-pound boy. The delivery was a tricky one, as the umbilical cord was found to be partially wrapped around the baby's neck. John was still on the road with Tommy Roe and Chris Montez, and did not manage to get to the hospital until a week later. By this time, local Beatles fans had received seismic intelligence of the event and were staking out the front entrance, so he had to be smuggled through a service door in disguise. Unfortunately, Cynthia had been given a room with a glass partition looking on to the main maternity ward. John's reunion with his exhausted and still pain-racked young wife and first meeting with his newborn son thus took place before a grinning audience of patients and nurses.

The baby was named John Charles Julian, after his father, his maternal grandfather, and, indirectly, John's mother, Julia. In fact, he was always to be known as Julian. Yet again showing supportiveness far beyond any ordinary manager, and heedless of religious complications, Brian Epstein immediately volunteered himself as godfather.

John was as entranced and excited as any other young father by the tiny edition of himself he held in his arms that day. On his visits home, he liked to have baby Julian put into his arms, fresh from the bath, smelling of milk, new blanket, and talcum powder. He also liked to boast that Julian would not be brought up to be good-mannered, like him and his cousins Mike and David, but would be "a free spirit." However, the practicalities of parenthood had little appeal for him. When Cynthia changed a nappy, he had to leave the room; otherwise, he warned, he would vomit.

Cyn had hoped Julian's arrival would create more of a bond between Mimi and her during John's absences. Alas, Mimi's baby-caring days were now too remote for her to feel much empathy with her great-nephew—especially when he revealed a pair of lungs almost powerful enough to rattle the Royal Worcester on its shelves. To make matters still more tense, Cyn's mother, Lilian, was home from Canada for good, and naturally wanted to spend as much time as possible with Julian and her. Mimi and Lilian had not met since their row at the Powells' house three years earlier, and showed little more enthusiasm for each other now—but Lilian could not be denied access to Mendips and her grandson whenever she chose. Family visitors grew accustomed to finding them in the front lounge and Mimi in her first-floor bedsit, muttering about the "two fat, lazy lumps downstairs, quaffing bottles of Guinness."

Despite all the witnesses both inside and outside Sefton General, not a word about Julian's birth reached the ears of a single journalist, national or local. Round-the-clock monitoring by Brian and Tony Barrow ensured that John gave nothing away. And, once back on the road with Paul, George, and Ringo, he seemed to *Boyfriend* magazine's Maureen O'Grady as much "a free agent" as ever.

On April 21, the Beatles appeared as a special attraction in the *New Musical Express*'s annual poll-winners' concert at Wembley Empire Pool, for the first time actually sharing a stage with John's particular bêtes-noires, Cliff Richard and the Shadows. Before starting their third all-Britain tour in four months, there was time for a short holiday. Paul and George went to stay with their Hamburg friend Klaus Voormann at his family's vacation home in Tenerife. And John provoked amazement—and speculation that continues to this day—by going off to Spain alone with Brian Epstein.

Their ten-day trip has passed into legend as the point when Brian finally came clean about his alleged homosexual passion for John—and when John may fleetingly have reciprocated it. Whether or not one accepts that interpretation, the whole episode was bizarre in the extreme. Whatever Brian's private feelings, it was an inexplicable step out of his normally shy and decorous character, especially at a moment when John's first duty was so obviously to Cynthia and their newborn son—Brian's godchild. And John himself clearly needed little persuading, despite the furor it was bound to cause. "Cynthia [had had] a baby and the holiday was planned, but I wasn't going to break the holiday for a baby," he would recall. "I just thought what a bastard I was, and went."

But some believe he had a quite different agenda—notably Bill Harry, *Mersey Beat*'s founder-editor, who knew both John and Brian well at this time. According to Harry, Brian felt that to maximize the Beatles' teen appeal, Paul would have to be given the greater prominence onstage. "He wanted to change them from John's group into Paul's group. So he took John away to Spain so that they could have some privacy while he explained the whole thing to him." Paul McCartney, too, has come to believe the holiday had a political rather than sexual motive, but one dictated more by John than Brian. "John was a smart cookie. Brian was gay, and John saw his opportunity to impress on Mr. Epstein who was boss of the group. . . . He wanted Brian to know whom he should listen to."

John himself, while admitting to "a pretty intense relationship" with Brian during the ten days, claimed on the record to have been no more than a fascinated observer of his manager's very different lifestyle under the forgiving Spanish sun. "I watched Brian picking up boys, and liked playing it a bit faggy. We used to sit in a cafe in Torremolinos looking at all the boys, and I'd say, 'Do you like that one? Do you like this one?' I was rather enjoying the experience, thinking like a writer all the time, 'I am experiencing this. . . .'" One day, they unexpectedly ran into some visitants from a rather more wholesome summer holiday—Cliff Richard and the Shadows, who were making a record in nearby Sitges. "I turned around in a restaurant and saw Brian and John at a table on their own," Richard remembers. "We had no idea what they were doing there."

John later allegedly told his old schoolfriend Pete Shotton that Brian had made advances to him and that, out of a mixture of curiosity and pity, he had briefly responded. It was, in fact, not the first time he'd made such a claim, even though the young men who for years had shared rooms and even beds with him—not to mention the young women who had done likewise—all felt sure there was not a gay molecule in his whole body. Often it was done merely to shock, as with Horst Fascher back in April 1962, when Brian had personally delivered the Beatles to Hamburg to open the Star-Club. "I heard there was an English guy drunk in the next-door bar, who I first thought must be a musician," Fascher remembers. "But when I go in there, I find Brian Epstein sitting up at the bar, passed out cold with his head on the counter. So I go back into the Star-Club and tell John to come and help me get him out of there. When John comes into the place, he just picks up a half-empty glass of beer from the counter, pulls back Brian's collar and pours the beer down his neck. I asked him if that was any way to be treating the Beatles' new manager. 'It's OK,' John said to me. 'I already gave him one up the ass.'"

Brian himself seems to have given his version of the episode to one person only. This was his close friend Peter Brown, then manager of NEMS's Charlotte Street record store, later a crucial figure in the Beatles' retinue. Four decades later, Brown prefers still to maintain discreet silence, beyond the general observation that "Brian had a tendency to prefer oral sex." He disputes, however, that John accompanied Brian to Spain for political motives, to maintain his ascendancy within the Beatles. "It had nothing to do with advancement of career. John knew that he already had Brian as an ally; he knew that Brian liked him, was attracted to him and stimulated by his intellect. Anyway, I don't believe John was that manipulative. And the idea of going along with it, and trying to take advantage of it, just wouldn't have been Brian's way."

Years later, John finally came clean about what had happened: not to anyone who'd been around at the time, but to the unshockable woman with whom he shared the last decade of his life. He said that one night during the trip, Brian had cast aside shyness and scruples and finally come on to him, but that he'd replied, "If you feel like that, go out and find a hustler." Afterward, he had deliberately fed Pete Shotton the myth of his brief surrender, so that everyone would believe his power over Brian to be absolute.

On May 11, the *Please Please Me* album reached number one in *Record Retailer* magazine's chart, where it was destined to stay for virtually the rest of the year. A week later, the Beatles set off on yet another UK package tour with an imported American star as its theoretical headliner. The names originally mooted for this increasingly thankless task had included Duane ("Mister Twangy Guitar") Eddy, the Four Seasons, and—a particular idol of John's—Ben E. King, the Drifters' former lead singer. In the end, it was Roy Orbison, the Texan singer-songwriter whose suboperatic ballads had inspired John to write "Please Please Me." Even Orbison's giant voice, however, could not hold the audiences hungry for Beatles. After a few days, they were given his place at the top of the bill, an affront he took like a perfect gentleman. "You can't measure success," John would later reflect, "but . . . the moment I knew [Paul and I] were successful was when Roy Orbison asked if he could record two of our songs."

June saw the start of *Pop Go the Beatles*, a weekly radio show on the BBC Light Programme, transmitted live on Tuesdays at 5:00 p.m., the time-honored slot for *Children's Hour*. Its theme song, performed by the Beatles themselves, was a burlesque version of "Pop Goes the Weasel." Between numbers came some crunching verbal collisions between John and a hapless announcer named the Lee Peters, known behind his back as "Pee Litres."

ANNOUNCER: Something you may not know is that the boys are responsible for their own arrangements. Tell me, John, how did you get on to this next one?

JOHN (*in comically thick Liverpudlian-Irish*): Well, ye just git yer gitar and strrroom it like . . . ye know Mister . . . rrrock and rrroll loike . . .

ANNOUNCER: John, what's your secret?

JOHN (*in stage whisper*): We've got the box, Harry.

ANNOUNCER (*baffled*): Well, Harry, I hope you're very happy with the box. And now, in case I get "boxed in," here's a request from . . .

On the June 6 program, John led a chorus of "Happy Birthday to You" for Paul McCartney's twenty-first, twelve days later. To accommodate both Paul's friends and his large extended family, and also escape fans lying in wait on the doorstep, the party was not held at 20 Forthlin Road but in a pavilion in his Auntie Jin's back garden in Huyton. Among the guests were his new actress girlfriend, Jane Asher, fellow Merseybeat stars Gerry Marsden and Billy J. Kramer, the Cavern club's deejay Bob Wooler, and two of the Shadows, Bruce Welch and Hank Marvin, who were appearing in a summer show in Blackpool.

During the evening, Bob Wooler came up to John and made a teasing reference to his and Brian's recent Spanish "honeymoon." John reacted with an unthinking fury he had seldom shown even in Hamburg, punching Wooler repeatedly around the face and body. Alcohol undoubtedly took Wooler's gift for the mot juste a step too far. But it was still an extraordinary assault on one of the Beatles' greatest allies, as well as on an older and much weaker man.

John later claimed to have been "out of my mind with drink . . . Bob was saying 'Come on, John. Tell me about you and Brian—we all know. . . .' You know when you're twenty-one, you want to be a man. If someone said it now I wouldn't give a shit, but I was beating the shit out of him . . . and for the first time I thought 'I can kill this guy.' I just saw it like on a screen: if I hit him once more that's going to be it."

Paul's twenty-first had been ruined—and the Beatles' future might well have been also. The area in which Fleet Street did cover pop music was that of antisocial behavior. Every national paper would leap on the story of a hit-parader who at one moment played "Pop Goes the Weasel" in the BBC's *Children's Hour* slot and at the next beat up deejays in drunken frenzies. No one realized the possible disastrous consequences more clearly than did John himself. "I was [feeling] so bad the next day," he remembered. "We had a BBC appointment in London . . . and I wouldn't come. Brian was pleading with me to go and I was saying, 'I'm not. . . .' I was so afraid of nearly killing Wooler."

Wooler, who had suffered bruised ribs and a black eye, was dissuaded from suing for assault by an ex gratia payment of £200 and a contrite telegram sent by Brian in John's name: REALLY SORRY BOB TERRIBLY WORRIED TO REALISE WHAT I HAD DONE STOP WHAT MORE CAN I SAY?

The attack had far greater psychological effect on a shy, vulnerable character into whose life John and the others had brought the only genuinely bright spot. To the end of his life, he would never quite get over it.

In a skillful damage-control move, Tony Barrow did not try to suppress the story but instead fed a damped-down version of it to a friendly Fleet Street contact, the *Sunday Mirror*'s pop columnist, Don Short. Under the headline BEATLE IN BRAWL—SORRY I SOCKED YOU, Short obligingly wrote a story of anguished remorse: "Guitarist John Lennon . . . leader of the Beatles pop group said last night 'Why did I have to go and punch my best friend? I was so high [drunk], I didn't realise what I was doing. . . . Bob is the last person in the world I would want to have a fight with. I can only hope he realises that I was too far gone to know what I was doing. . . .'" No other paper bothered to investigate the story, no eyebrow even twitched at the BBC, and in a few days, amazingly, the whole affair had blown over.

"I had to agree John's quotes with him before I dictated them over the phone to Don Short," Barrow remembers. "He was muttering that he wasn't sorry at all, that he hadn't really been all that pissed, and that Bob deserved it." Groveling apologies against his will, for the general good, were something he would have to get used to.

PART III

A
GENIUS
OF THE
LOWER
CRUST

14

LEATHER TONSILS IN A THROAT OF STEEL

It just happens bit by bit, gradually, until this complete craziness is surrounding you.

n the midsummer of 1963, John was just another successful British pop musician among many. Within barely a year, he had become one of the four best-known faces on earth.

No strides to the front rank of fame—and then dizzyingly beyond it—were ever so quick or seemingly effortless. On October 13, the Beatles topped the bill in Britain's most prestigious TV variety show, *Sunday Night at the London Palladium,* and the condition known as Beatlemania entered the national vocabulary. On October 31, returning from a Swedish tour, they caused their first mob scenes at London Heathrow Airport. On November 4, at the Prince of Wales theater, they were the hit of the Royal Variety Show, captivating the Queen Mother and Princess Margaret and upstaging a galaxy of international talent, including Marlene Dietrich and Sophie Tucker. Two months later, America fell; by the year's end, they had mopped up the rest of the world.

Where Britain and Europe were concerned, the springboard was their fourth single, "She Loves You," released on August 23, which became their third consecutive UK number one. Ironically for a song destined to be almost inaudible in live performance, its lyric was somewhat of an experiment. Rather than the usual direct appeal of boy to girl, a well-meaning third party acted as go-between from a girl to a boy who mistakenly thought she had broken up with him. It was doubly ironic, therefore, that the tempests of female excitement were created by males singing to a *male*. The message intended to be whispered in someone's ear was perversely pounded out at top volume, its affirming cliché-cry of "Yeah!" given brand-new spin by being brazenly uttered in triplicate. With even less conversational logic, the chorus ended in the Little Richard–ish falsetto "Ooo!" that had already been tested in the middle eight of "From Me to You."

Though the song was full of recognizable Lennonisms (for instance, the meticulous scansion of "apol-oh-gise to he-er"), John always gave Paul full credit for a story line that might not readily have occurred to him. "[Paul] would write a song about someone. I'm more inclined to write about myself."

In any news-film miscellany of 1963, they are always there—the four little figures onstage in their knife-sharp suits and boots; the tiers of immature female faces contorted in rapture, adoration, or anguish; the screams that reach a new zenith each time the front three go "Ooo!" and shake their hair like manic feather dusters. There was, of course, hysteria on a similar scale when Frank Sinatra opened at the New York Paramount in 1942 and Elvis first shook his hips and curled his lip in 1955. Beatle-generated screams are not only louder and wilder but at a decibel level that can seem barely human, more like the squeal of navy bosuns' pipes a million times magnified. Half joyous, half dolorous, the awesome racket never ceases from the moment the four appear until long after they disappear: an atonal, almost rhythmic "eeeee! eeeee! eeeee!" that takes no account of anything they do or say and obliterates almost every sound they make.

But unlike the transports that greeted Sinatra and Presley, Beatle screams have no sexual element. This is not the noise of adolescent femininity, torn by confused desire and frustration, but of little girls keening over a deceased pet hamster or celebrating a brand-new teddy bear. Frank and Elvis had each performed under bombardments of scribbled telephone numbers and pairs of panties; at John, Paul, George, and Ringo, the fans throw jelly babies.

Fleetingly audible in the tearful eye of the hurricane will be John singing "Twist and Shout"—now lifted off the *Please Please Me* album to become the title track of an EP (a four-track mini-album) that reached number two in the UK singles chart. The audience has only to hear its slowed-down "La Bamba" bass riff to erupt into fresh frenzy, goaded by more hair-shaking *Ooo*'s and barnyard whoops and yelps. It is the dumbest as well as most unoriginal song the Beatles will ever perform, and John conveys his full appreciation of that fact even while giving it the same larynx-ripping intensity he did on record. "[He] must have grown leather tonsils in a throat of steel," says Tony Barrow's EP sleeve note, "to turn out such a violently exciting track." Often as he sings the dippy words, celebrating the passé dance—"C'mon, twist a little closer now"—his eyes take on a stony blankness, like some marble knight lying with folded hands for eternity in the hushed transept of a cathedral.

Several factors, working in strange harmony, transformed the Beatles from a purely adolescent preoccupation to a national talking point, then a national treasure. Of no small significance was that in 1963 the immemorial grip of Britain's upper classes finally appeared to loosen. All summer, the developing revelations of the Profumo scandal had shown those with posh accents to be just as capable of debauchery and dishonor as their basest social inferiors. Against the backdrop of randy Cabinet ministers, call girls, Russian spies, property speculators, and seedy "Society" osteopaths, the doddering complacency of Prime Minister Macmillan and his ministers, the constant smutty sniping of *That Was the Week That Was* and *Private Eye* magazine, newly chic northern honesty and plainspokenness seemed more refreshing than ever, especially when allied to youthful energy and charm. The social climate could not have been more auspicious for the Beatles to appear in the Royal Variety Show or for John's quip, as he introduced "Twist and Shout" to the boiled-shirt-and-tiara set, to delight the whole nation: ". . . people in the cheap seats, clap your hands . . . and the rest of you, if you'll just rattle yer jewellery."

Britain's national press was at last waking up to youth culture, its growing importance to the national economy and the power of its idols to stimulate circulation. And at this exact moment, providence delivered a pop group who were not the traditional grunting Neanderthals but unprecedentedly articulate and funny, who delivered good quotes in natural profusion rather than obliging reporters to manufacture them. They were also perfect comic relief from an otherwise unremitting diet of hard and often grim news: not only the continuing fallout from the Cuban missile crisis, the Profumo scandal, and Harold Macmillan's resignation, but also Britain's abortive efforts to join the European Common Market, the Greville Wynne spy case, and the Great Train Robbery.

Fleet Street coined the term Beatlemania and, from late 1963 onward, had a vested interest in its perpetuation. Here we are not speaking of tabloids in the modern sense but of "popular broadsheets," as the *Daily Express* and *Daily Mail* both still were: Tory trumpeters with enormous readerships throughout Middle England, which had never previously needed to pay attention to anyone under twenty-one except the teenage Derby-winning jockey Lester Piggott. Back in February, the *Express* had been particularly censorious over the Beatles' little brush with Carlisle's Young Conservatives, dwelling on the unsavoriness of their black leather jackets as though they were reincarnated Nazi storm-troopers. Now the same paper claimed credit for first putting "Beatlemania" into a headline, as if it were the scoop of the century.

Their second album, *With the Beatles*, was as much a social milestone as a musical one. The *Please Please Me* LP cover, a straight color portrait by Angus McBean, had shown four lads manifestly from pop's usual artisan class, grinning down over a balustrade in the stairwell at EMI House. On the cover of *With the Beatles*, those cheeky provincial interlopers were no more. Four serious, self-possessed faces cupped in high turtlenecks floated on a plain black background, each half in shadow like light and dark sides of adjacent moons. All of them, rather than just one, might have been sometime art students, if not male models straight from the pages of *Vogue* or *Town* magazine.

Here was an LP that could be carried as a fashion accessory, and whose authentic hard-core rock and soul ingredients (Chuck Berry's "Roll Over Beethoven," Barrett Strong's "Money," the Miracles' "You Really Got a Hold on Me") contrasted irresistibly with its aura of existentialist cool. From here on, the aura of proletarian vulgarity and shoddiness that Elvis and the Teddy Boys had given rock in 1955 vanished forever. Not only girls serving behind the counter at Woolworths but also girls preparing for their first London "season," not only boys sweating over factory lathes but also boys in their studies at ancient public schools or ivy-clad Oxbridge were now with the Beatles.

The album's release date, Friday, November 22, found the Beatles in Stockton-on-Tees, preparing for a one-nighter at the Globe Cinema. Around six p.m., a fellow musician came to their dressing room with the news, just flashed on the BBC, that President John F. Kennedy had been killed by a sniper as his motorcade passed through cheering crowds in Dallas, Texas. Kennedy was an inspirational figure to the British hardly less than to his own people, not merely for facing down Russia over Cuba but for his youth and glamour and the sense of idealism and optimism he had given the new decade. John would later remember how numbed with shock all four of the Beatles were, although that night's show still had to go ahead as planned. For the first time—but alas, not the last—America and Britain had lost a hero in common, millions on each side of the Atlantic feeling such unified grief and disbelief that they would always remember exactly where and in what circumstances they first heard the news.

Even Britain's mourning for Kennedy cast no serious shadow on Beatlemania. A week later, the fifth Beatles single, "I Want to Hold Your Hand," instantly went to number one on advance orders of a million copies, finally ending the long supremacy of "She Loves You." The same happened in the album charts, where *With the Beatles* and *Please Please Me* stood at number one and two respectively. With these unprecedented statistics came an equally astounding critical accolade. The *Times*'s classical music critic, William Mann,

named Lennon and McCartney as "the outstanding English composers of 1963," and commended them for having "brought a distinctive
and exhilarating flavour into a genre of music that was in danger of
ceasing to be music at all."

Mann's unsigned eight-hundred-word article created a sensation
matched by few other pieces of twentieth-century criticism. Never
before had the world of classical music regarded that of chart-busting
pop with anything but snobbish incomprehension. It was all the
more extraordinary for appearing in the "top people's paper," an
establishment bulletin board so wedded to stuffy tradition that the
front page was still covered with classified ads for domestic servants
and prep schools.

The most widely quoted passages would be those where Mann
gave musicological definitions to vocal and instrumental effects John
and Paul had hit on by instinct or accident—the "major tonic sevenths and ninths," the "flat submediant key-switches," the concluding "Aeolian cadence" in "Not a Second Time," which, so they now
learned, had the same chord progression as the end of Mahler's *Song
of the Earth*. But Mann was also strangely clairvoyant—predicting
the Beatles' American conquest weeks before it was even remotely
on the cards. And both his higher-tuned powers of aural perception
and his command of English resulted in a far more vivid, thought-
provoking critique than any pop reviewer had yet managed. He was,
for instance, the first to notice the greater complexity and subtlety
of Beatles B-sides than their million-selling A-sides, as if a Graham
Greene–like decision had been made to separate experimentation
from pure entertainment.

No analysis could have been sharper of "the . . . often quasi-
instrumental vocal duetting, sometimes in scat or falsetto, the me-
lismas with altered vowels ('I saw her yesterday-ee-ay') which have
not yet become mannered, and the discreet, sometimes subtle, vari-
eties of instrumentation—a suspicion of piano or organ, a few bars of
mouth organ obbligato . . . the translation of African blues or American western idioms into tough, sensitive Merseyside."

Mann, at this stage, had not met John and Paul or seen them in
live performance, yet somehow understood the balance of power

between them. "How Lennon and McCartney divide their creative responsibilities I have yet to discover," he wrote, "but it is perhaps significant that Paul is the bass guitarist of the group."

What captivated and fascinated Britain in late 1963 was not just a pop group more extraordinarily and unstoppably successful than any before. It was the new definition of "pop group" they had created, something closer to the Marx Brothers than any forerunners like the Blue Caps or Shadows—a gang laughingly on the run from overblown adulation and desire, a brotherhood that in the brightest glare of publicity still kept its own intriguing secrets, the ultimate impenetrable clique. And within that magic circle were four individuals who might have been handpicked by central casting to appeal to every shade of temperament in their public: the clever one; the sweet, pretty one; the shy, serious one; the haplessly adorable runt of the litter.

Later eras of mindless celebrity worship and voyeuristic tabloid journalism would see nothing like the British media's first obsession with the Beatles. Day after day came stories of their new feats in the charts and the shrieking and mobbing of their fans, and still the public clamored to know more: how barbers throughout the land were besieged by demands for Beatle cuts; how sales of toy plastic guitars and black turtleneck sweaters were booming; how, thanks to them, the nearly defunct corduroy-manufacturing industry had experienced a renaissance; how their private Liverpool slang—"fab" and "gear" for *good*, or "grotty" (a contraction of "grotesque") for *bad*—now tripped off tongues from the salons of Mayfair to the remotest Outer Hebridean island.

To whatever was going on, however far from the haunts of screaming youth, they were an infallible touchstone. Any publicity-seeking parliamentarian, any vicar composing a parish newsletter, any headmaster's speech-day pep talk had only to mention their name—only quote the "Yeah yeah yeah!" from "She Loves You"—to be certain of attracting headlines. No one was immune from their spell, or wished to be. Public figures from the Duke of Edinburgh to Earl Montgomery of Alamein stood in line to voice an opinion of them. Psychologists wrote learned articles about their effect on teenage

girls and the significance of jelly babies as "an unconscious preparation for motherhood."

Naturally there were dissenters—retired army colonels in the
shires who lamented that a world war had been fought and won for
this; boys' schools that outlawed Beatle cuts on pain of expulsion;
left-wing intellectuals who contributed essays called "The Menace
of Beatledom" to rarified weekly reviews. But the mass-circulation
press had entered into an unspoken covenant to print nothing negative about them. Besides, whatever the controversy, it tended to
evaporate in the face of the Beatles' own personal qualities: their
innocent high spirits, their enthusiasm, their honesty, their modesty,
the unfailing quick wit that never overstepped the bounds of politeness. You can see them working almost telepathically together in
a primitive video clip, as yet another middle-aged, plummy-voiced
inquisitor thrusts a microphone toward Ringo and poses the same
old question: just why are they called the Beatles?

RINGO: John knows, and he'll tell yer . . . now.

JOHN: Erm, well it's just a name, isn't it? Like "shoe."

PAUL: There you are, we could have been called the Shoes for all
you know . . .

What we now know as pop "culture" was still years in the future.
The setting for the Beatles first fame was the red plush darkness of
theaters and cinemas that still offered their customers live "variety"
in addition to films. As much as rockers, they were minstrels that
John's namesake grandfather would have recognized, albeit white-
faced and electrified. One of the earliest marks of their success was
a Beatles Christmas Show staged by Brian Epstein at the Finsbury
Park Astoria cinema, in which they performed spoof Victorian
comedy sketches besides rolling out their hits. A television appearance with Morecambe and Wise on December 3 had them in striped
blazers and straw boaters, joining the comedy duo for a rendition of
"On Moonlight Bay." Before becoming the world's most adored rock
band, they were Britain's last great music hall turn.

While his shows rocked the roof and his songs burned up the charts, John's domestic arrangements remained as make-shift as ever. Though he now spent the greater part of each week in London, his wife and son were still up on Merseyside, officially nonexistent and leading a life as different from his as chalk from Camembert.

The situation had, indeed, become so riven with female politics that John preferred to emulate other retiring menfolk in his family and keep out of it as much as possible. At Mendips, tensions between Cynthia and her mother downstairs and Aunt Mimi upstairs had finally become too much for everyone concerned; Cyn and Lilian had removed baby Julian to their home territory of Hoylake, leaving Mimi in peace and order once again with her Coalport china and her cats.

By now in Fleet Street, a story that had not raised a flicker of inter-est six months earlier loomed large on every popular paper's news list. Cynthia and her mother had scarcely regained possession of their old home when they were doorstepped by journalists seeking to discover if the love object of a million British schoolgirls really had gambled his future by taking a wife. The *Express* finally managed to corner Cyn and put the challenge directly; though she admitted nothing, there was corroboration enough for the banner headline BEATLE JOHN IS MARRIED.

To soften this supposed devastating blow to the Beatles' core audi-ence, John formally owned up via a "life story" in *Mirabelle* magazine on October 12. Though clearly ghostwritten, it was stronger stuff than the usual teen-mag pap, leading off with the "awful tragedy" of losing his mother "before my fourteenth birthday" (it had been before his eighteenth), paying tribute to Mimi for raising him, and painting a fond picture of "her frilly curtains and her apple tree." Cynthia was slipped in anonymously, between Hamburg and Ringo joining the group.

I think by the way Paul's eyes kept flashing he too liked the German girls but me, I had different ideas. My girl was at home in Liverpool . . . A little while later we were married. I love her. As I'm away such a lot, she lives with Aunt Mimi. I'd like to tell you more about her but I've this old-fashioned idea that marriage is a private thing, too precious to be discussed publicly. So forgive me and understand.

For months it had been obvious that all the Beatles needed to settle permanently in London, to be as close as possible to Brian's transplanted NEMS Enterprises office, George Martin, Abbey Road, the BBC, the beckoning world of filmmaking, and the jumping-off point for overseas ventures soon to come. With Cynthia's Hoylake cover blown, there was no reason for John to delay the move any longer, much as he might have preferred to. His life in the metropolis would have to become a family man's.

To save on hotel expenses, Brian had rented his boys a mews flat in Green Street, Mayfair, a few doors from the elegant block where he himself was about to take up residence. This was, however, just a crash pad, suitable only for the two most undemanding and unattached Beatles, George and Ringo. After a brief, discontented stay there, Paul found an alternative address providing both an almost impregnable refuge from fans and a quantum leap up the social ladder. The father of his girlfriend, Jane Asher, was a consultant psychiatrist whose home as well as office was a Regency house in Wimpole Street, Marylebone. Here Paul now lived as a nonpaying guest, sharing the top floor with Jane's brother, Peter. Her mother, an accomplished musician who'd once given oboe lessons to George Martin, also made the basement available for Lennon-McCartney songwriting. Strange to think of those early London-era tracks gestating in the street where Robert Browning wooed Elizabeth Barrett, set about by brass plaques for expensive dentists and urologists.

John, by contrast, ended up in busy, noisy, tourist- and student-ridden South Kensington. He owed the choice to Robert Freeman, the young photographer who (with an obvious debt to Astrid Kirchherr) had created the half-shadow group head shot for the cover of *With the Beatles*. Freeman lived in Emperor's Gate, one of the warren of faded grand Victorian terraces between Hyde Park and Cromwell Road. During a house-hunting visit to London by John and Cynthia in late 1963, he mentioned that the flat above his was vacant. The

pair viewed it and, despite several all-too-obvious drawbacks, took
it immediately.

The accommodation would now be termed a duplex but in those
days was called a maisonette: two floors at the top of a porticoed
house, accessible only by winding communal stairs. The bedroom
overlooked the West London Air Terminal; at the rear lay an open
stretch of Underground line, with noisy trains passing constantly in
both directions.

Socially, however, the location could hardly have been better. As
an in-demand photographer—an occupation fast acquiring some of
the glamour of pop stardom—Bob Freeman knew everyone who
was anyone around town, from Peter Cook to the editor of the
Sunday *Times*'s color magazine, Mark Boxer. Freeman's wife, Sonny,
was a model, with impish looks and a rangy physique that perfectly
set off the new "fun" fashions of young designers like Mary Quant.
In 1964, photographed by her husband in a man's blue denim shirt,
she would become one of the first images in the groundbreakingly
erotic Pirelli calendar. Sonny had been born in Berlin but, growing
up in Britain in postwar years, preferred to say she was Norwegian.
The Freemans' apartment, it so happened, was mostly paneled in
wood.

Bob and Sonny Freeman gave John and Cynthia their first entrée
to new London clubs, nothing like the brown leather mausoleums
of Pall Mall and St James's, whose entry requirement was not to be
an earl or an archbishop, but young, famous, and fashionable. The
four went out together almost every night, joining the small coterie of actors, fashion models, painters, and photographers who were
changing the word *in* from a preposition to an adjective.

Above the Prince Charles Cinema, just off Leicester Square, was
the Ad Lib, the first club to cater specifically to moneyed young pop
stars, with a resident disc jockey and a sound track of hard-core R&B.
One night, the in-crowd included John's boyhood heroes the Everly
Brothers and his Dovedale Primary schoolmate Jimmy Tarbuck,
now exploiting the nation's infatuation with Scouse humor to brilliant effect as a stand-up comedian. With an echo of his old Teddy
Boy truculence, Tarbuck told John to "bow down and worship" Don

and Phil Everly as the inspiration for the Beatles' vocal harmonies. "Yeah," John readily agreed. "I love the Ev's."

Sonny Freeman remembers John as "very cheeky but very impressionable. . . ." One of the things that impressed him a lot was that Bob had been to Cambridge University. John seemed almost envious of that. He loved to discuss books and films and art, and I realised that under the clowning and joking he was really quite deep." Often after a night's clubbing he still wouldn't be tired, but happily sat up until dawn in the Freemans' wood-paneled apartment, talking to his beautiful faux-Norwegian neighbor "about things like life and death, the way you always do when you're young."

In fact, Sonny had no reason to be secretive about her German birth. During the war, her father had been the stoutly anti-Hitler Mayor of Breslau, and had paid for his courage with his life. "One night I told the story to John, how my father had been shot dead by a Nazi gauleiter. During the same conversation, I remember John saying he didn't think he was going to live very long—that he had a premonition he'd be shot, too."

There were also outings to restaurants, if not with Brian then with George Martin and his secretary, soon to be wife, Judy Lockhart-Smith, whose top-drawer accent was a source of endless delight to John. The urbane Martin tried to break down some of his northern gastronomic prejudices, urging him at least to try more exotic menu items and see if he liked them. One such evening brought his first, suspicious encounter with sugar snap peas, the miniature variety you eat in their pods. "I'll try them," he told Martin, "but put them over there . . . not near the food."

Being rich was as yet only a vague sensation in comparison with the daily, oppressive reality of being famous. Like all the Beatles, John still had no clear idea of how much he had earned, was earning, or might be expected to earn from the huge gross income accruing to the Beatles in performance fees, record royalties, and the labyrinth of merchandising deals set up by Brian for everything from Beatle jackets to Beatle-themed cupcakes, not to mention the separate royalties John divided with Paul as sole suppliers of material to Northern Songs. All his major living expenses were taken care of by

Brian's office, from which—somewhat recalling pocket-money days with Aunt Mimi—he received £50 in cash per week. Like the hero of Mark Twain's story "The £1,000,000 Bank-Note," he discovered the strange truth that the richer one becomes the less obligation there seems to pay for anything. Clubs he visited pressed free drinks on him, restaurants automatically waived bills, guitar makers sent him their choicest new models simply for the glory of his patronage.

He bought himself presents all the time, seldom looking twice at them at the point of sale, let alone afterward, usually directing that the bill—if there was one—be sent to that comforting, auntlike entity, "the office." Like royalty, he had no need to carry money and, as a result, had no sense of rolling in it. "I never see more than £100 [about £1,000 today]," he told one interviewer. "I never use money because I'm always being taken around."

Some evenings he preferred to forsake the in-crowd for more traditional celebrities whom he'd met through *Sunday Night at the London Palladium* and the Royal Variety Show, and continued to meet simply by hanging out with his manager. Though now the dominant force in British teen culture, Brian saw himself essentially as a West End impresario in the tradition of Lew Grade and Bernard Delfont. His headquarters were in Argyll Street, right next door to the Palladium Theatre, and his support team included London's top show-business lawyer, David Jacobs. Since Jacobs was of the supersmooth legal breed whose clients become personal friends, this put John into the same social circle as Liberace, Judy Garland, Eartha Kitt, and Zsa Zsa Gabor.

Chief among such older showbiz pals was Alma Cogan, a singer who had topped Britain's pre-rock-'n'-roll hit parade, billed as the Girl with the Giggle in Her Voice. (At art college, John loved to parody her 1958 single, "Sugartime," accompanied by his worst village-idiot grimaces.) Though the hits were long gone, she remained a vibrant and popular figure, living with her mother in Kensington High Street and keeping more or less permanent open house for fellow entertainers in a flat stuffed with kitsch red glassware and Spanish flamenco dolls. All the Beatles loved these soirees with Sara Sequin, as John nicknamed her, when they would hobnob with the likes of

Lionel Bart and Bruce Forsyth, be served tea and dainty sandwiches by her mother, and often end the night with an old-fashioned party game like charades.

Though most male suitors were kept firmly at arm's length, Alma's younger sister, Sandra, now says that John and "Sara Sequin"had a passionate affair—mostly conducted at West End hotels, where they would register under aliases like "Mr and Mrs Winston"—and that Cyn never found out about it. To complicate matters, Brian also developed an infatuation with Alma, to the point of wavering back toward heterosexuality; he took her to Liverpool to meet his parents and talked openly of marrying her and "settling down." That would have spelled a very different future for him and possibly John also; however, nothing came of the idea, and Alma was to die from cancer in 1966, aged thirty-four.

The closely guarded secret of John's new London address did not last long. Within only days of his arrival in Emperor's Gate, a permanent picket of girls had formed outside the Grecian portico of number 13. No matter what time John and Cynthia went out or came home, the same chorus of squeals and thicket of autograph books would be there to greet them. Downstairs, the house's only other tenants, Bob and Sonny Freeman, acted as unwilling concierges, answering dozens of rings on the doorbell each day or expelling unauthorized intruders from the communal hallway. Unfortunately for Sonny, she had blonde hair similar to Cynthia's and a small son, Dean, who was the same age as Julian. Often when she took Dean into nearby Hyde Park, she would find herself followed and Dean's stroller mobbed in mistake for that of the Beatle baby.

In these days, celebrities were not dogged night and day by scandal-ranking press columnists and paparazzi even in London, never mind outside. As the virtually open affair with Alma Cogan demonstrated, John could philander as much as he liked, secure in the knowledge that it would never get back to Cyn. On the road, his conquests included Maureen Kennedy, lead singer with the Vernons Girls, a sexy song-and-dance troupe originally formed by Vernons Football Pools in Liverpool. "While John was onstage, Mo would make me stand in the wings and hold her hand while she watched him," fellow Vernons

Girl Frances Lea remembers. "When he sang "This Boy" in that slow, smoochy way, her nails used to dig into my palm until it hurt."

On a tour of the Channel Isles, just before Beatlemania broke in earnest, he ran into an interesting old acquaintance, the poet and erstwhile paperback writer Royston Ellis. According to Ellis, he, John, and a female third party ended up bed together for a sexual romp featuring black oilskins and polythene bags, so planting the seed—as it were—of a song destined to emerge five years later. More prosaically, the poet offered a remedy for an infestation of crab lice John had picked up in the unhygienic toilets of theater backstages and cheap hotels.

Not all his amours were so tactfully far-flung. He also began a casual affair with Sonny Freeman, which Cynthia never suspected even though they were all living in the same house—one that would remain secret even after Sonny's Norwegian connection and her wood-paneled flat had been transmogrified into a classic Beatles track.

Those whom Fate decides to make rich and famous discover sooner or later it is not the storybook happy ending they had always thought but merely a threshold to unimagined new problems, pressures, and dissatisfactions. And for John, once he had all the recognition he could ever seek, all the sex he could ever desire, all the expensive food and drink he could ever consume, all the shiny new guitars he could ever play, and all the many-colored, vari-collared shirts he could ever wear, the promised land was quicker than usual to reveal its drawbacks.

Being greeted by wilder acclaim than any other musical performer in history every time he stepped onstage might appear the ultimate artistic satisfaction. Initially, as any other twenty-three-year-old would, John found the mayhem of Beatles concerts exhilarating and the antics of the fans hilarious. But after a while, the sheer mindlessness of it all—the moronic perverseness of people claiming to love his music, lining up for hours to hear it, then drowning it in shrieks—turned his amusement to bafflement, frustration, and finally anger. It so happened that, for the very first time since he took the stage at the Woolton fete, he was seeing his audience without the help of glasses. Back in April, on the Roy Orbison tour, an Orbison band member named Bobby Goldsboro (later a successful singer-songwriter) had introduced him to the modern ophthalmic marvel of contact lenses.

Though he mostly kept up his blank marble-effigy look, there were moments when he showed his opinion of his fans' intelligence level in the way his former Quarry Bank classmates and fellow art students knew so well. Amazingly, no one among the thousands present was offended, indeed no one even seemed to notice when, in place of the regulation bow, he responded with a toothless village-idiot leer, stomping one leg on the stage as if it were malformed and clapping his hands with both sets of fingers curled into "spassie" claws.

Backstage, too, there were ordeals that had never existed when the Beatles were straightforward teenage idols. The most wearisome part of every show for John was the procession of local dignitaries and VIPs Brian would usher into the dressing room beforehand or afterward. No matter how overbearing, condescending, or plain ridiculous their behavior, he always had to be Beatlishly charming and polite. "It was awful—all that business was awful," he would remember. "One has to completely humiliate oneself to be what the Beatles were, and that's what I resent. . . . I didn't know, I didn't foresee; it just happens bit by bit, gradually, until this complete craziness is surrounding you and you're doing exactly what you don't want to do with people you can't stand; the people you hated when you were ten."

The Royal Variety Show, seemingly the Beatles' highest point to date, was for John the most distasteful bout of knuckling under yet forced on him. His perfectly pitched "rattle-yer-jewellery" line to the assembled Royals and bigwigs, in his own mind, represented only cowardice and compromise. "I was fantastically nervous," he would recall, "but I wanted to rebel a bit and that was the best I could do." In fact, he had been tormenting Brian with a threat to say "rattle yer fuckin' jewellery." On the old video recording, as the delighted applause ripples out, you see him almost pull one of his "spassie" faces, then obviously think better of it. Significantly, although the Beatles were approached every subsequent year until almost the decade's end, they never appeared in another Royal Variety Show.

For the most part, as their former press officer Tony Barrow recalls, John gritted his teeth and did whatever PR stuff was necessary, putting the good of the group as a whole before his own feelings. The good nature and impulsive kindliness of which he was capable could sometimes rescue the dodgiest PR stunt, as when *Boyfriend* magazine's readers were offered a "date" with the Beatles as a competition prize. It was meant to be at a secret rendezvous, the Old Vienna restaurant in Bond Street, but inevitably the word got out and the place was besieged by screaming fans. "John turned up very late, with soaking wet hair and obviously in a foul mood," *Boyfriend*'s Maureen O'Grady remembers. "But once he saw the rather scared little girls who were supposed to have 'won' him, he couldn't have been nicer."

As always, the danger-zone loomed when he had one too many of the exotic new drinks, the fine wines, vintage Cognacs, Scottish malts, and Russian vodkas pressed on him everywhere he went. As always, just one or two hits turned friendly, kindly, generally reasonable John into moody, bellicose, and cruel John, oblivious of how much noise he made, whom he insulted, or how innocent and defenseless might be the victim of his cat-o'-nine-tails tongue. "When we came home late at night, there was always a girl waiting for John who was a bit disabled," Sonny Freeman remembers. "If he was drunk, he'd just tell her to piss off. I'd say, 'John, be nice. You could at least give her an autograph.' He'd say, 'But I've given her twenty-five already.'"

There was also the thoughtlessly malicious John that the Australian entertainer Rolf Harris encountered as emcee of the first Beatles Christmas Show. "Before they came on, I did my Australian routine, telling the audience different Aussie words and explaining what they meant," Harris remembers. "One night while I was on, John was standing in the wings, and had somehow got hold of a live mike. With everything I said, his voice would come booming over the PA: 'Is that right, Rolf? . . . Are you sure about that, Rolf?' It fair knocked

me through a loop. As soon as I came off, the Beatles went on, so I
had to wait to the end of their show to have it out with John but I was
still so mad, I was spitting chips. I said, 'Look, if you want to fuck up
your own act, that's your prerogative, but don't fuck up mine.' John
just turned on the charm: 'Ooh, look . . . Rolfie's lost his rag. . . .'
Being angry with him was like trying to punch away a raincloud."

If the pressures on John were colossal and unremitting, no newly
minted young megastar could have had—and none since has had—a
better support structure. Brian was not only unique as a manager
in integrity, conscientiousness, imagination, and good taste; he also
collected around him people for whom running Britain's biggest-
ever musical money-spinner was not a business (as their uniformly
modest salaries proved) but a vocation.

The prime example was their record producer, George Martin,
by a long way the greatest altruist and—other than Brian—the most
all-round gentleman in pop music history. From his initial position
of absolute power at Abbey Road Studios, there were any number of
ways in which Martin could have exploited the Beatles. Other producers with far less input into the music would have claimed a share
of Lennon and McCartney's songwriting credit and thus a third of
the royalties, or sneaked B-sides written by themselves onto the reverse of each chart-busting A-side, or (with Brian's other main Liverpool acts also on board) sought personal glory for having invented
the Mersey Sound. Instead, Martin remained a background figure
who selflessly devoted his musical skills to nurturing and developing
John and Paul's unschooled talent, pruning and shaping the rough
material they brought him, translating their ideas into reality, turning the precious ore into perfectly cut diamonds.

In contrast with the huge retinues of modern bands, the Beatles
traveled with just two roadies—then more formally known as road
managers. The loyal, overburdened Neil Aspinall had now been
joined in the task by Mal Evans, a Liverpool Post Office engineer
and part-time bouncer at the Cavern club. Between them "Nell"
and gentle giant Mal took care of everything a small army would
nowadays be deployed to do in getting the Beatles to gigs, through
the crowds, and on and off stage: they drove the vans, humped

the equipment, liaised with house managements, supervised security, checked the (rudimentary) sound and lighting, set the stages, brought in food, drink, and whatever else their charges required, and, most crucially, policed the backstage areas and dressing rooms. Friends but not equals, servitors but never servile, Neil and Mal would stay with the Beatles as long as there was any kind of road to be managed; they were the little bit of down-to-earth Liverpool the four carried with them to inconceivable summits, trusties where no one else could be trusted, a breath of sanity and normality even where the madness seemed most overwhelming.

But the most vital defensive resource they had was their own friendship. Whereas extreme fame tends to blow rock bands apart, it only welded the Beatles more tightly together. There were disagreements, even fights, but, at this stage, no politics; as with D'Artagnan and the Three Musketeers, or William, Ginger, Henry, and Douglas, it was "all for one and one for all." Eyewitnesses recall moments when they would close ranks against some overintrusive journalist or guest VIP, all with never an impolite word spoken or a slackening of their friendly, charming Beatleness. A signal would be sent to one of the road managers—usually blunt-spoken Neil—and the offender would be shown the door with all four moptops seemingly mortified to see him go.

After years of sharing bedrooms—and often beds—they had the innocent physical intimacy of puppies sprawled over each other in a basket. Paul McCartney recalls how on one nighttime van journey northward in freezing fog, with Mal Evans at the wheel, a stone shattered the windscreen. Mal simply punched a hole through the broken glass and pressed on at about three miles per hour through the fog with only the curb to guide him. The sole defense the four Beatles had against the resultant icy wind was a bottle of whiskey. Finally, the cold became so bad that they lay on top of each other in a vertical pile, warming themselves with their own collective body heat. When the one on top was nearly frozen, he would change places with somebody lower in the pile.

When the four performed badly onstage or in the recording studio, rather than recriminate against one another, they would turn on

their roadies, blaming some, usually nonexistent, fault in the lighting, sound, or equipment. "That was what I called Road Manager's
Syndrome," Neil Aspinall said. "Soaking up the aggravation and not
answering back was part of our job." New to the business as Mal
was, he committed some serious blunders, including losing John's
precious Gibson Jumbo acoustic guitar at Finsbury Park Astoria. "An
outsider watching John sometimes mightn't have thought he was
the most likeable person," Aspinall conceded. "But I'd say to them,
'Could you get up on a stage and do what he did?' And if he blew up
over something, he'd always apologise. It might take him two years,
but he'd do it."

As Beatlemania grew, another kind of backstage duty became increasingly common. Audiences generally included groups from local
children's hospitals and institutions, many of them severely disabled,
who would be placed in the front rows directly in the Beatles' sight
line. Often, too, they would be expected to meet and greet teenagers
or children in wheelchairs who heartbreakingly incarnated John's
"spassie" act. "No one used to ask if it was all right beforehand,"
Neil remembered. "When we got to the theatre, the dressing room
would be full of wheelchairs." It was perhaps not too great a price to
pay for their own abundant health and wealth—though their fellow
NEMS artiste Cilla Black recalls one occasion, at least, when their
good nature was abused in the most cynical way. "At the Christmas
Show, I saw people using children in wheelchairs just as a trick to get
in to see them."

Aghast at becoming some peripatetic Lourdes shrine, the other
three sought refuge in John's unrepentant mockery and mimicry of
"cripples." The word became code for anybody who outstayed their
welcome: one of the Beatles had only to say "Cripples, Neil" for the
dressing room to be cleared forthwith.

From the moment the four entered the national spotlight, there
had been awareness of John as a pungent character in his own
right. As early as June 1963, he was invited to appear without the
others on *Juke Box Jury*, a BBC television show where a celebrity panel
voted new single releases a hit or a miss. To transport him from BBC

Television Centre in London to that night's Beatles show in Wales, Brian spent £100 to charter a helicopter, even though the gig paid only £250. Much to the viewers' delight, John voted every record a miss, saying of Elvis Presley's "Devil in Disguise" that the King was "like Bing Crosby now."

He also stood out from his fellow moptops by starting to sport a black leather peaked cap reminiscent of male headgear in the 1917 Russian Revolution. Though other young Britons already possessed such caps, and thousands more now rushed to buy them, John wore his in a distinctive way, slightly tipped back with a faint but discernible revolutionary air—Lennon half wanting to be Lenin.

His media interviews at this time often suggest someone trying—usually in vain—to show he has a mind with more on it than guitar chords, screaming girls, and new shirts. Unlike the decorous, diplomatic Paul, he would answer any question that was put to him, so long as it was sincere, with a directness his interlocutors seldom expected or knew what to make of. ". . . I don't suppose I think much about the future. I don't really give a damn. Though now we've made it, it would be a pity to get bombed [he means the hydrogen bomb]. It's selfish but I don't care too much about humanity—I'm an escapist. Everyone's always drumming on about the future, but I'm not letting it interfere with my laughs. . . . I get spasms of being intellectual. I read a bit about politics but I don't think I'd vote for anyone. No message from any of those phoney politicians is coming through to me."

Attached to the Beatles in late '63 and early '64 was Michael Braun, a young American who would later turn their life on the road into arguably the first piece of serious pop journalism. A surprising feature of Braun's account is how much of John and Paul's offstage chat concerns avant-garde French cinema. John continually throws out puns on his childhood radio and film favorites, like a motor that can't be switched off: "One more ciggy, then I'm gonna hit the sack; 'hit the sack' being an American thing we got off Gary Coople as he struggled along with a clock in High Goons. . . . You can sack Rome or you can sack cloth or you can sacrilege or saxophone, if you like, or saccharine. . . ."

To Braun he confesses how "unnerved" he feels now that his cousin Stanley Parkes—the boyhood hero from whom he inherited that wonderful Dinky car collection—feels obliged to treat him "like royalty." He is even willing to discuss his father, usually a no-go area to his closest friends, let alone the media. Braun remarks that it can be a handicap to have a famous father, but John demurs: "I could have stood a famous father rather more than the ignoble Alf, actually." The dirt-digging *News of the World* has discovered how his father walked out of his life all those years ago, and claims to have traced a friend of Alf's—by implication, a prelude to unearthing Alf himself. "I don't want to think about it," John says. "I don't feel as if I owe him anything. He never helped me. I got here by myself, and this [playing music] is the longest I've ever done anything, except being at school."

That Christmas, the Beatles sent a thank-you to their British fans via a flimsy plastic disk, recorded at Abbey Road, with tinkling sleigh bells, nonsense carols, and a spoken message from each in turn. Paul's was a model of appreciativeness, wide-eyed wonderment, and tact; even while asking concertgoers to desist from throwing jelly babies (unpleasant missiles to receive continuously in the face), he stressed that he wasn't denigrating their generosity and that the Beatles still loved jelly babies, along with other kiddy sweets like chocolate drops and Dolly Mixture. John read the words that had been written for him in an ironical monotone: "Our biggest thrill of the year well I suppose it was being top of the bill at the London Palladium. . . ." At any risk of sounding too obsequious, he broke into parody Jewishness or Goon German. Here was someone taking all possible pains to distance himself from Dolly Mixture.

His favorite journalist, out of a very small field, was Maureen Cleave, pop columnist for the *London Evening Standard*, who had first interviewed him in Liverpool just before the Helen Shapiro tour. Cleave was a quintessential product of new London—a diminutive young woman whose chic outfits and Mary Quant bob contrasted with a precise, almost schoolmistressy manner. She was not particularly a pop music fan (not even owning a record player until the *Standard* bought her one), but covered it as an objective outsider, in sardonically grown-up prose that had never been used on it before.

Maureen Cleave was the first to observe that John had "an upper lip that is brutal in a devastating way," and to find his cast of mouth and "the long pointed nose he peered down like an eagle" (mainly thanks to nearsightedness) reminiscent of Britain's famously humorous and cruel monarch, Henry VIII. Though knowing nothing about his childhood and background, she instantly saw the connection with Richmal Crompton's William; that, for all their exotic Liverpudliana, he and his fellow Beatles were essentially William and the Outlaws, meeting an unpredictable, unreasonable adult world head-on and doing their best to make sense of it. For John, Cleave's astringent style awoke echoes of Richmal Crompton's own; he even told her she was like "that woman who wrote William."

She quickly realized that, with an interviewer he liked—especially one associated with his most cherished author—there were no boundaries to what John would discuss, no limits to what he would say, and no question of anything being "off the record," much as he might later wish it had been. She even got to see his flat in Emperor's Gate, a place usually off-limits to press. "He showed me an Elvis Presley album that had Stu Sutcliffe's name on it, with his own name written over the top, I remember, he kept looking at Elvis's picture on the cover and saying, 'Isn't he beautiful?' He said he'd felt disloyal to Elvis when he started liking Little Richard but because Little Richard was black, that made it all right."

Six months earlier, while the Beatles were still purely a teenage obsession, Brian had been approached by a twenty-nine-year-old Russian émigré entrepreneur and filmmaker named Giorgio Gomelsky with a plan to make a fly-on-the-wall documentary about them. Gomelsky also ran a blues club, the Crawdaddy, in Richmond, Surrey, whose star attraction was a group he informally managed called the Rolling—sometimes Rollin'—Stones. Though nothing came of his documentary idea, the Beatles liked the sound of Gomelsky's Crawdaddy Club and agreed to drop by there and catch the Rolling Stones one spring Sunday night after taping *Thank Your Lucky Stars* at ABC-TV's studios in nearby Teddington.

The Stones at this point were very much like the Beatles eighteen months earlier: a group with a fanatical following at a tiny venue—in their case the back room of a pub called the Station Hotel—but without management of sufficient vision or resources to take them any higher. The differences were that (still with pianist Ian Stewart) they numbered six, not four; that they played Chicago and Delta-style blues unpolluted by any pop influences; and that their vocalist, a London School of Economics student then known as Mike Jagger, audaciously faced his audience without the bluesman's traditional prop of a guitar.

The Beatles loved what they saw in Surrey and, big shots though they were by comparison, instantly chummed up with Jagger and the other two principal Stones, rhythm guitarist Keith Richard and lead guitarist–harmonica player Brian Jones. A week later, when the Beatles appeared in the BBC's Great Pop Prom at the Royal Albert Hall, the Stones received front-row tickets, hung out with them backstage, even lent Mal and Neil a hand in carrying their equipment. Brian Jones, who had founded and named the group, was then its most magnetic figure, an oversexed blond leprechaun with command of an extraordinary range of instruments, from guitar and bluesman's "harp" to saxophone, flute, and marimba. Watching Jones play blues harmonica at the Crawdaddy not only thrilled John; it also, typically, made him feel his own gold-spinning performances on the instrument to have been amateurish, even somehow fraudulent, by comparison. "You really play that thing, don't you?" he said to Jones almost wistfully. ". . . I just blow and suck."

By late 1963, the Stones had found their visionary manager in NEMS Enterprises' former PR man, nineteen-year-old Andrew Loog Oldham, and had been signed to the Decca label by the very same A&R executive who turned the Beatles down. After making little impact with their debut single, Chuck Berry's "Come On," they reached number thirteen with a Lennon-McCartney song, "I Want to Be Your Man," written for the *With the Beatles* album, which the composers obligingly turned over to them on learning that they were stuck for a follow-up. As a result, the Stones left purist R&B to become the Beatles' main rivals in the pop charts, and Jagger and Richard were motivated to form their own songwriting partnership, ultimately with huge success.

Oldham's inspired gambit was to market the not naturally aggressive Stones as British pop's first antiheroes, aimed at teenagers for whom the Beatles were in danger of becoming too glossy and parent friendly. For an older generation barely reconciled to neat bangs and round-necked suits, their unkempt hair, ungracious scowls, and unmatched stage clothes would create almost the terror of an Antichrist. The rebellious, don't-give-a-damn image manufactured by Oldham was, in truth, very much what the Beatles had genuinely been in Hamburg and at the Cavern, before Brian cleaned them up and got them bowing and smiling. As the Stones grew ever more anarchically successful, so did John's angry regret deepen for having—as he thought—sold out to mainstream show business too easily.

Nor could any outsider have guessed what insecurity underlay even the greatest of the Beatles' triumphs in 1963. As with every other pop hitmaker back to Bill Haley, the assumption was that sooner or later their novelty must inevitably wear off and fickle teenage taste move on to something else. It was the media question put to them most often, after the ones about their name and their hair: how long could all of this possibly last? John's answer was always direct and self-deprecating. "You can be big-headed and say, 'Yeah, we're going to last ten years,' but as soon as you've said that you think . . . we're lucky if we last three months."

As the Beatles knew, as their manager and producer and publicists knew, as every last fan who bought their records and screamed at their concerts knew, being big in Britain, even on such a scale, left massive heights unconquered. America still represented the world's most boundlessly lucrative pop music market, still dictated pop's every fashion and mood, still poured toxic apathy on almost any foreigner who tried to sell it facsimiles of its own inimitable product.

Of no help at all was the fact that a major American label, Capitol, was actually owned by British EMI. Each of the Beatles' first three UK number ones had been submitted to Capitol by George Martin, and snootily declined as "unsuitable" for the U.S. market. An incredulous Martin had been forced to make deals with two tiny independent labels, Veejay and Swan, for "Please Please Me" and "She Loves You" respectively. Neither had made any impression on the American charts or, it seemed, on American teenage consciousness.

"I Want to Hold Your Hand" (written by John and Paul in the Ashers family's Wimpole Street basement) was something of a last-ditch attempt to crack America, with a sound as stylishly "black" and a sentiment as ingratiatingly "white" as possible. The quality of the end product distracted attention from its essential implausibility: John Lennon being content with holding someone's hand?

Even at the height of British Beatlemania, the Beatles themselves were always looking nervously over their shoulders for competitors who might knock them off the charts, maybe for good. Brian's other two main Liverpool acts, Gerry and the Pacemakers and Billy J. Kramer and the Dakotas, also with three hit singles apiece, frequently resembled such a nemesis. Then there were the Liverpool groups managed by other hands and signed to other labels, like the Searchers, the Swinging Blue Jeans, and the Fourmost. There were the harbingers of the rival sound from Liverpool's old commercial adversary, Manchester: the Hollies, Freddie and the Dreamers, and Wayne Fontana and the Mindbenders. There were the bands now emerging in a retaliatory wave from London and the south, like Brian Poole and the Tremeloes, who had passed the Decca audition the Beatles failed and had made the Top 10 with a souped-up version of "Twist and Shout."

John and Paul's extraordinary success rate as songwriters generated insecurities of its own. To soak up all possible profit before the craze evaporated, George Martin demanded a new single every three months, a new album every six. What if their next effort didn't reach number one? What if it only reached number two? What if the magic knack should desert them as mysteriously as it had come? The pair spent hours trying to analyze just what had made their latest hit a hit, so they could be sure to repeat the formula next time around. For a while, they believed the crucial ingredient was simply the word *me* or *you*, hence not only "Love Me Do," "Please Please Me," "From Me to You," and "She Loves You," but also "P.S. I Love You," "Do You Want to Know a Secret?" "Thank You Girl," "I'll Get You," "Bad to Me," and "Hold Me Tight." In the wake of "She Loves You," the word *yeah* assumed a similar talismanic quality. The chorus of "It Won't Be Long," the opening track on *With the Beatles*, features six *yeah*'s in two lines; "I Want to Hold Your Hand" has an *oh yeah* before the lyric even begins.

Despite the relentless pressure to be commercial and formulaic, they were also managing to write songs that had nothing to do with the feverish ebb and flow of the charts, songs that on very first hearing seemed like old favorites—instant standards. There was, for instance, nothing else around remotely like John's "This Boy," the slow ballad on the B-side of "I Want to Hold Your Hand." Nothing like its economy and neat antithesis—this boy loves you; that boy will hurt you. Nothing like the harmonizing of John, Paul, and George—as close as only three could be who'd kept each other warm in the back of a freezing van. Nothing like John's bravura solo vocal—the heart-on-sleeve passion and tenderness that so impressed William Mann in the *Times*, and made Vernons Girl Maureen's fingernails dig so agonizingly into her friend's palm.

Indeed, as 1963 moved to a close, both John and Paul began hinting that songwriting would be their safety net once Beatlemania had blown over. Giving "I Wanna Be Your Man" to the Rolling Stones was not only a typically openhearted gesture; it also looked like insurance for the future, even if John did always dismiss the song as "a throwaway."

With the New Year, all those wise predictions seemed to be coming true rather sooner than expected. A three-week stint of concerts at the Olympia theater in Paris received a muted reception, suggesting that Beatlemania had not even crossed the Channel. Back in Britain, meanwhile, "I Want to Hold Your Hand" was pushed from the number one spot by a London group, the Dave Clark Five, and their so-called Tottenham Sound. The *Daily Mail* published a cartoon of a teenage girl being regarded with pity by her friends. "She must be really old-fashioned," the caption said. "She remembers the Beatles." Having built them up, Fleet Street seemed to be preparing, in time-honored fashion, to knock them down again.

Then America fell.

15

THE BIG BANG

We knew we would wipe you out if we could just get a grip.

O n the cold, snow-flecked afternoon of February 7, 1964, the Beatles' Pan Am jet touched down in New York before a crowd of ecstatic humanity such as had never greeted any foreigner setting foot on American soil. It was an airport scene as jubilant, in its way as epoch-making, as Charles Lindbergh's arrival in Le Bourget after the first solo Atlantic flight or Neville Chamberlain's "peace in our time" return from Munich. For millions of young Americans, it would be the moment when the Sixties finally got going in earnest. What tends to be forgotten is how dumbfounded the Beatles themselves were by their reception.

A few days before departure, yet another plummy-voiced television reporter had asked John how he rated their chances of success where so many other British pop acts had failed. His obvious unease came out in a tone of heavy sarcasm. "Well, I can't really say, can I? I mean, is it up to me? No!" Then, with a hasty backpedal to Beatle niceness: "I mean, I just hope we go all right."

Much later he was to admit, "We didn't think we stood a chance. Cliff [Richard] went to America and died. He was fourteenth on the bill with Frankie Avalon. We knew Brian had plans . . . but we thought at least we could hear the sounds [new music] when we came over. That's the truth. . . . We just went over to buy LPs."

The visit originally set up by Brian in late 1963 had been no more than a low-key promotional exercise. Capitol Records, having passed up the first four Beatles singles, had, rather grudgingly, agreed to release "I Want to Hold Your Hand" early in January. The four were booked to appear on NBC-TV's *Ed Sullivan Show*—which had famously introduced Elvis Presley to America—and to give two performances at New York's illustrious Carnegie Hall. Though all undoubtedly feathers in Brian's managerial cap, none of these was a guarantee of cracking the record charts.

But fate once again seemed to be working as their press agent. In the national gloom following President Kennedy's death, American news organizations cast around for some light relief and lit upon the four funny-haired Liverpudlians who were apparently sending Britain barmy. By Christmas, both *Time* and *Newsweek* and just about every American paper with a European bureau had published extensive accounts of Beatlemania. Even the parochial *New Yorker* interviewed Brian and quoted his prophecy that "the Beatles . . . will hit this country for six. . . ." On December 31, all-powerful *Life* magazine gave them a seventeen-page cover story; four days later, they made their first American television appearance via a film clip on CBS's *Jack Paar Show*.

In the face of this surprise publicity gusher, Capitol hastily multiplied its pressing of "I Want to Hold Your Hand" by five, to one million copies. The company also printed whole rain forests' worth of promotional matter, ordered its strategists to make 1964 the Year of the Beatles, and readied its sales force for a mass wearing of Beatle wigs. Strangely, the Beatles themselves knew nothing of the gathering storm until late on January 25, when they returned to their suite at the George V Hotel in Paris, disgruntled with their performance at the Olympia and fearing annihilation by the Dave Clark Five's Tottenham Sound. Then came the transatlantic call to Brian, saying that in *Cash Box* magazine's Top 100, "I Want to Hold Your Hand" had jumped from nowhere straight to number one.

When the four left London-Heathrow on February 7, they were regarded not as pop musicians out to make a quick dollar but as ambassadors at the level of senior politicians or Test cricket teams. Even the least pop-friendly of their countrymen and -women shared a sense that they were batting for Britain, that national pride as well as private ambition demanded they should return victorious.

The situation in the American record charts by now verged on the farcical. Not only was "I Want to Hold Your Hand" still number one and selling ten thousand copies per day in New York alone, but Capitol's former rejects "Please Please Me" and "She Loves You" had been remarketed by their respective pickup labels, and both instantly shot into the Top 10. The Polydor label had looked into its vaults, found the tracks the Beatles had recorded pseudonymously long ago in Hamburg with Tony Sheridan, and issued their version of "My Bonnie Lies Over the Ocean," which, as George said bitterly, was "a laff." Even that was surfing up the Hot 100, not far behind "From Me to You" and the album track "I Saw Her Standing There."

In addition to four thousand screaming, finger-crossing fans, the media pack who saw them off received an unexpected bonus story. Among the Beatles' party was a shy-looking young woman, dressed up for traveling after the northern manner in a coffee-colored PVC coat and a white hat with a brim, clearly meant as a companion to John's Lenin cap. It was, indeed, Cynthia Lennon, released from purdah at long last. Why he chose this moment to bring her into the limelight, violating the rock-'n'-roller's first principle of "no wives on the road," puzzled everyone in his circle. Tony Barrow thinks he did so purely on impulse, to make a power point with Brian. "None of the others was allowed to bring a female companion, so John said, 'Fuck it, I'm having Cyn.' But it was a decision he came to regret— and so did she."

Less sought after by photographers, though not from choice, was a sharp-faced young American who, even on this bleak winter's day, wore sunglasses both outside and indoors and displayed all the showy furtiveness of some master criminal on the run. Twenty-three-year-old Phil Spector was the prototype of an entirely new species, the boy pop tycoon. As a songwriter, his hits had begun with John's old Cavern standby "To Know Her Is to Love Her"; as a producer, he had created the tumultuous Wall of Sound, resembling a hundred car crashes in harmony, behind chart-topping girl groups like the Crystals and the Ronettes.

Spector was returning to America, after watching the Ronettes on a British tour with the Rolling Stones. Through the Stones and their own would-be boy tycoon, Andrew Oldham, Spector had gotten to know the Beatles, thus connecting John with a mighty influence on his music, past and to come. Spector then brought the Beatles and Ronettes together at a party given by promotion man Tony Hall. "My girls," as their producer jealously called them, were two sisters, Ronnie and Estelle Bennett, and their cousin Nedra Talley, all three stunning stick insects with piled-up hair and Cleopatra eyes. John and an equally besotted George lost no time in asking the trio to join the flight to New York. Spector, however, insisted that his girls should return home on an earlier plane, while only he traveled with the Beatles. Already legendarily neurotic, he believed that no aircraft carrying such a lucky quartet could possibly crash.

The other passengers were mostly favored journalists like Maureen Cleave (whose *Evening Standard* editors remained far from convinced that her trip would be worthwhile) and British businessmen hoping to do merchandise deals with Brian in the relative privacy of midair. The Beatles' nonstop in-flight clowning masked inner trepidation, even superconfident Paul reflecting, "They've got everything over there. What do they want us for?" While the "monk" side of John was in heartfelt agreement, the "performing flea" felt an illogical optimism. "On the plane . . . I was thinking, 'Oh, no, we won't make it,' but that's that side of me," he later told an American interviewer. "We knew we would wipe you out if we could just get a grip."

Many pioneers in the black art of hype would later claim credit for the spectacle at JFK Airport—the tiers of banner-waving girls who made British Beatlemania a silent movie by comparison, the screaming that multiplied Spector's Wall of Sound to infinity. It's certainly true that by the time the Beatles hit New York, seventeen different promotion men were involved in pumping up the event to maximum volume. But the pandemonium that broke loose as the aircraft nosed to a final stop and its door opened was way beyond any PR artifice or manipulation. It remains perhaps our happiest image of John as he pauses on the stairs, airline bag on shoulder, black leather cap pushed back, as laughingly lost for words as everyone else.

They were not quite home free. At Kennedy Airport they faced a hard-boiled New York media corps, most of whom had come with the avowed intention of slaughtering them. They triumphed with what was perhaps the earliest known deployment of the sound bite, John's the most biting of all. Would they play something? "We need money first." What was it about them that excited young girls so much? "If we knew, we'd form a group ourselves and be managers." Were they really wig-wearing baldies? "Oh, we're all bald, yeah—and deaf and dumb." America was more sensitive than Britain about physical disability, and that final little flourish might have been expected to offend somebody among the packed newspeople, if not among those who watched it or read it. But no one even seemed to hear.

Among the lens-leveling hordes were the brothers Albert and David Maysles, two soft-spoken Bostonians already noted for the distinctive cinema and TV documentaries they produced in partnership. Only hours before the Beatles' touchdown, British Granada Television had contacted the Maysles brothers, requesting footage of New York's welcome, or otherwise, for rush transmission on the home network. In the end, they tagged along with the Beatles' media retinue for the whole visit. Dispensing with any crew but themselves, using the latest small handheld cameras, they achieved a degree of invisibility and intimacy with their subjects that even the most favored of British chroniclers could not. The resultant black-and-white film shows Sixties pop life at its simplest and most innocent, just as a later Maysles production, *Gimme Shelter*, would show it at its ugliest.

The Maysleses' narrative begins in earnest inside the Beatles' suite at the Plaza Hotel, as crowds even wilder than at the airport heave against chains of blue-coated police twelve floors below. We can see John and the others, still crumpled and dazed from their flight, absorbing the special atmosphere of a New York grand hotel, the Versailles-splendid brocades and chandeliers, the gleaming, towel-stuffed bathrooms, the flesh-colored telephones that ring with a single polite purr, the gold-crested pens, ashtrays, notepads, coasters, and matchbooks, the outsize tumblers of ice water, the real-life voices uttering phrases heard a thousand times from the cinema screen: "Room service," "Valet," "You're welcome," "Aw-righty!" "Have a nice day."

We share their wide-eyed amazement at the sumptuous choice of New York entertainment media in comparison with Britain's miserly one: the six or seven television channels and scores of radio stations—almost all of the latter playing their music virtually nonstop. Children on Christmas morning could not be more thrilled as they discover it is possible to call up a radio show in midbroadcast, then hear themselves on air via the transistor radios shaped like Pepsi Cola vending machines that have been artfully product-placemented into the suite. We see John on the line to *Saturday Club*'s Brian Matthew back in London, evidently concerned lest British Beatles fans' ardor should cool even in this short absence. "Tell 'em not to forget. . . . We're only away for ten days . . . We're thinking of 'em."

We join the first outdoor photo op, across the road in Central Park: just John, Paul, and Ringo (George was confined to bed with a sore throat) doing "Hello, New York" poses for a gaggle of tabloid lensmen in short overcoats and Cossack hats, who address them as "You . . . the fellow on the right" or "Hey . . . Beatle!" Hindsight gives this routine scene a horrible irony. Just across the park lies a craggy Gothic pile known as the Dakota Building where, it so happens, the elder Maysles brother, Albert, has an apartment. Mugging dutifully for the cameras in the icy-fingered cold, John has no inkling of the place where he will one day live, and die.

In contrast with the crowds on the street and the deejays on the air, the Plaza reacted in horror to its twelfth-floor VIPs, lodging an almost immediate demand for them to settle their account, even making radio appeals for any other Manhattan hotel to take them over. During the endless photo sessions up in their suite, one cameraman requested John to lie on a bed, the better to show off what

Americans termed his "pixie boots." A hovering Plaza official protested this was not the image the hotel wished to project, and besides, the coverlet might be damaged. "It's all right," John reassured
him, "we'll buy the bed."

One essential ground rule imposed on the Maysles brothers'
documentary was that Cynthia Lennon must be kept out of frame.
Although John's British fans might know he was married, his new
American ones were to have their illusions preserved for as long as
possible. Now and then, a sequence of him on the phone to some
radio show accidentally includes Cynthia, wearing a neat white
blouse and dark glasses, never saying a word or having one addressed
to her, pretending stoic indifference to the "beautiful, willowy girls"
(including Ronnie of the Ronettes) who had surrounded John and
the other three from the moment they arrived.

Apart from hotel suites and television studios, John saw almost
nothing of the city that had towered over his imagination since
childhood. Capitol Records laid on a brief limo trip of major uptown
landmarks, which, at the Beatles' request, was extended to the safer
part of Harlem. Their disc jockey–guardian, Murray the K, organized a night at the Peppermint Lounge, home of the New York
twist and Joey Dee and the Starliters, where the house band had
already switched to Beatle mimicry. Returning to their Plaza suite
in the small hours, John and Cynthia were ambushed by photographers, whom they thwarted by putting John's coat over both their
heads and scuttling round a corner. For those few moments, giggling
under cover together as of old, Cyn had fun.

The Beatles' appearance on the *Ed Sullivan Show* of February 9
was to place them in American history in a way that never quite happened back in Britain. Effectively, it signaled the end of mourning
for Jack Kennedy, through an event as hugely harmless as the one of
November 22 had been hugely horrible—a heartening reminder to
the whole nation of its unique ability to give its whole heart; living
proof there could be happier ways of always henceforth recalling exactly where one was at a particular moment.

The events of that Sunday night have passed into national folklore: how some seventy-three million people, the largest U.S. televi-

sion audience ever known, tuned in at 8:00 p.m. to watch the live show—on which, technically, the Beatles were not even top of the bill. How, just beforehand, a good-luck telegram arrived from the last Sullivan attraction to win comparable Nielsen ratings: ". . . We hope your engagement will be a successful one and your visit pleasant. . . . Elvis and the Colonel." How the crustiness of Ed Sullivan, normally the most misanthropic man ever to host a prime-time TV variety show, melted like puff pastry as he paid tribute to these "fine youngsters from Liverpool." How New York's criminal element were so transfixed that throughout all the city's five boroughs not even a car hubcap was reported stolen. How in those few flickering black-and-white moments, young girls from coast to coast forgot homegrown pinups named Frankie or Bobby, amateur bands stopped playing surf music and began practicing vocal harmonies, and boys with crew cuts could almost feel their hair start to grow.

The appearance was in two segments, one beginning the show with the Beatles on a set composed of giant white, inward-pointing arrows; the other, with a backdrop of Plexiglas rectangles, at the very end, after appearances by Tessie O'Shea, Frank Gorshin, and the Broadway cast of *Oliver*. The surprise delivered by an umpteenth watching of the famous videotape is how slight John's presence initially seems. The opening number, the one that says "Hello, America, we're here!" is "All My Loving," sung by Paul with George's help, followed by Paul's Peggy Lee ballad "Till There Was You"; then "She Loves You," which, thanks to a inept sound mixing, again chiefly features Paul and George. The linking announcements, too, are by Paul. At the point when each Beatle in turn is helpfully captioned, JOHN (with the subtitle SORRY GIRLS, HE'S MARRIED) comes last.

The two-song second segment seems to continue this Paul bias, starting with "I Saw Her Standing There." Only for the final number, "I Want to Hold Your Hand," as the sound stabilizes, does John come into complete definition. The watching seventy-three million could now fully appraise that splay-legged, slightly hunched stance, those minimally moving lips, that expression under the Beatle bangs which somehow made instant contact with hitherto conformist, literal-minded young Americans in every state of the Union. Among thousands who never forgot the epiphany was singer-songwriter Billy Joel, then aged fourteen and living in Hicksville, Long Island. "I remember noticing John that first time on the Sullivan show," Joel would say fondly almost three decades later. "He's standing there, looking around him as if to say, 'Is all this corny or what?'"

It was not a tour in the later sense of the word—rather, a cultural mission that became an almost royal progress. In two weeks, the Beatles gave only three concert performances, the two prearranged at Carnegie Hall and an extra one at the Washington Coliseum arena, under conditions the least cosseted modern touring band would not tolerate. For this, their first-ever live American show, they played on a stage like a boxing ring with shrieking fans banked up all around them, yet a security cordon numbering no more than about five. To give every ticket holder a frontal view, the microphones had to be continually repositioned on different sides of the stage, and Ringo's drum podium rotated laboriously by hand. Keeping up his front-man role, Paul requested the crowd to clap along while a shambling, grimacing John demonstrated how a "spassie" would do it, to spectators both before and behind him. And still no one seemed to take offense.

Nor would any modern UK rock band in Washington be expected to call on the British ambassador like some visiting trade delegation—let alone endure what the Beatles did at their country's most prestigious overseas embassy, following their Coliseum show on February 11. The invitation to attend a charity ball was clearly meant to capitalize on their unofficial diplomatic triumph; the four themselves made no protest, even though it would mean exposure on a major scale to the kind of people John most detested. The Maysleses' film shows disaster already building as he follows Ambassador Sir David Ormsby-Gore down a staircase into the assembled crowd of braying Hooray Henrys and Henriettas. Sucking in cigarette smoke through tightened lips, he glares around him like some Garston Ted, ready for a rumble.

Soon afterward it transpired that, without consulting them, the Beatles had been scheduled to draw the winning tickets in a raffle.

When John showed reluctance to leave the anteroom where he had sought refuge, he was surrounded by young Foreign Office types and officiously ordered to "Come on and do your stuff." Fortunately, the emollient Ringo was on hand to prevent a major Lennon blow-up. In fact, what made John finally lose it was an insult to Ringo: a woman came up behind him with some nail scissors and gigglingly snipped off a lock of his hair. "I just walked out, swearing at all of them," John remembered. "I just left in the middle of it. . . ." After such an incident today, blame would automatically fall on the temperamental, foul-mouthed pop star; back then, questions were asked at the highest official level about the discourtesies the Beatles had suffered.

In the Maysleses' film, too, there is great significance to be read into hair. While Paul's Beatle cut remains as shapely and glossy as one of Aunt Mimi's pedigreed cats—indeed, he himself can hardly stop stroking it—John's already hangs in a tangle on his forehead and reaches downward in shaggy sideburns, Significant, too, is a scene (cut from the final film) aboard the train that took the Beatles back through the snows from Washington to New York. John is being interviewed by the journalist Al Aronowitz, a bulky, black-bearded figure noted for his close friendships with bohemian celebrities such as the beat poet Allen Ginsberg. The talk takes a dangerous turn, which John, as a dutiful Beatle, realizes may not be welcome to British viewers of Granada TV:

JOHN: I know, OK, OK we're all drug addicts.

ARONOWITZ: I don't know about you, but I'm one [*makes loud inhaling noises*].

JOHN (*to camera*): Here we have a drug addict—can't get it off . . . what is it? . . . can't get off a line. [*Slightly nervous.*] That's enough about drugs. Let's talk about Woodbines.

The only other stop on the itinerary was Miami, Florida, where the second *Ed Sullivan Show* of their triple commitment went out on February 16 from the Deauville Hotel. (A third, prerecorded in New

York, was screened after their return home.) Now John spent no time out on the margins: "This Boy" was number two on the playlist. Before the Beatles' second segment, their new Uncle Ed read out congratulatory sentiments from another giant of American popular music, the composer Richard Rodgers. The coauthor of songs like "My Funny Valentine" and shows like *South Pacific* called Beatlemania "harmless" and said it would be "a wonderful thing" if young people "continue all their lives to get that enthusiastic about anything."

Paul's former gosh-thanks solo announcements now became more of a double act, with John ordering the 3,500-strong studio audience to "shut oop while he's talking" in the accent of some dour old northern music-hall comedian like Robb Wilton or Norman Evans. The 70 million who tuned to this Sullivan show also received a glimpse of the "spassie" routine that the first one's 73 million had been denied. Yet again, the brief paroxysm of leering and claw-handing seemed to go unnoticed, none dissenting from Uncle Ed's further eulogy to "four of the nicest youngsters we've ever had on our stage."

Florida's gorgeous winter climate, warm ocean, and ubiquitous palm trees seemed like paradise to young men nurtured on the drab, Mersey-washed sands of New Brighton. The Miami visit was treated as a holiday as much as work, with Brian procuring visa extensions to allow them four extra days. George Martin and his fiancée, Judy Lockhart-Smith, also joined the party, having made their own way from Britain to catch the East Coast dates. Brian, rightly considered them a civilizing, stabilizing influence, especially where John and Cynthia were concerned.

Fans besieged the Deauville as noisily as they had the New York Plaza, their numbers swollen by the more clement weather and the adjacent surf-fringed beach. Even when vacation time officially began, the Beatles remained cooped up for long periods in their suites, increasingly bored with room service and the radio, gazing down almost longingly at the well-wishers' messages scrawled in huge patterns like crop circles on the sand twelve floors below. Miami's police department had provided a twenty-four-man, round-the-clock "Beatle Squad," commanded by a tough sergeant named

Buddy Bresner and as much concerned with the hotel's good name as with its star guests' protection. Bresner later reported how in his nightly bed check of the Beatles' quarters, he found "no women in their rooms, no drugs, no way, shape or form . . . these were the cleanest kids."

The Deauville's owner, Morris Lansberg, lent them his yacht for a day's swimming and deep-sea fishing away from prying eyes and press cameras; wealthy locals offered free use of swimming pools, convertibles, and Olympic-class motorboats. Their police protector, Buddy Bresner, took them home to meet his family and share a family roast beef dinner (for which John later wrote a polite thank-you letter, as his Aunt Mimi had always taught). These rare tranquil moments, at sea or the poolside, produced some of the most relaxed pictures ever taken of John and Cynthia, even if he is mostly shown asleep or staring abstractedly off into the distance.

In commercial terms, America was like a courtesan lying back on a couch and murmuring "Take me." New York promoter Sid Bernstein, who had staged the Beatles' Carnegie Hall shows, could have booked them into Madison Square Garden and sold out every seat in minutes. From coast to coast, top-flight impresarios were holding out giant venues and sacks of money. Nevertheless, Brian chose to end it here, for the present, amid the sand crop circles and the palms. His boys were due back in Britain for EMI recording sessions and, early in March, to start work on their first film. For Brian, whatever tempting better offers might arise, a deal was a deal.

The initial phases of shooting *A Hard Day's Night* did not impress Richard Lester overmuch with John's potential as a screen actor. "Paul was the one obviously making an effort," Lester remembers. "John didn't try at all. I noticed this quality he had of standing outside every situation and noting the vulnerabilities of everyone, including myself. He was always watching."

The film had been set up late in 1963, with little thought of quality or originality. America's United Artists corporation, the project's backers, saw it primarily as a way to cash in on European Beatlemania before the bubble burst. For UA, the real moneymaker was the sound track of new Beatles songs, which could subsequently be put out as an album. What went on the screen was intended to be a pop exploitation vehicle in the banal tradition stretching back to *Rock Around the Clock*, with risible plot and paper-thin characters merely providing an excuse for music. The budget was a rock-bottom £180,000.

However, in this apparent bargain-basement atmosphere, the Beatles once again got lucky. Rather than some nameless, jaded hack director, they got Lester, a young American who had worked in Britain for several years, building a reputation in the comedy genre dearest to John; he had been responsible for transferring the *Goon Show* from radio to television and had directed Peter Sellers's surreal comedy short, *The Running, Jumping, Standing Still Film*. Equally fortunate casting was the scriptwriter, Alun Owen, a fellow Liverpudlian whose plays, notably the TV drama *No Trams to Lime Street*, had been in the vanguard of rain-on-cobblestones northern chic. Thus in one package came American know-how, lineage with the Goons, and a reassuring breath of home.

Alun Owen's screenplay depicted the Beatles just being the Beatles, perpetually on the run from screaming fans and coming into occasional conflict—always victoriously—with stuffy representatives of the British establishment. The film's main opening sequence was a train journey, much like the real-life New York–Washington one documented by the Maysles brothers. A press reception crowded with strident upper-class twits (Q: "How did you find America?" John: "Turned left at Greenland.") clearly owed something to the British Embassy in Washington. As in life, the Beatles were guarded by two roadies, renamed Norm and Shake, and kept virtual prisoners between performances.

Owen was to win praise for catching the flavor of the Beatles' private repartee. But to John, the film's dialogue seemed artificially cute. His very first line is "Who's that little old man?"—in reality, he said, it would have been "Who's the old crip?" Although an admirer of *No Trams to Lime Street*, he became exasperated with his Boswell, whose persona tended to switch between Welsh and Scouse according to the company. "Why should I listen to you?" he once growled at Owen. "You're nothing but an amateur Liverpudlian." Owen riposted: "Do you think that's better than being a professional Liver-pudlian, John?"

Film acting may seem glamorous but is, in fact, an arduous busi-ness, involving punishingly early mornings, long periods of wait-ing around, and strict regimentation and obedience. John began the seven-week shoot apparently as intent on flouting rules as he had been at school and college. In front of the camera, he insisted on wearing his own clothes, including the Lenin cap, thereby playing havoc with continuity. One scene in the finished film shows him run-ning for a taxi in a shirt and tie; the next has him looking back from its rear window in a turtleneck. And his ability to cause laughter where strict silence was needed, and mislay scripts within minutes of receiving them, would have driven a lesser director to despair.

He had met his match, however, in the elegant, unflappably pa-tient and polite Richard Lester. His attitude changed as he realized Lester's dedication to putting the Beatles onscreen with the same stylishness and unpredictability with which George Martin recorded them. "It took me a while to get through to John, but after that there was no problem," Lester says. "The surprising thing about him was just how normal he sometimes could be."

The production called for a batch of Lennon-McCartney songs, some recorded preshoot for the sound track, others afterward for the tie-in album. Somehow finding time in Paris and then Miami, John and Paul had produced a rich crop for Lester and the film's (also American) producer Walter Shenson to cherry-pick. The half dozen chosen numbers were integrated into the action with a panache that pop video directors would still admire forty years later. "I Should Have Known Better," a John vocal-with-harmonica, was performed inside a metal cage in the train's freight compartment while a group of nubile uniformed schoolgirls (a detail no one then thought ques-tionable) gazed rapturously through the bars. "If I Fell"—a plaintive John ballad that made grannies go gooey long before anything of Paul's—was busked during time-out at a TV studio, to cure Ringo of the sulks. "Can't Buy Me Love" pealed over the breakout sequence, in which the quartet escape their guards to hold kiddy races on a sports field, speeded up like Cuban-heeled Keystone Cops.

Each Beatle received his fair share of camera love—Paul the

charming, George the laconic, Ringo the sad-eyed, put-upon puppy dog. John's moments usually came when Lester needed a nonsensical or surreal touch. One sequence, largely ad-libbed, shows him in a bubble bath, still wearing the Lenin cap, playing with a toy submarine and mimicking a U-boat captain in the Heil Hitler accent he loved so well. Called to duty by roadie Norm, he tries to escape by sinking beneath the bubbles. When Norm runs the water away, nothing remains but smears of foam and the Lenin cap. Later in a theater corridor, John is mistaken for someone else by a neurotic-looking woman in a so-1964 cashmere sweater and chunky beads. Though never told whom he's supposed to be, he plays along just as he would have in real life. "Oh, wait a minute . . . don't tell me. No! Oh you are! You look just like him." "Do I? You're the first one that's said that, ever . . ."

Throughout, he is portrayed as an unremitting thorn in Norm's side, even though he does nothing much worse than put on funny voices. One exchange between the roadies seems more a comment on his real-life dealings with Brian:

NORM: This is a battle of nerves between John and me.

SHAKE: John hasn't got any.

NORM: Sometimes I think he enjoys seeing me suffer.

The film ends with Norm hustling the Beatles on to their next gig and John protesting that they're being pushed too hard. The script's final line is Norm's rejoinder: "Now there's only one thing I've got to say to you, Lennon . . . you're a swine." The word is used with a twinkle of affection; even so, it's hard to imagine any modern pop star vehicle ending on such a note

Until its final production stage, the film was to have been called *Beatlemania*. Then Ringo happened to describe a recent bout of burning the candle at both ends as "a hard day's night" (a phrase actually coined by John some months earlier in a piece of comic writing named "Sad Michael.") So the obvious teen flicky *Beatlemania* became the subtle, allusive, faintly Goon-flavored *A Hard Day's Night*.

Although John and Paul had already turned out more music than the film needed, they now also had to concoct a song of the same name to play over its opening credits. The two shut themselves away, and within twenty-four hours had come up with the goods.

When John went to Abbey Road for the recording session, he was accompanied by the *Evening Standard*'s Maureen Cleave. During the taxi ride, he showed her the lyrics, which he'd written out on a fan's birthday card to his son, Julian. The opening verse ran, ". . . when I get home to you, I find my tiredness is though . . ." Cleave, in her privileged role as surrogate Richmal Crompton, suggested that the last four words were too clunky. There and then, John changed them to "I find the things that you do . . ." In the studio later, she was amazed by how quickly the track took shape. "John and Paul just seemed to hum at one another with their guitars, and it was done."

Commentators who suggested (and maybe hoped) that the American triumph would be a short-lived fluke were quickly silenced. "Can't Buy Me Love"—a Paul-weighted song with a crucial George Martin edit—sold two million copies in the United States in its first week, earning a Gold Record even before release and becoming the first British single at number one simultaneously on both sides of the Atlantic. Here was no play-safe retread of "I Want to Hold Your Hand" but a determinedly left-field production with its retro jive beat and alternately furious and fainting harmonies, the incantatory "yeah" abolished in favor of a defiant "No, no, no . . . NO!"

Publicity in both markets was boosted by a loud but not lethal burst of controversy: did the reference to "buying" love mean prostitutes? In fact, it was Lennonesque wordplay of a kind even the most nonverbal fans were starting to recognize; dropping the word *money* from the title made it less a trite truism, more like a Liverpudlian endearment, "me love" as in "me darling" or "me duck." To top the American charts, "Can't Buy Me Love" had to leapfrog four other still-active Beatles singles—"I Want to Hold Your Hand," "Please Please Me," "She Loves You," and "Twist and Shout." By early April, they had created a seemingly impenetrable blockage at numbers one, two, three, four, and five.

John's distinctive way with words had always been part of the collective Beatle charm, though until now limited to seemingly artless malapropisms. On March 19, the four took a break from filming to be honored as Show Business Personalities of the Year (still no rock culture even dawning!) by the Variety Club of Great Britain. Their awards were presented by the opposition Labour Party's new leader Harold Wilson, who happened also to be MP for the Merseyside constituency of Huyton. The Variety Club's presiding official was known as Chief Barker—a "barker" being fairground parlance for front-of-tent showman. Confusing Mr. Wilson with this personage, and thinking of Barker and Dobson sweets (a superior brand his Aunt Mimi had always favored), John called Britain's soon-to-be prime minister "Mr. Dobson." The awards themselves were heart-shaped plaques. "Thanks for the purple hearts," John said as the recipients went through their naughty-but-nice-boys act at the microphone. His audience tittered indulgently, unsure whether he meant the American military decoration or the pep pill.

While interviewing him in late 1963, the American author Michael Braun had picked up some of the nonsense writing he still compulsively turned out in spare moments between composing, recording, and performing. Braun's publishers were the old established house of Jonathan Cape, at that time being shaken up by a new young editorial director named Tom Maschler. When Braun happened to show him a selection of John's output, Maschler instantly spotted a potential literary chart topper.

Rather than over the boozy lunch with which publishers traditionally woo prospective authors, he met John at a convention of the Beatles' Southern Area Fan Club. The Beatles stood behind a metal grill while the fans lined up to pass autograph books and gifts through an aperture at the bottom. John was amazed that anyone, other than his old *Mersey Beat* mates, would want to publish his work. At the same time, he made Maschler feel rather foolish, as the publisher has recalled, "for taking his frivolity seriously." A contract was drawn up through Brian Epstein, whom Maschler expected to demand some impossibly vast advance against royalties; instead, the sum agreed was just £10,000.

The backlog of poems, parodies, and playlets in John's possession did not constitute enough for even the slimmest hardback book. He therefore had to buckle down to a new, unavoidable kind of homework as well as do more concentrated drawing than he had since leaving art college. Maschler acted as his editor, making regular trips to the Lennons' flat in Emperor's Gate. Though the place, in his recollection, always seemed "full of noisy children," John took the consultations seriously and always found a quiet corner where they could work. One day, Maschler brought a new book on Cape's list by the cartoonist Mel Calman, hoping that John might supply a quote for its jacket. John's only comment was, "Why don't you suggest he takes up the guitar?"

They finally settled on thirty-one pieces, illustrated by the same octopoid grotesques that had once populated Quarry Bank school's "Daily Howl." Through the blizzards of Goonery could be discerned pastiches of Enid Blyton's Famous Five ("Gruddly pod, the train seemed to say . . . We're off on our holidays. . . .") and Robert Louis Stevenson's *Treasure Island* (featuring "Long John Saliver" and "Blind Jew"), even fragments of Bible-study inculcated by St. Peter's Sunday School ("Yea, though I walk through the valet of thy shadowy hut I will feel no Norman. . . .")

Favorite targets cropped up everywhere and, in that pre-PC era, remained free of editorial blue penciling—Partly Dave, who "leapt off a bus like a burning spastic"; Eric, who "lost his job teaching spastics to dance"; Michael, who was "debb and duff and could not speeg"; the "coloured man," who "danced by, eating a banana or somebody"; Little Bobby, whose "very fist was jopped off and he got a birthday hook." There was even a description of a drug trip, still in the voice of an objective satirist: "All of a southern, I notice boils and girks sitting in hubbered lumps, smoking Hernia, taking Odeon and going very high. Somewhere 4ft high but he had Indian hump which he grew in his sleep. . . ."

John drew up a list of possible titles, among them *The Transistor Negro*; *Left Hand, Left Hand* (a play on Osbert Sitwell's autobiography, *Left Hand, Right Hand*, which he was probably the only pop musician to have read); and *Stop One and Buy Me* (ice cream carts in his boyhood used to carry the invitation Stop Me and Buy One). In the end, Maschler opted for the more straightforward *John Lennon: In His Own Write*. The book was produced in an elegant pocket hardcover format, designed by Robert Freeman, its dark blue cover showing John in his trademark cap. Paul McCartney contributed a foreword, affectionately recounting how he had first met the author, "drunk" at St. Peter's Church fete.

The book was a simultaneous popular and critical triumph, selling out its first printing of fifty thousand copies on publication day, March 23, and spurring even the most highbrow reviewers to Beatlemania of their own. As a writer, John was compared with Lewis Carroll, Edward Lear, and James Joyce, and as an illustrator, with James Thurber and Paul Klee. The *Times Literary Supplement*, a separate publication from the daily *Times* and normally even stuffier, said *In His Own Write* was "worth the attention of anyone who fears for the impoverishment of the English language and of the British imagination." In America, where it was published by another prestigious house, Simon & Schuster, equally high-flown comparisons gushed forth. Tom Wolfe, writing in *Book World*, called John a "genius savage" like Artemus Ward, Mark Twain, and Brendan Behan and, later in the same article, a "genius of the lower crust."

As with song lyrics later, John firmly resisted all attempts to find classical literary influences or cerebral subtexts in his stories and verses, even where they were most obviously present. But he could not hide his pleasure at so resounding an independent achievement. "There's a wonderful feeling about doing something successfully other than singing," he admitted. "Up to now [the Beatles] have done everything together, and this is all my own work."

The critiques that flooded in from every intellectual compass point even included one in *Hansard*, the daily official record of parliamentary debates. In the House of Commons, Charles Curran, Conservative MP for Uxbridge, read out three verses of "Deaf Ted, Danoota and Me" in support of an attack on current standards in state education. The author, Curran acknowledged, had "a feeling for words and storytelling" but was in "a state of pathetic near-literacy" comparable to H. G. Wells's Mr. Polly. The Conservative member for Blackpool, Norman Miscampbell (his real name, not a John coinage), responded with a fellow northwesterner's loyalty: "It is unfair to say that Lennon of the Beatles was not well educated. I cannot say which, but three of the four went to grammar school, and as a group are highly intelligent, highly articulate and highly engaging."

As might be expected, John's new status as a published author impressed his literary-minded Aunt Mimi more than all the Beatles' musical triumphs put together, even if the book in question did consist of drawings and poems like those she once used to fling into the dustbin. Mimi herself was never interviewed by the Beatle-media and only very rarely photographed: such was her nature that she seldom spoke of John's extraordinary rise to anyone outside her immediate family circle. One remarkable exception was a thirteen-year-old John fan named Jane Wirgman, from Kingston-on-Thames, Surrey, who in April 1964 discovered Mimi's address and decided to write to her. "I knew that, with all the thousands of girls around John, there wasn't a chance that he'd never notice me," Jane says now. "But I thought that maybe it might happen somehow if I made friends with his aunt."

Wisely, she enclosed a stamped, self-addressed envelope with her letter, and, despite the drifts of fan mail always piling up at Mendips, Mimi did reply. It was to be the start of a correspondence extending over the next two years, in which Mimi expressed her pride in John to an unknown Surrey schoolgirl as she never would or could have to his face. Her letters, written in a neat, sloping hand, are pure Mimi: brisk yet friendly, humorous, and occasionally even a little auntlike toward her young correspondent; full of the glamour and luxury John has given her, yet complaining as much as ever about his hair and clothes; still achingly missing him from her life, yet ready to start another of their ding-dong rows whenever they make contact.

19 April, 1964

Dear Jane

Thanks for your letter. I saw [the Beatles] on TV Saturday night & by now I gather you like John!! They are all nice, but of course John's my boy. Didn't he look great (and the others) with their straw hats?

No, I don't think you are a Silly or Sentimental Ole Slob.

Remember, if you girls hadn't liked them, well . . . where would they be? and they do appreciate that fact.

He has always been funny at home to, and the latest thing is that he's been calling me—"Me Old Aunty.' Wait till I see him. Here's Ringo's address . . .

The next letter from Mendips contained a surprise enclosure—a Hofner guitar string, which John had bought for his Club 40, still coiled in its packet.

Dear Jane

Looking through John's old rubbish, his room was always full of things all boys seem to collect, I found this old string. It has been here for years. I think he uses more expensive ones these days, but this one belongs to his Art College days. I thought you might like it . . .

When *In His Own Write* was published, Jane sent a copy to Mimi with a request for John to autograph it. Back came the reply:

Thanks for letter, Jane.

John's in Scotland at the moment. I'll try to get the book signed, but as you know, I don't see so much of him. Anyway, I'm glad you are happy with it. He tells me he may do another one later in the year.

By the way, he promised me one and I am patiently waiting, although I have read it, & laughed.

All the best
Mimi Smith

To set the seal on literary London's acclaim, John was invited to be guest of honor at a Foyle's lunch on June 18. These gatherings, sponsored by the self-proclaimed "world's greatest bookshop," were held at the Dorchester Hotel in Park Lane and previously had been graced by authors such as Winston Churchill, Charles Chaplin, and Noel Coward, all of whom repaid the honor with a gracious and witty postprandial speech. For the John Lennon event, six hundred people bought tickets and the head table was carefully planted with sympathetic-minded celebrities, among them the violin virtuoso Yehudi Menuhin, the designer Mary Quant, the *Daily Express* cartoonist Osbert Lancaster, the composer Lionel Bart, the comedian Arthur Askey, and the ex-Goon Harry Secombe, as well as John's, and Brian's, great friend Alma Cogan.

John initially expressed willingness to make the traditional speech, but as the day approached he became increasingly uneasy about it, even admitting "I durn't" to a radio interviewer in his thickest faux-naif Scouse. On the eve of the lunch, Brian telephoned Foyle's to say that there would, after all, be no speech from John but that he, Brian, was more than happy to say a few words instead. Unfortunately, no one passed on Brian's message to the organizers, and six hundred literati and celebs waited agog for Lennon witticisms à la Royal Variety Show. Instead, he got to his feet, mumbled, "Thank you, it's been a pleasure," then sat down. Once again, the media could not find it in their hearts to criticize him. Some reports helpfully reworded his mumble into a more Beatly "Thank you . . . you've got a lucky face."

He was not the only one currently bursting into print. Earlier that year, Brian had been asked to write his autobiography by Souvenir Press, a publisher somewhat lower in prestige than Jonathan Cape. Rather than foster authorial fellow feeling in John, it inspired a put-down that even then rocked bystanders, like George Martin, back on their heels. What should he call his life story, Brian wondered aloud one day. *"Queer Jew,"* replied John without missing a beat. Its eventual title, in oblique acknowledgment to the Cavern club, was *A Cellarful of Noise.* John referred to it, if at all, as *A Cellarful of Boys.*

The second half of 1964 was to be spent mainly in satisfying the international Beatle hunger that the first half had created, with visits to Denmark, Holland, Hong Kong, Australia, New Zealand, and finally back to America. Since this time it was positively "no wives on tour," John felt obliged to make amends to Cynthia in advance for his impending long absences. The two therefore arranged an Easter weekend break at the Dromoland Castle Hotel, a baronially grand establishment in Ireland's County Clare. With them went George Harrison and his new date Pattie Boyd, a pretty blonde fashion model in the John-approved Bardot mold who had played one of the schoolgirls in *A Hard Day's Night*. Despite elaborate security, the foursome were immediately tracked down by press photographers and after only one night decided to abandon their visit and return home. To avoid the cameras, Cynthia and Patti disguised themselves as hotel maids, then were smuggled off the premises in an outsize laundry hamper.

The world-circumnavigation was planned in two phases: Europe to Australasia in June, trans-America in August. On the eve of the first phase, seeming disaster struck when Ringo was hospitalized with acute tonsillitis. Few, if any, modern bands would consider making so important a trip across the globe without their regular drummer: in this case, despite some mutterings from George, a session player named Jimmy Nicol was hired on salary, put into a Beatle suit and bangs, and sent out on half a journey of a lifetime.

In Amsterdam, the second stop, shrieking Dutch fans perched on top of high lampposts, even jumped into the canals to pursue the Beatles' open-top launch. Europe's most sexually liberal city after Hamburg also demonstrated how little they needed professional PR people to safeguard their wholesome public image. At the first opportunity, all four left their hotel and made a beeline for the red-light district, by repute second only to the Reeperbahn. "Just as we got there, the police rolled up," Neil Aspinall remembered. "They literally tapped us on the shoulder and said, 'Naughty Beatles, back to your hotel' as if we were schoolboys. We said, 'OK, fine.' They took us to the hotel—then John and I went straight out again and back to the red-light district. When we came out again, it was dawn and all the people were on their way to work."

For the Hong Kong–Australasia leg, their entourage had an extra member: Aunt Mimi. It was entirely John's idea, as Tony Barrow recalls, born of the same impulse that had catapulted Cynthia to New York: "He wanted the people closest to him to see how important he was." Mimi needed little persuading because the trip would allow her to visit her relations in New Zealand—the ones she might have joined permanently but for John's mother's death. Aunts on tour might have been even less welcome to his companions than wives on tour. "But we all knew Mimi and how much she meant to John," Aspinall said. "There was no problem."

So Mimi prepared to leave Mendips for the longest time since John's babyhood, deputing her two nephews, Michael and David, to move in during her absence and look after the garden and the cats. During her meticulous packing, she found time to write to thirteen-year-old Jane Wirgman in Surrey, returning the copy of *In His Own Write* that Jane had sent her, hoping to get it autographed by John.

> I will not see him until I join him at the airport for the Australian-New Zealand tour. [The Beatles] have one night in Hong-Kong, but I have to go on. He's afraid I may be nervous if there is a crowd there. He's right too!
>
> You will get the book signed by John later.
>
> You're very nice, too—Mimi Smith

The atmosphere was still nearer a Royal tour than a rock one. At Hong Kong's Kai Tak Airport, the Beatles crossed the tarmac ringed by colonial police in peaked caps and shorts and later performed to an audience entirely made up of British military personnel and their families. Wherever crowds of Chinese onlookers closed in on Mimi, a path was instantly cleared for her with cries of "John Mama! John Mama!" Landing at Sydney's Mascot Airport in an almost monsoon-strength rainstorm, they found they were scheduled to parade around the airport on a flatbed truck, with only short capes and flimsy umbrellas for protection—which, amazingly, they did. The lashing rain made all the dye run out of their capes and soak through the garments beneath so that when each undressed later, his skin was mottled royal blue.

Ringo rejoined the lineup in Melbourne, and Mimi parted company from it to visit her Stanley relatives in New Zealand. "I was bewildered by the unexpected deluge of photographers, reporters, flash-bulbs etcetera," she would later write to Jane Wirgman. "I'm Sure the reporters thought I was a half-wit. I didn't let anyone know

I was with them. I had left them (thankfully) in Australia & arrived alone in N.Z., expecting only the family to meet me."

A Hard Day's Night received its premiere at the London Pavilion cinema on July 6, before a VIP audience including John's Royal targets "Princess Margarine" and "Bony Armstrove," aka Princess Margaret and Lord Snowdon. As he exchanged receiving-line banter with the princess, his face wore an expression only describable as Washington embassy-itis. Nonetheless, the trendy Royals were so charmed that they could hardly be persuaded to leave the after-show party and go on to their next engagement.

The film won ecstatic reviews in the United Kingdom and, later, when it opened across America. Andrew Sarris in the *Village Voice* dubbed it "the Citizen Kane of jukebox musicals," though most reviewers found more obvious parallels in Mack Sennett's silent-screen Keystone Cops and, of course, the Marx Brothers. Some months afterward, Richard Lester bumped into Groucho Marx, the brothers' cigar-chewing wise guy—so presumably John's counterpart—and found him less than flattered by this comparison. "At least," he grouched, "you could tell us apart."

On July 10, the film also had a special charity premiere in Liverpool, combined with a civic reception for its stars. Despite having carried their home city's name into the stratosphere, all four were uneasy about this homecoming-in-state—specifically about their welcome, or lack of it, from all the fans they'd left behind. Through various channels, they'd heard they were "finished" at the Cavern club, which, for John in particular, took some of the shine even off having played Carnegie Hall. But Liverpool knows how to do crazy enthusiasm as well as cool antagonism. On their drive into town from Speke Airport, cheering crowds lined every roadside. Among the welcoming delegation was Bob Wooler, the Cavern deejay John had beaten up at Paul's twenty-first birthday party for insinuating he'd had an affair with Brian. "Hello, Bob," John greeted him. "Has anyone given you a black eye lately?"

At the Town Hall, the Beatles were presented with ceremonial keys to the city by the lord mayor, then made an appearance on the balcony overlooking Castle Street to wave at the multitudes below. Framed among beaming dignitaries in fur-trimmed robes and chains of office, John could not resist adding a few Nazi-style salutes. Once again, a bit of potentially catastrophic devilment seemed to go over everyone's heads. For Brian, in any case, that day's main problem had nothing to do with John. Someone among the crowd was found to be circulating leaflets with a paternity claim against Paul. Working feverishly to trace and neutralize this saboteur, Brian and his PR team had no time to worry about the odd, reckless Lennon Sieg Heil.

Among the guests at the civic reception, and in the Odeon cinema audience later, were most of the extended family in which he had grown up: his Aunts Harrie and Nanny and Uncle Norman, his cousin Stanley, and his young cousins Michael and David and half sisters Julia and Jackie. "Trouble was that John had been his usual disorganised self admin-wise, and we stood around, not really knowing what was going on," his cousin Michael says. "I remember him saying from the Odeon stage, 'Where was my family?'" The Beatles returned to London immediately after the film, so that was all his relatives would see of him.

Mimi, however, missed the occasion. She was still in New Zealand, enjoying a reunion with her Stanley kinfolk, which eventually lasted almost all summer. "She only came home when she did because some man out there had started to show an interest in her," Michael says. "She wasn't having any of that."

Waiting for her at Mendips were the usual piles of fan mail for John, of which only one, with a Kingston-on-Thames postmark, demanded a reply:

251/29 October 64

Dear Jane

I quickly recognised your writing—thousands of letters waiting here. Oh dear!

I arrived home about two weeks ago, but have since been up to Edinburgh and Glasgow to see John, as I haven't seen him since Wellington, New Zealand.

I gather [the Beatles] are to be in pantomime Christmas time. I may go up, or sooner, to see them. However, he will be home on 8 November. I'll see what's what.

. . . You will simply love boarding school. I know—you see. . . .

Lovely big party travelling out [on tour] with the boys, and what do you think! I sat behind the Pilot when we landed at Darwin, 2 AM, and I really think Pilots are the 'tops'.

Enjoy the Show, what an excitable little girl you are.

love Mimi

Traveling rock shows were, of course, nothing new in America. But the Beatles' return there in August, to remedy the coitus interruptus of February, imposed unprecedented new demands on what had been a relatively straightforward process. The result was the first-ever rock tour as we now understand the term, a blueprint for the thousands more that were to come but also unique in its combination of excess and innocence. Five weeks later, when it was all over, even John could not summon up a snide or cynical word. "It's been fantastic," he told radio reporter Larry Kane. "We'll probably never do another tour like it . . . it could never be the same."

No previous mobile spectacle of any kind, other than political, had ever aspired to so vast a catchment area. In thirty-four days, the Beatles appeared in twenty-four cities, from Jacksonville, Florida, to Vancouver, British Columbia, traveling 22,441 miles, an average of over 600 per day. In every city, they performed at the principal arena, including the famous Hollywood Bowl, to audiences of between twelve thousand and thirty-five thousand. Gone, too, were the snub-nosed silver buses and overloaded station wagons in which troubadours had always been accustomed to wander the continent. This four and their retinue traveled in a private Lockheed Electra jet aircraft hired by Brian for a staggering $37,000. As much as a sensible practical measure, it was a piece of calculated symbolism on his part, taking his boys off the tour bus forever and putting them into the cloud-borne company of presidents and potentates.

In a farewell nod to package-tour tradition, they had a supporting bill of American acts: the Righteous Brothers, the Bill Black Combo, the Exciters, and singer-songwriter Jackie DeShannon. And their own stage show was still the one they had been giving at British theaters, a rerun of their chart hits, plus the odd album track, lasting only thirty minutes.

This was Beatlemania in a jumbo-size cup, its every manifestation a hundred times more extreme than the European variety. Here young girls were not content to sit and scream in their seats, but rushed the stage to hug a Beatle for a desperate few seconds before being batted away by security men, or threw themselves like lemmings from high balconies. Here they did not pursue Beatle-bearing vehicles pathetically on foot, but in their own cars, turning almost every overland journey into a demented drag race. Here they did not merely congregate hysterically outside hotels, but found their way inside and up to the Beatles' quarters, often by means that would not have disgraced Houdini. Even the confectionary love tokens with which they bombarded their idols had a new, aggressive edge. Rather than soft, sugar-coated British jelly babies, these were hard-shelled American jelly beans that volleyed out of every auditorium like arrows at Agincourt and stung like buckshot. Many other types of adoring missile also had to be dodged, such as lighters, whole cartons of cigarettes, even shoes.

Whereas British fans had commemorated the Beatles merely in corduroy jackets or plastic guitars, America demanded more potent souvenirs, and American entrepreneurism hastened to meet the demand. After they checked out of one Midwestern hotel, all the bed linen they had used was bought by two local businessmen for $750. The unlaundered sheets and pillowcases were then cut into three-inch squares and each square offered for sale at $10, accompanied by a legal affidavit that a portion of one or another Beatle truly had rested on it. Efforts were made to buy up residues of their shaving cream and bathwater; in New York, supermarkets reported a brisk trade in canned "Beatle breath."

The sums of money swirling in the Electra's slipstream were sometimes too enormous to be taken quite seriously. At the start of the tour in San Francisco, Brian had been approached by a Kansas City businessman named Charles O. Finley, who offered an unheard-of $100,000 if the Beatles would give a single show in his home city over and above their existing schedule. Tempted though Brian was, he had to reply that there was no slot available in the entire five weeks. But Finley was not about to lose face with Kansas City: he kept coming back and upping his offer until it reached $150,000. Brian then put it to the Beatles as a possibility only if they sacrificed one of their few precious rest periods. John, speaking on the others' behalf, replied they would do whatever Brian thought best. So the city they had hymned so many times in Liverpool and Hamburg got in on the act yet again.

But Finley was to discover even that kind of money could not buy him love. To round off his triumph in Kansas City's eyes, he also wanted the Beatles to play for an extra five minutes above their usual thirty. This time, unfortunately he was overconfident in the power of his wallet, breezing into their hotel suite in a shiny silk suit and addressing them presumptuously as "Boys." Though Brian was in the room at the time, negotiations went on solely between Finley and John. Finley offered $5,000 for the extra five minutes; John merely shook his head. Finley kept raising the bonus by units of $5,000 until it reached $50,000, but still received the same dismissive turndown. Finally losing his temper, he called the Beatles "a bunch of boys" with a small *b*, and stormed out. Later, backstage at the Municipal Stadium, it became clear that for all Finley's efforts on Kansas City's behalf, the shows were rather less than a sellout. John grinned at him and said, "You shouldn't have spent so much money on us, Chuck."

Despite the deep-pile red-carpet treatment they received, the Beatles were constantly aware of a society more dangerous and unpredictable than their own at that time, whose police carried rifles, even for the task of holding back teenage girls, and whose president had been gunned down before similarly welcoming crowds only ten months earlier. Bomb threats were made before two of their shows, one in Las Vegas, the second in Dallas, where nerves were already jittery enough. One reporter asked John if any of these serial queasy moments had scared him. He replied that being onstage with the others gave him a strange sense of invulnerability: "I feel safe as long as I'm plugged in. I don't feel as though they'll get me."

As their on-the-road PR man, the Beatles now had Derek Taylor, a thirty-three-year-old fellow Merseysider with the chiseled good looks and immaculate grooming of an Italian movie star. Hoylake-raised, a former *Daily Express* journalist, Taylor had ghostwritten Brian's autobiography, *A Cellarful of Noise*, then joined NEMS, initially as his personal assistant. By the Amsterdam visit, this had developed into handling press for Brian's boys under the usual conditions of Brian watching critically over his shoulder, at one moment leaving everything to him, at the next bawling him out for overpresumptuousness.

Taylor proved to be a perfect fit with the Beatles as well as an ideal intermediary with reporters, who until recently had been his colleagues. Though his greatest friendship within the group would be with George, he and John found an instant rapport, thanks to their shared love of words and fondness for the more obscure British music-hall comedians. Normally, the least likely person to observe a star's better nature is his PR man. But it was to Derek Taylor that John most consistently showed the side of himself that had nothing to do with rock-'n'-roll image and everything to do with his upbringing by Aunt Mimi—the quality Taylor would later sum up as "grace."

A small party of journalists, British and American, rode on the Beatles' plane, filing daily reports from the campaign trail. They included thirty-five-year-old Art Schreiber, a senior correspondent for the Westinghouse Broadcasting System, whose usual beat was politics and national affairs. Schreiber initially wondered how to get a handle on this very different subject matter; then in a conversation with John, he happened to mention that he enjoyed playing Monopoly. At this, John's sardonic cool melted into schoolboyish enthusiasm. "I've got a board!" he said.

So, while the rest of the Beatles' party whiled away in-flight hours with their usual poker game, John and Art Schreiber would play Monopoly, sometimes joined by George Harrison. "George would hardly say a word for the whole game," Shreiber remembers. "But John always got really involved and excited. He always stood up to throw the dice. And if he got Park Place and Boardwalk, he'd be triumphant. He didn't care if he lost the game so long as he had those two properties. We played so late sometimes that I'd doze off to sleep. Then I'd feel a dig in my ribs and hear John's voice: 'Come on, Art . . . it's your move.'"

Schreiber's past assignments had included covering John F. Kennedy's presidential campaign and state funeral; he came to Beatlemania directly from reporting on the civil-rights campaign and its inspirational leader, Dr. Martin Luther King. Though his role was to ask questions of John, he found that more often John would quiz *him* about the domestic and foreign problems that currently darkened America's horizons: the vicious attacks on Dr. King's peaceful rallies and marches, and the increasing scope of U.S. military involvement in a far-off, little-known Asian country called Vietnam. "What really surprised me was what a helluva lot John already knew about this country," Schreiber remembers. "The thing he couldn't understand was the violence . . . the murder of Kennedy, the police brutality against innocent marchers in the South, the guns he saw being carried everywhere. I could see the soul of an activist building up in him."

The mass hurling of jelly confectionary was not all that America's Beatlemaniacs had picked up from Britain's. Children and young people in wheelchairs filled the front rows at every performance, and afterward were brought to the Beatles' dressing rooms as if to some healing holy shrine. Here, too, they were often ruthlessly exploited, serving merely as a passport through security for able-bodied Beatle hunters. But somehow in America, the degree of physical and mental affliction seemed more terrible, the exploitation more grotesque. "Most of those poor kids were in such a bad way, they wouldn't have known who the hell the Beatles were," Art Schreiber says. "John hated going through that, but it had nothing to do with callousness or indifference. 'What do I say to them?' he'd often ask me afterwards—and the guy was really despairing."

There were, of course, some things these embedded tour correspondents could not report if they wished to keep their seats on the plane. They could say nothing about the provision of sex for all the Beatles, which was carried out with a practicality General Hooker would have approved, sometimes drawing on the oceans of all-too-eager fans, sometimes using the higher-class call girls to be found in each stopover city. Still less could they mention the offers of sexual favors they themselves routinely received from females desperate for any introduction to a Beatle. Rather like servants in an Edwardian country house, they hovered in the background, seeing and hearing everything yet prevented by their terms of employment from telling it to anyone but one another.

Realizing what a charmed life they led, the four Beatles scarcely bothered to maintain their public image in front of these omnipresent media butlers and footmen. "These things are left out, about what bastards we were," John remembered. "Fucking big bastards, that's what the Beatles were. You have to be a bastard to make it, and that's a fact. And the Beatles were the biggest bastards on earth. We're the Caesars. Who's going to knock us when there's a million pounds to be made, all the hand-outs, the bribery, the police and the hype?"

There were also incessant diplomatic duties, either as standard-bearers for Britain or trophies of Capitol Records, to which he submitted with the same resignation as the other three. After their Hollywood Bowl show on August 23, they had to attend a charity cocktail party organized by Capitol's president, Alan Livingstone, for which leading Hollywood stars had clamored to buy tickets at several hundred dollars each. Faces that John had once ogled on the screen at the Woolton picture house now stood reverently in line to meet him, among them Edward G. Robinson, Jack Palance, Hugh O'Brien, Shelley Winters, Dean Martin, and Jack Lemmon. Even so, he quickly became bored by the whole affair, commenting later that it was "natural for us to play and sing but . . . unnatural to sit on a stool and shake hands" and that he'd expected Hollywood to be "more fun."

Only once on the whole tour did he come near to a compromising headline. Among Hollywood's new Beatlemaniacs was Jayne Mansfield, the phenomenally endowed platinum blonde who had made even milk bottles have orgasms in her film *The Girl Can't Help It*. Mansfield turned up at a private party at the Beatles rented Bel Air mansion, and spent most of the evening exercising her busty, breathy allure on John. The following night, they went to the Whisky a Go Go club, traveling in an obliging policeman's cruiser and—by a fellow passenger's account—"making out like kids" in its backseat. At the club, Mansfield hogged the assembled cameras, seated with one hand on John's thigh and the other, for good measure, on George's.

Fortunately, George then created a diversion by throwing his drink over a too-intrusive photographer. So no mischievous report about The Girl Helping Herself to a Beatle found its way back to Cynthia.

The following week brought John a double encounter that was to have profound consequences for both his music and his life. On August 28, when the Beatles returned to New York, he was introduced simultaneously to Bob Dylan and marijuana.

Dylan, then twenty-three, was the most spellbinding new voice in American music—the traditional voice of the dissident folk singer, endowed with unprecedented energy, passion, and range. His songs, phrased like biblical psalms and spat out with a heckler's venom, had become a rallying cry for the civil-rights movement, for left-wing activists of every kind, above all for the conviction spreading like brushfire through once-peaceful colleges and schools that America was not the perfect place it had always been painted. Though Dylan was a folkie and John was a rocker, and the twain were never supposed to meet, they had many unrealized points of contact. Both were in flight from their upbringings (Dylan's by respectable Jewish parents in Minnesota); both hid bottomless wells of anger and aggression; both were compulsive writers of prose and poetry; both wore horn-rimmed glasses in private and Lenin caps in public; both played mouth organs, John's hidden in a pocket, Dylan's suspended before his mouth on a metal frame. When Dylan's journalist friend Al Aronowitz talked to John back in February, he had instantly seen "[Bob's] English reflection through the looking-glass and across the sea in the land of left-hand drive."

The Beatles had all been fans of Dylan since George had bought his second album, *The Freewheelin' Bob Dylan*, featuring "Blowin' in the Wind," "Don't Think Twice, It's All Right," and the nuclear apocalyptic "A Hard Rain's a-Gonna Fall." For John, it had brought a total rethink of his approach to songwriting. "I had a sort of professional . . . attitude to writing pop songs," he would recall. "[Paul and I] would turn out a certain style of song for a single. . . . I'd have a separate songwriting John Lennon who wrote songs for the meat market, and I didn't consider them to have any depth at all. To express myself I would write . . . *In His Own Write*, the personal stories which were expressive of my personal emotions. Then I started being me about the songs, not writing them objectively but subjectively." It was already starting to happen, albeit in lyrics still ostensibly stuck in the realm of boy-meets-girl. "You Can't Do That," the B-side of "Can't Buy Me Love," gave romance a threatening tone that only Cynthia had heard before; "I'll Cry Instead," originally intended for the *Hard Day's Night* sound track, found its author casually disclosing: "I've got a chip on my shoulder bigger than my feet."

Before starting out on tour, John had asked Aronowitz to fix a meeting between Dylan and him, rather nervously stipulating it must take place on his territory. The appointed place was the Beatles' New York hotel, the Delmonico, after the first of their two performances at the West Side Tennis Club stadium in Forest Hills, Queens. That same evening, as it happened, Brian was hosting a lavish reception at the hotel, to which other, more anodyne American folk artistes, like Peter, Paul and Mary and the Kingston Trio, had been invited. Dylan turned up outside, escorted only by Aronowitz and a roadie named Victor Maimudes, and called the Beatles' suite from a phone booth across the street. Neil Aspinall was dispatched to escort him up, bypassing the fellow folkies who were so soon to regard him as a traitor.

A few minutes later, John was shaking hands with the tousle-haired, full-faced, cold-eyed youth who could get as much power from a single acoustic guitar and wired-up mouth organ as the Beatles could through their three Vox amps. Obviously fascinated by one another but equally unable to admit as much, they exchanged greetings and superficial pleasantries in a manner later described by Aronowitz to Allen Ginsberg as "demure." Brian Epstein's hospitable diplomacy also badly misfired. Invited to have a drink, Dylan made his usual solidarity-with-the-hoboes request for "cheap wine." Brian had to reply apologetically that there was only vintage champagne.

Things began to loosen up when Dylan—secretly a keen observer of commercial pop—revealed that he knew the Beatles' songs well, though their British accents had produced one major misunderstanding on his part. In "I Want to Hold Your Hand," he thought the line "I can't hide, I can't hide" was "I get high, I get high"—i.e., a reference to smoking marijuana. Rather shamefacedly John and Paul had to confess that, far from smuggling it onto a hit single, they'd never even tried pot in any serious way. "We may have had a bit up in Liverpool," Neil Aspinall says. "But that was only twigs . . . not real leaves."

The omission was quickly rectified in an adjacent bedroom, Aronowitz producing the stash, Dylan himself attempting to roll an introductory joint but messing it up; his roadie, Victor Maimudes, then taking over to fashion individual roll-ups for each Beatle in case the squeamish Britons balked at the usual practice of passing a single one from mouth to mouth. John refused to sample his until Ringo went first as his "royal taster."

Within a few moments, those misheard words from "I Want to Hold Your Hand" had come true. Brian Epstein, deprived of his managerial dignity and poise, could do nothing but slump on a sofa, repeating, "I'm so high, I'm on the ceiling . . ." Paul, in one blinding flash, understood the whole meaning of life and ordered Mal Evans to follow him around, making a careful note of everything he said. On John and Ringo, the sucked-in draughts of sage-scented smoke had a rather simpler effect: neither of them could stop laughing. From here on, John's code for suggesting they repeat the experience would be "Let's have a laugh."

A further and more relaxed meeting between Dylan and him took place at the tour's last-stop hotel, the Riviera Motor Inn, close to Kennedy Airport. Later, accompanied by Neil Aspinall, they managed an incognito visit to a neighborhood diner. "If ever Bob got together with the Beatles after that, John was always the one he zeroed in on." Aspinall said. "He knew who was the leader of the band."

16

THE TOP OF THE
MOUNTAIN

I was crying out for help. It's real.

The only truly invented part of *A Hard Day's Night* is that onscreen Paul has a grandfather, a disreputable Irish Scouser (played by Wilfred Brambell, from Britain's beloved TV comedy *Steptoe and Son*) who turns up out of nowhere and becomes a source of hideous embarrassment to all the boys—drinking, stirring up trouble, and chasing women half his age. Toward the end of the film, having repeatedly landed them in the soup, he receives a little homily from John: "You know your trouble. You should have gone west to America. You took a wrong turning and what happened? You're a lonely old man from Liverpool."

The words were to prove ironic, their tone of kindly disinterest even more so. For it was during the filming of his scenes with this fictitious old reprobate that John's father, Alf Lennon, walked back into his life.

377

Seventeen years had gone by since the summer day in Blackpool when Alf had let Julia take back six-year-old John, and then, losing all appetite for seafaring, had disappeared into Britain's landlocked underclass. In all this time, he had made no effort to see or communicate with John, not even after Julia's death in 1958. His thinking had the same mixture of fatalism and quixotic pride that had so often torpedoed his career afloat. With the transference of John into Aunt Mimi's care, Alf decided he could no longer play any meaningful part in his son's life or hope to correct the negative image of himself retailed to John by Mimi. His decision caused him great pain, so he later said, and in the decades that followed, he often wondered how his "little pal" was getting on. Then in late 1963, the headlines of every newspaper, magazine, and news broadcast in Britain let him know.

Alf was by now past fifty but, in all his own time "on the road," had not advanced a single step in status or income. He still worked as a kitchen porter—a euphemism for dishwasher—in pubs and small hotels in the midlands and south, usually choosing jobs where room and board were provided. Since 1946, he had acquired neither property nor savings, put down no roots, nor found any relationship to erase the memory of Julia. Even so, he remained a jaunty figure, standing barely five feet four inches on the legs that childhood rickets had stunted; his long hair swept back like an old-fashioned musical maestro. He was the life and soul of every kitchen where he worked, performing his menial tasks with gusto, singing at the top of his voice, as content as ever with the transitory satisfactions of a drink and a laugh. Somewhere along the way, he had stopped calling himself Alf and instead adopted his second Christian name, shortening it to Fred or the more debonair Freddie.

Freddie Lennon was working at a pub called the Grasshopper, near Caterham, Surrey, when John Lennon first began to be written and talked about on a national scale. Not until several people had commented on their identical surname and city of origin did Freddie suspect he might be this famous young Lennon's father. Without consulting him, so he later claimed, the pub's chef shopped him to the *News of the World*—hence the exposé that the author Michael Braun reported to be hanging over John's head in late 1963. But this one did not reach fruition. So incensed was Freddie by the chef's action that he quit his job and took off before the *NoW*'s sleuths could get to him.

By his account, he originally had no intention of contacting John, knowing that any approach would inevitably brand him as a sponger. He therefore did his best to avoid notice, taking a new KP post at a hotel in the south coast resort of Bognor Regis. By this time press stories were starting to appear about how John had been abandoned by his father as a small boy and had not seen nor heard from him since. The first part, at least, was a calumny: Freddie's only "abandonment" had been going away to sea, latterly on war service. He had abducted John to Blackpool intending to make a new life for the two of them in New Zealand; by his own lights, he'd had only John's interests at heart in allowing Julia to reclaim him.

The two Lennon uncles, of whom grown-up, famous John was hardly conscious, also played their part in breaking Freddie's cover. His oldest brother, Sydney—who had cherished hopes of adopting John prior to the Blackpool episode—considered Freddie almost as much a ne'er-do-well as did Aunt Mimi. Now, as Beatlemania set in, Sydney wrote to Freddie, sternly warning him not to bring "shame" on John by attempting to cash in on his wealth and celebrity. On the other hand, his ever-loyal younger brother, Charlie, urged him to put the record straight about the circumstances that had brought John into Mimi's care rather than Sydney's. An outraged Freddie returned to Liverpool, accompanied by Charlie, and publicly berated Sydney outside his place of work. As a result, the two brothers never spoke to each other again.

By a bizarre coincidence, while John was actually filming some of the later *Hard Day's Night* scenes with Wilfred Brambell, the real-life "lonely old man from Liverpool," who might well have "gone west to America" like his own Kentucky minstrel father, and certainly had taken the mother of all "wrong turnings," was only a matter of yards away. Freddie had come to London in search of work and was drinking tea in a café near the Scala Theatre, where the film's climactic Beatles concert takes place—including an unintentionally prophetic moment when Brambell pops up through a trapdoor among the four as they play. The sight of screaming fans around the theater, so Freddie later said, helped decide him to put his side of the story into print.

His chosen platform was the *Daily Sketch*, the milder of the two weekday tabloids then circulating in Britain. Predictably, the *Sketch* was less interested in putting the record straight than in the live-action scoop of actually confronting John with his missing father. Freddie was stowed away in a hotel under guard, to prevent any rival paper getting to him, and liberally plied with alcohol. Each day, in cloak-and-dagger fashion, he was driven to the Scala Theatre and kept waiting in the car while the *Sketch's* people negotiated with the Beatles' for access to John.

The meeting, as Freddie later recalled it, was brief and initially glacial. John showed no emotion at seeing him, merely asking point-blank what he wanted. Freddie replied that he was not after money or any other kind of share in the Beatle bandwagon: all he sought, after years of character assassination, first by Julia's family, then by journalists, was a chance to defend and explain himself. Once this assurance was given, he said, John's attitude seemed to soften. Freddie told his tale: how Julia had left him for another man but how nonetheless he had been willing to take her back, how he had not deserted John but had been emotionally blackmailed into relinquishing him. Father and son exchanged some reminiscences of times together back in the gray war years—even managed to share a laugh or two. After twenty minutes or so, Freddie departed, feeling that the reunion had not gone badly, though John was later to recall: "I saw him and spoke to him, and decided I still didn't want to know him."

Mimi, too, had received advance warning that Freddie was about to resurface. When the press stories about him first began circulating, he sent her an aggrieved letter, reminding her of the true facts as he saw them, which Mimi marked "return to sender" without reading. Though Freddie no longer had power to take him away, Mimi still "felt a shock go right through my body to my fingertips and the tips of my toes" when John telephoned and told her of the meeting and the resultant *Daily Sketch* story. He reassured her—as he himself believed—that Freddie would not trouble them further.

Even without errant fathers turning up on his doorstep, living in London had become more trouble to John than it was worth. The fans besieging his rented flat in Emperor's Gate continued to increase, in number and agitation, their ranks now swollen by converts from America, Europe, and Australasia; the telephone rang almost nonstop day and night, both in the Lennons' duplex and Bob and Sonny Freeman's ground-floor flat. Little though John wanted to leave the city's ever-blossoming scene, he recognized that Cynthia and Julian had a right to some peace and privacy. Another factor way well have played its part in the decision. Freeman, the Beatles' invaluable photographer, still seemed unaware of John's trysts with his Pirelli calendar-girl wife—and Cyn certainly was. Better, then, to quit while one was ahead.

Too busy and disorganized to find a new home for himself, John handed over the problem, as usual, to Brian Epstein. Brian in turn passed it to his accountants, the Albemarle Street firm of Bryce, Hanmer and Isherwood, which also channeled his boys' income and living expenses. As it happened, the head of the firm, Charles Isherwood, lived in Weybridge, the heart of the Surrey Stockbroker Belt. Isherwood suggested the town's St. George's Hill estate, an enclave of baronial-style properties that already harbored several big show-business names, among them Charlie Drake and Spike Milligan. John voicing no objection to the area, a short list of available houses was drawn up for Cynthia and him to view.

They chose the third one they saw, a twenty-seven-room mansion situated on a grassy hill among several acres of landscaped garden. The house was mock-Tudor in style and named Kenwood after the famous Robert Adam–designed stately home in North London. If John had consciously set out to find a southern counterpart to Woolton and a magnified Mendips, he could hardly have done better. The house was bought on his behalf for £20,000 in the early summer of 1964. Pending extensive renovations both to the building and grounds, John, Cynthia, and Julian took up residence in a staff flat in the attic.

Happily, buying Kenwood coincided with acquiring wealth he could actually see. Nor was his quarter share of the Beatles' worldwide performance fees and record royalties anywhere near the end of it. In February 1965, Northern Songs, the publishing company whose creation solely to handle Lennon-McCartney compositions had seemed like pure swagger two years earlier, was floated on the London Stock Exchange. Never before in Britain had pop songs become a commodity like oil and grain, nor had stockbrokers and City analysts turned to the *Melody Maker* Top 20 chart as hungrily as they did to the *Financial Times*. The flotation was a spectacular success that saw Northern's two-shilling (10p) shares rocket in price to 7s 9d (almost 40p) and the value of Dick James's original £100 company reach almost £3 million.

Prior to flotation, John and Paul sold 85 percent of their respective shares, a transaction that netted them each £94,270, between £2 million and £3 million by today's values. Their work for Northern Songs had previously been assigned through a company named Lenmac Enterprises Ltd., which they now sold to Northern for another £140,000 apiece. From here on, their songs would be supplied through a new company, Maclen (Music) Ltd.—a little-noticed instance of Paul's name coming first. City investors, at least, no longer considered pop a passing fad. The guarantee of Northern Songs' stability and growth was that, via Maclen, John and Paul were contracted to supply it with material until 1973.

Thus no expense was spared to make John's new home a showpiece rivaling any of the millionaire hideaways round about. Brian's interior designer, Ken Partridge, was hired to sweep away Kenwood's old-fashioned décor and provide its already-immaculate grounds with new adornments, including a Hollywood-size swimming pool. Given carte blanche by John, Partridge knocked down walls, inserted new staircases, laid vistas of black carpet—bruiseable by the lightest footfall—and put in a state-of-the-art kitchen so complicated that the supplier had to send someone from London to teach Cynthia how to use it. John had barely glanced at Partridge's original plans and now took violent exception to much of what had been done. Further large sums were spent in undoing and replacing the designer's handiwork—for example, exchanging his hard red-leather couches (which Ringo Starr inherited) for softer velvet ones.

Despite John's far-from-constant presence there, the house was always preeminently a reflection of his character and ever-changing taste. At ground-floor level, the main room was a den—dens being as much a feature of twentieth-century British suburbia as morning rooms—containing his books, two Stuart Sutcliffe paintings, and an impressive desk where he planned to sit and write like any great author from literature. Another room had three Scalextric miniature racecar sets combined into one vast layout; another had slot machines, table football games, and a jukebox of rock-'n'-roll classics. In the attic was a music room filled with his guitars, pianos, and tape recorders. A Mellotron organ which proved too difficult to manhandle up the final narrow stairs, stood on a half landing below.

The latest craze was for Victoriana and Edwardiana: brass bedsteads, flowered chamberpots, fringed lamps, enamel signs for Oxo or R. White's lemonade, sepia photographs, and mementoes of the Boer War and World War I, which had been familiar fixtures in the childhood of John's generation but now suddenly assumed a delicious quaintness and irony. Kenwood rapidly filled up with such "fun" objects, each representing a brief, costly burst of enthusiasm on John's part—a huge altar crucifix rescued from some condemned church, a Victorian family Bible, a suit of armor named "Sidney," a gorilla costume, which he liked to say was the only thing in his gigantic wardrobe that really fitted him. In the book-lined front hall hung a Great War recruiting poster, with Lord Kitchener pointing a stern forefinger above the famous slogan "Your Country Needs YOU." John positioned it so that anyone approaching the front door was greeted by Kitchener's baleful, mustachioed stare through an adjacent window.

Amid the rather impersonal tailor-made luxury were unmistakable reminders of the smaller mock-Tudor house, and the region, that had nurtured him. If careless of all his other impulse-bought possessions, he arranged his books in meticulous order: Swift, Tennyson, Huxley, Orwell, the well-thumbed red cloth bindings of Richmal Crompton's William stories. Half a dozen cats—including one named Mimi—padded around the designer rooms, making messes on the pristine black carpet and tearing at the costly fabrics with their claws. Domestic life, such as it was, centered on a small sunroom opening onto the garden, rather like Mendips's old morning room.

While the servants' bells at Mendips had been merely a relic of past times, Kenwood required a staff of at least three to maintain it properly, including a full-time chauffeur to take John to concerts and up to London for his recording sessions. Though still unqualified to drive, he'd lost no time in buying himself a black Rolls-Royce Phantom V, equipped with a cocktail cabinet, television set, and telephone, its windows darkened to prevent curious fans from peering inside. After the Rolls came a Radford Mini Cooper, a customized and souped-up version of the ubiquitous Mini Minor that had originally been created for Peter Sellers. In February 1965, John passed his driving test, an event that made headline news across the nation. Within hours, every luxury car dealership in the Weybridge area, hoping for his business, jammed the road outside Kenwood's security gates with Maseratis, Aston Martins, and Jaguar XK-E's. John strolled out to inspect this gleaming smorgasbord, eventually selecting a £2,000 light blue Ferrari.

A woman named Dot Jarlett, who had worked for the house's previous owners, agreed to stay on with an expanded role as housekeeper, child-minder, and companion for Cynthia. But the quest for further domestic help initially met nothing but problems. A married couple hired to act respectively as chauffeur and cook quickly caused domestic chaos: the man ogled anything in skirts, his wife squabbled with Dot, and their daughter, on the rebound from a broken marriage, moved into the staff flat with them.

One day while Brian was down from London on a visit, he strolled past the house next to Kenwood as its chauffeur, a six-foot-four former Welsh Guardsman named Les Anthony, was washing a vintage Rolls-Royce in the front driveway. Impressed by Anthony's dapperness and bodyguard proportions, Brian asked if he would consider leaving his present employer to enter John Lennon's service. Thirty-two-year-old Anthony jumped at the chance, especially upon viewing the selection of cars he would get to drive. "John's Rolls was all black—even the wheels," he remembers. "The only bit of chrome on it was the radiator. He told me he'd wanted that to be black as well, but the Rolls people wouldn't do it. And his Mini-Cooper had so many gadgets inside, I had to take the arm-rests out before I could sit at its wheel."

Despite having somehow scraped through his test, John was a hopelessly bad driver: too myopic to read traffic signs until they were almost on top of him, too vague to follow the simplest route, however many times previously traveled, too impractical to deal with or even recognize the smallest mechanical problem. The result was that, for £36 per week (John was never a munificent employer), Les Anthony found himself on more or less permanent call, to the detriment of his private life and ultimately his marriage. Whatever the time of day or night, he was always in parade-ground order, including black-braided chauffeur's cap, and addressed John punctiliously as "Mr. Lennon."

Two other Beatles also now had need of some domestic seclusion and, prompted by Brian and the accountants, followed John into Stockbroker Land. In February 1965, Ringo married his pregnant girlfriend, a Liverpool hairdresser named Maureen Cox. After staying a few months at Ringo's Montagu Square flat, they too arrived on the St. George's Hill estate, settling in a low-rise mock-Tudor extravaganza named Sunny Heights, just a few hundred yards from Kenwood. George, who had recently begun living with his soon-to-be wife Pattie Boyd (they would marry in January 1966), bought a luxury bungalow on the Claremont Estate in nearby Esher. Brian himself wanted the castellated house next door to John but, understandably—having already been robbed of their chauffeur—the owners refused to sell. Only Paul McCartney, the quartet's last remaining bachelor, stayed on in central London.

But if the three migrant Beatles had hoped to escape fan-madness in suburbia, they were quickly disillusioned. Renovation work was still in progress at Kenwood when the first girls were discovered on the grounds, gathering twigs and blades of grass as souvenirs. John fans had a complex message to send him: they were not the sort of mindless hysterics he would mock and despise; they also read books, looked at art, and resisted conformity; and they understood about his marriage, sympathized with Cynthia, and took an interest in Julian. They did more than worship him, they appreciated him. All of which was a tall order to get across in the few seconds when a black-windowed, black-wheeled Rolls swept past.

George's and Ringo's arrival in John's neighborhood was more than just a neat corralling measure on Brian's part. Despite weeks and months of suffocating proximity on tour, the three knew no better company than one other during their time off. For John, having Ringo just down the road and George a ten-minute drive away was rather like his Outlaws being close at hand long ago in Woolton. "John really loved Ringo," Maureen Cleave remembers. "And he often said how much he loved George, which was a slightly unusual thing for a man to come out with in that era." He tended to socialize much less with Paul; theirs was always first and foremost a professional relationship. When new material needed to be written, Paul would come down from London by appointment, usually driving himself in his Aston Martin. One day when he happened to use a chauffeur, the man complained en route that he'd recently been obliged to work "eight days a week." When Paul reached Kenwood, he repeated this phrase to John, who instantly came up with the line "Ooh, I need your love, babe"; so another song was born.

Paul recalls working methods that had changed little since their truant afternoons in his Forthlin Road living room. "John would get up when I arrived, I'd have a cup of tea and a bowl of cornflakes with him and we'd go up to a little room, get our guitars out and kick things around. It would come very quickly, and in two or three hours time I'd leave." They seldom bothered to tape a song-in-progress, keeping up the old rule that if both could remember it next day, it worked.

To Julian, John continued to be a mysterious, uninvolved figure who usually came home at dawn, slept until late each afternoon, then spent his time mostly stretched on a sofa in the sunroom, alternately looking at newspapers and the ever-murmuring television screen, in the condition Cyn defined to herself as "present but absent." "What day is it?" he once asked Maureen Cleave, quite seriously, when she telephoned.

He tended to enjoy Kenwood the most when fellow Beatles and members of their inner circle were visiting, or when he could show the place off to members of his family. He was an especially thoughtful and genial host to the younger generation he had grown up with—his Edinburgh-based cousin, Stanley Parkes, his half sisters, Julia and

Jackie, his Aunt Nanny's son, Michael, his Aunt Harrie's son, David. Julia and Jackie were taken shopping in London by Cyn and saw a Beatles concert at the Finsbury Park Astoria, traveling up with John in the Rolls. Michael and David, who arrived together, were taken to the Beatles Christmas Show and an evening preview of the Boat Show at Olympia, and sent off to buy new gear at the trendy clothes boutiques of Carnaby Street. Roaming around Kenwood during their stay, the boys found one of John's guitars and begun plunking out some of his early Beatles hits on it. John heard them, and good-humoredly came to join in.

A frequent house guest from the beginning was Pete Shotton, John's old partner in crime at Quarry Bank High School. Pete's career in the Liverpool Police had not lasted, and he'd become part owner of a small café near Penny Lane named the Old Dutch. When this proved less than a rip-roaring success, John sought various ways of helping out. On one trip home to Liverpool, he made Pete accept his entire—unopened—Beatle wage-packet of £50 in crisp, blue £5 notes. At another point, a plan was mooted to make the ex–beat bobby and greasy spoon proprietor Brian Epstein's personal assistant.

In 1965, John lent Pete £20,000 to buy a small supermarket in the Hampshire seaside resort of Hayling Island. The new venture being just two hour's drive from Weybridge, Pete could drop around almost as easily as he used to from Vale Road to Menlove Avenue. For John it was the best possible respite from Beatledom to hang out with such a familiar old mate, playing with the one-arm bandits and Scalextric cars, and recalling their boyhood exploits as Shennon and Lotton. To Cynthia, Pete's stays seemed overlong but, as usual, she said nothing.

Robert and Sonny Freeman would occasionally come for the day, bringing their son, Dean, to play or swim in the pool with Julian. John's affair with Sonny had still apparently not been discovered by their respective spouses; otherwise, such family occasions would hardly have been possible. Freeman remained a crucial member of the Beatles' backup team, photographing their album covers and de-signing the graphics for their forthcoming second film, none of this compatible with being an outraged, cuckolded husband. Though the

Freemans' marriage did break up shortly afterward, Sonny is ada-mant that John was not a factor. As for Cyn, even in the second and more recriminatory of her two autobiographies, published in 2005, she would voice only the vaguest, uncorroborated suspicion that he might have been involved with Sonny.

She had received a confession, however—in code decipherable to everyone but herself. In January 1965, she and John went on a winter sports holiday to Switzerland, accompanied by George Martin and Judy Lockhart-Smith. "It was Brian who suggested that Judy and I should go with them," Martin remembers. "I suppose he thought we were decent, respectable people who could be trusted." The trip was low-key—with, surprisingly, no press intrusion: the four stayed at the Palace Hotel in St. Moritz, spending all day on the ski slopes and quiet nights drinking hot chocolate and playing Monopoly. John had brought along a guitar and, during one such cozy après ski interlude, began strumming and singing a new song he was working on. "I re-member hearing the words, and not believing my ears," Martin says. "They went 'I once had a girl / Or should I say / She once had me. . . .' He was owning up to having had an affair, obviously not very long previously. And Cyn was sitting a few feet away, not understanding any of it."

Cynthia's chief ally was her widowed mother, Lilian, a woman who for John personified every mother-in-law joke ever told by his fa-vorite northern comedians, and then some. "He couldn't stand her," his cousin Michael Cadwallader remembers. "Neither could Mimi." Despite John's success, Lilian remained as convinced her daughter had thrown herself away on him as Mimi was that he'd thrown him-self away on Cynthia. Voluble and pugnacious herself, she was horri-fied by the conditions Cyn accepted so uncomplainingly as his wife. After the move to Surrey, she left Hoylake and arrived at Kenwood ostensibly to help Cynthia with Julian, implicitly to keep her son-in-law in line.

Although hostile to John, Lilian did not mind partaking in the fruits of his success. Still antiques mad, she toured local salerooms, spending his money on "finds" for the house that later received only a dubious welcome. A couple of times each month, Les Anthony would drive her in the Rolls back to Hoylake, where she still kept up her old home, sometimes accompanied by Cynthia and Julian, sometimes in queenly majesty on her own. Even John's purchase of a house for her in Esher, for which he also paid the upkeep, plus a weekly allowance of £30 (the same as Mimi received), did not greatly lessen her vigilant presence at Kenwood. A family visitor recalls her "flopped on a couch, stuffing glacé fruits into her mouth," while John—with uncharacteristic gloomy resignation—"passed through without comment."

The person on whom he most wanted to spend his wealth, however, had little taste for luxury or high living—and, indeed, responded to most of his attempts with stern lectures on the virtues of frugality. "John was so naïve with money, all his life," Mimi would recall. "He just never had any idea of its worth, probably because he never had to work hard for it like some people. He was a soft touch. He would listen to a sob-story and then just give his money away to some hanger-on who had spun him a yarn.

"He was always trying to make me buy new clothes or things for the house when he became famous, but I'd tell him, 'No, I'm not the kind who goes out spending for spending's sake.' John once insisted on buying me a fur coat from Harrods. I didn't want it. I told him so. When I went on tour with [the Beatles] to New Zealand, I did buy myself a new coat, but then I wore it for the next fifteen years. I looked after my clothes. John could never understand that."

Mimi was now nearing sixty, and, though she remained as energetic and self-reliant as ever, the strain of living alone at Mendips, under round-the-clock pressure from Beatles fans, was beginning to tell. "John was always nagging on at me to move," she would remember. "I think he was worried about me living there on my own. I had a dizzy spell one day and fainted after I had to answer the phone . . . it was always ringing . . . there would be girls wanting to speak to John, asking if he was in. And if I went out for five minutes and left the back door open, there wouldn't be a single cup or spoon left in the kitchen when I came back."

In fact, Mimi accepted that her life in Woolton had become untenable and, as it happened, knew roughly where she would like to establish a new home. She had always fancied living beside the sea, preferably in one of the genteel South Coast holiday resorts which, by good luck, all lay within easy reach of Weybridge. But for several months, no location, let alone property, could be found that suited her exacting tastes. On March 3, 1965, she mentioned the search in passing to her thirteen-year-old correspondent, Jane Wirgman, who had written for some signed Beatles photographs for her sister Liz and herself.

Dear Jane

So nice to hear from you. I didn't answer before because I wouldn't like your parents to think you were too interested in the Beatles at the expense of the all-important School work.

However, I was in the Beatles' Press Office the other day & got a few photographs. So I'm sending two of each, one for Liz. (My sister's name is Liz.) You may already have the smaller one. They look 'Horrors' to me, but you may like them . . .

I was in Bexhill [Sussex] the other day, looking at some houses, one 'The Moorings' which was lovely, but I didn't want to live at Bexhill.

So in about three weeks I'm going to have a look around Hove, Worthing etc.

I was staying with John for a few days before he went away.

He wants me to live nearer to him but—He Can't Come and See me until he does Something with that 'Mop' and I Mean it.

He said he would have it cut on the [film] Set. I asked him if he was trying to look like a Yorkshire Terrier. Now Jane—you must agree. Those 'Mops' are getting out of hand.

I'm So Cold, I can hardly write . . .

All the best to Liz and yourself.
Mimi.

The following month, she had second thoughts about Bexhill, as she confided to Jane in a letter that began as another lamentation about John's hair, and went on to include several revealing family vignettes:

Yes, I saw the Beatles on Lucky Stars. John's cousin David was here, otherwise, if not reminded, I always forget. But not David.

That hair, it was the very limit, the absolute end. I was almost a Screaming Auntie, much to David's amusement. I could contain myself not one minute more, & promptly phoned him & a good old time battle royal followed, no holds barred & two receivers were banged down. So that was that. He phoned me on Monday, saying he couldn't help it—too busy—same old excuse, but that I would see it has been cut for the Eamonn Andrews Show on Sunday night. Well, we'll see, a Gimmick is all right, but that's going too far. I honestly thought at first it was a wig, he was being funny, fully expecting it to be pulled off. However, we are friends again—at the moment.

He says he has written another very good song, not the one just released, he thinks it's a much better one but it's for the [new] film. Title for the film just one word up to now.

Just had surveyor's report on The Moorings . . . thought I would have another look at it after all, but a lot of woodworm in it . . . So I'm on the lookout again. May have a look at Bournemouth.

No, John did not go to boarding school, a big mistake on my part . . . Now [he] blames me for keeping him at home, & look what I've got——a long-haired rebel! My Sister phoned after Lucky Stars, from Edinburgh—and said, or yelled—"Did you see him?"—Shouting—"You are to blame for all this nonsense.' So poor old Mimi. What can one do with a highly intelligent, in his own way, clever rebel—answer—nothing.

No photographs of Self. I get enough Shocks without Seeing myself.

Have a nice holiday. John's half sister Julia is coming tomorrow. She's working like mad on A Levels. She's 18, is taking Russian as an extra, and definitively not interested in the Beatles, much to John's annoyance, and he's not interested in her Russian—so—

Bye to you and love
Mimi

Mimi did subsequently have a look at Bournemouth, accompanied by John, Cynthia, and Julian in the all-black Rolls, but again could find nothing she liked in the town itself. They were about to give up and return home when an real-estate agent steered them to Canford

Cliffs, a suburb of expensive modern homes that overlooked neighboring Poole Harbour. Here in Panorama Road, a luxurious bungalow named Harbour Edge had just come on the market, priced at a
hefty £25,000. "There were still people living there, so I didn't want
to go in, but John did," Mimi remembered. "I was shocked because
he had his old jeans on with holes in, and a silly cap on; he looked
a mess, but in he went, bold as brass, and 'Do you mind if I look
around?' John liked the place straight away. He said to me 'If you
don't have it, Mimi, I will,' and then he rang his accountant and that
was that."

Harbour Edge was, in fact, an ideal choice, secluded and peaceful,
yet with the busy panorama of Poole Harbour a few feet away to
provide constant interest and banish any feeling of loneliness. By the
time Mimi let Jane Wirgman know her new address, the wrench of
leaving Merseyside had already begun to fade:

> . . . Still looking for different things, which somehow seem to have
> gone astray, including letters, my own fault of Course.
>
> This is a Semi Bungalow, in Some ways not as nice as my own
> house in Woolton. I miss the lovely trees, especially the two big
> Elm Trees in the back garden, there are plenty of trees here, but
> they are mostly tall Pines.
>
> But the view over the Harbour here is lovely, with the Purbeck
> Hills in the distance. The Harbour is very deserted now, of small
> boats anyway, mostly tankers and fussy little tugs bustling about.

After her move south, as she grew older and more overtly dependent on John, a new note entered their relationship. Often it was if
their former roles have been reversed: now he had become the over-
solicitous, scolding parent and Mimi the stubborn, rebellious child.
In another letter to Jane she wrote:

> . . . I am trying to get ready for a holiday in Florence & Venice.
> John insists . . . & I have always wanted to See Michael Angelo's
> Boy David Sculpture & others. So I'm trying to Sort out my rags
> etc. I leave London about 10 AM 3 May & return 17 May when
> John's Car will meet me & I am to go on to Weybridge. "You

Know Who" was on the phone for an hour yesterday morning, bossing me about Something awful. I Say 'Yes dear, oh of Course dear" & go on my own way, which saves a lot of trouble, but the dear boy, I'm quite Convinced, wonders how I'm walking without Crutches! So old, so old. Ah well!

The Beatles' third consecutive British and American number one single, released in November 1964, had given no hint of anything amiss with John. As well as writing the track and singing lead, he also partnered George in the two-handed guitar riff that ran through it. The guitars sounded more like keyboards and seemed set at two different volume levels; the intro began with an echoey groan of feedback, originally produced when John happened to lean his switched-on guitar against a live amp. Despite these founding experiments in sonic novelty and distortion, his lyric was one of pure, simple euphoria. Fresh from a triumphant American tour and elevation to the Weybridge landed gentry, what else could his message possibly be but "I Feel Fine"?

Somewhat different signals were to be read in the album *Beatles for Sale*, which also had instantly gone gold a month earlier. In contrast with clear-cut, upbeat Paul songs like "Eight Days a Week" and "I'll Follow the Sun," John explored grayer areas of self-doubt, mourning, and embarrassment—"No Reply," "Baby's in Black," "I Don't Want to Spoil the Party"—though, as usual, he had made essential contributions to Paul's lightness, just as Paul had to his darkness. His spirits seemed highest in the cover versions that still interspersed Lennon-McCartney originals: Chuck Berry's "Rock and Roll Music," Doctor Feelgood and the Interns' "Mr. Moonlight," and a faithful copy of Buddy Holly's "Words of Love." The album cover showed the four still with their Stu Sutcliffe art-student look, swathed in thick black knitted mufflers. John's face had a strangely drawn, affronted look, as if the snap of the camera shutter had coincided with some mortal personal insult.

It was a strange and wholly new kind of creative frustration he was discovering: to have his every new song awaited so hungrily yet listened to so inattentively, his least predictable themes greeted with the same shrieks of undiscerning rapture, his bleakest thoughts submerged and transfigured by the Beatles' collective joie de vivre. Watch him in early '65, performing a showstopper from *Beatles for Sale*, ducking between his lead vocal and the mouth organ he now has on a frame like Bob Dylan's. Would you believe such energy, and ecstasy, could be generated by a song called "I'm a Loser"?

The follow-up single to "I Feel Fine," released in April 1965, found him in nothing like the same mood of euphoric well-being. "Ticket to Ride" was, on the face of it, a traditional waving-farewell-at-the-station song, rooted in characteristic Lennon wordplay. Paul McCartney's cousins, Mike and Bett Robbins, good friends to the former Nurk Twins in their struggling days, now ran a pub in the small seaside town of Ryde, Isle of Wight. John had been with Paul to stay with the Robbinses, a journey necessitating a "ticket to Ryde" by ferry across the Solent.

But the song contained no echo of that pleasant visit, still less the brave optimism traditionally expressed to departing loved ones by those they leave behind. The tone in which John saw off his anonymous "gerl" was one of glum passivity and self-deprecation: "She said that living with me was bringing her down / That she would never be free when I was around . . ." Whereas previous chart-aimed Beatles tracks had all been bouncy and toe-tapping, this was slow, somnolent, almost hypnotically repetitive—embryonic heavy rock, even heavy metal. Had such a term yet existed, it might almost have been called "druggy."

"Ticket to Ride" was a foretaste of the second Beatles feature film, on which work had begun in February. Once again, the producer was Walter Shenson and the director Richard Lester. Thanks to the global success of *A Hard Day's Night*, this sequel had received a heftily increased budget from United Artists and an upgrade from black-and-white to color. Rather than just playing themselves, the Beatles now played parodies of themselves; no longer shut away under guard but having adventures in the outside world like characters in a cartoon strip. The script—by American screenwriter Marc Behm and British playwright Charles Wood—concerned the efforts of a fanatical Eastern sect to retrieve a sacred ring, which has somehow wound up with the other trademark chunky baubles on Ringo Starr's fingers.

An impressive supporting cast included distinguished actors like Leo McKern and Patrick Cargill and two modish new faces from the satire boom, Roy Kinnear and Eleanor Bron. The provisional title, combining Hinduism's most familiar deity with Beatle jokiness, was *Eight Arms to Hold You.*

Overall, however, neither lavish budget nor living color resulted in anything half as engaging as *A Hard Day's Night.* The complexity of the plot and overnumerous supporting characters meant that the Beatles were often marginalized except in their set-piece performance sequences. Leo McKern, in particular, as the sect's high priest, who takes time out from murderous plotting to discuss theology with a Church of England vicar, ruthlessly upstaged everyone in sight. John was later to complain with good reason of feeling "like extras in our own film."

Much of the interest lies in the eerie accuracy with which Behm and Wood's silly knockabout plot foreshadows real events soon to follow. The Indian theme, with sitars plunking Beatle tunes, is the most obvious but no means only example. At one point, ordinary police protection having failed to shield the foursome from Goddess Kaili's turbaned hit squad, they are shown hiding out inside Buckingham Palace. At another, they try to foil their pursuers by flying out of Heathrow Airport in disguises intended to make them unrecognizable as Beatles. John's round glasses and long, flowing beard are precisely what this particular Beatle will be wearing in earnest four years hence.

A sequence was filmed on location in the Bahamas—not because the plot demanded it but simply as a quid pro quo to that celebrated tax haven for sheltering some of the Beatles' earnings. The islands were still a British Crown Colony, and, in an echo of the Washington episode, the four found themselves pressured into attending a formal black-tie dinner at Government House in Nassau, along with Brian Epstein, Walter Shenson, and Richard Lester. "We'd spent the day filming at what was supposed to be a deserted army barracks," Lester remembers. "When we got there, we found it was a psychiatric institution where old people and children were crowded together in the most terrible conditions. All of the Beatles were sickened by it."

Incensed by the contrast between that and the governor's glittering soiree, John rounded on the nearest official, who happened to be the Bahamian minister of finance. "He really tore into this guy," Lester says. "In front of Walter, Brian, me . . . everyone." The minister protested feebly that he was doing his best and, in fact, received no payment for his job. "In that case, you're doing better than I thought you were doing," John snapped back.

Among his fellow cast members, he found a special empathy with Eleanor Bron, the actress-comedienne cast as the Kaili sect's reluctant handmaiden. Thirty-one-year-old Bron was currently famous for her appearances on the BBC satire show *Not So Much a Programme . . . More a Way of Life*. Intensely beautiful, intensely clever, and intensely private, she awoke all John's well-concealed love of intellectual women and chivalry toward vulnerable ones. One day on a remote Bahamian island, she and the Beatles found themselves cornered by a mob of press photographers, who demanded that Bron should strip and pose for "bikini shots" with the four. "John dealt with them in no uncertain manner," Lester recalls.

The new elements in the Beatles' sound on "Ticket to Ride" did indeed reflect a new element in their lives. Since their initiation by Bob Dylan the previous summer, all four had become regular marijuana users, avid for any chance to seek a place apart and pass around the thin, loosely packed cigarettes whose laughter-giving powers had proved so instant and infallible. And, despite Brian's paranoia over their public image, they carried generous supplies of the drug with them wherever they went. Before each tour, the two roadies Neil and Mal would empty out a full-size carton of two hundred regular cigarettes, then fill each pack with prerolled joints, resealing the cellophane outer wrapper with a warm iron so that no customs official would suspect it had been opened.

Though pot had been illegal in Britain since 1920, most police officers as yet had little or no experience of it. One day when Les Anthony was driving all four Beatles along Exhibition Road in Kensington, a police car pulled him over for a routine traffic offense. "When John wound down the back window to see what was going on, all this pot smoke came billowing out," Anthony remembers. "But the coppers seemed to have no idea what it was. When I went home after a day round and about with John, my clothes used to reek of it."

By the time John turned his mind to writing a title song for the film, some seven weeks into production, it had been renamed *Help!* Initially working alone at Kenwood, he embarked on a formula that seemed straightforward and superficial enough, a Beatly love song conveying the film's cartoon-strip terror and confusion. Into the mix also went the chorus from Bob Dylan's "My Back Pages," a song John had played and replayed since its appearance a year earlier: "Ah, but I was so much older then / I'm younger than that now."

The lyric that emerged was not boy talking to girl so much as patient to psychotherapist, or lost soul to Samaritan: "Help me if you can I'm feeling down . . . I'm not so self-assured . . . Every now and then I feel so insecure . . . Help me get my feet back on the ground . . . Won't you please, please, help me?" These might seem astonishing admissions by the supposedly hard, cynical John Lennon, though to one perceptive American reporter they can have come as no surprise. The future feminist crusader Gloria Steinem, who interviewed him for *Cosmopolitan* magazine, recorded a telling exchange amid the melee at New York's Riverside Motor Inn. "The tall girl leaned over to Lennon and told him that his skin was looking mottled again. 'I know,' he said, and looked embarrassed. 'It's nerves.'"

At the time, even John himself did not realize how much his "Help!" words came from the heart. ". . . later I knew, really, I was crying out for help," he would recall. "The whole Beatle thing was just beyond comprehension. I was eating and drinking like a pig, and I was as fat as a pig, dissatisfied with myself, and subconsciously I was crying for help . . . You can see the movie: he—I— is very fat, very insecure [there are, in fact, no visible traces of either] and he's completely lost himself. And I was singing about when I was so much younger and all the rest, looking back at how easy it was, but then things got more difficult. . . . Anyway, I was fat and depressed and I was crying out for help. It's real."

Paul McCartney, who joined the composition process at an early stage, admits to having had no idea of the song's true motivation. "There was some pessimism in John's songs, but "Baby's in Black" was one we wrote together, and we liked heavy, black, bluesy songs because many of the [American] songs we liked were rooted in the blues and R&B. . . . It probably is true that John might have identified a little more than I did with those. To me—to both of us—they were essentially just the blues genre, which we loved, but it did transpire later that John was having a harder time with his emotions."

In the studio, John's solitary cri de coeur turned into another joyous Beatles A-side, its title merely emphasizing how little help they needed from anyone. A two-part lead vocal and speeded-up tempo further defused the message: while John's impassioned top line grabbed listeners by the lapels, Paul's buoyant countermelody reassuringly patted their heads. "The real feeling of the song was lost because it was a single," John said later. "We did it too fast, to try to be commercial . . . I remember, I got very emotional at the time, singing the lyrics. Whatever I'm singing, I really mean it. I don't mess around." The B-side was a Paul composition, almost parodying the same SOS theme with a cheerful call-and-response chorus of "I'm down . . . I'm really down . . . Down on the ground. . . ." Has any other million-selling double-sided disk ever been so jam-packed with depression?

The *Help!* sound track album, released in August, showed a John not influenced by Bob Dylan so much as possessed by him. The standout Lennon contribution was "You've Got to Hide Your Love Away," a somber ballad about rejection and alienation, couched in more "literary" language (". . . head in hand, turn my face to the wall . . .") than he'd ever previously tried, and played in folkie acoustic style, without overdubbing. His voice, too, had taken on a Dylanesque quality: harder and more nasal than before, its phrasing more adventurous, its tone laced with bitter irony as much as bleak self-pity.

The best-remembered *Help!* album track, however, did not feature in the film nor—amazingly—in the current British charts. This was a tune that Paul had awoken one day to find running through his head, a pensive little melody so fully formed and inevitable in its pattern that he assumed it must be some well-known air he was simply recollecting. Only after playing it to several expert arbiters, including George Martin and Alma Cogan, did he accept that it truly was his own invention and add some lyrics, changing the rough title "Scrambled Eggs" to "Yesterday." Since it was outside anything in the Beatles' canon, sounding more Anglican hymn than anything, Martin decided to recorded it as a solo by Paul, replacing John, George, and Ringo with a classical string quartet. Nevertheless, it went onto the Beatles album of the moment and, according to usual practice, its composition was credited to Lennon and McCartney. Though John may have criticized Paul's later forays into the mainstream, he did not object to this one, even praising a "bluesey note" in the cello passage.

Over the next thirty years, "Yesterday" would break the record of Irving Berlin's "White Christmas" as the most-recorded song of all time. Such were the musical riches pouring from John and Paul in 1965 that Parlophone didn't bother to release it as a single.

In October 1964, a general election had brought the Labour Party under Harold Wilson back to office after thirteen years of Conservative rule. As prime minister, Wilson did not promise to be much fun. Although only forty-nine, the youngest British premier since Rosebery, he seemed a good ten years older with his silver hair, stern cherub face, and flat, prim Yorkshire vowels. In stark contrast to the tweedy aristos who had preceded him, he wore a rubberized Gannex raincoat, holidayed no farther abroad than the Scilly Isles, and smothered his food in proletarian HP Sauce. His aura was that of some cold, practical efficiency expert dedicated to sweeping away the complacent inertia of Toryism and creating a modern, "dynamic" and "purposive" nation, as he ringingly expressed it, "forged in the white heat of the technological revolution."

But Wilson's John Blunt exterior was deceptive. While in public he drank bitter beer and smoked a homely briar pipe, his private preference was for brandy and cigars. Under the seeming high-minded asceticism lay a fascination with show business glamour and an insatiable hunger for personal publicity not seen at 10 Downing Street since the days of Winston Churchill.

The true tone of the Wilson era was set on June 11, 1965, with publication of the Queen's Birthday Honours list. Though billed as the sovereign's personal choice, the recipients are nominated by the prime minister's office and traditionally receive automatic Royal assent. The Beatles were each to receive the MBE: membership of the Most Excellent Order of the British Empire. Those selected for any honor first receive a letter asking if they are willing to accept it (which some are not). The Beatles' letters came in brown official envelopes, outwardly indistinguishable from banal missives like income tax demands or—until a few years previously—conscription into the army. When John's envelope arrived, he later said, he thought he was being "called up" [for military service] and so "chucked it in with the fanmail."

It was the first time such recognition had ever been given to anyone under the age of twenty-five, let alone to rowdy pop musicians. Although the media were generally enthusiastic (SHE LOVES THEM YEAH YEAH YEAH! ran one banner headline, as if it were all the Queen's idea), many among the older generation bewailed the cheapening and vulgarization of the honors system, little guessing how much further that process still could, and would, go. Several existing MBE-holders returned their decorations in protest at being bracketed, as one put it, with "a gang of nincompoops. The four recipients themselves were at first equally dubious, unsure whether they wanted to be sucked into the Establishment quite so far. "We all met, and agreed it was daft," John would remember. 'What do you think?' we all said. 'Let's not.' Then it all just seemed part of the game we'd agreed to play. We'd nothing to lose, except that part of you which said you didn't believe in it."

Following the success of *In His Own Write*, John had contracted with Tom Maschler at Jonathan Cape to produce a sequel for publication the following year. Having now used up all his student and *Mersey Beat* material, he had to start this second book from scratch, which gave the project an unpleasant flavor of school homework. To limber up, he began reading Chaucer, Edward Lear, and his other supposed stylistic influences, even making a stab at James Joyce's nonsense epic, *Finnegans Wake*. "It was great, and I dug it and felt as though [Joyce] was an old friend," he reported. "But I couldn't make it right through the book."

Cape duly received a further batch of prose, verse, and black-and-white illustrations, mostly wrought amid the splendor of his Kenwood den. However painfully extracted, the material this time was both more ambitious and funnier, with noticeably less schoolboyish harping on physical disability or race. "The Singularge Experience of Miss Anne Duffield," featuring the great detective "Shamrock Wolmbs," caught the authentic tone of a Conan Doyle Sherlock Holmes story as well as turning "Elementary my dear Watson" into "Ellafitzgerald, my dear Whopper" and "recuperated" into "minicoopered." "Cassandle" was a well-observed parody of the *Daily Mirror*'s columnist W. F. Connor, aka Cassandra, even down to the line drawing of Connor that headed his column. A poem, "The Wumberlog (or The Magic Dog)," evidently inspired by Lewis Carroll's "The Hunting of the Snark," ran to seven printed pages.

There was a topical commentary on the "General Erection," in which "Harrassed Wilsod" had defeated "Sir Alice Doubtless-Whom" (Sir Alec Douglas-Home, pronounced "Hume") and the "Torchies" (Torchy the Battery Boy was a children's television character) "by a very small marjorie." No great faith in the new prime minister was evident, despite his generosity with MBEs: "We must not forget to put the clocks back when we all get bombed, Harold. . . ." The book was called *A Spaniard in the Works* after another of its prose offerings, the story of Barcelover-born car mechanic Jesus El Pifco (a foretaste of larger sacrilege to come). The cover picture showed John in a cape and wide-brimmed Spanish hat, somewhat resembling the trademark for Sandeman's Port. Lest the pun in the title should not be clear enough, his right hand flourished a large spanner.

British publication was on June 24, coincidentally just after a Beatles European tour that had included shows in two Spanish bullrings. To promote the book, John made the rounds of highbrow arts programs, both radio and television, often reading extracts as well as answering questions. He admitted that *A Spaniard in the Works* had been hard work of a very different kind from touring, songwriting, and recording. "I could only loosen up to it with a bottle of Johnnie Walker. . . . We [the Beatles] are disciplined but we don't feel as though we are. I don't mind being disciplined and not realising it."

Had he plans to try writing at greater length, say in a novel? "The Sherlock Holmes seemed like a novel to me, but it turned out to be six pages. . . . I couldn't do it, you know. I get fed up. And I wrote so many characters in it, I forgot who they were."

Help! opened in British cinemas with a Royal charity premiere on July 29 at the London Pavilion, attended by Princess Margaret and Lord Snowdon. John's Aunt Mimi was also there, and later sent a report to Jane Wirgman that showed her as capable of "rattling their jewellery" as her nephew:

> So you liked 'Help'. Well I didn't, although the Colour was very good. I went to the Premiere & it was like a mad house at the Show. I Sat immediately behind P. Margaret, & when the Beatles came in I was panic Stricken, almost anyway. The girls in top balcony yelled & leaned over the edge & only for an attendant—one of them was nearly over. Everybody, it seemed, in the film world & a lot of Stage Stars too, were selling programmes, & Some of the most outlandish dresses and hair dos—all there to be Seen, not to See the film. It was for Charity, So did good. At the dinner at the Dorchester later also Some Funny Sights, but John was in great form & our table was in an uproar and Jane Asher is really a delightful girl. One thing I'll always remember was the Sight of a woman, 80 if she was a day, yellow wig on, low cut dress, face a mask under heavy make-up, mass of wrinkles, doing the rumba & up for every dance & whats more a good dancer. I thought at first She was a 'Comic Turn', & could not take my eyes off her. Ah Well, funny people these days to be Seen—and John Says I'm funny looking, So there you are.

Both the single and the album went straight to the top of their respective charts, the pattern being repeated in America with the same predictable double-click when the film opened there a month later. John had scarcely concluded his trip around literary London— which this time, significantly, did not include a Foyle's lunch—when he was swept away on a second Beatles tour of North America, the last the four would make without their hearts either in their boots or their mouths.

Brian had been crafting the itinerary since the previous February, choosing just ten venues for his boys' two-week journey, each a nationally or regionally celebrated arena or sports stadium with the highest standards in spectator comfort and security and a sound system of proven quality. The opening one, on Sunday August 15, was to be the most memorable of all: the newly opened William A. Shea Stadium in Flushing Meadows, Queens, home of the New York Mets baseball team.

The original plan had been for the Beatles to arrive by helicopter, touching down on the baseball diamond in front of the specially built stage. However, for safety reasons they had to land on the roof of the adjacent World's Fair Building, then travel the remaining hundred yards inside a Wells Fargo armored truck. It was still a heart-stopping moment as they dipped low over Shea's pristine blue, white, and orange bowl, and the capacity crowd of 55,600 roared up a greeting, mingled with skyward camera flashes like wartime anti-aircraft flak. Brian's copromoter, Sid Bernstein, remembers a phrase John used to him, which, in the clamorous urban twilight, had an almost biblical ring: "It's the top of the mountain, Sid . . . the top of the mountain."

The four that day unveiled a striking new stage look: pale fawn jackets with epaulets and brass buttons fastening to the neck like British Army tunics from the Boer War period. Each in addition sported the official badge of a Wells Fargo agent, earned by their brief journey in the company's security truck. And, as the film of the performance shows, they had their best time onstage together since Hamburg. "It was the high point of a vintage year," remembers NEMS's chief press officer, Tony Barrow, who accompanied the tour. "Real wealth had started to come through to them, their music was advancing by leaps and bounds, they were enjoying themselves beyond belief. They'd come up playing in places like the Liverpool Cavern where the audience was so close, you could reach out and take a half-smoked ciggie from a girl in the front row. At Shea Stadium, even though the front row looked miles away, they managed to create that same feeling of intimacy."

On this occasion John made some of the linking announcements, Boer War tunic gaping open at the neck, his hair sweat-glued to his forehead, his words progressively less coherent: "We'd like to do a slow song now . . . It's also off *Beatles Six* [a U.S. album] or something . . . I don't know what it's off . . . I haven't got it. . . ." Toward the end of the eleven-song set, he exchanged his guitar for the Vox Continental organ he had used on "I'm Down," the burlesque-depressed B-side to "Help!" Feeling "naked" without the Rickenbacker, he launched into a wild parody of Jerry Lee Lewis, dragging one finger cacophonously up and down the keys, playing with his elbow, even his foot. "John cracked up on that show," Ringo would remember. "[He] just went mad. Not mentally ill . . . just got crazy."

There was something else waiting at the top of the mountain. Twelve days after Shea Stadium—ten years after first hearing him and coming properly alive as a result—John met Elvis.

It was, of course, not quite the same Elvis whom that transfigured fourteen-year-old had force-fed his protesting aunt "for breakfast, dinner and tea" in 1956. Now thirty years old, Presley had abandoned not only rock 'n' roll but live performances of any kind, instead turning out a series of increasingly bland and forgettable Hollywood movies, otherwise leading a sequestered existence at his Graceland mansion with the troupe of hangers-on and ex–service buddies known as the Memphis Mafia. Though he still had occasional chart hits, they were middle-of-the-road pop, devoid of his old sneering sexual magic. In America, he was as embarrassing a symbol of a craze-gone-by as bobby socks or the hula hoop; in Britain, even his most loyal fans had given up hope that he'd ever return to form.

Nor was it a given that the former King would wish to meet the young British invaders who had stolen his crown. The good luck telegram that so thrilled the Beatles before their second *Ed Sullivan Show* had, in fact, been sent as a PR gesture by Presley's wily manager, Colonel Tom Parker. Initially, Presley had been baffled by their music and repulsed by their hair and clothes, complaining with old-fashioned Southern puritanism that they looked like "a bunch of faggots."

There had been talk of a summit meeting during the Beatles' main 1964 American tour, but schedules on both sides had proved too hectic; in the end, only Paul had spoken briefly to Presley by telephone from Atlantic City. This year, when the Beatles reached Los Angeles, the King also happened to be in town, fresh from filming on location in Hawaii. Fortuitously, too, Brian had scheduled some free time before the shows at Balboa Stadium in San Diego and the Hollywood Bowl. After intense negotiations with Colonel Parker, brokered by the *New Musical Express* journalist Chris Hutchins, the meeting was set for the evening of August 27.

Despite the Beatles' ascendancy, there was no question as to who was the monarch and who the supplicants: they went to Elvis, driving from their rented mansion in Benedict Canyon to his in Perugia Way, Beverly Hills, accompanied by Brian, Tony Barrow, and roadies Neil and Mal. Secrecy was meant to be absolute, but Parker had tipped off a local radio station in advance. Consequently, a flotilla of press cars followed in hot pursuit, and dozens of screaming non-Presley fans were waiting outside the King's gate. Racked with pre-audience nerves, the four had taken advantage of their thirty-minute journey to "have a laugh," and so tumbled out of their limo giggling and uncoordinated, as though in some extra sequence from *Help!*

Presley received them seated on a sofa, watching television with the sound turned down—exactly as John always did—and thumbing softly at a bass guitar plugged into a live amp. Such was the Beatles' emotion that they registered only odd details of this modern Versailles: the Sun King's brilliant red shirt; a jukebox playing "Mohair Sam" by Charlie Rich; the fact that Elvis did not have to rise nor even lean forward to adjust his TV set, but possessed a revolutionary handheld device that enabled him to do so without stirring on his throne.

John later recalled the weirdness of meeting someone whose face was almost as familiar to him as his own, but who was nonetheless a stranger, a million miles away even when shaking hands. "At first we couldn't make him out. I asked him if he was preparing any ideas for his next film and he drawled: 'Ah sure am. Ah play a country boy with a guitar who meets a few gals along the way, and ah sing a few songs.' We all looked at one another. Finally Presley and Colonel Parker laughed and explained the only time they departed from that formula—for *Wild in the Country*—they lost money. He was just

JOHN LENNON: THE LIFE

Elvis, you know? . . . He seemed normal to us, and we were asking about his making movies and not doing any personal appearances or TV. . . . He was great: just as I expected him."

Things warmed up still more when guitars were produced for John and Paul, and they reprised some of the Elvis songs they once used to smuggle into the Cavern's all-skiffle program, while the true, honest-to-God, flesh-and-blood, in-this-room Elvis smiled indulgently and thumbed his bass, and the body servants of both factions hovered bonhomiously near. Later came games of pool and roulette, and a fleeting sight of Priscilla Beaulieu, the doll-like teenage beauty in training to become Presley's wife. As the visitors left, seen off personally by their host, John turned and shouted "Long live the King!"

Subsequently, plans were discussed for Elvis to return the compliment and visit the Beatles at their Benedict Canyon hideaway. It never happened, even though an advance guard of Memphis Mafiosi came to check out the house. While they were doing so, John asked one of them, Jerry Schilling, to convey a further message of appreciation: "Tell [Elvis] if it hadn't been for him, I would have been nothing."

After the twin peaks of Shea Stadium and meeting Elvis, the remaining tour dates—each a display of industrial-strength Beatlemania in its own right—inevitably seemed rather a letdown. Resilient though the Beatles were (and no young men could possibly have led such a life without enjoying A1 health), all four, in their different ways, were starting to feel the strain. John in particular, at a moment that should have seen his self-esteem at its zenith, was overcome by the same inexplicable depression and loneliness that had permeated *Help!* Five thousand miles from Kenwood, under the balmy California sun, he suddenly began to reflect on his shortcomings as a family man and especially as a father; how, in the whirlwind of the previous three years, he had missed out on almost all Julian's steps from baby to little boy. These feelings were poured out in a surprisingly emotional, contrite letter to Cynthia, saying how much he missed Julian and regretted "those stupid bastard times when I keep reading bloody newspapers and other shit while he's in the room with me. . . . I really want him to know me and love me, and miss me like I seem to be missing both of you so much. . . ."

So from the King to the Queen: on October 29, the Beatles went to Buckingham Palace to receive their MBEs at the sovereign's hands, causing larger crowds outside her London home than any since her coronation day. Normally, the sequel to each Royal investiture is the recipients' emergence into the palace yard, showing off their decorations with their proud families. As if to underline the Beatles' status as pet aliens—nowhere more so than here—they arrived without any family members in support. Even Cynthia and Julian could not publicly share John's triumph but had to be content with watching TV news reports at home in Weybridge.

Despite his skepticism, John found himself impressed by "Buck House's" glittering grandeur and swept along by the pomp and protocol of the investiture ceremony. The Royal moment, when it came, had much the same unreal quality as beholding Elvis. "[The Queen] said something like 'ooh ah blah blah' we didn't quite understand. She's much nicer than she is in the photos . . . I must have looked shattered. She said to me, 'Have you been working hard lately?' I couldn't think what we'd been doing, so I said, 'No, we've been having a holiday.' We'd been recording, but I couldn't remember that." After the ceremony, the Beatles signed autographs for their fellow awardees, then posed for the press with their decorations: four modest little medals in presentation boxes. John afterward gave his to Aunt Mimi, pinning it on her in a parody of the palace ceremony because, he said, she deserved it far more than he did.

Years later, he would say that, to calm their preinvestiture jitters and express a little covert defiance of those officious Royal stewards and chamberlains, the four managed to escape to a palace washroom for a few minutes and there sneak a few puffs of marijuana. But according to Paul McCartney, they had a laugh only in the literal sense. "I remember that smoking was not allowed generally and we went sneaking off to the bog, as we called it, for a ciggie and giggled a lot at the sheer cheek of us smoking a ciggie in Buckingham Palace. I don't think it was a joint."

17

REAL LIFE IN CINEMASCOPE

I don't want to know what it's like to be dead.

To begin with, making records was something the Beatles did when they could find time. Their sessions at Abbey Road Studios with George Martin had to be slotted into the breakneck schedule of touring, filmmaking, television, and radio, and, like everything else, were arranged over their heads. "If it was time for a new single or album, I'd have to get in touch with Brian," Martin remembers. "He'd look through his diary and say 'I can give you May 19th and perhaps the evening of the 20th.' I had to grab them whenever I could."

Their producer in these early days was an all-powerful boss figure, combining the authority of the label head and the gravitas of a classically trained musician. From the raw material submitted to him, Martin chose the songs he considered worthwhile; he altered tempos, switched verses or choruses around, prescribed the ratio of vocal to instrumental. In short, he performed all the functions of a good editor, whose discreet structural amendments and corrections in grammar or punctuation help brilliant copy speak for itself the more eloquently.

The first Lennon-McCartney compositions to be recorded were submitted as combined efforts, invariably written in spare moments in hotels or dressing rooms and sung and played on acoustic guitars by both authors together while Martin sat on a bass-player's stool, listening with elegant impassivity. By 1965, John and Paul had taken to working mainly apart, usually developing most of each new lyric and melody before turning to each other for criticism and advice. Their individual composing techniques, Martin remembers, were utterly different.

"Paul would think of a tune and then think 'What words can I put to it?' John tended to develop his melodies as the thing went along. Generally he built up a song on a structure of chords which he would ramble and find on his guitar until he had an interesting sequence. After that, the words were more important than anything else. They used to come out sometimes as a monotone, just one note punctuated by the rhythm of the words. He never set out to write a melody and put lyrics to it. He always thought of the structure, the harmonic content and the lyrics first, and the melody would then come out of that.

"However good the song was, John never seemed that confident about it. In all the time we worked together, I never heard him hype his own work in any way. After he'd played over something to me, his first question was always 'What do you think?' The second was 'What shall we do with it?' After a time, I realised that he was actually embarrassed by his own voice. Whenever we did a vocal, he always insisted on wearing cans [headphones] and told me to put lots of echo through them, so that he couldn't hear what he really sounded like. When we got into slap-echo, like on Presley's "Heartbreak Hotel," he loved that and his voice always went through the cans like that, though not onto the record. It was like an ointment for him. It smoothed out all the things in his voice that he didn't like.

"But then, you see, John didn't like much. It wasn't just his voice;

everything in his mind was much better than reality, always. And he was always somewhat disappointed with the results of what we did. In the beginning, I was in charge and no criticisms were voiced. But as he grew more powerful and more aware of what was going on, he grew more critical of everything. He was always searching for something he couldn't quite grasp. His wonderful dreamland in there [inside his head] never really reached reality."

In many ways, Martin remembers, John was more easygoing than the perfectionist, workaholic Paul. "If we were doing a song of Paul's, he'd get hold of his guitar and tell George what he wanted him to play in the middle; he'd get on the drums and show Ringo what he wanted. And that used to irk the piss out of them sometimes, obviously. When John recorded a song, he let other people do what they were going to do: Paul would work out a bass line, maybe add a little bit here and there, and George would do his guitar solo, and Ringo would take care of the beat. John would be entirely focused on his part of things, and leave the others to get on with theirs. As long as the end result was up to standard, he'd be happy.

"Paul was his sounding-board, of course, and George had a huge amount of input, which, to my eternal regret, I didn't sufficiently recognise at the time, but Ringo's opinion was always important to John, just because he knew that with him there'd never be any bullshit. He'd often turn to Ringo and ask what he thought and if Ringo said, 'That's crap, John,' he'd do something else."

He took his role as rhythm guitarist with extreme seriousness, learning new chords as diligently as he ever had, sometimes even proudly announcing, "I'm playing a G minor seventh here, Paul!" But all other musical disciplines bored him. "George would work away like a Turkish carpet-maker at whatever it was, whether mending a car or constructing a song," Martin says. "John couldn't be bothered even to tune his guitar. He was a completely impractical man. And if there was someone around to do it for him, why not? That was his attitude.

"Remember that my focus was on the Beatles, not just on John, though inevitably how he was feeling dictated the general mood. He could get irritated by lots of things. Paul used to irritate him . . . and

George often did as well. But in the studio generally we all got on like a house on fire. Because he and Paul were turning out such wonderful material. No matter what kind of pressure they were under as live performers, they always came up with a fresh idea; they were never content to use a cliché, but always gave me something slightly different. Each song was a jewel on its own, and I used to bless them for that."

Paul McCartney remembers how, in those days, even the fiercest dispute with his collaborator seldom lasted long. "One of my great memories of John is from when we were having some argument. I was disagreeing and we were calling each other names. We let it settle for a second, and then he lowered his glasses and he said, 'It's only me . . .' and then he put his glasses back on again. To me, that was John. Those were the moments when I actually saw him without the facade, the armour which I loved as well, like anyone else. It was a beautiful suit of armour. But it was wonderful when he let the visor down and you'd just see the John Lennon that he was frightened to reveal to the world."

In a life otherwise plagued by intruders and distractions, recording sessions became the Beatles' one precious oasis of privacy. As EMI's greatest-ever moneymakers, they enjoyed privileged treatment at Abbey Road that the greatest names of the past, Caruso or Sinatra, had not. Studios One and Two, each large enough to house a symphony orchestra, were set aside for Martin and his sacred quartet in open-ended sessions that were as much about exploration and rehearsal as actual recording, and habitually continued far into the night. Gone were the technicians' white coats and the forbidding force field around the control room; gone even was the formality of rolling tape for a take. Such were the gems to be picked up at every moment that tape rolled all the time.

Wives and girlfriends, it went without saying, were totally excluded. Even Brian himself looked in only occasionally and was careful to make his visits as brief and businesslike as possible. This followed an unhappy incident when he had appeared in the control room unexpectedly late one night while the Beatles were hard at work on the cable-strewn floor below. Unusually for the public Brian, he was slightly drunk and, still more unusually, accompanied by one of his gay friends.

This gratuitous reminder of the lifestyle he usually concealed from his boys would have been faux pas enough, but alcohol and a desire to impress his companion led to an even worse one. At the end of the take, he switched on the intercom and slurrily announced that something or other hadn't sounded "quite right." There was a horrible pause, then John's voice came back with a line he had used before but which never failed to slice off its victim's legs at the knees: "You look after your percentages, Brian. We'll take care of the music."

October and November of 1965 found the Beatles back at Abbey Road for the second UK album of their yearly quota, as usual timed to catch the Christmas market. However, the frenetic summer of touring, meeting Elvis, and joining the Most Excellent Order of the British Empire had left John and Paul almost no time to replenish the stock of songs used up by *Help!* Nor was it possible any longer to use rock and soul cover versions as a makeweight. They would have to write the whole album to order, and in double-quick time to make the December release date.

The competition out there had never looked more formidable. In Britain, half a dozen bands originally formed as ersatz Beatles with bangs and round-collared suits had proved themselves robust individualists and brought glory to other cities and suburbs once thought unmentionable—the Hollies, from Manchester; the Animals, from Newcastle-upon-Tyne; the Who, from Shepherds Bush in the west of London; the Kinks, from Muswell Hill in the north. Nor was exposure any longer as easy and assured as simply turning up at good old "Auntie" BBC. In mid-1964, a bold young entrepreneur had realized he could legally break the corporation's government-enforced broadcasting monopoly by transmitting programs from a ship moored outside British territorial waters. There had since been a proliferation of such pirate radio stations, transmitting continuous pop record shows in Americanized formats with commercials, station IDs, and jingles. Besides their "old mate" Brian Matthew at the Beeb, a new Beatles track must tickle the fancies of seasick deejays unsteadily at anchor between the Thames Estuary and the Firth of Clyde.

At home, the main threat was posed by the five former R&B purists who ironically owed their first major chart success to John and Paul. Under the guidance of Brian Epstein's former PR man Andrew Loog Oldham, the Rolling Stones had achieved monster fame with a delinquent image as carefully crafted and as illusory as the Beatles' one of blandness and cuddliness. Fired by Lennon and McCartney's example, the Stones' Mick Jagger and Keith Richard were now writing songs together and, in their darker, sourer way, showing an almost equally sure golden touch. In July 1965, they outraged the singles charts with "Satisfaction," a title fraught with masturbatory innuendo though, in fact, it was a hymn of hate against the penalties of pop stardom, the ineffable boredom of adulation and luxury, that John endorsed with all his heart. But, gallingly, he was not the first to say it.

The Beatles' American triumph brought still greater pressures and insecurities in its wake. Thanks to them, the land that had once been so fiercely resistant to British pop now wanted nothing else, provided it came in squads of four or five, with fringed faces, skimpy suits, and oddball limey accents. Musical Anglomania had reached such a height that any new American band took care to look and sound like as much like a British one as possible, filtering their own indigenous music through the sensibilities of Liverpudlians, Londoners, Mancunians, or Tynesiders. Some of these, in turn, bounced Beatle-influenced American music back to Britain, with added dividends of skill and invention that could make the most feted of their transatlantic exemplars feel like beginners again. The two John considered the most talented—and, therefore, worrying—both happened to have names also beginning with a B. The first were the Beatly misspelled Byrds, whose soaring, sighing voices and twangly electric twelve-string guitars owed as much to traditional American folk as to mid-Atlantic Merseybeat. The second were the Beach Boys, former exponents of the simplistic "surf" sound, who took Beatlish harmonies into new realms of echo and multitracking, as different from John, Paul, and George's homely fusions as a cathedral from a beach hut.

But the greatest challenger, so far as John was concerned, took some time to show his full hand. In May 1965, Bob Dylan had visited London to appear at the Royal Albert Hall. He was still singing protest songs alone with acoustic guitar and suspended mouth organ, though his stylish Mod clothes and ever-enlarging curly pompadour hinted that the days of kinship with ragged-assed folk heroes were numbered.

Still warmly grateful for their initiation into pot, the Beatles hastened to Dylan's suite at the Savoy Hotel, unusually taking their womenfolk along to share the reunion. However, the atmosphere proved markedly less cordial than at the Delmonico in New York the previous summer. John felt that on their home territory, it would have been more mannerly for Dylan to call on them; he in turn seemed cold and, in the new word, uptight, though this may not have been all his visitors' fault. Since their previous encounter, he had graduated from marijuana to sniffing heroin, and during his London debut was to spend three days in a hospital, reportedly suffering from "a cold."

To lighten the tension, Dylan summoned his friend the beat poet Allen Ginsberg, who also happened to be staying at the Savoy. John had read Ginsberg's verse epic *Howl*, intrigued by the echo of his own "Daily Howl" at Quarry Bank school. But the sight of the thirty-eight-year-old poet in person, bald, black-bearded, overtly gay, and strenuously clownish, proved rather disconcerting. When Ginsberg perched on the sofa arm beside him, John asked sarcastically why he didn't get a bit closer. At this, Ginsberg flopped into his lap, gazed up at him, and asked if he'd ever read William Blake. "Never heard of him," replied John; such a willful untruth that even his usually diffident spouse could not let it pass. "Oh John, stop lying," Cynthia chided. "Of course you have."

Ginsberg stayed on in London after the Dylan concert and, a couple of weeks later, invited John and George, with Cyn and Pattie, to his thirty-ninth-birthday party at a mutual friend's flat in Fitzrovia. They arrived to find their host naked, with a pair of underpants decorating his bald head and a hotel "Do Not Disturb" sign dangling from his penis. Nervous of being photographed in such company, the two

Beatles quickly made an excuse and left. Even Hamburg-hardened John seemed shocked. "You don't do that in front of birds," he was heard to complain.

Dylan, meanwhile, had returned to America to detonate his long-fizzing bombshell. That July, his audience at the Newport Folk Festival broke into scandalized cries of "Traitor!" when he took the stage backed by the electrified Paul Butterfield Band. Over the summer, he released two pop singles—"Subterranean Homesick Blues" and "Like a Rolling Stone"—each a mold-shattering blend of verbal virtuosity and supercharged beat. He would later attribute his conversion to another British band, the Animals, and their cover of an old blues lament, "The House of the Rising Sun." But John always begged to differ. "Dylan liked to say how much the Beatles learned from him," Neil Aspinall remembered. "John used to mutter, 'He learned a bit from us, too.'"

Despite the little time available, John and Paul were equally determined to make this sixth Beatles album a conclusive answer to Dylan and all the other rivals snapping at their heels. One innovation they discussed with George Martin (but would not employ until four years later) was leaving out the spaces between tracks, so that one song merged into another with only the briefest pause, like movements in a classical symphony. They also deliberately put behind them the small-group arsenal of guitar-bass-drums, which until now had served them as well on record as in live performance. In Abbey Road's Studio One, under the long open staircase to the control room, there was a cabinet full of exotic instruments left behind by other musicians who had worked there down the decades. The four had always enjoyed rummaging through this miscellany of tambourines, sleigh bells, and Moroccan hand drums; now it became an ally in the fight to prove themselves top dogs again, as did Martin's classical background and every possible resource of the studio itself. Implicitly, from the very start, this was not stuff intended to be played live onstage.

John was later to call the end result "the pot album," implying that the whole thing had taken shape amid sage-scented clouds of the stuff. He certainly intended it to be that way, lighting up a joint as his Rolls left Weybridge for the nightly trip to Abbey Road, passing it to Ringo and George as each came aboard. Unfortunately, the billowing fumes in the Rolls's heated interior tended to produce an effect inimical to "having a laugh": often by the time they reached London, all three would be feeling thoroughly nauseous. Out of respect for Martin, they did not smoke in the studio but withdrew to toilets or unfrequented stairwells like schoolboys skulking behind the bike sheds. As Ringo has since recalled, anything they tried to record under the influence always proved unusable: "It didn't do for the Beatles to be too demented while making music."

Eight of the eventual fourteen tracks were enough on their own to have put clear blue water between the Beatles and every home and foreign competitor, and reconfirm Lennon and McCartney as creators of the catchiest, classiest, edgiest pop around. "You Won't See Me," "I'm Looking Through You," and "Wait" were grade-A, Paul-dominated productions in a steady line of ascent from "A Hard Day's Night" and "Help!" "Drive My Car" followed a tradition of novelty motoring songs, down to the "Beep-beep, yeah!" chorus and surprise punch line. John's "Run for Your Life" (its opening line, "I'd rather see you dead, little girl, than to be with another man") slipped unchallenged into a world not yet disturbed by feminism or concerns about domestic violence. Two songs by George ("Think for Yourself" and "If I Needed Someone") and a token hillbilly vocal by Ringo ("What Goes On?") reinforced the irresistible image of a foursome whose greatest joy still came from being together.

But the remaining seven songs were of an order so different, so vastly superior, it was hard to believe they sprang from the same musicians, the same studio, or moment in time. These owed nothing to any other current pop sound and fitted no known categories. In them, John's and Paul's individual creative voices first come clearly into counterpoint: one that of a matchlessly artful, perfectly focused commercial songwriter, the other torn between the impulses of a poet, journalist, autobiographer, satirist, sloganeer, nostalgic, and melancholic.

For John, composing under pressure, like some reporter chasing an edition, at first seemed to have negative effects. He would later recall a day at Kenwood when he spent five fruitless hours trying to think of something clever until finally, "cheesed off," he went for a lie-down. Stretched on his king-size bed in his mock-Tudor mansion, with his myriad possessions all around, he suddenly thought of "a Nowhere Man . . . sitting in Nowhere Land." With this as a peg, the song took only minutes to write itself.

"In My Life," another superlative achievement, began with similar brain-cudgeling and false starts. Since the publication of *In His Own Write* and *A Spaniard in the Works*, various interviewers—notably the challenging Ken Allsop—had asked John why his song lyrics did not have the same highly individual stamp as his prose. He himself was aware of having "one mind that wrote books and another mind that churned out things about 'I love you and you love me.'" Accordingly, he sketched out a song that would use poetic observation in the style of Wordsworth or Tennyson, recalling the Liverpool he had known as a child and lamenting how, even over his short lifetime, that old, solid world of ships and docks had all but vanished.

The choice of subject can have been no accident. His Aunt Mimi was soon to leave Mendips for Harbour View, finally closing the long-extended chapter of his boyhood. His original lyric was a wistful return to years gone by, reliving the bus journey he had taken countless times from Menlove Avenue into central Liverpool, via Penny Lane, Church Road, "the Dutch and St Columbus, and the Dockers' Umbrella [elevated railway] that they pulled down."

Somehow, this first attempt to immortalize Penny Lane refused to jell, so John cut the "travelogue" part of the song, making it instead a personal requiem for "friends and lovers . . . people and things that went before." Even with an "I love you" payoff, it broke new ground. In the onward-and-upward-thrusting mid-Sixties, nostalgia was still comparatively rare. A twenty-five-year-old pop superstar was the least likely person to be looking back over his life as if time were already growing short.

John's laissez-faire attitude in the studio provided the track's final winning touch. As usual, the vocal was recorded first, with space for an instrumental break to be added later. While the Beatles were out having dinner, George Martin devised a piano solo in the style of Bach, then fiddled with the recording speed so that on playback it had the spindly quiver of a harpsichord. He wondered how John would react to so pretty and demure an interpolation. John loved it.

Also on the agenda was that other scrap of autobiography Martin had heard in the rough at the Palace Hotel, St. Moritz, while Cynthia Lennon sat nearby, listening in happy incomprehension. Now titled "Norwegian Wood (This Bird Has Flown)," its purpose seemed to combine one existing trendy craze with another soon to dawn. All over Britain, people were transforming their once-cluttered kitchens and living spaces with austere tracts of Scandinavian stripped pine. And, rather than a guitar, as if in perpetuation of *Help!*'s comic sub-plot, George Harrison played a jangly Indian sitar.

But no one who knew John—other than his wife—could fail to recognize the situation the song described or wince at its ring of absolute truth. Here he was in some arty dolly bird's stripped-pine flat, talking and drinking wine into the small hours in hopes of se-ducing her, but at the crucial moment losing his nerve and slinking off to sleep the night in her empty bathtub, much like some over-flow visitor long ago at Gambier Terrace. In the unnamed girl, most of John's circle thought they recognized Maureen Cleave, the *Eve-ning Standard* writer whose appeal for him plainly went beyond her Richmal Crompton-esque prose style. However, Cleave says that in all her encounters with John there was "no pass." And Sonny Free-man, then wife of the Beatles' favorite photographer, has always taken the lyric as an oblique reference to her. Circumstantial evi-dence seems compelling: her preference to be known as Norwegian rather than German, her wood-paneled flat under John's in Emper-or's Gate, the late-night assignations they used to make under every-one's noses.

Classic pop tracks are a synthesis of words, music, and production; in general, the most effective lyrics turn to lead on the printed page. John's for "Norwegian Wood" are among very few that can also be read as poetry or even drama. In twenty-six skillfully rhymed, per-fectly scanned short lines, a scene is set, two characters are created and converse, a farcical climax is reached, followed by a slightly sin-ister epilogue. The ambiguous ending, "So I lit a fire . . ." (to com-fort his bruised ego on waking to find the "bird has flown"? Or to torch the pristine timbers in revenge?), is almost worthy of Beckett or Pinter.

However unlike the material Lennon and McCartney wrote on their own, they instinctively tuned in to each other's wavelength, often supplying some final touch that turned a good song into a superb one. As John previewed the unfinished chorus of "Nowhere Man" and came to "making all his nowhere plans . . . ," Paul extemporized the little twist of "for nobody." John in turn supplied the plaintive "I love you I love you I lo-ove you" bridge in Paul's "Michelle," modeling it on Nina Simone's soul classic, "I Put a Spell on You." Their closest collaboration was "The Word," a song foreshadowing a whole era with its advocacy of "love" as a cure for all ills, and John's promise to "show everybody the light."

"Nowhere Man" is generally viewed as a self-portrait, expressing John's frustration and self-disgust at his exile in the Stockbroker Belt. In fact, he distances himself from the Nowhere Man (". . . isn't he a bit like you and me?"), leaving us with a character who could have stepped from some modish black-and-white TV play. No, the real window on his emotions—the raw anguish that, decades later, still rises up and batters you with a brick—is in the innocent-sounding "Girl." John himself always insisted the song had no real-life model, that the girl in question was "just a dream." God knows what kind of dream it could have been to provoke such aching misery, such dark visions of male enslavement and humiliation. In contrast with the Frenchified romanticism of "Michelle," "Girl" has a zithery, Viennese-café, film-noir sound, punctuated by sharp hisses that could be pain or disbelief. Only once ever again will John sing thus, as if his heart is breaking inside him.

"We've written some funny songs—songs with jokes in," Paul somewhat misleadingly informed a journalist as the album neared completion. "We think that comedy numbers are the next thing after protest songs." Its title was a pun on soul music and a sly dig at their archrivals (and private best mates) the Rolling Stones. A black American musician had recently commented that British groups like the Stones, for all their invasive power, played only "plastic soul." The Beatles decided on *Rubber Soul*, implying that their variety at least was stamped out by a good strong northern Wellington boot.

The cover was originally to have been a straight Robert Freeman group photograph, showing off their latest suede and leather Carnaby gear. To help them decide which image would work best, Freeman projected each color transparency onto a cardboard square the same size as an album cover. As a close-up head shot appeared, the cardboard slipped askew, distorting their features and making John dominate the frame like some cruelly impassive, suede-collared Tartar prince. All four loved this "fisheye" effect and unanimously picked it as the cover shot.

John had scarcely delivered his lyrical tribute to "people and things that went before" when he found himself facing the most unwelcome of all possible examples. After a silence of more than a year, his father, Freddie, again reappeared in his life, this time even more publicly and embarrassingly.

Early in 1965, Brian Epstein received a letter from a firm of literary agents announcing that they had "Mr Alfred Lennon, father of John," under contract to write his life story. Their client, they said, was "deeply resentful of letters he has received from relatives and others, accusing him of trying to exploit the now famous son he neglected as a child." Before starting the project, he wished Brian to arrange a meeting with John "so that he can give his own explanation of what happened when the family split up." Brian wrote back a dismissive couple of lines saying he could not get involved in so private a family matter. The life story—really an extended interview—was duly sold to downmarket *Tit-Bits* magazine for £200.

The genie was now well and truly out of the bottle. Following the *Tit-Bits* article, Freddie struck up an acquaintance with a Liverpudlian wheeler-dealer named Tony Cartwright, who was then working for Tom Jones's manager, Gordon Mills. Cartwright was intrigued to discover what hotel workers up and down Britain already knew: that John Lennon's errant father had had a lifelong ambition to become an entertainer himself. He offered to become Freddie's manager and, on the strength of the Lennon name, had little trouble in getting him a recording contract with the Pye Piccadilly label. The two then set to work to write a song for the novelty market that had previously seen such money-spinners as Rolf Harris's "Ringo for President" and Dora Bryan's "All I Want for Christmas Is a Beatle."

The result was "That's My Life (and My Love and My Home)", a title uncomfortably though quite accidentally close to John's "In My Life." A monologue with instrumental accompaniment, it combined romantic allusions to Freddie's seafaring years with self-justification about his failings as a father. The chewy Scouse voice (which not all of Pye Piccadilly's technical resources could make a jot like his son's) intoned sonorously against a background of violins and crashing waves: "It started in Liverpool where I was born . . . No father to advise me, but I carried on . . . I saw a lifetime of love go wrong . . . Pity was my partner all along . . . I'll make no excuses for my own abuses . . . Because life makes us all that way . . . I could blame the cruel sea for taking me away . . . It could be the end of my story, but my story will never end."

The record came out in December 1965, unfortunately coinciding with the release of *Rubber Soul*. Freddie was caught up in a whirl of promotion that included performing his monologue live on Dutch television. But in the United Kingdom, it quickly sank without trace. Far from making Freddie's fortune, it left him £20 in debt. Anticipating a life in the spotlight, he had undergone extensive private dental work for which he was left holding the bill.

Though the record palpably never stood a chance, some journalists and disc jockeys undoubtedly did boycott it out of loyalty to John. Freddie later claimed to have heard from music-business insiders that Brian Epstein had brought pressure to starve it of coverage and airplay. A kitchen porter once again, he happened to find work at a pub in Hampton, just a mile or so from Weybridge. One day, he impulsively decided to call on John and ask point-blank whether the rumors of sabotage were true. Unfortunately, only Cynthia and Julian were at home. Cyn had never met Freddie and scarcely even knew she had a father-in-law, but was her usual kindly, hospitable self, introducing him to his grandson, making him tea, even trimming his untidy locks for him in Kenwood's huge, incomprehensible kitchen.

He returned a few days later when John was at home, but this time did not succeed in penetrating the house. Still convinced there had been skulduggery over his single, he unwisely brought along his erstwhile manager, Tony Cartwright, for support. There was a brief exchange among the three in Kenwood's front porch as Lord Kitchener looked on balefully from his recruiting poster; then John retreated inside and slammed the door.

A few months earlier, John and Cynthia had driven into London with George Harrison and Pattie Boyd for what promised to be a fairly low-key evening out. It began with dinner at the flat of John and George's dentist, John Riley, in Strathearn Place, Bayswater. The only other person present was Riley's twenty-two-year-old Canadian-born girlfriend, Cindy Bury, who worked at the recently opened Playboy Club in Park Lane. As the guests took their seats in the candlelit dining-room, Cynthia noticed a curious decorative touch: arranged along the mantelpiece with evident care were six sugar cubes.

Riley was one of London's leading celebrity dentists, and already such a pal of John and George that he had flown out to join them in the Bahamas while they were filming *Help!* The plan this evening was that, after dinner at his flat, he and Cindy would accompany the Beatle foursome to the Pickwick Club, where Brian's latest acquisition for NEMS Enterprises, a trio named Paddy, Klaus and Gibson, were appearing live. Since Klaus was John and George's old Hamburg friend Klaus Voormann, there could be no begging off or showing up late. Riley insisted that they must have coffee before leaving, and dropped a sugar lump from the mantelpiece into each of their cups. A few moments later, John turned to George and tersely announced "We've had LSD."

The thirty-four-year-old Riley was no career drug pusher; nor was he one of those sleazy people who get a kick from turning on celebrities. Both John and George had previously expressed curiosity about LSD, and, through medical connections, Riley had obtained some from a source in Wales. His girlfriend Cindy knew he planned to give it to them without their knowledge, but not that he'd chosen this particular evening or that she—and he himself—would be taking it for the first time along with them. "We were six friends and we were young, and if you were young in those days that's what you did. You tried everything." For Marcel Proust, a tea-soaked biscuit provided a springboard into the past. For John—and many more than him—the future was changed by sugar in his coffee.

Cynthia Lennon, who had never heard of LSD and had been un-wontedly happy and relaxed up to now, was the first to feel the drug's effects. "It was as if we suddenly found ourselves in the middle of a horror film," she recalls. "The room seemed to get bigger and bigger. This man [Riley] who'd been so nice and charming until then, seemed to turn into a demon. We were all terrified. We knew it was some-thing evil—we had to get out of the house." Cindy's version is that they left quite normally to go on to the Pickwick Club as planned.

That evening, it so happened, they did not have John's Rolls wait-ing outside but had come up from Surrey packed into George's Mini Cooper. By the time they reached the West End some fifteen min-utes later (Riley and Cindy following by taxi), their first LSD trip was kicking in with a vengeance. Normally lighted theater and cinema marquees seemed to blaze with unearthly radiance and the pave-ment crowds to surge and roar like multiple Royal film premieres. All four were in a state hovering between dazzled stupefaction and hysteria; Pattie, as a rule the sanest of young women, was seized by a desire to smash shop windows. "We were cackling," John would recall. "We were just insane. We were out of our heads."

None of them would afterward recall arriving at the Pickwick or watching Paddy, Klaus and Gibson's debut. Klaus Voormann has no recollection of seeing John at all that night. John Riley and Cindy were left behind somewhere along the way, and neither John nor George ever saw them again. The next concrete collective memory was getting to the Ad Lib, just off Leicester Square, where they had arranged to meet Ringo. The Ad Lib was reached by an elevator that, as it carried them upward, suddenly seemed to burst into flames.

As they sat in the club, telling Ringo about the fiery lift, it seemed that their table began to alter shape, lengthening and widening into the dimensions of an airport runway. But while the others reacted in panic or hysteria, John experienced a moment, if not of déjà vu, then of déjà lu. He had, after all, grown up on *Alice's Adventures in Wonderland*, in which Alice had only to drink or eat something for everyday objects to magnify on this same gargantuan scale. Alone of the group, too, he had read *Confessions of an Opium-Eater*, Thomas de Quincy's 1822 record of drug hallucinations in which "a theatre seemed suddenly opened up and lighted in my brain [presenting] spectacles of more than earthly splendour" and "buildings, land-scapes etc. were exhibited in proportions so vast as the bodily eye is not fitted to receive. . . ." Whereas the usually dour and stand-offish George experienced a sudden urge to tell everyone that he loved them, John felt de Quincy's sensation, in more benign opium trances, of being "at a distance and aloof from the uproar of life," when "crowds became oppressive . . . music even." Sometime that night, a fellow musician came up and asked permission to sit beside him. "Only if you don't talk," he replied.

Later, George somehow managed to drive back to his house in Esher, keeping the souped-up Mini at a cautious 18 mph the whole way, with Pattie still suggesting mad escapades beside him and John manically telling jokes in the back. Unable to manage the further couple of miles to Weybridge, the Lennons decided to crash out at George's, thinking that whatever ailed them would recede with a few hours' sleep—little suspecting that LSD, unlike alcohol, does not cause drowsiness, and can take up to twelve hours to run its course.

Cyn spent the rest of the night in extreme distress, unable to sleep or make herself vomit up the poison. But for John, the continuously unfolding visions—although sometimes so terrifying that they made him bang his head against the wall—were also like watching the most exciting and gorgeously colored movie while simultaneously starring in it. In the trip's most memorable phase, he later recalled, George's house became a giant submarine, which he piloted single-handedly through another de Quincy vista of "chasms and sunless abysses . . . depths below depths . . . a sea paved with innumerable faces, upturned to the Heavens." As Cyn suffered in the bathroom, he also began turning out drawings at a furious rate. One showed four of the sea faces turned to him gravely and saying—as faces in real life so seldom would—"We all agree with you."

The substance to which that generous tooth fairy introduced John had actually been around, in various, little-publicized forms, since his early childhood. In 1943, a Swiss chemist named Albert Hofmann stumbled on the psychoactive properties of ergot, or rye fungus, while seeking a cure for migraine. From ergot Hofmann compounded lysergic acid diethylamide, a drug combining all the illusions of opium eating, and more, with the hazards of Russian roulette. For it had the power to tap directly into its user's subconscious, conjuring unrealized fears and insecurities from the darkest corners of the psyche, at some times creating euphoria but at others anxiety or terror, intensifying light and color and altering physical dimensions in ways that could unpredictably enchant or repel, bringing on hallucinations that could be heavenly or hellish. Odorless, colorless, and flavorless, it was so strong that optimum results could be produced by the smallest dose, usually in liquid form on a piece of bread or a sugar cube.

Until the late fifties it was purely a tool of doctors and psychiatrists, used to treat alcoholics and as a truth serum for criminal psychopaths. Then a Harvard psychology professor named Timothy Leary pronounced it beneficial to all humankind: "medicine for the soul" that need have no adverse effects if taken in the proper way. Leary's conviction was strengthened by Aldous Huxley, the visionary British novelist (whose works had always been to the fore on Aunt Mimi's bookshelf). Huxley's *The Doors of Perception* described how using a mescaline, a drug with effects like those of LSD produced by the peyote cactus, had allowed him to see "what Adam saw on the first morning of his creation—the miracle, minute by minute, of naked existence." He believed that, through Leary's proselytizing, LSD could make mystical experience available to millions and bring about "a revival of religion which will be at the same time a revolution."

LSD was not yet illegal but classed merely as an experimental drug. It was nicknamed acid; taking it was "dropping acid," after the custom of absorbing its minuscule doses into bread or sugar, or "turning on," implying instant access to a more exciting and vibrant mental wavelength. The unpredictable journey under its influence was known as a trip, no more portentous than some little outing by motorboat, though the distinction had to be made between good trips and bad. Its dual effect on mind and vision was termed *psy-*

chedelic, a word coined in 1956 by psychiatrist Humphrey Osmond from the Greek words *psyche*, "mind," and *deloun*, "to reveal or make manifest."

John's first, inadvertent trip having turned out a good one (like "CinemaScope in real life"), he could not wait to repeat the experience as soon as a nondental source of supply could be found. To his surprise, he found that the desired substance could be picked up around London with little more difficulty than aspirin. Generous consignments regularly crossed the Atlantic in the baggage of Leary's American converts, notably his "high priest," Alan Hollingshead, who arrived with five thousand doses and an almost evangelical mission to turn on Britain. Hollingshead would later found the World Psychedelic Centre, in Pont Street, Chelsea, where LSD-dipped fingers of bread were handed out gratis, much as today's supermarkets offer free samples of cookies or salad dressing.

Since George Harrison's first trip had, in its own way, been as good as John's, the two conducted much of their further exploration together. Unlike other drugs, acid involved a degree of forethought and unselfishness: users were advised to take it only among friends in comfortable, familiar surroundings, and had an obligation to provide mutual support if adverse reactions set in. For George, as he later said, this one-to-one caring and sharing finally broke down the barrier he felt had existed between John and him since he first joined the Quarrymen. "After taking acid [we] had a very interesting relationship. That I was younger or smaller was no longer any kind of embarrassment with John. . . . [He] and I spent a lot of time together from then on, and I felt closer to him than all the others . . . just by the look in his eyes, I felt we were connected."

When the Beatles had reached California on their '65 American tour, John and George were both carrying foil-wrapped sugar cubes with the intention of turning on Paul and Ringo at the earliest opportunity. In the event, Paul demurred and only Ringo partook, with Neil Aspinall loyally volunteering to keep him company. The occasion was an afternoon party at their rented mansion in Benedict Canyon, attended by, among others, David Crosby and Jim McGuinn of the Byrds, and the *London Daily Mirror* journalist Don Short. Ensconced by the pool, well supplied with food and alcohol, Short was blissfully unaware of the tripping going on under his nose.

The crowd who dropped by and turned on that afternoon also included a gangly young man named Peter Fonda, son of the Hollywood legend Henry and brother of Jane, who would himself one day make the most memorable film to emerge from Sixties drug culture. At one point, he buttonholed John with the rambling tale of how once, while playing with a gun, he had accidentally shot himself. "I know what it's like to be dead, man," he kept mumbling, as if it were a special, exclusive acid dividend. "Don't tell me," John protested. "I don't want to know what it's like to be dead."

To begin with, John had no idea of the mystical edifice growing up around LSD—hence its first, purely flippant appearance in Beatles music, the single "Day Tripper," cowritten by Lennon and McCartney and released in Britain alongside the *Rubber Soul* album in December 1965. The acidy title was merely to show how with-it they were; "Day Tripper" actually is a song about sexual frustration, similar to the Rolling Stones' "Satisfaction" (even down to its guitar riff) but expressed in terms far more brazen—"half the way there," "one-night stands," "big teaser" deliberately sung to sound like "prick teaser." George Martin had earmarked it as the A-side of the new single until Paul came up with a country-influenced ballad, "We Can Work It Out." When John refused to have "Day Tripper" relegated to the B-side, a compromise was formulated: a "double A-side" single. As the waltz-time middle eight of "We Can Work It Out"—for which Paul had called on John's help—so aptly put it, "Life is very short and there's no ti-i-i-i-ime / For fussing and fighting, my friend. . . ."

"Day Tripper" could equally have expressed John's view of himself in relation to London since his flight into the manicured Surrey countryside. Despite its easy accessibility by Rolls-Royce, he felt cut off from the pulse of life in the capital; out of step with fashions and obsessions that, as the decade passed its halfway point, seemed to change by the month, the week, the day, even the hour.

Clubs, restaurants, and shops were not the only things he missed, living so far from "the Smoke." The visual arts were flourishing as never before in his lifetime: painting, sculpture, printmaking, ty-

pography, collage, and all kinds of eye-catching new alliances between them. A brilliant young generation of Pop artists had wrested
the genre back from the American Andy Warhol and his glorified
Campbell's soup can, and given it a uniquely British slant. Most
were of John's generation, brought up during the dull fifties, in the
same Victorian-shadowed suburbia. Now they turned the mundane
devices and designs of that era into cherishable icons ranging from
matchbox labels and seaside slot machines to comic-book heroes like
Korky the Cat and Desperate Dan. More populist by far than Warhol,
their works spilled off gallery walls onto posters, magazine covers,
and book jackets. Here was the first distillation of what would be the
essential Sixties aesthetic—nostalgia for childhood combined with a
sense of reinventing the whole world.

The new spirit of America's hippies—young people who rejected
their country's long-sacred consumer society, "turned on" to acid,
and "dropped out" of formal education and conventional lifestyles—
was also blowing into London and germinating like so much drug-
charged pollen. Fashionable young people—upper-class ones, for
some reason, most eagerly of all—were abandoning their Carnaby
Street bell-bottoms and miniskirts for hippie caftans, sandals, head-
bands, and mystical amulets. The *in* quarters of Chelsea and Notting
Hill were filled with the sound of Indian ragas, the musk of smoldering incense, and the ever-strengthening voice of protest.

Initially, it must be said, Britain's would-be hippies did not have
overmuch to protest about. The country was currently involved
in no foreign war nor overt acts of tyranny in its few remaining
overseas possessions, and, unlike America, had no military draft.
Students left school for university assured of full financial support
from their local authorities and without any obligation to repay it.
Far from being oppressed, British teens and twenties were positively
adulated, the papers brimming with eulogies to the young painters,
young actors, young photographers, young writers, young journalists, young couturiers, and young entrepreneurs who now poured
through the breach the Beatles had first opened. Never before had
putative rebels been so achingly without a cause.

Lacking any suitable outrage on home territory, they were obliged

to choose one many thousands of miles away, in a land of which hitherto they had known nothing. America's military support of South
Vietnam against the communist north, begun under President John
F. Kennedy, had rapidly grown into independent military action and,
by 1965, included the bombing of North Vietnam's capital, Hanoi.
The U.S. military then knew nothing of news management and gave
the world's media unrestricted access to its operations, which inevitably included onslaughts on thatched villages by high-tech helicopters
and the immolation of women and children by a jellied petroleum
incendiary called napalm.

Overnight, Britain's former young worshippers, and beneficia-
ries, of American culture turned into its bitter opponents. Though
Harold Wilson's Labour government sent no British troops to par-
ticipate in the arduous, vicious—and unwinnable—conflict in South
Vietnam's jungles and paddy-fields, it refused to condemn America's
actions there. The result was an outbreak of antiwar marches and
demonstrations in support of those taking place, with somewhat
more relevance, on the college campuses of America. A new term,
the underground, encompassed all these modish new forms of dissent—for British ears, a dual echo of wartime anti-Nazi movements
and London's subterranean transport network. Protest, rock music,
and still-unbanned LSD increasingly came together in events billed
as freak-outs or happenings. And all the time, if not touring inside
the Beatles' hermetically sealed bubble, John was stuck away among
lawn sprinklers and garden gnomes in Weybridge.

By contrast, Paul McCartney, the only Beatle still based in London,
was gallingly close to this ever-developing scene. Lodging as he did
with Jane Asher's family in Wimpole Street, he had the West End
and all its myriad amusements just a few minutes' walk away. Jane's
doctor father and musician mother were cultivated people who fostered their celebrated young boarder's awareness of classical music,
theatre, ballet, and art as well as giving him an entrée into their top-
drawer social circle. He also formed a close friendship with Jane's
brother, Peter, who played guitar and sang in close harmony with a
Westminister schoolfriend named Gordon Waller. When EMI signed
the duo as Peter and Gordon in 1964, Paul gave them an unused

Lennon-McCartney song, "World Without Love," which took them to number one on both sides of the Atlantic.

Through Peter Asher, Paul—and therefore John—acquired other friends at the new frontier of pop music and the underground. The most crucial to this story was John Dunbar, a handsome twenty-two-year-old who had been a teenage acquaintance of the Rolling Stones' manager, Andrew Loog Oldham, studied fine art at Churchill College, Cambridge, then made national headlines by marrying Oldham's latest recording protégée, Marianne Faithfull. Equally appealing to John's quieter side was Barry Miles, known simply as Miles, a soft-spoken but sharp-minded young bookseller who, coincidentally, had grown up with the Rolling Stones' guitarist, Brian Jones, in Cheltenham, Gloucestershire.

In 1965, with £2,000 starting capital from Peter Asher, Dunbar and Miles set up a combined art gallery and bookshop named the Indica, in Mason's Yard, St. James's. Paul was an enthusiastic supporter of the project, even helping to repaint the premises before their official opening. Once the Indica was in business, he thoughtfully asked Miles to keep his suburbanized fellow Beatles informed of anything interesting that came in, either artworks or literature. John became a frequent customer at the bookshop, though, Miles remembers, he always seemed a little defensive and prickly, as if conscious of being an out-of-towner. "One day, the subject of Nietzsche came up, and John pronounced it 'Nicky.' When I corrected him, he got quite annoyed."

On another visit, Miles showed him a book that had appeared in America a few months earlier: *The Psychedelic Experience* by Timothy Leary, Ralph Metzner, and Richard Alpert (later known as Ram Dass). With an abruptness that his Aunt Mimi would have recognized, he took the slim volume, curled up on the couch in the middle of the shop and read it from cover to cover.

The book transformed what he had regarded merely as a new game into an alternative religion, with foundations as ancient as Christianity or Islam. To support their vision of LSD as "a journey into higher consciousness," the authors had based their manual on *The Tibetan Book of the Dead*, a Buddhist text traditionally read aloud to the dying to prepare them for the intermediate stage between extinction and reincarnation. In order to reach acid's higher consciousness, they said, one must first make the same renunciation of worldly aggression, competitiveness, and, above all, self-importance that Buddhism had been teaching for centuries. In Buddha-esque language, with a touch of the vaudeville hypnotist, there followed step-by-step instructions for attaining "an ego-free state in which all things are like the void and cloudless sky." "Do not struggle. . . . Do not cling in fondness and weakness to your old self. Even though you cling to your old mind, you have lost the power to keep it. . . . Trust your divinity, your brain and your companions . . . When in doubt, turn off your mind, relax and float downstream. . . ."

Amazing as it may seem, money was never the Beatles' prime objective. They saw themselves always as artists on a continuous upward curve of experimentation and innovation. After creating an album like *Rubber Soul*, it was galling to have to run back onstage with their same old matching suits and hair, and blast the same old thirty-minute repertoire into the same vortex of mindless screams. In late 1965, the four had a meeting at which all agreed their in-concert standards had gone to hell, simply because no one was listening. As John said: ". . . we could send out four waxwork dummies of ourselves and that would satisfy the crowds. Beatles concerts are nothing to do with music any more. They're just bloody tribal rites."

Modern rock stars on tour are insulated from the outside world by dozens of aides, fixers, security staff, and PR people. But the Beatles, despite their hugely enlarged performance venues, still traveled with much the same small entourage that used to accompany them around northern dance halls: Brian; the two roadies, Neil and Mal; and press officer Tony Barrow. Whenever they went, they were available—and vulnerable—in ways that no headliners today would tolerate. For John, the whole process had become a repetition of school, except that now there could be no playing truant. "He got to the point where he just hated the audience," says his old Hamburg friend and confidant Klaus Voormann. "He couldn't stand that this herd of cows was just screaming. He was angry about those people's reactions; he found it terrible. It was a complex with him. He'd gone from pretending to be this tough rock-'n'-roller into being a Beatle, which was also all about pretending. With all that he had, he wasn't happy because he hadn't come to terms with his own personality. He was a Beatle, and he knew that a Beatle doesn't really exist."

Britain had already, unknowingly, seen its last-ever Beatles tour, back in December 1965. Brian's original plan had been the traditional countrywide trek, ending with a second Royal Variety Show appearance and yet another of their metropolitan Christmas pantos. However, the four had flatly refused to do either the Royal or Christmas show, and raised so many other objections to their itinerary that the whole thing was almost called off. Eventually, they compromised with a nine-date circuit of key cities, including the Liverpool Empire and ending in Cardiff on December 10.

Despite the shortness of the tour, John was in an overtly rebellious mood, emerging from the Beatles' Rolls into the dank night fogs of Newcastle and Manchester, jacketless, in a white T-shirt—the new kind with a picture or slogan printed on the front—and greeting the stage-door media contingents with jeers and sarcasm (though in one-to-one interviews, even with the most obscure local journalist, he remained as open and honest as ever). Onstage, like the other three, he had virtually given up trying to make himself heard against the screams. Yet sometimes even now he would crash both forearms down on his organ keyboard in sheer fury and frustration.

Whatever his private feelings, the treadmill of his life as a Beatle for the moment seemed unstoppable. In the coming summer, the four were committed to an overseas tour, finishing up in America, whose only threat at this point was the tedium of being worshipped and adored. Meanwhile they had to turn out another album that would simultaneously confound all their rivals on a creative level and maintain their primacy in the charts. With barely two months to pull this off, they reassembled at Abbey Road Studios with George Martin on April 6.

John later called what emerged "the acid album," forming a book-end, as it were, with "the pot album," *Rubber Soul*. In fact, acid was just one of the elements that would make this, for many people, the

Beatles' finest achievement on record. With the new complexities and ambiguities of rock, it combined the old simplicity and certainties of pop, as well as the eclecticism and self-indulgence of studio despots; it had the energy and self-discipline of a band still on the road and under the cosh. It showed John moving off alone in a wholly new direction and (literally) finding a wholly new voice, yet still content to function inside a group, apply all his concentration to improving someone else's work, play rhythm guitar, sing backup harmonies, and simply have fun.

In four of the five new songs he brought to Martin, his senses appeared as lucid and his competitive edge as keen as ever. "Doctor Robert" took an objective, satirical view of drug use, lampooning a well-known New York physician who supplied wealthy Manhattan socialites with amphetamine-laced vitamin shots. "And Your Bird Can Sing," for all its enigmatic air, merely borrowed a titling device from Paul ("And I Love Her") and ended up as a message little more complex than "keep smiling." "She Said She Said" used the "I know what it's like to be dead" line with which Peter Fonda had simultaneously bored and unsettled him in California six months earlier. But Fonda's dirge was now ringingly upbeat, full of competitive left-field chord changes. Even the dozy mood of "I'm Only Sleeping" suggested a familiar John Lennon, who could be "miles away" and "in the middle of a dream," yet never ceased vigilantly "keeping an eye on the world going by my window."

Whether or not due to their shared acid experience, John and George found an empathy on this album that they never had before, although its first expression was hardly in the realm of the mystical. For all four Beatles, the thrill of acquiring real wealth had been marred by the discovery of top-rate British income tax, which, under Harold Wilson's Labour government, could reach 97.5 percent. Brian Epstein's attempts to hive off some of their earnings into an offshore fund in the Bahamas had lately ended in disaster, obliging each to pay a hefty capital sum in back tax and interest. The result was George's song "Taxman," a hymn of hate breathing John's influence—and input—in its vision of new taxes on streets, on shoe leather, even on the old penny pieces traditionally placed on the eyelids of corpses laid out in northern front parlors. John actually named the guilty man, that benign, pipe-smoking distributor of showbiz awards, crooning the name "Mister Wilson" and, for good measure, his Tory opponent "Mister Heath," in the place usually occupied by "Shang-a-lang" or "Bop-shoowop."

Paul's contributions represented a major leap forward on his own, very different, course: the euphoric "Good Day Sunshine," the uncharacteristically vulnerable "For No One," and the soul-influenced "Got to Get You Into My Life." While ordering in still more extra instrumentalists (a French horn on "For No One," a brass section on "Got to Get You Into My Life") he also provided a track that showed how little the Beatles needed anyone but themselves. "Here, There and Everywhere," a love note to Jane Asher, was recorded in almost a cappella style by voices as close-knit as the friends who once shared even their body warmth. Of all Beatles vocals, it remains the most intimate and sweet. Paul had first played it to John on a tape of rough song drafts by both of them, while they were sharing a hotel room on location for *Help!* "You know," John told him, "I probably like that better than any of my songs on the tape."

It was Paul's idea to include the first Beatles number overtly for children, in the spot traditionally occupied by Ringo Starr. The theme for "Yellow Submarine" came one night as he drowsed in bed, and its words and music were almost complete by the time he got up next morning. The notion of a yellow submarine was quintessential comic-book Pop Art, although—as would quickly be noted—the term was also slang for Nembutal or Pentobarbital downers. The recording turned into a miniature *Goon Show*, with Pattie Harrison, Rolling Stone Brian Jones, Marianne Faithfull, George Martin, Neil Aspinall, Mal Evans, and sundry Abbey Road employees providing subaquatic sound effects and joining in the choruses. John blew bubbles in a bucket of water, shouted out commands from an imaginary conning tower ("Aye, aye, Mr. Captain, full speed ahead!"), and echoed Ringo's vocal in a Neddy Seagood-ish shriek. When the tape stopped running, Mal strapped a bass drum on his chest and everyone danced round the studio behind him in a conga line.

From Paul, too, came a ballad that was as much a short story, the first of a trilogy that would take his talent to its zenith. The subject matter, a solitary woman wistfully picking up celebratory rice in "a church where a wedding has been," had no precedent in pop; if anything, it evoked the more melancholy reaches of Irish Catholic literature, particularly James Joyce's *Dubliners*. The central figure in this tender hearted lament for "all the lonely people" received her baptism in a roundabout way. Paul decided on the Christian name Eleanor, so he thought, after the actress Eleanor Bron; then, on a visit to Bristol, where Jane was appearing in a play, he happened to see the surname "Rigby" above a shop front.

In fact, Eleanor Rigby was embedded in his subconscious—and, even more deeply, in John's—thanks to a family gravestone in St. Peter's churchyard, Woolton. As a small boy, John had seen its weather-stained inscription to the "beloved wife of Thomas Woods and granddaughter of the above, died 10th October, 1939, aged 44 years" countless times on his way to and from church or choir practice. Racked by childhood's premature terror of the grave, he always found comfort in thinking she was not really dead and moldering under the ground but only, as her epitaph said, "Asleep."

John claimed that while the song that would immortalize her was worked out between Paul's grieving solo voice and a classical string octet, he and the other Beatles merely sat around "drinking tea." However, both George and he were involved in the vocal harmonies, and all four had contributed to the lyric (Ringo coming up with the vision of Father McKenzie, who was originally to have been called McCartney, "darning his socks in the night when there's nobody there.") Significantly, throughout all the creative disputes to come, John never rated Eleanor Rigby as other than a masterpiece, nor felt other than proud of his part in it, however peripheral. "It was Paul's baby," he would say. "But I helped with the education of the child."

The track chosen to end the album—rightly, since it hardly seemed to belong there at all, but already to be leaping off into the future— was an all-John number, initially known only by the code name "Mark 1." When he first played it to George Martin on acoustic guitar in his usual way, Martin was puzzled. The opening C major chord did not, as usual, form a threshold to some catchy sequence, but just went on, and on and on. With this strummed monotone came words that sounded like no John his producer had heard before: "Turn off your mind, relax and float downstream . . . Lay down all thought, surrender to the void . . . Listen to the colour of your dreams . . ." They were, in fact, almost verbatim quotations from *The Psychedelic Experience*, which he had devoured in one gulp at the Indica Bookshop. Here now was a fifteen-line lyric encapsulating the LSD apostles' creed that human existence was but a meaningless game, and the only way to salvation was "turn on, tune in and drop out."

John's sole guideline to Martin and the studio engineers, delivered with wonderful, dictatorial simplicity, was that he should sound like the Dalai Lama chanting from some Himalayan mountaintop. Their solution took the singing voice he so disliked into unprecedented realms of echo and distortion. The beginning of his vocal track was recorded on Abbey Road's newly installed ADT (Automatic Double-Tracking) system; the rest was put through a Hammond organ's Leslie speaker, whose rotating mechanism produced a wah-wah effect. The result was a flat, reedy, almost dehumanized tone, very much like that associated with mystics in holy trances. He loved it, of course—and instantly suggested a variation on the Leslie speaker technique whereby he would hang upside-down from the ceiling and slowly revolve while a fixed microphone picked up the erratic volume of his voice.

Although the track was John through and through, it owed a massive debt to Paul McCartney, still at this stage the most avant-garde Beatle as well as the one most dedicated to cultural self-advancement. The classical music learning curve, which for Paul began while living with Jane Asher's family, had since progressed far beyond simple Beethoven or Brahms. He also knew about John Cage and Karlheinz Stockhausen and their revolutionary conception of music as unpredictable sonic "events" rather than fixed patterns of notes. He knew about Pierre Schaffer's musique concrète, which was created solely by the manipulation of electronically generated sound and thus removed any need for talent or training in the performer.

Paul had by now left the Ashers' and, still resisting the call of the suburbs, had moved into a handsome town house in Cavendish Avenue, St. John's Wood, just around the corner from Abbey Road. There, at the stimulus of Barry Miles and other arty underground friends, he had tried out a seminal musique concrète technique with analog recording tape, in these days still mainly used on reel-to-reel machines. By joining the two ends of a tape and removing the machine's erase mechanism, one created a loop that repeatedly superimposed the same track on itself, so turning the most commonplace sound into an unearthly cacophony.

The sense of Himalayan height and space, combined with acid-induced rapture and spiritual mass-awakening, that John sought for "Mark 1" was created by five tape loops playing simultaneously. Following Paul's lead, John, George, Ringo, and Barry Miles all made their own loops at home by multiple rerecording of scraps of classical music, studio guitar outtakes, or even just laughter. The loop makers were stationed in studios all over the Abbey Road complex and, at a given signal, relayed their surreal sonic squibbles to George Martin's mixing console. Such ad hoc commandeering and unorthodox use of EMI resources being strictly against company rules, there was a touch of Quarry Bank naughtiness about it all.

Playback produced exactly the sound picture John had imagined—that of hundreds of monks in robes as yellow as a submarine, beating and plucking on strange instruments and chanting of the joys of his mental Shangri-La. Typically, he was disappointed, saying he wished they'd used real monks instead. Typically, too, when choosing a title, he passed over all Leary's mystic verbiage in favor of "Tomorrow Never Knows," a pet phrase of Ringo's, sensing it was just right "to take the edge off those heavy philosophical lyrics."

The album cover obviously needed to be something very special, an image as adventurous as the music it heralded, reaching into the same uncharted realms of Pop Art and psychedelia. The person who could have realized this to perfection, unfortunately, had died at twenty-one in a German girl's arms and was buried in Liverpool alone with his name. But if Stu Sutcliffe was no longer around, a powerful echo of his era, and his talent, still was.

Klaus Voormann's career as a Brian Epstein discovery had proved an unrewarding one. Paddy, Klaus and Gibson, the trio in which he played bass, had been signed to NEMS Enterprises by Brian in a burst of enthusiasm but, finding no success on record, had quickly fallen apart. Rather than return to Hamburg, Klaus stayed on in London, not seeing his old Beatle mates as much as he would have liked for fear of looking like a sponger. He would soon join the highly successful Manfred Mann group, but at this point, with no music gig in prospect, he had serious thoughts of resuming his original career as an artist and designer. One day, out of the blue, John telephoned and invited him to do a cover for the new album, now scheduled for release in August.

The moment was serendipitous: six years earlier, at Hamburg's Kaiserkeller club, Klaus had first plucked up courage to talk to John by showing him a design for an album cover. And, despite their long friendship—and the supposedly ego-softening power of acid—he found that prickly English boy-rocker could still readily resurface. "When John asked me to design the album, I hesitated for a moment before saying yes, I'd do it, and suddenly he gets very angry, very uptight: 'What's the matter? You don't want to do it or what?' He's still the old, intimidating John."

Klaus's chaste black-and-white design seemed to belong on the wall of some avant-garde gallery rather than in the finger-hurried racks of a record store. Four Beatle heads, sketched in pen and ink, spilled forth a collage of photographic images through the mingling, seaweedy tangles of their hair. John's face, at top right, had the almond eyes and long vertical nose of a Modigliani. The title, *Revolver*, was a sly Lennon pun, suggesting the action of a record on its turntable as well as a weapon that, for him, still belonged to the world of make-believe.

John with Julia in her sister Nanny's garden.

John's father, Alf—later "Freddie"—
during his years as a ship's steward.

John and his cousin Liela in the front garden at Mendips.

John's first inspiration for getting up and playing: the Lonnie Donegan skiffle group, 1957.

The Quarrymen play on a coal truck at the Rosebery Street party, 1957.

Painting of John in his hated glasses by fellow student Helen Anderson.

John, painted by fellow student Ann Mason after blowing his student grant on a black jacket and olive suede shoes.

Post–Hamburg look onstage at the Cavern: leather jacket, suffocatingly hot wool turtlencck, and Rickenbacker guitar.

Front-page attraction in new all-color *Mersey Beat*.

Stu Sutcliffe and John performing live onstage at Hamburg, 1960.

Two mentors meet: a rare picture of Brian Epstein and Astrid Kirchherr together.

John, photographed by Astrid: in their photo sessions he was always
"dead professional."

Four on a pedestrian crossing: this one in Liverpool in 1963, six years before the iconic *Abbey Road* shot. (Paul is behind Ringo.)

John with Mimi Smith—the aunt who raised him in suburban gentility. Even after he was world famous, she still complained about his hair.

John in Lenin cap shares the others' bemusement at their welcome to America.

Press conference in the U.S. where the Beatles created the sound bite—John's the most biting of all.

Working in the studio with George Martin. For Martin, John was the "lemon juice" against Paul's "virgin olive oil."

John and George with Maharishi Mahesh Yogi. Even the Queen complained: "The Beatles are turning awfully funny, aren't they?"

John pleads guilty to possessing cannabis, a decision that will come back to haunt him. Yoko has just had her hair brutally yanked by a hostile Beatles fan.

Loudhailer Lennon: John takes to the streets in support of *Oz* magazine, 1970.

Tittenhurst Park, the Georgian house and seventy-two-acre estate where John got off heroin, underwent primal scream therapy, and recorded the *Plastic Ono Band* and *Imagine* albums.

New York, mid-seventies: the short-lived craze for floppy clothes and berets. "John thought he was considered unhip for not doing the same androgyny thing as the Stones . . . he wanted the gay crowd to love him."

Onstage with Elton John, Madison Square Garden, 1974.

The devoted househusband with baby Sean: "I remember that around the house he always wore a blue-and-white floral patterned *yukata*, . . . and he always had a ponytail."

Showing off the green card that the U.S. government finally granted him in 1976: "Now I'm going home to crack open a tea-bag and start looking at some travel catalogues."

Outside the Dakota, December 1980.

18

A MOST
RELIGIOUS FELLOW

You might as well paint a target on me.

The world tour Brian had scheduled to begin in June 1966 was supposed to have eased the pressure on his boys. Their only European shows were three in West Germany. Hong Kong, Australia, and New Zealand were bypassed in favor of single-city visits to Japan and the Philippines. Following those hopefully unexacting appearances in Tokyo and Manila, they would have more than a month's break before returning to the ever-reliable embrace of America.

Behind them they left a new single that was like an hors d'oeuvre for the banquet to come on *Revolver*. The undisputedly more commercial A-side was Paul's "Paperback Writer," a satire on pulp fiction and Fleet Street, finally making use of a phrase that the poet Royston Ellis had dropped into his and John's consciousness in 1960. On the B-side, John's "Rain" was a celebration of acid's transfiguring power at its most benign, when a wet leaf could appear to blaze brighter than gold and a raindrop coursing down a windowpane to reveal all the mystery of Creation. "Can you hear me?" the voice of the new apostle repeated over and over. "I can show you . . ." Multitrack harmonies and varispeed tempos created an effect both dense and liquid, as of a sonic tropical monsoon. For the fade-out, George Martin had the idea of playing John's vocal opening backward. John loved the result, and from then on wanted everything played backward.

After such a creative surge, the thought of returning to a thirty-minute stage repertoire of dusty old hits was hardly bearable. And, what with putting the finishing touches to *Revolver*—and the certainty that no one out there would be listening anyway—the Beatles scarcely even bothered to rehearse before starting out on the road. During their opening concert, at Munich's Circus-Krone-Bau, John, George, and Paul simultaneously forgot the opening of "I'm Down," and had to stop and confer about it. Even after this, the usually meticulous Paul managed two further slipups in the lyric; then George mistakenly introduced "Yesterday" as a track from *Beatles for Sale.* Not since earliest Quarrymen days, and rarely even then, had they shown such blatant unprofessionalism.

The third West German concert took them back to Hamburg for the first time since January 1963 and provided a clearer-than-usual measure of how far they had risen since. The former illegal laborers, suspected arsonists, and police detainees now arrived at the city's central station aboard a luxury train fitted with velvet drapes and marble bathtubs, which had been used to transport Queen Elizabeth II during her state visit a year before. The former all-night ravers at the Kaiserkeller and Star-Club now played just two shows of thirty minutes each in the 5,600-seat Ernst Mercke Halle, although, as if to keep up Reeperbahn tradition, police arrested forty-four spectators for violence.

Numerous old friends were granted instant dressing-room visas, among them Astrid Kirchherr; Bert Kaempfert, the Beatles' first record producer (whose song "Strangers in the Night" had stopped "Paperback Writer" from reaching number one in the United Kingdom); and Bettina Derlien, the Star-Club barmaid who had always known just how to help John when he was feeling down. After their second show, the four Beatles took a nostalgic midnight stroll through St. Pauli, John showing particular pleasure—as a less enraptured George would later recall—in spotting other familiar faces among the strippers, bouncers, gangsters, and cross-dressers from the still-thriving Bar Monika. There was no happier memory for him, nor ever would be, than that of blasting out simple rock 'n' roll under crazy neon in this dangerous, sordid but also sheltering and tolerant place where, so unaccountably, he had once belonged.

For the first time, the support team traveling with the Beatles reflected the scale and scope of the journey. Besides Neil, Mal, and Tony Barrow, Brian had brought along Peter Brown, the ex-Liverpool record-shop manager who had become his most trusted lieutenant at NEMS Enterprises and closest friend outside it. Also in the party was Vic Lewis, an old-school London theatrical agent whose company had recently been acquired by NEMS, and who was about to join its board. These extra executive layers were meant to cushion pressure on the four, though, alas, the very opposite would happen.

From the moment they left West Germany, in Barrow's words, "everything started to go pear-shaped." A hurricane warning forced their Japan-bound flight to divert to Anchorage, Alaska, for a nine-hour stopover. When at long last they reached Tokyo, they found themselves the first pop group, possibly the first entertainers in any sphere, to receive death threats. The Nippon Budokan arena, where they had to give five shows, was normally a venue for Sumo wrestling and martial arts displays—in Japanese tradition regarded as religious rites as much as spectator sports. A group of extreme right-wing students had threatened vengeance for such defilement of hallowed ground with decadent Western music. From such cultural purists, this could only mean something very unpleasant with a long, curved sword.

It was later estimated that around thirty-five thousand police and security staff had been mobilized to guard the Beatles during their four-day stay in Tokyo. Paradoxically, Japanese Beatlemaniacs were the most peaceable they ever encountered. Five successive houses at the Budokan watched in almost complete stillness and silence, with any sign of exuberance instantly photographed by the police who thronged the side aisles. Between performances, they were kept under virtual house arrest in the top-floor suite of the Tokyo Hilton. Despite the numerous guards on twenty-four-hour watch, John and Neil Aspinall managed their usual trick of sneaking out and hailing an ordinary cab for some incognito sightseeing. "We found a local market, and got out to have a look around," Neil remembered. "But within a few minutes, the police turned up and sent us back to the hotel."

So paranoid was security that even shopping in central Tokyo was banned; instead, the city's leading stores sent selections of merchandise up to the Beatles' suite. Among the cameras, electronic gadgets, and *happi* coats were some painting and calligraphy sets and blocks of superfine Japanese art paper. Having nothing else to do, the four set to work on a large communal painting. Barrow remembers how, as soon as John picked up a paintbrush, all his usual aggression and impatience seemed to melt away. "Never before or after did I see [him] concentrating with such contented determination on a non-essential project." Interesting that the culture that provided this brief, unexpected respite from Beatle-slavery was Japan's.

The Philippines, their next and final Far Eastern stop, were not a usual destination for traveling pop groups and had seemed like a brilliant territorial move on Brian's part. Under the seemingly immovable dictatorship of President Ferdinand Marcos and his clothes-horse wife, Imelda, this was the most willingly Americanized nation in southeast Asia. Filipinos were renowned for their charm and friendliness and empathy with Western culture. The government-controlled press had whipped up feverish expectation over the Beatles' visit, portraying it as yet another benefit of Marcos's rule.

Before their departure from Tokyo, Brian had politely declined an invitation to the Beatles to call on President Marcos and the First Lady during their brief stay in Manila, explaining that they had only a brief rest-time between shows and it was now policy for them not to act as their country's emissaries while on the road. None of the Beatles' party appreciated that *no* is a word Asian dictators do not understand. On the morning after their arrival, before they were even awake, a party of government officials arrived at their hotel with a fleet of limousines and motorcycle outriders. They were expected within the hour at Malancañang, the presidential palace-cum-fortress. Sticking to his guns, Brian refused to let them be disturbed.

When the quartet finally surfaced a couple of hours later, they were able to watch live television coverage of the function they were supposed to be attending: not the private luncheon mentioned in Tokyo but a garden party hosted by Mrs. Marcos for four hundred children of government apparatchiks and senior military personnel.. Lingering close-ups were provided of the First Lady's puzzled pout and the children's disappointed faces as the wait grew increasingly hopeless.

The Beatles thus found themselves in the surreal position of being simultaneously VIP guests and pariahs. That evening, after giving two shows to a total of eighty thousand at Manila's Rizal Memorial Stadium, they found all police and security cover withdrawn without explanation. Next morning, they awoke to outraged newspaper headlines that they had "snubbed the First Family," and reprisals began in earnest. The Filipino promoter refused to hand over their share of the concert takings; government treasury officials threatened not to let them leave the country unless Brian paid a hefty cash sum in income tax. Their hotel joined in the attack, responding to room-service orders with trays of inedible food. Brian nobly took responsibility for the debacle, and went on Manila TV to explain that it had all been a misunderstanding, with no slight to the First Lady intended. As soon as he appeared onscreen, a blizzard of technical interference broke up the picture and drowned out his carefully rehearsed words. Mysteriously, as soon as his segment was over the interference ceased.

The party's departure for home next day, July 4, was a meticulously orchestrated nightmare. At Manila International Airport, no porters were available to handle their luggage; then every escalator came to a synchronized stop, forcing them to struggle up flights of stairs with the bags in subtropical heat. In the departure area, they were jeered, jostled, and even kicked by airport staff and bystanders. Crossing the open tarmac to the plane, everyone was in real fear of sniper fire from the heavily armed troops guarding the terminal. Moments before departure, Barrow, Brian, and Mal Evans were ordered off the aircraft again to sort out some nitpicking immigration point. Yet, amazingly, no Filipino customs official thought to search their luggage, which still contained most of the pot stash they had brought into the country with them.

Back in Britain, they played down the episode, though much could be read into John's expert mimicry of airport officials screaming "You just ordinary passenger!" "I was very delicate, and moved every time they touched me," he told journalists at Heathrow Airport. "I could have been kicked and not known . . ." Privately, he made a vow "never [to go] to any nuthouses again." On a copy of the tour itinerary next to Manila he scrawled, "Nearly fucking killed by the Government . . . and it's just another Beatle day. . . . George said 'They should drop an H-Bomb on Manila' and we all silently agreed."

Already in 1966, an American public-relations disaster, for which John bore no individual blame, had been narrowly averted. In June, Capitol Records had issued an album entitled *"Yesterday" . . . And Today*, comprising tracks from *Rubber Soul* and *Help!* plus three from *Revolver*. Its cover, shot in London by Australian Robert Whitaker, plumbed levels of bad taste that Punk Rock, ten years later, would scarcely equal. Four smiling—nay, chortling—Beatles were shown in long white butchers' coats, festooned with bloody joints of meat and naked, dismembered dolls. The outtakes were even more gruesome. One had George seemingly hammering nails into John's head; in another, all four were joined to a woman by a string of sausages like an umbilical cord.

Though the original concept was Whitaker's, they all willingly embraced it, as John later said, through "boredom and resentment" at having to do "another Beatle thing," and to subvert their cuddly moptop image: "There we were, supposed to be sort of angels. I wanted to show that we were really aware of life." The image was later interpreted as a deliberate one-fingered gesture to Capitol's management, whom John in particular resented for issuing too many such cobbled-together albums without their permission or approval. If such a gesture was intended, it was completely lost on Britain, where the picture appeared in advertisements for "Paperback Writer" and on the cover of the *Melody Maker*.

Capitol also noticed nothing amiss, put the cover into production as a "Pop Art experiment," and had shipped a first pressing of 750,000 copies to record stores across America by the time alarm bells belatedly started ringing. Most of the albums were called back from the retailers before they could be displayed for sale, and a new cover picture was shot of the Beatles, grouped now very unsmilingly around an old-fashioned steamer trunk. Rather than manufacture a whole new cover, Capitol simply pasted this image over the existing "butcher" ones and shipped them back to their original consignees. Ever since then, memorabilia hounds have been carefully peeling the steamer trunk picture off *The Beatles—"Yesterday" and Today*, hoping to find the censored bloodbath underneath.

With American Beatle fans spared the sight of their darlings seeming to exult over decapitated and limbless babies, arrangements ran smoothly ahead for the seventeen-day tour, due to begin in Chicago on August 12 and as yet regarded by no one as the Beatles' last ever. Recovered from their mauling in Manila, the four settled down to enjoy a summer that would enter British mythology rather like the long Edwardian picnic before World War I. That spring, America's mass media had finally noticed the explosion of pop music, fashion, art, and design in London, which a small in-crowd had had almost to themselves for two years. In April, *Time* magazine had published a cover story on this new "style capital of Europe," listing all the ways in which it was suddenly "swinging." The result was to bring millions of young people pouring across the Atlantic to experience London's boutiques, clubs, and alfresco fashion parades, and the ancient monuments, red buses, black taxis, and trotting Horse Guards that had, inexplicably, become their accessories. The very Union Jack was suddenly groovy: no longer a symbol of dusty imperial yesterdays, but a fashion statement flaunted by every young today-person on T-shirts, coffee mugs, or plastic shopping-bags.

One might have thought national self-esteem could rise no higher, yet it did. On July 30, at Wembley Stadium, England beat West Germany in the final of the soccer World Cup, proving World War II had not been a fluke after all. The final grace note in this sun-soaked symphony should have been the Beatles' departure on yet another bonanza American tour just over a week later. Instead, without warning, the heavens opened.

Back in March, the *London Evening Standard* had published yet another series of articles by Maureen Cleave, the Beatles' most trusted chronicler. Cleave's theme was that they had now risen above all competition and changes in fickle teenage taste to "a secure life at the top" otherwise enjoyed only by the Queen. Thanks to her equally good relationship with Brian, she was granted instant access to each Beatle in turn, with none of the time rationing or PR supervision that would be imposed on modern interviewers. Paul McCartney came to her London flat and sang "Eleanor Rigby" to her; George and Ringo were equally accessible, friendly, and frank. John she saw during one of his spells of domesticity in Weybridge.

The article, headlined "How Does a Beatle Live? John Lennon Lives Like This," ran in the *Evening Standard* of March 4. Cleave reported John to be still uncannily like portraits of King Henry VIII, "arrogant as an eagle . . . unpredictable, indolent, disorganised, childish, vague, charming and quick-witted." He had given her a guided tour of his toy-crammed mansion, with three-year-old Julian at their heels, on the way, letting drop a remark with dire implications for the Beatles' "stable life at the top," never mind for his wife and son. "I'm just stopping [here] like a bus-stop. . . . I'll get my real house when I know what I want. . . . You see, there's something else I'm going to do—only I don't know what it is. All I know is this isn't it for me."

Framed in a paragraph about his seeming lack of any self-doubt was this fateful quote: "Christianity will go. It will vanish and shrink. I needn't argue about that; I know I'm right and I will be proved right. We're more popular than Jesus now. I don't know which will go first—rock 'n' roll or Christianity. Jesus was all right, but his disciples were thick and ordinary. It's them twisting it that ruins it for me."

The observation did not come out of nowhere, as it seems to in the story. Later, Cleave mentions the eclectic range of John's literary taste, citing titles such as *Forty-one Years in India* by Field Marshal Lord Roberts and *Curiosities of Natural History* by Francis T. Buckland (though not *The Psychedelic Experience*). She also says he has been reading "extensively about religion," without mentioning exactly what. He had, in fact, been deeply absorbed in Hugh J. Schonfield's *Passover Plot*, a nonfiction book currently topping the bestsellers. Schonfield, a leading biblical scholar, advanced the controversial thesis that Jesus was a mortal man who planned his miracles to fulfill Old Testament prophecies, and faked his own crucifixion, using his disciples as unwitting accomplices—hence John's perception of them as "thick." The idea of Timothy Leary and Buddha as harbingers of a brand-new faith, whose holy communion was dispensed on sugar lumps, also must have colored his attitude.

It should further be pointed out, with no disrespect to Maureen Cleave, that those notorious words may not have been exactly what John said. Even the most articulate interviewees can ramble or lapse into non sequitur, and reporters often paraphrase or conflate quotes without damaging their essential accuracy. Cleave had not been looking for sensationalism, and at the time thought no more about the statement than "it was just John being John." The fact was that her conversations with him had produced far more obviously explosive material, much of it impossible to print in the *Evening Standard* or any other paper, then or since. Once, for instance, he had talked about his mother, Julia, how he still missed her and how beautiful she had been. Seemingly in all seriousness, he added that before she disappeared from his teenage life, he only wished he'd taken the opportunity to have sex with her.

"Christianity" to British readers overwhelmingly meant the Church of England, an institution that, in the dawning new consciousness of 1966, fewer and fewer people took with any seriousness. Anglican cathedrals and churches might be cherished in the national heritage, but Anglican worship and Anglican clergy were the butt of every contemporary satirist from Alan Bennett to Peter Sellers (who, not long before, had recorded a cover version of "Help!" in the persona of the Archbishop of Canterbury, Dr. Michael Ramsay). That, in pure box-office terms, the Beatles were "more popular than Jesus" was clear at underattended C of E services every Sunday of the year, as it also was in the church's rather desperate efforts to liven up the proceedings with pop rhythms and guitars. Polemicists were constantly making the very same point, in pulpits ranging from the *Daily Mail* to the *Church Times*.

So unremarkable was John's viewpoint in British eyes that the *Evening Standard* subeditors did not headline it nor even highlight it in the layout. And, ready and waiting though the national media were to jump on anything a Beatle said, no news bulletin picked up on it, no mass-circulation editorialist commented on it, no popular columnist even seemed to notice it. The single note of dissent—and that a very mild one—came from John Grigg, the former Lord Altrincham, writing in the *Guardian*. Cleave's article was later syndicated to various overseas publications (including the *New York Times*) and again produced no reaction.

Not until four months had passed did the backlash finally hit. An American teenage magazine called *Datebook* resurrected the Cleave interview for a spread in which John was to feature, entitled "The Ten Adults You Dig/Hate." His comments on the Beatles' and Jesus's comparative drawing power appeared in isolation, with one sentence lifted out as a cover line: "I don't know which will go first—rock 'n' roll or Christianity." The spread appeared in *Datebook*'s August issue, which reached newsstands in mid-July, three weeks before the start of the Beatles' tour.

In cynical, agnostic Britain, buried in a paper unavailable outside Greater London, the words had barely raised an eyebrow. In God-fearing America, blazoned across the front of a magazine nationally available to young people, their effect was very different. Within hours of *Datebook* going on sale, the Associated Press reported that radio station WAQY in Birmingham, Alabama, the very heart of the Southern Bible Belt, had announced a ban on Beatles records forthwith. Radio stations serving devout communities in Kentucky, Ohio, Alabama, Georgia, Mississippi, South Carolina, Massachusetts, Connecticut, Utah, and New York instantly followed WAQY's lead—although no New York City deejay joined the ban and station

WSAC in Fort Knox, Kentucky, which had not previously played the Beatles, now began to do so "to show our contempt for hypocrisy personified." The more showmanlike and publicity-hungry of the banning brigade smashed the actual disks on air, sponsored disposal bins in public places, labeled PLACE BEATLES TRASH HERE, even built bonfires or provided wood chippers so that listeners could personally consign their fallen angels' singles and albums to purgatory or pulp. Churches, chapels, temples, and tabernacles across the land joined in as with one voice, calling down hellfire on the Beatles' heads and any of their flock who now bought Beatle music or attended Beatle shows with instant excommunication.

From there, the uproar ricocheted throughout Christendom. Racially segregated South Africa briefly enjoyed a feeling of moral superiority when its national broadcasting service joined in the Beatles music ban. Stations in Holland and Spain did likewise on behalf of Protestants and Catholics respectively; there was even condemnation from the Pope via the Vatican newspaper, *L'Osservatore Romano*, which commented that "some things may not be dealt with profanely even in the world of beatniks." Bounced back to Britain from all these foreign parts, the once-overlooked quotes became a subject for feverish debate in the press and on television, with John receiving almost unanimous criticism, if not quite for sacrilege, then for vainglory, naïveté, and astounding bad timing. Never before—not when Elvis Presley's pumping crotch outraged the mid-fifties, nor when Jerry Lee Lewis married his thirteen-year-old cousin, nor even when Chuck Berry went to jail—had a pop star been so publicly and relentlessly put on the rack.

From Brian Epstein the crisis called forth all the diplomatic skills that had somehow failed him in Manila. Impressively, no attempt was made to blame Maureen Cleave by claiming she had misquoted John or used remarks meant to have been off the record. Instead, Brian quietly contacted Cleave and asked her to make no comment on the matter from here on. Such was her respect for him and John—and her shock and bewilderment at what was happening—that she agreed. It's hard to imagine any modern pop writer at the center of a world sensation backing away from the limelight so readily.

Brian's first idea was that John should tape a statement to be played on U.S. radio and TV, apologizing for the offense that had been caused. But in the event, it was Brian himself who made the statement at a press conference at New York's Americana Hotel, using techniques of projection and timing learned long ago at the Royal Academy of Dramatic Art. No communiqué from a political summit could have been more measured or dignified, as the young Jewish manager strove to put the Christian hue and cry into proportion. John, said Brian, was "deeply interested in religion," but his views on the subject had been "misrepresented entirely out of context. . . . What he said and meant was that he was astonished that in the last fifty years the Church of England, and therefore Christ, had suffered a decline in interest. He did not mean to boast about the Beatles' fame. He meant to point out that the Beatles' effect appeared to be, to him, a more immediate one upon certain of the younger generation."

Though clearly a question mark the size of a mushroom cloud now hung over the Beatles' American tour, they flew out of Britain on August 11 to begin it in Chicago, as planned. Six days earlier, *Revolver* had had its British release, with "Eleanor Rigby"/"Yellow Submarine" as its accompanying single. For now, the brilliance of the music took second place to this far more burning question.

Before leaving, John gave a brief television interview, with Paul McCartney beside him in the very obvious role of verbal minder. Was he worried by what might be waiting for him across the Atlantic? "It worries me," he replied, unusually casting around for the blandest words possible. "But I hope it'll be all right in the end, as they say." Paul then stepped in, at his most smilingly emollient, insisting, "It'll be fine." Later, John would tell a reporter in America he had been "scared stiff" by the chorus of damnation, and had at first wanted to pull out of the tour. "I thought they'd kill me, because they take things so seriously here. I mean, they shoot you and then they realise it wasn't that important. So I didn't want to go, but Brian and Paul and the other Beatles persuaded me."

When the four reached Chicago, it was obvious that Brian's statement had not nearly quelled the outcry and that something would have to come from John personally. Their itinerary was to take them through several of the states where divine retribution was being called down on their heads and their music cast onto heretics' pyres. The white supremacist Ku Klux Klan, an organization normally dedicated to murdering and terrorizing black people, had appointed itself the avenger of outraged Christianity throughout the South. There was a real possibility of some attack on John, or the group as a whole. If the situation did not improve, Brian told associates, he would call off the tour here and now.

A meeting took place among John, Brian, and the Beatles' press officer, Tony Barrow, in Brian's suite at the Astor Towers Hotel. Remembering John's defiance after the Bob Wooler–bashing episode four years earlier, Barrow might have expected him to dig his heels in and refuse to take back a single word. Instead, he was distraught to think he might have ruined the tour, and desperate to make any amends he could. "He actually put his head in his hands and sobbed. He was saying 'I'll do anything . . . whatever you say. How am I to face the others if this whole tour is called off just because of something I've said?'"

Later, supported by his fellow Beatles, he faced the media assembled like some latter-day Spanish Inquisition in Barrow's suite a couple of floors below. With the stress of the situation, his face seemed to have become thinner, the contours of his nose sharper, his Beatle cut somehow alien, like a borrowed hat. Other stars in such a situation would have read from a brief statement, answered a couple of questions, and left as quickly as possible. John, however, stayed on the firing line until everyone who wished to had taken a shot at him. His replies turned into an extended monologue, which soon went far beyond what he had been coached to say, and, on the whole, hit as many right buttons as his original quote had wrong ones: "I'm not anti-God, anti-Christ or anti-religion. I was not knocking it. I was not saying we were greater or better . . . not comparing us with Jesus Christ as a person or God as a thing or whatever . . . I happened to be talking to a friend and I used the word 'Beatles' as a remote thing—'Beatles' like other people see us. I said they are having more influence on kids and things than anything else, including Jesus, and I said it in that way, which was the wrong way, yap yap. . . ."

Now and again, the Star Chamber dissolved into laughter as touches of the old free-range John showed through. "If I'd said, 'Television is more popular than Jesus,' I might have got away with it," he remarked at one point, an observation both witty and true. ". . . My views are from what I've read or observed of Christianity, and what it was, and what it has been and what it could be. I'm just saying it seems to be shrinking and losing context. . . . People think I'm anti-religion, but I'm not. I'm a most religious fellow . . ." The media wanted ritual penance, and this was made with a sincerity that could not be doubted: "I'm sorry I opened my mouth."

With the qualified forgiveness of America's press, Brian decided that the tour should go ahead after all. But out in Middle America, where crosses clustered as thickly as TV antennae, the transgression was not so easily wiped away At every stop, the screams that greeted the Beatles were now leavened with anger and reproach. The waving placards bore messages like BEATLES GO HOME and JESUS DIED FOR YOU, TOO, JOHN LENNON (with the occasional, apostate LENNON SAVES). Former besotted listeners to "I Want to Hold Your Hand" and "She Loves You" publicly broke or stamped on their copies, and devoted readers of *John Lennon: In His Own Write* tore the book into shreds. Hardened as the Beatles were to mass dysfunctionality, one image was to haunt them all: that of a little boy, running beside their escape bus until his legs gave out, his cries inaudible, his face a picture of bewildered betrayal.

At some venues, following Manila's example, police cover was withdrawn without explanation. Despite the high security surrounding the Beatles' interperformance flights—arrivals far away from terminal buildings where marksmen might lurk; departures, where possible, under cover of night—several bullet holes were later found in the aircraft's fuselage. In some places, there was even trading in the "rights" to mass Beatle record smashing or burning, which were usually acquired by supermarkets as attractions to be staged in their parking lots.

On August 19, the tour reached Memphis, a place that once would have excited John as Elvis Presley's hometown but now harbored nameless perils as the very heart of the Bible Belt. "It's John they want—send him out first," joked someone on the plane as crowds of banner-waving zealots came into view below. John gloomily concurred: "You might just as well paint a target on me."

Before their two shows at the Mid South Coliseum, a hulking young Ku Klux Klansman, minus his ceremonial tall hood, excoriated the Beatles on local television for claiming they were "more better than Jesus Christ," reminded viewers of the Klan's reputation as "a terror organization," and menacingly promised "surprises" when they went onstage later that day. So many people lined the streets to the Coliseum, and so many convenient windows for rifle muzzles yawned above, that the Beatles' limousines were sent ahead empty as decoys while they themselves rode to the venue in a Greyhound bus, crouched double on its floor. Before the afternoon show, there was a bomb scare; demonstrators were reportedly being bused in by the Klan and records being ceremonially burned in oil drums.

At the second show, the four had been performing only a few minutes when a firecracker exploded near them with the shallow "snap-snap-snap" of a real-life revolver. Tony Barrow still remembers the horror of that moment. "Every one of us [the tour entourage] and the other three Beatles looked at John, half-expecting to see the guy sinking down."

Shea Stadium, New York, on August 26 was nothing like the sweltered triumph it had been a year earlier; eleven thousand seats had remained unsold, prompting reports that "the bloom has gone off the Beatles." At their Manhattan press conference, all four were said to be looking "pale and tired," so very different from the wisecracking charmers who had wowed the city in 1964. Hungry for further headlines, some questioners tried to lure them into commenting on the Vietnam War. But they refused to be drawn beyond a collective murmur of "We don't like war. War is wrong." Paul said it would be better for them to express their views back in Britain, because "there, people listen a bit more. In America, they hold everything against you." "You'll have to answer for that tomorrow," John told him, only half joking

He himself was asked why he thought his words had created such a national furor. "There are more people in America, so there are more bigots also," he replied, then took care to add, "Not everyone in America is bigoted." Circumspect as he strove to be, the Henry VIII lip refused to stay totally buttoned. On a lighter note, someone asked Paul what had been the inspiration behind Eleanor Rigby. Before he could answer, John chipped in: "Two queers."

The tour's final stop could not have been a more appropriate staging post between what they had been and what they were about to become. On August 29, they reached San Francisco to appear at its Candlestick Park baseball stadium. Ringo Starr later remembered "a lot of talk" before the show about "how it all had to end" and John's firm declaration that "he'd had enough." There was no formal announcement of their decision (as there never would be) and not even the savviest among the U.S. Beatle press corps at Candlestick Park realized the significance of the moment. Despite their boredom and exhaustion, they could not say this covert farewell without a pang of nostalgia. Each of them had a camera surreptitiously parked atop an amplifier. Toward the end of the performance, Ringo left his drums, and all four turned their backs to the audience and photographed the stage and its furniture like school graduates taking nostalgic snapshots of a once-hated classroom.

The British media had equally little clue about the milestone that had passed—and, in any case, were still overwhelmingly concerned with John's American crucifixion. To fellow Brits, at least, irony could be employed to temper the iron in his soul. Fielding questions back in London, he adopted the resigned air of one whose slightest word was likely to trigger more worldwide religious controversy. Had he not been afraid that criticizing America over Vietnam, however obliquely, might stir up even more trouble over there? "You can't keep quiet about everything that's going on in the world," John replied, "unless you're a monk . . . Sorry, monks," he added hastily, as though picturing saffron-robed holy men all over the Himalayas rising up in protest. "I didn't mean it. . . ."

As much as he had grown to hate touring, the prospect of life without it initially filled him with something near panic. "I couldn't deal with not being onstage," he was to remember. "[For] the first time I thought, 'My God, what do you do if this isn't continually going on. What else is there?'"

Touring might have crushed his spirits and stultified his creativity, but it had also had its advantages. These years on the Beatlemania treadmill had spared him almost all the more tedious obligations of growing from adolescence into manhood and becoming a husband and father. But on another, typically contradictory level, they had also given a stem of duty and responsibility to his existence: when he donned his stage suit, it was in the spirit of a soldier going "over the top" with his comrades. For all the frustrations of the road, there was much that he realized he would miss: the laughs, the Just William japes, the sense of uniquely kindred spirits taking on the whole world. Outside the Beatles, he could not imagine ever finding such companionship again.

The other three found no difficulty in occupying their newfound liberty and leisure. Paul composed the score for a new British film, *The Family Way* (which later won a Novello Award) and continued his assiduous self-education in classical music and the theatre. He remained deeply involved with the avant-garde crowd around the Indica gallery and, in late 1966, provided financial backing for London's first underground newspaper, the *International Times*, of which the Indica's Barry Miles was a cofounder. George immersed himself in Eastern music and religion, visited India and conversed with gurus and swamis, as well as continuing to study the sitar under its master, Ravi Shankar. Ringo welcomed the chance to spend more time with Maureen, who shortly afterward became pregnant with their second child. Only John, the Beatle credited with the most individual potential—that acknowledged "genius of the lower crust"—had nothing in prospect but Weybridge, Cynthia, and Julian.

Comedy was one obvious area of development, the more so thanks to his firm friendship with Peter Cook. The foursome of Cook, Dudley Moore, Alan Bennett, and Jonathan Miller, with their stage show (and Parlophone album) *Beyond the Fringe*, had rewritten British comedy as completely as their Liverpool label mates later rewrote British pop. Since then, the lanky, languorous Cook had achieved stardom in his own right, opening London's first satirical nightclub, the Establishment, acquiring a controlling interest in *Private Eye* magazine, and creating a comic immortal to rival Hancock or Bluebottle in the sublimely banal park-bench philosopher, E. L. Wisty (though all the time, his secret ambition was to be a second Elvis).

In 1965, Cook and Dudley Moore had begun a new television comedy series on BBC2 entitled *Not Only . . . But Also*. The first episode featured a corduroy-dark, turtlenecked John, reciting passages from *In His Own Write*, assisted by Norman Rossington, who had played roadie Norm in *A Hard Day's Night*. As the closing credits rolled, John performed a spontaneous dance across the screen, which Cook and Moore reproduced at the end of every subsequent show. He enjoyed the experience so much that when a later episode was being rehearsed, he turned up uninvited and volunteered to take part again.

He and Cynthia were occasional dinner guests at Cook's Georgian house in Hampstead, joining a circle that included the actors Peter O'Toole and Tom Courtenay, the designer Mary Quant, the poet and *Private Eye* columnist Christopher Logue, and the journalist Bernard Levin. Cook's then wife, Wendy, was a celebrated hostess who thought nothing of serving her guests a whole roast boar. Here, at least, literary high society caused John no fits of inarticulateness. The evening would develop into a contest between Cook and him to top each other in lunatic free association. "They both had the same gift for ad-libbing," Wendy Cook remembers. "I wish I could remember some of their riffs, but all that comes back is being helpless with laughter—and that amazing nose of John's, the way he pushed his hair out of his eyes, and all the tension in his shoulders."

It was Richard Lester, director of *A Hard Day's Night* and *Help!*, who suggested a way for him to fill the post-touring void. Lester had lately been offered Hollywood's version of *Catch 22*, Joseph Heller's magisterial comic novel of the Second World War. Instead, he opted to direct a smaller, quirkier British production on the same subject called *How I Won the War*, based on a novel by Patrick Ryan and scripted by Charles Wood, the cowriter of *Help!* On the strength of John's performance in the two Beatles films, Lester offered him the supporting role of a British serviceman, Private Gripweed. The part was a purely dramatic one, with no singing onscreen or involvement in the sound track. Shooting on location was to begin in late October, first in Hamburg, then in Almería in southern Spain. Stirred by the challenge, and to postpone "going home to the wife" as long as possible, he instantly accepted.

How I Won the War is as much of its time as *Help!* or *A Hard Day's Night*, and cherished by many as an almost equivalent Sixties classic. Set in the North African campaign, it concerns a squad of British "musketeers" who are given the surreally daft assignment of establishing a cricket pitch behind enemy lines. In the mode of current British screen hits like *Tom Jones* and *Alfie*, the characters talk directly to camera as well as among themselves. When a musketeer gets killed, his place is taken by a soldier from World War I, a mute figure like a living statue in head-to-foot orange, green, or red. The photography alternates between color and black and white and is intercut with real footage of World War II events such as the D-Day landings. The overall effect is somewhere between *Oh What a Lovely War* and *The Goon Show*.

John was later said to have been attracted by the film's antiwar message, but actually this element is so slight as to be almost invisible. The Second World War everyone agreed then, as now, had been a necessary and just one. Britain's peacetime army had seen no significant overseas military action since the Suez crisis, and the Northern Ireland conflict was still three years ahead. Nor does Charles Wood's caricature of the military mind—witless subalterns, shrieking NCOs, generals exchanging bubblegum cards—stir the faintest resonance of current events in Vietnam. It is a Pop Art send-up of war films rather than war itself, still reflecting the myopic afterglow in which Nazi officers clicked their heels and played the game, and nobody mentioned the death camps.

Preparing for the role of Private Gripweed allowed John to cast off his Beatle look, forever as it would prove. His bangs disappeared, exposing his forehead to view for the first time in six years. Rather than a regulation military short back and sides, his hair was given a floppy Byronesque style that no enlisted man would ever have been permitted. Breaking the taboo that stretched back to early childhood, he also had to wear glasses. Ironically, these were the very same National Health type, with circular wire frames, that he'd rejected so vehemently as an eight-year-old.

The thought of being on location abroad, without the other Beatles to support him, was at first a daunting one. He worried, too, that his fellow cast members would look down on him for not being a real actor. So the loyal Neil Aspinall volunteered to go with him and stay on hand for the whole six weeks of the Spanish shoot.

The experience proved thoroughly pleasant for them both. Lester's cast of stalwart British character actors, like Michael Hordern and Robert Hardy, neither despised nor patronized John but respected the seriousness with which he took his role, his willingness to learn, and total lack of big-star airs and graces. He formed a particular friendship with Roy Kinnear, who had been in *Help!*, and Lee Montague, a misleadingly pugnacious-looking forty-year-old cast as the musketeers' sergeant major. In breaks between filming, John, Kinnear, and Montague would stand on the bridge over a nearby stream and play the game of Pooh Sticks immortalized in A. A. Milne's Winnie-the-Pooh stories. "You dropped a stick into the water so the current would carry it under the bridge," Montague remembers. "And the stick that came out first on the other side was the winner. John loved Pooh Sticks. Later he gave me one of his books, inscribed 'To my favorite uncle.'"

The film's nominal star was Michael Crawford, playing the dimwit squad commander, Lieutenant Goodbody, whom Gripweed serves as orderly. Crawford had brought his wife, Gaby, on location with him, and of an evening, the two would often drop in at the flat John shared with Neil for a drink or to play Monopoly. The Crawfords liked the flat so much that John offered to exchange it for their large rented villa, which had the—for him—irresistible attraction of a table-tennis table in its front hall. Soon after this accommodation swap, an NEMS emissary arrived from London, bringing John a large box of chocolates with hashish carefully packed among them. "When we tried to open the box, the lid flew off," Neil remembered. "All the hash fell into the shagpile carpet. We lost almost the whole lot."

A few days into the shoot, John's chauffeur, Les Anthony, turned up with his matte black Rolls Phantom V, recently equipped with further luxury accoutrements, including a fold-down bed and a set of external stereo loudspeakers. To maximize the shock value of these, John had supplemented his in-car record collection with "The Colonel Bogey March," Peter Sellers's parody of a party political broadcast, and assorted farmyard sound effects. There was also a microphone with which he could make his own broadcasts at shattering volume. One night in London, Brian Jones of the Rolling Stones was seated in a parked limo when he heard himself challenged by what he took to be a police bullhorn. Hopeless druggie that he was, the moment almost brought on cardiac arrest. But it was only John, pulling his leg.

The black Phantom with its thunderous sound track became a familiar sight around Almería, whose inhabitants nicknamed it *"El Funebre,"* or the Hearse. Neil Aspinall remembered mad journeys to and from the various outdoor locations, bouncing on rutted roads, with John and his fellow actors squashed into the back, Bob Dylan's voice wailing over the external speakers and rustic Spaniards staring in bafflement.

Near the end of the shoot, Cynthia came out for a holiday, accompanied by the ever-supportive Ringo and Maureen. In place of John and Neil's "damp and tatty" bachelor quarters, Cyn rented a much larger, more luxurious villa with its own swimming pool. This stood on the site of an old convent and was suspected of being haunted by its former occupants, though in an unthreatening, *Sound of Music* kind of way. One morning when Maureen awoke, the ribbons on her nightdress had all been mischievously tied in knots. And as the party held an impromptu singsong in the candlelit front hall, mysterious voices seemed to join in. Cyn for one had no doubt that the place was "full of beautiful spirits."

According to legend, *How I Won the War* revealed John to be a natural screen actor. With the increasingly successful Richard Lester for a mentor—so the story goes—he could easily have crossed over from music to a busy film career, like Frank Sinatra and Elvis Presley before him. He failed to do so because, at the last, he found it not

challenging enough and, more pertinently, realized a film star's life
could be even more confining than that of a Beatle.

Lester certainly believed he had potential, but this particular vehicle does not show overmuch evidence of it. Gripweed plays only a
minor part in the story and has little to say (although Charles Wood's
relentlessly absurdist dialogue gives every character a tinge of *John
Lennon: In His Own Write*). His asides are rather labored pseudo-
Lennonisms, as when he admits to having joined the British fascist
party: "I was a great mate of [Oswald] Mosley's. I used to hold his
voice for him when he lost his meetings."

There is, however, one moment of horrible prescience. As Gripweed crosses a field in a black-and-white sequence, hostile gunfire
catches him in the midriff. He looks down at himself, then incredulously at us. "I knew this would happen," he says. "You knew this
would happen, didn't you?" His face then appears in color, close up,
with a smear of blood at his mouth. "I'm not a thief really," is his
last, plaintive gasp. "I've never found anything worth taking." When
Cynthia saw the film, that scene reduced her to tears. For she felt it
was how John really would look at the moment of his death.

A century and a half earlier, Thomas de Quincy had recorded
how, for the habitual drug tripper, "the minutest incidents of childhood and familiar scenes of later years [are] often revived." So it was
for John when the songwriting urge returned to him during these
weeks of nonmusical filmmaking. The autumnal Spanish sun awoke
memories of July Saturdays long ago in Woolton, when the sound
of distant brass-band music would make him tug at his Aunt Mimi's
arm, desperate for coconut shies and cotton candy. In place of blinding white walls and terra-cotta roofs, he saw the sandstone orphanage whose annual fete had been the highlight of his boyhood
summers; he saw the iron front gates, the grimy Gothic casements,
the official signboard with its anomalous melt-in-the-mouth name:
Strawberry Field.

The lyric he now began to write (sitting on a powdery Mediterranean beach with Neil Aspinall a few feet away) turned "field" into
"fields," suggesting more the overgrown grounds that were once
part of his Outlaws' domain. What emerged was no nostalgic pic-

ture postcard, but an abstract painting in sound: mystical and ambiguous yet at the same time more revealing of its author than mere memoirizing could ever have been.

Its opening words are so familiar that one can easily overlook the layers of meaning, or rather mood, contained in them. "Let me take you down, 'cause I'm going to . . ." is a straightforward invitation to accompany him on the walk he took so often with Mimi and Uncle George. Then comes the Learyesque assertion that "nothing is real," then what should have been "nothing to get hung up about." (For pampered, privileged Sixties youth, "hung up"—mildly depressed or confused—was the very worst one could feel.) Unwieldy to scan, "hung up about" collides with "hang about," and maybe a touch of gallows humor, to end up as "hung about." Then we are back to childhood with a cry that might have come from the Sally Army orphans themselves as their team won the egg-and-spoon race: "Strawberry Fields forever!"

John himself always said the lyric was "psychoanalysis set to music" and declared it and "Help!" to have been "the only true songs I ever wrote." For him, the words signified how little he had really changed in the years since Strawberry Field was his adventure playground. "The second line [of the second verse] goes 'No one I think is in my tree.' What I was trying to say was 'Nobody seems to be as hip as me, therefore I must be crazy or a genius. It's the same problem I had when I was five.'" In fact, egotism is the last very thing that strikes you. The air of hippie wisdom and stoicism soon gives way to self-confessed mental muddle and perplexity, and finally outright incoherence ("I think I know I mean, er, yes but it's all wrong . . .") that nonetheless still rhymes true and has the correct number of feet per line. Other psychedelic songwriters produced druggy gibberish; John had to produce *crafted* druggy gibberish.

He also spent the time in Almería pondering what he might do with himself now that live concerts would no longer regulate his existence. "I was thinking, 'Well, this is the end, really,'" he later recalled. "'There's no more touring. That means there's going to be a blank space in the future. . . .' That's when I really started considering life without the Beatles—what would it be? And I spent that six weeks thinking about that. 'What am I going to do? Am I going to be doing Vegas? But cabaret?' I didn't even consider forming my own group or anything, because it didn't enter my mind. Just what would I do when it stopped?

"And that's when the seed was planted that I had to somehow get out of [the Beatles] without being thrown out by the others. But I could never step out of the palace because it was too frightening."

In the first and more forgiving of her two autobiographies, Cynthia Lennon dated the collapse of her marriage to the moment when John began to take LSD in quantity—to "eat the stuff," as he himself put it—and, as a result, turned into someone she no longer recognized or could communicate with. "There is an expression jazz musicians use when playing with a musician who is not quite in tune with the rest, 'He must be listening to a different drum,'" wrote Cynthia. "That particular expression adequately describes the way I was feeling. . . . John was still searching, whereas I thought I had found what I wanted out of life."

The thought was doubtless a consoling one amid the events that were soon to overwhelm her. But everyone else around John knew that the "different drum" had been beating ever more insistently long before acid came along and that, numerous as were its malefactions, Cynthia's loneliness, unhappiness, and ultimate humiliation could not be counted among them.

It was a source of general wonderment that John and she had stayed married for four years, and that none of the beautiful, bright women who incessantly threw themselves at him had yet consigned her to the well-supplied rubbish dump of show-business first wives. Her uncomplaining sweetness and mildness had earned the sympathy of the other Beatles, their partners, and their whole entourage, although there were some who thought that John also deserved a measure of sympathy. Nobody was fonder of Cyn than George Martin, yet John's situation was one Martin well understood, having himself been forced into a first marriage at the too-young age of twenty-two. "That marriage was doomed to failure." he says. "And so, I'm afraid, was John's to Cynthia."

Paradoxically, his former long absences on tour had kept things on a relatively even keel. Whenever domestic life grew oppressive, there was always that escape back into a world where he could live like a bachelor—and what a bachelor! At the same time, however much casual sex he had on tour, the pitiless spotlight that always shone on him as a Beatle prevented any more lasting involvements. "When he was travelling with the boys, there was no possibility of being seriously unfaithful to Cyn," George Martin says. "That couldn't happen until the treadmill finally stopped."

The physical attraction between them, once so overwhelming, had completely evaporated; in Cynthia's words, they lived together "like brother and sister." With the storms of John's jealousy and possessiveness long since blown out, their relationship settled into humdrum habit. "We never rowed," Cyn would recall. "We just rubbed along together without fireworks." This eerie equilibrium continued even after John's adventures with acid began creating mood swings between the comatose and the vicious. She had recently confided to him that she, too, felt creatively stifled and would like to return to painting or one of the other subjects in which she had shone at art college. John seemed sympathetic, so one evening while he was out, Cynthia devoted hours to painting a floral design on the white TV set in Kenwood's sunroom. Next morning, she found he had come in late, drunk or stoned, and had covered her handiwork with adhesive stickers all bearing the same slogan for the "drink more milk" campaign.

Cynthia's first, accidental encounter with acid, courtesy of dentist John Riley, had been more than enough for her. But John pleaded with her not to judge it on that one bad experience, promising that, if she tried it again in the comfort and security of their home, with himself and other initiates on hand to provide support and comfort, its wonders would be revealed to her. A pleading John by this time was such a novelty as to be irresistible. Thinking it would at least add to their small store of togetherness, she agreed.

A whole weekend was specially set aside for this "Operation Cynthia"—the longest period of time John had devoted to her since Hamburg days. Three-year-old Julian was packed off to stay with the housekeeper, Dot Jarlett, and a special support squad moved in to Kenwood, among them George and Pattie Harrison, Brian's associate Terry Doran, and an actress friend of Pattie's named Marie Lise. The den was prepared for the sacred ritual, with banked-up cushions, candles, smoldering incense, and atmospheric music. Cyn was still wondering how the acid would be given to her, whether on sugar cubes as before or in pill form, when she realized she was already slipping under the influence. It had been secretly put into her drink, in case she should chicken out at the last moment.

But this trip proved no better than her first. Stumbling into a nearby cloakroom a few moments later, she saw a skull grinning back at her from the mirror above the basin. John came after her and took her back into the supposed safety of the circle, but here, too, horrid visions soon closed in. When Terry Doran said something to her, he seemed to change into an alligator, then into a snake. One of the household cats that happened to be present became multicolored and multiform, its fur vibrating in time to the music. Even the pile in the carpet seemed to heave and twitch as if it had a life of its own.

The experience ended with a group hug and a chorus of congratulations to Cynthia, in which none seemed prouder or more loving than John. Much as she basked in this unwonted tenderness, she told him that for her LSD was "terrifying and dangerous" and she wanted nothing more to do with it. John, so she said, accepted this decision and put no further pressure on her; she, in turn, resigned herself to his growing immersion in the drug and alienation from herself and Julian.

In whatever John did, he still needed a special crony to act simultaneously as his mentor and follower. Where acid taking was concerned, this role was filled for some months by John Dunbar, the Indica Gallery's cofounder and director. Dunbar was a perfect companion, formidably well versed in avant-garde art yet equally at ease in the pop world through his marriage to Marianne Faithfull and friendship with the Rolling Stones. He was already a seasoned acidhead, having discovered it while hitchhiking around America as an undergraduate.

The two often took acid together at Dunbar's flat in Bentinck Street, Mayfair, where a whole wall of the living room ended up covered with their drawings of visions they had experienced. But John made no attempt to conceal his activities from Cynthia. "We did a lot down at his place in Weybridge as well," Dunbar remembers. "Cynthia would usually be there, but in another part of the house. You got the sense that their life together was over in any meaningful way . . . John just didn't happen to have moved on yet. Julian would often be around, too, but not getting a lot of attention from his father. I can remember John telling him, 'No, I'm *not* going to mend your fucking bicycle.'"

Terry Doran was his other main companion through these Thousand-and-One Acid Nights. A curly-haired Liverpudlian, easygoing and charming, Doran had come into the Beatles' circle as Brian's partner in a luxury car retail business, Brydor Ltd., based in Hounslow, Middlesex. He would later be George's personal assistant, but in this period belonged mainly to the Lennon camp, acting as a driver-protector to John and, equally, a friend, ego booster—even occasional escort—to Cynthia. So much a fixture was he at Kenwood that, even if John happened to be around, Julian would often prefer Terry to put him to bed.

Not everyone found the effects of drugs on John as deleterious as did his wife. "I thought he was someone whom pot and acid turned around in a good way," John Dunbar says. "To start with, they took him off the drink, which meant a lot of that old chippy aggression seemed to disappear. They also gave him a concern for other people that he'd never had to have as a selfish, self-centered pop star. I remember once, in the middle of a trip, he must have noticed me looking scared or worried. 'It's all right, man, don't worry,' he said to me. 'We're all the same, we're all scared. . . .' I don't think he'd have been capable of sensitivity like that before he took acid."

None of the Beatles now bore any resemblance to their former touring, smiling-and-bowing selves. On a recent trip back to Liverpool, Paul had been riding a moped around his old childhood haunts and had fallen off, badly gashing his upper lip. To hide the scar, he grew a mustache in the newly modish downturned style hitherto associated with Mexican revolutionaries. With their usual solidarity, the other three also instantly sprouted facial hair, in Ringo's case a matching "Zapata," in George's something closer to a Vandyke beard. John, however, opted for a mustache of more wayward shape whose ends meandered all the way down to his jawline. He had kept his hair short after playing Private Gripweed, and also retained the once-hated round-framed National Health glasses. The effect was not so much of a pop star or hippie mystic as some rather prim Victorian ledger clerk.

Underneath, he still seemed the same incorrigible japester, ever ready to undercut the most earnest hippiespeak with a daft pun, and turn even the sacred acid precept of "ego death" into slapstick. But when Klaus Voormann visited Kenwood, not long after designing the *Revolver* cover, he received a surprise glimpse behind the usually uncrackable Lennon facade. "John played me some music, then we went for a walk in the garden. He was really down, uptight, he was staring into the distance . . . then it all came pouring out. He had this wife he didn't want to be with . . . he said how he was in despair, how he wanted to disappear, just go into the ground. As he was telling me, he started to rip the leaves off a bush and throw them on the grass. He was so upset, he didn't realise he was tearing it to pieces. I said 'John, don't take it out on the bush, the bush didn't do anything . . .' He laughed at that, and seemed to feel a bit better."

As Paul had requested, John Dunbar still kept all the out-of-town Beatles informed about forthcoming events at the Indica Gallery. Not long after John's return from Spain, he received the catalog of an exhibition be to held there early in November. The artist already enjoyed enough renown to be billed simply as "Yoko at Indica," suggesting something rather more than merely paintings or static pieces of sculpture. "Dunbar told me about this Japanese girl from New York, who was going to be in a bag, doing this event or happening," John would recall. "I thought 'Hmm'"—you know—"'Sex.'"

His curiosity aroused, he arranged with Dunbar to drop by on the evening of November 9, 1966, the day before the show's official opening. Les Anthony was summoned to drive him up from Weybridge in his Mini Cooper, for once unaccompanied by any minders or followers. He was "in a highly unshaven and tatty state," he later said, having not slept for three nights previously. "I was always up in those days, tripping. I was stoned."

PART IV

ZEN VAUDEVILLE

19

BREATHE

That's when we locked eyes and she got
it and I got it, and that was it.

The woman destined to transform the rest of John's life was born in Tokyo on February 18, 1933. Japanese family names precede given ones, so until her late teens she was known as Ono Yoko. The kanji word *ko* means "child," and Yoko can translate as either Ocean Child or Positive Child. This particular infant, certainly, was to know little self-doubt and traverse many oceans, weathering tidal waves of hostility and misunderstanding along the way.

Like John's, Yoko's early years were dominated by class and, like him, she was to construct a public persona far removed from her true origins. Through her mother, Isoko, she belonged to one of Japan's four wealthiest commercial families, or *zaibatsu*, the Yasudas. Her great-grandfather Zenjiro Yasuda rose from poor samurai antecedents to make a fortune from currency dealing in the late nineteenth century, and eventually to found the Third National Bank of Japan. Zenjiro was a nationally admired figure, a gifted musician and poet, far ahead of his time in always acknowledging an equal partnership with his diminutive wife. They were so inspirational a couple that offices and shops throughout the country used to display a wood block etched with their likeness. Zenjiro's death in 1921 was to have a horrible resonance for the great-granddaughter he never knew. One day in his garden he spared a few moments to talk to a young man who was collecting funds for a workers' hostel. When Zenjiro declined to make a contribution, the young man assassinated him.

Yoko's father, Eisuke Ono, came from a family that had produced many notable painters, musicians, and academics—and also, in his mother, Tsuruko, one of Japan's pioneering feminists. Tall, handsome Eisuko was himself a gifted classical pianist, but chose a career in banking rather than the one he might well have had on the international concert stage. After his marriage into the Yasudas, his social status demanded that he should be taken to work each morning in a chauffeur-driven limousine. Embarrassed by such ostentation, he would stop the car a couple of blocks from his office and walk the rest of the way.

Isoko, Yoko's mother, was a stunning beauty, a much-praised painter, and a famous hostess whose photograph appeared constantly in Japanese society magazines. Both her family and Eisuke's were widely traveled, multilingual, and highly westernized, the men playing golf in plus fours and Argyll socks, the women chic in the latest Parisian gowns, hats, and furs. It was an era of seemingly unstoppable amity between Japan and America, with emigrants by the hundred thousand crossing the Pacific from the former to the latter, and ever-strengthening business and financial links. Just before Yoko's birth, Eisuke accepted a position in his bank's San Francisco branch, leaving Isoko behind in Tokyo. Yoko did not meet him until she was two, and for many years afterward only at long intervals. The transpacific journey in that era was most commonly made by ship. On the first voyage to see her father, she took part in a fancy-dress parade costumed as the moppet film star Shirley Temple, and won first prize.

As part of the Yasuda clan, she enjoyed a life of extraordinary privilege and luxury. Voluminous home movies still in her possession show a cute little girl with bobbed hair, immaculately turned out in sailor suits or Scottish kilts with matching tam o'shanters beside her fashion-plate mother. Because of the Yasudas' close relationships with successive emperors, she was allowed to attend the Gakashuin, or Peers' School, an establishment normally reserved for children of the imperial family or senior members of the House of Peers. The family kept thirty servants, including a governess to instruct her in all the labyrinthine points of social and feminine etiquette. Servants had to come into her presence on their knees, and depart from it on their knees backward. On excursions into the outside world, she was not allowed to sit on any public seat until a servant had cleansed it with disinfectant-soaked cotton wool.

Despite this cossetting, her childhood was solitary and insecure. Thanks to her family's wealth and eminence, few children her age were deemed suitable to play with her. Every summer, Isoko would pack her off to the family's big country house in the charge of her governess while her brother Keisuke, three years her junior, stayed in Tokyo with their mother. Like some medieval infanta, Yoko would eat her meals alone, with her governess seated nearby murmuring precepts about manners or deportment. Desperate for company, she would sometimes creep to the servants' quarters and eavesdrop on their conversations. Once she overheard a young housemaid describe the process of childbirth to workmates, complete with harrowing sound effects. The melodramatic shrieks and groans lodged in Yoko's mind, to surface many years later as her own special brand of singing.

Imagination became her only refuge in the big, lonely house. To stave off her terror of the dark, she would stage a play with chess pieces for characters or arrange objects on her coverlet in the same meaningless but reassuring patterns. But whereas most solitary children keep their fantasies secret, Yoko always felt a powerful urge to communicate hers. "When I was in this summer place by myself, the only playmate I had was the caretaker's daughter, who was about two years older than me," she remembers. "We would go to the fruit

orchard and I'd take an apple seed and a pear seed and plant them together, to see if the fruit that came up was half apple, half pear. Then
I would tell the girl to write it down. I was always thinking 'I have to
tell the world of my discoveries.'"

The outbreak of war with America, and consequently Britain, in
1941 was a traumatic event for cultured, Western-leaning Japanese
like the Onos. Although her father was still far from home, now
working in French Indochina, Yoko's life at first remained largely untouched by danger or hardship. She remembers parties given by her
mother, where beautifully dressed men and women danced to gramophones with the same hectic, damn-tomorrow gaiety as others far
across the seas in London, Berlin, and Liverpool.

By 1945, Japan had been defeated on every overseas front and the
Americans were bombing Tokyo in preparation for their finale over
Hiroshima and Nagasaki. In a single night, the waves of B-29 Super-
fortresses set sixteen square miles ablaze, killing a hundred thousand
people. Eisuke Ono was now in an internment camp in Hanoi. Reluctant to leave Tokyo herself, Isoko sent her children to safety in the
countryside with a handicapped servant who had escaped call-up to
essential war work. The country people exploited the city refugees
without mercy, forcing them to trade their expensive clothes and
possessions for meager portions of rice or vegetables, often taking
the possessions, then refusing to hand over the food. The servant,
as a fellow peasant, received kindlier treatment, the more so if she
distanced herself from her charges. Twelve-year-old Yoko thus found
herself effectively the guardian of her brother and her toddler sister,
Setsuko. Their mother tried to keep them supplied with basics, like
miso paste to make soup, but they often went hungry. To distract her
two siblings, Yoko would conjure sumptuous feasts from her imagination.

Despite having been hit with two atomic bombs, postwar Japan
under American occupation recovered with a speed that made Europe—especially threadbare, food-rationed Britain—gape in resentful disbelief. And despite losing overall grip on industry and finance,
the zaibatsu still retained much of their old power. When Yoko entered Gakashuin University, the combined prestige of the Yasudas

and intellectualism of the Onos seemed to guarantee her choice of brilliant careers. She was the university's first-ever philosophy student, was gifted in languages and literature as well as the visual arts, and, like her father, was an accomplished pianist. With a view to the performing career Eisuke had been denied, she also studied music, specializing in German lieder and Italian opera.

Unfortunately, this talented student also possessed a rebellious spirit still extremely uncommon among young Japanese women of her class. Although hugely self-confident on the surface, she remained haunted by childhood insecurities, in particular the guilt she had always felt about her privileged station in life. "My father wanted me to be a concert pianist, but I wasn't good enough. As a painter in the conventional style, I used to feel overshadowed by my mother. I knew I couldn't be a linguist like my uncles; I didn't like the way they put foreign phrases into everything they said. So all the doors were closed on me. I had to find my own way."

When she was eighteen, the family moved to America to join Eisuke, who had been appointed president of the Bank of Tokyo in New York. They settled in Scarsdale, and Yoko entered Sarah Lawrence College, near Bronxville, to continue her studies in philosophy, music composition, and literature. Sarah Lawrence, in those days an all-female college, had a reputation for fostering individualism and radicalism, positively relishing the idea that its alumnae might go out into the world as "troublemakers." But Yoko's developing theories about music, writing, and the visual arts soon had even this most liberal of young ladies' seminaries scratching its collective head. She dropped out after three years, having been advised by a friendly professor that she might find more sympathetic eyes and ears in the art world of downtown New York.

Her parents had hoped that art and music would be no more than graceful pastimes, and that in due course she would make a suitable marriage and turn into a conventional, dutiful Japanese American wife. One of Japan's wealthiest men wrote formally to her father, in the traditional manner, proposing his son as a husband for her. But Yoko would have none of it and, aged twenty-three, eloped with a Japanese-born composer-pianist named Toshi Ichiyanagi, who had been studying at the Juilliard School of Music. Without a backward glance, she exchanged her family's palatial homes for a cold-water artist's loft in Greenwich Village, and her extensive childhood wardrobe for allover bohemian black.

Here, as her college teacher had prophesied, she quickly found empathetic spirits. By the early Sixties, she had become associated with the Fluxus group, a multiethnic circle of artists unusual for that time in not confining themselves to a single medium but amalgamating the disciplines of painting, sculpture, photography, music, poetry, film, and theatre. Taking Marcel Duchamp as their god, Fluxus members abhorred so-called high art, choosing as their subject matter the most familiar, even banal, components of everyday life. Their moving spirit, Lithuanian-born George Maciunas, proclaimed their mission to "purge the world of bourgeois sickness, intellectual, professional, and commercialized culture . . . Purge the world of dead art, imitation, artificial art, mathematical art . . . Promote a revolutionary flood and tide in art. Promote living art, anti-art, promote NON ART REALITY."

Under this doctrine, the personality and political agenda of the artist became as important as the work, or more so, and the audience response a crucial part of its realization. Fluxus events combined shock with deadpan humor: spectators would find they had bought tickets simply to sit and watch an alarm clock tick on an empty stage or a group of artists make a salad together. The emblematic event was John Cage's *4',33"*, in which a pianist sat at a keyboard without touching it for exactly four minutes and thirty-three seconds. The "music" was the puzzled fidgeting and whispering of the customers as they waited in vain for something to happen.

Yoko became the epitome of Fluxus multimedia antiart. Her works tended to be sculpture, or rather three-dimensional collage, assembled from quotidian objects and usually inviting physical contact with the observer. Sometimes the creation would be a piece of theatre, with the role of the artwork played by the artist and the audience's reactions serving to illuminate some truth about the nature of art or the human condition in general. George Maciunas called her technique "neo Haiku theatre"; the art historian Ken Friedman defined it as "Zen vaudeville."

She began to acquire a reputation for audacity rivaling Cage's, and additionally spiced with a certain sexual frisson. In her *Cut Piece* event—first staged in Japan in 1964, and later at other important venues, including New York's Carnegie Hall—she sat alone onstage, motionless and silent, with a large pair of scissors in front of her. Audience members were invited to come up and each cut off a piece of her clothing until she was down to her underwear. The way in which each individual approached this mute sacrificial victim spoke volumes about human aggression and respect, crudity and delicacy, voyeurism and embarrassment. Also in 1964, she published *Grapefruit*, a book of haiku-length "instructional poems," which aimed to make words like the commands of musical notation: "Steal a moon on the water with a bucket. Keep stealing until no moon is seen on the water." "Draw a map to get lost." "Make all the clocks in the world fast by two seconds without letting anyone know about it."

Her marriage to Toshi Ichiyanagi did not last, although the two remained mutually admiring and supportive. Ichiyanagi returned to Japan, where he ultimately became one of the country's best-known composers. With his encouragement, Yoko, too, returned to her homeland to stage a series of shows and exhibitions. Her American press coverage had been generally friendly, but Japanese critics proved harder to impress, one in particular writing a review of devastating personal viciousness. Not accustomed in those days, as she puts it, to "being slashed," she suffered a breakdown and checked into a clinic for a complete rest. Instead, she was subjected to ceaseless harassment by journalists and commentators intrigued to see someone of her exalted connections in distress. The time was still far off when she would not mind the whole world peering at her in bed.

Among her visitors was a young American filmmaker named Tony Cox, a devotee of her work who had come from New York on the off chance of meeting her. Yoko refused to see him at first, but relented after he left a little pot of flowers every day with her nurse. Cox was extremely handsome, somewhat like the film star Anthony Perkins, and endowed with great charm and persuasiveness. He quickly convinced Yoko that life was worth living, encouraging her to cut down the heavy doses of Valium the clinic was administering and, eventually, to discharge herself. In 1962, she divorced Ichiyanagi and, later that same year, married Cox. Because of a legal technicality, the marriage was annulled in March 1963; they remarried the following June, and two months later Yoko gave birth to a daughter, Kyoko.

Cox put his own artistic ambitions largely on hold and became a tireless proponent of Yoko's work, seeking out sponsors to finance her, negotiating with galleries, and also looking after Kyoko, while she gave her whole attention to creating. But he was a volatile character, she was obsessed with her work above all else, and within three years this marriage, too, was breaking down. In September 1966, Yoko's friend Mario Amaya, editor of *Art and Artists* magazine, invited her to come to London to attend a symposium on "The Destruction of Art." Mainly to escape the growing pressures of her marriage, she accepted. "I thought, 'This [New York] is the Mecca of art,'" she remembers. "'Now I'm going to be going to nowhere.'" She meant it to be a clean break from Cox, but he insisted on accompanying her, so Kyoko had to be brought along, too.

The symposium over, Yoko decided to stay in London and persevere with marriage and motherhood. She and Cox took a flat in Hanover Gate Mansions, an Edwardian block just down the road from Lord's Cricket Ground (and not far from Abbey Road Studios), where their neighbors included the art critic Robert Hughes and the widow of the conductor Sir Henry Wood. Though impressively spacious, the flats rented for as little as £14 per week and backed on to a railway switchyard.

For the majority of Londoners in 1966, encountering a Japanese person was exceedingly rare. With the war only twenty-one years distant, attitudes remained colored by the ill-treatment that the "Japs" had inflicted on their British and Commonwealth prisoners in southeast Asia. However, the diminutive figure to be seen around Hanover Gate Mansions did not at first arouse hostility so much as bafflement. Her long, unstyled hair crowded in on her face so closely that her eyes and mouth seemed to merge seamlessly with it. In contrast with the vivid, skimpy female fashions of the hour, her clothes were always concealingly shapeless and funereal black. Two teenage sisters from the same block who occasionally babysat three-year-old Kyoko told their parents incredulously of a flat painted blinding white throughout, without carpets or furniture beyond a few brocaded cushions on the floor.

Her name might still be unknown to most of Britain, but in her own recondite world she was a star. Certainly, when John Dunbar heard she was in London he lost no time in offering her an exhibition at the Indica Gallery, which duly took shape as *Unfinished Paintings and Objects*, aka *Yoko at Indica*. There, just two months after she had arrived in London, and three after he stopped touring with the Beatles, John Lennon walked into her life.

At the time, she was still putting the last touches to her show before its opening the next day, so was not best pleased to see Dunbar bring in an early visitor. "I thought, 'What's he doing? Didn't I tell him I didn't want anyone to come until the opening?' I felt a bit angry about it, but I was too busy to complain or make a fuss. And, no matter what anyone said later, I didn't realise then who John was. He was an attractive guy . . . that's all that passed through my mind. Up to then, English men had all looked kind of weedy to me. This was the first sexy one I met."

She has no recollection whatsoever of the unshaven, bleary-eyed, half-stoned scruff that John himself always claimed to have been that evening. "He was shaved—and he was wearing a suit. He just came back from Spain, so he had a tan. I thought he was rather a dandy kind of person. I called it clean-cut; that's what we used to say at Sarah Lawrence. John hated that expression when I told him later how he looked to me that evening. 'Clean-cut!' he said. 'I was never clean-cut!' But he was going to a gallery in London, and he'd taken trouble to look good. He could do that dandy thing very well when he wanted to."

The exhibition combined works that Yoko had already shown in New York and Japan with others created specially for the occasion. Here was her *Eternal Time Clock*, showing only seconds and sealed inside a Plexiglas bubble attached to a stethoscope. Here was her *Ladder Piece*, a white stepladder up to a card on the ceiling, with the single word *Yes* written in script so tiny, it had to be read through a magnifying glass. Here was a large, empty black bag labeled WITH A MEMBER OF THE PUBLIC INSIDE, and a plain green apple bearing a price tag of £200. It was John's first serious exposure to antiart, and at first—without Dunbar at his elbow to prompt him—he assumed he was merely being had. "There's a couple of nails on a plastic box. Then I look over and see an apple on a stand with a note saying 'apple' . . . I was beginning to see the humour of it. I said 'How much is the apple?' '£200.' 'Really? Oh, I see. So how much are the bent nails?'

"Then Dunbar brings [Yoko] over, because The Millionaire is here, right? And I'm waiting for the bag. Where's the people in the bag? So he introduced me, and of course there was supposed to be this event happening, so I asked, 'Well, what's the event?' She gives me a little card. It just says 'Breathe' on it. And I said, 'You mean [exhaling]?' She says, 'That's it. You've got it.' . . . I got the humour—maybe I didn't get the depth of it but I got a warm feeling from it. I thought, 'Fuck, I can make that. I can put an apple on a stand. I want more.'"

Again, Yoko's recollection is somewhat different. "He said, 'I heard there's a happening or something . . . it's about a bag.' I said, 'No, today's event is this,' and I showed him the sign that said 'Breathe.' When he breathed out, he did it really hard and he came so near to me, it was a little bit flirty in a way. Then he went to the apple and just grabbed it and took a bite. I thought, 'How dare he do that?' I thought it was really gross, you know; he didn't know manners. He must have noticed I was so angry because he put it back on the stand."

The next exhibits to catch his eye really did invite spectator participation. ". . . I went up to this thing that said 'Hammer a nail in.' I said, 'Can I hammer a nail in?' and she said, 'No,' because the gallery was actually opening the next day. So Dunbar says, 'Let him hammer a nail in.' It was, 'He's a millionaire. He might buy it.' She's more interested in it looking nice and pretty and white for the opening. . . . There was this little conference and she finally said, 'OK, you can hammer a nail in for five shillings [25p],' so smart-arse here says, 'Well, I'll give you an imaginary five shillings, and hammer an imaginary nail in.' And that's when we really met. That's when we locked eyes and she got it and I got it and that was it.

"Then I saw this ladder on a painting leading up to the ceiling where there was a spyglass hanging down. It's what made me stay. I went up the ladder and I got the spyglass, and there was tiny little writing there. You really have to stand on top of the ladder—you feel like a fool, you could fall at any minute—and you look through and it just says 'Yes' . . . And just that 'Yes' made me stay in a gallery full of apples and nails instead of walking out, saying, 'I'm not gonna buy any of this crap.' "

Yoko, however, was quite unaware of the epiphany. "He came back down the ladder again, said 'Mm' or something and just left. I went downstairs, where there were several art students who were helping us. And one said, 'That was John Lennon . . . one of the *Beatles*.' I said, 'Oh, really? I didn't know that.' "

A fortnight or so later, she happened to be at the opening of a new show by an American rival—and friend—the Pop Art sculptor Claes Oldenburg. As she passed through a crowded space dotted with Oldenburg's giant plaster milk shakes and foam-rubber hamburgers, she remembers: "Somebody grunted. And in a corner there's a guy standing, looking so unshaven and pale-looking, a drugged-out-of-his-mind kind of guy. He'd been up with John Dunbar or someone, taking acid. And looking very angry . . . totally different from what I saw at Indica Gallery. And that was John. I think he always mixed up that night with the one when he came to my show at Indica."

Yoko moved on through the crowd to speak to Claes Oldenburg, but a few minutes later found herself back in the vicinity of John's corner. "Then Paul [McCartney] came up and started to talk to me, saying, 'My friend went to your gallery show. . . .' While we were talking, John walked over and said, 'We have to go now,' and just pulled Paul away. He seemed like an angry guy . . . an angry working-class guy."

The Beatles might have stopped performing onstage, but they still had to do so on record—and here there was no letup in the pressure to outdo their rivals on both sides of the Atlantic. Principally, this meant the Rolling Stones, who had become almost as big a concert attraction as the Beatles in their prime and who, having found fame as their polar opposites, now seemed to be muscling in on their territory. The Stones' 1966 *Aftermath* album was not the familiar raunchy R&B but a crafted song cycle, overtly modeled on *Rubber Soul* and showcasing the talents of lead guitarist Brian Jones, an instinctive musical genius whose sitar playing made George Harrison seem ploddy by comparison. It was mainly to prove they had not been eclipsed by *Aftermath* that John and Paul took their next quantum leap and created *Revolver*.

The Beach Boys' superb 1966 album *Pet Sounds* was an answer to *Rubber Soul* by their unstably brilliant leader, Brian Wilson. No sooner had the Beatles answered Wilson with *Revolver* than he answered back with "Good Vibrations," a single that took two months to make, cost a phenomenal $40,000, and packed in more layers of electronic and harmonic wizardry than many an entire album. The Byrds, too, those former Beatle look-alikes, had marked out their own unique territory athwart psychedelia and old-fashioned folk. Nineteen sixty-six saw the release of their *Fifth Dimension* album, containing the supremely weird and wonderful "Eight Miles High," the closest aural re-creation of an acid trip that anyone had yet dared commit to vinyl.

From New York's Greenwich Village came the Lovin' Spoonful—a play on the traditional, multihandled loving cup—whose singer-songwriter, John Sebastian, was like John and Paul rolled into one sunny smile. From the West Coast, where group names were growing as long as freight trains, came the Mothers of Invention, fronted by a dervish-headed, chin-bearded former advertising man named Frank Zappa. The Mothers' album *Freak-Out* presented Zappa polemics such as "Trouble Every Day" and "Who Are the Brain Police?" as a sequential performance on a common theme, like a classical symphony or oratorio. This new notion of the "concept" album was something else the Abbey Road songsmiths would have to take on board.

One competitor, above all, hovered constantly at the edge of John's consciousness; never more so than amid this creative meteor shower of 1966. In May, Bob Dylan released *Blonde on Blonde*, an album in the startling new format of two 33 rpm discs packaged together. Backed by a circle of talented session musicians (including the future personnel of the Band), Dylan synthesized folk and rock with avant-garde poetry and rumbustious vaudeville into a string of instant classics: "I Want You," "Just Like a Woman," "Visions of Johanna," "Sad-Eyed Lady of the Lowlands," above all the sing-along, oompah-pah-ing "Rainy Day Women # 12 & 35," with its incantatory chorus of "Ever'body must git *stoned!*"

When Dylan returned to Britain on tour later that summer, he and John again hung out together, although there was too much mutual uncertainty about who was inspiring and who copying whom for the friendship ever to be entirely relaxed. Dylan's UK performances were filmed by the American documentary maker D. A. Pennebaker as a color follow-up to *Don't Look Back*, his black-and-white chronicle of the previous year's tour. One scene in Pennebaker's sequel shows John and Dylan traveling together by car from Weybridge up to London. Both have clearly heeded the call of the Rainy Day Woman (traditional slang for a joint), though the effects on each are very different. Whereas Dylan stoned is a self-regarding bore, John remains lucid and humorous and even seems slightly embarrassed by his companion's ramblings. The sequence ends abruptly as the usual hazard of driving from Weybridge in a sealed limo full of pot smoke kicks in, and Dylan announces that he needs to throw up.

The Beatles therefore returned to Abbey Road Studios in late November with a daunting range of new possibilities to explore and competition to try to beat. The first potential new track that John played over to George Martin in their usual tête-à-tête manner was the song he'd written while away filming in Almería. "When I first heard 'Strawberry Fields Forever,' I was sidesmacked," Martin remembers. "Even with John singing it alone to his own acoustic guitar, I thought it was a wonderful piece of work. I said, 'What do you want to do with it?' and he said, 'You tell me.'"

The song that subsequently evolved in the studio was at first simple, light, and literal. Where John had originally begun with the first verse, "Living is easy with eyes closed . . . ," Martin suggested going straight into the chorus, "Let me take you down," that misleadingly plainspoken invitation to accompany him back to boyhood. Paul McCartney provided a crucial atmospheric touch, playing a Mellotron intro like some creaky, dusty harmonium in a 1950s church hall. Otherwise, the first takes featured the Beatles' playing unadorned, with John's voice artificially lowered by a semitone and sounding warm, nostalgic, even folksy.

Martin (whose schoolmasterly reserve had long since disappeared) pronounced himself "thrilled" with this version, and even John seemed satisfied. A few days later, however, he decided the song needed a heavier treatment. Martin wrote a formal orchestral score for cellos and brass, changing the key without telling John in order to reach the cello's dramatic bottom C, while George weighed in with a new instrument from his tutorials with Ravi Shankar, a swarmandel, or Indian zither. Further engineering work was done on John's voice, which drained away its former warmth and involvement and retracted its three dimensions to one.

For Martin and the other three Beatles, this new interpretation lifted the song to a thrilling new plane. But John, although pleased with its added complexities and ambiguities, decided that after all he liked the earlier, simpler arrangement just as much. Martin's solution was to splice the two different versions together, beginning in the dusty church hall then, after about a minute, plunging into the undergrowth of manic celli Cs and shivery Indian strings. This instrumental split personality exactly caught the contradictions in John's lyric: the oracular wisdom mixed with confusion and uncertainty, the mysticism and yet ordinariness, the carefully crafted incoherence. Listening to it now, one does not feel its author's new acid sensibility so much as his old, chronic nearsightedness: the picture of iron gates, weathered sandstone, and overgrown garden seems clear enough at first, then dwindles into the blurry perspective of the boy who never would wear his glasses. Martin summed up the effect perfectly as "dreamlike without being fey, weird without being pretentious—nostalgia with an air of mystery."

Paul, too, had been working independently on a song harking back to the Liverpool of his childhood. For him, the portal into Proustian remembrance was Penny Lane, that modest little thoroughfare in Liverpool 18, with its parade of shops and commercial buildings, where, in years past, he had changed buses and trams more times than he could count. Penny Lane was part of the other Beatles' childhoods, too, and also of Brian Epstein's. But for John—as that verse deleted from "In My Life" had already shown—it had the deepest resonance of all.

The whole district was woven into his family history, both the one he knew and the one that had been kept from him. His father, Alf, now Freddie, had been educated at the Bluecoat Hospital in nearby Church Row. His mother, Julia, was working at a café in Penny Lane when she met Taffy Williams, the young soldier who made her pregnant during Alf's wartime absence at sea. John had even lived in the immediate vicinity as a toddler, when his parents shared the Stanley family home in Newcastle Road. Later, in Aunt Mimi's care, he had taken the bus to the Penny Lane junction each morning on his journey to Dovedale Primary. The pre-McCartney Quarrymen had made their debut at St. Barnabas church hall, and in early Beatlemania days, Cynthia had been secreted in a bedsit in adjacent Garmoyle Road. The lane itself had also witnessed a tragedy for John's family in which history eerily repeated itself. Earlier in 1966, his mother's former lover, Bobby Dykins, the father of his two half sisters, Julia and Jackie, had crashed a car into a lamppost there. Like the elder Julia after another road accident eight years earlier, poor well-meaning "Twitchy" had been rushed to Sefton General Hospital, but had died soon after admittance.

In utter contrast with "Strawberry Fields Forever," Paul's recreation of Penny Lane was another short story in miniature, using photographic clarity and detail where John had fuzzy impressionism. McCartneyesque though the overall vision, almost every scene and character was like a snapshot from John's boyhood. The "barber showing photographs" was Bioletti, the elderly Italian who had cut his hair—and his father's before him—and whose shop window used to display sun-bleached pictures of customers proudly showing off their Tony Curtis or Jeff Chandler cuts. The "shelter in the middle of the roundabout" was where John had often lurked with his Outlaws, to gloat over stolen Dinky cars and, later, to grope girls. The "pretty nurse . . . selling poppies from a tray," though principally a memory of Paul's mother, was also a nod to John's arch-crony Pete Shotton, whose girlfriend, later wife, Beth Davidson, often used to perform that voluntary duty each November before Remembrance Sunday.

In the recording, Paul told George Martin he wanted a "clean sound," different in every possible way from the aural tangles of "Strawberry Fields Forever." Hence the feeling of breezy open air under those "blue suburban skies" and the piccolo trumpet solo, borrowed from the Brandenburg Concerto No. 2, as if Bach himself were strolling among the Saturday-afternoon shoppers, debating whether to buy a poppy or get a haircut. Though absent from the finished track, John provided crucial input, helping to write the third verse, about the "fireman with an hourglass" (whose fire station, strictly speaking, lay some way off, along Allerton Road). There was also a typical Lennon leer as well as typical Lennon surrealism in the second chorus's "four of fish and finger pies." "Four of fish" meant four old pennyworth, the price of a goodly slab of battered cod or hake at a Liverpool chippie when he was a child, while "finger pie" was the olfactory reward of groping inside a girl's crotch in a dark, windswept bus shelter. No pop song before had ever smuggled such arrant smut onto a million turntables—but at the time it was not even noticed, let alone challenged.

With these two disparately stunning autobiographical fragments in the can, John and Paul decided the concept album that everyone now expected from the Beatles would be all about their memories of Liverpool and childhood. But even now their prerogative was not absolute. Despite almost three months' intensive work at Abbey Road, they had not put together a second album for 1966, the one traditionally aimed at the lucrative Christmas market. George Martin therefore had no alternative but to make a selection from their past releases, stretching back as far as "She Loves You" and half apologetically entitled *A Collection of Beatles Oldies . . . but Goldies!* After Christmas, with no new album yet even remotely in sight, Martin decided to release "Strawberry Fields Forever" and "Penny Lane" as a double A-side single on February 17. He has since called it "the biggest mistake of my professional life."

Record buyers had never before, and have never since, been offered such superb value on one two-sided disk. Yet, such are the ways of the world, "Strawberry Fields Forever"/"Penny Lane" became the first Beatles single since "Love Me Do" not to reach number one in Britain. It rose to number two, but could not dislodge Engelbert Humperdinck's country ballad, "Release Me." For John, after so many effortless number ones, this came almost as a relief: in his new hippie love-all persona, he denied feeling any hostility toward Humperdinck or to a song that might ordinarily have made him stick his fingers down his throat. As if the Top 10 were now a commune rather than a greasy pole, he observed magnanimously, "There's room for everything."

The story of John and Yoko has always been represented as that of a scheming, self-aggrandizing woman who marked out the famous Beatle as her quarry at their first meeting—or even before it—and then pursued him with ruthless dedication until she got him. In fact, no other pair of famous lovers in history can have come together in quite so roundabout a fashion, nor with so many mutual misgivings.

Yoko admits to having been attracted to John at their first encounter, largely thanks to a penchant for "working class guys" that was part of her rebellion against her parents and background. Having just arrived in London as an unknown, she was also in urgent need of a wealthy patron to sponsor her work. Previously, the drumming up of such finance had been left to her husband, Tony Cox. But with their marriage now foundering, Yoko had to take on the task herself.

Following their meeting at the Claes Oldenburg show, she did send John a copy of *Grapefruit*, her collection of "instructional poems." But that had no ulterior motive, she insists: "I'd brought some books with me from New York because it wasn't out yet in Britain. I'd mentioned it to John when we talked and, like any author would do, I sent him a signed copy."

Grapefruit confirmed to John that this unknown woman from inconceivable other worlds was on a wavelength he'd always thought to be his exclusive preserve. He kept the chaste little white book beside his bed, suspending all his other omnivorous reading in favor of it, returning time and again to the single, unrhymed stanzas—

sometimes only single lines—that hovered so intriguingly between the mystical and mischievous: "Light a match and watch till it goes out." "Make a key. Find a lock that fits. If you find it, burn the house that is attached to it." "Listen to the sound of the earth turning." Conscious as he was of pop music's barefaced opportunism and ridiculously inflated values, he also loved the "Ono price-list," offering blank audiotapes said to be various types of "snow falling at dawn" at "25 cents per inch."

Cynthia Lennon would later claim that Yoko subjected John to a "determined pursuit" in which she bombarded him with letters and cards and "came to the house looking for him several times." According to Ray Coleman's 1980s biography of John, she turned up unannounced at Kenwood one day and, finding neither him or Cyn at home, persuaded the housekeeper, Dot Jarlett, to let her in to make a supposedly urgent telephone call. Later, she phoned John to say she had left "a valuable ring" beside the phone and would have to come back and collect it. Yoko says the whole story is pure fabrication. "I was never standing in front of the gate. That wasn't my style. And anyway, I didn't know where the house was."

Her only visit to Kenwood during this era was at John's invitation, for what she presumed would be a pop-star party. Instead, it turned out to be a lunch, prepared by Cynthia, with two members of a design group named the Fool—soon to loom large in Beatles business—as the only other guests. That day, John was no longer arrogant, as at the Indica show, nor surly, as Claes Oldenburg's, but a convivial host who talked animatedly about what he had enjoyed in *Grapefruit*. He was particularly struck by Yoko's idea for "A lighthouse . . . constructed from prisms which exist in accordance with the changes of the day"—an effect which, unbeknownst to her, was already being developed under the name *hologram*.

"John said to me, 'I thought maybe you could build this lighthouse in my garden,' she remembers. I said, 'It's just an illusion, it's not a built thing.' He looked a bit disappointed: 'Oh, OK—I thought the Americans had found out something we don't have yet. . . .' I thought it was cute. I laughed about it. But that was just an excuse, I know. He wanted me to be somehow involved in his life, and that was one way he might have done it."

During these first months of 1967, however, John had little time for anything but writing and recording. The premature release of "Strawberry Fields Forever" and "Penny Lane" had taken all the steam out of the Liverpool concept album idea, leaving George Martin to wonder remorsefully forevermore how great an album it might have been. Yet the need remained to come up with something that would knock Bob Dylan's, Brian Wilson's, and the Byrds' collective socks off.

On a recent solo visit to America, Paul had been struck by the fad among West Coast rock groups for ironically long and nonsensical names: Big Brother and the Holding Company, the Strawberry Alarm Clock, the Pacific Gas and Electric Band. Also in his mind was swinging London's current obsession with Victorian militaria, either picked up in original forms in Portobello Road antiques markets or mass-produced for a store chain called I Was Lord Kitchener's Valet. The result was a McCartney song for the still-unfocused new album, mixing these two trends together with nostalgia for north-country brass bands and a touch of "Eleanor Rigby" melancholy; its title was "Sgt. Pepper's Lonely Hearts Club Band."

Not until the Beatles were developing the track at Abbey Road did their roadie Neil Aspinall finally come up that elusive "concept." Why not record a whole album, not as themselves but under the alias of Sgt. Pepper's band, giving it all the atmosphere and spontaneity of a live show? They had recently been amused to read that Elvis Presley was sending out his gold-plated Cadillac to tour America, confident that the same crowds would gather to view this symbol of himself as once had for his living presence. With the question still constantly in the air of when the Beatles would play live again, a make-believe theater show on record could be their own Elvis Cadillac; instead of returning to the road themselves, they could send the album.

Keenly though they all embraced this idea, it soon bit the dust. Having recorded Paul's overture number as Sgt. Pepper's band with the atmosphere of a circus big top seething with excited spectators, they peremptorily abandoned their alter ego and returned to being the Beatles in real time and familiar order of precedence. A reprise of the overture near the album's end would be their only other nod toward thematic continuity. Not that it would ever matter, as

Ringo Starr later recalled: "A bunch of songs and you stick two bits of 'Pepper' on it and it's a concept. . . . It worked because we said it worked."

Certainly, John's most significant contributions had little to do with faux-Victorian fun and burlesque. They were products of yet another "trough," as he himself termed the dives into despair and self-disgust that he took every year or so, unknown to almost everyone around him. He had emerged from one circle of Beatle hell only to find himself in another, less crazily hectic but no less arid and unfulfilling, from which the only escape seemed to lie in drugs. A few rare pieces of art turn the bleakest negatives into radiant positives, telling you life is not worth living in terms which reassure you that it is. So now from the most unpromising elements—indolence, passivity, a sense of time ticking uselessly away—John made his masterpiece.

Lying on his undersize couch in the rear sun parlor at Kenwood, scanning newspapers and magazines with half an eye, watching almost-mute TV with the other half, he had absorbed two separate random news items. The first concerned a death among London's innermost in-crowd, where the highest class now mingled democratically with the lowest. Just before Christmas 1966, Tara Browne, the twenty-one-year-old son of brewing heiress Oonagh Guinness and friend of the Rolling Stones and Paul McCartney, had inexplicably driven his Lotus sports car through a red traffic light in South Kensington, crashed into a van, and been killed. The second was a *Daily Mail* snippet of the "Just Fancy That" variety John had always loved. In Blackburn, Lancashire, the Borough Surveyor's department had decided to count the number of potholes in its roads and announced there were exactly four thousand.

Few song titles were ever more confessional: not "In My Life" or "A Day in My Life" but "A Day in the Life," suggesting an existence almost too shameful to admit to. Here was the easily decryptable lament of someone who felt connected to reality only through newspapers and the media: reading about "the lucky man who . . . blew his mind out in a car"; learning only via the rushes of his own film that "the English army had just won the war"; speculating mindlessly, as in extreme stonedness or boredom, how many of the "4,000 holes in Blackburn Lancashire" might equal the volume of London's Royal Albert Hall. It was almost as if he were having an out-of-body experience, floating unseen above the wreckage of Tara Browne's wrecked Lotus and the horrified onlookers.

Early studio takes of "A Day in the Life" featured only Paul on piano, George on maracas and Ringo on bongos, John counting himself in by repeating "sugar plum fairy"—slang for a drug dealer. Those opening words "I read the news today oh boy," with their huge weight of apathy, sent shivers down George Martin's spine, as they would send shivers down spines ever afterward. He had told Martin to give him as much echo as Elvis had had on "Heartbreak Hotel"; as a result, his voice seemed to float from some cold, barren, lonely place, beyond the reach of all human help or comfort. He had written his very own "Heartbreak Hotel," or maybe *De Profundis*.

For his second great achievement on the album, he seemed to cut himself off completely from everyday things, retreating with relief into a mental hideout that for him long predated LSD. His two favorite books in all the world were still Lewis Carroll's *Alice's Adventures in Wonderland* and *Through the Looking-Glass*; indeed, using acid only sharpened his delight in the surreal fantasies that a nineteenth-century cleric apparently conjured from stimulants no stronger than weak China tea and cucumber sandwiches.

"Lucy in the Sky with Diamonds," as John would later insist, was inspired by a specific scene in *Through the Looking-Glass*. Alice walks into a shop to find a talking sheep in a poke bonnet knitting behind the counter; then, all at once, the two of them are drifting downriver in a skiff, using the knitting needles as oars. The book's verse epilogue also played its part: "A boat, beneath a sunny sky / Lingering onward dreamily. . . . / Still she haunts me, phantomwise, / Alice moving under skies / Never seen by waking eyes. . . ." Filtered through yet another of George Martin's electronic strainers, John's voice took on an almost childlike quality, as if the seven-year-old who had first followed Alice into the White Rabbit's burrow were speaking through him.

Time being short as usual, other songs had to be improvised from any ingredients at hand. "Being for the Benefit of Mr. Kite" was suggested by a Victorian circus poster he bought in a Kentish antique shop while shooting a promotional film for "Strawberry Fields" in the grounds of a stately home called Knole. His lyric simply repeated the poster's list of attractions, the trampolining Hendersons, "late of Pablo Fanques Fair," the "hoops and garters and . . . hogshead of real fire," adding an occasional grace note like "Henry the Horse dances the waltz." The farmyard-themed "Good Morning, Good Morning" borrowed the slogan crowed by a cartoon rooster on Kellogg's corn-flakes packets. Though just "a throwaway" to John, it shed bitter sidelights on the Kenwood breakfast table (". . . time for tea and meet the wife . . .") and his own sense of intellectual sterility ("I've got nothing to say but it's okay"). And of whom could he have been thinking in his obvious eagerness to be "in town . . . now you're in gear . . . go to a show you hope she goes"?

John was never closer to Paul than during these weeks. Though hotly competitive in songs they wrote individually outside the studio, they remained a matchless team within it, each working unselfishly to set off the other's latest brain wave at its best. Paul composed a piping intro for Lowry organ that established the drowsy riverbank atmosphere of "Lucy in the Sky with Diamonds" before John had sung a word; he also contributed to the lyric, supplying "Cellophane flowers" and "newspaper taxis" to set alongside John's "tangerine trees" and "marmalade skies." A half-finished song in the McCartney bottom drawer became the urgent, real-world middle passage of "A Day in the Life" ("Woke up, fell out of bed . . .") that is so inspired a contrast to its out-of-body languor. John and Paul together devised the lyric's final touch: the drawn-out, syllable-stretching sigh of "I'd love to tu-u-rn you-ou-ou-ou o-o-on . . ." Paul remembers how at the microphone they exchanged a glance, as if to say "Should we really go on with this?" The "nice" Beatle was as sure as the "rebel" one that they should.

Not the least of Paul's contributions was realizing John's typically apocalyptic but vague wish for "a sound like the end of the world" to link the song's contrasting movements and also bring it to a cli-mactic finish. This was achieved by a forty-one-piece symphony or-chestra, playing under no directions but to go from the lowest note on their instruments to the highest—a conception worthy of Cage or Stockhausen. The recording session, on March 10, was a gala occasion, with the classical violinists and woodwind players decked out in carnival hats, red clown-noses, and gorilla-paw gloves, and Studio Two's usually barred doors thrown open to a crowd of friends and colleagues, including Brian Epstein, Mick Jagger and Keith Richards of the Rolling Stones, Marianne Faithfull, and Donovan.

Lennon and McCartney still composed together, as in hotel rooms of old, for instance hammering out "With a Little Help from My Friends" as a vocal for Ringo (who otherwise spent most of the prodigal studio time learning to play chess). And the light and shade of their respective natures could still grab perfect harmony out of thin air. One day John happened to walk into the studio while Paul was at the mike, singing "It's getting better . . ." "It couldn't get much worse," his partner ad-libbed in counterpoint, and the line stuck.

Whatever John's later opinion of Paul's "soft" numbers, he threw his whole weight behind them now with backup vocals that remained totally faithful to their intent while adding a dash of vinegar to the honey. In "She's Leaving Home," his is the gently empathic voice of the parents who awake in horror to find that their daughter has eloped with the "man from the motor trade": "We . . . sacrificed most of our lives . . . we gave her everything money could buy. . . ." In "When I'm Sixty-four," his responses to Paul's George Formby-esque visions of "a cottage in the Isle of Wight" and grandchildren named Vera, Chuck, and Dave seem no less rapturous than their creator's. "Lovely Rita" would not be half the song it is without John's almost atonal background drone of "Lervly Rrrreeta Meetah-Maid! . . ." The same half-mocking, half-sleepy chorus echoes distantly in the finale of "A Day in the Life," like the Cheshire Cat's grin still floating in midair after every other bit of it has vanished.

Ironically for an album that would be so much identified with LSD, the Beatles took almost no acid while making *Sgt. Pepper*. The sense of forging into new territory each day, and infallibly conquering it, gave a high that no drug ever could. The only lapse that John would remember happened purely by accident: one night he swallowed a tab of acid by mistake for an upper to keep him going. Later, while recording vocals for "Getting Better," he suddenly felt over-whelming panic. George Martin noticed him looking "a bit pecu-liar" and suggested he got some fresh air. With fans besieging every street door, Martin had no option but to take him up onto the roof. The producer still knew nothing of mind-expanding substances, so could not understand why John should wax so ecstatic about a seem-ingly normal London night sky. When he rejoined the others, he had become atypically meek and reticent, telling them to carry on with-out him and he'd just sit and watch. It was the only time Martin ever saw him incapacitated in the studio.

Since he was clearly in no condition to return to Weybridge, Paul took him home for the night to nearby Cavendish Avenue. Though by now also initiated into LSD (by that "lucky man," Tara Browne, as it happened), Paul had never taken a trip with John, and decided this was the moment. John insisted that Neil Aspinall should also be there, but not turn on "in case of emergencies." They stayed up most of the night, Paul remembers, and "hallucinated a lot . . . John [was] sitting around very enigmatically and I had a big vision of him as a king, the absolute Emperor of Eternity . . . in control of it all." Finally Paul decided to turn in, despite John's warnings from long experience that he wouldn't be able to sleep. Sure enough, the vi-sions pursued him into bed. Every so often, roadie Mal Evans came in like a night nurse to check that he was all right.

For three years, Britain's Establishment had looked on its frolick-ing youth culture with bemused indulgence. But by early 1967, things were starting to change. It had become clear that horrifying numbers of young people were turning on to drugs, encouraged ever more blatantly by the music they listened to and the musicians they idolized. Police forces up and down the land therefore began system-atically targeting the main culprits, spurred on by savage envy of their quarries' lifestyles and armed with draconian powers of search and entry. In February, an eighteen-strong task force raided a week-end house party given by Rolling Stone Keith Richards, from which Beatle George Harrison and his wife had departed just a few hours earlier. Richard and Mick Jagger were both charged with drug pos-session along with their friend, the art dealer Robert Fraser.

Searching official scrutiny also fell on London's underground press, whose whole raison d'être was the promotion of drug use, anti–Vietnam War protest, and sexual nonconformity. In December 1966, one of the founders of the *International Times*, John "Hoppy" Hopkins, was busted for possessing cannabis and subsequently jailed for nine months. The following March, John's and Paul's friends at *IT* printed an interview with the black American radical Stokely Carmichael, which included the word *motherfucker*. Police instantly swooped on the paper's offices, confiscated documents and reference books (even telephone directories), and charged its editors under the Obscene Publications Act.

To raise funds for their legal defense, a gigantic happening was held at Alexandra Palace, North London, on April 29. Billed as the 14 Hour Technicolor Dream and promising "kaleidoscopic colour and beautiful people," the night-long mixed-media marathon featured music from bands like Pink Floyd, Soft Machine, the Move, and the Crazy World of Arthur Brown, readings from poets like Christopher Logue and Michael Horovitz, films, lightshows, and the performance art of Yoko Ono. Thousands of hippies converged on the hilltop entertainment complex, paying £1 per shaggy head, and BBC television provided live coverage throughout the evening. John was watching with John Dunbar in Weybridge and on a sudden impulse decided to drive up to "Ally Pally" and take part.

Yoko's contribution was to have been *Cut Piece*, in which she sat or knelt motionless onstage while audience members cut off pieces of her dress. However, the sight of the deranged throng, ingesting everything from outsize "banana joints" to STP (a psychedelic even stronger than LSD), caused her an uncharacteristic fit of stage nerves. A female stand-in therefore did *Cut Piece*—with the snippers using scissors wired to an amplifier—while Yoko watched from the sidelines. John had no idea that she was there, and she did not see him. After mingling with the spectators for a few minutes, he and Dunbar retreated to the gardens outside to share a more secluded joint, then were chauffeured back to Weybridge. "Nobody told me he'd been in the place," Yoko remembers. "People were too high, I'm sure, to care if a Beatle was there or not."

Throughout that portentous spring of 1967, John looked in several other directions to cure his boredom and restlessness. Just before the 14 Hour Technicolor Dream, he had read that a tiny, uninhabited island off western Ireland named Dorinish was for sale at £1,700. The following day, as the culmination of an almost weeklong acid bender, he and John Dunbar flew to Dublin, traveled by rental car to Clew Bay in County Mayo, then took a boat out to the rocky, wave-lashed outcrop that was available at such a bargain price. Fired by visions of a hippie existence close to nature, John used Dunbar's sketchbook to draw a lighthouse-like structure, which he planned to build and inhabit, apparently alone. Dorinish duly became his, and he never set foot on it again.

His Rolls-Royce provided another short-lived burst of enthusiasm. During the car's visit to Almería for *How I Won the War*, its black paintwork had been ruined by abrasive sand particles. Prompted by Ringo, John had the idea of repainting it in psychedelic style, like a full-size gypsy wagon caravan that he had recently installed in Kenwood's garden. Since the Rolls-Royce company itself would never commit such sacrilege, a private coachbuilder named J. P. Fallon in nearby Chertsey—where John's chauffeur, Les Anthony, happened to live—agreed to undertake the work. The Rolls was resprayed pale yellow and its radiator covered with Art Nouveau tendrils of red and green. The side panels were decorated with rose clusters reminiscent of Aunt Mimi's best chinaware, while John's astrological sign, Libra, covered the roof. The final touch was a still-unusual personalized license plate, WEYBRIDGE 46676. Crowds lined Chertsey's streets to witness Anthony collect the transformed vehicle—as many as ever flocked around Elvis's touring Cadillac.

For John, keeping boredom at bay required a constant turnover of people as well as things. This past year his favored sidekick had been John Dunbar, the most serious "art person" he had known since college days. Dunbar's wife, Marianne Faithfull, had by now decamped to live with Mick Jagger and had been present at the Rolling Stones' February drug bust. (A rumor was currently sweeping the country that, when the police arrived, Jagger had been licking a Mars bar lodged in Marianne's vagina.)

Living with Dunbar at his Bentinck Street flat was a twenty-one-year-old Greek named Ianni, or Alexis, Mardas, whom he had gotten to know through the wife of the Greek sculptor Nicholus Takis. Though Mardas currently worked as a television engineer, his true vocation was inventor of electronic gadgets, both for corporate and private use. So much did he impress Dunbar that the two formed a business partnership meant to combine their respective aesthetic and technological gifts. Despite the recent theft of his wife, Dunbar remained close to the Rolling Stones, and the pair duly won the job of lighting designers on a Stones European tour.

Hanging out at Dunbar's, Mardas soon met John and found opportunities to outline his proposed inventions to him. Some anticipated soon-to-be telecommunication developments, like a phone that dialed automatically by voice recognition and displayed the numbers of incoming callers. Others seemed more in the realm of science fiction: an X-ray camera, a protective force field that surrounded a house with colored smoke, or a building that could hover in midair. To John, whose practical knowledge was nil—who could not so much as change a lightbulb—all seemed equally, life-transformingly wondrous. Dunbar was suddenly out and Magic Alex, as John dubbed him, was in. He became the first serious interloper into the Beatles' inner circle, even turning up with John for one of their meetings at Paul's house and being proudly introduced to the others as "my new guru."

Having taken four months and cost an astounding £25,000, *Sgt. Pepper's Lonely Hearts Club Band* was almost ready to meet its public. The final touch was shooting an album cover, designed by Peter Blake and destined to go down in Pop Art as well as pop music history. The Beatles, dressed as psychedelic bandsmen, were surrounded by a collage of cultural icons, high and low, from Bob Dylan and Marlon Brando to Karl Marx, Carl Jung, W. C. Fields, Edgar Allan Poe, Oscar Wilde, Dylan Thomas, Marilyn Monroe, Fred Astaire, Laurel and Hardy, Tommy Handley, and Diana Dors. John's nominations of Jesus Christ and Adolf Hitler were vetoed as "too far out," though he was allowed the occultist and so-called Great Beast Aleister Crowley. Stu Sutcliffe's image also made an appearance, beside Aubrey Beardsley's and Max Miller's. So did the Beatles' Madame Tussaud's waxworks as they had looked four years earlier, to the left of John in his yellow, red-frogged satin hussar coat with a French horn under his arm. Strange to reflect what anathema those quiet gray stage suits had once been to him.

On May 27, Brian hosted a prerelease party for selected music journalists, attended by all four Beatles. According to the next week's *Melody Maker*, "Lennon won the sartorial stakes with a green-flowered patterned shirt, red cord trousers, yellow socks and what looked like cord shoes. His ensemble was completed by a sporran. With his bushy sideboards and National Health specs, he looked like an animated Victorian watchmaker . . ." Close friends from the media pack noted that he was unshaven and haggard.

His verdict on the finished album was typically downbeat and self-derogatory: "I actively dislike bits . . . which didn't come out right. There are bits of 'Lucy in the Sky' I don't like. Some of the sound in 'Mr Kite' isn't right. I like 'A Day in the Life,' but it's still not half as nice as I thought it was when we were doing it. I suppose we could have worked harder on it, but I couldn't be arsed doing any more. 'Sgt. Pepper' is a nice song, 'Getting Better' is a nice song, and George's 'Within You Without You' is beautiful. What else is on it musically, beside the whole concept of having tracks running into each other?"

That weekend, Brian threw an even more lavish party to celebrate *Sgt. Pepper*, this time at his newly acquired country house near Crowborough, Sussex. As well as three Beatles and their consorts (Paul failed to arrive), the guests included Mick Jagger, Marianne Faithfull, the songwriter Lionel Bart, London Philharmonic conductor Sir John Pritchard, and—most appealingly to John—the Beatles' former press liaison man, Derek Taylor. Since quitting his job after a tiff with Brian on the '64 American tour, Taylor had gone on to a successful career as a PR consultant in Hollywood. Brian now regretted his loss, and had backed up the party invitation with two first-class round-trip air tickets.

When Taylor and his seven-months-pregnant wife, Joan, flew into Heathrow Airport on the morning of the party, they were met by John, Ringo, and Terry Doran, all in full hippie regalia, strewing flowers and ringing little bells. Joan Taylor, who had always been nervous of John's unpredictable moods and lashing tongue, now found herself warmly hugged by him. "This is the new thing," he explained. "You hug your friends when you meet them and show them you're glad to see them. Don't stand there shaking hands as if everyone's got some disease. Get close to people."

The Taylors stayed the weekend with him and Cynthia at Kenwood, and they all traveled down to Brian's in the newly psychedelic Rolls. During the party, John offered Joan a tab of acid, telling her that Derek had already accepted one from George. Despite the advanced state of her pregnancy, she took it. "John and George looked after Derek and me for the rest of the night," she remembers. "They couldn't have been kinder or more attentive."

Sgt. Pepper was released on June 1, 1967. With its sumptuous packaging and giveaway novelties—paper mustaches and sergeant's chevrons the buyer could cut out and wear—it was itself a party invitation, perfectly timed for the golden season that would become enshrined as the Summer of Love. It topped the UK album chart for twenty-seven weeks, selling half a million copies in its first month, and in America stayed number one for nineteen weeks, selling 2.5 million by August. A whole generation, still used to happy landmarks through life, would always remember exactly when and where they first played it, and their amazed delight as the needle bit into its grooves.

A further innovation was providing the lyrics of each song in full on the album's back cover. Lennon and McCartney's words would therefore be read and reread by more millions of people than any modern author, certainly any poet, could hope to reach in a dozen lifetimes. However, that also meant they could be studied at leisure by moral guardians whom past purely verbal reference to "prick teasers" or "finger pie" had completely escaped.

"Lucy in the Sky with Diamonds" was instantly banned by the BBC for spelling out the letters of the drug that increasingly dominated newspaper headlines. John retorted that the song had nothing to do with LSD but was simply the title of a painting his son Julian had done at school—a story which Paul would later corroborate. It is a plausible enough explanation if one accepts that John never took acid or encouraged its use, that he was completely word blind, and that he took an ongoing and responsive interest in Julian's schoolwork.

Nonetheless, "Lucy" managed to be heard throughout the British Isles, and ultimately would prove the most influential track on the whole album. For it set the pattern for British psychedelic rock as a marriage of self-consciously poetic language with the visions of earliest childhood. Thus Pink Floyd's concept album *The Piper at the Gates of Dawn* would borrow a chapter heading from Kenneth Grahame's *The Wind in the Willows*, Keith West would make the Top 10 with an Enid Blytonish song about children mourning a village grocer, and Traffic's *Hole in My Shoe* use a lisping Alice voice-over to evoke "a place where happiness reigned all the year round and music played ever so loudly." At times the UK charts would seem positively silted up with dragons, magic spells, rocking horses, smiley-faced kites, and tin soldiers.

"A Day in the Life" also was banned by the BBC, and many U.S. radio stations, although that provocative "I'd love to turn you on" was just one cause of its exclusion. The man who "blew his mind out in a car" was assumed to have been on an LSD trip and the "4,000 holes in Blackburn, Lancashire" to represent needle puncture marks; the middle section (by Paul) about having "a smoke" and going into "a dream" was taken to be about pot; even the instrumental "sound like the end of the world" was accused of suggesting narcotic delirium. Indeed, every song on the album was to be put through the X-ray machine and set alarm bells ringing, if not for drug advocacy then for sexual innuendo. "With a Little Help from My Friends" earned double notoriety, for its reference to getting high and the unspecific (but obviously grubby) "What do you see when you turn out the light?" "Fixing a Hole" was interpreted as yet another injection metaphor, where Paul had been thinking only of home improvement. The "man from the motor trade" in "She's Leaving Home"—a reference to Brian's car-sales partner, Terry Doran—was said to be a synonym for an abortionist.

The transatlantic media were now in full cry for a Beatle to admit to using drugs. But the first one to break cover was the last anybody had expected. In a *Life* magazine interview with the Beatles, published on June 19, Paul admitted in having taken LSD "about four times" and enthused about its power to unlock the brain's hidden creative potential. As a result, this normally infallible PR man for the group unleashed a storm of criticism and reproach almost on "bigger than Jesus" level: The *Daily Mail* branded him "an irresponsible idiot" for giving out such a message to youth, while the American evangelist Billy Graham offered up intercessionary prayers. However, the Beatles were still considered such a national treasure that no police action resulted. And Paul handled the furor adroitly, saying that he'd just given an honest answer to a direct question, and that if the media were worried about publicizing drugs to the young, they could simply not have printed and broadcast his words.

The Beatles preserved traditional solidarity, John and George admitting (along with Brian himself) that they, too, had tried LSD, albeit only "half a dozen times" back in the era when it was still legal. Privately, both were annoyed that, having virtuously resisted turning on for something like eighteen months, and while still a rank beginner in comparison to themselves, Paul should now step forward as the Beatles' resident acidhead. Years from now, after the bitterness between them had cooled, John would pay wry tribute to Paul's knack of hogging the limelight, good or bad: "He always times these big announcements right on the letter, doesn't he?"

In fact, John himself was about to make an announcement of far greater magnitude. The same BBC that had lifted its skirts in horror at "A Day in the Life" and "Lucy in the Sky with Diamonds" was also still a matchless public-service broadcaster, with a global mission to enlighten and unite. June of 1967 saw the corporation inaugurate the first truly international television program, using the new communications satellites that now orbited the earth. Entitled *Our World*, it involved eighteen different overseas broadcasting systems and was to be transmitted simultaneously by three satellites across five continents (though not in the Soviet Union, which pulled out at the last moment). For the BBC's own segment, there could be only one subject, irrespective of the recent terrestrial scandals they had stirred up.

On the evening of Sunday, June 25, Studio One at Abbey Road suffered its greatest invasion to date. Thanks to those beeping orbs in the far heavens, a total of 350 million people across Europe, Africa, Asia, Australasia, the United States, and Latin America could join the

Beatles as they recorded a brand-new song (actually just singing to a backing track) watched by a live audience of full-dress flower children, including Mick Jagger, Marianne Faithfull, Keith Richard, Eric Clapton, and Keith Moon of the Who. The song had been written by John as a distillation of the hippie creed, the Beautiful People's prescription for anything and everything that ailed the watching planet: "All You Need Is Love." As simple in form as "Three Blind Mice" on the offbeat, with lyrics more like slogans than sentences ("Nothing you can do that can't be done . . . Nothing you can sing that can't be sung . . .") it was the first instance of his power to create anthems that transcended language, culture, or religion. However calculated, and laughably simplistic, it was not a bad first message for satellite broadcasting.

The famous black-and-white footage of the transmission shows a serious John the world had never seen before, seated on a stool, with a single headphone speaker clamped to one ear, singing expressionlessly between chews on a wad of gum. Yet several irrepressible Lennonisms undercut the virtuous mood. The song opens with trumpets sounding "La Marseillaise," theme-song of the French Revolution, an episode not best known for propagating love. And in its closing instrumental maelstrom of classical brass and 1940s swing, we feel him cast off earnestness like a chafing sandal: "Al-to-ge-ther . . . ev'ry-bo-dy," he exhorts with mock booziness as if his 350 million watchers are sharing some Saturday-night pub sing-along. He even throws in a sarcastic "She loves you yeah yeah yeah"—the last rites for that hated distant past of four years ago.

"It's ea-sy," he says of love, through gum-chews, though for him, as he must already guess, it will be anything but.

20

MAGIC, MEDITATION, AND MISERY

I was scared. I thought, "We've fuckin had it now."

On the August Bank Holiday weekend of 1967, the Beatles were together in Bangor, north Wales, being initiated into transcendental meditation by their new spiritual teacher, Maharishi Mahesh Yogi. Two days into the course, they heard that Brian Epstein had been found dead at his London home of an alcohol and barbiturates overdose, aged thirty-two. The enduring image of that moment is John's face, blank with horror amid popping flashbulbs as the massed media clamor for a reaction. "I dunno what to say. . . . He was a beautiful feller and it's terrible."

Despite numerous other projects and preoccupations, Brian had retained exclusive managerial responsibility for the Beatles and Cilla Black, the only other of his original Mersey Beat stable to inspire anything like similar dedication. And in their off-road state, the

Beatles still relied heavily on him, collectively and as individuals. The previous January, he had concluded a new deal with their UK record company, EMI, replacing the minuscule royalty rate they had had to accept as newcomers in 1962 with a whopping 10 percent of retail price. He had been closely associated with the *Sgt. Pepper* project while simultaneously fielding a plan (abortive, as it would prove) for the playwright Joe Orton to script their next film. In September, his own five-year management contract was due to expire, and there seemed little doubt about its renewal, albeit possibly for a smaller commission than his previous 25 percent.

His relationship with the Beatles during these final months was that of a parent bird watching its newly launched fledglings with a mixture of concern and amusement, ready to swoop to their aid at the first faint cheep for help. After Paul's admission to *Life* magazine, Brian came forward alongside John and George to say that he, too, had taken acid and found its effects beneficial. From then on, he stood shoulder to shoulder with them and other British musical and cultural luminaries in pleading the harmlessness of soft drugs and protesting against the ferocity of the police's crackdown. A few days after chorusing "All You Need Is Love" on the Beatles' *Our World* telecast, Mick Jagger and Keith Richard each received an absurdly harsh prison sentence for the minor drug offenses committed six months earlier. Set free after a media outcry, the two Rolling Stones celebrated their liberation with a new single entitled "We Love You," a sarcastic riposte to the British judiciary, on which John and Paul featured anonymously as backup singers.

On July 14, a rally calling for the legalization of pot drew five thousand supporters to London's Hyde Park. Eight days later, the *Times* published a full-page advertisement headed "The Law Against Marijuana Is Immoral in Principle and Unworkable in Practice" and signed by Brian (who had paid for it), the four Beatles, and sixty other distinguished names, including Graham Greene, David Hockney, Jonathan Miller, David Bailey, and Kenneth Tynan.

In his private life, Brian remained as troubled and unstable as he had ever been. That same month, Parliament introduced a new Sexual Offences Act, which decriminalized sex between consenting males over the age of twenty-one. Although the day was still far off when most gay men would feel able to come out, the new legislation brought an end to fear, persecution, and victimization for thousands. But unluckily for Brian, his sexual tastes still lay well outside the law. On the evening before his death, he had left a group of friends at his Sussex house and returned to London alone, bored and frustrated because a party of rent boys had failed to materialize for his entertainment. His homosexuality, though still unexposed by the media, was well known to those who pulled the strings of public life; it can have been the only reason why, for all his vast contribution to Britain's economy, culture, and international prestige, he had never received an honor from the Queen or any other official recognition.

To the very end, he never lost his infatuation with John, nor the hope that, some glorious day, his feelings would be requited. One of the few people to whom he admitted—or half admitted—as much was Jonathan King, a rising young singer-writer-producer who had had a number one single, "Everyone's Gone to the Moon," while still a Cambridge undergraduate. Throughout the centuries of oppression, gay men had learned to communicate almost telepathically. So with Brian, King remembers, there would be no more than an expressive eye flutter behind John's back or when his name was mentioned—"a sense of 'he may come over to us one day.' "

Since their ill-advised Spanish holiday in 1963, John had never given the smallest grounds for such hope. But he was always conscious of this power over the man on whom, paradoxically, he also relied so much. His public cruelties to Brian, usually jibes at his race if not his sexuality, were legendary within their common circle. Once, while Brian was away in America, John said it was to sign up "a rhythm and Jews group." The B-side to "All You Need Is Love" was a hippie-debunking Lennon song called "Baby You're a Rich Man," ostensibly mocking the Beautiful People but providing a coded double dig at Brian. In practice sessions (some say on the finished track also), John sang its chorus of "Baby, you're a rich man, too" as "you're a rich fag Jew."

John had been no more aware than the other Beatles of Brian's turbulent parallel life, his excessive drinking and pill taking, his ad-diction to gambling, and the disastrous sexual liaisons that had even caused him to miss their last-ever stage performance in San Fran-cisco—a lapse for which he excoriated himself ever afterward. "I didn't watch him deteriorate," John would later admit. "There was a period of about two years before he died when we didn't hardly see anything of him. . . . I felt guilty because I was closer to him earlier, and then for two years I was having my own internal problems . . . and I [had] no idea of the kind of life he was living. . . . I introduced Brian to pills—which gives me a guilt association with his death—to make him talk, to find out what he was like. . . . [He used to have] hellish tempers and fits and lock-outs and he'd vanish for days . . . the whole business would stop because he'd been on sleeping pills for days on end and wouldn't be awake . . . or beaten up by some docker in the Old Kent Road."

The first serious warning sign came early that summer, when Brian checked into the Priory clinic in Putney in a desperate—and, it would prove, fruitless—attempt to get clean. The news came as a great shock to John, and brought out all the "grace" that the percep-tive Derek Taylor saw in him. A vast floral bouquet was dispatched to the Priory for Brian with a handwritten card saying, "You know I love you . . . I really mean that, John." When Brian read it, he burst into tears.

The Brian problem was thrust aside in late August, however, when John met the Indian mystic known as Maharishi ("Great Seer") Mahesh Yogi. George Harrison's wife, Pattie, had lately joined the Maharishi's worldwide "Spiritual Regeneration movement," and she told George that this most celebrated of all Hindu holy men was to address a meeting of his London disciples in the unlikely surround-ings of the Hilton Hotel, Park Lane. George in turn passed the word to his fellow band members. "Everybody going to the Maharishi was like everyone ending up with moustaches on Sergeant Pepper," Neil Aspinall recalled. "A lot of it was follow-the-leader, whoever the leader was at the time."

Tiny in stature with lank shoulder-length hair, a parti-colored, forked beard, and a giggly falsetto voice, the Maharishi might have stepped straight out of John's Quarry Bank cartoon book. What he preached that day at the Hilton to the caftaned and beaded Beatles was much the same Buddhist wisdom they had been absorbing and regurgitating since "Tomorrow Never Knows." But this was mysticism in a tabloid form, instantly appealing to young earthly gods for whom real self-denial was unthinkable and whose powers of concentration on anything outside music were virtually nonexistent. The Maharishi's route to spiritual regeneration involved no special training, no memorizing of complex prayers or incantations, and next to no personal inconvenience. To attain the state of inner joy and repose he described—to rise above mundane pressures and anxieties to a state of "pure awareness"—it was necessary to meditate for only half an hour each day.

Despite hundreds of trips, LSD had never quite lived up to John's expectations as a relief from the toils of everyday superstardom. Nonetheless, he still clung to his belief in a single "secret" or "answer" that would simultaneously explain the universe and put him at ease inside his own skin. And suddenly on this random afternoon in Park Lane, a comical little Indian yogi seemed to offer it. Quarry Bank classmates of yore would hardly have known the respectful floral-shirted pupil, seated as close to his teacher as possible and raptly drinking in every word.

The other Beatles—who all, to some extent, shared John's malady—were equally captivated by the Maharishi's promise of bliss without effort. After this one short encounter, in true William and the Outlaws style, all four signed up to the Spiritual Regeneration movement, which obligated its members to tithe one week's wages and act as transcendental meditation teachers and proselytizers. They further agreed to study at the Maharishi's ashram, or retreat, in the Himalayas and, as an introduction, to join his ten-day Spiritual Guides course, due to begin that very weekend at a teacher-training college in Bangor. Next day, they traveled to north Wales in the holy man's retinue, accompanied by Pattie, Jane Asher, Maureen Starkey, Mick Jagger, and Marianne Faithfull. In Beatle terms, it was an act of almost Buddhist asceticism to exchange their usual black-windowed limousines for an ordinary, dingy British Rail train from Paddington; as John remarked, it felt "like going somewhere without your trousers." Cynthia Lennon had also been asked along but, in the melee of press and fans, was left behind in tears on the platform. Far from feeling threatened by the new guru, Brian had wished them well—indeed, had promised to try to join them later in the course.

For one Beatle, at least, the moment of numbing shock from a clear blue sky was all too horribly familiar. It had already happened three times to John—when his Uncle George suffered a fatal hemorrhage on the stairs at Mendips, when his mother had stepped in front of a speeding car in Menlove Avenue, and when Stu Sutcliffe's brain had seemed to detonate in Hamburg. As with those previous losses of incalculably important people, his initial reaction, he admitted, was not weeping but laughter, "a sort of hysterical tee-hee-hee, I'm glad it's not me. . . ." And once again, grief and disbelief were tempered by something like reproach that he should be thus abandoned yet again. "I've had a lot of people die on me," he said in one interview, as if their deaths had been almost a dereliction of duty.

Fortuitously, the Maharishi was on hand to soften the raw anguish with comforting Eastern homilies about the pettiness of earthly existence and the liberating power of death. John received this counseling eagerly, later passing it on to the media with a fervor that left no doubt about his absolute conversion. ". . . Meditation gives you confidence enough to withstand something like this, even after the short amount we've had," he told reporters. "You don't get upset when a young kid becomes a teenager or a teenager becomes an adult or when an adult gets old. Well, Brian is just passing into the next phase. His spirit is still around and always will be."

After returning from Bangor, all four Beatles went together to Brian's house in Chapel Street, Belgravia, to offer condolences to his mother, who recently had also lost her husband of thirty-four years. "Come to India with us and meditate," John, not very realistically, suggested. Glad of any diversion, Queenie Epstein asked what meditation involved.

"Well, you just think of something," John said. "Like a carrot . . ."

Mrs. Epstein could not help smiling. "When I think of a carrot, I think of tomorrow's lunch," she replied.

The four did not attend Brian's funeral for fear of the media orgy it would provoke. Afterward, they had a meeting with Neil Aspinall, Mal Evans, and Brian's closest lieutenant, Peter Brown, to discuss where they went from here. Brown remembers how, stricken by the loss of his best friend as well as employer, he found it hard to sit around and talk cold-blooded business strategy. "After a few minutes, John came to me and put his arms around me and asked in the gentlest of voices if I was all right. He knew that the two people most emotionally affected by Brian's death were him and me, and only he understood how totally devastated I was by Brian's death because he felt the same way, too." John's special bond with Brian, says Brown, came from "sharing and seeing in each other complicated personalities which were often unhappy and frequently frustrated. They, perhaps as no others, understood each other."

There was no obvious candidate to take Brian's place, at least where the Beatles were concerned, which was all that interested the world's media. Robert Stigwood, his recently acquired partner in NEMS, initially looked like his heir apparent, but was roundly rejected by all four Beatles and left the company with a sizable chunk of its talent, including the Bee Gees, soon afterward. The helm at NEMS was taken over by Brian's younger brother, Clive, a decent, well-meaning man, but devoid of Brian's imagination and flair. Brown, Aspinall, Alistair Taylor, and the other key figures in Brian's original Liverpool team were all loyal, dedicated, and practiced at Beatle maintenance, but none felt qualified to step into his shoes. For the first time since Brian had walked into that Cavern club lunchtime session in 1961, the Beatles were on their own.

"It's up to us now, to sort out the way we and Brian wanted things to go," John said with apparent self-assurance. "He gave us the strength to do what we did, and the same urge is still alive. We have no idea of whether we'll get a new manager. We've always been in control of what we're doing and we'll have to do what we have to now. . . ."

Years later, he would admit: "I knew we were in trouble then. I

didn't really have any misconceptions about our ability to do anything other than play music, and I was scared. I thought, 'We've
fuckin' had it now.'"

The loss of this nearest to a father figure in John's life had the
effect of turning his thoughts back to his real father. Six days
after Brian's death, perhaps from a sense that life was too short to bear
grudges, he wrote to Freddie Lennon, suggesting they should meet
and promising to get in touch again "before a month has passed."
At a loss for a suitable mode of address, he began with every one he
could think of, even the Latin tag his educated aunts had taught him
as a toddler: "Dear Alf Fred Dad Pater whatever . . ." The note ended
with a plea not to talk to the press. ("I don't want Mimi cracking
up!") On the back of the envelope, he scribbled a half-playful, half-
embarrassed "Guess who."

It had been eighteen months since Freddie's dip into the world of
celebrity and his last, acrimonious meeting with John. He had made
no money from his short career as a pop singer and only very little
from selling his story to the newspapers. When Fleet Street lost interest in him, he had returned to his old life as an itinerant hotel
worker, resigned to having no further contact with the son he had so
mortally offended and to living among dirty pots and scummy water
for the rest of his days.

But at the age of fifty-four, after decades without a female of any
significance in his life, an astounding thing had happened to Freddie.
Christmas of 1966 found him employed on his accustomed bottom
rung at a hotel named the Toby Jug in Tolworth, Surrey. Here he
met an eighteen-year-old Exeter University student named Pauline
Jones, who had a vacation job in the hotel kitchen. His recent disap-
pointments had not quenched Freddie's ebullient humor or his habit
of singing lustily as he worked. Thanks to his recent exposure to
pop culture, moreover, he now kitchen-portered in an eye-catching
getup of red trousers, a yellow T-shirt, and a leather waistcoat.

It was never a question of guileful older man hypnotizing impressionable teenager; for all his other foibles, Freddie was no lecher and,
to begin with, could neither understand nor believe his appeal to

an intelligent and pretty young woman thirty-four years his junior. Only after long confusion and misgivings did he come round to Pauline's view that the Grand Canyon of an age gap between them did not matter. They began a romance initially consisting of long talks, with the occasional chaste kiss, in the Toby Jug's kitchen between meal services. Underlining that innocence, Freddie nicknamed Pauline "Polly" after his mother, the redoubtable Grandma Lennon whom John had visited so seldom at her spotless home in Copperfield Street, Toxteth.

The odds against any more serious relationship at first seemed insuperable. Pauline's widowed mother, understandably, was horrified to discover what was going on, and forbade her to see Freddie again. She returned to her studies in Exeter, but at term's end rushed back to the Toby Jug, where Freddie went down on one knee and proposed to her in the kitchen. Neither of them, however, dared take it seriously. When Pauline went back to Exeter, Freddie followed, hoping to find scullion's work on the university campus. He was unsuccessful, and ended up sleeping rough, first in a college chapel, then in an empty train in a railway siding.

As a last attempt to please her mother and follow convention, Pauline took a job as a children's tutor in Paris; Freddie, meanwhile, drifted back to Surrey, finding work again at the Greyhound pub in Hampton, just a couple of miles from Weybridge. Pauline's tutoring post did not work out, and, lonely and confused, she went into a Parisian church to pray for divine guidance. As she knelt there, a voice seemed to whisper the age-old proverb *amor vincit omnia*: love conquers all. With all her money gone, she threw herself on the mercy of the British Consulate, which subsidized her passage back to Britain, and Freddie.

Throughout all these rootless years, Charlie Lennon, Freddie's younger brother, had never wavered as his ally and defender. As an eyewitness of Julia's misadventures—he had helped track down the Welsh artilleryman who made her pregnant—Charlie was outraged by the press stories about Freddie's alleged desertion of her and six-year-old John. The last straw was reading of Freddie's visit to Kenwood in 1966, which had ended with John slamming the door in his face. Charlie therefore sat down and wrote a long letter to the nephew he had not seen in more than twenty years, and who probably would not even recognize him now if they were to meet. In it he explained that Freddie's "desertion" had simply been that of a merchant sailor in wartime (which it had, even if magnified by bad judgment and accident-proneness) and that Julia had been the one to stray, first with the Welsh gunner, Taffy Williams, then with Bobby Dykins.

Amazingly enough, Charlie's letter found its way to John, and was couched in terms convincing enough to make him question the version of events his Aunt Mimi had drummed into him since toddlerhood. Soon afterward, Brian Epstein died and, with atypical good timing, Freddie himself sent John a short, sincere note of sympathy. The result was the half-embarrassed, half-hopeful letter addressed to "Dear Dad, Alf, Fred, Pater, whatever . . ."

About a month later, Freddie received written instructions from Brian Epstein's office to be outside the Post Office in Kingston-on-Thames at a certain date and time. There he was met by John's chauffeur, Les Anthony, who handed him an envelope full of money, then put him into the back of the psychedelic Rolls and drove him to Kenwood.

John did not return home from the recording studio until late that night, but from the outset it was clear that his attitude to Freddie had totally changed. He enfolded him in one of the hugs that now came so easily, calling him Dad rather than Alf, Fred, Pater, or "whatever," and saying they must both put the past behind them. Furthermore, in his abrupt way, he had decided this newly dubbed Dad must join the family circle forthwith. A gobsmacked Freddie was told he would spend that night in the guest room, then tomorrow the Rolls would collect his possessions from the Greyhound, and he would move in permanently.

So Freddie took up residence at Kenwood, occupying the former servants' flat at the top of the house, where John and Cynthia had camped out during its overlong refurbishment. If he had thought that living with John meant spending more time with John, however, he was soon disillusioned. For the most part, he found himself playing his new role of paterfamilias to an audience comprising only Cyn and his grandson, Julian—who, it transpired, had rather liked his ill-fated single, "That's My Life." Father and son did manage one heart-to-heart, in which Freddie reiterated that he had not wanted to walk out of John's life that day in 1946, and at long last felt himself believed. He felt secure enough even to chide John for having accepted an MBE, which, to an old Liverpool leftie like himself, signified kowtowing unforgivably to the Establishment.

Cushy as his new billet was, Freddie found himself missing the bustle, variety and, above all, companionship of bar and kitchen work. With Julian at school and Cynthia pursuing an increasingly independent social life, he found himself alone for long periods— to such a gregarious, exhibitionistic soul, a refined form of torture. Les, the chauffeur, and Dot Jarlett, the housekeeper, both regarded him with unconcealed disdain. He could not drive and didn't like to ask Les or Dot to run him anywhere in one of the expensive cars on hand. When he tried walking to the nearest pub, a mile away, he got lost among the estate's private roads and driveways, and attracted suspicious stares from John's neighbors. As he would later recall, it began to feel as if John were keeping him shut away "like a mad relative in the attic."

An unlikely ally materialized in Cynthia's mother, Lilian Powell, who had remained a regular visitor to Kenwood despite John's pointed provision of quarters for her elsewhere. Finding Freddie moping dejectedly around the house one day, Mrs. Powell declared in her forthright way that he looked "like a hen in a coop," and should ask John to set him up in a place of his own where he could enjoy some independence. John proved amenable, and Freddie was provided with a flat in nearby Kew, plus a television set, some sheets and blankets, and £10 per week, paid via the Beatles' accountants and calculated as the equivalent of his earnings as a kitchen porter. Only after leaving Kenwood and moving into his new home did he hear from a third party that John had been upset by his decision to leave.

The revelation that Freddie had a nineteen-year-old girlfriend, whom he was apparently set on marrying, caused John none of the shock and furious disapproval it was creating elsewhere. On the contrary, he was hugely tickled by his father's late-flowering romance and intrigued that it seemed as much a surprise to Freddie as everyone else. Since returning from Paris, Pauline Jones was back living with her mother, under strict orders to stay away from Freddie but sneaking off to him whenever she could. Curious to meet someone who could fall for a penniless, fifty-four-year-old washer-up, John invited her to spend a weekend at Kenwood, offering her the attic quarters just vacated by Freddie.

For most nineteen-year-olds in this era, staying at John Lennon's house would have been a prize beyond the dreams of *Boyfriend* or *Mirabelle* magazine. Pauline, however, was resolutely unawed. Her chief impression of John was his "atrocious" table manners, though on the plus side, he seemed to accept the validity of her feelings for his father and to see no reason why they should not marry if that was what they both truly wanted. Pauline's grown-up air so impressed Cynthia that during the weekend she offered her a job as nanny to five-year-old Julian. John was initially dubious, but warmed to the idea when Cyn pointed out that they also needed someone to deal with the incessant telephone calls and the piles of fan mail that silted up the house. So, while Freddie remained in his new quarters at Kew, Pauline took over Kenwood's servants' flat.

One of Brian's last executive acts had been to sanction an authorized biography of the Beatles. Such things already abounded for the teenage fan market, but Brian, typically, had put together something much classier: a "real" book to be written by the *Sunday Times* journalist Hunter Davies and published in hardcover by the prestigious house of William Heinemann. Davies received generous access to each Beatle and interviewed their respective families, in return for paying them a third of his royalties and allowing his manuscript to be vetted by all four before publication.

In John's case, "family" now not only meant his Aunt Mimi but also a newly emancipated dad. Hunter Davies therefore talked at length to Freddie, who willingly provided a colorful account of his education at Liverpool Bluecoat Hospital, his courtship of Julia, his adventures and misadventures at sea, and the circumstances behind his sudden exit from John's life. According to Pauline, John was anxious that the story should be published in its full and correct form. "No question that he wanted Hunter to portray the truth about his parents—after all, he had just learned via Charlie what really happened—and this had been corroborated and further explained by Freddie, and I truly believe he wanted to do his father justice."

In 1967, the Beatles knew nothing—literally nothing—about the vast business they had created and continued to generate. Brian had always taken care of everything, periodically bringing them contracts or agreements, which they always signed without question, often without even reading. After his death, therefore, extensive detective work was necessary to disentangle the Beatles from his other complex enterprises and construct a full financial graph of their career to date. When this was finally accomplished, it revealed anything but the infallible young tycoon they, and the outside world, had always taken him for. As often as Brian had been astute, he had also been naïve; as well as prescient, he could be shortsighted; among the breathtaking deals he had done for his boys were others of almost laughable inadequacy.

Their two globally successful feature films, for example, had earned them only a pittance in comparison with the makers and distributors, and the rights for both had somehow ended up with the producer, Walter Shenson. Even worse was the maladministration of the merchandising opportunity—for Beatle wigs, toy guitars, bubblegum, and such—which, after their American conquest, had been virtually limitless. Not foreseeing the market potential, Brian handed over responsibility for granting merchandise licenses in the United States to a group of young British opportunists on a 90–10 percent split in their favor. Then, realizing his error, he began a lawsuit against his British partners, creating such confusion among the manufacturers involved that orders worth millions of dollars were canceled. As a result, the biggest marketing bonanza since Walt Disney created Mickey Mouse had dwindled to dribs and drabs, and a present and future fortune beyond computation was lost.

For some time before Brian's death, the Beatles had been discussing how to extend the creative control they enjoyed over their music output into the ancillary spheres, like films, publishing, and fashion, which earned such colossal sums off their name. John coined a bitter phrase, "the men in suits" for what he saw as the dull-spirited, dully clad oldsters ruling over those areas (though, in truth, it was besuited older men like George Martin and Dick James, not to mention Brian himself, who had given him his unprecedented degree of artistic freedom and also refrained from ripping him off in a thousand and one possible, permissible ways).

With Brian's full support, a first step toward greater autonomy had been taken before the release of *Sgt. Pepper's Lonely Hearts Club Band*. A Victorian house had been acquired in Baker Street, central London, and a small music publishing company established there, to be run by Terry Doran, "the man from the motor trade." As it chanced, the art dealer Robert Fraser had lately supplied Paul McCartney with René Magritte's painting of a green apple, entitled *Le Jeu de Mourre* (*The Guessing Game*). This image perfectly expressing the freshness and simplicity of the Beatles' corporate intentions (as well as coincidentally recalling John's first encounter with Yoko), the company was named Apple Publishing.

One of Brian's more mysterious failings, given all the high-powered accountants on his payroll, was in the area of investments and tax efficiency. Since the Beatles began making big money, there had been almost no systematic attempt to mitigate the Labour government's punitive income tax rates, either by channeling their earnings into offshore accounts or investing in business or property within the United Kingdom. The one serious attempt to go offshore (which explained why *Help!* was partially shot in the Bahamas) had ended by leaving them in a worse tax hole than before. Brian's view seems to have been that, as national treasures, it ill behooved them to spirit money abroad or otherwise try to sidestep their 90 percent–plus tax bracket.

Whatever Brian's fiscal miscalculations, they also learned that he'd left them more cash-rich than ever before in their career. In April 1967, the replacement of their original company, Beatles Ltd., by a partnership called Beatles & Co. allowed them to sell themselves to themselves for a capital gain of around £200,000 apiece.

Also, EMI had been holding some £2 million in back royalties, which were paid only after the signing of the new recording contract in January. During Brian's last months, they conceived one scheme to buy a Greek island and found a tax-exiled hippie commune there, then planned another to invest in property at home by owning their own private village of thatched cottages around a traditional green.

With no new manager yet remotely in sight, the investment of their capital now had to be decided by the four themselves. "Our accountants came up and said, 'We've got this amount of money. Do you want to give it to the Government or do something with it?'" John would recall." So we decided to play businessmen for a bit . . . we really didn't want to go into fucking business but the thing was 'If we have to go in, let's go into something we like.'"

Clive Epstein suggested that, harking back to Brian's first success in management, they should open a chain of record shops. But this excellent idea seemed too stodgy and predictable and, moreover, would put them in the anomalous position of selling their rivals' products. With millions of young Britons, female as well as male, now trying to look like Beatles, the most obvious option was clothes and lifestyle retailing. John had vague notions of a kind of alternative Marks and Spencer, gratefully recalling the inexpensive V-necked sweaters, in black or charcoal lamb's wool, which used to bulk out his beatnik wardrobe in the late fifties. Paul, more upscale as usual, favored a version of Terence Conran's Habitat shops with the difference that everything on sale would be white.

In the end, it was decided to start with a single boutique, selling predominantly female fashions and accessories and modeled on Barbara Hulanicki's hugely successful Biba shop in Kensington. Fortuitously on hand were the Anglo-Dutch design group collectively known as the Fool, who had designed and made extravagant hippie raiment for the Beatles, their womenfolk, and close friends, and also decorated John's upright piano and the gypsy caravan in his garden. Without further ado, the Fool received £100,000 (more than £1 million in today's values) to create a boutique located under the publishing company in Baker Street—and likewise named Apple. John's electronics guru, Magic Alex Mardas (lately their guide in acquiring

offshore Greek real estate) was hired to design and install the lighting, while John's old school crony Pete Shotton, who had previously
been running a small supermarket in suburban Hampshire, became
shop manager.

High on the independence agenda was the making of a film: not
another slick United Artists production in which the Beatles felt
"like extras," but one giving them the same total control they enjoyed on record—and hence the same power to make masterpieces.
What was more, they had a subject ready and waiting. Its origin was
an outtake from the *Sgt. Pepper* sessions, written by Paul in the same
homely, nostalgic spirit as "When I'm Sixty-four." A feature of both
his and John's fifties childhood was the holiday "mystery tour" by
bus, setting out from Liverpool with a blank destination board and
an air of great secrecy and anticipation, though invariably ending
up at some familiar locale like Prestatyn or Blackpool. A Magical
Mystery Tour was to have been among *Sgt. Pepper*'s attractions, its
passengers summoned on board by John, enunciating his *r*'s like a
Scouse Edith Piaf: "Rroll up! Rroll up for the Mysterrry Tour! . . ."
However, once the track was recorded, it sounded too close to the
album's existing overture, so it was set aside.

Subsequently, Paul came across the story of the Merry Pranksters,
a troupe of American hippie entertainers and exhibitionists, led by
the novelist Ken Kesey, who in 1964 had updated mystery tours for
the oncoming flower-power generation. Aboard a Day-Glo-painted
school bus, the Pranksters traveled across America, filming their
own epic consumption of still-legal LSD, which they would administer in Kool-Aid to unsuspecting victims. Their journey was already
an underground legend and would soon reach the mainstream in
Tom Wolfe's book *The Electric Kool-Aid Acid Test*. For the Beatles'
first independent film project, Paul proposed a British version of the
Merry Pranksters' journey, using the Magical Mystery Tour concept
that had failed to make it onto *Sgt. Pepper*. Financing it, as they could,
with no outside help, they would not merely star in the film but also
write, produce, cast, and direct it.

Only one person had ever been able to organize John, and it was
still difficult to believe he was no longer around. "I still felt every
now and then that Brian would come in and say, 'It's time to record'

or 'Time to do this.' And Paul started doing that . . . 'Now we're going to make a movie. Now we're going to make a record.' And he assumed that if he didn't call us, nobody would ever make a record. Paul would say, well, now he felt like it—and suddenly I'd have to whip out twenty songs."

Whatever his private feelings, however, John offered no objection to the *Magical Mystery Tour* project, accepting, with a touch of almost royal noblesse oblige, that the Beatles "had a duty to the public to do these things." Though it would go down in history as Paul's pet project—and mostly Paul's fault—John seems to have played an equal part in such planning as was done.

The formula seemed straightforward enough—simply charter a luxury coach, repaint it in psychedelic colors, hire a film crew, recruit a cargo of prankish cotravelers, then just take off into the Summer of Love's golden afterglow. Professional actors were employed to portray a tour courier and his curvaceous assistant; the thirty-five-odd remaining passengers were a kind of living *Sgt. Pepper* collage, selected to evoke old-fashioned music hall schmaltz mixed with seaside-postcard vulgarity. They included the eccentric Glasgwegian songwriter-poet Ivor Cutler, the rubber-limbed comedian Nat Jackley, a childhood favorite of John's, and, equally Lennonesque, a "fat lady" and a midget. More up-to-date humor and eccentricity were represented by the Bonzo Dog Doodah Band. Paul was a huge fan of the Bonzos' musical parodies and invited their three leading lights, Viv Stanshall, Neil Innes, and "Legs" Larry Smith to join the company, despite surprising resistance from John. (In recognition of this, Stanshall was to spend much of the trip in a T-shirt inscribed LUMP IT, JOHN.) The coach left London on September 11, setting a course for the westerly counties of Devon, Somerset, and Cornwall, which are considered Britain's most "magical" region, with their ancient burial mounds, chalk figures etched on downland, and legends of King Arthur's Camelot.

Filmmaking of any kind requires extensive forethought and extreme precision; in general, the more spontaneous the style, the greater the planning and organization behind it. But the *Magical Mystery Tour* was achingly devoid of either. No locations had been reconnoitered in advance, no permits and clearances had been obtained from nervous local authorities, nothing was explained to the cast, and there was no script. Throughout the bus's four-day odyssey, it was followed by a convoy of media vehicles sometimes stretching back almost a mile. Police forces turned out in strength to hold back the roadside crowds and deal with the unremitting traffic chaos. An emblematic scene (one of many cut from the finished film) showed the coach stuck halfway across a narrow bridge, hemmed in by vehicles in front and behind, and an infuriated John jumping out and tearing the Magical Mystery Tour placards off its sides.

While developing their dual role as movie magnates and shop owners, the Beatles saw no anomaly in discussing their conversion to transcendental meditation and commitment to spreading a gospel founded on the unimportance of worldly things. For John, especially, meditation seemed as much a wonder cure as Bile Beans or Ovaltine in the newspaper advertisements of his childhood: "You feel more energetic, you know, just simply for doing work or anything. You come out of it and it's 'Who-o-oaah, let's get going!' "

He took just as seriously the duty now imposed on him to spread the Maharishi's teaching in places where no TV lights or cameras would be waiting, to convert others as he himself had been converted, and advertise transcendental meditation as a complete antidote and alternative to drugs. "We'll ask for money from anyone we know with money," he promised. "Anyone that's interested in the so-called establishment—who's worried about kids going wild and drugs and that." To the media, the most interesting obligation for him and the other three was contributing a week's wages, which clearly would add many thousands of pounds to the Maharishi's coffers. John replied that it was no more than fair for them to give what other disciples did, that only a single joining fee was levied and that this lack of discrimination between rich and poor "[is] the fairest thing I've ever heard of."

On September 29, just back from the Magical Mystery Tour, he and George together submitted to gentle probing about their conversion on David Frost's ITV chat show. Despite the earnest matters under discussion, John remained his familiar droll, artless self—a knack that eluded George and, alas, always would. At one point, George explained to Frost that some spiritual leaders, like Buddha and Krishna, are born divine, while others manifest divinity later in life. "So Maharishi's one of them," John chipped in. "He was born quite ordinary, but he's working on it."

For most journalists, the Maharishi was irrevocably cast as a pint-size Rasputin, casting his unhealthy spell over four gullible modern czarinas. And concern for those once-uncomplicated moptops reached the highest levels. Not long after the Frost interview, the Queen held a levee at Buckingham Palace for the chivalric Order of Knights Bachelor, whose members included Sir Joseph Lockwood, chairman of EMI. As she shook Lockwood's hand, Her Majesty commented, "The Beatles are turning awfully funny, aren't they?"

October finally saw the release of *How I Won the War*, John's debut as a serious screen actor. The film was marketed largely on his name and attracted an initial surge of his music fans, though this rather tailed off as word got around that he neither sang nor played guitar in it. After the London premiere, Cilla Black hospitably gave a party for John and his costars, plus an assortment of mutual music-business friends, at her flat in Portland Place. As Cynthia had attended the premiere, John had no choice but to bring her on to the party. During the evening, Cilla was approached by a fellow hit-parader, Georgie Fame, with an embarrassed look on his face. "Did you know," he said, "that Cynthia Lennon is hiding in your wardrobe?"

"I went upstairs," Cilla recalls, "and sure enough there inside my wardrobe was Cynthia. When I asked what she was doing, she said, 'I'm waiting to see how long it is before John misses me and comes looking for me.'" Though unaware of the developing crisis in their marriage, Cilla knew John well enough to realize what a mistake this was. "I told Cyn, 'You'd better face it, kid—he's never gonna come.'"

Yoko Ono, meanwhile, popped up intermittently in the British press with art projects that seemed quintessential examples of Swinging Sixties wackiness. One was a short black-and-white film, directed by her husband, Tony Cox, officially entitled *Number 4*, but known forevermore as *Bottoms*. In it, consecutive pairs of nude buttocks, female and male, in tight close-up, undulated rhythmically as their owners walked on a treadmill and discoursed in voice-over about the experience (an extremely rare one for Britons then) of publicly baring one's behind. Another work, first attempted in late 1966 but not accomplished to Yoko's satisfaction until almost a year later, was a performance art event called *Wrapping Piece*, using as props the massive stone lions that recline on plinths at the foot of Nelson's Column in Trafalgar Square. These sacred Victorian monuments now found themselves enveloped by her in billowing white canvas—the first British national treasure, as it were, to go into the bag.

Her relationship with Cox had by now broken down beyond repair, though the two remained professionally interdependent and their five-year-old daughter kept them theoretically together. Kyoko was an enchantingly pretty child, if somewhat resigned to her parents' erratic lifestyle and stormy relationship, and a sense that she was already more grown-up than either of them. As she recalls now, her only glimpses of normal family life came through the friends and neighbors in whose care she was often left. "I had no experience of the popular culture other girls of my age were exposed to." Some friends of Cox's with whom she often stayed in Brighton took her to the cinema one day, to see *The Sound of Music*. The film's visions of childhood so transfixed Kyoko that she made them take her back to see it six times more.

While shooting the *Bottoms* film, Yoko was interviewed by Hunter Davies, the Beatles' authorized biographer. It made a perfect item for Davies's tongue-in-cheek *Atticus* column in the *Sunday Times*—a weird Japanese woman seeking to elevate the fundamental feature of British low humor into high art. The headline was "Oh No, Ono," and an accompanying photograph brought out all the contrast between Yoko's funeral-black clothes and unsmiling face and the earthy eroticism of her subject matter.

Yoko knew about the Beatles, of course, but, fixated on her own art as she was, took no interest in their music and had no idea of John's creative powers. To her at the outset, he was just "an attractive guy" whose vast celebrity came from a world alien to her and who, ethnically, culturally, temperamentally, above all aesthetically, seemed her total opposite. Then one day in a London bookshop she was checking the O section for her poetry collection, *Grapefruit*, and in the adjacent L section found *John Lennon: In His Own Write* and *A Spaniard in the Works*. Flipping through the pages, she noticed a random sentence, "I sat belonely" and then a picture of an ugly woman whose naked body was covered with flies. As it happened, a similar image haunted Yoko's mind as a possible film idea. "The book showed me John's soul," she would later write. "A witty, funny and relentlessly romantic spirit with a taste for the grotesque."

In John's case, the revelation had come much sooner. From his earliest adolescence, an equivalent fantasy to sex-kitten Brigitte Bardot had been "a woman who would be a beautiful, intelligent, dark-haired, high-cheekboned artist." Originally his ideal had been the deep-voiced, guitar-playing Juliette Greco, reputed descendant of the painter El Greco; then, on a Beatles-tour stopover in India, the vision changed to that of "a dark-eyed Oriental."

Most fascinatingly of all, Yoko was a "real" artist, the first with whom John had had any serious dealings since Stu Sutcliffe's death. In her tiny frame were all the audacity and imperviousness to criticism and mockery that Stu had possessed—and that he himself so much longed to. He would later describe her as "the only woman I'd ever met who was my equal in every way imaginable. My better actually. Although I'd had numerous interesting affairs in my previous incarnation, I'd never met anyone worth breaking up a happily married state of boredom for. Escape, at last! Someone to leave home for. Somewhere to go. I'd waited an eternity. Since I was extraordinarily shy (especially around beautiful women) my daydreams necessitated that she be aggressive enough to save me i.e., 'take me away from all this.'"

In that time before cell phones, e-mails, texting, and faxes, the only way they could surreptitiously keep in touch was by mail. When Yoko organized a thirteen-day dance festival that was to take place entirely "in the mind," she sent John the same enigmatic instructions that its other participants received. "Cards kept coming through the door, saying 'Breathe' or 'Dance' or 'Watch the lights until dawn,'" he remembered, "and they'd upset me or make me happy, depending how I felt."

One morning, Yoko awoke at her flat in Hanover Gate Mansions to find that Cox had not returned home the previous night. The melancholy sight of their half-slept-in double bed inspired her to create what would later become known as an installation—an entire room consisting of half a bed, half a table, half a chair, half a cup, half a saucer, etc. This went on display at the tiny Lisson Gallery in North London on October 11, entitled *The Half a Wind Show*. John provided financial backing for the project, although Yoko, atypically, was at first reluctant to seek his sponsorship. "I realised he was a sensitive artist," she says. "I felt bad about hitting on him for money, so I said 'Why don't you put something in, too?'" John suggested adding bottles in which the missing other halves of the exhibits were allegedly corked up. "I thought that was great," Yoko says. "That's when I knew we were totally on the same wavelength."

His name was to have appeared on the poster alongside hers, but at the last minute he was overcome by fears of the gossip and press speculation this might unleash. Instead, in tune with the theme of missing other halves, the show was credited to "Yoko and Me." To prevent the slightest whisper reaching his official other half, John did not even view it in situ.

Soon afterward, he finally plucked up courage to take their relationship to a different level. But the clumsy way he did so almost ended it for good. As Yoko recalls, she was invited to Abbey Road Studios during a Beatles recording session—at this point, a disinterested onlooker in the space reserved for privileged guests. When John joined her, he remarked that she looked tired and asked if she'd like to "lie down." One of the Beatles' entourage then drove the two of them to a nearby flat and, without preamble, began folding out a sofa into a bed. It was clearly established procedure for John's conquests, and the fastidious Yoko was deeply offended. "Maybe he thought we were two adults, we didn't have to pretend. But it seemed so crude; I rejected it. Probably I was a snob—something I got from my upbringing. The minute a guy came on to me in a way I didn't like, I would just shut the door on him."

A few days later, she was invited to show her *Bottoms* film at an arts festival in Knokke-le-Zoute, Belgium. Thinking she had blown the relationship with John, she decided to go without even mentioning it to him. After the Knokke festival, she traveled to Paris to explore possibilities of showing her work there. "I thought I would never go back to London."

There was still room in John's mind for other new commitments and partnerships. That autumn, still unaware that Yoko had left Britain, he began working with the actor Victor Spinetti on a stage adaptation of *John Lennon: In His Own Write*. An ebullient Welsh-Italian, Spinetti had contributed a memorable cameo to *A Hard Day's Night*, as the paranoid TV producer, and was popular with all the Beatles for his abounding energy and good humor. "Don't waste it on Vic," John would tell anyone who offered Spinetti a joint. "He's permanently stoned on fuckin' life."

With Vic, John made none of the homophobic cracks he used to with poor Brian; on the contrary, he seemed to find the actor's cozy campness reassuring and, when introduced to Spinetti's partner, Graham, was charm personified. "He knew all the grace-notes," recalls Spinetti in an echo of Derek Taylor. "When he met Graham, he was wearing dark glasses. Graham said, 'I bet you've got the most beautiful eyes, but it's impossible to see them under those fucking glasses.' John carefully took them off, then leaned forward and kissed him on the forehead."

John had offered Spinetti the role of courier on the Magical Mystery Tour bus, candidly admitting over the telephone that "there's no fookin' script." Spinetti had prior work commitments when the journey was to take place, but agreed to film a separate vignette as a nonsense-spouting army sergeant major, a character he'd originally played in Joan Littlewood's *Oh, What a Lovely War!* "PS, got any uppers?' were John's parting words on the phone.

Shortly afterward, Spinetti received another, more surprising Lennon-related call. It was from Kenneth Tynan, formerly the *Observer*'s brilliant drama critic, the first man ever to say the word *fuck* on British television, and now dramaturge, or literary manager, for the newly constituted National Theatre. The National planned to stage an adaptation of *John Lennon: In His Own Write* at its then home, the Old Vic theatre in Waterloo Road. Would Spinetti care to direct it?

The adaptation was by a respected black American dramatist, Adrienne Kennedy, and had initially been intended for Glasgow's Citizens

Theatre. When problems developed there, Tynan had snapped the
play up for the adventurous, often controversial program that he and
the National's supremo, Laurence Olivier, were developing together.
Olivier, Britain's greatest twentieth-century actor, was enthusiastically behind the project and personally recommended Spinetti as its
director. However, Kennedy's script, drawn from both *In His Own
Write* and *A Spaniard in the Works*, simply turned John's prose-squibs
and poems into dialogue, as had already been done in a limited way
on Peter Cook and Dudley Moore's television show.

Spinetti decided to make it more directly autobiographical—"a
story of personal growth"—and persuaded John to collaborate with
him on writing a new version. They worked mainly at Spinetti's flat
in Manchester Street, just a stone's throw from the soon-to-be Apple
boutique in Baker Street. "John was wonderful to work with," Spinetti says. "He was totally focused, no big-star airs and graces and, oh
my God, so quick. He'd ad-lib something in a second and it would
work beautifully." Feeling a need to go "somewhere warm" as a relief
from chilly, autumnal London, he spirited away his collaborator—
and Cynthia, much to her surprise—for a flying visit to Morocco.

The new treatment centered on a character named Me—the same
half-coy entity as had figured on Yoko's *Half a Wind* poster—who
was discovered in a bedroom just like John's boyhood one at Mendips. Me's life then followed the same early milestones as John's,
from being "bored when I believe the Nasties were still booming us,
led by Madolf Heatlump," through school, cinemagoing, and tedious
church sermons (quoting "St Alf, chapter 8, verse 5.") Along the way
came walk-on appearances by the great detective Shamrock Wol-
mbes, Bobby "who got a birthday hook," and Deaf Ted, Danoota,
and Me. Three years after original publication, there was still no objection to Deaf Ted, "cripples," or lines like "Well, Mr Wabooba . . .
may I call you Wog?"

It was, in fact, a defining moment for British theatre. In a few
months there was to be an end to the age-old official censorship,
wielded by a bizarre Royal functionary called the Lord Chamberlain,
which forbade any overt reference to sex onstage. In preparation for
this great day, the subversive Tynan was assembling a revue to be entitled *Oh! Calcutta!* (a pun on the French *Oh, quel cul tu as*, "Oh, what

an ass you've got") in which every former sexual no-go area was to be visited. At one of Tynan's famously starry parties, John happened to mention the boyhood group masturbation sessions when his schoolmates would stimulate each other by groaning names like "Brigitte Bardot," and he would spoil the mood by calling out "Frank Sinatra!" Tynan instantly proposed he should write it as a sketch for *Oh! Calcutta!* with the provisional title "Liverpool Wank." He even provided a written synopsis of sorts: "You know the idea, four fellows wanking—giving each other images—it should be ad-libbed anyway—they should even really wank, which would be great."

The Lennon-Spinetti script, entitled *Scene Three, Act One*, was accepted by the National Theatre and quickly went into rehearsal with Ronald Pickup as Me, a fifteen-person cast, and a sound tape specially recorded by George Martin at Abbey Road. Its writing credit was shared with Adrienne Kennedy, who had originally developed the project, but when subsequently published (in hardcover) by Jonathan Cape, its overall title was *The Lennon Play*. It received a single Sunday-night performance at the Old Vic early in December, when the reception was so positive that Tynan and Olivier agreed to give it a longer run early the following year.

The hour-long *Magical Mystery Tour* film had meanwhile been snapped up by BBC television and was to receive its world premiere on Boxing Day, December 26, in a prime-time evening slot guaranteeing a viewership rivaled only by the Queen's Christmas Day broadcast. In advance of this presumed triumphant follow-up to *Sgt. Pepper's Lonely Hearts Club Band*, the Beatles threw a fancy-dress ball at London's brand-new Royal Lancaster Hotel. Harking back to the first fancy dress he'd ever worn, John went as a Teddy Boy in velvet-collared drape jacket, drainpipe trousers, and brothel-creeper shoes, his once Beatle-fluffy hair greased and swept back in a duck's arse as it used to be in his teens. Cynthia went as an early Victorian lady in a crinolined ball gown, George Martin as the Duke of Edinburgh in a full-dress admiral's uniform, and Pattie Harrison as an Eastern belly dancer in not very much at all.

The occasion marked John's first public appearance with his father—and also with the nineteen-year-old whom Freddie intended to make his stepmother. Freddie decided to go as a garbage collector, allowing John to incarnate the Lonnie Donegan song "My Old Man's a Dustman." Pauline went as a schoolgirl, in the tunic she'd worn for real only a couple of years previously. The tunic was with some clothes she had left behind at Kenwood and on the eve of the ball she came over from Freddie's rent-free flat in Kew to pick it up. John happened to be at home and, to her surprise, was friendlier than at any time when she had been his employee and boarder. As they chatted in the kitchen, Pauline reiterated that she truly loved Freddie and was determined to marry him. John seemed to have no personal objection but warned of the consequences she and Freddie would have to face: the prurient stares, pointing fingers, and sniggers behind their backs. He could have been describing the very scenario that lay ahead for himself.

For Cynthia, the fancy-dress ball was a night of knuckle-whitening humiliation. John had always made a thing of fancying Pattie Harrison, but tonight her diaphanous Eastern houri's costume caused friendly joshing to harden into something more. He danced with Pattie time after time while Cynthia, in her Quality Street crinolines, sat neglected and miserable. This finally proved too much for her good friend Lulu, who was decked out as the child star Shirley Temple, complete with outsize lollipop. Onlookers were treated to the sight of superstar Teddy Boy receiving a spirited telling-off from ringletted Thirties moppet for being so mean to his wife.

Afterward, John, Cyn, Freddie, and Pauline went on to a club with Lulu and Maurice Gibb, of the Bee Gees, whom Lulu was going out with; then the four were driven home together in the psychedelic Rolls. During the journey, John fell asleep; his head slipped down into Freddie's lap and Freddie began stroking his hair. For a few minutes, it was as if the years, with their cargo of blame and guilt, had rolled away: Steward Alf and his "Little Pal" were once again as close as when they'd run away to Blackpool together, supposedly en route for New Zealand. Then the car stopped in Kew to let Freddie and Pauline out, and the spell was broken, never to be recaptured.

21

THERE'S A GOOD
LITTLE GURU

To tell you the truth, I was hoping he might slip me the Answer.

F ew films have ever received a more universally venomous initial reception than *Magical Mystery Tour.* Certainly it marked a watershed: before it, everything went right for the Beatles, creatively speaking; afterward, almost nothing did. From first to last it could be held up as a textbook example of how not to make a movie. But for modern audiences, who have grown up with pop video and the unstructured comedy style of *Monty Python's Flying Circus,* it is very far from the "blatant rubbish" that one outraged 1967 reviewer called it.

The irony is that it should have been made as an antidote to *Help!* and *A Hard Day's Night,* in which John had felt "like an extra"—for on the Magical Mystery Tour the Beatles are little more than that. The only one with lines to speak on the actual coach trip is Ringo, playing the nephew of the "fat lady," Jessie Robbins. John is spasmodically visible among the other passengers, wearing a high-crowned black hat with two long feathers, which gives him somewhat the look of a Native American medicine man. The Beatles' ensemble dialogue is limited to a studio-filmed sequence in which they appear as long-robed, conical-hatted wizards in a laboratory, looking down on the coach's progress like deities from Olympus in a Ray Harryhausen B movie. John adds the homey touch of a coffee mug to his wizard's outfit and speaks in a tone of surprising campness. He also provides a fragmentary voice-over commentary, a device that lends the story some cohesion and also suggests that, had he lived, his speaking voice might have become as beloved across the English-speaking world as his singing one.

The oddest touch is the inclusion of the Bonzo Dog Doodah Band's three leading lights, Viv Stanshall, Neil Innes, and "Legs" Larry Smith, all giant-size extroverts, hogging limelight that seems to have been ceded to them without a murmur. The only real Lennon moment comes where the ill-matched lovers, Buster and Jessie, go to a restaurant. John is their waiter, with slicked-back hair and a small mustache, looking much as Freddie Lennon must have done in the first-class saloons of prewar cruise ships, as he dumps mounds of spaghetti onto their plates with a shovel. The whole sequence had come to him in a dream—or a nightmare, perhaps—of ladling out flavorless stodge to an indifferent public (never mind turning into his father).

But the film is essentially a vehicle for Beatles music, which certainly reaches *Sgt. Pepper* standard and several times goes a step higher. As a serial pop video, a tour through three rapidly emerging solo talents, it has all the magic which that effortful bus trip somehow missed. There is Paul singing "The Fool on the Hill," an almost "Yesterday"-size future standard, on a Provençal mountainside, all big brown eyes and turned-up overcoat collar. There is George, seated cross-legged in incense-heavy twilight, intoning "Blue Jay Way" as if it is a new mantra from the Maharishi rather than a street in Hollywood. There are the four Beatles in identical white tailcoats descending a curved staircase painstakingly in step—as they would soon cease to be—for another McCartney vaudeville number, "Your Mother Should Know." And, vindicating the whole enterprise on its own, there is John's "I Am the Walrus."

Like "A Day in the Life," this runner-up for the title of his masterpiece came from two unconnected and seemingly unconnectable sources. At Kenwood one day, the distant sound of a police-car siren stoked up his anger over the recent persecutions of good friends like Mick and Keith and the boys at *International Times*. On another occasion, Pete Shotton happened to mention that at their old school, Quarry Bank, senior English students were now made to dissect and analyze the lyrics of "Strawberry Fields Forever" and "Tomorrow Never Knows," just as they themselves once had analyzed the poems of Wordsworth and Shelley.

The result was a string of random images, fulminating against the repressive forces of law and order, with a sideswipe at credulous souls who pored over his words as if they were Holy Writ. By the time he had finished, the lyric was almost a miniature *Oh! Calcutta!* in the number of taboos it sought to shatter. But the habit of role-playing was still a hard one to break. For his first anti-Establishment rant, John therefore chose an alter ego from his favorite poem in Lewis Carroll's *Alice* oeuvre, "The Walrus and the Carpenter." "Later . . . I realised the Walrus was the bad guy in the story and the Carpenter was the good guy," he would remember. "I thought, 'Oh shit, I've picked the wrong guy.' But that wouldn't have been the same, would it: I Am the Carpenter?"

The opening lines ("I am he / As you are he / As you are me . . .") seem so quintessentially Lewis Carroll that one checks the dictionary of quotations to see if they figure alongside "Will you walk a little faster . . . ," "Tweedledum and Tweedledee . . . ," and "You are old, Father William . . ." Carroll is there, too, in the juxtaposition of "policemen" with "pigs" and "flying." (One of the Walrus's philosophical musings is "whether pigs have wings.") A Carroll-saturated childhood is there, too, in the varying riff from "Three Blind Mice" ("see how they run" . . . "see how they fly"); in the memory of 1950s school food and the immemorial playground chant of everything disgusting ("Yellow-matter custard / dripping from a dead dog's eye.") John's own current lifestyle is there, too, drenched in the same contempt as everything else, from "sitting in an English garden" to "singing Hare Krishna" and even "Lucy in the sky": no longer a riverbank goddess but an inciter of urban mayhem.

The forces of censorship are challenged with "stupid bloody Tuesday," "pornographic priestess," and (God save us) "you let your knickers down." The "expert texperts," agog for hidden meaning, get "sitting on a cornflake," "corporation T-shirt," "crabalocker fishwife," "elementary penguin," and "semolina pilchard climbing up the Eiffel Tower," with a recurrent lapse into pure baby-talk ("Goo-goo G'Joob") lest they be in any doubt that "the joker laughs at you." Surprisingly, or perhaps not, the other insistent refrain through this aria of fury and derision is "I'm crying."

George Martin provided a wonderful score of sawing, grinding, bottom-register cellos, like sarcasm made melody, in which further insults, irony, and smut were hidden below the waterline. The Mike Sammes Singers, radio's coziest middle-of-the-road vocal group, were hired for the play-out chorus of "Oompah-oompah, stick it up your jumper!" and "Everybody's got one!" The multilayered sound effects even included a snatch of Shakespeare's *King Lear* lifted from a BBC Third Programme performance starring Sir John Gielgud (the scene where Oswald is fatally stabbed and cries, "Oh, untimely death!").

It was clearly a song far beyond the powers of any four-piece rock group, so that is how the Beatles perform it in *Magical Mystery Tour*—first in their familiar stage formation, with flower-power shirts and beads replacing round-collar mohair suits; then cavorting in walrus costumes of the crudest pantomime variety. John himself ends up with his head bound in white linen like the denizen of some eighteenth-century Bedlam as his fellow inmates dance the conga behind him, linked together by what looks like an outsize surgical bandage. Pop video would never get wilder or weirder than this.

The Beatles' 1967 Christmas single had Paul's cheerily unverbal "Hello Goodbye" for an A-side with "I Am the Walrus" relegated to the flip. The BBC instantly banned the song from radio play, citing the "knickers" reference from the wide choice available, but still went ahead with prime-time transmission of the film as planned. It had been shot in color, but at this time the overwhelming majority of UK television viewers still received only black and white. The effect was thus of a home movie, with all the self-indulgence as well as ineptitude that implies. Its mistakes seemed to loom larger than CinemaScope while the good things vanished into murky gray haze. During the psychedelic "Clouds" scene, for instance—one of the few well-thought-out and effective blends of magic with the everyday—the nation's screens seemed to go completely blank.

By long tradition, there is no hard news in Britain over the Christmas holiday; the papers therefore fell on *Magical Mystery Tour* like starving wolves, and word of the Beatles' first flop beamed across a surprised and deeply offended world. The accompanying album reflected no such disappointment, however, selling a million copies in America and five hundred thousand in Britain.

As 1968 dawned on this sour, recriminatory note, it was Freddie Lennon's domestic situation rather than his son's that stubbornly continued to hold center stage. Right after Christmas, momentarily dismayed by the prospect of becoming Freddie's wife, not to mention acquiring a Beatle as a stepson, Pauline Jones returned home to her mother and made a conscientious effort to live the life expected of a nineteen-year-old. But her feelings for Freddie proved irresistible. At the end of January, she moved into his flat in Kew and soon afterward became pregnant. To keep this news out of the media as long as possible, John agreed to provide Freddie with new accommodation in a locale unknown to any Fleet Street newshound. He and Pauline were therefore resettled in a one-bedroom flat in Brighton, fifty miles to the south.

Yoko, meanwhile, had more or less decided to continue her career in Paris. Yet she found her thoughts continually turning back to John, his clumsy seduction attempt, and her dismissive response. "I kept thinking, not 'I really fucked up' because I didn't know the word 'fuck,' but 'I really messed up.' Because, always being in the public eye, he couldn't have done it any other way, we couldn't have had a regular date. So I realised I must be falling in love with this guy."

Among the admirers her work attracted in Paris was Ornette

Coleman, the great American saxophonist and exponent of classically influenced "free jazz." It happened that Coleman was about to
visit London to appear at the Royal Albert Hall, and he suggested
that Yoko should join him onstage there. So she returned to London,
resolved not to say no if John asked a second time, however he might
ask it. When she tried to open the front door of her flat at Hanover
Gate Mansions, it was blocked by a deluge of letters on the hall mat.
All of them were from John, who had never realized she was out of
the country. The single postcard she'd sent him had obviously not
penetrated the protective screen. "I said to him later, 'When you
wrote me all those letters, weren't you worried I'd run to a newspaper or something? You're a married man.' He said, 'I used to write
long letters like that to Stu Sutcliffe.' 'Oh,' I thought, 'I'm a replacement for Stu, am I? He was a guy and I'm a woman. . . .' I thought
that was a little bit strange."

In February, the Beatles finally kept their six-month-old promise to
study transcendental meditation under Maharishi Mahesh Yogi at
his ashram in India. The emergence of a new object of worship in
John's life during that time had not dimmed his enthusiasm for the
Maharishi and determination to make the group standard-bearers
for TM. "This is how we plan to use our power now—they've always
called us leaders of youth, and we believe that this is a good way to
give a lead," he said. "The whole world will know what we mean,
and all the people who are worried about youth and drugs and all
that scene—all those people with the short back and sides—they can
all come along and dig it, too."

True to his word, he took everyone he could round up to meet the
Maharishi, including his actor friend and playwriting partner, Victor
Spinetti. To Spinetti's surprise, the "giggling guru" lampooned by
Fleet Street proved insightful, even witty. "A woman in the audience
stood up and asked, 'Tell me, your Highness, how do you teach chil-
dren the process of Transcendental Meditation?' 'My dear lady,' the
Maharishi said, 'They invented it.'"

Since the previous August, many other pop and show-business figures had followed the Beatles into the Maharishi's flock. As a result,

they were to lead a virtual celebrity package-tour out to India, also including the folksinger Donovan, Mike Love of the Beach Boys, and the young American film actress Mia Farrow (fresh from shooting the scary *Rosemary's Baby* with Roman Polanski in a strange old Manhattan apartment building named the Dakota). Since the pilgrimage included wives and girlfriends, John had no choice but to take Cynthia. She had, in fact, embraced the Maharishi's teachings as wholeheartedly as had Pattie Harrison, viewing them as a means to get John off drugs and restore some peace and stability to their marriage. What she did not know was that John had also invited Yoko to join the party under the guise of a celebrity fellow-traveler. Yoko was game enough, and even attended a preliminary briefing in London. But when John raised the idea with the others, he met such resistance that he lost his nerve and had to tell her he'd been unable to swing it.

He, George, and their wives flew to Delhi on February 15, followed by Ringo, Maureen, Paul, and Jane Asher four days later. In their absence, the Beatles' nonmeditative public had been provided with a new single, "Lady Madonna"—an oddly Catholic note to strike at such a moment—written by Paul and borrowing the "See how they run" motif from "I Am the Walrus." But where John had used it to evoke blind-mice panic, Paul was simply referring to a sluttish earth mother's laddered tights.

Rishikesh is situated two hundred miles north of Delhi on the banks of the River Ganges, looking toward the snow-flecked Himalayas. A little apart from the town stood the ashram where the Beatles were scheduled to spend three months. John later remembered it as "a sort of recluse holiday camp. . . . It was like being up a mountain, but it was in the foothills hanging over the Ganges, with baboons stealing your breakfast and everybody flowing round in robes. . . . It was a nice scene. Nice and secure, and everyone was always smiling." Living conditions, though simple, were far from Spartan: the students lived in substantial stone bungalows equipped with hot water and Western plumbing, and the all-vegetarian food—the best kind in any part of India—was appetizing and plentiful. Nor was their guru too insistent that they led lives of absolute purity. In addition to the squads of servants with which India provides every foreign visitor, they were allowed their own personal retinue. Roadie Mal Evans lived with them at the ashram, his main job buying and cooking eggs for Ringo, whose delicate stomach could not stand spicy food. A constant stream of telephone calls and cables kept them in touch with their parallel existence as heads of the ever-growing and diversifying Apple organization. Neil Aspinall flew out and spent a week with them while another trusted aide, Tony Bramwell, was based in Delhi to receive and forward letters from home, the week's music-trade papers (for news of "Lady Madonna"), and any significant new record releases by their rivals. Even "behind the wire," as they soon learned, a handful of two-rupee notes bought extra home comforts, from chocolate bars and camera film to booze and hash.

For all the Beatles, it was an enforced slowdown from the lunatic pace that had not let up since their departure from Liverpool to Hamburg seven years earlier. Day after day, there was literally nothing to do but sit and think. At first, the effect on John was anything but tranquilizing. No matter how he tried to make his mind a blank, ideas for lyrics and chord changes kept scribbling themselves across it. "I couldn't sleep and I was hallucinating like crazy—having dreams where you could smell," he would remember. "The funny thing about the camp was that although it was very beautiful and I was meditating about eight hours a day, I was writing the most miserable songs on earth. In 'Yer Blues,' when I wrote 'I'm so lonely I want to die,' I wasn't kidding. That's how I felt . . . up there, trying to reach God and feeling suicidal."

The songs never stopped coming—some of his very best, so he later thought—but their misery quotient dropped sharply as the gentle, reassuring daily routine and the gorgeous weather of northern India's winter began to take effect. The former hypercritical group leader became content to be just one of a crowd, walking to and from meals and seminars along dappled paths or sitting and strumming guitars with Paul and George in the balmy sunshine. There was even mindspace to think about his fellow students and their own problems in adjusting from the outer to the inner world. Mia Farrow's young sister, Prudence, for example, became so obsessed with meditating that she refused to emerge from her bungalow at all for several days. It was John who eventually coaxed her forth by writing her a song, "Dear Prudence," the most charming of entreaties to come out and play, which he and Paul then sang together under her window.

Amid the droning mantras, orange garlands, and tinkly bells, he remained irrepressibly John. If any long-distance press lens managed to get him in shot, he would obligingly wave, pull a grotesque face, or do a little dance. At his instigation, the four Beatles held a daily contest to see who could meditate longest. Even his reverence for his spiritual teacher could occasionally slip. Leaving the Maharishi's presence one day, he patted his head, like a whiskery domestic pet, and said, "There's a good little guru."

A young Canadian backpacker named Paul Salzman, to his astonishment, became part of the Beatles' circle and was allowed to take color photographs of them, which the press outside the gate would have killed for. These show a white-clad John with several days' growth of beard, invariably looking happy and relaxed. In many he is holding hands with Cynthia, whose Indian clothes and simpler hairstyle give her a new beauty and serenity. To begin with, they shared a bungalow equipped with a four-poster bed, but after a few days, John insisted on moving into separate quarters so that he could better concentrate on his meditation. Even so, Cyn felt convinced their marriage was entering a new phase of companionship and mutual tolerance.

All the time, he was receiving postcards from Yoko, which his guardians now had strict orders not to deflect. They were sent to Tony Bramwell in Delhi, who forwarded them to Rishikesh in plain brown envelopes so that Cynthia would suspect nothing. Often they consisted of a single thought, in Yoko's tiny, arty script: "Watch for me—I'm a cloud in the sky." John's Rishikesh songs in lighter vein included one called "India, India," anomalously written as a calypso, in which he talked of "the girl I left behind me." During a heart-to-heart with Paul Salzman, the young Canadian mentioned having recently been dumped by a long-standing girlfriend. John's response indicated just how intently he was watching for that cloud. "Love can be tough," he said. "But then you get another chance, don't you?"

What kept him in Rishikesh for these eons beyond his normal attention span was not meditation or beauty or peace or the glorious
weather. From the Maharishi, he hoped finally to receive the "secret"
or "answer," that magic key to understanding both the universe and
his own place in it that acid had not provided. It annoyed him that
others among the Maharishi's flock already seemed to have been
granted this revelation, yet refused to share it. Pattie Harrison, for
instance, returned from an early TM meeting to report, "They give
you a word, but I can't tell you. It's a secret." John had been the first
to write, "Say the word and you'll be free." Now everyone seemed to
be conspiring to hide it from him. "What sort of scene is this, if you
keep secrets from your friends?" he asked Pattie, much offended.

Yet time passed, and still the Maharishi uttered only vague, benign
generalities. Finally John decided that if hanging on to his every
word did not produce the spiritual jackpot, then guile would have
to be employed instead. One day, a helicopter landed at the ashram,
lent by one of TM's wealthy Indian supporters to fly the Maharishi
to Delhi for a meeting. The Beatles' party were offered a quick joy-
ride with their guru, which for space reasons must be limited to one
person. John took it, as if by right. "I asked him later, 'Why were you
so keen to get up with the Maharishi?'" Paul would remember. "To
tell you the truth," John said, "I was hoping he might slip me the
Answer."

Ringo abandoned the course after two weeks, unable to stomach the food, and returned to Britain with Maureen amid general
goodwill from the others for having given it a whirl. Paul left with
Jane and Neil Aspinall two weeks later, but intimated he might come
back for more at a later stage. In his place came Magic Alex Mardas,
reportedly with plans for a telecommunications system to beam the
Maharishi's message around the world in the tracks of "All You Need
Is Love."

By the fifth week, John and George still showed no signs of flag-
ging. John sent Ringo a postcard with a message for Dot, the Kenwood housekeeper, to have his videotape machine ready for his
return, but gave no indication this might be sooner than scheduled.
"We've got about two LPs worth of songs now," he wrote Ringo. "So
get yer drums out. . . ."

Despite their elevated spiritual state, the Rishikesh disciples were as prone as any small, self-contained community to rumor and gossip. Besides, under an unwritten but immutable law, the Maharishi's time as a Beatle fad was starting to run out. A story began circulating that, although purportedly a lifelong celibate, he had made sexual overtures to a young woman known to all the celebrity inner circle, a former nurse from California. Although famous Indian holy men would later be exposed as lechers—some on an epic scale—this was the only such accusation ever made against the Maharishi, nor was there ever a scrap of real evidence to support it.

But John's mood had now changed completely: he still had not received the Answer and was becoming increasingly preoccupied by that "cloud in the sky." The obvious gusto with which the Maharishi organized constant photo ops made him feel his "good little guru" was a little too interested in celebrity and money. Those rumors of sexual impropriety were a perfect excuse to cut the visit short, especially when even George showed signs of going off the Maharishi and decided to leave for a trip through southern India.

Without the usual retainers on hand to do their dirty work, the two had no choice but to lead a deputation to the Maharishi's bungalow, where John bluntly announced their decision. "I said, 'We're leaving,'" he remembered. "[The Maharishi] said, 'Why?' [I said], 'Well, if you're so cosmic, you should know why.' Because all his right-hand men were always intimating that he did miracles. . . . He said, 'I don't know why, you must tell me.' And I just kept saying, 'You ought to know.' And he gave me a look like 'I'll kill you, you bastard.'"

When the time came to leave, the Maharishi was seated alone in one of the outdoor arbors where his superstar disciples had so recently clustered so raptly at his feet. He made a last appeal to John to come and sit and talk things over, but received no response. Cynthia was touched by how sad and bewildered he looked, but both John and George feared he might have some sinister retribution up his sleeve. On the five-hour drive to Delhi, John began writing a foul-mouthed lampoon of a song around the word *Maharishi*. George persuaded him to change the title to "Sexy Sadie" and take out the swear words, just to be on the safe side.

But the Maharishi cast no evil spell, nor did he long repine in his arbor. Shortly afterward, he flew to New York, checked into the Plaza Hotel and went on tour with the Beach Boys.

"We made a mistake there," John told the press back in Britain. "We thought [the Maharishi] was something other than he was. But we were looking for it and we probably superimposed it on him. We were waiting for a guru and along he came. But he was creating the same kind of situation . . . which he's giving recipes out to cure." Amazingly, it occurred to none of the international Beatle press corps to pursue the inside story of this speedy disillusionment, or even to coax John into being a little more explicit. So great was the relief that the Beatles had come to their senses, no further questions needed be asked.

George would later regret their behavior, renew relations with the Maharishi, and become one of the TM movement's most faithful mainstays. For John, there was to be no going back, though in time he acknowledged the positive effects of his stay in Rishikesh. "I don't regret anything about meditation. I still believe in it and occasionally use it. India was good for me. . . . I met Yoko just before I went to India and had a lot of time to think things out there. Three months [*sic*] just meditating and thinking, and I came home and fell in love with Yoko and that was the end of it."

Actually, it was not quite that simple. Returning home to Kenwood meant more than he had expected—sharing Cynthia's ecstatic reunion with Julian, seeing the little boy's excitement at the presents they'd brought him, including a set of intricately carved wooden figures from the Maharishi. On the long flight back from Delhi, something had prompted John to give Cynthia a detailed account of all his infidelities down the years—all, anyway, that he could remember. Shaken by the Sears Roebuck–size catalog though Cyn was, she felt comforted that, at least, they seemed to be communicating again. A couple of weekends later, he went on his own to stay with Derek Taylor, who had returned from California to become press officer for the new Apple organization and was temporarily based with his family at a house named Laudate, belonging to Peter Asher, in

Newdigate, Surrey. The sight of the Taylors' large brood stirred up strange, unfamiliar emotions in John: when he came home, he told Cyn they ought to have more children to keep Julian company. She burst into tears and replied that he'd be much better off with someone like Yoko Ono. He still professed incredulity at such an idea.

He was about to fly with Paul to New York to unveil Apple—which now encompassed a record label as well as films, publishing, retail, and electronics—to the American media. Cynthia asked to go with him, remembering their fun time at the Plaza in 1964, but he refused. Instead, it was arranged that she should go on holiday to Greece for two weeks in a group of former ashram students comprising Magic Alex, Jenni Boyd, Donovan, and his manager, a raffish character known only as Gipsy Dave. Having only just welcomed his parents home, Julian was packed off stay with Dot, the housekeeper, yet again. "John was lying on our bed when I left," Cyn would remember. "He was in the almost trance-like state I'd seen many times before, and barely turned his head to say goodbye."

In New York, John faced the American press for the first time since the "bigger than Jesus" furor two years earlier. Paul and he were as effective a double act as ever, explaining how Apple would be the first business aimed at young people to be run by young people and informed by the hippie ideals of love, peace, and sharing, "a kind of Western Communism," as Paul put it. "We're in the happy position of not really needing any more money, so for the first time the bosses aren't in it for the profit. We've already bought all our dreams, so now we want to share that possibility with others."

John was in agreement all the way: "We want to set up a system whereby people who just want to make a film about anything don't have to go down on their knees in somebody's office. The aim . . . isn't really a stack of gold teeth in the bank. We've done that bit. It's more of a trick to see if we can get artistic freedom within a business structure, and to see if we can create nice things and sell them without charging three times our cost." Elsewhere, he likened Apple and all its mold-breaking ideals to an old-fashioned spinning top: "You set it going and hope for the best." The same might have been said of the other, private venture he was about to begin.

When he returned from New York on May 16, Cynthia was still away. To keep him company at Kenwood, he invited Pete Shotton to come to stay for a few days. It was as if he needed the cover of their old "Shennon-Lotton" school partnership for what he was finally daring to do.

Two nights later, after Pete had gone to bed, he screwed up all his courage, telephoned Yoko in London, and asked her to come down right away. The hour was late and the journey a long one, but she kept her resolution not to say no a second time. "John told me he didn't have the car, so I'd have to come in a taxi," she remembers. "He said he'd meet the taxi at the gate and pay it off. Usually, he didn't handle money at all, so I was really impressed that he had the whole thing so carefully worked out."

She arrived at Kenwood sometime around midnight. Now that the moment was finally here, both found themselves overcome by shyness. "I didn't know what to do," John would recall, "so we went upstairs to my studio and I played her all the tapes that I'd made, all this far-out stuff, some comedy stuff, and some electronic music. There were very few people I could play those tapes to. She was suitably impressed, and then she said 'Well, let's make one ourselves,' so we made Two Virgins. It was midnight when we started . . . it was dawn when we finished, and then we made love at dawn. It was very beautiful."

Once the top was spinning, all John's doubts melted way, although Yoko's were to linger a while yet. "This is going to work," she remembers him assuring her. "You're a wonderful creative artist . . . and I'm rich."

For all Cynthia's nervous premonitions, she was totally unprepared for what awaited her on her return from Greece. Arriving back at Kenwood with Magic Alex Mardas and Jenni Boyd, she found the house strangely quiet, with no sign of Julian or Dot the housekeeper. In the rear sun parlor, that former small oasis of family togetherness, John and Yoko were seated on the floor together—wearing identical bathrobes according to Cynthia but "work-clothes" according to Yoko. John showed no signs of guilt or even surprise, merely looking round with a casual "Oh . . . hi." Upstairs, a pair of Japanese slippers stood neatly outside the guest bedroom, although the room showed no signs of occupancy. Cynthia simply turned and fled.

When she nerved herself to return to Kenwood a couple of days later, Yoko had gone, Julian and Dot were back, and John greeted her as though nothing had happened. According to Cynthia, when she brought up the scene in the sunroom he insisted that it meant nothing of importance and it was still her whom he loved. He even made love to her that night, after a physical estrangement now running into years.

In the days that followed, however, he seemed to grow cold and withdrawn once again. There was much going on in his professional life, what with the launch of Apple and the run-up to a new Beatles album. As fearful for her marriage as Cynthia was, a Beatle wife's duty not to create a nuisance or distraction still took precedence. She therefore asked permission to go on holiday again, this time to Pesaro in southern Italy, accompanied by Julian, her mother, and an uncle and aunt. A worldlier soul might have scented danger in the promptness of John's agreement.

Within hours of Cynthia's departure, Yoko had left Tony Cox and Kyoko and moved into Kenwood with John. "We both knew this was it," she remembers. "We were both so excited about discovering each other, we didn't stop to think about anyone else's feelings. We just went ahead, gung-ho; what we had was more precious than anything else."

The creative union that had come before their sexual one now went into instant, multimedia overdrive. The brief time they spent together at Kenwood was largely devoted to making two films celebrating their newfound love. The first, officially titled *Number 5* but known as *Smile*, showed John's face in close-up, smiling, grimacing, and waggling his eyebrows. Taken with a camera that recorded 20,000 frames per second, this animated snapshot could be stretched out to almost indefinite length; Yoko originally intended it to last four hours, but eventually whittled it to fifty-two minutes. The second of these so-different Kenwood home movies was called *Two Virgins*, after the music they had made together in John's studio. Compared with the visuals that music would ultimately inspire, it was an innocently lyrical sequence of faces merging and separating, and hazy silhouettes wrapped in an embrace.

Together with making films in which he was indubitably not "an extra" came John's first essay into sculpture since he'd helped Stu Sutcliffe build a driftwood collage on the beach near Hamburg. Yoko had recently been invited to contribute a work to London's newest experimental gallery, the Arts Lab in Drury Lane. At John's suggestion, and with his collaboration, this became a piece called *Build Around*, a wooden base covered with chunks of broken glass and plastic, to which spectators could add their own contribution. One day when both Paul and Ringo were driving through London with him, John suggested they might like to stop off and see the exhibit. But both turned out to have pressing previous engagements.

Fleet Street took some time to wake to the hottest Beatle-related story since "Bigger than Jesus." On May 22, Apple launched yet another offshoot, a bespoke tailoring business (described Sgt. Pepperishly as "Civil and Military") in Chelsea's King's Road. When John arrived for the press-packed opening party at nearby Club Dell' Aretusa, Yoko was by his side and never left it.

They had, in fact, chosen exactly when and where to unveil their partnership. In three weeks, the prestigious National Sculpture Exhibition was to be held in the precincts of Coventry Cathedral (along with Liverpool, Britain's most famous martyr to wartime bombs). Through her contacts in the art world, Yoko arranged that she and John should contribute something. John proposed that it should be two acorns, which they would then ceremonially bury, one facing to the west, the other to the east, to symbolize their meeting and the merging of their two cultures. The exhibition organizers naturally jumped at the chance of John Lennon's participation but were less keen to include something called *Acorn Event* in the catalog, so instead the pair produced their own. To describe their piece, John simply wrote, "This is what happens when two clouds meet," a sentiment that so impressed Yoko that for her own entry she merely repeated it. He also ordered a white wrought-iron garden seat to mark the site of the acorns, and a silver plaque inscribed JOHN BY YOKO ONO, YOKO BY JOHN LENNON, SOMETIME IN MAY 1968.

The *Acorn Event* was to take place on the exhibition's preview day, June 15. Early that morning, John and Yoko set off for Coventry in the psychedelic Rolls with Les Anthony at the wheel and a trailer bearing the garden seat hitched on behind. On reaching the cathedral, they received a first taste of the disapproval and hostility that lay ahead. An officious cleric told them their acorns could not be buried on the exhibition site because it was consecrated ground. Straying from his ecumenical brief, the cleric added that, in any case, acorns were "not sculpture." An irate Yoko then gave the names of several prominent British sculptors, insisting that any one, if contacted, would vouch for her standing in the art world. A phone call was actually made to Sir Henry Moore, but he was not at home.

Eventually, a compromise was reached: John and Yoko could bury the two pots containing their acorns in unconsecrated ground a little distance away, and mark the spot with the garden seat and silver plaque. Within a couple of days, the acorns had been dug up and carried off by Beatle souvenir hounds. A fresh pair were interred by proxy and a round-the-clock security guard was mounted over them.

Possibly because of its esoteric nature, the *Acorn Event* attracted comparatively little press coverage. But when John's stage play returned to the National Theatre three nights later (no longer entitled *Scene Three Act One* but *John Lennon: In His Own Write*) the wolf pack was out in force.

Strictly speaking, only a third of the evening belonged to John. The dramatization of his two books evolved by Adrienne Kennedy, Victor Spinetti, and him ran less than an hour, not nearly long enough in 1968 (though it would be today) for a stand-alone commercial production. The National's director, Lord Olivier, therefore decreed it should be bolstered by two other short plays from earlier centuries, both of which, in a nod to Spinetti, would also be directed by an actor. The first of these makeweight minidramas was *The Covent Garden Tragedy* by Henry Fielding, noteworthy only for the truism "Enough is equal to a feast." The second—its title prophesying headlines soon to come—was John Maddison Morton's nineteenth-century comic interlude, *A Most Unwarrantable Intrusion.*

Also, for the first time ever, John's words had been subjected to a blue pencil. In one of the dying gasps of theatrical censorship, a parody Queen's speech he had written specially for the play was ordered to be cut. (It would be reinstated later in the year, after censorship ended.) Spinetti wondered how this might affect John's view of their collaboration, but he should not have worried. On the morning of the premiere, a gift arrived at the flat where they had worked so many nights together. It was a huge rubber elephant with a label I'LL NEVER FORGET VICTOR SPINETTI SAYS JOHN LENNON.

For all the National Theatre's tripartite billing, no one imagined it was Henry Fielding or John Maddison Morton who brought crowds and massed photographers to the Old Vic theater that rainy night of June 18, 1968. John and Yoko sat in the front row of the dress circle in matching white outfits, flanked by the other Beatles and their usual consorts. Mixed with laughter and applause for the production came heckling cries of "Where's your wife?" and "Where's Cynthia?" To limit such awkward moments, the after-show celebration was low-key. "There was no party," Spinetti remembers. "We all just went round the corner to a pub."

Next morning, every front page in Britain trumpeted the month-old fact that John Lennon had left his wife and begun an affair with Yoko Ono. The unanimous public response was blank incomprehension. Despite recent travails, John still lived a life that was the envy of millions. He could have anything in creation that he wanted. With such clothes and cars and mansions and beautiful dolly birds at his disposal, what could he possibly want with a fiercely unglamorous-looking Japanese woman from the art world's lunatic fringe?

Cynthia was still on holiday in Pesaro, unaware of all these developments. It also happened that, for the first time in ten years' unbroken dedication to John, she was enjoying the company of another man. This was an Italian named Roberto Bassanini, two years her junior, whose parents owned the hotel where she was staying. According to Cynthia, it was no holiday romance—she was there with Julian; her mother, Lilian; and two other relatives. Bassanani simply supplied the kindness and attentiveness that had so long been lacking at home. One evening, on her return from a family outing with Bassanini, she found Magic Alex Mardas awaiting her at the hotel. As she would recall: "[Alex] said, 'I've come with a message from John.

He is going to divorce you, take Julian away from you and send you back to Hoylake.' "

Mardas could not, or would not, add any explanation to this shockingly bald statement. Cynthia began preparations to return home immediately but—no doubt partly a result of her traumatized state—was stricken by laryngitis and a high fever and pronounced unable to travel. It was while still confined to bed in Pesaro that she finally read English newspaper reports of John's "new love."

Once bitten, twice shy, Cynthia did not return to Kenwood with Julian, but instead sought refuge with her mother, who by now was living in central London in a flat owned by Ringo Starr. She at once tried to contact John via the Beatles office, but met the same defensive shield that any ordinary female supplicant would have. Eventually she was notified that John intended to sue for divorce on the grounds of her adultery with Roberto Bassanini. Again she begged Peter Brown, the Beatle aide most like Brian Epstein, to persuade John to talk to her face-to-face. Civilized, sympathetic Brown tried his best, but had to admit failure. Eventually a message came that John and Yoko had left Kenwood, so Cynthia could make use of it, if she chose, pending divorce negotiations. Having nowhere else to go and only £1,000 in the bank, she accepted this offer, taking her mother with her. The house was still just as she had last seen it, with all John's myriad possessions, and even his books, in their usual place.

A week or so later, he finally agreed to a meeting with Cynthia at Kenwood. Even for this most agonizingly private of encounters, he and Yoko turned up together, clad in the matching allover black that had already become their trademark. Cynthia was supported by her staunch ally—and John's old adversary—her mother. In vain she protested that she was not and had never been involved with Roberto Bassanini; John merely switched tack and accused her of fancying a young American actor who had been among the meditators at Rishikesh and to whom she'd barely even spoken. When Cyn still failed to scream at him, Lilian Powell weighed in, giving full vent to the anger and contempt she had felt on her daughter's behalf for so long. Les Anthony, waiting by the Rolls outside, remembers "all hell breaking loose."

Cynthia remained at Kenwood throughout the summer, in a limbo of grief and foreboding that only a cast-off wife of Henry VIII could have understood. Dot, the housekeeper, was still there; Les Anthony still for drove her, as well as John. Otherwise, she felt she had been amputated from his life "like a gangrenous limb." Not long after his final visit, a photograph was taken of Cynthia sitting on the patio, with Julian's head in her lap. The little boy smiles for the camera, the way little boys always must. But, as with every child whose parents break up—as with John two decades earlier—his childhood has been stolen.

Out of loyalty to John (or fear of him, Cynthia believed), George and Ringo both kept their distance; so, more woundingly, did the two other Beatle wives, Pattie and Maureen, whom she had always regarded as friends. But one day she received a surprise visit from Paul McCartney, alone and bearing a single red rose. As Yoko confirms, Paul had been among the first people John told officially that he and she were now together. "We stopped the car outside his house and I waited while John went inside. It was partly a macho Liverpool thing, I think, in case Paul had been thinking of making a play for me."

Paul's life, too, happened to be in a state of flux. The previous Christmas, after five seemingly perfect years together, he and Jane Asher had announced their engagement. Seven months later, Jane ended their relationship on discovering him in flagrante with an American girl named Francie Schwartz. Still shaken by her departure, he identified with Cynthia's plight—and, in any case, felt no need to kowtow to John. That afternoon at Kenwood, he was kindly and supportive, offering Cynthia the single rose he had brought and joking that now perhaps the two of them should get married. On his drive down from London, he had begun writing a song in his head, intended to give words of comfort to Julian and provisionally called "Hey Jules."

He made no secret of the visit afterward, nor did John react in any way adversely. It was proof of the strength of their friendship in this, the last year they would be friends.

22

BACK TO VIRGINITY

We are here, this is art.

For now, John had no idea where he wanted to live with Yoko; all he knew was that Weybridge wasn't it. After abandoning Kenwood, the two spent several weeks with no fixed address, first staying at Paul's house, then hiding out with trusted members of the Beatles' entourage like Derek Taylor, Neil Aspinall, and Peter Brown. In early July, they moved into Ringo's London flat at 34 Montagu Square—the same place where, a few weeks previously, Cynthia had sought shelter with her mother.

John was later to maintain that Yoko had, in the most literal sense, saved his life. "The king is always killed by his courtiers, not his enemies. The king is over-fed, over-drugged, over-indulged, anything to keep [him] tied to his throne. Most people in that position never wake up. They die mentally or physically or both. And what Yoko did for me was to liberate me from that situation . . . she showed me what it was to be Elvis Beatle and to be surrounded by sycophants and slaves who were only interested in keeping the situation as it was. . . . She didn't fall in love with the Beatle, she didn't fall in love with my fame. She fell in love with me for myself, and through that brought out the best in me. [I realized], 'My God, this is different from anything before. This is more than a hit record. It's more than gold. It's more than anything.'"

They were, of course, not quite the runaway orphans of the storm, living on love alone, that such imagery might suggest. Whatever John's triumph at having finally "broken out of the palace," he was still connected to courtiers ready and waiting to fulfill his slightest whim, a seemingly bottomless bank account, and a chauffeur-driven Rolls. With all these cushions in place, it was heady to return to a makeshift, camping-out existence such as he hadn't known since art college.

The real change was in the attitudes imbued in him by his north-country upbringing and hardened by years of veneration as an earthly demigod. "I was used to being served by women, whether it was my Aunt Mimi—God bless you—or whoever, served by females, wives, girlfriends," he would admit. "Yoko didn't buy that. She didn't give a shit about Beatles. 'What the fuck are the Beatles? I'm Yoko Ono, treat me as me.' From the day I met her, she demanded equal time, equal space, equal rights. I didn't know what she was talking about. I said, 'What do you want, a contract? We can have whatever you want, but don't expect anything from me or for me to change in any way.' 'Well,' she said, 'The answer to that is that I can't be here. Because there is no space where you are. Everything revolves around you, and I can't breathe in that atmosphere.'"

Yoko also had to do her share of adjusting. No man she had ever met before, certainly neither of her two husbands, had impinged on her consuming preoccupation with her career or mitigated the sense of being essentially a loner and outsider, which she had carried with her since childhood. Now here she was with someone who wanted—demanded—to spend every minute of every day with her, to be involved in every aspect of her life and to involve her in every aspect of his. Relatives back home in Japan who had so long bewailed her refusal to conform would have been astonished by the old-fashioned domestic roles she now accepted without a murmur. One night, John and she turned up at Derek Taylor's home, where they were hospitably given the use of the Taylors' marital bed. "Next morning, I asked what I should make them for breakfast," Joan Taylor remembers. "Yoko told me that she was the only one who prepared John's breakfast for him."

All this still wasn't enough for John. Indeed, the frantic adolescent jealousy and possessiveness that had characterized his first wooing of Cynthia ten years earlier now seemed mild by comparison. Soon after he and Yoko got together, he asked her to write out a list of everyone she'd ever slept with before they met. Thinking it was just a game, she began jotting down names in lighthearted fashion—then realized that John took it with deadly seriousness.

He regarded every man who crossed their combined path as an active and dangerous rival for her affections, and methodically set about cutting her off from all her existing male friends in avant-garde art and music, however elderly or gay. Anything that took Yoko's attention away from him, even for a moment, counted as a threat. Though she lived her life in English, there were occasions when she spoke to Japanese compatriots, either in person or on the telephone, and glanced at Japanese-language books, newspapers, and magazines. John hated this, as it represented a part of her that he could not share. "He'd always be saying, 'What are you thinking? Why aren't you looking at me?' I always had to look at him in the right way, straight into the middle of his eyes, or he'd start to get upset."

Though she had left her husband for him, he still regarded Tony Cox as an ever-present rival who might walk in and reclaim her at any moment. He accepted, however, that contact with Cox had to be reestablished so that Yoko could see Kyoko and discuss plans for a divorce. Paradoxically, when they did meet at last, John took an instant liking to his perceived deadly rival. And Kyoko charmed and captivated him as his own five-year-old never had. "My parents had an open marriage, so I was used to seeing them both with other people," she remembers. "But even I could tell that John was something different. He was always very sweet. He never lost his temper with me, though I knew he had a temper. Later on, he and my mom and dad would have very bad rows in front of me. All of them believed in really letting it go."

· Yoko was only beginning to learn what insecurity, even timidity, coexisted with John's rock-star egotism. That summer, he had to keep his promise to write the "Liverpool Wank" sketch for Ken Tynan's *Oh! Calcutta!* revue. An exercise he once would have tossed off in a few seconds, so to speak, for "The Daily Howl" or *Mersey Beat,* now reduced him to agonies of indecision and self-doubt. Yoko asked him to tell her the story, and responded just as wholeheartedly to the idea of schoolboys group-masturbating amid cries of "Brigitte Bardot!" as John had to her imaginary "Snows of Kos." With her standing at his shoulder, the way Paul McCartney once used to, the sketch was finally typed and submitted.

Behind her own art-star egotism, Yoko was not without hang-ups either. "I'm not an insecure artist, but as a woman I had all kinds of hesitations about myself. When I met John, I was self-conscious about my appearance. I thought I was too short, my legs were the wrong shape, and I used to cover my face with my hair. My hands are so stringy in a way, my fingers and all that. I was always hiding my hands. John said to me 'No, you're beautiful. You don't have to hide your hands, your legs are perfect, tie your hair back and let people see your face.'"

Before meeting John, she maintains, she never used the word *fuck.* "He told me once, 'You're too Asiatic, too Japanese, you should say 'fuck.' And a beautiful woman saying 'fuck' is really very attractive. I told him, 'I'm not beautiful enough to say that,' but I went to the mirror and practised going 'Fuck, fuck, fuck.'"

Despite years among artists in Greenwich Village, she had never taken drugs of any kind, not even nicotine, before coming to Europe. At the Knokke festival with the *Bottoms* film, she was given her first tab of LSD; in Paris shortly afterward, among Ornette Coleman's jazz crowd, she tried heroin. Acid-guzzler though John was, he had always steered clear of smack, terrified by its association with needles and the physical degradation so harrowingly portrayed onscreen by Frank Sinatra in *The Man with the Golden Arm.* Yoko had merely inhaled rather than injecting it, and reported no such calamitous after-effects. "John kept saying 'That must have been so interesting—what was it like?'" she recalls. "He never stopped hounding me about it."

During their short stay together at Kenwood, she had been startled by the quantity and variety of lesser drugs in his possession. "He was on everything by then. Next to his bed, he had a huge glass jar of pills, acid, Mandrax, I don't know what that blue one was called. . . . In the morning when he woke up, he used to just grab a handful at random." His current craze was for Mandrax (methaqualone, or Quaalude); he urged Yoko to try it but did not pressure her when she declined.

She could do nothing about his heavy consumption of French Gitanes cigarettes and—nonsmokers still swimming much against the social tide—speedily joined him in the habit as a further mark of togetherness. She was more successful against the junk food he still mainly lived on, despite Brian's and George Martin's attempts to educate his palate. Yoko was a convert to the vegetarian, nondairy, and preservative-free macrobiotic diet with which more serious hippies proclaimed their abdication from the material world. One of her few male friends unthreatening to John was a young American expat named Craig Sams, who had pioneered macrobiotic cuisine in London virtually single-handedly. Together they became regulars at Seed, Sams's tiny basement restaurant, off Westbourne Grove, where dishes were priced in shillings rather than pounds. As with all initiates, the regimen of brown rice and vegetables, and the elimination of sugar and preservatives, brought John a surge of energy and well-being. He could not get over how "brown rice and a cuppa tea [are the] biggest high I ever had."

Domestically, as opposed to creatively, the new tenants of the basement-and-ground-floor duplex at 34 Montagu Square might not have appeared a perfect macrobiotic balance of yin and yang. Yoko was accustomed to a habitat as chastely minimalist as one of her installations. John was a musician, a calling synonymous with dark, fetid rooms, dirty shirts, empty bottles, and cigarette butts floating in cold tea. It was therefore a pleasant surprise for her to discover his passion for domestic order, his fastidiousness about personal hygiene and fragrance, the care he took over the smallest aesthetic detail. One little trick he taught her would stay with Yoko long after he had gone. When putting on a baggy shirt, he would tuck it into his belt, then raise both arms at once so that its folds billowed out symmetrically all the way around.

He was completely open and uninhibited with her, as she learned to be with him, owning up to his deepest sexual fantasies—like one of making love to a woman in her eighties, or even older, whose veined and wrinkled hands would be covered in diamonds. Over time, she became accustomed to his particular style of backhanded compliment. "Do you know why I like you?" he remarked on one occasion. "It's because you look like a bloke in drag. You're like a mate." Yoko laughingly replied that she thought he must be "a closet fag."

John would later sum up his situation with a favorite song of his mother's, "Those Wedding-Bells Are Breaking Up That Old Gang of Mine." "When I met Yoko [it was like] when you meet your first woman and you leave the guys at the bar and you don't go play football any more, and you don't go play snooker and billiards. Once I found the woman, the boys became of no interest whatever other than that they were old friends. . . . That was it. That old gang of mine was over the moment I met her. As soon as I met her, that was the end of the boys. But it so happened the boys were well known and weren't just the local guys at the bar."

In reality, wedding bells were not yet even remotely on the cards, and the "old gang" had no sense of breaking up. To Paul, George, and Ringo, Yoko seemed no more than yet another of John's passing fancies, which sooner or later—sooner rather than later—would pass away just like all the others. And whatever John's inner thoughts, he remained a fully paid-up Beatle, subject to the remorseless manufacturing cycle, which, in late May, had summoned them back to Abbey Road Studios. With them they brought a much larger than usual song cache, mostly written during the weeks of enforced tranquility at Rishikesh. John had been the most productive, with fifteen potential new tracks as against Paul's twelve and George's six. And at the back-to-school session on May 30, his initial intention became clear: not to break up the old gang, but to augment it.

"He wanted me to be part of the group," Yoko says. "He created the group, so he thought the others should accept that. I didn't particularly want to be part of them. But by that time, he had got all the avant-garde friends of mine out of my life, so I had nobody else to play music with. I couldn't see how I would fit in, but John was certain I would. He kept saying 'They're very sensitive guys. . . . You think they're just Liverpool gits, but no, they're very sensitive. . . . Paul is into Stockhausen . . . They can do your thing. . . .' He thought the other Beatles would go for it: he was trying to persuade me."

So when John settled himself on his stool with his guitar in the sacred vault of Studio Two, there beside him on a matching stool, in matching allover black, sat Yoko. It was a moment worthy of the great 1920s cartoonist H. M. Bateman, who portrayed monumental social gaffes and the reeling shock of bystanders: "The Man Who Lit His Cigar Before the Loyal Toast," "The Boy Who Threw a Snowball at St Moritz," and "The Guardsman Who Dropped His Rifle on Parade" might now have been joined by "The Beatle Who Brought a Chick to a Recording Session." However, while there certainly was Batemanesque jaw-dropping and eye-popping among the Beatles' retinue, this "most unwarrantable intrusion" left the other three—to begin with—relatively unfazed. "I think John told them some kind of sob story, like she was depressed or she was in pain, so he wanted me to be there to cheer me up or something like that," Yoko says. "So George came over and said, 'Hello, how are you?' They were all treating me like this depressed woman they had to cheer up."

This summer of 1968 was to be altogether different from the happy, hazy twelvemonth ago whose apotheosis had been *Sgt. Pepper's Lonely Hearts Club Band*. A word that had haunted European politicians for decades after the Bolshevik uprising in 1917, and which the postwar world believed to be extinct outside Latin America, was displacing *love* and *peace* on young lips everywhere. The word was *revolution*. In late 1967, China's despot, Mao Tse-tung, had launched his so-called Cultural Revolution by inciting mobs to turn on liberal and intellectual elements who threatened to soften his totalitarian regime. Conversely, a few months later, a popular revolt in Czechoslovakia, led by the liberal Alexander Dubček, threw off the repressive rule of Communist Russia to establish a "Prague Spring" of democratic self-determination until its brutal extinction by Soviet tanks the following August.

In parts of the world where no dictators ruled, the call for overthrow was no less urgent, the demagoguery no less frenzied, the street fighting no less ugly, the bloodshed no less random. Paris's fabled springtime brought the worst civil unrest since the Liberation, as college students rose up jointly against the Vietnam War and the landslide reelection victory of France's wartime savior, Charles de Gaulle. In London, a savage antiwar riot outside the American embassy in Grosvenor Square ended with three hundred arrests and ninety police casualties. As America itself saw its armies humiliated by guerrillas in southeast Asia, its name reviled throughout the so-called free world, its once idyllic college campuses in turmoil, its once pacific black communities in open revolt, it also had to face the realization that the dreadful event in Dallas on November 22, 1963, had not been a one-off tragedy, but the beginning of a trend. In April, the great civil-rights leader Martin Luther King was killed by a sniper as he stood on the balcony of a hotel in Memphis, Tennessee. Two months later, John F. Kennedy's younger brother, Bobby, would be ambushed and shot dead in a Los Angeles hotel kitchen, having just launched his own presidential campaign with a pledge to end the Vietnam slaughter.

But revolution no longer signified its old hot blood: revolution was cool. And for the first time ever, *classless*. Middle-class British students were among the fiercest converts to Marxism, Leninism, Trotskyism, or Maoism, often flitting from one to the other and back again, and seeing no contradiction between their new beliefs and the comfortable capitalist lifestyle, which the system they professed to hate still allowed them. A range of institutions, from the London School of Economics to Hornsey College of Art, followed the Czech example in declaring themselves breakaway states, but with the important distinction that no tanks came to meet them. Emergent leaders of this Europe-wide academic insurrection, like France's Daniel Cohn-Bendit and Britain's Tariq Ali, received worship almost on a par with rock stars. It was an untrendy flat indeed where posters of Lenin or Mao did not compete with the new psychedelic individual head shots of the Beatles. When a new club opened in London, more plushly luxurious than any before, and more dedicated to excluding the lower orders, it was called—what else?—the Revolution.

The first track laid down by the Beatles for their next album was one of John's titled with this suddenly omnipresent buzzword. "I wanted to put out what I felt about revolution," he would explain. "I thought it was about time we spoke about it, the same as I thought it was about time we stopped not answering about the Vietnam War. I had been thinking about it up in the hills in India. That's why I did it. I wanted to talk."

Actually, John's "Revolution" was not a call to take to the streets so much as a satire on all the well-fed young revolutionaries with their hotheaded desire to "change the world" and the iconic "pictures of Chairman Mao" hanging up behind their bathroom doors. It explicitly declined to give either moral or financial support to "minds that hate," warning those bent in mere mindless destruction that "you can count me out." By the time the song was ready to record, John seems to have felt he had taken altogether too soft a line. There was also the point that "destruction" could mean knocking down stubborn attitudes as well as buildings. So the crucial declaration became an equivocal "Count me out . . . in."

This first version (later to be known as "Revolution 1") was performed at a slowish tempo and in an almost pensive tone, with John's fuzzy lead guitar kept at low level and "Shooby-dooby" background vocals almost reminiscent of the Cavern club. It took up a total of forty hours' studio time, including one session where, trying as ever to alter the timbre of his voice, John lay prone on the floor and sang into a microphone suspended from a boom. The most revolutionary element was Yoko: not simply being there but also taking part. The track lasted more than ten minutes, of which the last six consisted of John screaming "All right!" or just screaming, while Yoko moaned, hummed, chirruped, and intoned random phrases like "You become naked."

George Martin was more mystified than anyone by John's decision to bring Yoko into the studio, felt "terribly inhibited" by her presence, but knew that to remonstrate with him "would rupture our relationship." Similar diplomacy had to be exercised in regard to his other new songs which, in Martin's view, came nowhere near "Strawberry Fields Forever," "A Day in the Life," or "I Am the Walrus." Almost all were satirical in tone, with long, complicated titles that automatically excluded them from the singles market, and subtexts that would be lost on anyone who hadn't shared his life over recent months. The voice was just as potent as ever, the craftsmanship just as meticulous ("revolution" carefully scanned with "evolution," "real solution," "contribution," "constitution," and "institution") and the chord work just as ear-catching; the problem was with the mood. If Martin had not realized before, he did now: John was great only when totally serious.

There were snapshots from Rishikesh to set alongside "Sexy Sadie," his coded yah-boo to the Maharishi, and "Dear Prudence," the ballad with which he'd sweet-talked Mia Farrow's sister out of hiding. "The Continuing Story of Bungalow Bill" memorialized another fellow student who would take time off from meditation to go tiger hunting, rather implausibly accompanied by his mother. "Everybody's Got Something to Hide Except Me and My Monkey" was at once a name-check for the baboons that used to steal his breakfast, an oblique reference to Yoko—and a lingering complaint about that unrevealed Answer. "I'm So Tired" was a more unkempt version of "I'm Only Sleeping," recalling hours of insomnia and chain-smoking alone in his quarters, and cursing Sir Walter Raleigh ("He was such a stupid git!") for ever having discovered tobacco. "Yer Blues," written at the very bottom of that same depression, transposed the idiom from south to north, although its apocalyptic visions of despair and decay ("The eagle picks my eye / The worm he licks my bone . . .") belong less to Muddy Waters and Blind Lemon Jefferson than to some acidhead King Lear.

"Happiness Is a Warm Gun" came from the cover line on an American hunting magazine, horribly apposite to the current promiscuous shooting of beloved public figures in that country. It began as an elegiac love song and wandered through surreal terrain that apparently included a sports day at a nunnery ("Mother Superior jumped the gun") before ending as a satiric soul barnstormer whose background chorus of "Bang! Bang! Shoot! Shoot!" is difficult to listen to today. "Glass Onion" taunted the overly earnest fans who ransacked his lyrics for hidden messages and meanings. References back to "Strawberry Fields," "Lady Madonna," and "The Fool on the Hill" lead to a spurious revelation: "The Walrus was Paul." The sense of writing off the past was deliberate, as John later acknowledged. "I thought, 'Well, I'll just say something nice to Paul, that it's all right and you did a good job over these few years holding us together.' He was trying to organize the group. . . . so I wanted to say something to him. I thought, 'Well, he can have it. I've got Yoko.'"

If the other Beatles managed to reserve judgment on Yoko, the British public's hatred and resentment of her for having abducted one of its four favorite sons grew daily more virulent. This was an era when racism still flourished unchecked at every level—the peculiar, sly British racism expressed in behind-hand jokes and farcical stereotypes, but none the less poisonous for that. In Yoko's case, the "Jap" and "River Kwai" jibes were also tinged with ancient innuendo concerning the supposed sexual artfulness of Asian women. *Private Eye* magazine, still heavily influenced by John's old friend Peter Cook, caricatured him as "Spiggy Topes, leader of The Turds singing group"; in a pun on the *Kama Sutra* word for vagina, Yoko was cast as "Okay Yoni."

But there was more than hostile print to endure; there was also the live animosity of female fans who waited for John endlessly outside Abbey Road Studios, and somehow managed to turn up wherever else he happened to go. When Yoko appeared with John, she was greeted by screams of "Chink!" or "Yellow!" One day, a bunch of yellow roses was thrust at her stems first, so that the thorns would prick her hands. Hitherto, John always had people protecting him; now he was obliged to shield Yoko from the mobbing, the name-calling, the ill-natured jostling, the voyeuristic leering.

Being abused by complete strangers was nothing new to Yoko. She had become hardened to it as a child during the war, when her mother sent her out of Tokyo with her two siblings and the country people would shun or victimize them for their high caste. Later, too, when her family first settled in America, local children used to throw stones at her. "I'd always felt like an outsider, so this was kind of a familiar feeling—"The natives are stirring up again,'" she recalls. "There's a narcissistic side of me that was totally in love with my work and had nothing to do with those pitiful people who were ignorant about me and saying things. And an incredibly romantic side of me thought, 'This is a test. Fate is testing me to see if I'm going to give up this love affair.' I thought of it almost as a Greek tragedy, because I was losing my daughter, I was losing my artistic credit, all because of my love for this man. I sensed that it would be a very difficult life for me—and I did sense that if I got involved, some terrible tragedy was waiting."

Few journalists at this stage bothered to talk to Yoko rather than abusing her from a distance. One who took the trouble was Anne Nightingale, a British music writer who became the first female disc jockey on the BBC's new Radio 1 pop network. Behind the forbidding exterior, Nightingale discovered a friendly woman who talked about herself with the same instant openness that John did about himself, and whose weird ideas would have a eerie way of eventually coming true. She talked, for instance, of siting film cameras on Oxford Street to record the crowds that came and went every day—a vision of future closed-circuit TV surveillance. And to Nightingale she confided a clairvoyant terror of "ending up alone and shaking in a New York apartment."

Aside from Paul, George, and Ringo, only one other person's opinion really mattered to John. Well before the story of him and Yoko was generally known, he took her to the bungalow overlooking Poole Harbour, where pedigreed cats padded over the well-vacuumed carpet and his MBE medal stood proudly on the TV set. "[He] had rung to say he was bringing someone down," Aunt Mimi later recalled. "He came in all bright and breezy—typical John—and she followed behind."

Mimi's response was one of pure horror, though the conventions of hospitality prevented her from voicing it as explosively as she would have liked. "I took one look [at Yoko] and thought, 'My God, what is that?' Well, I didn't like the look of her right from the start. She had long black hair, all over the place, and she was small—she looked just like a dwarf to me. I told John what I felt while she was outside, looking across the bay. I said to him, 'Who's the poisoned dwarf, John?'"

Very different was Yoko's first impression of Mimi. "I thought she was beautiful, so tall and slim, with beautiful skin and bone structure. When John went to the bathroom and left us alone together, Mimi told me how she'd brought him up to be very good mannered, and always stand up when a woman came into the room."

In Yoko's presence, Mimi contented herself with warning John of the effect their relationship would have on his popularity, citing the famous episode from her own youth where a young man close to the nation's heart had sacrificed everything for an unsuitable woman. "She started saying how the Duke of Windsor had been so popular, but he lost it when he married Mrs. Simpson," Yoko remembers. "He thought that he could get away with it because he was so popular," Mimi said. "But he lost his popularity, and John, you'd better know that.' Which meant she was saying it right in front of me, that I'm the Mrs. Simpson."

"John just laughed," Mimi remembered. "He laughed it off, but he knew I didn't like her and he knew I was a good judge of character. I couldn't see what he saw in her and I thought it was wrong and nothing good would come of it."

Despite John's recent adventure with acorns, he remained wholly committed to Apple as an expression of the Beatles' collective will. To be sure, its official designation as Apple Corps—pronounced "core"—brought a breath of Lennon punnery wherever it cropped up. The company had moved into a large open-plan office at 75 Wigmore Street, just a few minutes by psychedelic Rolls from Montagu Square. John went in almost every day, determined to show himself every bit as much a director as Paul and happy to turn his mind to the smallest administrative matter, provided that Yoko was never more than a couple of centimeters away.

The flagship division was, of course, the Apple record label on which henceforward the Beatles would appear with their own personally selected roster of artistes. A high-powered executive named

Ron Kass was brought from the Liberty label to take charge, with Jane Asher's brother Peter as head of A&R. And the first acquisitions certainly seemed to bear out Apple's promise to foster talent from any quarter. Paul signed up Mary Hopkin, an eighteen-year-old Welsh folksinger who had won a television talent contest, and the Black Dyke Mills Band, a century-old brass band recruited from west Yorkshire mill workers. George brought in Jackie Lomax, a fellow Liverpudlian whose singing and songwriting he rated equally highly. No expense was spared in grooming these discoveries or on the media campaigns with which PR director Derek Taylor prepared to launch them. Further thousands were spent on the label's logo, a green Granny Smith apple that might have been handpicked by Magritte for the A-side, a sliced-in-half one for the B-side. London's most famous graphic artist, Alan Aldridge, was hired to write the copyright line in heartbreakingly beautiful italic script.

The openness of the Beatles' door—and wallet—was reiterated by a full-page newspaper advertisement, composed by Paul, urging anyone who believed they had musical talent and wanted to own a Bentley limousine to send their tapes to Apple. The result was an almighty deluge, not just of tapes by aspirant singers and bands but requests for finance across the whole creative field on which Beatles might be expected to smile, from impoverished poets in the Welsh wilds to seaside Punch and Judy men. Hundreds of applicants turned up to make their pitch in person; all but the most obviously certifiable were given a sympathetic hearing and many went away with large wads of Beatle cash, though few would ever be heard of again.

As much as a business, Apple set out to become a kind of alternative welfare state. Plans were announced for an arts foundation that would award regular stipends to deserving applicants, even an "Apple school," where the Beatles own children and those of their followers would be educated side by side. John took a particular interest in the school project, insisting it must bear no resemblance to the disciplined academies he and Paul had both attended, and bringing in their mutual childhood friend Ivan "Ivy" Vaughan, now a noted educationalist, to develop it. John's other main protégé or charitable interest—depending on one's point of view—was Magic Alex, by now established in a well-equipped workshop under the banner of Apple Electronics and supposedly at work on life-transforming inventions of every kind.

Apple Films also acquired its own chief executive and burgeoning staff, and continued to issue grandiose mission statements— although, after the mauling given to *Magical Mystery Tour*, potential follow-up projects were being sifted with understandable caution. Fortunately, its obligations did not include supplying the third feature production that the Beatles owed to United Artists. In 1967, Brian had sanctioned a feature-length cartoon, translating their children's song "Yellow Submarine" into a psychedelic fantasy in which their characters were voiced by soundalike actors. The plot conflated the song's lyrics and *Sgt. Pepper*, with the cartoon Beatles voyaging by canary-colored submersible to a place called Pepperland to defeat a tribe of music-hating trolls called the Blue Meanies.

A quartet of writers were involved, including the future bestselling novelist Eric Segal; even so, additional input had to be frequently sought from John. "Brodax [the producer] got half of *Yellow Submarine* out of my mouth," he would recall. "[The writers] used to come to the studio and chat: 'Hi, John old bean, got any ideas for the film?' And I'd just spout out all this stuff, and they went off and did it."

The Beatles' only direct involvement was with the music sound track, and that was hardly onerous. In addition to its iconic title song, the film recycled "All You Need Is Love" and demothballed three unreleased tracks from the *Sgt. Pepper* period, Paul's "All Together Now" and George's "It's All Too Much" and "Only a Northern Song." The rest of the score consisted of orchestral pieces composed and conducted by George Martin. Fearing that all this looked rather thin, the producer begged an original composition from John, who obliged with "Hey Bulldog," "a good-sounding record," so he later said, "that means nothing." Genuinely witty and charming, the film managed to create Beatle magic by proxy and became a must-see that summer for anyone under thirty. However, its less-than-bumper-value sound track album was held back from release to prevent any conflict with the new song cycle still arduously taking shape at Abbey Road.

By June, Apple had outgrown its Wigmore Street office and moved into a £500,000 Georgian town house at number 3 Savile Row, the heart of Mayfair's bespoke tailoring district. The interior was painted white, carpeted in thick-piled apple green, filled with expensive furnishings, pictures, and fabrics, and equipped with a Cordon Bleu kitchen. A doorman in a gray frock coat was engaged to control the knot of girls—nicknamed Apple Scruffs by George—who instantly formed a round-the-clock guard beside the front steps. The basement was earmarked for a recording studio where the Beatles and other Apple talent could work in privacy and comfort. Laughing to scorn the comparatively simple technology that George Martin still used at Abbey Road, Magic Alex set to work designing a recording desk with a promised seventy-two-track capability.

Mayfair also provided the setting for John's first-ever solo art exhibition, which opened at the Robert Fraser Gallery in Mount Street on July 1. Since turning Paul McCartney on to Magritte, the gay Old Etonian Fraser had risen to even greater eminence among rock 'n' roll's demimonde. In 1967, he had been jailed for drug offenses alongside Mick Jagger and Keith Richards, but unlike them—the drug in his possession having been heroin—he had served his full term.

The Fraser Gallery show, which John dedicated "to Yoko with love," was saturated in her influence yet also as much a reflection of his childhood as any song he'd ever written. Its title, *You Are Here*, was a phrase familiar from map boards in the sprawling Liverpool parks of his boyhood, now given extra resonance by his sense of finally having found his way to himself. Spectators first encountered a series of charity collection boxes, among them the plaster orphan girl with one leg in braces who had stood outside so many High Street shops in the 1950s. As much as conceptual art, it seemed like self-prescribed therapy, finally laying to rest the fear and loathing he had always felt toward "cripples."

The exhibition proper consisted of a white canvas circle inscribed "You are here" in John's handwriting, and an upturned hat with a handwritten card: "For the artist. Thank you." At its opening, 360 helium-filled white balloons were released over Mayfair's rooftops, each with a label repeating "You are here" and inviting its finder to write to John care of the Fraser Gallery. (A large number of replies subsequently came back, many expressing disappointment in his recent conduct or making racist comments about Yoko.) In a sarcastic comment on the show, a group of students from Hornsey Art College left a rusted bicycle outside, which so amused John that he instantly set it among his other exhibits.

There seemed to be nothing that could distract his attention from Yoko, but, late one afternoon just before Apple's move to Savile Row, something did. Yoko happened to be otherwise occupied, and John was at 75 Wigmore Street, discussing with Derek Taylor how to fill the next few hours, when a telephone call came through from the Mayfair Hotel. Brigitte Bardot was in town and would love to meet the Beatles or any individual one who might be available. John and Taylor each took a "sparkle" of acid, just enough to make the world shimmer hilariously, then went over to the Mayfair Hotel in John's Rolls.

But, as he had already found with Elvis, meeting an idol seldom lives up to the dream—or, in this case, wet dream. The Bardot of 1968 was no longer the bewitching "sex kitten" of ten years before. The ponytail had been replaced by an unkempt blonde mane, the dew-fresh face had coarsened, the once-mischievous eyes were thickly outlined in black. With her, even more disappointingly, were two male companions who took turns in acting as her translator.

The encounter grew increasingly sticky, with John seated guru-style on the floor, dragging on endless Gitanes, while Derek Taylor and Bardot's two minders struggled to keep the flow of pleasantries alive. Bardot proposed going out to dinner, but John declined to move, and he and Taylor were left alone in the suite. When Bardot's party returned some hours later, they found their guests still there, rendered oblivious to passing time by the usual chemical means. Taylor was vaguely aware of John singing a song for Bardot, then soon afterward passed out on her bed. So all those group wanks at the sound of her name turned out to have been as exciting as it got.

With the move to Savile Row came the first casualty in Apple's commercial Garden of Eden. Seven months after its bravura launch and massive media send-off, the Apple boutique in Baker Street had conspicuously failed to become another Biba, Bus Stop, or I Was

Lord Kitchener's Valet. By July, losses had reached such a level that the only option (other than recruiting hated "men in suits" from the mainstream retail trade to halt the endemic shoplifting) was to close it. In the spirit of Apple's "Western Communism," it was decided to give away the entire stock. Derek Taylor counseled against such an ignominious end, but in vain. "I was running the office at the time," John remembered. "Paul had called me up one day and said, 'I'm going away. You take over.' It was as stupid as that."

On the eve of the closeout, July 30, the Beatles and their partners and favored cronies went through the boutique helping themselves to the choicest items. "It was great . . . like robbing," John said, even though he'd robbed nobody but himself. Next day, print and television greedily recorded the frantic public scrimmage for what was left, with flower children fighting fiercely over the same Buddhist tract on brotherly love and cabbies leaving their motors running while they gathered armfuls of embroidered cushions or tore kaftans from racks. It was left to Paul, that consummate PR man, to suggest that the Beatles had not so much lost a fortune as withdrawn in the nick of time from an activity far beneath them; they were, he said, "tired of being shopkeepers."

The boutique balls-up vanished from memory on August 11, when the first fruits of the Apple record label were simultaneously released. In addition to a new Beatles single, these comprised Mary Hopkin's "Those Were the Days," produced by Paul; the Black Dyke Mills Band's "Thingumybob," written (for a TV series) by Paul; and Jackie Lomax's "Sour Milk Sea," written and produced by George. The four disks came packaged together in a shiny black presentation box, emphasizing the Beatles' kinship with their protégés, and the democratic all-inclusiveness of the target audience was made clear from the start. On release day, boxes were hand-delivered to the Queen at Buckingham Palace, the Queen Mother at Clarence House, Princess Margaret at Kensington Palace, and the prime minister, Harold Wilson, at 10 Downing Street.

At the time, it struck no one as odd, to say the least, that four musicians ranked as Members of the Most Excellent Order of the British Empire should send their sovereign, not to mention her mother and sister and chief minister, a song entitled "Revolution." This was not, however, the version of John's song that he'd taken forty hours to record in June. Neither George Martin nor the other Beatles had been happy with that long, chaotic, Yoko-assisted performance, thinking its tempo too slow and the distortion on John's lead guitar too extreme. In July, therefore, he had cut a new, shorter, and obviously more commercial version. On this one, his intro was a two-note electric scrawl, echoing a childhood radio favorite, Khachaturian's "Saber Dance." The six-minute playout of screams with Yoko disappeared, and the ambiguous final message crystallized into "Count me in." But even in this form, Revolution was deemed fit only for the sliced-apple B-side of the Beatles first release on their own label, the whole-fruit A-side going to Paul's "Hey Jude."

John had not only lost pole position on arguably the Beatles' most important singles release since "Love Me Do"; he had lost it to a song about his private life, and one that—albeit very obliquely—criticized his behavior. For "Hey Jude" had started out as "Hey Jules," Paul's consoling message to the five-year-old son who had been left behind at Kenwood, apparently without a backward glance. Though the name had since changed to the more Hardyesque and gender-ambiguous "Jude" and the lyric evolved into a conventional love song, Paul's original, good-hearted intention still colored every line: to comfort and reassure and cheer up Julian and, in however small a way, "make it better."

As John saw it, "Hey Jude" was all about his relationship with Yoko, and Paul's feelings about being superseded as his creative other half. "'Ah, it's me,' I said when Paul first played it,' he would recall. "If you think about it, Yoko's just come into the picture. . . . The words 'go out and get her' . . . Subconsciously he was saying 'Go ahead, leave me.' But on a conscious level he didn't want me to go ahead. The angel inside him was saying 'Bless you.' The devil in him didn't like it at all because he didn't want to lose his partner." Whatever its subtext, John recognized the song's potential as a crowd-pleaser, even if its length of more than seven minutes (possibly in a competitive spirit with the ten minutes of "Revolution 1") might be daunting to many radio deejays of that time. In its initial tryouts, one verse still had an unwritten line, which Paul filled in with "The movement you need is on your shoulder." At John's urging, the words stayed on the finished track.

Two television appearances with David Frost in the space of a couple of weeks gave notice where his priorities now lay. On August 24, Frost was granted the first interview with Yoko and John together, on condition that it dealt with his new artistic consciousness, not his private life. When Frost announced them, the two loped onto the set hand in hand, in matching all-black outfits, like latter-day Quarry Bank truants. The encounter included a demonstration of Yoko's *Hammer a Nail In* exhibit, with volunteers from the studio audience, and finally Frost himself, hammering their own nail into a board and describing the emotions they felt—in every case, less than overwhelming. There was also a clip from *Smile*, the filmed close-up of John's barely moving face. "The thing is, there's no such thing as sculpture or art," he explained. "We're all art, art is just a tag. . . . Sculpture is anything you care to name. This is sculpture, us sitting here, this is a happening, we are here, this is art."

In *New Musical Express*, the Alley Cat's back-page column called his performance "boring"—the first time that word had ever been used of him. Even the Beatles' official fan magazine reported dismay and disgruntlement among its readers. "I only wish John would stick to things he's good at," was a typical reaction." I don't mean just music because I think his writing is brilliant. . . . There's no meaning to the things he's doing with Yoko Ono. A film of someone smiling isn't art. Nor can we appreciate knocking nails into a slab of wood. Well, I ask you, surely John is losing his touch if he really thinks we ought to be praising him for that!"

Then on September 8, Frost's program was used to launch "Hey Jude" on its way to an eventual three-million sale. It was, in effect, the Beatles' first live performance since August 1966, filmed in front of a three-hundred-strong audience with an introduction by Frost to make it seem like part of his regular show. "The world's greatest tea-room orchestra," as their host announced them, played sitting down, with Paul at an upright piano and John and George together on his left. John contributed almost nothing to the opening badinage with

Frost, and barely seemed to be either singing or playing. From the emollient opening chords to the final, extended sing-along chorus, Paul buttonholed the camera with his shiny hair, red velvet coat, and commiserating brown eyes.

If "Hey Jude" was a return to lovability for the Beatles, "Revolution" awoke the gladdest expectations in those whose hatred of the system did not include pop music and for whom John, Paul, George, and Ringo still ranked alongside Lenin and Mao. Young revolutionaries across two continents expected John to declare solidarity with them; instead, the message was "Count me out." The song had barely gone on sale when the ugliest conflagration yet erupted in Chicago. Encouraged by the city's corrupt mayor, Richard Daley, police went on the rampage, beating up demonstrators in full view of TV cameras, even turning their fury on innocent delegates to the Democratic Party convention. For apparently copping out when it came to the crunch, John was denounced as a "traitor" to the counterculture and, by implication, a tool of its deadliest foes. The militant soul singer Nina Simone recorded an answer to "Revolution," urging him to "clean" his mind.

September also brought publication of *The Beatles*, the authorized biography by Hunter Davies. During the book's preparation, Brian Epstein had died, the Beatles had discovered and discarded the Maharishi, Apple had begun, and John had gone off with Yoko: in the whole realm of nonfiction there was no hotter topic, and Davies had it all to himself.

For its time, the book seemed extraordinarily frank and open, especially about the Beatles' childhoods and their early days in Hamburg. The lengthy interviews with each one were also unprecedentedly candid, John's most of all, as he owned up to his failure at school and college and his belief that he was just "conning" the fans who regarded him as an oracle. However, the text had been thoroughly vetted in proof by the Beatles, their chief minders, and respective families. Brian's homosexuality was not mentioned, beyond a sly reference to him as a "gay bachelor"—*gay* still generally meaning "lighthearted"—nor was there any hint of his fixation on John and John's often brutal treatment of him. The book's deadline meant that Yoko was absent from the narrative, which ended with John still at Kenwood, swapping apparently empathetic banter with Cynthia.

Another thread in the continuing story which remained unpursued was that leading to Freddie Lennon and his pregnant twenty-year-old fiancée at their tiny flat in Brighton. Here, Freddie and Pauline Jones had hoped for the peace and seclusion to enjoy a relationship in its way as controversial as John and Yoko's. Pauline's widowed mother remained implacably opposed to the match, and determined to end it by any possible means. When maternal appeals, reproaches, and threats to Pauline proved useless, Mrs. Jones began legal proceedings to have her declared a ward of court, so making Freddie liable to criminal prosecution if the threatened marriage went ahead.

The resultant stress affected Pauline so severely that she suffered a miscarriage, and on the day of the court hearing she was still too weak to attend. To the surprise of both sides, the judge refused Mrs. Jones's application, ruling only that Pauline could not marry Freddie until she was twenty-one.

Throughout all this, John remained one of their very few allies. After Pauline's miscarriage—which happened while he was still nominally with Cynthia and Julian—he sent a sympathetic handwritten note from Kenwood, giving a new private telephone number but making no other reference to his own domestic situation. In a short time, Pauline became pregnant again. With the ban on their marriage still in force, she and Freddie decided to follow countless other star-crossed English lovers and elope to Scotland, beyond the jurisdiction of English courts. John not only knew about the plan in advance but paid their traveling expenses and sent a note wishing them good luck. They duly took a train to Edinburgh, where they married by civil ceremony on Pauline's twentieth birthday. John continued to be generous, buying a house in Brighton to replace their rented flatlet and making over the deeds to Freddie.

No Beatles fan awaited their authorized biography more eagerly than Freddie Lennon. After what he had told Hunter Davies a year previously, he was expecting the full story of John's early childhood to be finally on record. Freddie did not hope to be painted as an ideal husband or father, but he expected credit, at least, for having tried to preserve his relationship with John's mother, Julia, despite her two-fold adultery. Above all, John would see enshrined in print that his father had not willingly abandoned him, but turned him over to Julia in what then seemed his best interests. Taken with the fact that by now John also had a forsaken son on his conscience, Freddie believed this would create new understanding between them.

The book began by outlining each Beatle's childhood in order of precedence, which meant its opening passage was devoted to "Fred" Lennon. A detailed account was given of Freddie's education at Liverpool's Bluecoat Hospital, his wooing of Julia, his career as a ship's steward, and the wartime "lost weekend" that took him away from his family to wander around America and North Africa for eighteen months. But there was no mention of Julia's having become pregnant by another man while Freddie was at sea, nor of her later extramarital relationship and two children with Bobby Dykins.

John was later to call Davies's book "a whitewash," claiming that his Aunt Mimi had insisted "the truth bits about me mother and that" should be cut, and he had "copped out" and agreed. Mimi did indeed receive a set of proofs, to which she reacted so explosively that John wrote to Davies, asking him to go and see her and calm her down. ("Do yer duty, lad," the note ended.) But in a postscript to later editions of the book, Davies wrote that what upset Mimi were references to schoolboy rebelliousness and swear words. To appease her, Davies inserted the not inaccurate statement that after she took John over from Julia, he had been "as happy as the day is long."

Not until 2006, with the publication of Davies's memoir *The Beatles, Football and Me*, was a little more light shed, albeit unwittingly. The section on the biography contained a hitherto unrecorded background detail: that John had vetoed a passage "about a Welsh boyfriend of his mum's." This, surely, was none other than Taffy Williams, the soldier by whom Julia became pregnant and whose baby girl was given up for adoption despite Freddie's offer to take her in. With the near-sacred memory of Julia that John cherished, he might well have felt squeamish about having the episode made public. Or perhaps he was simply doing Mimi's bidding, or anticipating it. At all events, a story to his father's indisputable credit remained untold.

After five troubled months, work on the Beatles' next album finally seemed to be nearing completion. As it had evolved, it was less the product of a band than of individual talents, still umbilically joined by name but frequently hostile and—perhaps even worse—apathetic toward what their colleagues were doing. During the strung-out recording process, different Beatles at various times were absent from the studio, sometimes even from the country—an unthinkable situation in the *Sgt. Pepper* or *Revolver* era. Previously, George Martin had been able to watch brilliance beget brilliance from a single control room; now he often found himself shuttling between John, Paul, and George, at work on separate tracks in three different studios.

It had quickly become clear that having Yoko with him at Abbey Road was no mere passing fad of John's and that here, as everywhere else, he now regarded her as his muse. "The Beatles were getting real tense with each other," he would recall. "Because they were upset over the Yoko thing and the fact that I was again becoming as creative and dominating as I was in the early days, after lying fallow for a couple of years [*sic*] it upset the applecart. . . . Everyone seemed to be paranoid except for us two, who were in the glow of love."

Nor did the revolution end with Yoko's presence at John's side for every minute of every session, throughout every related conference, conversation, tryout and playback, and every meal-, tea-, coffee-, telephone-, and cigarette-break, often with Kyoko playing on the sidelines. Even when he went to the toilet, Yoko went, too—proof enough to incredulous onlookers of how deep she had her hooks into him. According to Yoko, it was one more manifestation of John's jealousy and insecurity. "People said I followed him to the men's room, but he made me go with him. He thought that if he left me alone with the other Beatles even for a minute, I might go off with one of them."

Most unbelievably, at the end of a take, it was to Yoko rather than Paul or George Martin that he first turned for comment. And, being Yoko, she did not hesitate to give it. "John always said to me, 'If you notice anything, just whisper.' And I did notice a lot because in classical music where I was trained, you learn how to listen to all the instruments. So I'd say something like, 'The bass is not right,' but I didn't say it out loud. John was almost flaunting it, actually. He'd say, 'OK, Yoko, what rhymes with this?' and then say to the other three, 'It's fucking convenient to have her, right?'"

It says much for the affection in which he was held, and their tradition of loyalty and tolerance, that the other three did not simply lay down their instruments and walk out. Paul, true to character, tried diplomacy, which John later saw as underhandedness, accusing him of "gently coming up to Yoko and saying, 'Why don't you keep in the background a little more?' It was all going on behind my back. . . ." Ringo Starr was frankly baffled but, as always, managed to strike the right note with John when he confessed as much. "I used to ask [him], 'What's this about?'" Ringo later recalled. "He told me straight: 'Well, when you go home to Maureen and tell her how your day was, it takes you two lines, "Oh, we had a good day in the studio." Well, we know exactly what's going on. . . .' I was fine after that, and relaxed a lot around Yoko."

George by contrast, despite long marinading in soft-tongued Buddha-speak, was his most bluntly charmless. "[He] insulted [Yoko] right to her face in the Apple office," John would remember. "Just being straightforward, that game of 'Well, I'm going to be up-front because this is what I've heard, and Dylan and a few people said you've got a lousy name in New York and you give off bad vibes.' That's what George said to her and we both sat through it. And I didn't hit him, I don't know why."

To include all the material that had been recorded, the album would have to be in the new and still relatively unusual double-disk format. George Martin was opposed to the idea, arguing—in vain— that its several undoubtedly first-rate new songs should be arranged into a single-disk suite that would certainly be the equal of *Revolver*, if not quite *Sgt. Pepper*. The Beatles were agreed on one point at least: everything had to go in. For Martin, one track above all represented this unfamiliar spirit of indiscipline and self-indulgence. John had taken the extended finale to his original slowish performance of "Revolution" (now known as "Revolution 1") and, with Yoko's help, turned it into an eight-minute mélange of tape-looped sound effects, shrieks, moans, and random voices, including Yoko's command (or warning) "You become naked." The overall effect was rather like tuning a radio dial to a series of incomprehensible foreign radio stations. To distinguish it from its parent track, and acknowledge his approaching October birthday and overall lucky number, John called it "Revolution 9."

As the sessions continued fitfully into the summer, Yoko discovered that she was pregnant. The timing was not good, with divorce proceedings under way against Cynthia on grounds of her alleged adultery with Roberto Bassanini, and matters between Yoko and Tony Cox, specifically over custody of Kyoko, as yet unresolved. John, however, reacted with a joy and excitement that would have brought a sour smile to Cynthia's face, remembering his gloomy resignation before Julian's birth back in 1963.

Ringo had always been the glue that bonded the Beatles, and so— albeit in a negative sense—it still proved. One day, he went to John with the amazing news that he wanted out. "I said, 'I'm leaving the group because I'm not playing well and I feel unloved and out of it and you three are really close.'" he later remembered. "And John said, 'I thought it was you three.' Then I went over to Paul's . . . and said the same thing . . . and Paul said, 'I thought it was you three.'" Assuming his career as a Beatle was over, he took his family on holiday to Sardinia. The other three, genuinely mortified, put aside their conflicts with one another and sent a telegram after him: "You're the best rock 'n' roll drummer in the world. Come on home. We love you." When Ringo returned to Abbey Road a few days later, he found his drum kit covered with more flowers than the *Sgt. Pepper* cover. The episode concentrated everyone's minds, and from there on they buckled down until the job was finished.

On October 13, John recorded the album's thirty-second and final song, its most individual and independent piece of work—in effect, his first-ever solo track. It was a ballad called "Julia," after the mother he had never stopped thinking of since her death ten years before— and who had recently been conjured up afresh through the memories of old friends like Pete Shotton and Nigel Walley in Hunter Davies's biography. Indeed, it was less song than séance, with John alone in the studio but for his acoustic guitar, his voice free of any technical distortion, speaking rather than singing to that flighty auburn-haired spirit. Grief, yearning, shyness, and self-knowledge came together in language of which any contemporary "serious" poet might have been proud: "When I cannot sing my heart / I can only speak my mind. . . ." But in the months since he had made "Yer Blues," anguish and fury had softened into gossamer dreaminess, the former *King Lear* cataracts and hurricanoes dwindled down to the softest sea-shell sigh. For Julia now had an alter-ego—Ocean Child, the English translation of the name Yoko.

Five days later, John and Yoko's borrowed flat at 34 Montagu Square was raided by a seven-strong police task force, comprising two plainclothes detective sergeants, two detective constables, a po-licewoman, and two sniffer-dog handlers. At their head was Sergeant Norman Pilcher, an officer who already had several notable scalps to his credit in the war against drug-using pop stars.

It happened just before noon, as John and Yoko lay in bed together, clad only in skimpy undershirts. When Yoko refused to open the front door, the officers found their way to a rear window, which John initially tried to hold shut against them. He then agreed to admit them via the front door after warnings that otherwise it would be broken down. The sniffer-dog handlers did not have their dogs with them—the only two currently at the Drug Squad's disposal—and there was a half hour wait while the animals were sent for. Fleet Street had been tipped off in advance about the raid, and within a few minutes a crowd of photographers were baying outside. John was allowed to make one telephone call, and phoned Neil Aspinall at Apple. "Imagine your worst paranoia," he told Neil. "Well, it's here."

The bust was a shock but hardly a surprise. Some weeks earlier, John had been tipped off by an old Fleet Street friend, Don Short, that the police were out to get him. Ironically, when the raiders burst in, he and Yoko both considered themselves "very clean and drug-less." Prior to their tenancy of the flat, it had been rented to Jimi Hendrix, a musician whose epic consumption of drugs was matched by his carelessness about hiding them. John refused to move in until the whole place had been scoured for Hendrix's leftovers, then thoroughly spring-cleaned to vacuum up the smallest residue.

Believing the Montagu Square flat to be clean, John was dumbfounded when the police told him that the two dogs, Yogi and Booboo, had found cannabis in various hiding places, such as a binoculars case, a film can, and a cigarette roller, totaling 219 grains (about half an ounce) in all. Though the substance had nothing to do with him, he reacted almost with relief, thinking of what harder stuff the raiders could have found. By the time he and Yoko arrived at Marylebone police station to be formally charged, he was back to his usual flippant self, answering as "Sergeant Lennon" when a phone call was put through from the chairman of EMI, Sir Joseph Lockwood. "It was better when it happened," he would remember. "It [had been] building up for years. The Beatles thing was over. No reason to protect us for being soft and cuddly any more—so bust us."

For "Sir Joe," as John called the stately Lockwood, aghastness was only just beginning. Aside from the Beatles' imminent double one, John had a new album of his own to be released on the Apple label and distributed by EMI. It consisted of the tapes he and Yoko had made together at Kenwood during their first night together: a miscellany of the same electronic and vocal effects that eventually made up "Revolution 9." In a combination of Yoko's art-catalog style and Lennon irony, it was to be called *Unfinished Music No. 1—Two Virgins*. As well as being its sole performers, producers, and engineers, they also furnished the image for its cover: a realization of Yoko's "You become naked." Using a delayed action shutter, John had photographed the two of them nude, standing together in the Montagu Square flat with their arms wrapped around each other. The backcover shot showed them similarly in the buff but turned around and looking over their shoulders.

John's aim, so he later said, "was to prove we are not a couple of demented freaks, that we are not deformed in any way and that our minds are healthy. . . . What we did purposely is not to have a pretty photograph, not have it lighted so that we looked sexy or good. There were a couple of other takes . . . when we looked rather nice, hid the little bits that aren't that beautiful. . . . We used the straightest, most unflattering picture just to show that we were human. . . . We felt like two virgins because we were in love, just met, and we were trying to make something. . . . People are always looking at people like me, trying to see some secret. 'What do they do? Do they go to the bathroom? Do they eat?' So we just said 'Here.' "

By 1968, the age-old British concept of "private parts" was fast disappearing. With the end of theater censorship had come the opening of an American rock musical called *Hair*, its title embracing both the cranial and pubic variety, as its young, hippie-ish cast appeared full-frontally nude. But a recording artiste and his woman friend exposing themselves on an album cover was still an altogether different matter. EMI agreed to press *Two Virgins* but refused to have any part in marketing it, as did American Capitol. In Britain, its distribution was handled by the Who's record label, Track, and in America by a company called Tetragrammaton. The offending picture had to be concealed under a plain brown paper cover—something, ironically, that Brian Epstein had once proposed for the *Sgt. Pepper* album. Even in this form, they remained vulnerable to the forces of old-fashioned prudery. Thirty thousand copies being stored in a New Jersey warehouse before shipment were seized as "obscene material" by the local police.

The Beatles' double album was also having prerelease problems, of a less dramatic kind. Its original, Ibsenesque title, *A Doll's House*, had to be dropped when a rival British band, Family, put out an album called *Music in a Doll's House*. Working to that brief, Apple's pet designer, Alan Aldridge, had planned a cover like an Advent calendar, each window opening on a different image from the songs. When Aldridge's design proved too complex and costly for mass manufacture, the commission was handed over to the Pop artist Richard Hamilton, who encased the two discs in plain white, crookedly die-stamped with "The BEATLES" and with a serial number suggestive of some limited-edition print. Though never officially so called, the collection thus became known to posterity as the *White Album*.

It was, in fact, a blueprint for breakup. Track after track revealed Lennon and McCartney pursuing their own divergent paths: John with "Yer Blues," "Happiness Is a Warm Gun," and "Revolution" (the slower, "count me in" version); Paul with "Martha My Dear," an ode to his old English sheepdog, the sing-along "Ob-La-Di, Ob-La-Da," the sighing "I Will," the almost Elizabethan "Blackbird." Yet the two could still switch personalities, and in doing so make the whole band sound united and carefree once again. Paul's "Helter Skelter" and "Why don't we do it in the road?" were rockers as raw as John could wish, and his "Back in the USSR," a mixture of Chuck Berry, Soviet Russia, and the Beach Boys, was as wittily surreal. Conversely, there could not have been a more Paul-sounding track than John's "Good Night," a lushly orchestrated lullaby in the tradition of Jolson's "Sonny Boy," written for his own son Julian in who knows what burst of affection or remorse (but here vocalized by Ringo).

George Harrison's stronger-than-usual presence was a further sign of changing times. Since *Revolver*, spurred on by the two supertalents he was lucky enough to play with, George had made increasing strides as a writer. Four songs on the *White Album* were his, the best three in different ways pointing to the same mentor. "Piggies" had John's venom (remember "pigs from a gun"); "Savoy Truffle," listing the flavors in a box of Good News chocolates, had John's eye for mundane exotica; "While My Guitar Gently Weeps"—on which George brought in his own outsider, Eric Clapton, to play lead—had John's love of exact rhymes and John's melancholy.

The release date was November 22. As John geared up for a round of promotional appearances, Yoko's pregnancy developed complications, and she was admitted to Queen Charlotte's Hospital in Hammersmith. Unable to be separated from her, he put on a pair of pajamas and climbed into the vacant bed next to hers, clasping her hand tightly across the gap. When the bed he had commandeered was needed by a genuine patient, he slept beside Yoko on the floor. To spare them the horrors of hospital food, Greg Sams delivered macrobiotic dishes from the Seed restaurant, while John's actor friend Victor Spinetti smuggled in Craven A cigarettes. Yoko's condition continued to give such cause for concern that her doctors ordered a blood transfusion. To ensure that the blood would be as wholesome as possible, she stipulated that it should come from somebody on a macrobiotic diet. Sams toured London in John's Rolls, rounding up Seed's half dozen best customers, of whom one proved to share her blood type. But all in vain. On November 21, she suffered a miscarriage at six months. John's thoughts may have been dominated by his mother, but he could not stop his life running eerily in parallel with his father's.

The *White Album*'s release the following day brought no sense of impending doom to the Beatles' world public. It sold in vast quantities and received reviews, if possible, even more ecstatic than had *Sgt. Pepper*. The British critic and TV producer Tony Palmer wrote that Lennon and McCartney's only songwriting peer was Schubert, unmindful that no Schubert song exactly tripped off most people's tongues. Wherever questioned, John allowed himself more praise than for anything he had done before. "[It's] a complete reversal from Sergeant Pepper. . . . The music is better for me—because I'm being meself. I'm doing it how I like it."

On November 28, he and Yoko appeared at Marylebone Magistrates Court, charged with possessing the 219 grains of cannabis. Though no suggestion of planting evidence was ever made, the raid's dubious circumstances had not gone unnoticed in official circles. Its main arresting officer, Sgt. Norman Pilcher, subsequently had to explain to the Home Secretary, James Callaghan, why such heavy police resources had been deployed for so very modest a haul. Pilcher replied that pop-star premises were often full of people holding "unusual parties," implying he had expected to bust an orgy rather than a married couple in bed. It was also widely asked who had tipped off the press to arrive at exactly the same moment. There, alas, the good sergeant could shed no light.

The possession charge against Yoko was dropped, after John—in a move that was to have repercussions for him for years afterward— elected to plead guilty and take sole responsibility. "[The prosecutor] said, 'I won't get you for obstruction if you cop a plea,' " he remembered. "And I thought, 'Oh, it's a hundred dollars or whatever. It's no skin off my nose.' And he said, 'I'll let your missus go.' " Yoko being a foreign national, there was a risk that if convicted she might face deportation. The magistrates imposed a fine of £150 with 20 guineas

(£21) costs. Still weak and shaken from her miscarriage, Yoko was mobbed outside the court building, one female spectator taking the opportunity to give her hair a vicious yank.

The following day *Unfinished Music No.1—Two Virgins* was released in the United Kingdom, adding an unofficial charge of indecent exposure to John's indictment. The brown paper cover had an allure long proven in the dirty book trade, and thousands rushed to buy the album, not to hear what extraordinary new sounds the Two Virgins had created on their first night together, but for a look at her tits and his dick. To modern eyes, so assailed by manipulative sexual imagery, it is hard to believe what transports of disgust and derision their self-portrait unleashed. The effect is not smutty or suggestive, but strangely innocent and vulnerable. Even at the time, an Anglican clergyman, more humane than others of his calling, was moved to quote the Old Testament's Genesis: "And they were both naked, the man and his wife, and were not ashamed."

The revelation of Yoko's pregnancy put an end to John's divorce petition against Cynthia for alleged adultery with Robert Bassanini. Cynthia countersued on the same grounds, citing Yoko as corespondent, and was granted an uncontested decree nisi, with custody of Julian. As a financial settlement, John first offered £75,000, the mythical "first dividend" jackpot of Littlewoods and Vernons football pools. Although advised she could claim half his assets, Cynthia could not face a drawn-out and ugly legal fight, and agreed to £100,000 (£1 million in today's values) of which £25,000 was to buy a new house and the rest to support her and Julian until he reached twenty-one. A further £100,000 was put into a trust fund for Julian with a proviso that if John had any further children, the money would be shared with them.

At the same time, arrangements were discreetly made for Yoko's divorce in a suitably faraway spot, the American Virgin Islands. John had not grown any less insecure where Tony Cox was concerned and, despite all Yoko's protestations, still half expected her to go back to Cox at any moment. Cox was amenable to walking away without a legal battle but expected a cash settlement for the loss in income it would entail. He accepted £6,000, plus payment of his legal expenses and a supply of macrobiotic food from the Seed restaurant. Custody of Kyoko was to be shared between her parents, although, as Cox had always done the greater share of child care, she continued living with him. "We shared custody because that was the hippy thing—sharing," Yoko says. "Tony thought John had been an easy touch, but John could be tough over money. Once the custody thing was settled, he refused to pay Tony's legal expenses."

If John's public was appalled and mystified by his new partnership, fellow musicians seemed to have much less of a problem with it. On December 11, he and Yoko took part in the Rolling Stones' *Rock and Roll Circus*, a putative TV special transparently inspired by the Beatles' *Magical Mystery Tour*. Filmed under a circus big top with a live audience, the Stones headed a bill featuring the Who, Jethro Tull, Marianne Faithfull, and bluesman Taj Mahal in alternation with deliberately passé trapeze artists and tumblers and facetious chat by Mick Jagger in a ringmaster's tailcoat. John, as "Winston Legthigh," did a cross-talk act with Jagger, eating mush from a bowl with chopsticks and reminiscing in fruity American tones: "Those were the days . . . I wanna hold your man. . . ." Later—prophesying a familiar figure at political conferences and public speaking events—he announced the Stones in put-on sign language.

A more relevant prophecy was in his appearance onstage without the three musicians from whom he'd been inseparable since 1962. He performed "Yer Blues" fronting an ad hoc band called the Dirty Mac (traditional garb of the sexual pervert), comprising Keith Richard from the Stones, Eric Clapton from Cream, and drummer Mitch Mitchell from the Jimi Hendrix Experience, with Yoko beside them concealed inside a black sack. For their second number, "Whole Lotta Yoko," she came forth to scream and ululate into the microphone, accompanied by the virtuoso Israeli violinist Ivry Gitlis, while John and the two guitar giants behind her just played along.

It was a remarkable show of solidarity against the tide of abuse and ridicule. Unfortunately, the Rolling Stones did not like the way their *Rock and Roll Circus* turned out, and blocked the film's release until almost thirty years later.

23

BEDLAM

I don't believe there's any cause worth getting shot for.

The Beatles' big mistake, they now knew, was never having formally announced an end to touring after Candlestick Park in 1966. As a result, despite all the shows on vinyl they had given since, their return to live performance was still a source of endless media rumor and speculation. And, almost as if Brian's ghost were whispering diplomacy in their ears, they never quite liked to puncture that huge bubble of expectancy. However honest and unpredictable John might be on other issues, the question "When are you guys going on the road again?" was one even he could be relied on to sidestep or fudge.

But while he and George and even Ringo branched off on individual creative paths, Paul McCartney's commitment to the band, and pushing them onward and upward, still far outweighed any solo project. A compulsive showman, he still missed the buzz of live performance, which for the other three, John especially, had no more allure than a dentist's drill. Despite the achievements of their studio years, Paul felt that by severing their old intimate link with their audience, some vital creative spark had been extinguished. With the onus of leadership now on him, reestablishing that that bond—and with it, the Beatles' sense of unity, both as performers and people—became his crusade.

The two separate, brief live performances of "Hey Jude" and "Revolution" they had filmed as TV promos in July 1968, strengthened Paul's hand. Rather than the old mindless shrieking, it had been pleasant to face more mature, empathetic listeners who paid rapt attention and did not hurl a single jelly bean. So good was the feeling that the Beatles had jammed a few extra numbers, with John seemingly enjoying it as much as anyone. Citing this precedent, Paul secured his agreement, and George's, to an ambitious though quite logical and practicable strategy for early 1969. They would give one stage performance, to be circulated to their hungry public as a film made and marketed by their own Apple organization. As a prelude or trailer to the concert, there would also be a short documentary showing them in rehearsal.

Paul's initial suggestion was that Yoko might direct the film. To his tidy, pragmatic mind, it seemed an ideal way both of giving her the respect John demanded and prying her loose from his side while the Beatles were at work. But Yoko, the avant-garde filmmaker, had no interest in shooting a straight documentary—indeed, felt the offer to be as subtly insulting on a professional level as a personal one. Instead, the job went to Michael Lindsay-Hogg, a gifted young television director whose association with the Beatles dated back to their "Paperback Writer"/"Rain" promo film in 1966. He had also directed the live "Hey Jude"/"Revolution" sequences and the Rolling Stones' *Rock and Roll Circus*, featuring John's debut performance as a non-Beatle.

The setting for the comeback concert was to be no ordinary hall or stadium but some exotic outdoor location such as had never served as a backdrop for rock music before. Various grandiose ideas were suggested, like the Egyptian Pyramids, the Sahara Desert, and the deck of a liner in midocean. Lindsay-Hogg brought with him a more realistic suggestion; a two-thousand-year-old Roman amphitheater in Tunisia. "The Beatles were to start playing as the sun came up, and you'd see crowds flocking towards them through the day. It would have been fantastic."

While scouts from Apple Films evaluated the Tunisian location, Lindsay-Hogg began shooting the "Beatles at work" scenes that would precede the show. These were laid on a soundstage at Twickenham Film Studios, where in less complicated times they had done interiors for *A Hard Day's Night* and *Help!* Shooting began on January 2, 1969, just eleven weeks after the *White Album* had wound to its exhausted, divisive end. The Beatles were required to keep filmmaking rather than Abbey Road hours, which meant starting work at around ten a.m. rather than in the early evening. Moreover, a cavernous soundstage in midwinter was a cheerless place to make music, even had the musicians been in total accord. "It wasn't Minsk in January by any means," Lindsay-Hogg says. "But in the morning, people tended to keep their coats on. By afternoon, the lights and body-heat would have warmed the place up."

After the previous November's drug bust, and consequent exposure of their hideaway to well- and ill-wishers, John and Yoko had been forced to move on from Montagu Square. Pending the acquisition of a home of their own, they had the same Good Samaritan as before to thank for offering them a roof. Ringo had lately bought Peter Sellers's riverside mansion in Elstead, Surrey, but still owned his old Weybridge home, Sunny Heights. This he loaned to the runaways for as long as they needed it. John's flight had come full circle back to the St. George's Hill estate, just down the road from Kenwood.

From the outset of rehearsals at Twickenham, resentful reluctance floated like ectoplasm in the chill air. "It was obvious that Paul was the driving force behind the project, and that the other three didn't really want to be there," Michael Lindsay-Hogg remembers. "Paul would always be the one to check in on time every morning, and he was the only one I ever really discussed the filming with. The others would arrive between one and two hours late. On a couple of days, John didn't turn up at all."

The uncivilized hours, the intrusive cameras, even the abhorrent sense of having to, could not altogether suppress John's innate professionalism. "He was a musician," Lindsay-Hogg says. "Put him in a chair, give him a guitar and a cup of tea, and he'd do something. Even at his semi-best, he was still very quick . . . quick to be funny, quick to attack." The great change the director noticed was in Lennon and McCartney's creative relationship. "I'd seen how they worked together when we filmed Paperback Writer, and it was fascinating to see. Now one of them would write a song, bring it in and just tell the others how to play it as if they were session-men."

The anger finally surfaced after eight days, when George walked out, tired of the uncomfortable conditions and, as he saw it, being bossed and bullied by Paul. Prior to the sessions, he had been in America, hanging out with Bob Dylan and the Band and being treated as a respected equal. Now here he was again as a second-string Beatle, still regarded as the "bloody kid" who had tagged along all those years ago. He had had an angry confrontation with Paul, while the camera was running. But in an unrecorded exchange with John, things had gotten even worse. "They actually came to blows," George Martin says. "You'd think it would have been with Paul, but it was John. It was all hushed up afterwards."

Off camera, too, a far graver source of disharmony was starting to develop. Since the previous autumn, a flow of agitated memos from the Beatles' accountants had warned of the vast sums being swallowed up by Apple Corps. At their own rash invitation, Apple's headquarters in Savile Row had become a magnet for anyone hoping to get into the pop business, needing finance for some or other creative project, or, under the terms of "Western Communism," simply seeking a handout from supposedly bottomless Beatle coffers.

By Christmas 1968, even Apple's most utopian-spirited codirector was growing alarmed by the apparent orgy of begging, scrounging, freeloading, and time-wasting at 3 Savile Row. "Eighteen or twenty thousand pounds a week was rolling out . . . and no one was doing anything about it," John would recall. "All our buddies that had worked for us for 50 years were just living and drinking and eating like fucking [ancient] Rome." To mark that festive season, there had been a tea party for employees' children at which, like some paternalistic northern mill owner, he appeared as Father Christmas, accompanied by Yoko as Mother Christmas. The rosy-intentioned kiddiefest was turned into a brawl by some Hell's Angels from San Francisco whom George had invited to London. Those present would never forget the sight of Father Christmas trying to shield Mother Christmas from flailing fists and falling bodies with spilled tea trickling down his glasses.

During the first days of rehearsing at Twickenham, John was interviewed by a journalist he had known since the Beatlemania era, Ray Coleman of *Disc and Music Echo*. Coleman naturally inquired after the health of Apple, prepared for some anodyne boardroom-formulated response. Instead, John gave him the whole scoop: "We haven't got half the money people think we have. We have enough to live on, but we can't let Apple go on like it is. We started off with loads of ideas of what we wanted to do—an umbrella for different activities. But like one or two Beatles things, it didn't work because we aren't practical and we weren't quick enough to realise that we need a businessman's brain to run the whole thing. . . . It's been pie in the sky from the start. We did it all wrong—Paul and me running to New York saying, 'We'll do this and encourage this and that.' It's got to be a business first, we realise that now. . . . It needs a new broom and a lot of people will have to go. . . . It doesn't need to make vast profits, but if it carries on like this, all of us will be broke in the next six months."

In fact, this apocalyptic view was far from justified. Although Apple's original raison d'être had been to lose money, and though it certainly attracted spongers, con artists, and hangers-on like wasps around a honeypot, it was very far from just being (in George's phrase) "a haven for drop-outs." Its failure in the retail field and undiscriminating largesse were more than balanced by the instant spectacular success of its record label. Aside from the Beatles' own automatically chart-topping output, Mary Hopkin's single, "Those Were the Days," had been an international hit. The roster of talent being built by Ron Kass and Peter Asher promised solid growth across the musical board, from the illustrious Modern Jazz Quartet to the American singer-songwriter James Taylor.

The search had already long been under way for the "new broom" John had mentioned, to run both Apple and the Beatles. Recognizing that no other pop impresario could take Brian Epstein's place, the four were agreed it should be someone from the world of big business, whose role would be purely commercial and administrative. One such figure to be approached was Lord Beeching, who, three years earlier, had "rationalised" Britain's railway network by closing down huge stretches of it; another was the Queen's financial adviser, Lord Poole. John had also offered the job to Neil Aspinall, the Beatles' oldest and most loyal associate, urging, "Come on Nell . . . you may as well have the 20 percent." Though titular managing director of Apple, Neil had no wish to take on such a hugely magnified role. However, by the time *Disc and Music Echo* published John's cri de coeur on January 18, a solution to the problem seemed to have been found.

The last thing Paul McCartney ever intended or expected was to fall for a woman with the same intensity that John had. "I'm glad I'm not in love like that," he once remarked revealingly when John and Yoko were first together. But suddenly—as if the old Outlaw follow-your-leader spirit still held sway—he was. In mid-1968, he had begun seeing a rangy young New Yorker named Linda Eastman, then working as a freelance magazine photographer. The chemistry had been instantaneous; Linda now lived with him in London, arousing even fiercer hostility from his fans than Yoko did from John's.

Linda's father, Lee Eastman, was a respected Manhattan lawyer whose clients included many top show-business names as well as some of American's foremost painters. Her brother John also worked in the practice. Toward the end of the year, Paul accompanied Linda to New York, met Lee and John Eastman, and returned convinced that here were the rescuers Apple sought. It certainly seemed a neat and easy solution, answering the Beatles' need for experienced business hands on the tiller while they got on with being creative. John had a deep-seated dislike of faits accomplis, especially if they came from Paul, but even so, in the absence of any rival candidate, the Eastmans' path seemed clear.

Whatever the misuses of the Apple house, it came into its own as a refuge from those disagreeable rehearsal sessions at Twicken-ham. After George's walkout on January 10, the Beatles decided to abandon their cheerless soundstage and, after a short break, con-tinue work in the studio that Magic Alex Mardas had been install-ing in the basement of 3 Savile Row. George agreed to return on condition there was no more talk of concerts in Roman amphithe-aters or on the decks of ocean liners, and they simply concentrated on making their next album. Although this took away most of the point of a tie-in documentary, Michael Lindsay-Hogg's two cameras continued filming anyway.

The previous July, George's American friends the Band had taken time out from backing Bob Dylan to release *Music from Big Pink*, an album whose folkish simplicity was a conscious reaction to *Sgt. Pepper* and its countless intricately engineered imitators. Once more going with the flow of their own backwash, the Beatles decided on a similarly direct, intimate style, as close as possible to the way they used to sound in Liverpool and Hamburg. Restored to his accus-tomed role as producer, George Martin was briefed by John in terms that as good as wrote off the brilliant work they had created together at Abbey Road. "[He] came to me and said, 'On this one, George, we don't want any of your production crap. It's going to be an honest album, OK? I don't want any overdubbing, or any of the editing that you do. I want to do it so that when we listen to it I know we did it.' In this slighting spirit of regression and renewal, the album was pro-visionally titled *Get Back*.

Martin had been led to believe he would be working in a studio whose technological marvels would make Abbey Road seem prehis-toric. Instead, he found that only the control room was in a usable state. To begin recording when the Beatles demanded, on January 22, most of the sound equipment had to be hastily shipped in from EMI. A tight-lipped Martin had to deal with further problems, from an intrusively noisy air-conditioning unit to a lack of feed holes for cables onto the studio floor. After the bleakness of Twickenham, the Beatles demanded that their work environment be as homelike as possible, with comfortable armchairs and an open fire burning in the hearth. "When they listened to the first tracks, there was this mysterious crackling noise in the background," Neil Aspinall remembered. "Finally we realised it was the bloody fire."

Despite vastly pleasanter surroundings and a clearer objective in view, tension soon began seeping back. Playing whole tracks in one go, without editing or overdubbing, was something the Beatles had not done since Martin had wrung their first album out of them in a single day back in 1963. "And course it became terribly tedious because they couldn't give me what I wanted—a perfect performance," Martin remembers. "I'd say 'Okay, seventeen . . . John that was a lovely vocal, but Paul had a bit of a glitch on the bass.' . . . On the 61st take, John would say 'How was that one, George?' I'd say 'John, I honestly don't know.' 'No fookin' good then, are you?' he'd say. That was the general atmosphere."

Since Yoko had taken up station next to John, and Eric Clapton had played lead guitar for George on the *White Album*, no one any longer regarded the Beatles as an inviolably self-sufficient foursome. On the *Get Back* sessions, they acquired their first black American auxiliary in keyboards player Billy Preston, whom they had first met when he appeared at the Hamburg Star-Club with Little Richard. Preston fitted effortlessly into the music, while his happy-go-lucky personality did much to improve the problematical vibes. When not working on tracks for the album, they used up hours of tape and film in talking and jamming every kind of irrelevant number—fifties rock-'n'-roll classics, old Beatles tracks, current chart hits by other people, show tunes, comic songs, even nursery rhymes, around a hundred titles in all. "They didn't care what I filmed because they were the producers and could cut anything they didn't like," Lindsay-Hogg remembers. "It all began to feel like Sartre's play *No Exit* . . . characters trapped together in a room, uncertain why they were there and not knowing how to get out. There didn't seem to be any way of stopping it."

The only possible ending was for the Beatles to give the live performance they had originally intended, albeit at some venue nearer at hand than Tunisia or Egypt. Ringo suggested going back to their old Liverpool home, the Cavern club, but none of the others fancied such a sentimental journey. Weary of the whole subject, John was heard to mutter, "I'm warming to the idea of doing it in an asylum."

The least bad option seemed to be the Roundhouse, a converted tram shed in Chalk Farm, which had become the London counterculture's favorite auditorium. Then Lindsay-Hogg came up with an idea that combined maximum visual drama with minimum inconvenience. "One day when we were all having roast lamb in the Apple boardroom, I said why didn't they do the show here, from their own roof? As we were in midwinter, it would have to be quite early in the day, before the light started to fail. I told them they should aim to make so much noise that George Martin would hear it over in St. John's Wood."

The roof of 3 Savile Row included a good-size flat portion accessible via the main stairs (as more than one casual visitor had demonstrated by stealing portions of valuable lead insulation and making off with it unchallenged). A quick inspection confirmed that it could easily accommodate a makeshift wooden stage and the requisite camera and sound-recording equipment. Besides shooting from chimney level, Lindsay-Hogg planned to hire a helicopter for aerial views like those of Shea Stadium in 1965. "I went to Paul and asked if it was OK. He answered, 'That's a yes' with his thumb turned down and 'That's a no' with his thumb turned up. Then I looked at John, who just nodded. I took that to be the say-so that mattered."

The performance was scheduled to take place on the afternoon of Thursday, January 30. The day was unrelievedly dull and cold, with a biting wind and a suspicion of fog that ruled out the helicopter sequence. On Apple's roof, the stage was prepared, the cameras were in position and about thirty spectators, friends or employees, had taken up vantage points on the surrounding walls and parapets; five stories below, the streets were crowded with unsuspecting passers-by. "About 10 minutes before we were due to start, all the Beatles were in a little room at the top of the stairs and it still wasn't certain that they'd go ahead," Lindsay-Hogg remembers. "George didn't want to and Ringo started saying he didn't really see the point. Then John said 'Oh fuck—let's do it.'"

His interview with *Disc and Music Echo* had appeared twelve days earlier and had spun and echoed around the world. BEATLE BITES APPLE, FINDS WORM, said *Variety* in the spirit of its

famous 1929 headline, WALL STREET LAYS AN EGG. Far from trying
to tone down the vision of chaos and imminent insolvency he had
shared with Ray Coleman, John repeated it to the other reporters
who instantly besieged him, adding more and better particulars
all the time. The choicest were given to *Rolling Stone*, the "serious"
music paper that had recently begun publication from San Francisco.
Apple had become such a drain on his personal resources, he told
Rolling Stone, that he was "down to my last £50,000." Though £50,000
was an enormous sum in 1969, and the estimate patently unrealistic
(what about the constant top-up from songwriting royalties?), the
notion of a cash-strapped Beatle caused universal amazement and
consternation.

Paul, that tireless PR man, tried to downplay the story, fearful of
the damage it would do to Apple's credibility as a company, never
mind the morale of 3 Savile Row's many decent, conscientious employees. Bumping into Ray Coleman there, he berated the scoop
getter for not having realized it was "just John shooting his mouth
off" with customary disregard for consequences. On the contrary,
the revelation had been timed for the moment when Paul's chosen
new broom, Lee and John Eastman, were poised to sweep into Apple.
It could be read as an open invitation to rival candidates to step forward, if not a coded message to the one who actually did.

On January 28 John and Yoko kept a secret rendezvous at the
Dorchester Hotel with the Rolling Stones' manager, Allen Klein. A
thirty-seven-year-old accountant from New Jersey, Klein had made
a specialty of British pop acts with bankability in America, also controlling the Dave Clark Five, the Animals, Herman's Hermits, and
Donovan. In the transatlantic music world, he was renowned for the
ferocity with which he negotiated recording contracts for his artistes,
securing them large advances against royalties (something never
yet done for the Beatles) and pursuing his commercial adversaries
through the courts. Klein himself had no quarrel with his reputation
as—in one British newspaper's words—"the toughest wheeler-dealer
in the pop jungle." On his desk he kept a plaque, half-quoting Psalm
23: "Yea, though I walk through the valley of the shadow of death, I
shall fear no evil for I am the biggest motherfucker in the valley."

Short and pudgy, with greased-back hair, somewhat like the forties comedy star Lou Costello, he seemed the very last person with whom John could ever strike up a rapport. "But Allen was very clever," Yoko says. "He knew all the lyrics of John's songs. He just kept on quoting lyrics. He'd memorised them all. And that got John."

Klein's proposition, expressed in blunt, colorful New Jersey-ese, was simple. He would go into Apple, stem the hemorrhage of waste, and, by reorganizing the Beatles' contracts in his usual style, make all four wealthier than they'd ever dreamed—wealthy enough, as he put it, to say, "F.Y.M., Fuck You, Money." After the Eastmans' Park Avenue preciousness, he seemed to John like the honest, unpretentious whiff of a downtown kosher deli. Nor was he one of the hated "men in suits," being addicted to turtleneck sweaters (despite being severely challenged in the neck department) and cardigans with leather facings. The vibe grew still better when it emerged that his parents had separated when he was very young and that, just like John, he had spent much of his childhood in the care of an aunt. At the end of a couple of hours, John had made up his mind, and there and then dashed off a note to EMI's chairman Sir Joseph Lockwood: "Dear Sir Joe—from now on, Allen Klein handles all my stuff."

His Apple codirectors were not informed of his decision until a board meeting on the day after the rooftop concert. Paul was hopeful this might have reawakened the others' appetite for playing together, and suggested they might follow it up with some further appearances at selected small venues on the ground. John bluntly told him to forget any such ideas, then went on to capsize the new-broom strategy the others regarded as virtually a done deal. "I don't give a bugger what anyone else wants," he said. "I'm having Allen Klein for me."

John would not back down, and Paul could not. He was irrevocably committed not only to the Eastman law practice but the Eastman family, through his involvement with Lee Eastman's daughter, Linda. Ironically, a year or two before, he had been strongly in favor of hiring Allen Klein to light a fire under EMI Records on the Beatles' behalf. Now, after a hostile briefing on Klein from all three Eastmans, he would sooner have put himself in the hands of Jack the Ripper. With John resigned and forbearing no longer and Paul angry

that the Beatles' traditional democratic spirit was being ignored—
and atypically passionate and outspoken—this first-ever real quarrel
between them was to prove fatal.

Despite John's belligerently unilateralist tone, he knew that having
one management for himself and another for the rest of the Beatles
would be unworkable. The crucial question was how George and
Ringo would take to Allen Klein. In the event, both were equally
captivated by Klein's down-to-earth manner and "Fuck You, Money"
pledge, withdrawing their support from the Eastmans and aligning
themselves behind John.

For now, an uneasy compromise was agreed to. John Eastman and
Klein both moved into 3 Savile Row, ostensibly handling separate
aspects of Apple business but in evident daggers-drawn competition.
While their respective champions beavered away, John and Paul
maintained an appearance of amity, though new tensions were bub-
bling under the surface. John clearly did not care overmuch for Linda,
whom he regarded as little more than a spy for a hostile power. Paul
thought that most unfair, considering the friendliness he felt he had
shown to Yoko. Linda and Yoko found little in common, despite both
being New Yorkers and divorcées with small daughters of similar
ages. In contrast with John and Yoko's low-key comings and goings,
Paul liked to make an entrance with Linda, usually carrying her little
girl, Heather, on his shoulders. "Here comes the Royal Family," John
would mutter as the stir of their arrival floated upstairs.

Klein played a clever game, always scrupulously giving Yoko the
same respect and attention he did to John and putting their work
together on the same level as the Beatles'. Though a veteran of a
thousand bloody boardroom scraps, he refused let John Eastman
rile him. The first meeting he had with Lee Eastman and the three
in-the-bag Beatles, at Claridges Hotel, broke down when Eastman
senior began shouting at him. The outburst had, in fact, been skillfully provoked by Klein to make Eastman look like a hysteric and
himself like a stolid underdog. George, Ringo, and especially John
sided with the underdog.

Klein also quickly found an arena in which to employ his fabled
deal-making techniques and put the Eastmans' noses out of joint.

Despite the establishment of Apple, the Beatles' earnings continued to be paid into NEMS, the management company Brian Epstein had built around them—and in which he had given them a 10 percent stake. Late in 1968, faced by punitive taxes on Brian's estate, his brother, Clive, and mother, Queenie, had no choice but to sell NEMS. John Eastman had put together a plan for the Beatles to acquire the company, helped by a £1 million loan from EMI. The Epstein family felt a moral obligation to consider no other offer, and the deal seemed a foregone conclusion.

With Klein and his reputation added to the mix, however, Clive and Queenie Epstein took fright and on February 17 sold out to a firm of London merchant bankers. There followed a protracted battle in the High Court over whether the Beatles' earnings in future should be channeled through NEMS's new owners or paid directly into Apple. Klein managed to sideline John Eastman and conclude a settlement that, if it did not win NEMS for the Beatles, at least broke its hold over them. The new owners would buy out their 10 percent share and cease receiving their income, and levying commission, in exchange for a lump sum to be paid from future EMI royalties.

The brickbats thrown at Klein by the British press during the NEMS affair only hardened John's support and loyalty. Friends in the music business who begged him to think again all received equally short shrift. Even that least altruistic of pop stars, Mick Jagger, phoned one day and offered to brief him on the Rolling Stones' growing disillusionment with their manager. But when Jagger arrived in Apple's boardroom to see John, he found Klein also sitting around the table. Never one for confrontation, Mick departed without unburdening himself.

Having tried various forms of facial hair since *Sgt. Pepper* and India, John now grew a long, bushy beard, weirdly similar to his joke disguise in *Help!* Its effect was to transform a face that never looked serious into one that looked nothing else. Framed by shoulder-length hair, it gave him a permanently tragic and aggrieved expression, like the stylized Christs in religious imagery of his boyhood—though he had only to open his densely whiskered mouth for the same old John to be instantly resurrected.

With Yoko he was discovering a new kind of live performance, arousing reactions very different from the joyous, uncritical Beatlemaniac screams that so used to disgust him. The two had made their debut together at the Alchemical Wedding, a Christmas party for London's avant-garde art community at the Royal Albert Hall on December 18. They appeared onstage together hidden inside a large white sack, making no sound but writhing energetically. This was Yoko's concept of "Bagism," inspired by the dictum of Antoine de Saint-Exupéry's cult novel *The Little Prince*: "It is only with the heart that one can see rightly. The essential is invisible to the eye."

They were fully visible in an experimental music festival held at a Cambridge college on March 2. Yoko occupied the foreground, screaming and keening as she'd once heard her family servants do when discussing the horrors of childbirth, while John stood in the shadows behind her, vamping guitar chords with heavy feedback. The arty Cambridge crowd were as shocked and affronted to discover a pop star in their midst as the Beatles' constituency had been by Yoko.

On March 12, Paul married Linda Eastman at Marylebone Register Office in London, amid scenes of hysterical grief from his female fans. None of the other Beatles was present. The news reached John as he and Yoko were driving down to visit Aunt Mimi in Poole. Yoko's divorce decree had become final a few weeks earlier, and, in a resurgence of Beatle copycat spirit, John told her they, too, must get married as soon as possible.

Initially Yoko was far from enthusiastic. "I'd never really wanted to be married the other two times," she recalls. "It was just something I'd fallen into. Having a child wasn't something I'd wanted either, but had all come from Tony. I didn't particularly like the thought of limiting myself to one guy again. And I still had that strange thought at the back of my mind that if I stayed with John, some terrible tragedy was waiting."

He won her agreement by promising that, unlike Paul's, their marriage would be the quickest, simplest, and most private of ceremonies. For his initial plan, he had to thank his upbringing in a seaport and knowledge of the powers traditionally invested in master mariners. "On the drive down to Mimi's, John slid back the partition and told me they wanted to be married at sea by a ship's captain," his chauffeur Les Anthony remembers. " 'Can you get us on a ship, Les?' he said. 'I don't care where it's going. And don't say anything to Mimi.' " While the pair were at Mimi's, Anthony drove to nearby Southampton and discovered there was a P&O Line cruise to the Bahamas departing at eight that evening. "Book us on it," John ordered. But by that time, P&O's reservations office had closed for the day.

It then struck John that any ship's captain must be empowered to perform weddings, even those commanding the humdrum ferries that plied across the English Channel to the Continent. He and Yoko drove posthaste to Southampton and tried to book tickets on a Sorensen Line ferry to France, intending to seek out the skipper and persuade him to marry them as soon as the vessel left dock. But because of an irregularity in Yoko's passport, they were turned away. What made it doubly galling was that when Paul had gone to France to film "The Fool on the Hill" for *Magical Mystery Tour* two years earlier, he had forgotten his passport but been allowed to travel anyway.

Having failed to reach France as a humble day-tripper, John said, "Fuck it," hired a private jet, and took Yoko to Paris, hoping that instant nuptials might be procurable somewhere or other in continental Europe. It so happened that Peter Brown, the Beatles' fixer-in-chief, was spending that same weekend in Amsterdam. At John's request, Brown tried to arrange a quickie wedding there, but found that Dutch law required a minimum two weeks' residency beforehand. After further research, he reported back that the only place in Europe where such regulations did not apply was Gibraltar, off the south coast of Spain. Not only did it grant instant marriage licenses but it was an historic British possession and military base. To be granted entry, John would not even need a passport.

The plan was kept secret from everyone at Apple but Neil Aspinall. A photographer named David Nutter, whose brother Tommy lived with Brown, was flown to Gibraltar under cloak-and-dagger conditions, having no idea why. On March 20, 1969, John and Yoko, clad in matching white, made the three-hour flight from Paris by private jet. They drove straight to the British Consulate, where they were joined in matrimony by the elderly Registrar, Cecil Wheeler, with Peter Brown as best man. David Nutter did some quick pictures of them on the Consulate staircase surrounded by bemused staff, and on their own outside, with Yoko steadying her wide-brimmed hat in the Mediterranean wind. In less than an hour, they were heading back to Paris to reveal their coup to the world's media. John explained they had picked Gibraltar because it was "quiet, British and friendly. . . . Intellectually, we knew marriage was a stupid scene, but we're romantic and square as well as hip and aware." Looking down from their hotel window on the French newspaper placards that trumpeted the story, Yoko burst into tears to think Kyoko might see similar ones in English.

If the wedding had been quiet, the reception would be something else. Les Anthony was waiting in Paris with John's Rolls-Royce and, next day, drove them two hundred miles north through the Low Countries to Amsterdam, where they had originally hoped to tie the knot. There they dispatched Anthony back to England with the Rolls, checked into the ninth-floor Presidential Suite of the Hilton hotel, and announced they would hold a weeklong "bed-in for peace." "Yoko and I decided that we knew whatever we did would be in the papers," John later explained. "We decided to use the space we would occupy anyway with a commercial for peace. We sent out a card 'Come to John and Yoko's honeymoon. . . .' The press seemed to think we were going to make love in public because we made an album with us naked—so they seemed to think anything goes."

The reporters and cameramen of every nation who stampeded through the doors of suite 902 certainly received a jaw-dropping surprise. Instead of the expected two Virgins–style nude bacchanal, they found the newlyweds propped up by side by side in the double bed, decorously pajama-clad, surrounded by flowers and hand-lettered placards saying BED PEACE, HAIR PEACE, I LOVE YOKO, and I LOVE JOHN, with a normally clad Derek Taylor as Groom of the Bedchamber. His thick beard oddly in contrast with his pristine sleep attire, John explained the rationale. Rather than march and fight with the militant counterculture to make a better world, he had resolved to "do it Gandhi's way," but using a power to command attention that the Mahatma had never known.

"Marching was fine and dandy for the Thirties. Today you need different methods—it's sell, sell, sell. If you want to sell peace, you've got to sell it like soap. [The media] have war on every day, not only on the news but on the old John Wayne movies and every damn movie you see, war war war, kill kill kill. We said 'Let's get some peace, peace, peace on the headlines, just for a change.' . . . For reasons known only to themselves, people do print what I say. And I'm saying 'Peace.' " Along with Gandhi, another, perhaps even more surprising, spiritual ally was invoked. "We want Christ to win. We're trying to make Christ's message contemporary. What would he have done if he'd had advertisements, records, films, TV and newspapers? Christ made miracles to tell his message. Well, the miracle today is communications, so let's use it."

For seven days, the couple held court in this eighteenth-century salon manner, John talking almost nonstop to the relays of interviewers or over TV and radio hookups, with frequent promptings and interjections from Yoko. They had all their meals in bed, leaving their nest of pillows under the panoramic window only for essential ablutions or when brisk Dutch maids needed to change the sheets.

In later years, pop stars who used their headline-grabbing power to preach humanitarianism, such as Bob Geldof or Bono, would be admired and honored. Yoko and John's Amsterdam bed-in was the first time such a thing had ever occurred, and they paid the usual price of pioneering. The world's commentators were at one in dismissing it as fatuous, presumptuous—above all, sublimely pointless. The pajama-Mahatma begged passionately to differ: "In Paris, the Vietnam peace talks have got about as far as sorting out the shape of the table they're going to sit round. Those talks have been going on for months. In one week in bed, we achieved a lot more. . . . A little old lady from Wigan or Hull wrote to the *Daily Mirror* asking if they could put Yoko and myself on the front page more often. She said she hadn't laughed so much for ages. That's great! That's what we wanted. I mean, it's a funny world when two people going to bed on their honeymoon can make the front pages in all the papers for a week. I wouldn't mind dying as the world's clown. I'm not looking for epitaphs."

The perambulation around European capitals was not over yet. Five months earlier, in the aftermath of Yoko's miscarriage, she and John had coproduced and codirected their most ambitious film to date. This was a seventy-five-minute piece entitled *Rape* and featuring twenty-one-year-old Hungarian actress Eva Majlata. The rapist was a television camera, which followed Majlata's character everywhere with the same remorselessness that such devices once had stalked the Beatles—and now did the newlywed Lennons—almost hounding her to her death in front of a truck, finally cornering her in an apartment, impervious to her whimpers for mercy. The film had been commissioned by Austrian television and went out immediately after the Amsterdam bed-in, on March 31.

That same evening, John and Yoko held a press conference in the Red Room of Vienna's famous Hotel Sacher. Once again, the media found them hidden inside a sack. Despite a chorus of pleas, John declined to come out, explaining "This is a Bag Event—total communication." Some questioners asked if such reticence wasn't a little odd for a man who had just invited the world's press into his bedroom. "We're showing how all of us are exposed and under pressure in the contemporary world," he replied. "This isn't just about the Beatles. What's happening to this girl is happening in Vietnam, Biafra, everywhere." The bag-in generated considerably more seriousness than had the bed-in. *Rape* was subsequently shown at the prestigious Montreux Festival and received a glowing review in the *London Evening Standard* from the German-born critic Willi Frischauer, who wrote that "it does for the age of television what Franz Kafka's *The Trial* did for the age of totalitarianism."

Unfettered though John might now seem, he was still tied to the Beatles' annual life cycle, which carried on under Apple just as it had under EMI. Spring meant a new single, just ahead of an album that would set the tone of the summer for millions. But the *Get Back* project was in no state to meet either demand. When the sessions in Apple's basement studio had finally ground to a halt, none of the band—not even Paul—could face sifting through the thirty-odd hours of tape with George Martin to find twelve serviceable tracks. Instead, the whole lot were turned over to Glyn Johns, their engineer at Twickenham Studios, to put into the best shape he could.

The Beatles single released on April 11 offered two of the songs they had played in that reluctant alfresco concert on Apple's roof. Neither gave any hint of a band reaching for a simpler, more "honest" style. The one actually called "Get Back" was a catchy but unmeaningful McCartney A-side about characters in a pastiche American West—Jojo and Sweet Loretta Martin. On the B-side, John's "Don't Let Me Down" spoke directly to Yoko with heart-whole commitment of an extra marriage vow: "I'm in love for the first time . . . It's a love that lasts forever / it's a love that has no past."

On April 22, the Apple roof was pressed into service again for a ceremony reaffirming his commitment to Yoko. Up there among the Mayfair chimneys and burbling pigeons, in front of a Commissioner for Oaths, he discarded his war-baby middle name of Winston and became John Ono Lennon to her Yoko Ono Lennon. Afterward, he noted with pleasure that between them they now mustered nine letter o's—his lifelong lucky number. "The simplest way of saying what Yoko is to me and what I am to her is that before we met we were half a person. You know, there's no myth about people being half and the other half being in the sky or in Heaven or something or the other side of the universe or the mirror-image bit . . . We were two halves and together we are a whole."

Another Lennon song was on the drawing board that had even less to do with getting back to where he once belonged. His lyrics always been a kind of journalism, drawn as much from passing headlines as from the heart and soul. Now he decided to file his own version of the story that had been eating up newsprint this past month. The result was "The Ballad of John and Yoko," a piece of reportage laced with satire and double entendre, structured like a short story and with dialogue like a play. It retraced the couple's European odyssey, from "standing in the dock at Southampton" to flying into Paris and Peter Brown's discovery that they could "get married in Gibraltar, near Spain"; from the Amsterdam Hilton and "talking in our bed for a week" to Vienna and eating chocolate cake (the Hotel Sacher's famous, decidedly nonmacrobiotic *Sacher torte*) "in a bag." A chorus of pursuers and persecutors played walk-on parts: immigration officers, hostile questioners at the bed-in, newspaper commentators muttering snidely that "She's gone to his head" and "They look just like two gurus in drag."

The middle eight featured a metaphysical quotation from Yoko, here cozily depicted as "the wife," while the chorus of "Christ! You know it ain't easy!" and the prediction that "They're gonna crucify me" overtly dared the religious zealots of three years earlier to rise up again.

None of it had anything to do with the other Beatles, yet John still looked for no other collaborators to bring his combined travelogue, PR job, and cry of protest to fruition in the studio. At that point in mid-April, however, George had gone abroad; Ringo was making a film, *The Magic Christian*; and only Paul was in London. Despite the rift between them over business, John asked him to help finish and record "The Ballad of John and Yoko." And, despite Paul's lack of engagement in the subject matter, it was an appeal he could not refuse. John came to his house in St. John's Wood; they discussed the song while walking in the garden, then went around the corner to Abbey Road Studios to cut it. They settled on a laid-back, almost Latin beat, dividing the roles of the two absentee Beatles between them—John on lead guitar as well as lead vocal, Paul on drums as well as bass, piano, and maracas. The track was finished in a single session amid much good-humored mutual joshing about their surrogate roles. "Go a bit faster, Ringo," John called out at one point. "Okay, George," Paul replied.

Thus, the song that represented John's first break for freedom ended up being credited to Lennon and McCartney and released in the United Kingdom as an extra springtime Beatles single on May 30, while "Get Back" was still number one. Thus, thanks to pairing with an indifferent George Harrison song, "Old Brown Shoe," the truant had his first A-side with the band in two years, and a hit on both sides of the Atlantic. And thus it seemed that in his escapades with beds and bags, the other three stood as solidly behind him as ever.

Lennon and McCartney's truce over "The Ballad of John and Yoko" ended well before the single came out. Early in May,

John went to Paul, backed by George and Ringo, and asked for his signature alongside theirs on the management contract Allen Klein had drawn up. Paul conceded defeat but, reluctant to let Klein reel them in with such apparent ease, suggested trying to reduce his commission from the 20 percent he was asking. The deputation said there was no time for further argument, as Klein had to fly back to New York that same day and present a fully ratified contract to his "board." Paul saw this as just a ruse to pressure them: Klein was a virtual one-man band in his company, ABKCO Industries, and, anyway, they were just coming up to a weekend, so nothing needed be done until the following Monday. There was a heated argument, which ended with Paul saying "Fuck off" and the other three walking out.

The following week, discussions reopened on a calmer note. Paul accepted the majority decision to hire Klein, with the proviso that his 20 percent would not extend to the Beatles' earnings from Capitol Records in America. When he negotiated a new royalty rate with Capitol, later that year, he would receive 20 percent only on the increase. Even now, Paul did not actually sign the management agreement. Nor did he acknowledge that Klein had any personal sway over him as an individual and—emphatically not—as a musician. For such advice and guidance as he sought in these areas, he continued to turn to his new father-in-law and brother-in-law, Lee and John Eastman, and, increasingly, to his wife, Linda.

The immediate effect was to make him lose all interest in the organization he above all had wanted to bring into existence and had worked so hard, on so many fronts, to maintain. His pride hurt more than his smiley face ever let on, he retreated with Linda and little Heather behind the walls of his London house or to his Scottish farm near the Mull of Kintyre.

With all opposition now removed, Klein went through Apple like a Rottweiler through a basket of newborn puppies, slashing costs, axing idealistic or unproductive projects like the Apple school, the Apple Foundation for the Arts, Apple Films, and Apple Electronics, firing all staff members he deemed nonessential, creating an atmosphere of terror and insecurity that was normal to American business

but still almost unknown in Britain. That many marked for termination considered themselves personal friends of John or George, as
much as large-salaried and expense-accounted employees, made no
difference. Apple Records' top man, Ron Kass, was instantly let go,
even though his division represented the company's one undoubted
commercial success. The head of A&R, Peter Asher, resigned out of
loyalty to Kass, taking with him a soon-to-be monster moneymaker,
James Taylor. Concerned that, here and elsewhere, Klein seemed to
be throwing out the baby with the bathwater, Neil Aspinall protested
to John, but even he received short shrift. Back came a telegram that
seemed to take little account of Neil's longtime loyalty and selflessness. "Don't bite the hand that feeds you," it said.

Klein's powers turned out to have some limits. Derek Taylor, the
Apple press officer, was too much beloved of John—never mind the
press—for Klein to try to unseat him or seriously curb the daily carnival that went on in his office. And Aspinall soon found that his
years of loyalty were not as undervalued as he had thought. "One
day in the boardroom, Klein tried to make me sign a contract while
John and Yoko were sitting at the table," he would remember, "I'd
never had any kind of written contract with the Beatles, and I wasn't
going to start now. I got up and started dodging round the table and
Klein chased me, waving this piece of paper. When he got to John
and Yoko, John put out a hand and stopped him. 'Look at all the
trouble I got into, signing bits of paper.' John said. 'He's not stupid.
Leave Neil alone!'"

Ron Kass's departure had left vacant an elegant, high-ceilinged
office on the ground floor, looking into Savile Row. This now became
a self-contained headquarters for John and Yoko where the pair
would develop their own film and musical projects and continue the
momentum of their recent European travels. They formed a company named Bag Productions, hired their own art adviser, a critic
and exhibition organizer named Anthony Fawcett, and announced
open house.

After the bed-in, every pacifist organization in the world was avid
for John's suggestions on how to publicize their message with similar effect. Among those who requested his input was the Campaign

for Nuclear Disarmament (CND), whose mass rallies and marches on nuclear bases had made headlines in the late fifties, but had since greatly declined in newsworthiness. John suggested a promotional strategy that certainly would have won it more attention: "You've got women in your movement. Sell sex for peace." He received countless invitations to address conferences and seminars, but declined them all because formal speechmaking had never been his bag, and also on the perfectly sincere grounds that "I'm a shy guy under all this madness."

Apple's staff were expected to work for Bag Productions also, carrying out assignments that sometimes made Beatle whims seem almost routine. Picking up the theme of their Coventry Cathedral exhibit, John and Yoko decided to present every major world leader with two acorns to bury as a symbol of peace. Since this was springtime and oak trees do not yield their crop until autumn, a nationwide search for secondhand acorns had to be made. Leading philosophers and thinkers, among them the nonogenarian Bertrand Russell, had to be contacted and asked for support. "Think of it as a pop song," John said. "You've got to have a great catchphrase and the catchphrase is 'Acorns for peace.'"

He was aware of the jokes and cruel nicknames that Yoko inspired around Apple and, on his angrier days, believed the whole house to be colluding to undermine their projects. On May 9, they released a second album of sonic experimentation, *Unfinished Music No. 3—Life with the Lions*. This nod to John's childhood radio favorite, *Life with the Lyons*, was the only lighthearted touch. The contents included a recording of his gig with Yoko at Cambridge in February, and the brief heartbeat of the baby they had lost four months earlier. The front cover showed Yoko in bed at Queen Charlotte's Hospital, with John next to her on the floor where he had slept. The back-cover image was a press photograph of them being mobbed outside Marylebone Magistrates Court after John's drug conviction.

Life with the Lions did not come out on Apple but on Zapple, a subsidiary label dedicated to poetry- and prose-reading, run by the Indica Gallery's Barry Miles and miraculously still unmauled by Klein. It clearly was never going to get much radio play beyond John

Peel's esoteric *Night Ride* program on the BBC. Nonetheless, John was furious with Apple's promotion department for not doing more to plug it.

He might have merged his name with Yoko's, mingling letter *o*'s like red corpuscles, but in the public's mind it was still indivisibly joined to that of his former creative other half. The Lennon-McCartney song catalog was the richest storehouse of universally adored music ever created. Northern Songs, the public company that controlled it, ranked with Shell Oil, Ford Motors, and the other most enduring chart-toppers on the London Stock Exchange. Behind that simple, rain-on-cobblestones name were 129 Lennon-McCartney song copyrights, many now ranked as classics alongside the best of Cole Porter or Irving Berlin.

Northern was still run by Dick James, the small-beer publisher who had set it up around John and Paul after a single hearing of "Please Please Me" in 1962. So long as Lennon gave an appearance of being as house-trained as McCartney, the future of Northern Songs was rosy. But once John's individuality asserted itself and a threat to that golden stream of hits was perceived, the share price began to wobble alarmingly. In March 1969, Dick James's nerves could stand no more and, without any advance warning, he sold his 23 percent stake for £1 million to the television mogul Lew Grade, whose ATV corporation already owned 12 percent. With 35 percent now under their belt, Grade and ATV had announced a £9.5 million bid for the rest of the company.

The news had come when John was in bed in Amsterdam and Paul enjoying a more conventional honeymoon in America. Despite their disagreement on other issues, they were united in fury against James for having sold them down the river without even the courtesy of a warning. The managerial duel between John Eastman and Allen Klein at this point was still far from resolved, but once again Klein took the initiative, putting forward a strategy for Apple to snatch Northern Songs from Lew Grade's open jaws. At present, John and Paul each owned 15 percent of the company, and another token 1.6 percent was held jointly by George and Ringo. Klein's plan was to offer £2 million for the 20 percent that would secure them a

hair's-breadth majority stake. The money was to come from a firm
of merchant bankers on collateral including John's entire holding
in Northern, 650,000 shares. While these arrangements were going
forward, it emerged that, on Eastman's advice, Paul had quietly increased his own holding to 750,000 shares, which would form no
part of the collateral. John was vociferously upset by what he saw as
Paul's underhanded behavior and selfishness.

By mid-May, it seemed as if they were going to win. Apple had
found enough allies to secure that vital extra 20 percent, most crucially a City consortium that currently held 14 percent. A delicate
deal was in place, stipulating among other things that Klein would
have no part in the new Northern's management structure and that
John and Paul would extend their creative involvement beyond the
present expiration date of 1973. Then, at a crucial meeting with the
consortium's representatives, John lost his temper and announced
he was "sick of being fucked around by men in suits, sitting on their
fat arses in the City." The offended suits instantly switched allegiance
to ATV, Lew Grade gained control of Northern Songs, and Lennon-
McCartney's catalog became a pass-the-parcel prize that would be
handed down the decades, increasing stupendously in value each
time it was unwrapped.

Between May 26 and June 2, John and Yoko staged a second bed-
in. They originally planned to do it in America on a mission
that would also include visiting the country's new Republican president, Richard Nixon, and presenting him with two acorns to bury
for peace. The rest of that painstakingly gathered crop had been put
into little boxes, labeled with the names of other world leaders, such
as China's Mao Tse-tung and the Soviet Union's Leonid Brezhnev,
who were likewise to be invited to forget warfare and oppression,
choose a plot of earth, unwrap their acorns, pick up a spade, and
get digging. John wanted to take the boxes to the United Nations
building in New York where the emissaries of every leader, except
China's, could be found "in a pile." Those that could not be handed
over personally at the UN would be mailed.

The original plan was for him and Yoko to cross the Atlantic on the Cunard company's brand-new *Queen Elizabeth II* liner, with Ringo and Maureen Starr, Derek and Joan Taylor, Peter Sellers, and the writer Terry Southern as fellow voyagers. En route to Southampton to board the *QE2*, John was called on his car telephone and told that, because of his drug conviction, he had been refused an American visa. As Joan Taylor remembers, he shrugged philosophically and told Derek and her to go on without him, little guessing how much more of this was to come.

Even then, he suspected the reason was not his—very mild—drug offense so much as his widely quoted criticism of the Vietnam War and, still more pertinently, the fact that he'd written a song entitled "Revolution." At the time, other British pop stars with drug convictions were being granted American visas with little or no problem, most recently the folksinger Donovan. "The States are afraid we're going to go over there and rouse the kids up, which we don't intend to do at all," he insisted. "We intend to calm it down, you know. I think the States needs us, and we can help."

Barred from mainland America, the peace missionaries decided to "do a Cuba" and beam in their message from the nearby Bahamas—which, being a British territory, presented no passport difficulties. They traveled to Freeport on Grand Bahama Island but were repulsed by the heat and the unpleasantness of the hotel offered to them, so decided on Canada instead. Not only was it next door to America, but its British heritage would, hopefully, make it a more tolerant and relaxed host. In the event, Canada refused John's visa application on the same grounds as had the United States, but there at least he would be allowed entry and several days grace to lodge an appeal. He and Yoko flew to Toronto, accompanied by Kyoko and Derek Taylor, then made their way to their chosen venue, the Queen Elizabeth Hotel in Montreal.

An early opportunity arose for John to prove he had not come to North America to "rouse the kids up." At the University of California, Berkeley, students were in open revolt and heavily armed police had been sent onto the campus to restore order. A radio link was arranged between some of the protest's leaders and the giver of that blanket promise, "You can count me in." But instead he delivered a passionate appeal to them not to resort to violence and to maintain self-control, whatever the police provocation. "Sing Hare Krishna or something, but don't move around if it aggravates the pigs. Don't get hassled by the cops and don't play their games."

Early in the week, a journalist asked for a capsule summary of what he and Yoko were trying to do. "All we are saying," John replied, "is give peace a chance." It was a phrase with inbuilt rhythm, like "Honi soit qui mal y pense" or "Now call we this the field of Agincourt," and within hours, prompted by Yoko, he had turned it into a song—or, rather, a mantra like those he had learned in India. The verses were pure nonsense, spinning off rhymes from "Bagism" ("Shagism, Dragism, Madism . . .") and "Revolution" ("Evolution, mastication, flagellation, regulations, integrations . . .") and listing some of the people who had joined the bed-in, together with others he wished had done so ("Timmy Leary, Rosemary, Tommy Smothers, Bobby Dylan, Tommy Cooper, Derek Taylor, Norman Mailer, Allen Ginsberg . . ."). "I sort of cheated," he later admitted. "The word 'masturbation' was in it but when I wrote in the lyric-sheet— because I'd had enough of all the bannings . . . I copped out and wrote 'mastication.' It was more important to get it out than be bothered by a word."

Aside from the bedlam of those eight days, Yoko remembers quiet and intimate moments. "After we finished doing interviews and talking to people and everyone else had gone away, it was the nicest time in our lives. One night, there was a beautiful full moon in the sky and no clouds and John said 'Well, we're going to keep on writing songs together and our songs are going to be played all over the world. That's our life. That's how it's going to be.' It was just the moon and us. It was great." Yet even here, John was still looking over his shoulder, half expecting Tony Cox to come along and take back Yoko. One day when Kyoko was with them, Cox telephoned long-distance to talk to her. "Tony was only on the line for a couple of minutes," Yoko says. "But John was really uptight about it."

On the final day, they recorded their song "Give Peace a Chance," still in situ, using a borrowed eight-track machine and enlisting the vocal help of some who were roll-called in its lyric, Timothy and

Rosemary Leary, Tommy Smothers, Allen Ginsberg, Derek Taylor, plus the British singer Petula Clark, the black comedian and activist Dick Gregory, and every reporter, TV person, and casual gawker who happened to be in the room. The track featured Yoko singing in conventional Western style, her voice not at all untuneful and strangely childlike against the lemon-squeezed tartness of John's. By now, his appeal against the Canadian government's refusal to grant him a visa had failed: next day, the couple were deported and put on the first flight out of Montreal, which happened to be bound for Frankfurt.

The companionable bedside choristers who joined him on "Give Peace a Chance" had suggested an exhilarating new concept of recording and performing to John. Back in London, he and Yoko decided to keep alive the idea of a performing group that was not limited, like the Beatles, to a sacred four; not introverted, formula-bound, and hostile to outsiders, like the Beatles, but open to anybody, regardless of musical ability, appearance, age, or gender, and with as many or as few members as suited the moment. Its nucleus, moreover, would not be egotistical, quarrelsome humans, like the Beatles, but conceptual artworks which might have stepped straight from one of Yoko's shows.

To play the roles of unsinging, unplaying, unproblematic anti-Beatles, they designed four acrylic towers, two tall and rectangular, one tall and cylindrical, one short and cube-shaped. Like intestines inside their transparent bodies, the robot quartet contained all the latest sound and vision technology: a tape recorder, a record player, a closed-circuit TV camera and monitor, and a lightshow projector. The constitution of this revolution in pop-group evolution—allied to the name that was now his as well as Yoko's—led to their instant baptism as the Plastic Ono Band. The same label would be given to any configuration of human performers who appeared alongside them.

The open-door ethos was announced in press advertisements showing an acrylic robot's electronic innards silhouetted against a random page of the London telephone directory. "You are the Plastic Ono Band," promised the caption beneath. John stressed that the new entity was not a replacement for the Beatles but simply a diversion to keep his hand in as a performer. Nor, even now, did he rule out the chance of the Beatles going on the road again. "The Plastic Ono

Band's going to be pretty flexible—because it's plastic. The Beatles playing live is a different matter—we've got that great thing to live up to, it's a harder gig—but just for Yoko and me to get out there, we can get away with anything." Although "Give Peace a Chance" was billed as the first incarnation of the Plastic Ono Band, it was still cataloged according to longtime Beatle practice as a Lennon-McCartney composition. He would later bitterly regret "[being] guilty enough to give McCartney credit as co-writer on my first independent single instead of giving it to Yoko, who had actually written it with me."

Privately, he seemed to think the Beatles no longer had any viable future even in the studio. After devoting months to the mess of tapes from January's confused and acrimonious Apple basement sessions, plus some made later at Trident Studios, engineer Glyn Johns had pieced together an album's worth of material and submitted it to the four for approval. All of them hated it. John was the most appalled by what he described as "the shittiest load of badly-recorded shit with a lousy feeling to it ever." Yet a new Beatles album was long overdue, and wheels were turning to package and market one called *Get Back*. A cover photograph had already been shot, reflecting that supposed nostalgia for simpler times: the present-day Beatles, bewhiskered and tense, looked down from the very same balcony that their clean-shaven, optimistic young selves had on their debut album in 1963.

Much as John loathed the Glyn Johns compilation, he was all for releasing it anyway. "I thought it would be good . . . because it would break The Beatles," he remembered. "It would break the myth . . . [It would say], 'That's us with no trousers on and no glossy paint over the cover and no sort of hope. This is what we are like with our trousers off, so would you please end the game now?'"

George Martin had played little part in trying to salvage *Get Back* and, after the tetchy atmosphere in the Apple basement, felt his long association with the Beatles had ended on the sourest possible note. He was thus astounded to be rung up by Paul in mid-June and told that the band wanted to get back with him at Abbey Road and make a new album from scratch "like we used to." Martin replied that he wasn't prepared to repeat the experiences of January, with John telling him there must be "no production shit." "'No, it won't be like that.' Paul told me. 'John's come around and realises how much we need you.' So, against my better judgement, I agreed."

After the final break with Cynthia a year previously, John had been too frantically preoccupied even to remember that he had a six-year-old son, let alone feel many stirrings of paternal affection or remorse. But in the lull that followed the Montreal bed-in, he was seized by a sudden wish to see Julian. Cyn was by now in a relationship with the Italian Roberto Bassanini and was living in Kensington, West London, where Julian attended an ordinary state school. She invited John to her housewarming party and, much to her amazement, he turned up, accompanied by Yoko, and had an apparently friendly talk with Bassanini. Soon afterward, he notified her that he finally wished to exercise his court-awarded rights of access to his son. Les Anthony duly appeared in the Rolls and took Julian off alone to spend the first of what would be regular weekends at Ringo's Sunny Heights.

Against all precedent, John seemed to relish his role as paterfamilias. Toward the end of June—only a few days before work with George Martin and the Beatles at Abbey Road was scheduled to begin—he decided to show Yoko and Kyoko the Scottish Highlands where he had spent so many happy holidays as a small boy. In his enthusiasm, he announced that the trip would not be by chauffeured Rolls but that he would drive them himself in his supercharged, lavishly customized Mini Cooper. Julian happened to be visiting and was included on the trip without any consultation with Cynthia.

Since passing his driving test in 1965, John had rarely sat behind the wheel of a car and, on those few excursions, had terrified passengers by his myopic unawareness of other traffic, tardy reflexes, and almost nonexistent navigational skills. Nonetheless, he managed the first leg to Liverpool without mishap. There he realized the Mini Cooper was too small to carry two adults and two children on such a marathon journey, and telephoned Les Anthony to bring him up a larger car, an Austin Maxi. Anthony then took the Mini back to Weybridge.

A secondary purpose of the trip was to introduce Yoko to his three other aunts, Nanny and Harrie on Merseyside and Mater in Scotland. He spent several days showing his charges around Liverpool, staying first with Aunt Nanny and Uncle Charles in Rock Ferry, then with Aunt Harrie and Uncle Norman in Woolton. Nanny and Harrie had been as baffled and appalled by recent events as their sister Mimi but, despite their own significant part in John's upbringing, did not share Mimi's prerogative to tell him so. As Nanny's son Mike Cadwallader remembers, they confined themselves to expressive looks when Yoko commandeered their kitchens to prepare John's macrobiotic meals, and to surreptitious tut-tutting to each other about his drastically changed appearance. "I overheard a lot of 'He can't just eat beans . . . needs a proper meal . . . he's fading away . . . he's all skin and bones.' The comments weren't necessarily anti-Yoko or pro-Cynthia. but just anti-anyone who got their hands on one of 'their' children." When Mike's girlfriend, Linda, produced a bag of jelly beans, those once-hated symbols of Beatlemania, John's dietary principles wavered. "He grabbed them and scoffed quite a few before being told off," his cousin recalls.

His intended final destination was Aunt Mater and the remote Highland croft, near Durness, Sutherland, which he had helped his Uncle Bert to renovate as a fifteen-year-old during that life-changing "Heartbreak Hotel" summer of 1956. Here, the welcome was a little cooler. Stately, elegant Mater was as forthright a character as Mimi and, moreover, the only one of John's aunts who had actively liked Cynthia. And near here, his luck behind the wheel finally ran out. On July 1, the day that work on the new album officially began, he was driving his brood near the small town of Golspie. On a stretch of providentially empty road, he lost control of the car, and it veered into a roadside ditch. He, Yoko, and Kyoko each suffered cuts to the face and Yoko an injured back. They were rushed to Golspie's Lawson Memorial Hospital. John's facial injuries required seventeen stitches (and left a permanent scar), Yoko's fourteen, and Kyoko's four, and the unharmed but tearful Julian received treatment for shock.

Cynthia's first inkling that Julian was not in Weybridge was a telephone call informing her that he'd been in a car crash in northern

Scotland. With the help of ever-sympathetic Peter Brown, she caught the first plane up there. John, Yoko, and Kyoko were still detained in the hospital, but Aunt Mater was caring for Julian back at Durness. When Cyn tried to see John and demand an explanation for what had happened, she was told he didn't wish to talk to her.

When John and Yoko finally joined the other Beatles at Abbey Road Studios, both still bore the marks of the accident. Yoko's back injury gave her constant trouble, and to save her the discomfort of sitting for hours on a stool beside him, John had a bed delivered from Harrods and set up on the studio floor. There she spent several sessions, propped on pillows à la Amsterdam and Montreal, with a microphone rigged above her head so that she could comment on the proceedings at will.

After this unpromising start, something marvelous, one might almost say magical, was to happen. Now that they had stopped trying—and now that it was far too late—the Beatles finally got back to where they once belonged. Got back to working together without grumbling and bickering. Got back to George Martin's indispensable influence. Got back to taking as much trouble over each other's songs as they did with their own. Got back to having fun. Got back to sounding as if no power on earth could come between them.

The album that took shape between July and August turned out to be one of the easiest as well as, arguably, one of the three best they ever made. When all was said and done, no better vibe existed than in this leafy North London boulevard with its turreted mansion flats, nor around these familiar institutional EMI corridors where echoes of *Beatles for Sale* and *Rubber Soul* mingled with those of Caruso, Sinatra, and the London Philharmonic Orchestra. Abbey Road pardoned the truants their defection and gave them back their infallibility. Existing tracks that had been virtually written off as irredeemable messes at Twickenham and in the Apple basement now coalesced without further struggle. New tracks were developed and perfected in short order. Such was the Abbey Road effect that, despite all his other preoccupations and his burning desire to be up, up, and away, John performed more brilliantly within the Beatles than at any time since *Sgt. Pepper*. "We all knew this was the end," George Martin says. "There was an unspoken feeling of 'Let's make it the best we possibly can.' I'm sure that's why John was so collaborative."

The three principal songs he brought to the table, while reflecting his absorption in Yoko and new dedication to world enlightenment, also showed his love of nonsense and trivia and instinct for a catchy hook to be working as strongly as ever. "Come Together" had originated as a theme song for Timothy Leary's abortive 1968 campaign to become governor of California. With its slow, stoned, hissing beat, it was at once a caricature of Leary, a "free your minds" tract, a cornucopia of private jokes ("Ono sideboard," "Bag production," "juju eyeball," "walrus gumboot," "toe jam football") and a dispatch straight from the bedroom. "I Want You (She's So Heavy)" testified to a passion almost beyond words, switching from anguished blues to orgasmic hard rock and back again. At previous sessions, repeated unsuccessful attempts to play it in the "honest" one-take way that John demanded had made everyone, including himself, sick to death of it. Now Abbey Road administered a French kiss of life, via what he no longer scorned as "production shit." The final version was an amalgam of the best three of thirty-five takes, which then received extensive further overdubbing and remixing.

Significantly, his most impressive contribution was not a solo vocal but a chorale for Paul, George, and himself, which no bedroom full of Montreal friends or acrylic robots could ever have attempted. It had begun with Yoko, that trained classical pianist, who one day happened to be playing the introductory chords of Beethoven's *Moonlight* Sonata. "Give me them chords backwards," John demanded. The result was "Because," a paean of pure erotic rapture, with George Martin on harpsichord and the three divergent Beatle voices overdubbed twice to create a nine-part harmony closer, purer, and sweeter than any they had made since "Here, There and Everywhere."

In reality, the old balance had gone forever. As though in corroboration of his new minority status, Paul ended up with only two full tracks, the unmemorable "Oh! Darling" and the uncharacteristically dark and vicious "Maxwell's Silver Hammer." George, meanwhile, had come up with a brace of compositions, "Something" and "Here Comes the Sun," that, for the very first time, stood comparison with any under the Lennon-McCartney imprint. Ringo, too, was making strides as a writer and now chipped in a country-flavored children's song called "Octopus's Garden," meriting production values almost at the level of "Yellow Submarine."

Ever since *Sgt. Pepper*, George Martin had tried to persuade John and Paul to think in terms of symphonies and concertos rather than three- and four-minute pop songs. "Paul wasn't unamenable," he remembers. "But John always used to say 'I'm a rock-'n'-roller. I can't do clever stuff like that.'" For their present album, Martin resurrected the idea in a less intimidating form. He knew how many unfinished songs lay in both of their bottom drawers, and proposed making the second side a medley of such fragments, running into each other like a purpose-written suite. "As soon as we started, John got into the spirit of it. He kept coming along and saying 'I've got another bit here. Do you think you can find room for it?'"

Though not technically their last appearance together on record, this was to be the Beatles' formal farewell to their listening public. So how richly appropriate that it consisted of John and Paul, bouncing half-developed ideas off each other, much they used to as teenagers across the fireplace in Jim McCartney's front room. Only Paul's overture, "You Never Give Me Your Money," with its mention of "negotiations," "funny paper," and "breakdown," hinted at the late conflict between them. The rest of the thirty-minute medley, beginning with John, then shading into Paul, not only celebrated their partnership at high tide but somehow managed to take it to a new levels of competitive empathy.

John's three unfinished songs added up to a kind of backward voyage from the flower-power era to the unflowery city and culture that had raised him. First came "Sun King," a hippie incantation subverted by a chorus of spoof-Spanish nonsense like "chickaferdy" and "cake-and-eat-it'; then "Mean Mr. Mustard," a remnant of mid-Sixties enamel-sign Victoriana; then "Polythene Pam," inspired by a long-ago sex game in a threesome with his poet friend Royston Ellis. Sung in rabid Scouse calculated to chill his Aunt Mimi's blood, it even broke into "yeah yeah yeah" as if some disgusting adolescent habit had got the better of him.

Paul took over with "She Came In Through the Bathroom Window," picking up John's last theme almost psychically, as with the middle section of "A Day in the Life"; then "Golden Slumbers," an adaptation of Thomas Dekker's seventeenth-century lullaby; then "Carry That Weight," a prophecy that for both of them was already coming true. As much as a trawl through their past, the medley was a glimpse into a future never to be—the ground they could still have broken together, the symphonies and operas they might have gone on to write. But no one by now was under any illusions. Its wrap-up track was called "The End" and featured guitar solos by John and Paul as well as George and an unprecedented drum solo from Ringo. As a surprise bonus there was a tiny Paul oddment called "Her Majesty," a kind of postscript to the 1963 Royal Variety performance and "just rattle yer jewellery," when a Beatle could get away with anything.

In acknowledgment of its resuscitator—and of reliable good vibes back to 1962—the album was named *Abbey Road*. For a front cover, the Beatles were photographed walking single file over the zebra pedestrian crossing a few yards south of the studio gate at a brief moment when no traffic was passing and mansion flats and horse chestnut trees slumbered in midsummer sun. Compared with *Sgt. Pepper's* excesses, the image was simple to the point of banality (though destined to be imitated and parodied forevermore). A white-suited John was first in line, as ever, shoulders hunched, hands thrust into trouser pockets, his hirsute profile irradiating boredom and impatience.

24

WITHDRAWAL SYMPTOMS

I started the band. I disbanded it—it's as simple as that.

The previous May, John and Yoko had finally found a home that satisfied all—or almost all—their exacting joint requirements. A hideout where they could enjoy some privacy and recharge their batteries between one public foray and the next was only one of several needs to be met. They also planned an operations center for their professional partnership, which would free them from dependence on Apple, with a recording studio, art workshops, photographic darkrooms, and film-processing and editing facilities. And John stipulated that the garden must have a lake.

They looked at properties all over southern England, including a house in Churt, Surrey, which had once belonged to the Great War statesman David Lloyd George, and a disused church in Hertfordshire. The winning candidate was Tittenhurst Park, a white Georgian mansion near Ascot, Berkshire, which had formerly belonged to the industrialist Peter Cadbury and was on the market for £145,000.

With the house went a seventy-two-acre estate, including spectacular gardens, a row of former servants' cottages, and a mock-Tudor
villa as big as the one in which John had grown up. Wherever he
went, Mendips always seemed to follow.

The whole upper part of the house became a private sanctum for
Yoko and him, with its own separate kitchen as well as a huge master
bedroom, his and hers walk-in closets, and a circular bath. Most of
the ground floor was opened up into a single long, white room lined
with French windows facing onto the garden.

The various ancillary buildings were also expensively refurbished
to provide quarters for employees or friends in temporary need of a
roof. First in this pecking order came a young American mime artist
and choreographer named Dan Richter, who, with his English wife,
Jill, had been Yoko's and Tony Cox's next-door neighbor at Hanover
Gate Mansions, and who had since become John's de facto personal
assistant. Two of the former servants' cottages were combined to
make an apartment for the Richters and their small son, Sasha. The
gatekeeper's lodge was turned over to John's chauffeur, Les Anthony
and his woman friend, who brought with her six young children
from a previous relationship. After the Amsterdam bed-in, the ex-
guardsman had been told to dispense with his official chauffeur's
cap, grow his hair longer, drop the punctilious "Mr. Lennon," and
call his two charges by their first names.

The lake that meant so much to John was created on sloping
greensward below the house, despite the unsuitable sandy soil and
in defiance of the local planning authority's refusal to grant permission for anything larger than a pond. Fired by childhood memories
of Robert Louis Stevenson, he also specified that there should be an
island in the middle. Nearby stood one of the garden's stranger new
ornaments, an Austin Maxi estate car with a badly crushed front,
mounted on a concrete pedestal. It was the rental vehicle John had
wrecked on his family trip to the Scottish Highlands the previous
July. Afterward, he bought it from the rental company and had it
transported to Tittenhurst and installed on its plinth in exactly the
same condition that the accident had left it, with traces of his and
Yoko's blood still on the seats.

Among the pantheon of European surrealists, John had always felt a special affinity with Jean Cocteau, whose genius spilled over from art into writing, filmmaking, and theatre design and whose drawings were everything he wished his own could be. While camping out with Yoko at Montagu Square, he became immersed in Cocteau's book *Opium: The Story of a Cure.* "He was fascinated by Cocteau's experiences with opium and how he got clean of it," Yoko remembers. "The story was all about Paris in the Twenties, Picasso, Diaghilev, Eric Satie and people like that. John couldn't put the book down." Cocteau's illustrated reminiscences spurred him to fresh interest in Yoko's own Parisian encounter with opium's most powerful derivative two years earlier. "He started asking me again what taking heroin was like, saying how interesting it must have been."

Despite their devotion to pot and acid, British pop stars at this time still largely steered clear of junk—aka smack, Henry, or just plain H. Along with fear, snobbery managed to play a part: trendy acidheads looked down on smackheads with their unaesthetic sunken eyes, skeletal frames, and needle-pitted skin. Other musicians of the first echelon would later fall victim to the drug, notably Keith Richards and Eric Clapton. But John was ahead of them all.

His squeamishness about injections was soon allayed. Heroin could be taken as painlessly as pot, either snorted or swallowed in pills, called jacks. When he decided to take it, there was no question but that Yoko should join him. And for both, the seduction was instantaneous. Compared with pot's fuzziness and acid's unpredictable magic carpet ride, this seemed the easiest of trips, neither disorienting nor distorting—on the contrary, seeming to focus the mind and sharpen the senses to a wondrous new degree. Dan Richter was already a user, further reason for his welcome at Tittenhurst Park.

Heroin was to have been John's secret ally against the scorn and vituperation of the media and the infighting at Apple. But, as always, reality failed to live up to his expectations. "It was not too much fun," he would later admit. "We sniffed a little when we were in real pain. We got such a hard time from everyone, and I've had so much thrown at me and at Yoko, especially at Yoko. . . . We took H because of what the Beatles and others were doing to us."

The drug can imprint its death's-head on its victims with horrible swiftness. In January, during a break at Twickenham Studios, Canadian TV had interviewed a John showing all the signs of what heroin users call "pulling a whitey"—deathly pale face, slurred speech, jumbled thoughts. After a few minutes, he jumped out of his canvas director's chair and vomited just off camera. When his cousin Liela Harvey, now a qualified doctor, called at Apple to see him that summer, she was horrified by the change in his appearance. "He looked about 90, his eyes were staring. He was a sick boy," she remembers. Underneath, though, he was still the Just William character who used to keep her "in tucks" when they were children. "We talked about my career and I told him I was specialising in anaesthesiology. 'I'd rather be doing the operations,' John said.'"

According to Yoko, they kicked the habit before any serious damage could be done. They still hoped to have a child together, and had been warned that heroin could increase her chances of a second miscarriage or could addict the baby she bore. "John said, 'Right, that's it. We cut it here,'" she remembers. "'And we can't go into any clinic or the press will find out. So we have to do it ourselves.'"

It is a peculiarly vivid twist of language that withdrawal from heroin should be nicknamed "cold turkey," its horrible physical symptoms—fever, palpitations, insomnia, nausea, diarrhea, alternate sweats and goose-bump chills—equated with the gruesome leftovers of a Christmas feast. For John and Yoko, cold turkey was the housewarming of Tittenhurst in late summer, 1969. The task was made a little easier than it might have been because John used an inferior dealer who had often diluted their supplies with talcum powder. "It was still a battle for him much more so than for Yoko," Dan Richter remembers. "Yet he still managed to be supportive of me as I was trying to deal with my habit. I owe a lot to both him and Yoko."

Where Cocteau had kept a diary, John wrote a song named after the ordeal he was putting himself through, detailing its manifestations and his own reactions as precisely as a chart at the foot of his bed: "temperature rising . . . fever is high . . . 36 hours rolling in pain . . . body is aching . . . goosepimple bone . . . Oh, I'll be a good boy. Please make me well. . . ." "It took courage enough for John to go cold turkey on his own," Richter says. "But to admit it, and tell you everything about it, how he wanted to be a baby again, how he wished he were dead . . . that took real guts."

In an afterglow of Abbey Road togetherness, he immediately offered "Cold Turkey" to the other Beatles. ". . . I said, 'Hey, lads, I think I've written a new single,'" he recalled. "But they all said 'Umm . . . aah . . . well,' so I thought, 'Bugger you, I'll put it out myself.'" The track thus became a second single for the Plastic Ono Band, in this instance consisting of John, Yoko, Klaus Voormann, and Ringo Starr, with John acting as producer as well as singing and playing shuddery, feverish lead guitar. The B-side was given to Yoko and a song about her daughter, "Don't Worry Kyoko (Mummy's Only Looking For A Hand in the Snow)."

As if in step with John's peace campaign, young people everywhere continued to demonstrate their power to gather in huge numbers and worship their heroes without doing harm to one another. The fashion for giant open-air rock festivals, begun in Monterey in 1967, seemed to work just as well however far-flung from sunny California. On June 7, Eric Clapton's new "supergroup," Blind Faith, played for free to 150,000 in London's Hyde Park; a month later, the Rolling Stones performed gratis to around 500,000 in the same venue. Between August 15 to 18, another peaceable half million bivouacked on muddy farmland near Woodstock, New York, to watch an Anglo-American bill including Jimi Hendrix, the Who, the Grateful Dead, Jefferson Airplane, and Creedence Clearwater Revival, and send up a shout of contempt for the insatiable U.S. military draft to Vietnam. The organizers had written to John, offering the Beatles any fee they cared to name if they would appear; his counteroffer of just him with the Plastic Ono Band had been declined. Despite this snub, he found Woodstock hugely exciting—a giant response to the crusade he and Yoko had launched from bed. "[The festival crowds] were . . . getting together and forming a new church . . . saying, 'We believe in God, we believe in hope and truth and here we are, 20,000 or 200,000 of us, all together in peace.'"

The most amazing visitation was reserved for a sleepy British offshore island that Sixties pop culture had hitherto left almost untouched. A week after Woodstock, 250,000 hippies trekked south to the Isle of Wight for a three-day festival headlined, unbelievably, by Bob Dylan and the Band. Like the Beatles, Dylan had seemingly retired from live performing in 1966, in his case following a serious motorcycle accident. What brought him to the Isle of Wight when all other lures had failed were its associations with one of his favorite poets, Alfred, Lord Tennyson. John and Yoko attended the festival, and afterward George Harrison brought Dylan to Tittenhurst just as John was preparing to record "Cold Turkey." There was a fleeting idea that Dylan should join the Plastic Ono Band on piano, but nothing came of it. "I remember, we were both in shades and both on fucking junk," John remembered. "And all those freaks around us, and Ginsberg and all those people. I was as nervous as shit."

On September 10, the Institute of Contemporary Arts in London staged the first of two evenings devoted to John and Yoko's films. The program comprised *Two Virgins*, *Rape*, *Smile*, *Honeymoon*, and a new offering called *Self-Portrait*, a twenty-minute study of John's penis achieving semierection in slow motion. Beside the screen stood a large white sack containing two people, assumed to be the filmmakers but actually stand-ins, or crouch-ins. The second evening featured a single production entitled *Apotheosis*, an extended study of clouds, shot in color with the aid of a helicopter and a hot-air balloon. Despite the prestigious venue, no mainstream film critic could be persuaded to attend either night, and the coverage inevitably centered on *Self-Portrait*—a form of self-portrayal for which, it was widely pointed out, sad men in dirty raincoats got arrested on Clapham Common. In reply, in typically quotable and homely terms, John stated the principle Yoko had developed with the Fluxus group; that shocking an audience into any kind of strong emotion could do only good. "People are frozen jellies. It just needs somebody to turn off the fridge."

However, defrosting a few dozen jellies at the ICA hardly compared with the communicating that Dylan, Jagger, and the rest were now doing through rock festivals. And there was a further temptation to play truant from "pure" art. At Woodstock, one of the best-received acts had been an American vocal group called Sha Na Na, affectionately pastiching rock-'n'-roll and doo-wop hits of the fifties. Long-dormant giants from that era, like Chuck Berry, Little Richard, and Jerry Lee Lewis, were emerging from their sepulchers and proving that no one had ever surpassed them in energy or anarchy. Elvis Presley himself had shaken off the shroud of Hollywood and, at a barely conceivable thirty-four, been restored to his old place as sexiest dude on the planet. The X-rated songs that had once turned John and his schoolfriends into pariahs were reincarnated as harmlessly hilarious family favorites, adding a layer of nostalgia for the Fifties to that for the departing Sixties. Ten years on, and several universes away from Litherland Town Hall and the Kaiserkeller, there was still no music John loved more.

Coincidentally, at this very moment, the first festival dedicated to the rock-'n'-roll revival was being put together in Toronto, Canada, with a lineup including Little Richard, Chuck Berry, Fats Domino, and Bo Diddley. Just two days before its opening on September 13, John received an invitation for Yoko and himself to attend. "They were inviting us as the king and queen to preside over it, not play," he remembered. "But I didn't hear that bit. I said, 'Just give me time to get a band together,' and we went the next morning."

It was a perfect opportunity to unveil the Plastic Ono Band as a unit that could instantly meet any challenge, like World War II pilots dashing for their Spitfires. To accompany Yoko, the four acrylic robots, and himself to Toronto, John recruited his old Hamburg friend Klaus Voormann on bass, Eric Clapton on guitar, and Alan White, later of Yes, on drums. He also asked George Harrison, but George was the last person to jet off at a moment's notice to a gig about which almost nothing was known.

There was no time for rehearsal other than during the flight and backstage at Toronto's Varsity Stadium a few minutes before showtime. Having been so desperate to get there, John was now so overcome with terror at competing with so many of his boyhood idols at once that he threw up violently backstage. "We're going to do numbers we know 'cause we've never played together before," he told the audience. "But here goes—and good luck." He sang three old Cavern showstoppers—"Blue Suede Shoes," "Dizzy Miss Lizzy," and "Money"—followed by "Yer Blues," Give Peace a Chance," and a first live preview of "Cold Turkey." Yoko then emerged from a white bag to unveil two new compositions, "Don't Worry Kyoko (Mummy's Only Looking For A Hand in the Snow)" and the thirteen-minute "John, John (Let's Hope for Peace)." Little of it counted as rock-'n'-roll revivalism, but nothing could mar the crowd's joy at seeing John live again, in whatever eccentric and synthetic company. "The buzz was incredible," he remembered. "I never felt so good in my life."

Before leaving London, he had finally made up his mind to resign from the Beatles, but the whirl of departure had left no time to break it to the other three. "I told Eric Clapton and Klaus I was leaving and that I'd like to probably use them as a group," he would recall. "I hadn't decided how to do it . . . to have a permanent new group or what. Later on, I thought, 'Fuck, I'm not going to get stuck with another group of people, whoever they are.' So I announced it to myself and the people around me on the way to Toronto. Allen came with me, and I told Allen it was over."

It was the last thing Klein wanted to hear. He had just negotiated the Beatles a hefty increase in royalties from their American record label, Capitol, bludgeoning Capitol's chief executive, Bob Gortikov, into conceding an unprecedented 25 percent of retail price. Even his archenemies, Lee and John Eastman, having scrutinized the deal on Paul's behalf, admitted it was impressive. Now he was faced with the appalling prospect of having no clients to receive these bumper new rates or pay his 20 percent commission. It was, of course, nothing new for the mainstay of a successful band to get bored after a time and seek fresh challenges, either by forming a new one or going solo. If any other top-echelon act lost a member, he would simply be replaced, as the Rolling Stones had replaced Brian Jones with Mick Taylor. But that the Beatles might continue without John never crossed anyone's mind.

On September 20, Klein called a meeting in Apple's boardroom for the formal signing of the Capitol contract. Paul's presence in the building for the first time in months meant that John had all his fellow Beatles on hand to hear his news. But initially he held back, confining himself to a generalized complaint about Paul's dominance of the band since the *Magical Mystery Tour* album. "I didn't write any of that except Walrus . . . You'd already have five or six songs, so I'd think, 'Fuck it, I can't keep up with that.'" His tone was more hurt than accusatory. "So I didn't bother, you know, and I thought I don't really care whether I was on or not, I convinced myself it didn't matter, and so for a period if you didn't invite me to be on an album personally, if you three didn't say, 'Write some more songs 'cause we like your work,' I wasn't going to fight."

The insecurity and fatalism revealed in this outburst were surprising enough. But John did not stop there. Warming to his theme—though still wounded rather than angry—he accused Paul of always having overshadowed him, not only by writing more songs but also by inveigling the lion's share of studio time. It was not a row, more like the airing of mutual grievances before a marriage counselor. Surprised, and not a little hurt himself, Paul conceded that he might have "come out stronger" on recent albums, but pointed out that often when they went into the studio, John would have only a couple of songs ready to record. John agreed his inertia had been a factor: "There was no point in turning 'em out—I didn't have the energy to turn 'em out and get 'em on as well."

Now that the cards were on the boardroom table, he took a swipe at what he termed Paul's "granny music," the cute, tuneful family-pleasers that, to be fair, had been part of the Beatles' repertoire since Cavern days. Had fairness entered into it, he might have paused to reflect that, of the two songs he singled out for denigration, "Ob-La-Di Ob-La-Da" and "Maxwell's Silver Hammer," one featured a rousingly committed Lennon piano solo and the other was too Lennonishly sick to please any granny alive.

He also called on Paul to share the belated guilt he himself was feeling over their treatment of George. Previewers of Abbey Road unanimously rated its two George songs, "Here Comes the Sun" and "Something," as highly as anything on the album, including the Lennon-McCartney suite. "Something," especially, was far beyond George's recent range: passionate, sophisticated, and devoid of his usual Indian preachiness. It had got him onto the A-side of a Beatles single at long last and would ultimately attract more cover versions than any Beatles hit since "Yesterday." John repeatedly cited it as the best track of the collection.

Still, no one but Klein had any idea what was afoot. Paul was all for burying hatchets and pressing forward, convinced all would be well if they could free themselves from balance sheets and office politics and return to a place that—he almost pleaded with John and George to remember—had not always been so very terrible. "When we get in a studio, even on the worst day, I'm still playing bass, Ringo's still drumming, we're still there, you know. . . ."

It was the cue for John's bombshell at last. "He hadn't even told me he was going to do it," Yoko remembers. "Paul was saying 'Why don't we do it this way and that way . . .' John said 'You don't seem to understand, do you? The group is over. I'm leaving'"

"I started the band, I disbanded it. It's as simple as that," John himself would recollect. "When I finally had the guts to tell the other three . . . they knew it was for real—unlike Ringo and George's previous threats to leave. I must say I felt guilty at springing it on them at such short notice. After all, I had Yoko; they only had each other." According to Paul, he added that he'd originally planned not to tell the others until after they signed the Capitol deal. "Good old John, he had to blurt it out. I remember him saying 'It's weird, this, telling you I'm leaving the group, but in a way it's very exciting.' It was like when he told Cynthia he was getting a divorce."

Capitol's new royalty rate was not all to have been suddenly put in jeopardy. According to music-industry wisdom in 1969, not even the Beatles could split up and expect to continue selling records in significant quantity afterward. It was therefore vital that no word of John's resignation should leak out until the *Abbey Road* album had realized its full market potential. "Paul and Klein convinced him to keep quiet," Yoko remembers. "We went off in the car, and he turned to me and said, 'That's it with the Beatles. From now on, it's just you—okay?' I thought, 'My God, those three guys were the ones entertaining him for so long. Now I have to be the one to take the load.'"

In fact, the outside world needed no telling that the end of the Sixties also meant the end of the Beatles. The international media seethed with predictions of an official split any day now, and speculation as to whether the eventual breaking point had been Yoko, Linda Mc-Cartney, Allen Klein, or the problems with Apple. Paul's continuing unexplained absence from the spotlight fueled a worldwide rumor, supported by ever more ingeniously specious "evidence," that he was dead.

Along with the general dismay and disbelief could be felt something close to panic. For Britain's war babies in particular, whose astonishing inheritance this decade had been, the Beatles were as essential to enjoying life as the sun on their shoulders. The Beatles had led them through every change in their lot since 1963, from blazers and balloon dresses to caftans and beads, from hairdos to hair-don'ts, from lemonade shandy to Bacardi and Coke, from fish-and-chips to beef Stroganoff and coq au vin, from cod-liver oil to patchouli oil, from Children's Favourites on the BBC Home Service to Ravi Shankar and Stockhausen, from Brighton and Margate to Torremolinos, Ibiza, and Katmandu, from Woodbines to Acapulco Gold, from "I Want to Hold Your Hand" to "Come Together," from "I Feel Fine" to "Revolution." A future without these companions, who were as potent as gods yet closer than closest family, hardly bore thinking about.

The *Abbey Road* album, released on September 26, brought a brief surge of hope that things might not really be so bad as the newspapers said—even that the likeliest instigator of the breakup might have relented after all. How could a band falling apart create harmonies as close and warm as they were on John's "Because"? How could a band said to be irredeemably darkened by anger and bitterness make a track as radiantly optimistic as "Here Comes the Sun"?—written and sung by George, but saturated in John's influence, down to its recurrent little sigh of "And I say . . ." The publicity photograph, taken at Tittenhurst Park a month earlier, put all such illusions to rest. It was a portrait of four people going through the motions without a gleam of enthusiasm or conviction, unable to summon up a smile among them.

With renovations at Tittenhurst still not complete, John and Yoko continued to use the front ground-floor office at 3 Savile Row as headquarters for Bag Productions and their peace campaign, watched over by a taciturn robot from the Plastic Ono Band. Throughout dozens of media interviews each day, John kept his word not to drop the smallest hint about his resignation from the Beatles. His line was that Apple's troubles had all now been successfully sorted out by Allen Klein and that, in its new, rationalized form, the company would be going forward, with himself as much its enthusiastic proponent as ever. "The circus has left town," he told *Melody Maker*, "but we still own the site."

On October 20, "Cold Turkey" was released as a single in the United Kingdom, coupled with "Don't Worry Kyoko (Mummy's Only Looking for Her Hand in the Snow)" and credited to the Plastic Ono Band. When it appeared in the United States four days later, many radio stations took it to be about drug use rather than withdrawal and denied it airplay, but it still charted at number 30 (14 in Britain), giving John his second out-of-Beatles hit in four months. A week later, he and Yoko released their third LP collaboration under the title *Wedding Album*. On side one, they were heard calling each other's names with varying intensity against a background of their own heartbeats; side two comprised interviews, conversations, and random sounds from the Amsterdam bed-in. The record came in an opulent white box, accompanied by old-fashioned matrimonial trappings—a facsimile of their marriage certificate and a photograph of a slice of wedding cake. It made no impression on the UK album chart, but in America was briefly logged at number 178.

Though the term *helpline* had yet to be coined, that is essentially what John and Yoko made themselves in late 1969, not only to likeminded antiwar campaigns and pressure groups but to any victim of oppression, injustice, or discrimination. Each week, they received hundreds of pleas to lend their support to causes for which there was no established lobby or which had exhausted all other avenues of appeal. They could rarely resist an underdog, whether represented by Britain's gypsy population or Hispanic immigrants working for slave wages in California vineyards. The more obscure and hopeless the petition, the likelier was John's heart to be stirred. A group of hippies needing a home were astounded to be given rent-free, indefinite use of Dorinish, the rocky islet off Ireland's west coast where he had once planned to build a tower and live as an artist-hermit.

Near the top of his campaign agenda this winter was the James Hanratty case. Twenty-six-year-old Hanratty had been hanged in 1962 for the infamous A6 murder, so becoming one of Britain's last victims of capital punishment. Doubts had always surrounded the case, partly because of Hanratty's well-substantiated alibi, partly because a more hardened criminal had subsequently hinted he was the real killer. Hanratty's father was a decent man who believed passionately in his son's innocence and had fought to clear his name in an era when such miscarriages of British justice were almost unthinkable. Worn down by resistance from the judiciary and the police, he turned as a last resort to John and Yoko. They immediately pledged their support, promising to make a film about the case, meanwhile adopting the slogan "Britain murdered Hanratty" with the same fervor that they accused America of murdering Vietnamese.

Each new cause they took up inevitably brought a fresh onslaught of mockery and excoriation for dabbling in matters they did not understand. To John, being regarded as figures of fun was a positive asset in the arena they had chosen. "Laurel and Hardy, that's John and Yoko," he admitted. "And we stand a better chance under that guise because all the serious people like Martin Luther King and Kennedy and Gandhi get shot."

Although the British government sent no troops to America's aid in Vietnam, it remained equally culpable in John's eyes for never opposing or explicitly condemning the war. And in 1968, Britain once more seemed a willing party to mass murder, this time within its so-called Commonwealth. When part of Nigeria seceded under the name of Biafra, Harold Wilson's Labour administration supported the Nigerian regime's brutal repressive measures, which resulted in the slaughter of thousands and the starvation of millions more. John's protest marked his final escape from the old, conformist self that had accepted a public honor via the same prime minister three years before. He retrieved his MBE from the top of his Aunt Mimi's

TV set and, on November 25, dictated identical short notes to Buckingham Palace and 10 Downing Street, saying he was returning it as a protest against Vietnam, Biafra, and "Cold Turkey slipping down the charts."

Not for a long time had any recipient of a Royal honor repudiated it; not since 1965, in fact, when sundry apoplectic colonels and civil servants had disowned MBEs in protest against the Beatles' investiture. And now that John had resigned from the order, several of those former members clamored for reinstatement. An elderly ex-policeman who wrote to Buckingham Palace for his medal back was told that it had been lost. When John heard this, he sent word that the applicant was welcome to the one he'd just returned.

As Christmas loomed, only the most optimistic fans, shivering at the doorstep of 3 Savile Row, could delude themselves that the Beatles had any future together. If Paul's intentions were still a mystery, both George and Ringo seemed to be following the trail John had blazed and preparing for life on the outside. Early in December, George took his first tentative steps back to live performance by touring with Eric Clapton and a band Clapton had put together around the American rockabilly duo Delaney and Bonnie. Ringo had played cameo roles in two big-budget feature films, *Candy* and *The Magic Christian*, the latter alongside Peter Sellers, and was considering several further offers. Ironically, after so many years of near-muteness, he had beaten both John and Paul in releasing a solo album, a collection of standards entitled *Sentimental Journey*.

On December 11, the premiere of *The Magic Christian* took place at the Odeon cinema, Kensington, graced by those stalwart Beatlemaniacs Princess Margaret and Lord Snowdon. John and Yoko arrived in a limousine decorated with a large placard reading BRITAIN MURDERED HANRATTY. They took care to draw up right behind the Royal car, so their message would be seen by as many photographers as possible. But the next morning, no paper even mentioned it. Three days later, Hanratty's father appeared at Speakers Corner in Hyde Park, calling for a public inquiry into his son's conviction. On the ground beside him was a writhing white sack labeled A SILENT PROTEST FOR JAMES HANRATTY. This time, the occupants really were John and Yoko, as they proved later by accompanying Hanratty senior and other campaigners to hand in a petition at 10 Downing Street.

As if John did not already have enough product on offer, the Plastic Ono Band's debut at the Toronto rock-'n'-roll festival was released as an album, *Live Peace in Toronto*, on December 12. To promote it, the band took to the stage once more, this time at London's Lyceum ballroom, with John, Yoko, and the robots augmented by a vast lineup, including George Harrison, gigging with John for the first time since 1966, as well as Eric Clapton, Delaney and Bonnie, Billy Preston, Keith Moon from the Who, and disc jockey Jeff Dexter on tambourine. The performance was filmed by the *International Times*'s John Hopkins and was meant to have been shown simultaneously on the video monitor inside one of the robots—an idea later adopted by rock acts everywhere—but unluckily the equipment malfunctioned. "The sound was atrocious," Dexter recalls. "But no one seemed to care." Yoko began the show inside a white bag, then emerged to sing "Don't Worry Kyoko," punctuated by screams of "Britain murdered Hanratty!" It was to be John's last-ever live performance in Britain.

Back in the summer, he and Yoko had begun discussing ways to link their peace campaign to the alleged season of goodwill. One short-lived idea was to persuade newspapers to run the headline PEACE DECLARED with the same prominence that WAR DECLARED usually received; another was to beam it out over the Telstar space satellite rather like a follow-up to "All You Need Is Love." Finally they settled for the handbill-posting technique Yoko had often used for her art shows, but taken up a few notches by John's wealth. On December 16, a huge white billboard appeared amid the hyperactive neon in Times Square, New York, and identical ones simultaneously at the hubs of London, Paris, Los Angeles, Rome, Athens, Berlin, Montreal, Toronto, Tokyo, and Port of Spain, Trinidad. Their message spelled out in plain black type was "WAR IS OVER if you want it, Happy Christmas, John and Yoko."

As news organizations everywhere prepared reviews and retrospectives of the past year and past decade, one voice above all was sought to provide definitive commentary on both. BBC television made a documentary entitled *The World of John and Yoko*, to be

screened on December 30, filming their subjects over five days, at
Apple, in the recording studio, and in bed. *Rolling Stone* magazine
named John "Man of the Year," opining that "a five-hour talk between John Lennon and [President] Nixon would be more significant
than any Geneva summit conference between the USA and Russia."
The greatest accolade came when Britain's ATV company (the same
that had snapped up Northern Songs) invited three eminent intellectuals to make a short film on their respective choices as "Man of the
Decade." The veteran broadcaster Alistair Cooke chose John F. Kennedy; the left-wing American writer Mary McCarthy chose North
Vietnam's leader, Ho Chi Minh; the anthropologist and sociologist
Desmond Morris chose John.

Strolling through the grounds of Tittenhurst Park with Morris,
Yoko, and a camera crew, John could not have sounded more upbeat,
generally and personally. "Everybody is talking about the way
[youth culture] is going and the decadence and the rest of it. . . . Not
many people are noticing all the good that came out of the last ten
years . . . Woodstock . . . is the biggest mass of people ever gathered
together for anything other than war. Nobody had that big an army
and didn't kill someone or have some kind of violent scene like the
Romans or whatever, and even a Beatle concert was more violent
than that, you know. . . .

"I'm full of optimism because of the contacts I've made personally
throughout the world . . . knowing there's other people around that
I can agree with, you know. I'm not insane and I'm not alone. That's
on a personal level and of course the Woodstock, Isle of Wight, all
the mass meetings of the youth [are] completely positive for me. . . .
And this is only a beginning. The Sixties bit was just a sniff. The
Sixties was just waking up in the morning and we haven't even got
to dinner-time yet and I can't wait, you know. I just can't wait. I'm
glad to be around and it's gonna be great and there's gonna be more
and more of us and [peering humorously into the camera] whatever
you're thinking there, Mrs. Grundy of Birmingham on toast, you
know you don't stand a chance."

Sadly, rock festivals could no longer boast their impressive record
of nonviolence. On December 6, at a free concert by the Rolling

Stones in Altamont, California, Hell's Angels "stewards" had attacked spectators with pool cues, and a young black man been knifed to death a few feet from the stage. Undeterred, the organizers of the Toronto rock-'n'-roll festival were planning a follow-up event, "bigger than Woodstock," to take place in Mosport Park, Montreal, over two days the following July. To distance it from the ugliness at Altamont, John's participation was clearly a sine qua non. He agreed to make it in effect the John Lennon Peace Festival and, despite the imminence of Christmas, flew to Canada with Yoko on their third visit in six months to join in the planning.

Their first stop was Toronto, where they stayed on a ranch belonging to the veteran rock-'n'-roller Ronnie Hawkins. Hawkins and his wife, Wanda, gave up their marital bed, and chefs were brought in to provide macrobiotic meals. "Despite the diet, I caught John and Yoko down at the fridge a couple of times in the middle of the night, having a quick slice of bologna," Hawkins remembers. There had been thick falls of snow and, between conferences with the festival organizers, John spent hours dashing around the ranch on a six-wheeled open buggy called an Amphicat. As well as a depleted fridge, the Hawkinses were left with a collapsed living-room ceiling after their guests' bath overflowed.

To the reporters who dogged his every step, John repeated the mocking mantra that great world leaders like President Nixon were frightened of the acorn peace symbols he and Yoko had wanted to give them. Inevitably there were fresh waves of questions about his future with the Beatles and relationship with Paul, George, and Ringo. Still keeping his promise, he said he was merely "on holiday" from the band and there was no dissent between him and the other three, least of all over his peace crusade. "George is as big a peacenik as I am. Paul's the same on a more intellectual level—and Ringo's a living acorn."

He dismissed any idea that he was setting himself up as a figurehead, either for antiwar activists or insurgent youth. "I'm not a leader; I'm just John Lennon who happens to think this way." And if President Nixon's doors remained barred, other eminent "squares" were lining up behind Desmond Morris to acknowledge the extraor-

dinary, and undeniably positive, influence he wielded. Before leaving Toronto, he and Yoko had a meeting with Marshall McLuhan,
guru of the new science of communications, whose famous axiom
"the medium is the message" might have been coined especially
for them. Why choose Canada as their arena rather than London,
McLuhan asked. "Whenever we've done anything, we've done it out
of London, 'cause they don't take it seriously in England," John replied. "They treat us like their children. . . . 'It's that mad, insane
guy,' you know. 'He should be tap-dancing on the Palladium rather
than talking about war and peace.'"

McLuhan observed that in the eyes of America's government—
especially the new Republican one personified by Nixon—anyone
who inspired dissent on the scale that John did risked being branded
"a long-haired communist." "In Europe, it's a joke, you know," he replied, little dreaming how carefully his words were being monitored
over the nearby border, nor how they would one day come back
to haunt him. "I mean, we laugh at America's fear of communists.
It's like, the Americans aren't going to be overrun by communists.
They're going to fall from within, you know."

The climax of the four-day visit was a train journey to Ottawa on
December 23 for a fifty-minute audience with Prime Minister Pierre
Trudeau, at that time the youngest and hippest leader on the world
stage. John was consumed with nerves beforehand and, as if at Aunt
Mimi's invisible prompting, wore a formal dark suit and tie. Trudeau
proved to be a fan of his books as much as of Beatles music, and
promised full support for the Montreal Peace Festival. Later, John
commented drily that his only contact with Britain's prime minister
Harold Wilson had been a photo-op handshake at an awards ceremony in 1964.

New Year's Day 1970 found him and Yoko in Allberg, northern
Denmark, where Yoko's ex-husband, Tony Cox, was now living with
Kyoko and a new Texan girlfriend named Melinda. The four spent
almost a month together, in apparently perfect domestic harmony.
A kitten named Miso was acquired for Kyoko, and John took special pains to prepare fish meals without bones that might stick in
its throat. During their stay, he and Yoko both had their hair shorn

down to matching crew cuts to mark what they dubbed "Year One for Peace." John also abandoned his Old Testament beard in favor of a bristly, jaw-hugging model that restored the animation to his face, if never quite its old derisive smile. The symbolism was obvious: the Sixties were behind him, as unmourned as sweepings around a barber's chair.

He expected his Aunt Mimi to be pleased after all the years she had harangued him to get his hair cut. Instead, Mimi was appalled by what she called a "horrible skinhead style" and declared it was "too short."

I f the Beatles or the Sixties had a message," John would later say, "it was learn to swim. Period. And once you learn to swim, swim. The people who are hung up on the Beatles' and the Sixties' dream missed the whole point when the Beatles' and the Sixties' dream became the point. Carrying [it] around all your life is like carrying the Second World War and Glenn Miller around. That's not to say you can't enjoy Glenn Miller or the Beatles, but to live in that dream is the twilight zone."

Certainly the dawn of the new decade found him swimming at top speed into waters he had once thought way out of his depth. The previous year, his art adviser, Anthony Fawcett, had suggested he try his hand at creating lithographs, which could be both exhibited and sold in a limited edition. To save him the art-college drudgery of etching onto stone blocks, Fawcett supplied special drawing paper from which more patient hands could transfer his work onto sensitized zinc. By this method he had produced fourteen images, some of recent milestone events like his wedding and the Amsterdam bed-in, others erotic studies of a nude, recumbent Yoko. Three hundred sets were produced at £550 apiece, all signed by John, embossed with a personalized red seal, or "chop," after the practice of Japanese artists, and packed in a white holdall inscribed BAG ONE.

The lithographs went on show at the London Arts Gallery on January 15, before John and Yoko had returned from Denmark. There would be further exhibitions at the Galerie Denise Renée in Paris and at the Lee Nordness Gallery, New York, where Salvador Dalí attended the private view with a pet ocelot on a leash. In London, they had been on display barely twenty-four hours when uniformed police strode in and confiscated the eight Yoko nude studies ("arresting pieces of paper," John called it) on grounds of an alleged complaint from a member of the public. Legal action was then taken against the gallery under the Obscene Publications Act. It was a ludicrous exercise; the images were not in the least obscene but skillful, tasteful, and rather touching, albeit adorned with forbidden bouquets of pubic hair. The result was to win huge publicity for *Bag One* and elevate John to the company of persecuted erotic geniuses from Gauguin to Aubrey Beardsley.

He had made up his mind that nothing in the seventies would be as before, least of all the process of making records. On January 27, he telephoned George Harrison (with whom his relationship still remained good despite everything) and asked him to join yet another mission for the Plastic Ono Band. The idea was to change the traditional slow, painstaking lithography of Beatles studio sessions and postproduction into an impulsive lightning sketch. "[John] . . . said 'I've written this tune and I'm going to record it tonight and have it pressed up and out tomorrow,'" George would recall. "'That's the whole point—Instant Karma, you know.'"

Klaus Voormann had also been summoned to Abbey Road's Studio Three that night, along with drummer Alan White and Billy Preston to play electric piano. "When I arrived, there was this little American guy in the control room, very busy, twiddling knobs and telling Alan, 'Turn your cymbal up,'" Voormann remembers. "No one had told me who was producing the session and I didn't know who this busy little guy was, except that on his shirt were the letters PS."

It was none other than Phil Spector, the first producer in pop history to become more famous—or, in his case, infamous—than the artistes he put on record. Since the mid-Sixties, Spector's legendary Wall of Sound had been all but washed away by the successive tides of psychedelia and folk rock. After the failure in America of his masterpiece, Ike and Tina Turner's "River Deep, Mountain High," he had closed his Philles record label, married the lead singer in his girl group, the Ronettes, and been reduced to taking small film parts, like the drug dealer in *Easy Rider*. Even so, he was top of John's wish list to mark the break from George Martin and all things Beatlesh. They had not met since 1964, when Spector had been among the copassengers on the Beatles' first flight to America. However, Allen Klein knew him well and had no difficulty in bringing him to London for what would be as significant a fresh start for him as for John.

"Instant Karma" was in the minimalist, sing-along style John had developed with the Plastic Ono Band, similar to "Cold Turkey" in tempo but far more relaxed and humorous. Indeed, one of the effects of Spector's production was to give his voice a taut expressiveness it had not had since "Norwegian Wood." The idea was quintessential Lennon—the age-old Buddhist law of cause and effect turned into something as modern and synthetic as instant coffee and, simultaneously, into a bogey under the stairs that can get you if you don't watch out. Its warning, couched in the hippie catchphrase of the moment, was obviously not to be taken literally: "You better get yourself together / Or pretty soon you're gonna be dead. . . ." The chorus returned to peace campaigning and nonviolent, optimistic togetherness. Henceforward, any group of young dissidents, menaced by batons or water cannons, could draw strength and unanimity from its chant of "We all shine on / Like the moon and the stars and the sun."

The track was finished in just ten takes, with background vocals provided by Yoko, Mal Evans, and several complete strangers who, on a sudden whim of John's, had been rounded up at Hatchetts, a West End club. It was released on Apple just six days later, with PLAY LOUD printed across the label. (The B-side, a Yoko vocal called "Who Has Seen the Wind?" was inscribed PLAY QUIET.) It went to number five in the United Kingdom and number three in America, becoming the first single by a solo Beatle to sell a million copies there. As John played it on BBC-TV's *Top of the Pops*, Yoko sat beside him, wearing a white blindfold and knitting.

This new epoch also saw John's one-man crusade on behalf of the oppressed and disadvantaged increasingly focus on those rendered so by the color of their skins. It was perhaps the greatest of all mental turnarounds for someone raised on the idea of black people as comical inferiors, who not long since had been getting laughs at the expense of "Negroes" and "Mister Wabooba." Part of the reason was the vicious racism that underlay so much public hostility to Yoko. A significant part was the rise of America's militant Black Power movement and the emergence of highly articulate and literate demagogues like Stokely Carmichael and Eldridge Cleaver. Nearer home there was the racist apartheid regime in South Africa, a member of the British Commonwealth, which, despite growing condemnation and isolation, continued to send its all-white national sports teams on overseas tours. In February, heavy fines were imposed on a group of antiapartheid protesters who had disrupted a rugby match between a Scottish side and the South African Springboks the previous December. All the fines were paid by John.

The gesture inevitably brought him into the sights of Britain's nascent Black Power movement and its chief spokesman, Michael Abdul Malik, aka Michael X. Born Michael de Freitas in Trinidad, Malik had dominated black politics in Britain since the mid-Sixties, converting to Islam in emulation of his American counterparts and styling himself X after their charismatic young leader Malcolm X, who had been assassinated in 1965. A would-be writer and poet and a dedicated social climber, Michael X was adept at raising funds from affluent whites by playing on their guilty liberal consciences. This gambit paid off handsomely when he approached John and Yoko for money to support the Black House, a welfare center for delinquent teenagers that he ran in Holloway, North London. He announced that the Beatles' music had "stolen the rhythms of black people," and it was payback time. A remorseful John offered him an advance to write a book called *A Black Experience* and also agreed to help fund a soup kitchen at the Black House.

After John and Yoko's drastic barbering in Denmark, they had gathered up all their shorn hair and brought it home with them. Now they presented it to Michael X, to be divided into small portions, put into boxes, and sold in aid of the Black House. He in return gave them a pair of bloodstained boxing trunks allegedly belonging to another celebrity pal, Black Power Islam's most famous convert, Muhammad Ali. They made an appearance together on ITV's *Simon*

Dee Show, and John was seen around the Black House so much that he took to calling it "Black Apple."

His major commitment in the first half of 1970 was to have been the two-day Montreal Peace Festival in July. With his personal endorsement, the festival promised to out-Woodstock Woodstock several times over. An audience of between one and two million was projected, to hear a roster of performers headed by John and some if not all of his fellow Beatles, plus Bob Dylan, even possibly the resurgent Elvis Presley. There was talk of a stage shaped like a giant bed, commemorating John and Yoko's bed-ins, and of a "peace vote" in which every festivalgoer would register opposition to the Vietnam War.

But by spring, the epic project had hit trouble. Though initially content for the promoters to charge reasonable admission—as several previous festivals had without detracting from their mystique—John suddenly changed his mind and insisted it must be free. With commercial sponsorship of rock events still unknown and merchandising only in its infancy, that virtually guaranteed a horrendous financial loss. In addition, Montreal's city council had vetoed Mosport Park as a site, and no alternative had yet been found. The last straw was the involvement of two wacky friends of Tony Cox's, who announced that, to vary the musical program, real flying saucers would land. John pulled out, and the festival was canceled forthwith.

He and Yoko were both still struggling to stay off heroin, a relatively easy task amid bed-ins and prime-ministerial summit conferences when every moment brought its own "rush," but harder now they had time on their hands. During March, the journalist Ray Connolly met up with them in London, while Yoko was briefly an inpatient at a Harley Street clinic. "She's a junkie, you know," John told a startled nurse who came in with some medication. Connolly deduced that they were both taking the heroin substitute methadone and that, for John at least, the rigors of cold turkey were being alleviated by his new connection to the Black Power movement. During the journalist's increasingly off-the-record visit, Michael X arrived with a friend, bringing a large plastic bag of marijuana hidden in a suitcase. However, even Connolly did not cop the next printable

Lennon headline, nor did anyone in Fleet Street. On March 29, John sent a telephone message of support to eight thousand people taking part in a nuclear-disarmament rally in East London. In the course of it, he revealed that Yoko was pregnant again.

Sharing one's history is a part of any new relationship, all the more necessary if the partners come from widely different cultures. But with John and Yoko, the process was almost entirely one-sided. After months together, he still knew almost nothing of Yoko's early years in Japan, the privileged loneliness of her life surrounded by genuflecting servants, or the wartime hardships when she was left virtually alone to fend for two younger siblings as well as herself. She, on the other hand, knew every twist and turn of his infancy in gray, bomb-torn Liverpool: how his father had disappeared from his life when he was six, and his mother, Julia, had handed him over to Aunt Mimi, then gone on to have two children out of wedlock with John "Twitchy" Dykins.

More than anything else, he talked about Julia: how beautiful, fascinating, and funny she was, how she had stayed close to him throughout his boyhood yet never properly been "his," and what a horrendous gap had been torn in his eighteen-year-old life when a car knocked her down just yards from Mimi's front gate. To the unshockable Yoko he repeated a confession that had only ever slipped out once before, in conversation with his "Richmal Crompton woman," Maureen Cleave. "He told me that when he was in his teens, he sometimes used be in Julia's room with her when she had a rest in the afternoon. And he'd always regretted he'd never been able to have sex with her. . . . "At that point, I didn't know that he needed so much therapy as he did. I knew there was a crazy side of him, but I was like Peggy Guggenheim—thinking Jackson Pollock is great because he's crazy. At the opening of his show, Pollock would pee all over his painting or something. I didn't think of John as someone who should be boxed in and get therapy. I thought that fame had relieved the pressure for him a little bit. But that Liverpool childhood was still very scary for him."

One late-March morning, the post brought a bulky packet from the American publishers G. P. Putnam's Sons. It was a new book by a California therapist named Arthur Janov, which Putnam's was circulating to various big names, hoping to garner some prepublication endorsements. Its title was *The Primal Scream: Primal Therapy, the Cure for Neurosis.* When John saw the first three words, he instantly thought of Yoko's vocal technique. "He passed me over this book," she remembers, "and said 'Look . . . it's you.' "

Janov's thesis was that almost all neurotic behavior derived from the traumas of childhood. Adults who had been denied the child's basic, crying need for love, security, and attention tended to blot out the memory, finding apparent consolation in the sweets of adulthood—fame, wealth, or sex. But as long as those long-ago, unfulfilled needs were suppressed, their behavior remained essentially unreal and thus prone to neurosis in every form. Primal scream therapy was designed to break down "the force of years of compressed feelings and denied needs" by taking the patient back to childhood to confront the pain, articulate it as "primally" as babies do on first leaving the snug womb for the cold world, and so finally be cleansed of it.

John read the book in a single gulp, after his usual fashion, and decided he must meet Arthur Janov and undergo primal scream therapy without delay. A few nights later, Janov was telephoned at his California home by Yoko and asked to come to England to administer the treatment. He replied that he had a busy practice and could not abandon his other patients for the sake of just one, however famous. "Then afterwards when I told my two children, they said, 'Are you kidding? That's John Lennon!' " Janov remembers. Since generous travel expenses were offered, he decided to make it a family trip, taking both children out of school and including his then wife and professional partner, Vivian. In the usual spirit of togetherness, John wanted Yoko to have the therapy also, so it was agreed that Vivian Janov would take charge of her.

John's psychological state came as a profound shock to Janov. "The level of his pain was enormous . . . as much as I've ever seen. He was almost completely nonfunctional. He couldn't leave the house, he could hardly leave his room. He had no defenses, he was decompensating [falling apart], he was just one big ball of pain. This was someone the whole world adored, and it didn't change a thing. At the center of all that fame and wealth and adulation was just a lonely little kid."

To maintain professional distance, Janov stayed at the Inn on the Park hotel in London, traveling down to Tittenhurst each day with his wife by chauffeur-driven limousine. While Yoko's sessions with Vivian took place in the main house, John elected to have his in the still-unfinished recording studio, hoping its insulated walls would muffle the noises he had to make. From the title of Janov's book, he imagined himself rolling on the floor and shrieking uncontrollably, much like teenage girls had once done for the Beatles. "He told me he didn't know how to scream," Janov remembers. "He'd had to ask Yoko to give him lessons."

In fact, the sessions merely consisted of long talks with a ruggedly good-looking, curly-haired man whose quiet voice and low-key questions stripped away his past, layer by layer, almost without his realizing it. "[Janov's] thing is to feel the pain that's accumulated inside you ever since your childhood," he would later recall. "In the therapy you really feel every painful moment of your life—it's excruciating. . . . There's no way of describing it . . . what you actually do is cry. Instead of penting up emotion or pain, feel it rather than putting it away for some rainy day. It's like somewhere along the line, we were switched off not to feel things. . . . This therapy gives you back the switch, locate it and switch back into feeling just as a human being, not as a male or a female or a famous person or not famous person, they switch you back to being a baby and therefore you feel as a child does. . . ."

They talked about his abandonment, as he saw it, by his father that sunny Blackpool day in 1946 when he had been forced to choose either Mummy or Daddy. They talked about Julia, her beauty and magnetism, about his feeling that she had never fully belonged to him and that she, too, had left him just when he needed her most. They talked about the two other great tragedies in his young life, the deaths of Uncle George and Stu Sutcliffe—to both of which at the time he could respond only with hysterical laughter but which both now encouraged healthy, healing tears. They touched on the sexual feelings he had had for his mother, which to Janov squared perfectly with his choice of Yoko as a wife. "I'd had other patients with very seductive mothers who ended up with non-Caucasian wives, so as not to be too close to the incestuous thing." They talked about Mimi ("a lot," according to Janov): about the magnificent care and protection she had given, but her lack of the quality John craved most. "He'd had a seductive mother who was more like a girl friend, a father he viewed as just a bum, and an aunt who did the right thing by him, but who always seemed very tough and unfeeling. There had been a terrible lack of softness in his life."

They talked, too, about Brian Epstein, the fourth and last crucial figure whom John felt had, almost neglectfully, "died on him." "He knew Brian had adored him, and there was a lot of guilt there about the way he'd depended on Brian yet mistreated him," Janov recalls. They talked about John's notorious Spanish holiday with Brian in 1963 and the (to John) insignificant physical encounter that had resulted. The more Janov heard about Brian, the more he longed to have had him as a patient. "God, that was a tragic story. There was someone who needed therapy even more than John did."

The workmen still around the studio created intermittent noise and distraction, so after a few days John suggested moving to the house and continuing the sessions around the long rustic table in the kitchen. As their talk widened from his personal history into generalities, Janov was struck by his "amazing mixture of complexity and simplicity. . . . He could see right into people, the way some schizophrenics can. He was all right-brain [instinctive and intuitive, not analytical]. He would say, 'What about religion?' and I would say something like, 'People in pain usually seek out religion.' And John would say, 'Oh—God is a concept by which we measure our pain.'"

John himself believed the most important service Janov did for him was to break down "the religious myths" he had been absorbing all his life, from St. Peter's Church Sunday School in Woolton to the Maharishi's Indian ashram. "You are forced to realise that your pain, the kind that makes you wake up afraid with your heart pounding, is really yours and not the result of someone up in the sky. It's the result of your parents and your environment. As I realized this, it all started to fall into place. This therapy forced me to have done with all the God shit. . . . Most people channel their pain into God or masturbation or some dream of making it . . . [I started] facing up to reality instead of always looking for some kind of Heaven."

The Janovs made it a firm rule not to develop personal friendships with their patients. But they both recall the trouble that John took to make their stay in England pleasant. "While Vivian and I worked with John and Yoko, our children were sent tickets to all the best rock shows that were on," Arthur Janov says. "One day there was some mix-up over the schedule and I had to take my son, Rick, down to Tittenhurst Park with me. John was incredibly nice to him and took him out to play Frisbee in the garden." After three weeks, even though the treatment was not nearly over, Janov felt he could no longer neglect his patients back in America. He urged John and Yoko, and they agreed, to complete it at his Primal Center in Los Angeles that summer.

On April 1, Great Marlborough Street Magistrates' Court ruled that John's erotic lithographs of Yoko were not liable to "deprave or corrupt" under the letter of the Obscene Publications Act. In the artist's defense, a lithograph and a catalog of drawings by Picasso were shown to the magistrates. The prosecution was so fatuous, and the verdict so predictable, that John did not have to testify or even attend the hearing. (Three decades later, a set of the lithographs would be on permanent display at the Museum of Modern Art in New York.) By now, no fan or journalist in the world mistook him for a Beatle, despite Apple's vehement protestations to the contrary. "Spring is here!" began a rather desperate press release from Derek Taylor, "and Leeds play Chelsea tomorrow and Ringo and John and George and Paul are still alive and well and full of hope. The world is still spinning and so are we and so are you. When the spinning stops, that'll be the time to worry. Not before."

Though the Beatles were unable to work together anymore, they still had one major unreleased product, the album recorded early in 1969 under the title *Get Back*. Since Glyn Johns's failed attempt to give its voluminous tapes some coherence, the project had been in limbo—and, with it, the "Beatles at Work" documentary film directed by Michael Lindsay-Hogg. Such waste was anathema to Allen Klein, especially with a new Capitol contract entitling him to 20 percent commission. Unfortunately, even John, his strongest advocate in the band, could not be persuaded that *Get Back* was other than irredeemable "shit."

Klein's solution was to hire Phil Spector—a producer revered as much by Paul, George, and Ringo as by John—to attempt a further remix of the album. Spector worked on the tapes intensively at Abbey Road Studios for several weeks, adding extra vocal and instrumental effects to what in some cases had been barely more than run-throughs. When Paul heard the first pressing, he was appalled to find both his main vocal appearances melodramatically embellished with strings, brass, and celestial choirs. He registered an angry protest, but once again was overruled by the other three. To add insult to injury, the album was retitled *Let It Be* after one of those "Spectorised" McCartney tracks, an elegiac ballad built on a phrase all the Beatles had grown up with, and which now seemed strangely appropriate. In Liverpool, when small boys quarreled or nursed grievances, their parents would tell them (as Mimi often had John) to "let it be." Lindsay-Hogg's documentary received the same name, and album and film were finally scheduled for release in April.

Outvoted, marginalized, now widely believed to be dead, Paul had suffered a drop in self-esteem more vertiginous than any of his erstwhile colleagues could have guessed. His therapy—the only kind he would ever need—was to spend time with his new baby and start making a solo album of his own. In compensation for his loss of control on *Get Back/Let It Be*, this was a defiantly one-man enterprise, recorded in his private studio, with every instrument played by himself, and nobody else involved but his wife, Linda, on backing vocals (for which she received the same cobilling that John now gave Yoko). Titled simply *McCartney*, its front cover a head shot by Linda, the album was handed to Apple Records without reference to the other Beatles or Klein, and a release date set of April 10.

The trouble was that three other Beatle-related albums had been scheduled for around the same time: *Let It Be*, Ringo's *Sentimental Journey*, and a compilation for the American market entitled *Hey Jude*. Since the most obvious mutually detrimental clash was between *Let*

It Be and *McCartney*, one or the other would have to be postponed. With Paul refusing to talk to Klein, and no one at Apple Records possessing real executive clout anymore, it fell to John to deal with the problem. On March 5, he handwrote a note to Paul, with George as cosignatory, announcing that they'd told EMI to put back *McCartney*'s release date to June 4. "We thought you'd come round when you realised the Beatles album was coming out on April 24th," the note continued. "We're sorry it turned out like this—it's nothing personal. Love John and George (Hare Krishna)."

The letter was delivered to Paul at Cavendish Avenue by Ringo Starr, normally an infallible pourer of oil on troubled Beatle waters. But this time, even Ringo's emollience had no effect. Paul, understandably, could not bear his precious solo debut to be elbowed aside, particularly by a Beatles album containing work of his that he felt had been mutilated. His long self-schooling as Mr. Nice Guy forgotten, he lost his temper and ordered poor, blameless Ringo out of the house. Ringo, that unchangeable Mr. Nice Guy, returned to John and George and talked them into backing down. *McCartney* kept its April 10 release date while *Let It Be*, the album and film, were pushed back to May.

It says much about his demoralized state of mind that the Beatles' former tireless PR man now shrank from doing media interviews on his own behalf. Instead, press copies of the *McCartney* album came with a printed Q & A sheet, put together in consultation with Derek Taylor, which vented all the resentments and frustrations of recent months and finally confirmed what had been so long suspected.

Q: Will Paul and Linda become a John and Yoko?

A: No, they will become a Paul and Linda. . . .

Q: What do you think about John's peace effort? The Plastic Ono Band? Giving back the MBE? Yoko's influence? Yoko?

A: I love John and respect what he does—it doesn't give me any pleasure.

Q: Are you planning a new album or single with the Beatles?

A: No. . . .

As he would later explain: "I couldn't just let John control the situation and dump us as if we [were] the jilted girlfriends."

Just before the release of *McCartney*, he telephoned John and announced, "I'm doing what you and Yoko are doing and putting out an album. And I'm leaving the group, too." John's initial response was relief, that this most stubborn resuscitator of the band was finally giving up. If he felt anger with anyone, it was with himself for having heeded those appeals to his team spirit and kept his own exit under wraps so effortfully for so long. Now Paul had stolen the headlines yet again by grandly exiting a stage that John—and George and Ringo, too—had quietly left six months earlier. "[Paul] just did a great hype. I wanted to do it and I should have done it. I thought, 'Damn, shit, what a fool I was.' . . . I was a fool not to do it, not to do what Paul did, which was use it to sell a record."

After all its travails, the *Let It Be* film won an Oscar, and a Grammy for best original music sound track, while the album went to number one in both the United Kingdom and the United States, eventually spending more than a year on the charts. To John, there was never any doubt that Phil Spector had been its savior. "If anybody listens to the bootleg version . . . , which was pre-Spector, and listens to the version Spector did, they would shut up—if you really want to know the difference. The tapes were so lousy . . . that none of us would go near them. They'd been lying around for six months. None of us could face remixing them, it was terrifying. But Spector did a terrific job."

In interviews, he repeated that the breakup had been inevitable, that no one person or thing had been to blame, and that the worldwide mourners should keep a sense of proportion. "The Beatles were disintegrating slowly after Brian Epstein died, it was slow death and it was happening. It's evident on *Let It Be* although Linda and Yoko were evident then, but they weren't when we started it. It was evident in India when George and I stayed there and Ringo left. It was evident on the *White Album*. It's just natural. It's not a great disaster. People keep talking about it as if it's the end of the earth. It's only a rock group that split up. It's nothing important. . . .

"It takes a lot to live with four people over and over for years and years, which is what we did. We'd called each other every name under the sun. . . . We'd been through the mill together for more than 10 years. We'd been through our therapy together many times . . . It's just that you grow up. We don't want to be the Crazy Gang or the Marx Brothers being dragged onstage playing 'She Loves You' when we've got asthma and tuberculosis and when we're fifty."

25

BEATLEDÄMMERUNG

Our job is to write for the people now.

n May 1970, John finally managed to get back into America. After long negotiations with the U.S. Embassy in London, the Immigration and Naturalization Service (INS) waived the visa ban in force since his British drug conviction eighteen months earlier. Accompanied only by George and Pattie Harrison (and using the alias Chambers), he was permitted to fly to Los Angeles, then on to New York for business meetings with Capitol Records and Allen Klein. In July, he was again granted admittance to return to L.A. with six-months-pregnant Yoko for their second course of primal scream therapy under Arthur Janov.

Janov had warned that, to be effective, the therapy must proceed uninterruptedly for between four and six months—and in John's case might take even longer. He and Yoko came fully prepared for this, clearing their joint schedule of all commitments until September and renting a house in the film-star colony of Bel Air. They attended the Primal Center almost daily, continuing their respective one-on-one sessions with Arthur and Vivian Janov and also joining in group discussion and self-exploration with other patients.

Aware how beadily the eyes were trained on him, John kept a low profile, giving no media interviews, avoiding anyone who might drag him into compromising headlines. One exception was Jann Wenner, twenty-four-year-old editor and publisher of San Francisco's *Rolling Stone* magazine. Wenner was emerging as John's doughtiest press champion: *Rolling Stone* had reproduced the *Two Virgins* album cover in the teeth of American conservative outrage, sympathetically reviewed every John-and-Yoko album, and backed their peace campaign to the hilt. Now he wanted John to do one of the extended interviews for which his magazine was noted. That quest had already taken him to Britain, but, in the dark days just before meeting Janov, John could not contemplate such an idea. When Wenner arrived at Tittenhurst Park, Yoko said his prospective interviewee was "too paranoid" even to come downstairs and meet him.

Hearing that John and Yoko were receiving treatment at the Primal Center, Wenner invited them up to San Francisco for a weekend and gave them their first real tour of the city that first made *peace* a global buzzword. With Wenner's wife, Jane, they also saw an afternoon showing of *Let It Be* in an almost empty cinema. "After the show—moved at whatever level, either as participants or deep fans—we somehow cried," Wenner would remember.

Five or six more weeks with Arthur Janov convinced John that primal scream therapy was the Answer that neither God, rock 'n' roll, nor the Maharishi had been able to give him. And, as usual, he felt a need to share his feeling of redemption with the whole world. "He came to me and said he wanted to take out a full-page ad in the *San Francisco Chronicle*, saying, 'This Is It,'" Janov remembers. "I told him as politely as possible, 'John, this stuff is serious. It doesn't live or die on the approval of a rock musician.'"

Then, early in July, he suddenly announced that the INS was harassing him for overstaying his time, and he would have to leave America forthwith. He asked if Janov would assign him a personal therapist to continue his course in Mexico. "Just then, I had 5,000 applicants for treatment. I couldn't possibly spare anyone from my staff to go off with him like that," Janov says. "So the therapy had to end at what was a crucial point for John. We'd opened him up but we hadn't had time to put him back together again. A lot more work needed to be done to get right down to the root of his anger. I estimated it would take at least another year."

The solution was to employ a new therapist: himself. After his first sessions with Janov, he had begun work on a new batch of songs. These were polished, and new ones added, during his time at the Primal Center, and the minimum complement for an album—eleven tracks—finished off after his premature return to Britain. He had often written lyrics about himself, from "Help!" to "A Day in the Life," but always hitherto cloaked their message in poetic imagery or punning wordplay. Now all that seemed part of the repression that primal scream therapy sought to break down. "I had to look into my own soul," he would recall. "I wasn't looking at it from a mystical perspective . . . or from a psychedelic perspective or being-a-famous-Beatle perspective or making-a-Beatle record perspective. . . . This time, it was just me in a mirror."

The result was his first named solo album, *John Lennon/Plastic Ono Band*, recorded at Abbey Road Studios during September and October 1970. The Plastic Ono lineup this time was minimal, as if only trusted friends and colleagues could be allowed to hear the confessions in their raw state: Klaus Voormann on bass and Ringo Starr on drums, plus occasional keyboard contributions from Billy Preston. Production was credited jointly to Phil Spector, John, and Yoko, with Yoko receiving an additional credit for "wind." At the same time, Yoko made an album of her own with the same musicians, to be released alongside John's.

For the very first time, he was singing on his own, without backup harmonies or any of the sonic embellishment and distortion he habitually used with the Beatles. "It used to get a bit embarrassing in front of George and Paul," he would recall, "'cause we know each other so well: 'Oh, he's trying to be Elvis, oh he's doing this now,' you know. . . . So we inhibited each other a lot. And now I had Yoko there and Phil Spector there, alternately and together, who sort of love me, okay, so I [could] perform better. And I relaxed. The looseness of the singing was developed on 'Cold Turkey' from the experience of Yoko's singing—she does not inhibit her throat."

The opening song went straight to the core of his deepest-seated misery: it was called simply "Mother." By way of introduction, a church bell tolled slowly and sonorously, a summons to mourning rather than festivity. Though John had copied it from an old Hammer horror film, no sound was more evocative of the years that Janov's therapy had forced him to relive. That slow, ominous chime might have been from St. Peter's in Woolton, echoing through the silent winter Sunday evenings of his boyhood.

The lyric was a blunt accusation leveled at both the parents, whom he believed had so grievously failed him: one by giving birth to him, then giving him away; the other by walking out on him when he was a toddler. "Mother, you had me / But I never had you. . . . Father, you left me / But I never left you." The purpose of the song was what no one yet called *closure*—a final, liberating good-bye to the bewitching redhead who had loved him, but never quite enough, and the sailor who had always seemed to prefer the sea. Its ending was a repeated scream of panic that might have come from John's six-year-old self that sunny day in Blackpool when Julia and the father then known as Alf had forced him to choose between them: "Mama, don't go . . . Daddy, come home!"

The whole album was the same mixture of dam-bursting anger and haunting vulnerability. In contrast to the blind terror of "Mother," "Hold On" was a reassurance to Yoko, humanity in general, but, above all, himself, that "It'll be all right . . . we're gonna win the fight." "I Found Out" bitterly ticked off every nostrum he had ever tried, from "dope and cocaine" back through "Hare Krishna" and hippiedom's "brother, brother, brother" even unto wanking. "Isolation" owned up to the fear that he and Yoko often felt as "a boy and a little girl, trying to change the whole wide world," while "Remember" reflected that, however bad things might get, at least he was no longer small. "Look at Me" echoed his demand to Yoko that she must never for one second lift her attentive, adoring gaze from him. "Love" was haiku-brief ("Love is touch / Touch is love") sung in the wistful, fragile voice only previously used for "Julia" on the *White Album*—John with all his defenses down.

After "Mother," the most notable track, both for its self-lacerating emotion and its selectiveness with history, was "Working Class Hero." This one was squarely aimed at Aunt Mimi, Mendips, and the strainingly aspirant middle-class world that had put his childhood on terra firma but also, he now thought, destroyed his self-confidence and joie de vivre beyond rescue.

To repudiate this part of the past, he had turned to a genre he used to despise and written a folk song. He performed it alone with acoustic guitar, talking rather than singing the perfectly scanned rhyming triplets, resurrecting deprivations and grievances of twenty years ago (but forgetting the security, good cooking, and ample pocket-money): "As soon as you're born, they make you feel small . . . They hurt you at home and they hit you at school . . ." Big business and the military each received a swipe, as did even the Sixties generation and their mirage of being "clever and classless and free." But his iciest contempt was reserved for himself, as the fraudulent apotheosis of working-class "heroism" and dubious exemplar for all who aspired to it: "If you want to be a hero, well just follow me." He also did for pop albums what Kenneth Tynan had done for television four years earlier, premiering the F word not once but twice. Such was the virulence of every other word, it barely stood out.

His ad-lib to Arthur Janov, "God is a concept by which we measure our pain," triggered the climactic rite of renunciation in a song simply titled "God." Paradoxically framed in a slow gospel style, like the Anglican Creed in reverse, came a roll call of every once-awesome power he no longer believed in, Magic, I Ching, Bible, tarot, Hitler, Jesus, Kennedy, Buddha, mantra, Gita, yoga, kings, Elvis, Zimmerman [Bob Dylan], and finally, with almost audible nausea, Beatles. Spleen turned to softness again as he contemplated what was left: "I just believe in me / Yoko and me / And that's reality." The ending was a belated farewell to the world's Beatlemaniacs, apologetic, a little sad even, but irrevocable: "I was the Walrus but now I'm John / And so, dear friends, you'll just have to carry on. The dream is over."

It might have seemed impossible for him to twist the knife in himself anymore, but he did. The album's final, fragmentary track, "My Mummy's Dead," transposed his 1958 heartbreak into a nursery rhyme, sung in the voice of a dazed child and strummed on a tinny guitar that might have been the very Gallotone Champion Julia saved up to buy him. The broken words—"I can't explain . . . so much pain"—were like some psychic message; indeed, his handwriting in the original lyric has the jaggedly chaotic look of dictation from beyond the grave.

Like meditating in times past, the technique he had learned from Janov became part of daily life, converted into a verb: *to primal*. For Yoko, one positive effect was to curb his jealousy and possessiveness toward her. "If we were in bed and he'd start to accuse me of this and that, 'Why were you looking at that guy, why were you smiling at him?' he'd say 'Give me a pillow' and start to punch it. . . . It became a ritual for him to scream and shout. Then he'd immediately realise he was not angry at me but at something that happened long before he met me."

Yoko's baby was due in October, around the time of John's thirtieth birthday. They had stayed free of heroin and, with their cleaner and less frantic lifestyle of recent months, had every reason to hope this second pregnancy would be successful. Then, late one August night, an ambulance was called to Tittenhurst Park to rush Yoko to King's College Hospital in Denmark Hill, Dulwich. John went with her, and became so concerned by the bumpiness of the ride that a mile or so down the road he made the driver stop, then telephoned Les Anthony to bring the Rolls. As before, doctors ordered a blood transfusion, and Anthony had to round up donors whom Yoko considered trustworthy, like the disc jockey John Peel. But a couple of days later, she miscarried again. John was told that his sperm count could be part of the problem.

Janov had been uneasy at halting John's therapy before his reawakened anger over his early childhood could be fully laid to rest. The awful extent of this was revealed when, late in September, after an interval of more than a year, he heard from his father. Unconsciously adding insult to ancient injury, Freddie Lennon was no longer a rootless embarrassment but settled and happy with his young wife, Pauline, in the rent-free house provided by John in Brighton. After one miscarriage, Pauline had given birth to a son, David, granting Freddie an unexpected second try at fatherhood at the age of fifty-seven. His potential as a breadwinner being limited, Pauline went out to work while he—eerily foreshadowing his son's future role—looked after the baby, did the cooking, and ran the home. The arrival of a half brother had not seemed to interest John, however, and his always irregular letters ceased soon afterward.

Now Freddie had conceived the idea of writing his autobiography, and wanted John's consent to begin work. He knew John had been receiving some kind of therapy but had no idea how crucially his own life story figured therein, as also in the album being screamed and sobbed out in group sessions with the Plastic Ono Band. The encouraging response was an invitation to pay his first visit to Tittenhurst Park, with Pauline and eighteen-month-old David, on John's thirtieth birthday, October 9. Unaware that John had grown a beard since their last meeting, he took along a gift of aftershave lotion.

Freddie's hopes of a pleasant birthday reunion were soon dashed. On arrival at Tittenhurst, he and Pauline were stopped in the driveway as if they were trespassers and, their bona fides established, made to wait in the kitchen. When John finally appeared, he was utterly changed from the generally friendly, sympathetic person Pauline had known at Kenwood. His face, she recalls, was pale and haggard, the pupils of his eyes were contracted behind his granny glasses, his unfamiliar beard gave him the appearance of "a wild and primitive warrior," and he barely seemed to notice his new half brother playing on the floor. What happened next Freddie would later describe in a four-page handwritten statement, which he then deposited for safekeeping with his solicitor. Though highly melodramatic in tone, it is corroborated in every detail by Pauline:

. . . [John] launched into an account of his recent visit to America, and as the story unfolded, so the self inflicted torture began to show in his face, and his voice rose to a scream as he likened himself to "Jimi Hendrix" and other Pop Stars who had recently departed from the scene, ending in a crescendo as he admitted he was "Bloody Mad, Insane" and due for an early demise. It seemed he had gone to America, at great expense to have some kind of treatment through drugs, which enabled one to go back and relive from early childhood the happenings, which in his own case, he

should have been happier to forget. I was now listening to the
result of this treatment as he reviled his dead Mother in unspeakable terms, referring, also, to the Aunt who had brought him up,
in similar derogatory terms, as well as one or two of his closest
friends. I sat through it all, completely stunned, hardly believing
that this was the kind considerate "Beatle" John Lennon talking to
his Father with such evil intensity. But much worse was to follow,
I had cause to restrain my Wife in her efforts to defend me, as I
had perceived that she was only adding fuel to the fire, for I was
by now, convinced he would do us an injury if we tried to thwart
in any way, his evil intentions. It was when I once more alluded
to the fact, that I had never asked him for financial help, and was
quite prepared to manage without it, that he flew into another
abominable outburst, and accused me of using the "Press" to
force him to help me, and that, if I were to do so again, particularly about our present discussion, he would have me "done In."
There was no doubt whatsoever in my mind, that he meant every
word he spoke, his countenance was frightful to behold, as he explained in detail, how I would be carried out to sea and dumped,
"twenty—Fifty—or perhaps you would prefer a hundred fathoms
deep." The whole loathesome tirade was uttered with malignant
glee, as though he were actually participating in the terrible deed.
The week following this nightmarish interview with my son, furnished proof beyond doubt, that, not content with terminating the
weekly allowance, he had already begun proceedings, to force me
from the house we were living in, which I had presumed was already in my name, and was even prepared to pay for. This sort of
action, I could fight, but the threat, left me with no other alternative than to leave this full account with my Solicitor to be opened
only if I should disappear or die an unnatural death.

Signed:

Freddie Lennon

By then, Freddie had received a letter from Apple, demanding that
he sign a deed to transfer the Brighton house back to John. Also enclosed was his National Insurance card, which he had thought Apple
was keeping supplied with regular contribution stamps. It bore not a

single stamp, making him liable for some £300 in arrears. The lodging of the statement with his solicitor (and notification to John that he had done so) was no mere dramatic flourish. As Pauline recalls, he was genuinely in fear of his life—and so was she, given John's recent highly publicized association with dubious characters like Michael X. That threat of a watery grave was particularly terrifying because, as Freddie now confessed, in all his years at sea, he had never learned to swim.

The couple were not destitute, thanks to Pauline's work as a freelance translator and a recent win of £2,500 in the football pools. Shortly afterward, John relented a little, offering them £500 to help pay for fixtures and furnishings at a new flat in Brighton. This was on condition Freddie sign back the house, gave no further interviews to the press, and sent his statement about the Tittenhurst meeting to Apple to be destroyed (which he did, while keeping a photocopy). He and John were never to meet again.

On November 27, two weeks ahead of *John Lennon/Plastic Ono Band* (and *Yoko Ono/Plastic Ono Band*) George Harrison also came out with a solo album. Such was the backlog of songs he had been unable to place on Beatles albums that this debut took up three whole discs, packed in an Apple-chic box. Entitled *All Things Must Pass*, it converted George's rather ponderous Indian mysticism into lush, uplifting soft rock, produced by Phil Spector, with star backup musicians, including Ringo, Eric Clapton, and Billy Preston. The keynote track, *My Sweet Lord*, an anthem crossing all religious boundaries, from "Hare Krishna" to "Hallelujah," reached number one in America and spent thirty-eight weeks on the *Billboard* chart.

John could not but feel somewhat upstaged by that former tagalong "bloody kid." Despite the uncompromising bleakness of his own album, he intended it to be a commercial success and hoped a hit single would come from it. "I mean to sell as many records as I possibly can," he admitted, "because I'm an artist who wants everyone to love me and everybody to buy my stuff." "Working Class Hero" was obviously excluded from the singles market by its double *fucking*, while he thought "Mother" too raw and personal, and likely to fuel "suspicion that something nasty's going on with that John Lennon and his broad again." He considered releasing the evanescent "Love" but finally decided on "Mother." Released only in the United States in January 1971, it barely scraped into the Top 50. The album did better, making number six in America and eleven in Britain (where EMI ordered the *fuckings* to be asterisked out on its lyric sheet). At Arthur Janov's clinic in Los Angeles, it was played in full to an electrified gathering of patients, and thereafter became part of Janov's lexicon, renamed The Primal Album.

To promote it in the U.S. market, John went to New York, sat down with Yoko in ABKCO's boardroom, and gave Jann Wenner the *Rolling Stone* interview that Wenner had so long pursued. What he had to say was momentous enough to run over two issues of the magazine, on January 21 and February 4. By this time, news had come from London that Paul McCartney had begun legal proceedings to dissolve the Beatles' business partnership, so putting their breakup beyond all question. *Time* magazine headlined the double story with a nod to Wagner's epic opera about the twilight of the gods: "Beatledämmerung."

John's *Rolling Stone* interview was a further exercise in primal therapy, this time excavating a part of his life where the screaming had been done already. For the first time, he told what being one of the world's four most adored and envied young men had really meant— the infantile mayhem that had progressively stifled their desire to do live concerts, the enforced kowtowing to insufferable dignitaries and officials, the ban on expressing a view on any grown-up topic whatever, the backstage sex orgies ("like Fellini's *Satyricon,*" as he put it) belied by the front-of-stage squeaky-cleanliness, the sense of being trapped in ever-increasing, unstoppable madness. For the first time, he put on record that Brian Epstein had been gay, and how this and other uncomfortable "truth bits" about his childhood and his mother had been cut from Hunter Davies's authorized biography. Wenner asked point-blank whether he and Brian had had an affair on their notorious Spanish holiday in 1963. "No, not an affair," John replied. ". . . I watched Brian picking up the boys. I like playing a bit faggy, all that."

Now, too, he finally broke his silence about the two old comrades who had become his competitors. The massive success of George's *All Things Must Pass* and its spinoff single was understandably galling, as *John Lennon/Plastic Ono Band* moved rather effortfully up the album charts. "Every time I put the radio on, it's 'Oh My Lord.' . . . I'm beginning to think there must be a God." What others were hailing as a masterpiece, John rated no higher than "All right. . . . At home, I wouldn't play that kind of music. . . . George has not done his best work yet. His talents have developed over the years, and he was working with two fucking brilliant songwriters and he learned a lot from us. And I wouldn't have minded being George, the invisible man, and learning what he learned. And maybe it was hard sometimes for him, because Paul and I are such egomaniacs, but that's the game. So is George—just give him a chance and he'll be the same. The best thing he's done is 'Within You, Without You,' still for me."

About Paul, however, he was strangely muted, despite condemning the "Paul and Linda" *McCartney* album as "rubbish." "He's a good PR man, Paul. I mean he's about the best in the world, probably. He really does a job. . . . I was surprised [*McCartney*] was so poor. I expected just a little more because if Paul and I are sort of disagreeing and I feel weak, I think he must feel strong. . . . Not that we've had much physical argument. . . . So I was surprised. And I was glad, too." Their power to stimulate and goad one another still clearly existed for John, even if he now saw himself as the main stimulator. *John Lennon/Plastic Ono Band*, he hoped, would "scare [Paul] into doing something decent, and then he'll scare me into doing something decent, and I'll scare him, like that. I think he's capable of great work. I think he will do it. I wish he wouldn't. I wish nobody would, Dylan or anyone. I mean in me heart of hearts I wish I was the only one in the world. . . ."

His hardest words were reserved for the other Beatles' supposed hostility to Yoko (forgetting that, to begin with at least, they had shown considerable tolerance). He mentioned almost hitting George, but omitted to mention having actually done so. Wenner asked if the *McCartney* album cover, showing Paul with a new baby daughter, might have been intended to rub in the fact of Yoko's first miscarriage. "I don't think he did that," John said. "I think he was just imitating us, as [he and Linda] usually do, by putting out a family album. You watch—they do exactly what I do a year or two later. . . . They're imitators, you know."

Fresh from sharing supreme studio power with Yoko and Phil Spector, he dismissed George Martin as "a translator" whose expertise had mainly benefited Paul. "If Paul wanted to use violins and that, [Martin] would translate it for him. Like "In My Life," there's an Elizabethan piano solo on it. . . . And he helped us develop a language a little to talk to musicians. Because I'm very shy and for many, many reasons, I didn't much go for musicians. . . . That's nothing personal against George Martin; he just doesn't . . . he's more Paul's style of music than mine." Harsh judgment on the man whose "translations" had included seamlessly joining the light and heavy versions of "Strawberry Fields Forever," creating the fairground phantasmagoria in "Being for the Benefit of Mr. Kite," and arranging the casually requested "sound like the end of the world" as the climax of "A Day in the Life."

His view of the 1960s after almost a year's reflection was that their great cultural and commercial youthquake had changed little of real importance. "The people who are in control and in power and the class system and the whole bullshit bourgeois scene is exactly the same except that there's a lot of fag fucking middle-class kids with long hair walking around London in trendy clothes. And Kenneth Tynan's making a fortune out of the word 'fuck.' But apart from that, nothing happened [except] we all dressed up. The same bastards are in control, the same people are running everything. It's exactly the same. . . . We've grown up a little, all of us, and there has been a change and we are a bit freer and all that, but it's the same game . . . selling arms to South Africa, killing blacks on the street, people are living in fuckin' poverty with fuckin' rats crawling over them. . . . That dream is over, it's just the same only I'm thirty and a lot of people have got long hair, that's all."

He saw his creative future in protest songs, even though their simplicity and universality were even harder to bring off than multilayered masterpieces like "Strawberry Fields." "If I could be a fuckin'

fisherman, I would," he burst out at one point. "If I had the capabili-
ties of being something other than I am, I would. It's no fun being
an artist. You know what it's like, writing, it isn't fun, it's torture. . . .
I read about Van Gogh or Beethoven, any of the fuckers. And I read
an article the other day—'If they'd had psychiatrists, we wouldn't
have had Gauguin's great pictures.' And those fuckin' bastards [the
public], they're just sucking us to death. About all we can do is do it
like fuckin' circus animals. . . . I'd rather be in the audience really,
but I'm not capable of it. . . . I know it sounds silly, and I'd sooner be
rich than poor and all the rest of that shit. But the pain. I'd sooner not
be . . . I wish I was . . . ignorance is bliss or something. If you don't
know, man, there's no pain.

"I have great hopes for what I do, my work. And I also have great
despair that it's all pointless and shit—how can you top Beethoven
and Shakespeare or whatever? And in me secret heart I wanted to
write something that would overtake 'We Shall Overcome.' I don't
know why, that's the one they always sang. I thought 'Why isn't
somebody writing one for the people?' That's what my job is. Our
job is to write for the people now. So the songs they go and sing on
their buses are not just love songs . . . To me, I'm home. I'll never
change much from this."

Quoting a Beatles classic by other hands, Wenner asked if he had
a mental picture of "When I'm Sixty-four." "I hope [Yoko and I] are a
nice old couple, living off the coast of Ireland or something like that,"
John replied. "Looking at our scrapbook of madness."

This was his first visit to New York with Yoko, and her first trip
back since 1966. He reveled in being introduced to her old downtown
haunts, so different from previous stays besieged in the Plaza or the
Warwick, though he had no inkling yet that he would ever settle
here. "This is the first time I'm really seeing New York, you see,"
he told Wenner, "'cause I was always too nervous or I was a famous
Beatle . . . But it's so overpowering. . . . I'm too frightened of it. It's so
much and people are so aggressive. I can't take all that, you know. I
need to go home. I need to look at the grass. I'm always writing about
English garden[s] and that lot. I need that, the trees and the grass."

During their short stay, he also codirected two more films with

Yoko. *Up Your Legs Forever*, another production "for peace," showed 365 pairs of bare legs in succession, provided by, among others, Allen Klein, Jann Wenner, the filmmaker Donn Pennebaker, the actor George Segal, the journalists Al Aronowitz and Tom Wolfe, and the artist Larry Rivers. *Fly* was a twenty-five-minute color sequence of an ordinary housefly crawling over a young woman's prone, naked body. There was an initial hitch when none of the flies provided would act as required, even with the woman's skin thickly coated in honey. A fresh consignment, rounded up in neighborhood restaurant kitchens, were gassed with carbon dioxide until they were barely ambulatory. After almost a day's filming, one of them finally staggered its way to stardom.

Yoko's father, Eisuke Ono, had retired from his high-level banking job in America and returned with her mother, Isoko, to Tokyo. There she now took John to meet his new in-laws at last. Having visited Japan only once previously, as a captive Beatle, he had no real sense of the country or its culture, and expected all its inhabitants to be as diminutive as Yoko. "He said 'I bet your Dad is a real dwarf. Because all Japanese men are like that,'" she remembers. "So I said, 'Well, you'll see.' Because his Dad was a dwarf. And when we went there, he was so surprised that my father was taller than he was."

In fact, Yoko's family, especially its proud and socially prominent Yasuda side, had followed the adventures of the past eighteen months with no less dismay and embarrassment than had John's. After her appearance nude on the *Two Virgins* cover, the Yasudas even issued a press release, saying they were "not proud" of her but were of her cousin, a classical cellist who had won a prize in Sweden. At the family's ceremonial yearly get-together, her name was pointedly never mentioned. Most wounding of all was her mother's assertion—first made after her elopement with Toshi Ichiyanagi—that her behavior adversely affected her father's health.

She wondered how John would go down with the beautiful, cultivated Isoko, but need not have worried. "He said, 'Just leave it to me'"—and my mother adored him. There are pictures of her, holding his arm and gazing adoringly into his eyes." The formidable Eisuke, too, was won over, though not as unreservedly. "With both my parents, looks were everything. My father was wearing a velvet smoking-jacket, and John just his khaki tunic with the military insignia. And Tony, my first husband, had been very handsome. After meeting John, my father took me aside and said, 'The other one was better looking.'"

Though Apple continued to release all four ex-Beatles' solo records, it had shrunk to a wizened remnant of its former luscious self. Most of the staff at 3 Savile Row had been fired, the Georgian town house put up for sale, and the business transferred to a small, anonymous office in St. James's. The last two key executives of the pre–Allen Klein regime had finally resigned, Peter Brown to run Robert Stigwood's organization in New York, Derek Taylor to handle PR for the Warner/Elektra/Atlantic record label. From the Beatles' former support team, there remained only their original, irreplaceable roadies, Neil Aspinall and Mal Evans. Neil tended to assist George on developing film projects, while Mal continued his special role, halfway between bodyguard and nursemaid, mainly with John. On the *Plastic Ono Band* album, he receives a credit for "tea and sympathy."

With no press office to screen or program media interviews, John himself chose which publications and writers to engage with. And if their political credentials were right, prestige and circulation did not matter. In January 1971, he agreed to do an interview for *Red Mole*, a tiny ultraleft magazine edited by the Indian-born, Oxford-educated radical Tariq Ali, who had famously led the antiwar demo outside the American Embassy three years earlier. Ali's co-interrogator was Robin Blackburn, a future professor of sociology and editor of the *New Left Review*. While neither could believe their scoop, John was worried his presence might lower the tone of such a serious publication.

In a session almost as long as one given to *Rolling Stone*, he banished all memory of growing up in the comfortable, unoppressed bourgeoisie and declared himself a working-class hero for real. "I've always been politically-minded, you know, and against the status-quo," he said in a passage at once true and fantastical. "It's pretty basic when you're brought up, as I was, to hate and fear the police as a natural enemy and to despise the army as something that takes everybody away and leaves them dead somewhere. I mean it's just a basic working-class thing, though it begins to wear off when you get older, get a family and get swallowed up by the system. . . . But I was always political in a way, you know. In the two books I wrote, even though they were written in sort of Joycean gobbledegook, there's many knocks at religion and there is a play about a worker and a capitalist. I've been satirising the system since my childhood."

An important new strand in his thinking was also unveiled. Germaine Greer's *The Female Eunuch* had appeared the previous October, spurring women to demand liberation from age-old male dominance that the freedom-giving Sixties had somehow left out. Yoko, understandably, was in the vanguard of this Women's Lib movement, having been schooled in male dominance in Japan and continued to suffer from it throughout her artistic career. To her, female subservience was analogous to the enslavement of Africans a century earlier, and in 1967, to Britain's *Nova* magazine, she said so with a typically extreme metaphor: "Woman is the nigger of the world."

John may once have been the archetypal "male chauvinist pig," in Greer's scornful phrase, but love had brought about a remarkable transformation. "We can't have a revolution that doesn't involve and liberate women," he told *Red Mole*. "It's so subtle, the way you're taught male superiority. It took me quite a long time to realise that my maleness was cutting off certain areas for Yoko. She's a red-hot liberationist and was quick to show me where I was going wrong even though it seemed to me that I was just acting naturally. That's why I'm always interested to know how people who claim to be radical treat women. How you talk about power to the people unless you realise that 'the people' is both sexes?"

Next day, he phoned Tariq Ali to say he'd written a song around a phrase that had run through their discussion, "Power to the People." He was so pleased with it that he sang and played its instantly chantable refrain to Ali over the wire. Its proposition was the same as had been aired so tentatively on the Beatles' *White Album*: "You say you want a revolution . . ." However, the payoff was no longer "You can count me out," but "We gotta get it on right away." There was a call to "give the workers what they really own" and a searching question to his new brothers in the proletariat, "How do you treat your woman back home? . . . She got to be herself / So she can free herself. . . ." Released as a Plastic Ono Band single, it reached number seven in the United Kingdom and eleven in the United States. Communism and feminism came together in the charts for the first and last time.

Paul's original intention had only been to sue Allen Klein. But his lawyers' advice was that John, George, and Ringo's appointment of Klein against his wishes breached the partnership agreement they made as Beatles & Co. in April 1967, and his best means of protecting himself against Klein in the future would be to have it legally terminated. Since the other three opposed the idea, he would be suing all of them as well as Apple Corps, which owned 80 percent of the partnership.

The case opened in the Chancery Division of the High Court on December 31, 1970, while John was still in New York. Paul's counsel called for the dissolution of Beatles & Co., for impartial accounts of its dealings to be compiled, and for a receiver, or independent financial arbitrator, to oversee its finances henceforward. The judge, Mr. Justice Stamp, was told that the partnership's bookkeeping had been "lamentable," that despite income of between £4 million and £5 million per year, it might have insufficient reserves for outstanding income tax and surtax, and that Klein had been paying himself commission to which he was not entitled. The hearing was adjourned after undertakings from Apple's legal team that a substantial interim sum would be paid into the partnership and Paul's share released to him without delay.

When proceedings reopened on February 19, 1971, John, George, and Ringo's counsel, Morris Finer QC, counterclaimed that Klein's appointment had been a necessary measure to save the Beatles from "almost total bankruptcy." Klein had transformed their finances, doubling their income in the first nine months of his management and earning them just over £9 million between May 1969 and December 1970, of which £8 million was record royalties.

Paul was the only one of the partners to attend court and give oral evidence. Mr. Finer read out an affidavit from John, saying that before Klein's advent, Apple had been "full of hustlers and spongers," that two company cars had disappeared, and "we owned a house that no one could remember buying." Surprisingly, in view of his own longing to break free, he portrayed the partnership as something that had always had its discords but was nevertheless urgently worth preserving. "From our earliest days in Liverpool, George and I on the one hand and Paul on the other had different musical tastes. Paul preferred pop-type music and we preferred what is now called underground. This may have led to arguments, particularly between Paul and George, but the contrast in our tastes, I am sure, did more good than harm and contributed to our success. If Paul is trying to break us up because of anything that happened before the Klein-Eastman power struggle, his reasoning does not make sense to me."

In the witness box, Paul was questioned about another somewhat surprising statement in John's affidavit—that even when making their respective solo albums, "We always thought of ourselves as Beatles, whether we recorded singly or in twos or threes." He replied by quoting John's climactic assertion on the Plastic Ono Band album: "I don't believe in Beatles. . . ." Klein had not been a passive appointee of the other three, he maintained, but had actively tried to create dissent, sometimes even pretending to side with him against John. He instanced a telephone conversation in which Klein had allegedly confided, "You know why John is angry with you? It's because you came off better than he did on Let It Be." In another exchange about John, he recalled Klein observing, "The real trouble is Yoko. She's the one with ambition."

After an eleven-day hearing, Mr. Justice Stamp proposed appointing an arbitrator who would combine the roles of manager and receiver and would in turn appoint submanagers—including Klein—to run the Beatles' and Paul's financial affairs as separate entities. Neither side would accept this, so on March 12 the judge appointed Douglas Spooner, a partner in a firm of City accountants "as receiver and manager of the group's business interests pending trial of the main action." While concluding that their financial position was "confused, uncertain and inconclusive," Stamp found no evidence that Klein "had or would put partnership money into his pocket." An appeal on behalf of John, George, and Ringo was lodged, but dropped a few weeks later because "they considered it to be in the common interest to explore means whereby Mr. McCartney could disengage himself from the partnership by agreement."

Receivers being associated with business disaster and bankruptcy in the British mind, it was widely assumed that the Beatles had finally fulfilled John's prophecy and gone broke. However, this one was not only dealing with his clients' debts but also the massive income, mostly in record royalties, they continued to generate. All the Beatles received intermittent payouts from the receiver and had additional substantial sources of extra-partnership income not affected by the court judgment. Apple owned only 20 percent of Maclen, John and Paul's music-publishing company, and John's 40 percent of the proceeds from cover versions and worldwide radio play continued to flow in from Northern Songs under its new owners, ATV. Even after a receiver was appointed for Maclen also, the Lennon-McCartney royalties continued piling up on a Himalayan scale. Although technically superseded by Mr. Spooner, Klein remained John's manager in practice and was more than ready to advance him any additional capital he needed. In short, while plotting the end of the capitalist system with Tariq Ali and the *Red Mole* boys, he could go on spending as if there was no tomorrow.

This was just as well, since Tittenhurst Park and its motley collection of servitors and passing guests ate up money on an epic scale. Lavish open house was kept for John and Yoko's musical and artistic cronies, and anyone they considered a victim of establishment persecution or repression found generous sanctuary with them. In late 1970, for example, Michael X had been charged with robbery and extortion and, rather than face trial, had fled back to his native Trinidad. Despite the damning evidence, John remained his stalwart supporter and offered his wife, Desiree, indefinite rent-free use of Tittenhurst's Tudor cottage while she tried to sort out the legal and financial chaos he had left behind.

John's son Julian, by now a moon-faced seven-year-old, was a frequent weekend visitor, delivered by chauffeured Rolls from his mother's less-than-mansionlike home in West London. Tittenhurst was a seven-year-old's paradise (a "house of fun," grown-up Julian would call it), and father and son found their first sense of real togetherness racing over the hilly greensward on an Amphicat or rowing on the lake. Though an endearing little boy in many ways, Julian had none of John's precocious creativity and charm at the same age, and his relations with his new stepmother were—and would remain—uncomfortable. Yoko says she did her best to be nice to him, but admits she knew little about small boys or how to connect with them. Inevitably, Julian's visits reminded her of the problems she and John were experiencing in having a baby together. She also felt it keenly that, while his son had free run of their home, her daughter did not.

Until now, the shared custody arrangement whereby Kyoko lived with Tony Cox had seemed to work more or less to everyone's satisfaction. Cox had also somehow become part of John and Yoko's creative retinue—to the point where John even suggested they should form another breakaway band, with Cox's Texan girlfriend, Melinda, as its fourth member. Early in 1970, Cox had filmed John and Yoko for an intended documentary on Michael X's Black House, and shot further domestic sequences at Tittenhurst with John cuddling and petting Kyoko. As time passed, however, John began to suspect Cox of using his day-to-day control of Kyoko as a pressure point on Yoko and, more subtly, himself. When Cox invited them to Kyoko's seventh birthday party, John thought he was being set up, refused to go, and forbade her mother to do so either. "Can you imagine how I felt?" Yoko says. "I heard that Kyoko had been watching the door all afternoon, waiting for me to arrive."

In fairness to Cox, he was a devoted father who had always done the lion's share of parenting Kyoko, and felt deeply uneasy about her immersions in John and Yoko's unstable, unpredictable lifestyle. The constant media floodlight on them made it impossible for the girl to lead any kind of normal existence—sabotaging, for instance, her long-held wish to learn ballet. Often, too, when Cox tried to contact Yoko or John on some matter connected with Kyoko, he would be blocked by one or other of their assistants. Their car accident with Kyoko and Julian in the Scottish Highlands made Cox "freak out," according to his former neighbor, Dan Richter. From then on, he ruled that whenever Kyoko spent time with them, he must be there, too.

The various mystical manias of the Sixties had a profound influence on Cox. During their stay together in Denmark, he introduced John and Yoko to an American named Don Hamrick, a leading light in a cult known as the Harbingers. Both underwent hypnosis by Hamrick in attempt to cure their heavy smoking habit and, secondarily, to relive their former existences on earth. He also claimed to be in communication with other worlds and, with a fellow cult member, had proposed bringing the real UFOs to the Toronto Peace Festival. Though Cox remained friendly with Hamrick, he had since moved on spiritually, becoming a convert to, of all things, the Maharishi Mahesh Yogi's Transcendental Meditation movement. Along the way, his view of John radically changed from "great fellow" and potential backer to drug fiend and threat to the moral welfare of his daughter. He became progressively more difficult about access and finally, in mid-April, without any warning, left his London flat with Melinda and Kyoko.

Initially there was no clue whatsoever either to his whereabouts or his intentions. Then his Harbinger friend Don Hamrick let slip that he was attending a TM course on the Spanish holiday island of Majorca, where the Maharishi now owned a house. With Dan Richter and a Spanish lawyer named Cesar Lozano, John and Yoko flew by private jet to Majorca and removed Kyoko from the kindergarten at Cala Ratjada where Cox had enrolled her. Before they could make their escape, Cox discovered what had happened and called the police. John and Yoko were arrested in their suite at the Hotel Melia Mallorca in Palma, parted from Kyoko again, and taken to police headquarters.

Kyoko still vividly recalls the cycle of her emotions that day amid the sunshine and flowers: from shock at being snatched from her classroom to pleasure at seeing Yoko and John again, to fear of what her father would say and dread that the grown-ups would have another of their screaming fights. A summary hearing of the case was convened at Palma courthouse, beginning at midnight and lasting almost until dawn. The judge ordered that Kyoko be taken into the room where John and Yoko were being held, then into the one where her outraged father waited with Melinda. In a chilling echo of what had happened to John at around the same age, she was then told to choose between them. Accustomed to Cox's care as she was, Kyoko picked him. Cox ran out of the courthouse with her on his back and was driven away at top speed. A few days later, the adversaries gave a press conference and announced that the whole episode had been an unfortunate misunderstanding. Kyoko was even allowed to return with her mother to Tittenhurst Park.

John and Yoko had been released only on condition that they return to Majorca later in the month to face further questioning about the "abduction." The date of the hearing, however, clashed with that of the Cannes Film Festival, where their films *Apotheosis* and *Fly* were both premiered (the first to boos, the second to a standing ovation). Afterward, they had to honor a promise given months before to visit Michael X in his Trinidadian exile. So while Richter went to sort out matters in Palma, they spent a week loyally hanging out with the fallen demagogue and his family in the compound near Port of Spain, where he now planned—with John's patronage—to found an "alternative university."

On May 24 came the UK release of Paul McCartney's second solo album. Entitled *Ram*, it was credited to "Paul and Linda McCartney" in apparent imitation of John and Yoko; its cover showed Paul in Scottish sheepshearer mode, gripping the curled horns of a woolly coated ram. Although critically panned, it reached number one in America and two in Britain and spun off a hit single, "Uncle Albert/Admiral Halsey." Also included was a track called "Too Many People," clearly alluding to John's rejection of the Beatles for Yoko. "That was your first mistake," ran the refrain. "You took your lucky break and broke it in two."

As mild and oblique as the comment was, it seemed to cut John to the heart. On top of the questionnaire inside the *McCartney* album and the lawsuit, it was like the tipping point between a divorcing couple that turns love into savage, no-holds-barred hostility. Indeed, John's wounded anger was more that of an ex-spouse than ex-colleague, reinforcing a suspicion already in Yoko's mind that his feelings for Paul had been far more intense than the world at large ever guessed. From chance remarks he had made, she gathered there had even been a moment when—on the principle that bohemians should try everything—he had contemplated an affair with Paul, but had been deterred by Paul's immovable heterosexuality. Nor, apparently, was Yoko the only one to have picked up on this. Around Apple, in her hearing, Paul would sometimes be called John's Princess. She had also once heard a rehearsal tape with John's voice calling out "Paul . . . Paul . . ." in a strangely subservient, pleading way. "I knew there was something going on there," she remembers. "From his point of view, not from Paul's. And he was so angry at Paul, I couldn't help wondering what it was really about."

Just now, getting even with Paul had to take second place to the continuing saga of Tony Cox and Kyoko. After a short truce following the Majorca episode, Cox had once again vanished into thin air with his daughter and Melinda. In June, John's lawyers received information that the trio were now in America. He and Yoko returned to New York, hoping to pick up Cox's trail there, but the mission proved fruitless. Ironically, that week found Kyoko's distraught mother and John onstage with the Mothers of Invention, who were making a live album at the city's Fillmore East auditorium.

Back home, too, there was another urgent call on the John and Yoko agitprop helpline. In May 1970, the underground magazine Oz had published a "schoolkids issue," put together by schoolchildren, whose most striking feature was a pornographic cartoon strip with Rupert Bear heads superimposed on the characters. As a result, Oz's three editors, Richard Neville, Jim Anderson, and Felix Dennis, were charged with "conspiracy to corrupt public morals," ushering in the longest, most hilarious obscenity trial in British legal history. John issued a statement backing Oz, and he and Yoko joined a march protesting the absurd heavy-handedness of the prosecution.

By July, as the "Oz Three" stood in the dock at the Old Bailey, John was itching to make another album. To goad him, there was now even more than George's *All Things Must Pass* and Paul's *Ram* amidships. In April, Ringo had had a massive hit single, "It Don't Come

Easy," cowritten, produced, and lead-guitared by George, with Klaus
Voormann on bass and Stephen Stills on piano. No one was happier
than John to see Ringo start having solo hits, but he still could not
repress a twinge of competitiveness. He had done his therapy; now it
was time to try going commercial.

The studio at Tittenhurst Park was finished at long last, allowing him to work as he'd always wanted, free from the bureaucratic
annoyances of Abbey Road and Apple, with home comforts close at
hand and his beloved gardens all around him. Once again, the album
was to be jointly credited to the Plastic Ono Band and himself, and
coproduced by Yoko, himself, and Phil Spector. But this time, the
former spartan lineup of Klaus Voormann and a drummer was augmented by star session men, including George Harrison, pianist
Nicky Hopkins, and legendary saxophonist King Curtis, who had
once played with Buddy Holly. To give the "chocolate coating" John
desired, there was even a string section, billed as the Flux Fiddlers.

The recording sessions were filmed as part of a cinematic diary he
and Yoko had been keeping for some months past. This color footage, shot in the studio and around the house and grounds, shows a
very different Mr. and Mrs. Lennon from the hirsute near-look-alikes
of six months earlier. John has gone for seventies fashion at full tilt,
shaving off his beard (though keeping long sideburns to hide the scar
from his road accident), adopting a wheatsheaf haircut, exchanging his denim battle fatigues for skimpy Fair Isle sweaters, billowing bell-bottoms, and wedge-heeled shoes. Yoko has pulled her hair
back from her face and taken to figure-hugging jackets, hot pants,
jaunty French berets, and kinky boots. Both, in fact, look about ten
years younger. The only unchanged detail is the miasma of cigarette
smoke around them.

While providing a temporary home for session musicians and
technical staff, Tittenhurst was once again giving sanctuary to the
politically oppressed. The three Oz defendants had by now been convicted and sentenced to vicious prison terms. Pending their appeals
(which would be successful), two of them, Richard Neville and Jim
Anderson, had fled abroad, leaving their less affluent colleague, Felix
Dennis, to face the media fallout alone. Hearing of his plight, John

and Yoko offered him accommodation with Les Anthony and family in the gatekeeper's lodge.

As the new songs took shape, Klaus Voormann saw little resemblance to the "out-of-whack" John who had howled out his boyhood anguish and fury a year earlier. He seemed happy and relaxed and, like everyone emerging from therapy, anxious to make public what a mess he used to be. "Jealous Guy" ruefully owned up to the malady he had suffered since his first courtship of Cynthia and the low self-esteem that underlay it: "I was feeling insecure . . . You might not love me any more . . . I was shivering inside . . . I was swallowing my pain . . ." His whistled solo halfway through, almost lost in the backing, was somehow even more poignant than his words. "Oh My Love" was a new hymn of gratitude to Yoko in his Julia voice, because "for the first time in my life . . . my mind can feel." "Oh, Yoko!" admitted his need to be constantly reassured of her nearness ("in the middle of a bath," even "in the middle of a shave") with a country-and-western song of infectious jollity and an ebullient harmonica solo. "Yoko had an incredibly positive influence on the whole album" Dan Richter remembers. "She wasn't just sitting in the background and yowling occasionally. She could read and even write musical notation. If there was ever a problem, say over harmonies, Yoko as likely as not would come up with the solution."

Here and there, one bit through the chocolate coating to a rancid center. A perky little yee-haw hillbilly number, for instance, was called "Crippled Inside." The tolling, accusatory "I Don't Wanna Be a Soldier" came on as rock 'n' roll, with Link Wray–style bass guitar and an echoey "We-ell" that could have been Gene Vincent on "Be-Bop-a-Lula." "Gimme Some Truth" chose an almost Broadway show–tune style to pour scorn on "neurotic, psychotic, pig-headed politicians" and actually identify America's president Richard Nixon by his long-standing nickname of Tricky Dicky.

One track, however, made no attempt to candy-coat the message. "How Do You Sleep?" was a reply to Paul McCartney for that disparaging comment on the *Ram* album. Its title gave warning of the overreaction to come, for although Paul may have been self-serving and disloyal by John's lights, he had done nothing to lose sleep over.

Where his attack had been mild and sidelong, John's was violent and full-on, a nuclear missile answering a pinprick. It accused Paul of surrounding himself with sycophantic "straights" and being pussy-whipped by Linda ("Jump when your Mama tell you anything"). It called him "a pretty face" without staying power and trashed his songs as "Muzak to my ears." It worked in references to *Sgt. Pepper*, the "Paul is dead" rumor ("Those freaks was right when they said you was dead"), and, most unfairly of all, taunted, "The only thing you done was 'Yesterday.'"

Felix Dennis, who was around as the lyric took shape, remembers John's fellow musicians, including Ringo, telling him in vain that he was going way too far. In its original version, the line after the "Yesterday" reference was "You probably stole that bitch, anyway." Only when the album was being mastered in New York did Allen Klein persuade John to cut it on the grounds that Paul would probably sue. Instead, Klein suggested "And since you're gone you're just Another Day," a reference to Paul's recent solo single. Even the arrangement of "How Do You Sleep?" was subtly insulting, a melodramatic soul-funk suggesting that some risible Demon King might appear through a trapdoor at any moment. George Harrison played slide guitar, thereby endorsing every word.

The final insult was to Paul's new rustic life with Linda. In parody of the *Ram* cover's Highland sheepshearer, John had himself photographed in an identical pose straddling a pig. This was turned into a picture postcard, to be slipped inside every copy of the album. "I wasn't really feeling that vicious at the time," he would claim. "It was not a terrible, vicious, horrible vendetta . . . I used my resentment and withdrawing from Paul and the Beatles and the relationship with Paul to write a song. I don't really go around with those thoughts in my head all the time . . . I'm really attacking myself. But I regret the association—well, what's to regret? He lived through it."

It is part of the unending paradox of John that he could indulge in such puerile yah-boo stuff at one moment and at the next create the song regarded ever afterward as his solo masterpiece. Thanks to the album's film diary, we can follow the development of this, from rough talked-through version around the kitchen table ("Imagine no possessions . . . da-da-de-dah . . .") to first demo for the band and, finally, performance on film in Tittenhurst's long, white drawing room—an effortless, because unconscious, transition from the ridiculous to the sublime.

"Imagine" is, in many respects, one of his least inventive songs. As he would admit, it sprang from the "instructional poems" Yoko had been writing since the early Sixties—often a one-word command or exhortation like the "Breathe" that had transfixed him at her Indica show. He was also out to write something avowedly "spiritual" in response to George's "My Sweet Lord" and, for that matter, Paul's "Let It Be."

The vision he came up with is easily dismissible as hackneyed and can hardly be called alluring. We are called on to imagine a world set free from its ancient belief in both heaven and hell and cleansed of organized religion, war, and famine, with all national boundaries abolished to create "a brotherhood of Man"—a vista of purgatorial blandness, in fact, which would probably have sent John himself mad with boredom in five minutes. Nor are the lyrics anywhere near the standard he reached in, say, "Norwegian Wood." With Paul still looking over his shoulder, one cannot picture him rhyming "isn't hard to do" and "no religion, too," or repeating the same word in the chorus ("not the only one . . . world will be as one"). The little falsetto "You-oo" he uses as a bridge to the chorus seems too poppy—too Beatly—for such elevated subject matter.

Yet none of this matters. "Imagine" would touch millions while he was alive, and billions after he had gone, with its wistful passion and optimism and utter lack of pretension, conceit, or preachiness. As, equally, would the film clip of John performing it at his white grand piano—the burbling chords, his star-spangled seventies jacket and yellow-tinted glasses, those thin lips carefully shaping "Imagine all the pee-pul" while Yoko draws back one after another set of floor-length curtains and the room slowly floods with daylight. As the song ends, she sits beside him, they exchange a quizzical smile and, at the last moment, a bashful little kiss. Rock has never been more powerful, simple, or sad.

Even when dealing with themes such as these, John still resisted all attempts to treat him as a leader or visionary. The *Imagine* film also shows him talking to an American fan who has been caught sleeping rough on the grounds and marched before him like a poacher before the squire. The stalker—this time—is quite harmless—a leftover Sixties hippie with a strangely Christlike air that makes all the more pathetic his unshakable belief in John as his Messiah. "I'm just a guy, man, that writes songs," John protests. "You take words and stick them together and see if they have any meaning . . . I'm saying 'I had a good shit today and this is what I thought this morning and I love you, Yoko'" Finally, as exasperation turns to pity, we could almost be listening to stern, hospitable Aunt Mimi. "Are you hungry? Mm?" The boy beneath the man's whiskers nods miserably. "OK, let's give him something to eat."

"Imagine"'s wish list just then seemed a more than usually vain hope, especially "no need for greed or hunger." In the secessionist state of East Pakistan, renamed Bangladesh, a bloody war was raging between rebel forces and the avenging West Pakistan army. As refugees caught in the crossfire streamed toward the Indian border, torrential floods added to their plight. Though millions were starving, European governments declined to intervene in what they termed "an internal affair." It was a cause John and Yoko might have been expected to take up with vigor, but on this occasion they found themselves preempted. Briefed on the disaster by his friend and tutor Ravi Shankar, George Harrison set about recruiting superstar friends like Bob Dylan, Eric Clapton, Ringo Starr, and Leon Russell for a fund-raising Concert for Bangladesh at Madison Square Garden, New York, on August 1, and a live album to follow. It was an impressive occasion, which raised $250,000 for Bangladesh's refugees on ticket sales alone, gave the rock business a first injection of dignity, and paved the way for charitable spectaculars like Live Aid in the eighties and nineties. George later admitted he would never have thought of putting it together had not the trail of peace and humanitarianism, and using one's superstardom to take a moral stand, already been blazed by John.

John had naturally headed George's list of superstar sidemen and, conveniently, was in New York at the time. When George's call came, he and Yoko were having breakfast in their hotel suite and had just cowritten the song that would become "Happy Christmas (War Is Over)." Yoko was full of enthusiasm for the concert, not realizing George's invitation was to John only. "I kept saying, 'It's a charity event, we should do it,'" she remembers. "John got very angry, saying, 'Oh, you always want to sing at the drop of a hat,' and he just got up and left. I didn't realise at the time he was so angry and worried by the thought that my feelings would be hurt. Later he told me he hoped I would chase after him, saying, 'Oh, please don't go,' but I'm not like that."

A few minutes later, Dan Richter answered a knock at his door to find an agitated John there. "He couldn't swallow the idea that Yoko wouldn't be allowed to appear with him," Richter says. "And anyway, he was terrified the other Beatles were out to trap him. He thought he'd be onstage with George and Ringo, and then Paul McCartney would walk on, and headlines all over the world would say 'Beatles Reunion.'" Spurred by that hideous thought as much as the tiff with Yoko, he made Richter drive him to JFK Airport and caught a flight to Paris.

Yoko, still at their New York hotel, had no idea where he'd gone. "The next day, Allen Klein told me 'You gotta go home to Ascot. John's gonna be there, he's waiting.' Suddenly my brain, which had always tried to make myself so small in this relationship, opened up. I said 'Listen, I'm getting a rest from it, okay? He was the one who left me . . . and, anyway, this is *my* town.' He thought I would be lost on my own, but this was where I'd grown up as an artist. Then Allen said that John was calling him so many times during the night that Allen couldn't go to sleep; it was 'Please get Yoko to come, please get Yoko to come . . .' Allen told me that was the first time he realised I was not the one grabbing the relationship. Finally, I said 'Okay, I'll go back.'"

After all that, she expected John to meet her off the plane in London, but only their chauffeur, Les Anthony, showed up at Heathrow with the Rolls. "When I got back to Ascot, I thought John would be waiting at the front door—but still no John. And I went upstairs to our bedroom, I opened the door, the bag from my Bag Piece was on the floor and John was inside it. 'I'm sorry, Yoko' was all he said. And in Paris he had got me a heart-shaped diamond necklace. I thought it was so touching and sweet, because the heart was so small. He knew I didn't like anything too big and ostentatious. And so we got cosy in bed, and that was that."

But the pull of America was becoming ever more powerful. Though Yoko had never been granted U.S. citizenship, Tony Cox was an American national, which meant that their daughter was, too. Following the Majorcan debacle, John's lawyers advised Yoko to seek full custody of Kyoko in the American Virgin Islands, where her divorce from Cox had been granted. John applied for a twenty-four-hour U.S. visa to accompany her to the court hearing in St. Thomas, but was kept waiting for it in the nearby British Virgin Islands—then, to his amazement, issued with a visa for three months. The Virgin Islands court had no hesitation in granting Yoko custody of Kyoko, but stipulated that the child must be brought up in America. And clearly it was advisable for Yoko to base herself there for the present, in order to exercise her legal rights whenever and wherever Cox might resurface.

John, in any case, was growing tired of Britain. The racial slurs against Yoko, though not as virulent as formerly, had by no means gone away. And, for all its supposed social upheavals, the country seemed as stuffy and repressive as ever. A new Conservative government under Edward Heath was busy drawing battle lines with the trade unions. The Irish part of John was appalled that, in Ulster's worsening sectarian conflict, terrorist suspects could now be interned without trial. He was also upset that, after years of procrastination, decimal currency on the European model had finally arrived, sweeping away the familiar, clunky half crowns, florins, ten-bob notes, and threepenny bits that had been known as "LSD" long before mind-expanding drugs.

Further lengthy negotiations began with the U.S. Immigration and Naturalization Service (which paradoxically seemed rather miffed that John had not used his three-month entitlement after entering through the Virgin Islands). On August 13, he and Yoko were each granted new visas in the B2, or visitors' category, good until the following February. At the end of the month, they returned to New York without setting a firm date for their departure.

The only person John found it hard to leave behind was a brisk, self-sufficient woman, now in her late sixties, still living beside Poole Harbour with her books, her Royal Worcester china, and pedigreed cats. Aunt Mimi, of course, had no idea that he'd gone to America indefinitely—still less that she would never see him again. She expected him to turn up sooner or later, "like a bad penny" as she always said, maybe throwing pebbles at her bedroom window as on the night when he returned, broke, from Hamburg. Even after all these years, there was no doubt in Mimi's mind where he really called home. "He used to tell me that [the bungalow] was his haven," she would recall. "He could always come here, and have his own little room, and be waited on hand and foot. One summer, he came down for a week and sunbathed while I ran backwards and forwards for him, making cups of tea and cooking . . . just like the old days."

In times to come, Mimi would often look at his favorite spot on the back patio, where a flight of stone steps led down to the water, and yachts and excursion launches passed a few yards away. "He'd just sit there, dangling his feet in the water and watching the boats go by. The days always seemed sunny when John was here."

PART V

PIZZA

AND

FAIRY TALES

26

THE YIPPIE YIPPIE SHAKE

I fell in love with New York on a street corner.

John unpacked his bags in a country where the generation gap had turned into a blazing abyss. By 1971, the Vietnam issue divided America more bitterly than any since its traumatic Civil War a century earlier. Older people by and large still believed in the irreproachability of the U.S. Cavalry, while younger ones upheld the hippie ethos of love and peace, though sometimes with methods no longer loving or peaceable. Despite government noises about "de-escalation," the conflict had entered a horrific new phase in April 1970, when American forces first bombed, then invaded Cambodia, allegedly to disrupt North Vietnamese supply lines. The resultant explosion of youthful protest at home was met with a brutality more suited to Communist Eastern Europe. On May 4, at Kent State University, Ohio, four student antiwar demonstrators, two of them female, were shot dead by National Guardsmen, and nine were wounded.

For President Richard M. Nixon, it had become almost commonplace to look out from the White House onto horizonless seas of banner-waving protesters, invariably chorusing "Give Peace a Chance." Nixon was in many respects a visionary leader whose groundbreaking journeys to Moscow and Beijing signaled an eventual end to the Cold War. But long years of waiting for office had aggravated the secretiveness and paranoia that would be his eventual undoing. In mid-1971, a former Pentagon official named Daniel Ellsberg leaked a top-secret official dossier on the Vietnam War to the press, revealing among other things that it had long been regarded as unwinnable. When a federal court refused to ban publication of these Pentagon Papers, the government launched a covert plan to destroy Ellsberg, burgling his psychiatrist's office, even considering an assassination attempt. John, that insatiable newsprint addict, had followed every twist and turn in the saga, little imagining what similar treatment was in store for him.

He and Yoko started off at the plush end of New York, moving into the St. Regis Hotel, four blocks from that hallowed Beatle landmark the Plaza. Two adjoining seventeenth-floor suites were needed to house all their baggage and also serve as improvised offices, recording studios, and staff quarters so that they could pursue their numerous audio and visual projects without breaking step. The just-released *Imagine* album was climbing the American charts to its eventual high of number three (number one in Britain). At the St. Regis, they continued to accumulate footage for the documentary of the same name, recruiting fellow VIP guests in the hotel for cameo roles. One was the great Hollywood song-and-dance man Fred Astaire, who—despite being late for a plane—agreed to be filmed walking into a room with Yoko. Ever the perfectionist, Astaire asked to do a second take.

To interviewers John extolled the superiority of New York over London—the cheeseburgers, the malted milks, the freedom to go to a cinema or restaurant, buy a newspaper, or even visit a bookstore at whatever hour of the day or night he chose. "If I'd lived in ancient times, I'd have lived in Rome. . . . Today America is the Roman Empire and New York is Rome itself." The raucous, impatient rhythm of Manhattan daily life also awoke memories of Liverpool. "There's the same quality of energy, of vitality, in both cities. New York is at my speed . . . I like New Yorkers because they have no time for the niceties of life. They're like me in this. They're naturally aggressive, they don't believe in wasting time."

The pair's first public engagement in the U.S. was a major retrospective of Yoko's work, mounted by the Everson Art Museum in Syracuse, New York. Entitled *This Is Not Here* (after the framed motto above Tittenhurst Park's front door), the exhibit opened on October 9, John's thirty-first birthday. John featured as "guest artist" and catalog designer, and there were pieces by such luminaries as Andy Warhol and Willem de Kooning as well as friends like Bob Dylan, George Harrison, and Ringo Starr. John and Yoko chartered a plane to fly a large party up from New York City, including the Starrs, Klaus Voormann, Phil Spector, and Neil Aspinall. It was an expensively staged "water show," with even the invitations sent out in water-filled containers; when its costs overflowed the museum's budget, Apple had to make up the difference, which meant the other ex-Beatles subsidizing it, to their very mixed emotions. After the opening, there was a birthday party for John in his hotel room, with a jam session of rock-'n'-roll classics and Beatles oldies, including "Yesterday."

By the end of October, he and Yoko had left the St. Regis and moved downtown to 105 Bank Street in the West Village, renting a small two-room apartment from Joe Butler of the Lovin' Spoonful, with the great musical iconoclast John Cage as a next-door neighbor. They also acquired a building on Broome Street, mainly to serve as a headquarters for their film projects. "It was Yoko who sold me on New York," John would remember. "She'd been poor here and she knew every inch. She made me walk around the streets and parks and squares and examine every nook and cranny. In fact you could say I fell in love with New York on a street corner." They even bought bicycles—an English model, as close as possible to his old Raleigh Lenton for John, a high-tech Japanese one for Yoko.

If the city's toughness and scabrous wit reminded him of Liverpudlians, the district south of Houston Street—as yet barely gentrified into "SoHo"—almost reincarnated his home city in the years when he had loved it best. Often on his wanderings or bike rides with Yoko, he would stop and stare down a cobbled street of nineteenth-century warehouses, almost as if expecting to find the Cavern or the Iron Door around the next corner.

Under Yoko's guidance, he soon became acclimated, and addicted, to downtown life—the teeming markets of Chinatown, the trattorias and aromatic groceries of Little Italy, the oddball galleries, bars, and boutiques, the infinite tolerance of eccentricity, and respect for personal space that allowed them to stroll or cycle about largely undisturbed, as they never could in London. John's favorite comparison went over the heads of journalists except those who, like him, had read Dylan Thomas's *Under Milk Wood*: "It's like a little Welsh village with Jones the Fish and Jones the Milk, and everybody seems to know everybody."

His first real downtown buddy was David Peel, a songwriter and street entertainer whom he met one day at a St. Mark's Place clothes boutique called the Limbo Shop. Fronting a ragtag band, the Lower East Side, Peel mixed antigovernment, promarijuana polemics with wry satires on New York life among "the cockeroaches . . . living in a garbage can." John became a keen follower of the Lower East Side's street-corner happenings, which to him recalled skiffle gigs around Woolton in the late Fifties. Using expertise largely acquired from Phil Spector, he and Yoko produced Peel's third, almost universally banned, album, *The Pope Smokes Dope.*

The Bank Street apartment became a salon, conducted in a now familiar manner. "It was a very small place, two steps down from the street," Dan Richter remembers. "The back room had a skylight on the ceiling and a bed in the middle, and that's where John and Yoko would be when people came to visit. You'd have David Peel and the musicians, journalists and media crews and a lot of people who'd just walked in off the street to say 'Hello.' John would have his guitar and a bit of grass, and the TV going all the time."

This daily bedside throng produced two more friends of lasting loyalty and value. One was Bob Gruen, a curly-haired young photographer whose camera would record most of the crucial moments in John's life over the next eight years. The other was an aesthete and political activist named Jon Hendricks, who had known Yoko since her Fluxus group days, and who worked for John and her as an unpaid volunteer before joining their ever-fluid roster of personal assistants.

As composer of the protest anthem that had superseded "We Shall Overcome," John had already made the connection destined to cause him so much aggravation in the future. Abbie Hoffman and Jerry Rubin were joint leaders of the Youth International Party, or Yippies, the faction behind many of the headline-grabbing marches and rallies then convulsing America. Both had stood trial with the so-called Chicago Seven after the infamous 1968 Democratic Party Convention, and had since amassed a following comparable to that of Lenin and Trotsky in pre-1917 Russia. Campaigning for civil rights as much as disengagement from Vietnam and Cambodia, the Yippies worked in alliance with black radical groups, notably the ultra-militant Black Panthers through their cofounder, Bobby Seale. This coalition's objective was overthrow of the established order by any possible means; Rubin described their activities as "military" while Hoffman frequently declared, "We are at war."

John had initially been nervous about meeting such hell-bent extremists. But Rubin and Hoffman were young men of formidable charm who leavened their crusade with theatricality and absurdist humor after his own heart. The Yippies' most famous anticapitalist stunt—almost a piece of Yokoesque performance art—had been to scatter dollar bills onto the floor of the New York Stock Exchange, then film and photograph the resultant grabbing frenzy. Rubin was the author of a hilarious as well as inflammatory book entitled *Do It! Scenarios of the Revolution*, while his Black Panther cohort Bobby Seale harangued audiences in quasi verse, like a prototype rap star. "When I met [Hoffman and Rubin] I said 'You're like artists, man,'" John later remembered. "And they said [to Yoko and me] 'You two artists are like revolutionaries.'"

He was not long in declaring solidarity with these interchangeable revolutionaries and showmen. On December 2, Greenwich Village's weekly paper, the *Village Voice*, published a letter protesting against a recent attack on Bob Dylan in its pages by a writer named A. J. Weberman. The signatories were Jerry Rubin, David Peel, and John and Yoko, calling themselves the Rock Liberation Front.

Two issues currently dominated the Yippie–Black Panther coalition's agenda, one concerning a black woman, the other a white man, both exemplifying the Nixon regime's onslaught on the political counterculture. In California a year earlier, a young academic named Angela Davis, whose boyfriend was a prominent Panther, had been jailed on patently trumped-up charges of murder, kidnapping, and conspiracy. In Michigan, John Sinclair, the founder of a radical offshoot called the White Panthers, was beginning year three of a ten-year sentence for offering two marijuana joints to an undercover policewoman.

Led by Rubin and Bobby Seale, Sinclair's supporters staged a benefit rally and concert for him and Davis, in Ann Arbor on December 10, with appearances by Stevie Wonder, Bob Seger, and Allen Ginsberg. At Rubin's suggestion, John and Yoko also agreed to take part. John wrote a song about Sinclair, an Ozark Mountain–style country number ("It ain't fair / John Sinclair / In the stir for breathin' air . . ."), which he accompanied on a Dobro. The concert drew an audience of fifteen thousand and included a live telephone hookup with Sinclair in his cell. Three days later, he was freed on bail.

America's larger stage revealed for the first time what extraordinary power John's name possessed to transcend even the new spiky frontiers of race, gender, and political allegiance, and—more crucially here more than anywhere—to guarantee maximum media attention for any cause he supported. A week after Ten for Two in Michigan, New York witnessed a day of protest against the previous September's horrific Attica state prison riot, when security forces had killed twenty-eight prisoners and nine hostages. A benefit concert in aid of bereaved relatives took place that evening at Harlem's famous Apollo Theater, featuring some of the great names in soul music—yet the show's climactic moment was a surprise walk-on by John and Yoko.

To mark the event, and also publicize David Peel and the Lower East Side, they appeared on the open-forum television show that David Frost had been hosting in the United States since the late Sixties. While Peel performed a song called "I'm Proud to Be a New York City Hippie"—a retort to Merle Haggard's popular redneck taunt, "I'm Proud to Be an Okie from Muskogee"—John stood in the background, plunking a skiffler's one-string bass. Later, he returned to sit on the edge of the stage and unveil another new-minted protest song, "Attica State." When a middle-aged couple in the audience accused him of glorifying criminals (though the Apollo benefit was also for prison officers' and hostages' families) their neighbors angrily shouted them down.

As with Michael X in Britain, John seemed to feel it almost his mission to introduce figures like Rubin and Seale to a mainstream audience and show what intelligent and delightful people they really were. From January 14 to 18, he and Yoko acted as cohosts on daytime television's hugely popular *Mike Douglas Show*, introducing a series of guests chosen by them, including Rubin, Seale, and a five-piece group named Elephant's Memory, which Rubin had recommended to John as a new core for the Plastic Ono Band. When Rubin began to antagonize the conservative Mike Douglas, John's good-humored interjections saved face for both of them. Among the other surreal spectacles offered to Douglas's viewers was of rock-'n'-roll legend Chuck Berry sharing an apron with John in a macrobiotic cookery demonstration.

All these new causes and alliances, however, were incidental to his real reason for being in America—to help Yoko find Tony Cox and reclaim Kyoko in accordance with the Virgin Islands custody order. For two months, despite intensive inquiries, there had been no trace of Cox. Then, in mid-December, he reappeared in Houston, Texas, the hometown of his new wife, Melinda, and began legal action to restore his former equal access rights to Kyoko. The day after the Attica prison benefit, John and Yoko, accompanied by Jon Hendricks, flew to Houston for the court hearing.

Unlike in the Majorcan court battle, Kyoko was not asked to choose between her father and mother. Cox had hidden her away with Melinda's family, and ignored repeated orders from the judge to produce her, until finally—on Christmas Eve—he was charged with contempt of court, imprisoned for five days, then released on bail.

Meanwhile, Yoko's already airtight case was reinforced by a teacher who testified that in Cox's care, Kyoko had fallen three years behind the normal educational standard of an eight-year-old. The judge ordered that she be turned over to Yoko pending a final ruling. Cox's answer was to repeat his gambit of the previous summer: he, Kyoko, and Melinda once again disappeared without trace.

There was thus an unhappy subtext to "Happy Christmas (War Is Over)," the single John and Yoko had just released as a follow-up to the previous year's billboard campaign. In counterpoint to their alternating lead vocals, the "War is over / If you want it" chorus was provided by children from the Harlem Community Choir, many of them around Kyoko's age. For John, it was just another instant, disposable Plastic Ono project: he could not know that "Happy Christmas (War Is Over)" was to become as much a part of the Yuletide ritual as turkey or mistletoe. Equally ironic, as events would soon show, was his wish for the new year to be "a good one . . . without any fear."

He had inadvertently picked the worst possible moment to begin making waves in American public life. Nineteen seventy-two was a presidential election year, with Richard Nixon already assured of nomination for a second term by the Republican Party. Moreover, this election would see the franchise extended to eighteen-year-olds, thus creating some twelve million new voters. All his foreign policy triumphs in Russia and China had not lessened Nixon's persecution complex, and he feared that this youthful surge at the polls would cheat him of victory. He and his inner coterie were prepared to repeat all the dirty tricks Daniel Ellsberg had suffered—and more—against anyone who threatened to encourage that result.

A perfect hatchet man for Nixon was J. Edgar Hoover, director of the Federal Bureau of Investigation. Hoover had run the FBI since the twenties, accumulating such a dossier of dirt on public officials that he could neither be fired or retired, however gross his own abuses of office. In secret a homosexual transvestite given to frilly frocks, he ruled the bureau as if still combating Al Capone and John

Dillinger, and nurtured a ferocious hatred of "commies," "lefties," and their modern manifestation, rock stars.

John's ordeal at the hands of the U.S. government over the next three-and-a-half years might never have come to light but for a California academic named Jon Weiner, who was to dedicate himself to reconstructing it, armed with that most cleanly and enviable American law, the Freedom of Information Act. Even with this weapon, it would take Weiner three decades, spanning the regimes of four more presidents, to pry loose all the relevant official documents, the final ones not being released until 2006. It is a story of America at its worst and, ultimately, its best.

Weiner's investigation would show that the FBI's interest in John, on paper at least, dated back to the American release of his and Yoko's *Two Virgins* album. In March 1969, a congressman named Ancher Nelson sent J. Edgar Hoover an outraged letter from one of his constituents about the album's nude cover photograph and asked whether anything could be done to suppress it. With this in view, Hoover consulted the Justice Department but was told the cover "did not meet the criteria of obscenity from a legal standpoint." Before John's April 1970 visit to Los Angeles with George and Pattie Harrison, the bureau's West Coast agents were alerted to gather any evidence that the three were engaging in violent antiwar demonstrations or using narcotics. A dossier was even compiled on the Society for Krishna Consciousness, which he and George were said to support, lest it prove some kind of front for drug-taking or revolution.

With John's transplantation to New York and his open espousal of figures such as Abbie Hoffman, Angela Davis, and John Sinclair, the FBI finally had something substantial to chew on. The Sinclair freedom rally at Ann Arbor was heavily infiltrated by FBI informants, and detailed reports were compiled of the speeches made by Rubin, Seale, Allen Ginsberg, and others. One undercover FBI man who talked to John backstage claimed to have heard him speak in "antilaw enforcement tones" and pronounced him "a strong believer in the [Yippie] movement and in the overthrow of the present society in America today."

The attack, when it came, was not initiated by Hoover but by sixty-nine-year-old Strom Thurmond, Republican senior senator for South Carolina, an ardent segregationist and war enthusiast, and one of Nixon's most influential supporters on the party's far right. Early in February 1972, Thurmond wrote to John Mitchell, the attorney general and chairman of the Committee to Re-Elect the President (aptly known as CREEP). From his Senate Internal Security Subcommittee, Thurmond forwarded a staff memo warning that a group of anti-Nixon demonstrators planned to disrupt the Republican Party Convention that August, and that John was among its main supporters. The Thurmond letter implied that, with such a powerful agitator on hand, Nixon's renomination ceremonial could disintegrate into the same chaos as had the Democrats' catastrophic 1968 convention in Chicago. To head off this awful prospect, it proposed a "strategic counter-measure": that John be deported forthwith.

The warning was apparently based on a vague scheme of John's to go "out on the road" with Yoko later that year. "All our shows we do will be for free," he told a visiting crew from London Weekend Television. "All the money will go to prisoners or to poor people, so we'll collect no money for the performances. We hope to start touring in America and then eventually go around the world . . . possibly to China, too." He had also talked to Allen Ginsberg and others about using rock concerts to rally new young voters to the Democrats' cause. But he had no connections with the group mentioned in Thurmond's letter, the innocuously named Election Strategy Information Center, nor plans to go anywhere near the Republican Party Convention.

The letter was passed to J. Edgar Hoover, who in turn passed it to Richard Helms, director of the Central Intelligence Agency, as a matter potentially affecting national security. On February 12, 1972, Helms sent Hoover a coded teletype message, giving further sinister details of John's alleged plot to disrupt the presidential election. According to CIA investigators, he was involved in a project "which will involve the use of videotapes, films and special articles" and participation "by a caravan of entertainers." At this dire warning, the government's "strategic counter-measure" swung into action.

The B, or visitors', visas issued to Yoko and him the previous August were due to expire simultaneously on February 29. Usual practice was to allow visitors another fifteen days in which to apply for a renewal. Five days into the extension period, they heard a pounding on their front door, like the prelude to a police raid, then saw a slip of paper pushed underneath. It was from the Immigration and Naturalization Service, informing them that both their visas had been "recalled" and they must leave the country by March 15.

They needed a lawyer and, providentially, lit on the right one first time. Leon Wildes had fifteen years' experience in the immigration and naturalization field, and was just ending his tenure as president of the American Immigration Lawyers Association. An opera and classical music buff, he possessed none of John's records and had barely even heard of him before being approached—by Yoko—to fight their case. He visited them at 105 Bank Street, where, acknowledging the gravity of the occasion, they did not interview him from their bed. "Yoko talked to me first in the front room, then John came in and served tea."

Wildes was at first doubtful of being able to help. Obvious though it might be that John was being punished for his political views and choice of friends, there seemed no earthly chance of proving it. Nixon might be considered "tricky," but in early 1972 even his harshest mainstream critics would not have believed him this paranoid. Little was to be expected, either, from the INS system of review boards and courts that dealt with appeals against deportation—and rejected 95 percent of them. The only hope that Wildes could see was to fight the case through to the federal courts, whose judges were of higher caliber than the INS's in-house ones, and less likely to toe the government line.

With this in mind, Wildes turned up the 1968 drug-possession case that had gotten John banned from the United States for two years and had bedeviled all his visa applications since. John explained that he had pleaded guilty only to save Yoko from deportation from Britain, that the Montagu Square flat's previous tenant had been Jimi Hendrix, and that he had carefully swept it for Hendrix's drugs before taking up residence. Wildes at once spotted a gleam of hope. While marijuana was illegal in the United States, hashish, or purified cannabis resin, the substance found at Montagu Square, was not yet specifically named as prohibited under federal law.

Further hope lay in the fact that since John's case, UK law on drug possession had been amended. Unlike in 1968, the prosecution now had to prove a defendant had "knowingly" possessed an illegal substance rather than innocently occupying premises where it was hidden. Under American law, by contrast, John could never have been convicted without an opportunity to say whether he knew the cannabis was there. His suspicion that the police had planted the drug also looked more plausible now. The arresting officer, Sgt. Norman Pilcher, was now known to have consciously carved out a career in the headlines from busting pop stars, adding the scalps of Hendrix and Mick Jagger to his belt, often on equally dubious evidence. Before this year was out, Pilcher would be behind bars for conspiracy to pervert the course of justice. A case full of such holes, Wildes intended to argue, should never have been a basis for John's exclusion from America.

Through the spring and early summer of 1972, John made repeated appearances with Yoko at INS hearings, each time securing a temporary postponement of the deportation order against them as fresh submissions were made by Leon Wildes and the final decision was deferred once again. John compared it with being summoned to the headmaster's study at Quarry Bank School, except that he wasn't caned. Talking to the eternal clusters of reporters and TV cameras outside, he managed to hide his resentment of the whole draggy, squalid, humiliating, inconclusive process, merely repeating that he loved New York and wanted to stay, that he was trying to get his UK drug conviction overturned (though actually that formed no part of Wildes's strategy), that he needed to be in America with Yoko to recover Kyoko, and that they had no political agenda but the propagation of peace: "We're revolutionary artists—not gunmen."

On March 3, the Houston court upheld Yoko's solo custody of Kyoko and the Virgin Islands ruling that she should be brought up in America. The news was given to Yoko by Allen Klein as if it had been a personal deal-making coup on his part. But since there was still no trace of Tony Cox, Kyoko, and Melinda, the triumph fell rather flat.

Cox's strategy seemed to be to lie low until, as seemed inevitable,

John lost his immigration battle and was thrown out of the country. Since Yoko had no drug conviction, she should never have been threatened with deportation, and Wildes expected to sort out her case relatively easily. She would then have to choose between going with John or staying behind to continue the search for Kyoko. One of John's submissions to the INS was that, in all humanity, the two of them should not be torn apart like this: "I don't know if there is any mercy to plead for, but if so I would like it for both us and our child." He might as well have saved his breath. The latest allegation floating around in top-secret government documents was that he and Yoko were colluding with Tony Cox and that Kyoko's abduction had been a put-up job to give emotional leverage to his antideportation case. Houston's FBI office received orders to search for the hideout thought to have been agreed upon with Cox. If and when it were discovered, John would be charged with perjury.

Before meeting Leon Wildes, John had had no thought of seeking permanent residence in America. He assumed that with a drug conviction on his record, the permit known as a green card, which granted foreigners freedom both to live and work there, was automatically beyond reach. Wildes did not agree, and suggested that he and Yoko should apply for classification as persons of special artistic merit whose presence enhanced American cultural life. Such "third-preference" status would not only solve their immediate visa problems but also enter their names on the register of those deemed eligible for green cards. The application was duly made but, despite repeated letters and calls, the INS failed to deliver a verdict.

Preparing the case plunged Wildes into months of exhaustive research and investigation, in Britain as well as America. Meanwhile, it was essential that John cut a less controversial public figure than heretofore. "Rather than calling for Nixon's overthrow, I said he should confine himself to general statements of principle," the lawyer remembers. His commitment to the antiwar lobby remained as strong as ever. On April 22, he and Yoko attended a National Peace Rally in New York's Duffy Square, leading the crowds in the sine qua non chorus of "Give Peace a Chance." A month later, they added their names to supporters of a candlelight vigil in Washington, D.C., along with those of actor Eli Wallach, cartoonist Jules Feiffer, playwright Arthur Miller, and novelist William Styron. But there were no more overtly political appearances like the John Sinclair Freedom Rally. On Wildes's advice, the film Yoko had made of that event, *Ten for Two*, was also shelved indefinitely.

While the INS worked to get rid of John within the letter of the law, the FBI did so according to the personal doctrine of J. Edgar Hoover. The Bank Street apartment was put under surveillance, and tails were assigned to John and Yoko as they went about their daily business. Every lyric John had ever written was scrutinized for anti-government sentiment, every television appearance he made was watched, analyzed, and committed to memoranda headed "Revolutionary activities." There were plans for the Internal Revenue Service to investigate whether he had earned money while in the United States on a tourist visa, and for him and Yoko to be made to undergo psychiatric examinations. Contingency measures were even sketched out to meet his supposed threat to the Republican Convention, originally to be held in San Diego, California, but switched to Miami, Florida. These included the abduction of Jerry Rubin and Abbie Hoffman, the mugging of demonstrators by undercover government men outside the convention center, and the curtailment of John and Yoko's freedom to travel inside America.

Their telephone was bugged, as was their lawyer's. "We were told about a special number you could dial," Leon Wildes remembers. "If you got a busy signal your line was okay, but if there was a screeching noise, it was bugged. We both got the screech." Wildes's only guarantee of confidentiality was, where possible, to conduct his phone conversations in Yiddish. A tail was even put on John's personal photographer, Bob Gruen—"two guys in fedoras who looked like TV versions of G-Men." John tried to laugh off the situation, but no one around him, particularly not his American employees, found it at all amusing. "I was expecting him to be put in a bag at any moment and hauled off to the airport—or even to be assassinated," Dan Richter says. "It was scary."

Help was also enlisted from what, four decades later, could still be identified only as "a foreign intelligence service" but can have been none other than Britain's MI5. Well before John's departure for

New York, MI5 had him listed as a supporter of Republican terrorism in Northern Ireland; he had allegedly been seen carrying a banner against "British Imperialism" and had contributed to a civil-rights organization that was a front for the Provisionals. This dossier had been fattened by his and Yoko's participation in a demo by republican sympathizers outside the New York headquarters of Britain's national airline, BOAC. Coded teletypes from London to Washington chattered with further detail of his subversive activities in the United Kingdom, such as sending money to Scottish shipyard strikers and giving interviews to tiny-circulation radical magazines like *Red Mole*.

In Britain, John had written nothing about the worsening Ulster Troubles. But moving to New York had sharpened both his view of the conflict and his sense of his own Irish ancestry. American opinion on the Troubles ran largely against the British, even anglophile elements feeling a certain satisfaction that, after years of refusing outright support of the Vietnam War, Britain now had an analogously unwinnable conflict on its very doorstep. In New York, there were organizations openly dedicated to financing and purchasing weapons for the Provisional Irish Republican Army, who, against all evidence to the contrary, were seen as heroic young freedom fighters.

On January 30, 1972, a date known ever afterward as Bloody Sunday, British soldiers shot thirteen people dead during a civil-rights march in Londonderry. John's immediate response was a song called "Sunday Bloody Sunday," couched in a brogue that seemed more of the seventeenth than twentieth century: "Keep Ireland for the Irish / Put the English back to sea. . . ." Still more extreme sentiments permeated a companion ballad, "The Luck of the Irish," this time expressed with the same bitter sarcasm as "Working Class Hero." The British were depicted as "brigands" who had "raped" a "land full of beauty and wonder" and did wholesale murder "with God [i.e., Protestantism] on their side." Of the innocent Protestants daily bombed or shot in their own homes in front of their children, there was no mention: "Blame it all on the kids in the I.R.A. as the bastards [i.e., his compatriots] commit genocide."

The "kids in the I.R.A." were understandably delighted by this view of themselves, and for a time hoped to make John an even more useful advocate of their cause. In 2006, the writer Johnny Rogan revealed that a Provisional IRA activist named Gerry O'Hare visited John and Yoko at Bank Street, and that John talked seriously about doing a concert in Dublin for the Northern Aid Committee, a presumed IRA front, to raise funds for bereaved Catholic families. By this time, he had seemingly acquired a more balanced view of the conflict, making clear that he also wanted to give a similar show for Protestant victims in Belfast. The idea came to nothing, mainly because by now he feared that if he left America, he would not be readmitted.

As Jon Weiner would eventually discover, the anti-Lennon campaign was approved and closely monitored at the very highest level. On April 23, a few days after John's latest appearance before the INS, an FBI memo repeated the assertion from "a confidential source" that he had contributed $75,000 to a "New Left Group" that planned to disrupt the Republican Convention. It passed on John's statement to the INS hearing that he was being deported "for his outspoken views on United States policy in Southeast Asia" and listed two apparent ruses on his part to stall the process even further. According to other confidential sources, he had accepted a teaching post at New York University that summer, and was to join the National Commission on Marihuana and Drug Abuse. A footnote read: "This information is also being furnished to the Hon. H.R. Haldeman, assistant to the President at the White House."

The memo gives some flavor of the incompetence that underlay the whole operation. The bizarre belief that John was to be a member of the National Commission on Marihuana and Drug Abuse—a body recently set up by Congress at Nixon's behest—apparently derived from a statement to the INS tribunal that he and Yoko were planning a media antidrug campaign. Elsewhere, the mistakes and misinterpretations by Hoover's agents often tipped over into farce. Another report, conflating John's first two New York addresses and merging uptown with downtown, said he had resided at "the Saint Regis Hotel, Bank Street." In the event that he might follow Tony Cox's lead and go on the run inside America, a Wanted poster was drawn up—but using David Peel's photograph in mistake for his. The précis of a televised press conference he gave with Jerry Rubin noted portentously that "Rubin appeared to have his hair cut much shorter than previously shown in other photographs." Underneath, the nameless watcher printed in childlike letters "ALL EXTREMISTS SHOULD BE CONSIDERED DANGEROUS."

All the time, a simple solution to the problem lay under the bureau's nose. An early memo from the INS had admitted that only "a loose case" for deporting John existed on present evidence, and the best way to make it watertight would be to bust him for drugs, thus placing a second conviction on his record, which would guarantee his permanent exclusion from the country. FBI sources habitually mentioned his "excessive" use of substances stronger even than those favored by the Antichrist Rubin, and the New York Police Department had orders to swoop at the slightest suspicion of this or any other offense.

Yet it never happened, even though, in his daily and nightly rounds with Yoko and their musical, artistic, and political retinue, John disdained to exercise even the slightest caution. Rehearsal and studio bouts with Elephant's Memory always featured prodigal quantities of alcohol and drugs. "We called them the Tequila Sessions," Bob Gruen remembers. "There'd be maybe ten bottles of tequila between eight people—and that was every night. Then after working in the studio, we'd go out drinking; we'd have more shots of tequila, then a big steak dinner, then we'd have a lot of Cognacs—and beers throughout. And in most circles a lot of pot and other chemicals to keep you going. The cops could have come along and busted John any time they wanted. It wasn't like we were sneaking around. We were drinking and driving and smoking."

The government's crowning mistake was not appreciating what massive public support John could command. Jon Hendricks organized petitions calling for an end to his harassment, which soon collected tens of thousands of signatures; the *New York Times* ran an editorial backing him; the head of the national auto-workers' union sent a message of support. On April 27, New York's mayor, John Lindsay, appealed to the Commissioner of Immigration and

Naturalization in Washington for the deportation to be rescinded, calling it "a grave injustice" motivated not by John's drug conviction but the fact that "[John and Yoko] speak out with strong and critical voices on the major issues of the day." There was a similar appeal from Lord Harlech, Britain's former ambassador in Washington, making belated amends for the mistreatment the Beatles had suffered at his embassy in 1964.

Every TV talk-show host who interviewed John did so as an unequivocal sympathizer. "He had only to say 'Yes' and he could go on primetime and talk to a million people," Dan Richter says. "We didn't feel like we were underground people or outsiders. We represented reality—it was the politicians, the military and the people trying to deport John who lived in the world of fantasy."

His main ally in this arena was Dick Cavett, whose late-night show on ABC combined intelligence and literacy with overt sympathy for the counterculture. To Cavett on May 11, he revealed that the FBI had not been engaged in a covert operation so much as overt intimidation. "I felt followed everywhere by government agents. Every time I picked up any phone, there was a lot of noise . . . I'd open the door and there'd be guys standing on the other side of the street. I'd get in the car and they'd be following me and not hiding. . . . They wanted me to see I was being followed. Anyway, after I said it out on the air, on TV, the next day there was nobody there."

He also used the Cavett show to appeal to Tony Cox to come out of hiding with Kyoko. It was obviously better for a child to know both parents, he said, and Cox would be allowed fair access once a civilized dialogue had been restored. According to John, Yoko had been traumatized by Kyoko's disappearance; she could not bear to see children of the same age, even on television, and was having constant nightmares, which always came at the same time, five a.m.

On June 12 came the U.S. release of *Some Time in New York City*—which they had completed to coincide with their third wedding anniversary in March—coproduced by Phil Spector and with Elephant's Memory incorporated into the Plastic Ono Band. To underline Yoko's full creative partnership, the preceding single was a song built around her pioneering feminist slogan, "Woman Is the Nigger of the World," with the vocal delivered by John. Even used thus, to symbolize latter-day enslavement, the word *nigger* led to radio bans across America (though Britain still had no problem with it). John and Yoko appeared on television with representatives of two leading black magazines, *Jet* and *Ebony*, who said that in such an allegorical context the usage was justified. Dick Cavett defied his ABC bosses and sponsors and allowed them to perform it on his show, first giving his audience a detailed explanation of why he was doing so.

In contrast to Beatles albums that seemed to endure forever, John wanted this one to be as quickly assembled—and disposable—as a newspaper. Its cover was like a front page of the *New York Times*, each track-title appearing as a headline to a story and illustrated with gritty black-and-white news photographs. The contents might have been a checklist for the FBI of all the causes and individuals he had backed in the past ten months: "John Sinclair," "Attica State," "Angela" (about the Angela Davis case), "Sunday Bloody Sunday," and "The Luck of the Irish." In lighter vein, "New York City" added a fresh chapter to the "Ballad of John and Yoko," recounting their adventures since arriving stateside, with mentions of David Peel, Elephant's Memory, Max's Kansas City restaurant, their bicycles—and "the Man" who was trying to kick them out. As a live-performance bonus, the album included clips from their UNICEF gig at the London Lyceum and their Fillmore East guest spot with Frank Zappa.

Some Time in New York City was generally pronounced a failure, reaching only number forty-eight on the American chart and eleven in Britain (where its release was delayed until September). Even loyal *Rolling Stone* dismissed it as "incipient artistic suicide" and called the words "sloppy nursery rhymes." "We weren't setting out to make the Brandenburg Concerto . . . ," John retorted. "It was just a question of getting it done, putting it out and the next one's coming up soon. We needn't have done it. We could have sat on 'Imagine' for a year and a half, but the things . . . were coming out of our minds and we just wanted to share our thoughts with anybody who wanted to listen. The songs we wrote and sang are subjects we and most people talk about." Unconsciously he invoked the namesake grandfather who had crossed the Atlantic from Liverpool on an uncannily similar journey eighty years earlier: "It was done in a tradition of minstrels—singing reporters—who sang about their times and what was happening."

Today, the album is recognized to be much more than a soapbox rant. The mood of almost every track may be angry, but an artful range of commercial pop effects sweetens the harangue, including generous sprays of rock-'n'-roll chicken sax. To critics in 1972, it seemed the most unwarrantable intrusion yet that Yoko had equal time both as a songwriter and performer, that John sang her lyrics as well as his, and that in two songs, "Angela" and "Born in a Prison," he provided harmony for her just as Paul McCartney once had for him. Both duets, in fact, have an unexpected sweetness and delicacy—grim newsprint suddenly turning into Willow Pattern china. Yoko's words, more blank verse than lyrics, seem to stretch John's voice as even the most impassioned of his own never have. "Woman Is the Nigger of the World" gets a bravura performance rivaled only by "Twist and Shout."

This public affirmation that Lennon had found a successor to McCartney brought trouble in its wake. Since John began writing with Yoko, there had been problems in getting his British publishers, Northern Songs, to accept her name as a bona fide substitute for Paul's. So uncomfortable was Northern's new ATV management about billing "Happy Christmas (War Is Over)" as a John-Yoko collaboration that the single would not appear in Britain until the Christmas after its U.S. release. On *Some Time in New York City*, Yoko's publishing company, Ono Music, claimed half the copyright to four tracks she and John had cowritten: "Angela," "Sunday Bloody Sunday," "The Luck of the Irish," and "Woman Is the Nigger of the World." Northern and its associated Maclen company promptly filed a $1 million lawsuit against John in New York, claiming he had broken the 1965 agreement giving them exclusive rights to his work, whether solo or collaborative. John responded by countersuing for $9 million in allegedly unpaid foreign royalties.

Such an album was clearly not the most diplomatic thing to have released just as John and Yoko's lawyer, Leon Wildes, was trying to convince the immigration courts that they presented no threat to

America's internal security. While Wildes could not influence what John put on record, he urged him soften his persona by public charitable works in the mold of George Harrison's Concert for Bangladesh. An opportunity arose through a friendly TV reporter named Geraldo Rivera, who was helping to organize a fund-raiser for Willowbrook State School, a children's psychiatric hospital on Staten Island. John and Yoko volunteered to perform at the event at Madison Square Garden on August 30, alongside Steve Wonder, Roberta Flack, and Sha Na Na. Even for such an obviously respectable occasion, the FBI surveillance team turned out in force, ostentatiously photographing an audience that included Mayor John Lindsay, Princess Lee Radziwill, and the wife of the Democratic presidential candidate, George McGovern.

Backed by Elephant's Memory, John and Yoko played a chaotic medley, ranging from "Come Together" and "Hound Dog" to "Mother," which John introduced as "from one of those albums I made since I left the Rolling Stones." A famous film sequence shows him alone at the piano, in tinted glasses and olive-green shirt, screaming into the Garden's huge auditorium what most people would hesitate even to whisper secretly into their pillows: "Mother, you had me . . . but I never had you. . . ." However long ago and far away, it is still almost too painful to watch.

Back in Britain, what sent teenage girls crazy these days was glitter or glam rock. In reaction to the old decade's washed-out hippie smocks and quest for higher meanings, early seventies bands dressed in shiny suits and tottery platform heels, used female jewelry, hair dye, and even makeup, and gave themselves up to flashiness, triviality, and self-mockery. The latest to be hailed as "new Beatles" were T-Rex, whose lead singer, Marc Bolan, wore eye shadow and face paint; instead of Beatlemania, the press now talked about T-Rextasy. Bolan's run of self-penned hits like 'Ride a White Swan," "Telegram Sam," "Jeepster," and "Get It On," the *Melody Maker* said, made him "as important as Lennon or Dylan."

The statement brought swift reaction from a transatlantic migrant who had supposedly left all such considerations far behind. "I ain't heard 'Jeepster,' tho' I heard and liked 'Get It On' and [Bolan's] first hit," John wrote to the paper, trying—not very successfully—to adopt a benign elder statesman air. "Anyway, we all know where those 'new licks' come from—right, Marc?" Another correction came winging from New York after *Melody Maker* ran an interview with George Martin in which he said the Beatles' first British hit, "Please Please Me," had been cowritten by John and Paul and reordered a little by himself. "I wrote 'Please Please Me' alone. It was recorded in the exact sequence in which I wrote it. 'Remember?' love John & Yoko." Like its predecessor, the letter was meant for publication, even coming tagged with the words "LP Winner"—*Melody Maker*'s traditional award to the week's pithiest correspondent.

John's feud with his former other half staggered on for a little longer in this same arena. Late in 1971, Paul told an *MM* interviewer that the ex-Beatles' financial disputes would soon be resolved if the four of them got together, without Allen Klein, Yoko, or Linda, and simply signed a piece of paper—"but John won't do it. . . . Everyone thinks I'm the aggressor, but I'm not, you know. I just want out." At the time, the *Imagine* album had just appeared, with its anti-Paul-and-Linda tirade, "How Do You Sleep?" Paul laughed it off as "silly," though the jibe about "Yesterday" had obviously hurt him. "So what if I live with straights? I like straights. I have straight babies."

Claiming "equal time" on the letters page, John sent a lengthy reply (headed "Dear Linda, Paul and all the wee McCartneys . . .") from which nine lines had to be cut for fear of legal repercussions. The remainder was still headline-making stuff with its suggestion the other ex-Beatles might buy Paul's share of Apple, and brusque dismissal of the summit-conference idea.

For someone reputedly so dedicated to self-advancement, Paul had not fared nearly as well as John these past two years. Though the public smile never left his face, he had suffered a dark period immediately after the Beatles' breakup, starting to drink heavily and wonder if he really could go on without them. His decision to form a band named Wings with his wife in the lineup had been met with ridicule that even Yoko in the Plastic Ono Band never suffered. Unable to defeat the UK media's prejudice, he was reduced to touring

Wings in a small van, like pre-1962 Beatles, playing surprise gigs at provincial colleges. His post-Lennon-McCartney songs were increasingly criticized for being bland and cutesy, yet if he attempted to step out of character—as with his own comment on the Ulster Troubles, "Give Ireland Back to the Irish"—people threw up their hands in horror. While the Plastic Ono Band had hit after hit, Wings were far slower to take flight.

Dan Richter, for one, was always urging John to reopen communication with Paul. "I said, 'You guys have had your divorce, you did so much wonderful stuff together . . . you should be talking.'" But John still felt that Paul's attitude to Yoko created an unbridgeable gulf and that, anyway, Lennon and McCartney had both been too much changed by their respective spouses ever to find common ground again. "John used to say, 'Paul will always be a performer.'" Richter remembers. "'I've been a rock-'n'-roll star. I've done it. I want to move on.'"

Early in 1972, the two finally came face-to-face. Paul visited 105 Bank Street and they had a brief, guarded chat, agreeing not to dump on each other anymore, either in songs or through the media. But that slight thaw did not develop. When Paul was in New York, he would usually telephone John, sometimes to be greeted in friendly though distant fashion, other times by "Yeah, what the fuck do you want, man?" in an accent sounding more and more American. One way in which he continued to give offense, he recalls, was talking about his growing brood of young children, how he loved to read them bedtime stories and take them out for pizza. In a phrase that should have titled an album, John accused him of being "all pizza and fairy tales." During another such conversation, John's "vitriolic" mood caused Paul to lose his famous aplomb; he snapped, "Fuck off, Kojak," and slammed the receiver down.

Autumn was dominated by the presidential election. John pinned high hopes on the Democratic candidate, George McGovern, senator for South Dakota—an omen if ever there was one—who stood on an unequivocal pledge to end the Vietnam War. During the campaign, in what seemed a recurrent motif of American public affairs, a rival Democrat contender, Alabama's racist Governor George Wallace, was shot five times with a handgun by a twenty-one-year-old loner named Arthur Bremer, but survived, to be confined to a wheelchair for life. Despite McGovern's popular platform, the incumbent's diplomatic triumphs in Russia proved decisive. The voter surge of eighteen- to twenty-one-year-old voters, supposedly mobilized by John, failed to happen. Turnout was the lowest since 1948, and on November 7, Nixon won by a landslide.

John and Yoko had now been together for four years, spending almost every minute of every day in each other's company. Though they still constantly astonished and exhilarated each other on a creative level, their physical relationship had inevitably lost some of its initial blaze. John's sexual drive remained intense, but Yoko was finding herself less and less able, or inclined, to deal with it. "In lovemaking, I don't do much. John used to say, 'You're like one of those Victorian ladies—you just lie there and think of England.'"

They had often discussed the raging randiness which he freely confessed to, and which had been so easy to indulge during his years on the road with the Beatles. "Even when we first got together and were madly in love, John would say, 'I don't understand it, I'm madly in love, but why do I still keep looking at these girls on the street?'" Yoko remembers. "He always said that the difference with women was they could not separate sex and love. After we came to New York, I started to think there was a side of him that was feeling repressed a little."

The night of Nixon's reelection victory, they were invited to a party at Jerry Rubin's apartment. "John was totally out of his head with drugs and pills and drink because he couldn't stand the fact that George McGovern lost. He'd already started in the studio, when we were remixing something. . . . When we walked in to Jerry's, there was a girl there. She was the kind of girl you'd never think John would be attracted to, I don't want to describe her but anyway she was sitting there. She didn't come on to him at all, he just pulled her and went into the next room. And then they were groping and all that, and we were all quiet.

"Then one of the other guests was very kind and put a record on, Bob Dylan or something, so that we don't hear it. But we heard it anyway. And everybody had their coats in the next room, where John and this girl are making out, so nobody can go home. Then one girl was brave enough to get her coat, and the others followed her. And I was there and Peter [Bendry], our assistant, was there, and John and the girl were still in there. I said to Peter, 'Please take this flower to them and say to John I love him and don't worry.' I didn't like the situation. But I felt sorry for him. Peter said, 'No, I'm not going to bother them.'

"That situation really woke me up. I thought, 'Okay, we were so much in love with each other and that's why we sacrificed every-thing, my daughter, everything. It was worth it if we were totally in love with each other. But if he wants to make it with another girl or something, what am I doing?' And physically I was starting to feel like I didn't really want to get into it with him."

With so much else currently absorbing both their energies, the matter rested there for the present. Early in 1973, they came uptown to have lunch with Peter Brown, the former Beatles fixer-in-chief who was now running Robert Stigwood's New York operation and living in an elegant apartment building named the Langham, on Central Park West. John took an instant fancy to Brown's spacious pad with its sweeping views over the park and decided on the spot that he wanted to give up gypsy life in the West Village and move here. When the Langham proved to have no space available, he simply tried the building next door.

It was called the Dakota, but the place it suggested, even more pow-erfully than those cobbled SoHo alleys, was Liverpool. Some similar quasi-Gothic sandstone pile might have housed a bank or insurance company in North John, Tithebarn, or Water Street: the wealth and confidence of Mersey shipbuilders might equally have conceived its seven-story facade, embellished with balconies and terra-cotta mold-ings, its Germanic gables and steep copper roof, weathered to pale green, its street frontage of black iron lamps, flower urns, and deco-rative sea serpents. The very name suggested a touch of Liverpudlian sarcasm. When it was built, in the 1880s, this part of the Upper West Side was still so sparsely populated that fashionable people thought it as remote as North or South Dakota.

Though once the acme of luxury, the Dakota was no longer in Manhattan's premier real-estate league and had become the haunt of middle-range actors, film directors, and similar bohemian types. It had a slightly spooky ambience, the more so since being used as a location for Roman Polanski's satanic horror film *Rosemary's Baby*. Apartments were held on long, relatively inexpensive leases, and fell vacant only rarely. But it chanced that when John and Yoko's assistant, Jon Hendricks, made inquiries, the actor Robert Ryan was about to vacate number 72 on the seventh floor, owing to the recent death of his wife.

A single look at the Ryan apartment was enough to sell John on it. Running half the length of a block, it had four bedrooms, stunning views over Central Park's treetops and—the clincher for him—a distant view of the Lake. He loved the feel of the whole building, so like Victorian Liverpool with its heavy brass light switches, sit-down elevators, and mahogany, oak, and cherrywood paneling. In that crime- and violence-ridden metropolis, it seemed exceptionally well guarded: the entrance arch from West Seventy-second Street had an immense black iron gate and was watched around the clock by a security man in a copper sentry box.

For all the Dakota's bohemian ambiance, taking up residence there was not easy. The board of residents who ran the building maintained a blanket ban against diplomats (for their fly-by-night tendency) and rock stars. In parallel with the "Save John and Yoko" petitions he was compiling for their immigration case, Hendricks had to organize a campaign to persuade the Dakota's co-op board that they would not disrupt the place with wild parties or deafening music. Letters were submitted from character witnesses, including the head of the American Episcopal Church, Bishop Paul Moore, and they appeared before the board as neatly dressed and circumspect as in the immigration court. Eventually, they were accepted. The real-estate agent later admitted to Hendricks that he thought they hadn't stood a chance.

What did not already remind John of home in apartment 72, he was quick to add. The rather murky woodwork that had previously killed much of the Central Park light was replaced by brilliant white paintwork and some of the white carpets from Tittenhurst Park; the cramped kitchen was enlarged to one almost as spacious as Tittenhurst's. The main living room became a drawing room, as formal and spotless as Aunt Mimi's old one at Mendips, with huge white couches and ottomans and clusters of silver-framed family photographs—Mimi, his mother, his aunts and cousins, his beloved and never-forgotten Uncle George. Humorous brass plaques appeared on doors, identifying the kitchen as "Honey world" and an adjacent cloakroom-toilet as "Albert." Nor could it be a proper home for him until there were cats about the place. Yoko was not a cat person but, as ever, deferred to his wishes.

He remained in constant communication with the smaller counterpart of apartment 72 across the Atlantic, telephoning Mimi at least once a week and writing to her once a month or so. "I used to get to know by the way the phone would ring that it was John," she would remember. "When he rang, he would always say, 'It's Himself.' He would sign his letters like that, too." The calls were not mere dutiful check-ins. "He would always want to talk about what he had been doing and about the old days. He missed this country, of course he did." Now that he had a home in which he could entertain Mimi properly, he urged her to come and stay, but without success. "He was always on at me to go to New York," she would recall, "but I told him straight, 'I'm not going to a land where there's guns, John.'"

Safely returned to the White House for another four years (as he thought), Richard Nixon had nothing more to fear from the likes of John. The chief stoker of government paranoia, J. Edgar Hoover, had died in 1972, his penchant for wearing ladies' dresses still unrevealed. Nixon's first priority was to scale down the commitment to Vietnam, and on March 29, 1973, the last U.S. troops were withdrawn after a war that had cost 58,178 American dead—not to mention an estimated 3,800,000 Vietnamese, 800,000 Cambodians, and 50,000 Laotians. With virtually all the steam thus taken out of the national protest movement, FBI surveillance on alleged subversives, including John, was dropped.

But the Immigration and Naturalization Service continued to press for his deportation, seemingly deaf to any evidence his lawyer offered in his favor. The main plank of Leon Wildes's case was that since, unlike marijuana, cannabis resin was not illegal in America, John's 1968 conviction had no validity here. However, despite expert medical testimony, and even contemporaneous press reports of the case, the immigration judge refused to accept that the substance involved had not been marijuana under the letter of the law. On March 23, John was again ordered to leave the country, but granted a further limited stay pending appeal.

Months had now passed without any pronouncement from the INS on his and Yoko's dual claim for third-preference status, as creative artists whose presence benefited the nation's cultural life. Finally, Wildes went to the U.S. District Court and obtained a writ of mandamus, in effect compelling the INS's New York district director to do his duty and deal with the matter. It would later emerge that Immigration Commissioner Raymond Farrell in Washington had sent a confidential memo to the district director, ordering him not to adjudicate John and Yoko's application "until after we've gotten rid of them."

Remote though the chance of melting such officials' hearts with humor, they had a try. On April 1, the media gathered for a press conference at the office of the New York Bar Association, eager to know what John had devised to celebrate April Fools' Day. Flanked by Yoko and an indulgent Leon Wildes, he announced the creation of a "conceptual" country called Nutopia with "no land, no boundaries, no passports, only people." Its national flag was a Kleenex, and anyone who heard of its existence automatically became both a citizen and an ambassador. As ambassadors-in-chief, he and Yoko claimed diplomatic immunity from normal immigration procedure and legal process, and the prerogative to stay in America for as long as Nutopia's national interests should warrant. On the service door of their Dakota apartment kitchen appeared a plaque reading NUTOPIAN EMBASSY.

In ordinary circumstances, John's manager would have been expected to stand at his shoulder, providing aid and comfort throughout this whole ordeal. But Allen Klein no longer bore even a passing resemblance to a savior. Klein had dreamed of possessing the Beatles but had ended up running the careers of three ex-Beatles, not at all the same thing either in terms of money or mystique. And, as Brian Epstein might have warned, pleasing even three of his boys all the time was a task beyond the canniest operator. The watershed moment for Klein had been the Concert for Bangladesh, which he and George Harrison coproduced. John suspected him of backing George's refusal to allow Yoko onstage and never felt the quite the same about him afterward. George, too, had cooled on Klein, especially now that questions were being raised about how much of the concert and album proceeds had gone to Bangladesh's starving and how much been gobbled up by expenses, legal costs, and taxes.

March 31 brought the end of the management agreement that John, George, and Ringo had signed with Klein in 1969. Back in Britain, the Beatles' old roadie, Neil Aspinall, heard that John had renewed Klein's contract, but for one day only—a clear indication of how things stood between them. On April 2, a statement from Klein's ABKCO organization announced it was cutting all links with the three former Beatles and Apple forthwith. The next day, John talked to the media after filing an appeal against the INS's March 23 deportation order. Questions about Klein brought only the terse reply "We separated ourselves from him."

He unbent a little further a week later in Los Angeles, to an interviewer from London Weekend Television, saying there were "many reasons why we finally gave [Klein] the push. . . . Let's say possibly Paul's suspicions were right, and the time was right. . . ." With this bone of contention with Paul now removed, could a Beatles reunion be imminent? "The chances are practically nil," John replied. Since Aunt Mimi was bound to see or hear about the program, he signed off with a greeting to her: "Hello Mimi, how are you? We're eating well and I haven't given up my British citizenship. I just want to live here, that's all. . . ." On June 28, by way of limbering up for the legal marathon ahead, ABKCO filed suit against John for $508,000 allegedly paid to him in loans during Klein's tenure.

Outside the bedroom, John and Yoko's relationship seemed as frantically fruitful as ever. When the National Organization of Women invited her to perform at an international conference in Boston, he volunteered to go with her merely as her "band." Afterward, they visited Salem, Massachusetts, scene of the seventeenth-century witchcraft trials—a place with special resonance for Yoko after her experiences in Britain. Besides writing songs for a new album, John acquired an electric typewriter and began writing the short essays and reflections that would be collected (posthumously) as *Skywriting by Word of Mouth*. Yoko had also written a new album and, as it happened, was first into the recording studio. "Every day [he] waited for me to bring back a rough mix of what I had done. . . . 'You should call me in when you're ready,' he said, 'just like you would call in a session-guitarist, and I'll come and play.'"

With summer—a period when, as it happened, both were completely straight, not even smoking grass—the question of sex resurfaced again. "We made love here [the Dakota] and it was very good, he was very good and everything . . . it had nothing to do with the quality of the lovemaking," Yoko remembers. "I said, 'Look, John, it's getting a little bit like we're not passionate about each other. Are we just going to be one of those old conservative couples who are together just because we're married?'"

They agreed it would do their marriage no harm if John were to find other sexual partners. Promiscuity was, of course, nothing new in rock circles, but for him the conclusive factor was a book, *Portrait of a Marriage*, describing how the writer and diplomat Harold Nicolson and the poet Vita Sackville-West remained a loving, united couple while both having continual (homosexual) affairs. Apart from that one drunken lapse at Jerry Rubin's, John had never been unfaithful to Yoko, and had no idea how to go about it, even with her compliance. He talked enviously about a fellow British rock star who simply went to the Plaza Hotel's bar each night and sat there until some young woman picked him up and they adjourned to a suite. "John kept saying, 'It's that simple,'" Yoko recalls. I said, 'Okay, so do you want me to call the Plaza?' He said, 'Are you kidding? You're Mrs. Lennon, how could you think that?' I said, 'Well, what do you want, then?'"

There was even some discussion, albeit not very serious, of whether he should stick to his own gender. "John said 'It would hurt you like crazy if I made it with a girl. With a guy, maybe you wouldn't be hurt, because that's not competition. But I can't make it with a guy because I love women too much, and I'd have to fall in love with the guy and I don't think I can.'"

The new album he was currently making seemed to underline this desire to cut loose. It would be the first credited to John Lennon alone, without Yoko, Phil Spector, or the Plastic Ono Band; John acted as his own producer and arranger with a new studio lineup, including drummer Jim Keltner, who had played on two *Imagine* tracks, a talented young guitarist named David Spinozza, and a female backup group appropriately known as Something Different. Yoko's only credit in the liner notes was for "space." John also designed the cover, which showed him standing on a wide, grassy plain, suitcase in hand, with her upturned profile behind him like a distant mountain range.

The title, *Mind Games*, suggested a retreat from all the causes and victims they had championed together and a return to the therapist's couch, this time on the subject of marriage rather than parentage and childhood. Certainly, the polemical fire of *Some Time in New York City* seemed to have sputtered out, but for a few familiar nostrums, such as "make love nor war," "free the people now" (plus one heart-felt ad-lib of "jail the judges"). John's favorite press description of the album was *"Imagine* with balls," but, in fact, it is equally melodic and optimistic, even its psychologically suggestive title track—destined to become a first-echelon Lennon classic—pouring over the listener as reassuringly as a hot, scented shower. And adoring references to Yoko crop up throughout: "I was born just to get to you" ("Out the Blue"); "I'm a fish and you're the sea" ("One Day at a Time"); "Today I love you more than yesterday" ("Only People"); and "Wherever you are, you are here" ("You Are Here"). "Aisumasen"—"I'm sorry" in Japanese—might have been an apology for that night at Jerry Rubin's, or what was soon to come. The "Nutopian International Anthem" (three seconds of silence) acknowledged the tricky diplomatic mission they still faced together.

The question of giving John "space" outside the studio, however, remained unresolved. Though eager to accept the sexual freedom Yoko was offering, he felt squeamish about doing anything under her nose in New York. "So then I suggested L.A.," she remembers, "and he just lit up." The problem was that, since his earliest days as a Beatle, he had never traveled anywhere alone or had to fend in any serious way for himself. Somebody would have to be found to go with him.

With a view to bagging two birds with one stone, Yoko looked over the various young females in their circle. Her choice was May Pang, a twenty-two-year-old Chinese American who had worked as an assistant to both of them since before the move to America and who, in addition to being highly competent, was extremely pretty. "I said to John, 'What about May?' He said, 'Oh no, not May!'—it was like 'doth protest too much.' So I went to May and said, 'Look, I think you have to accompany John to L.A. I have things to do here, and I'm not a very good wife, you know.' I didn't say 'Do it' or anything. It was just to be an assistant, to go there. But I knew what might happen, because he was never without anybody."

On John's side, the possessiveness that had dominated his relationship with Yoko disappeared completely—or seemed to. He insisted that during their separation she must go out with other men so both of them would be equally guilty—and because he'd read that women who did not stay sexually active ran a higher risk of cancer. He also said he'd feel more comfortable if any affair she had was with a brother musician. They even discussed a possible candidate, the *Mind Games* guitarist David Spinozza, who had also played on Yoko's album *Feeling the Space*. As she recalls, Spinozza's extraordinary good looks seemed somehow to make him less of a threat. " 'David's so beautiful,' John said. 'I wouldn't mind having sex with him.' "

On September 18, he flew to Los Angeles with May Pang, for what May thought would be only a two-week stay. "I'd never been a bachelor since I was 20 or something, and I thought, 'Whoopee!' " he would recall. "But it was god-awful."

27

TROUBLE WITH HARRY

I'm in Lost Arseholes for no real reason.

ohn was to call these next fourteen months his Lost Weekend, borrowing the title of the most famous film ever made about alcoholism and urban loneliness. Billy Wilder's 1945 noir classic follows a young writer, played by Ray Milland, as he struggles through a solitary Friday to Monday in New York wrestling with demons of temptation and self-loathing. Alcohol certainly loomed large in John's West Coast version, as did loneliness and self-loathing, but the script would contain much else besides. "It wasn't by any means a lost weekend," his friend Elliot Mintz says. "Just a very long one."

Mintz had gotten to know John while working as a disc jockey on station KLOS in Los Angeles. His first contact was with Yoko, whom he interviewed on his show by phone from New York, proving so sympathetic that he afterward built up a friendship with her the same way. A face-to-face meeting did not come until the summer of 1972, when John and Yoko decided finally to kick their lingering methadone habit with the help of a Chinese acupuncturist in San Francisco. Feeling that they should take a proper look at the country from which they might soon be banished, they made the trip by road, chauffeured by their assistant, Peter Bendry. Rather than the usual limo, they chose an ordinary station wagon without the integrated stereo system John usually regarded as essential. Instead, he played singles on a portable record player whose needle jogged with a horrible scrunch whenever the car hit a pothole.

Some Time in New York City was just about to be released, with its eulogies to the Black Panthers and the IRA. When Elliot Mintz finally met John and Yoko in the flesh, John gave him an early pressing and said he was to have the privilege of breaking it in the L.A. area. Mintz played the entire album on KLOS without commercials or interruption, a bravura gesture that cost him his job at the station. He had since moved from radio to become an entertainment reporter for ABC-TV's *Eyewitness News*. This was to prove ironic, as the confidential nature of his relationship with John and Yoko would prevent many extraordinary scenes to which he was an eyewitness from finding their way onto the air.

Mintz was waiting at Los Angeles Airport when John arrived on the flight from New York, accompanied by May Pang and carrying $10,000 in traveler's checks, which he had borrowed from Capitol Records for their immediate subsistence. As Mintz recalls, there was no suggestion that he and Yoko had parted by mutual agreement or that their separation was other than permanent. "He said she'd kicked him out and he didn't know when or even if they'd be getting back together."

To all media interviewers he told the same story, as he would undeviatingly over the next twelve months: that Yoko and he were simply taking a break from each other, and there was nothing wrong with their relationship. "Now that she knows how to produce records and everything about it, I think the best thing I can do is keep out of her hair. We're just playing life by ear, and that includes our careers. We occasionally take a bath together and occasionally separately, just how we feel at the time."

As it happened, too, he had plausible professional reasons to be in Los Angeles. *Mind Games* was scheduled for release in November, and Capitol had scheduled various meetings with its West Coast marketing and promotion departments. Besides, L.A. had long since taken San Francisco's position as the happening place in white American pop, thanks to the new singer-songwriter breed headed by Joni Mitchell and James Taylor, and the modish country-rock style of Neil Young and Jackson Browne. If John wanted more hit albums, it was only wise to take careful soundings here.

Nor would he be friendless and neglected like the protagonist of *Lost Weekend*. Mal Evans, the Beatles' roadie who had always acted as nursemaid and bodyguard to him in particular, was now living in L.A., forgetful of a cash-strapped wife and children back in Britain. And Ringo Starr frequently came into town, as much a "bachelor" in his own marriage as John could wish to be. Despite the unresolved legal questions among them, the other three ex-Beatles could still put aside their differences in mutual fondness for Ringo: on his new, eponymous album, John had written one track, "I'm the Greatest," and sung harmonies with George playing lead guitar, while another, "Six O'Clock," featured Paul and Linda McCartney. Ringo had also recently bought Tittenhurst Park, in the same obliging spirit that a Liverpool pal might take over some old banger of a car. John hated the thought that his rolling parklands and lake had gone forever, and drew comfort from Ringo's promise that a bedroom would always be kept for him there.

He had been loaned a small duplex apartment in West Hollywood by Harold Seider, the lawyer representing him in the Allen Klein lawsuit. Soon after arriving, however, he bumped into an old friend from Beatlemania days, the Rolling Stones' former manager, Andrew Loog Oldham (who had many tales of his own about litigation with Klein). Oldham was staying at the Bel Air home of the record producer Lou Adler while Adler was away for an extended period. As he was about to return to Britain, he suggested that John and May should borrow the house in his place.

From the moment John reached L.A., according to Elliot Mintz, his one thought was returning to Yoko. "He called her every day, saying, 'When can I come home?' She'd also call me every day, to see how he was doing and check that he wasn't harming himself or making a fool of himself, though at that stage she certainly wasn't looking for steps to get him back. Most of the time, John was in denial. But when he got drunk or high, he couldn't stop talking about Yoko and how much he needed her. The sense with him all the time was 'What do I have to do to get out of here and back to her?' "

Yoko, too, found the separation hard, but was determined not to weaken. "For the first two weeks, my whole body was shaking, I couldn't stop. Because before that I was never without him, and now I was alone here [at the Dakota]. But I didn't want to tell that to John because then he would have come back. I thought, 'I have to get over this because I can't be in a position where my existence relies on being with somebody.'" On the telephone, John's mood would veer between euphoria at his newfound freedom and reproachful home-sickness. "In L.A., when things were going well, he'd say, 'Oh, you're such a great, great wife, I can't believe it,'" Yoko remembers. "When things were not going well, it was, 'How could you send me out here?'" A telegram he sent to Derek Taylor revealed the extent of his desperation amid the usual Lennon punnery: "I'm in Lost Arseholes for no real reason . . . Yoko and me are in hell but I'm gonna change it. . . ."

May Pang's precise role in the scenario would never be clear, least of all to May herself. Her later book, *Loving John*, portrays a young woman of strong Catholic scruples who was at first scandalized by the suggestion that she become John's mistress (even though, by her own account, they had been having a surreptitious fling in New York). She was indisputably his only public female companion during the Lost Weekend, sharing all the various temporary addresses he had in L.A., then back in New York. Without exception, everybody who knew them as a couple remembers May as a wholly positive in-fluence at a time when John most needed it: kind, sweet, and almost supernaturally unselfish.

Yet as Elliot Mintz recalls, she never quite attained the status of a rock star's "old lady"; one day John would be all over her in public, the next she would seem no more than his PA. And, as May would admit in her book, there was never a moment when she did not feel that Yoko, back in New York, was watching, even directing, the plot's development. "It wasn't like he left his wife for the mistress and then went back to the wife," says the photographer Bob Gruen. "He left his wife for wild times that his secretary oversaw. May talks about that period as if it was her time with John, but there are dozens of other women who can dispute that. It's fascinating to me that in all these years, not one of them has come forward or tried to cash in on their story. I tend to think they really treasure that hour, that ten minutes, that night with John Lennon, and they have their memory and it's private."

The great pop sensation in America that year was the British glam rocker Elton John, who had played a sold-out national tour recalling the Beatles in their heyday, and topped the charts with his album *Goodbye Yellow Brick Road*. Coincidentally, as Reggie Dwight from Pinner, Middlesex, he had been discovered by the Beatles' former music publisher, Dick James, proving that once-in-a-lifetime luck can strike twice. Twenty-six-year-old Elton stood for everything thirty-one-year-old John might have been expected to dislike, with his outsize glasses, flamboyant stage costumes, and seeming mission to kick the Fab Four into history. Yet he would be the one mainly responsible, not just for stabilizing the Lost Weekend, but eventually bringing it to an end.

They met in L.A. in October 1973, a couple of weeks after John's arrival. The intermediary was Tony King, who had been a song-plugger at Dick James's company, DJM, then gone on to work for Apple. Underneath his Liberace hubris, the glam rock icon was funny, honest, and self-deprecating, as well as a besotted Lennon fan, and John took to him immediately. If he found Elton's music a bit too kitschy and derivative, he envied his facility as a songwriter, his virtuoso piano playing, and, most of all, his stamina. Where a Beatles live set used to be twenty minutes, Elton was onstage for two and a half hours. "How the fuck do you do it?" John asked, apparently forgetting his own all-night sets with the Beatles in Hamburg.

Nor was he totally averse to the camp private world of Elton and his circle, where men were commonly referred to as "she" and nicknames like Sharon and Ada freely bestowed. A promotional film sequence was shot for *Mind Games*, in which Tony King, looking strangely like Queen Elizabeth II in a ball gown and tiara, danced an old-fashioned waltz with John while Elton looked on, calling them "Fred Astaire and Ginger Beer" (Cockney rhyming slang for "queer") and taking Polaroid photographs. "I'm gonna impound all those pictures till I get me green card," John was heard to mutter.

That prospect seemed as far off as ever. The threat of imminent deportation still hung over his head, and he had to make periodic trips back to New York to consult with Leon Wildes or make yet another appearance before the Immigration and Naturalization Service. Unaware that Nixon's reelection had ended the FBI surveillance, he believed he was still being watched and followed. "Often when I was driving John somewhere, he'd look in the rear-view mirror and say a car had been behind us for the last seven blocks, and I should make a hard right or left and try to shake it off," Elliot Mintz remembers. "I didn't tell him that in surveillance often two cars would be used, so that when you thought you'd lost one, the other would take over. It had become almost like a paranoia with John. And he remained very wary and secretive for the rest of his life."

He came to rely heavily on Mintz, who not only had entrée everywhere as an ABC show-business reporter but also shared his love of words and awareness of subjects outside rock. One night, Mintz took him backstage at the Roxy Theater to meet his great teenage rock-'n'-roll idol after Elvis, Jerry Lee Lewis. Instead of shaking hands, John fell on all fours and began kissing Lewis's cowboy boots. "Now, now, son," the discomfited idol protested, "that ain't necessary at all." There was a weekend trip to Las Vegas, where John devised an "infallible" system to win at roulette, betting a $10 chip on almost every number on the wheel. Within minutes, he attracted a crowd that the casino's highest roller could not. He also made Mintz go with him to see *Deep Throat*, the most explicit erotic movie yet shown in mainstream cinemas. But, despite his attendance record at such entertainments on Hamburg's Reeperbahn, he walked out, bored, after only twenty minutes.

Allen Klein was not the only litigant he had left behind back east. He had recently been hit by a suit for plagiarism, the first in eleven years as a superabundantly prolific composer. His multiallu-sional song "Come Together," on the Beatles' *Abbey Road* album, had opened with a Chuck Berry-esque line, "Here come old flat-top. . . ." which actually did figure in Berry's 1957 track, "You Can't Catch Me." Four years after *Abbey Road*, the New York publisher Morris Levy, who held copyright on the Berry song, suddenly noticed this fleeting homage and fired off a writ. The joke was that Levy—aka the Octopus—was notorious for ensnaring gullible young songwrit-ers and putting his own name on their work. Slight though John's offense, it was still unarguable and he had been forced to settle out of court. As part of the settlement, he undertook to record, and so pay royalties on, three songs owned by Levy, including "You Can't Catch Me."

Despite never writing a single word or composing a note, Levy had managed to stuff his back catalog with almost every rock-'n'-roll classic the embryo Beatles had ever played in Liverpool and Ham-burg, from Chuck Berry's "Sweet Little Sixteen" to Larry Williams's "Bony Moronie." John still loved rock-'n'-roll music better than any other kind, and so, rather than record three tracks in isolation, he decided to make a whole album of cover versions mostly drawn from Levy's accumulated plunder. After all those recent sermons to humankind, political tracts, and painful explorations of his psyche, it would be almost a rest cure to record "some 'ooh-ee, baby' songs that are meaningless for a change."

To set the seal on the project, Phil Spector lived in L.A. (in a fa-mously forbidding Bel Air mansion, ringed by barbed wire) and was currently in residence and available. After two albums at the cutting edge with the Plastic Ono Band, Spector, too, fancied a flight into nostalgia, the more so when John, for the first time, offered him full control, desiring only to be "a singer in the band." Time was booked at A&M Studios, and top session musicians were recruited, including Leon Russell, guitarists Steve Cropper and Jesse Ed Davis, and John's favorite post-Beatles drummer, Jim Keltner. Sessions began in mid-October, under the provisional title *Oldies and Mouldies*.

Let off the leash as he now felt, John "hit the bottle like I was 19, 20. . . ." And as ever, just a couple of drinks in the American

super size changed him in an instant from irresistible charmer and
jokester to surly, incoherent, venom-tongued, trouble-seeking, and
often violent drunk. "When we were out and about together and
John was in that state, it used to be quite pitiful if a fan spotted him
and came over for an autograph," Elliot Mintz remembers. "This
was the Beatle who had made us all think, the John Lennon who
lifted us onto a higher plane of consciousness with his lyrics, who
was always so witty and apropos. And here he is spilling a drink on
his pants and not able to form a coherent sentence. The look of letdown on people's faces was terrible."

He even drank in the recording studio, something he'd never
done during his whole career as a Beatle. "He'd sit there on a stool
in his headphones," drummer Jim Keltner remembers, "and down
on the floor beside him would be what you'd think was a joke-size
container of Smirnoff vodka."

Phil Spector, too, had changed from the respectful éminence
grise of the Plastic Ono Band albums. Back on his home turf, Spector began to live up to his most lurid Sixties legend, arriving for work
flanked by bodyguards and ostentatiously flashing a pistol in a shoulder holster. Sometimes he would be in fancy dress, costumed as a
surgeon in the operating theater, a karate champion, a priest, or a
blind man with dark glasses and a white stick; in answer to John's
vodka flagon, he kept a bottle of Courvoisier brandy always within
reach. Word quickly spread of the nightly party at A&M Studios,
and celebrities like Joni Mitchell, Warren Beatty, and Jack Nicholson
constantly dropped by. Meanwhile, Jim Keltner and the other session musicians became progressively more unhappy about what was
being put on tape. "There were some flashes of brilliance—with Phil
and John working together, there had to be. But mostly the music
crashed and burned."

Keltner and guitarist Jesse Ed Davis were called on to restrain
John one night when the cocktail of vodka and 100-proof rock 'n' roll
unlocked all his pent-up anguish over Yoko, and he went literally
berserk. "We had to hold him down in the back of the car to stop
him kicking the windows in, and the two of us could hardly do it,"
Keltner recalls. "He was lashing out at Jesse, and pulling my hair and

screaming Yoko's name." Back at the house he was borrowing from Lou Adler, the two musicians tried to immobilize him by trussing him up with neckties while May fled to seek refuge in the nearby Bel Air Hotel. Escaping his flimsy bonds, John went on a rampage through the house; he broke furniture, smashed Adler's prized collection of Platinum Albums (for chart toppers like the Mamas and Papas and Carole King) and uprooted a palm tree on the patio.

Even the slightly built, fastidious Elliot Mintz was not safe when these drunken paroxysms hit. "There were two occasions when I suffered physical abuse from John. On one of them, he grabbed me by the throat so hard, I thought he seriously meant to throttle me. A couple of other times, I was the victim of his verbal hatchets, and there were plenty of days when he was just low-level surly and mean. But against that I have to set two or three hundred instances of his selflessness, kindness, generosity and affection."

In the studio, Phil Spector's total artistic control was becoming ever more uncontrollable. One night, to emphasize that he would brook no arguments, he drew his pistol and fired it into the air. Jim Keltner, who had gone out to get a soda, returned to find Mal Evans standing on a metal cabinet and trying to pry the bullet from the ceiling. "Listen, Phil, if you're gonna kill me, kill me," John protested. "But don't fuck with me ears. I need 'em." Even for L.A. in the early seventies, this was going too far; A&M served an immediate eviction order, and the sessions had to move to another studio, the newly opened Record Plant West.

Insecure as ever, John was plagued by doubts about recording macho rock 'n' roll when all that young people seemed to want was camp, glittery glam rock. Even the Rolling Stones—who had managed to hang together when the Beatles could not—took the stage these days behind a lead vocalist in full makeup who danced like a Soho stripper. Just before Christmas, Mick Jagger blew through town: a married man now and a Somerset Maugham–ish tax exile in France. He stopped by the Record Plant and recorded a track, produced by John, called "Too Many Cooks." Ready as ever to look and learn, John had bought a ticket for a Stones East Coast gig but then had left for L.A., so he could only watch it on television. "It was a master performance," he told one interviewer, "and that's what Mick is—a master performer." Quite a change of heart from his gripe to *Rolling Stone* in 1970 about "Mick and all that fag dancing."

"John thought he was considered unhip for not doing the same androgyny thing as the Stones," Yoko says, "He was kind of tortured about that because he wanted the gay crowd to love him. But he picked up a little bit from Elton and the others in L.A. When he came back, they'd given him a woman's name, too. He was Catherine."

John's son, Julian, was now eleven. He had not seen his father for more than two years, and in all that time they had spoken only a couple of times on the telephone. His mother felt he had left childhood behind too quickly in his concern to protect her, and sometimes saw in his little moon face the abstracted sadness of a figure on a medieval tomb—the same look that John's used to wear, if she but knew, when private thoughts would carry him away from the hell of Beatlemania.

Life after John had not been easy for Cynthia. Her marriage to Roberto Bassanini had ended in divorce, and she had returned to her homeland, taking a small house in Meols on the Cheshire Wirral and trying to make a career as an interior designer. Reading of John's separation from Yoko, she wondered if it might presage a thaw in his relations with Julian—and herself. In February 1974, she was invited to join a group of friends crossing to New York on the liner *France*. Nervously she contacted John and asked if she could bring Julian over to see him. To her surprise, he not only welcomed the idea but offered to provide first-class tickets. Also on board was Elton John, who went out of his way to be charming to Cyn and invited Julian to his cabin to see his collection of enormous glasses.

John met them on the dock in New York, accompanied by May Pang and clearly in a state of trepidation almost equal to Cynthia's. It was Julian who broke the ice, flinging his arms around him as if the two-year gap had never been. May also helped to lighten the moment, having been Julian's occasional playmate at Tittenhurst Park, and clearly finding John's first wife a great deal easier to fathom than his second. The reunion passed off so well that John offered to take

Julian back to Los Angeles for a holiday while Cynthia stayed in New York with her old friend Jennie Boyd. When this arrangement fell through, he invited her to join the expedition to L.A. On the flight, however, her seat was at the rear of the cabin, as far as possible from John's, May's, and Julian's. Time had done little to harden Cyn and, in the privacy of her remote seat, she burst into tears.

May continued to be an emollient factor throughout the holiday, insisting, for example, that John should book Cynthia a suite at the Beverly Hills Hotel rather than boarding her out with his drummer, Jim Keltner, as he first intended. To build on the rapprochement with Julian, he had planned they should spend a day together at Disneyland—a wonder which, at that time, few British children had experienced. But Julian refused to go without his mother and grew so tearful that John had no choice but to acquiesce. Cyn, therefore, spent an uncomfortable few hours trailing around the rides with May and Mal Evans, aware of John's constant fear that they might lag behind the others and have to make conversation.

The ever-amiable "Big Mal" also helped matters by encouraging John to reminisce about old times in Liverpool and so again become somebody Cyn could connect with and understand. Additional healing infusions of normality came from Jim Keltner, a good-natured, unflappable man whose wife also happened to be named Cynthia and who had a son of Julian's age. There was little "Lost Weekend" about John's evenings at the Keltners' home, where he would be relaxed and charming, and praise Cynthia Keltner's dinner-table setting like a perfect guest from Emily Post's etiquette manual.

But etiquette could falter. One evening, about halfway through Julian's visit, John went with May and the Keltners to the Troubadour, the famous club on Santa Monica Boulevard that had given Elton John and many others their first big break. Headlining that night was Ann Peebles, a rather dour soul chanteuse whose single, "I Can't Stand the Rain," had lately been on the U.S. and British charts. Before going to the club, John's party ate dinner at Lost on Larrabee, a restaurant popular with the rock crowd. As they were leaving, he slipped into the women's room and rifled a cabinet full of Kotex sanitary pads. When he reached the Troubadour, he took a Kotex from his pocket and clamped it to the center of his forehead like an unwieldy Indian caste mark. (Even this may have been a symbol of missing Yoko. Not long after their first meeting in 1966, she had sent him an artwork called Mend Piece, consisting of some Kotex and a broken cup, which he'd unwrapped in the presence of both his then wife and mother-in-law.)

As Jim Keltner recalls, Ann Peebles's appearance onstage was slightly delayed, so the club's whole VIP section had ample opportunity to share in the joke. According to hallowed legend, John snapped at a dilatory waitress, "Do you know who I am?" and she snapped back, "Yeah, an asshole with a Kotex on his head." Neither May nor the Keltners recall any such words being said.

Its central component being unmentionable in print, the story did not reach the media, or the ears of Cyn and Julian. The holiday ended on a resoundingly successful note, with John taking Julian to Disneyland twice more and (at May's insistence) promising to phone him twice a week from now on. "Around this time, a radio interviewer asked John if there was anything about his life that he'd change if he had the chance," Elliot Mintz remembers. "John said there was nothing—then he paused, thought for a little and finally said that if he had his time over, he'd be different to Julian. He realised he should have been there more for him, but as he once said to me, 'some of us just can't handle that.' And I think when he realised it, a part of himself was able to forgive his own father, who hadn't been there for him."

For every day of drunken irrationality, there were dozens when, in Mintz's words, John was "as clear as a bell," scathingly observant and funny about his adopted city and determined to stay in touch with the world beyond its sun-soaked, brain-softening lifestyle. In this era before personal computers, the Internet, cell phones, CNN, and cable television, there were only limited ways of keeping up with current affairs. He read the *New York Times* from cover to cover each day, and waited impatiently for CBS's *Evening News*, fronted by Walter Cronkite (the same lordly anchorman who had grumped over the Beatles' American debut in 1964). When John was not lurching around with a Kotex stuck on his forehead, Mintz noted the rather

old-fashioned civility of his speech and his personal neatness and fastidiousness. "He prepared tea with utmost care, and didn't like to see
crumbs left on the kitchen-table or newspapers strewn on the couch.
If he was reading any kind of manuscript, all the sheets had to be
kept in alignment. I once asked him, 'Are all British people that way?'
John looked at me and said, 'What way?'"

Besides missing Yoko, he clearly missed Britain enormously; after
an interview with the *Melody Maker*'s L.A. correspondent, Chris
Charlesworth, he turned the tables and quizzed Charlesworth at
length about the Royal Family, what the new decimel currency was
like, and how much a bottle of milk cost nowadays. If no kindred-
spirited Brit happened to be in town, the next best thing was Sharon
Lawrence, an anglophile journalist–turned–PR rep, who had lived
in London and been a friend to many top musicians, notably Jimi
Hendrix. She was now running the West Coast arm of Elton John's
Rocket record label—an enterprise that in every way seemed to
have learned the lessons of Apple. In her office was a chintz love
seat, where John would curl up and talk for hours about byways of
British culture that few other Americans understood: music hall,
wireless soap operas of the 1950s, the Royal Worcester china that
was always the centerpiece of his Aunt Mimi's spotless household.

Once, the talk turned to Ringo Starr, and John revealed the almost
parental concern he felt for his old bandmate in this harsh post-Beatles
world. "He told me 'I'm always going to look after Ringo and make
sure he wants for nothing as long as he lives,'" Sharon remembers.
"I'd never thought John big-headed, but I was sometimes amazed at
his lack of confidence in himself. More than once, he sat there and
asked me, 'Do you think I'll ever have a hit record again?'"

Elliot Mintz believes John never really felt at home in L.A., and
certainly never considered settling there permanently. "There was
too much missing from the place for John. The people he was associating with didn't think about anything outside of music and getting
drunk and high, and never read anything more cerebrally demanding than *Rolling Stone*. And the relationship he'd left behind had so
many facets—intellectual stimulation, genuine love, a shared art-
istry. If there had been another Yoko out on the West Coast, things

might have ended very differently. But he didn't meet any woman who could hold a candle to her."

Yoko herself seemed to have had no trouble in adjusting to single life: besides producing art with her usual energy, she gave regular performances as a musician, appearing for a week at a fashionable Manhattan nightspot named Kenny's Castaways, fronting Elephant's Memory on the *Mike Douglas Show*, giving a Christmas Day concert at the Cathedral of St. John the Divine accompanied by David Spinozza, and later taking a Super Plastic Ono Band on a short tour of Japan. She and John still spoke constantly on the telephone; in a single day, May Pang once counted twenty-three calls, some running into hours. Via the "Karmic Messenger Service" of Elliot Mintz (in Mintz's own dry phrase) John continued to make clear how desperately he wanted to return, but the answer that always came back from Yoko was "He isn't ready yet."

On trips back to New York, he would often call at the Dakota but, she recalls, was always "too proud" to ask if he could stay. (Aunt Mimi could have cited a similar situation fifteen years earlier, after he had tired of his student flat and wanted her steak-and-kidney pie and his old bedroom at Mendips.) Forgetting his wish that Yoko remain sexually active, both to share the guilt and as a medical safeguard, he became more possessive than ever. Once when she was in Philadelphia, he returned to their apartment, found a new vase in her bedroom, and, assuming it was a gift from another man, smashed it to pieces, then disappeared again. Yoko's first act on returning home was to change all the locks.

Meanwhile, crisis had hit *Oldies and Mouldies*, the rock-'n'-roll covers album that John expected to be so relaxing. Having shown up at the studio in the varied guises of karate champion, surgeon, and trigger-happy cowboy, Phil Spector suddenly ceased showing up at all. He gave no explanation for his absence nor indication of when or if he intended to reappear. Telephone calls by the dozen were made to his office and his barbed-wire-encircled mansion near Sunset— many of them by John personally—but none was ever returned. On the musicians' grapevine, it was rumored that Spector had left the city, possibly even the country, or had suffered a horrendous accident and was lying somewhere in intensive care or maybe even dead. After two or three weeks of fruitless inquiry, John decided to take over producing the album himself, as he had done successfully with *Mind Games*, and called for the tapes of the sessions, which had been chaotically going on since the previous October. It then emerged that Spector had been in the habit of taking them home with him every night, and still had them. Short of starting again from scratch, nothing could be done until he chose to resume work or could be persuaded to hand the tapes over.

One dangerous accomplice had no sooner thus stepped out of John's life than another stepped in. He and May were currently staying at the Beverly Wilshire Hotel, in a duplex apartment that Ringo maintained there. Three fellow musicians were sharing the accommodation: Klaus Voormann, Keith Moon, and Harry Nilsson.

Nilsson—known professionally by surname only—was one of the more oddball characters in early-seventies pop. A New York–born singer-songwriter, he combined outstanding melodic and verbal talent with a voice whose operatic high register was matched only by Art Garfunkel's. Yet ironically, his two most successful singles, "Ev'rybody's Talkin'" (theme-song of the film *Midnight Cowboy*) and "Without You," had been written by other people, and the singer-songwriter wave seemed to have left him high, although not dry. Once beautiful and sylphlike, he was now paunchy, bearded, and apparently resigned to being (in Elliot Mintz's phrase) "the Orson Welles of rock 'n' roll."

He was already a crony of Ringo's and (like all three other ex-Beatles) had contributed to the hugely successful *Ringo* solo album. In the frat-house atmosphere of the Beverly Wilshire apartment, he and John now became inseparable. He was not only wildly funny but a brilliant mimic who could "do" John to the life—a novelty that John adored. And no one was better equipped to help lose a weekend, if not a lifetime. "The difference between the two was that Harry loved to drink and was good at it," Mintz remembers. "He could down triple Courvoisiers all night without any problem. John also loved to drink, but was no good at it. At the beginning of an evening with the two of them, the conversation would be brilliant, like being at Dorothy Parker's Round Table. Then suddenly it would flip, and the insanity would start."

On the evening of March 12, the two went to watch the Smothers Brothers begin a "comeback" engagement at the Troubadour. It was a glitzy occasion, attended by Hollywood royalty like Paul Newman, Joanne Woodward, and Peter Lawford. John that night had discovered Brandy Alexander—Cognac shaken with milk, ice cubes, crème de cacao, and nutmeg to taste as harmlessly refreshing as a milk shake. During the after-midnight wait for the curtain to rise, he began singing "I Can't Stand the Rain," the theme song of his recent Kotex fashion statement, in which Nilsson raucously joined. It so happened that, of the two Smothers Brothers, John liked Tommy but had never been able to stand Dickie—and in any case, understandably, was violently opposed to comebacks of any kind. When the brothers appeared, Dickie Smothers received a torrent of heckling from John. Their manager came over and began to remonstrate angrily; security people were called, John overturned a table, and he, Nilsson—and the blameless May—were ejected.

The fracas continued outside, with cameras unfortunately present. John grappled with a parking-lot attendant and wrestled him to the ground, then received such a look of hero worship from his supine victim that all his anger evaporated. Two other bystanders afterward claimed he had assaulted them—a club waitress and a photographer named Brenda Parkins. When Parkins brought charges, John settled out of court to avoid jeopardizing his immigration case, but maintained he'd never touched her—and anyway she hadn't been a bona fide press representative, just a pushy fan with "an Instamatic."

"OK, so I was drunk," he admitted later. "When it's Errol Flynn, all those showbiz writers say, 'Those were the days when we had Sinatra and Errol Flynn, socking it to the people.' I do it, I'm a bum . . . I was drunk in Liverpool and I smashed up phone boxes, but it didn't get in the papers. . . ." Next day, he and Nilsson sent flowers and a note of apology to the Smothers Brothers, who issued a diplomatic statement that "it was partly our fault." That night, a sober and penitent John was seen with May at an American Film Institute tribute dinner to James Cagney, prompting the first press reports of a "new girl in his life."

The ménage using Ringo's apartment at the Beverly Wilshire had by now worn out its welcome. Keith Moon was a past master in the seventies rock-star art of trashing hotels, and John (who seldom damaged so much as an ashtray in Beatle-touring days) was quick to emulate "Baron von Moon" as he admiringly dubbed him. Co-incidentally, the next-door suite was occupied by an old Swinging London crony, Jonathan King. One day when King used the elevator to the penthouse floor, he saw FUCK YOU scratched on its wood paneling in unmistakable Lennon capitals.

After several run-ins with the hotel management, the party moved to a large and well-secluded beach house in Santa Monica, where they were joined by Ringo, his new manager, Hilary Gerrard, and Klaus Voormann's girlfriend, Cynthia Webb. The house had once been used for Bobby Kennedy's assignations with Marilyn Monroe, and John and May were quartered in the very bedroom they were reputed to have shared. Here, mainly at the instigation of Baron von Moon, domestic life took on the semblance of a modern, multimil-lionaires' *Goon Show*. Every morning, for instance, Moon would live up to his name by appearing naked but for an ankle-length leather coat, split up the rear to show his bare bottom, a trailing white scarf, and ankle boots.

There still was no sign of Phil Spector and the *Oldies and Mouldies* tapes, so, rather than just sit around and wait, John decided to pro-duce an album for Harry Nilsson. This was to be entitled *Pussycats* and feature an eclectic song mix, from Bill Haley's "Rock Around the Clock" to Bob Dylan's "Subterranean Homesick Blues." Work began at Burbank Studios on March 28; John brought in session men like Jim Keltner from his own album lineup and even wrote Nilsson a track entitled "Mucho Mungo." "He was determined he was going to give Harry the breakthrough that no one else ever really had," Elliot Mintz says. "When he spoke about him it was almost in the vernacular of a manager."

During the first week of recording, Paul and Linda McCartney happened to be in L.A., and dropped by the studio to say what they expected would be only a brief hello. Paul by this time was finally enjoying solo success at the same level as John's; his wife-augmented band, Wings, had won credibility with the album *Band on the Run*, and he had written the theme song to a James Bond film, *Live and Let Die*, which was nominated for both an Oscar and a Grammy. Despite the thousands of miles between them, both geographically and spiritually, the old Lennon-McCartney symbiosis still occasionally revived. Paul, too, had been in hot water over a song about the Ulster Troubles, entitled "Give Ireland Back to the Irish," had been busted (twice) for cannabis possession, and was now having problems over U.S. visas.

The business disputes that had driven such a wedge between John and him were all now as good as settled. The Beatles partnership was on course for final dissolution in London's High Court in December. Both had ended their yoked-together contract with ATV/ Northern Songs in 1973, and were free to market their work through their own publishing companies. Most important, John admitted that if he'd followed Paul's advice in 1969, he, George, and Ringo would not now be battling Allen Klein in the U.S. civil courts with something like $19 million at stake. Consequently, when Paul visited one of John's sessions for *Pussycats*, the old partners greeted each other as if they'd never had a cross word. Within minutes, they had picked up guitars—left-handed and right-handed—and were jamming together on "Midnight Special," an old blues favorite from earliest Quarrymen days.

The following Sunday, March 31, John invited Paul and Linda to an all-day party at the Santa Monica beach house. Many other notable musicians were present, including Stevie Wonder, and another jam session soon started, with John on guitar and Paul on the absent Ringo's drums. In a medley of old favorites, from Little Richard's "Lucille" to Ben E. King's "Stand by Me," a matchless sour-sweet harmony took its final bow. "There were about 50 people playing," John would remember, "and they were just watching me and Paul."

Elliot Mintz believes he witnessed the end of the Lost Weekend, or at least the beginning of the end. One morning when he and John were having breakfast after an all-night studio session, a beautiful woman wearing an array of expensive bracelets stopped at their table and handed John a napkin with a telephone number written on it. "I don't want to disturb you," she murmured. "I just want you to have this. Use it when you're ready." Next day when Mintz arrived to collect John—it was during one of various breakups with May—he glimpsed the woman in the background, still with her conspicuous bracelets but otherwise wearing only a robe. John took him aside and asked him to get rid of her as quickly and discreetly as possible.

"Some people have bachelor parties; John had the Lost Weekend," Mintz says. "For him, it was the end of innocence and the start of growing up and being serious. And I think on that particular morning, he recognised the obvious. . . . He could spend a lifetime collecting phone numbers scribbled on pieces of paper. At age thirty-four, he knew that's how it might be forever. There would be a thousand amorous women in terry-cloth robes waiting around in the morning while he assigned someone or other the task of getting rid of her."

For John himself, the turning point was producing *Pussycats* for Nilsson, which by now had grown almost as much of a shambles as *Oldies and Mouldies*, with three different drummers (Ringo, Keith Moon, and Jim Keltner), a huge brass section, and a children's choir. The sessions had no sooner gotten under way than Nilsson's extraordinary, keening voice began to fail. "Harry told me he'd woken up on a beach somewhere after a night out with John," Keltner remembers. "They'd both been doing a lot of screaming the night before, which John was really good at, and the next morning Harry found his voice was completely shot." Afraid the album might be canceled, he tried to hide the problem from John, hoping that medication would cure it. "I [didn't] know whether it was psychological or what," John recalled. "He was going to the doctors and having injections and he didn't tell me till later he was bleeding in the throat or I would have stopped the session. . . . I'm saying, 'Well, where is all that yooo-deee-dooo-daaah stuff?' and he's going 'croak' , . . That's when I realised . . . I was suddenly the straight one amid all these mad, mad people. I suddenly was not one of them."

Those stricken vocal cords provided just the out that John was seeking. In mid-April, he brought Nilsson back to New York and checked into the Pierre Hotel on Fifth Avenue, ostensibly to finish *Pussycats* away from the distractions of their L.A. chums. It also happened that Nilsson's record company, RCA, had tired of waiting for another hit like "Without You" and was threatening to drop him.

John went to see RCA's bosses, talked up the brilliance of *Pussycats*, and hinted at a preparedness to sign with the label—bringing Ringo along, too—if Nilsson's contract were extended. Mesmerized by the prospect of owning two ex-Beatles (which, of course, would never happen) the RCA men fell over themselves to agree.

There was another, more pressing reason to be back East. For months past, the hundred or so total strangers per day who felt entitled to greet John like an old friend had invariably asked one of two questions. The foremost—which even a young L.A. cop, called to investigate yet another fracas in Bel Air, could not help blurting out—was "Will the Beatles be getting back together?" But a close second, especially beloved of cabdrivers, was "How's your immigration going?" By now, his virtual criminalization in the land the Beatles had once entranced was causing anger and puzzlement all over the world. In Britain, the outrage on his behalf posed the biggest threat to Anglo-American relations since Vietnam. Radio Luxembourg (as British an institution as warm beer or rainy summers) demanded a Royal pardon for the drug conviction that had started all his visa troubles, and delivered a petition with sixty thousand listeners' signatures to the prime minister, James Callaghan.

John's lawyer, Leon Wildes, had naturally been concerned about the bad publicity emanating from the West Coast (little dreaming how much more had been avoided). As a first step back to regaining his former moral high ground, Wildes counseled further involvement in charity events like the One to One Concert to benefit Willowbrook. So on April 28, John did a walk-on with Nilsson at a March of Dimes benefit concert in Central Park; for two days in mid-May, he broadcast as a disc jockey for station WFIL in Philadelphia during its "Helping Hand" marathon. All in vain, seemingly. On July 17, he heard from the Justice Department's Board of Immigration Appeals that his appeal against the previous October's deportation order had been rejected, and he had sixty days to leave the country.

But Wildes was proving a formidable adversary to powers that had always hitherto seemed faceless and invincible. His first major breakthrough was successfully taking the Immigration and Naturalization Service to New York's District Court over its calculated refusal to deal with John and Yoko's application for third-preference visa status. Diligent sifting of Yoko's personal papers revealed that she had actually been issued a green card, allowing her full U.S. residency, while married to Tony Cox. Though this had lapsed some years earlier, Wildes speedily established her status as a person of special creative merit, supported by testimonials from leading figures in the art world—and the fact that she had no drug conviction. The lawyer then used her case to strengthen John's, pleading that she needed his support in the continuing America-wide search for Kyoko and that kicking him out of the country would force her to make an unconscionable choice between her daughter and her husband.

Having proved the INS not invulnerable, Wildes launched two further actions against it in the district court. The first invoked the Freedom of Information Act to unearth files revealing that aliens with far worse drug records than John's were being allowed to live in the United States and that, in effect, a "secret law" discriminated between individuals the government did and did not like. The second action sued everyone in the anti-Lennon campaign's chain of command for "abuse of process" and violating John's constitutional rights, and demanded their personal appearance in court to explain themselves. Wildes began by subpoenaing New York's district director of immigration and his superior, the immigration commissioner in Washington, D.C., but he intended to move up the ladder to the attorney general in the relevant period, John Mitchell. Though he did not really believe it could happen, Wildes talked of bringing President Richard Nixon himself into court.

Before this extraordinary event could be mooted, however, the president simplified matters by committing hara-kiri. On the night of June 17, 1972, at the start of the presidential campaign—when the surveillance and wiretapping of John were at their height—five Republican party workers had been caught in the National Democratic Committee offices in Washington's Watergate Hotel complex, attempting to service bugging devices that had been planted there earlier. The burglars proved to work directly for CREEP, then headed by Attorney General Mitchell. Nixon could have escaped serious consequences by taking full responsibility and apologizing, but instead he and his senior officials consistently denied any involvement despite mounting evidence to the contrary. Two years later, the affair known simply as Watergate had turned into the political scandal of the century, with the president increasingly beleaguered and a special Senate committee conducting daily public investigations.

One of John and Yoko's last pre-separation outings together was to attend the Watergate hearings, accompanied by Jon Hendricks. Under interrogation that day, as it happened, was John Dean, the former White House counsel whose revelation of a secret taping system in the Oval Office destroyed all Nixon's claims that he knew nothing of his minions' grubby doings. "The metaphor was not lost on John and Yoko," Hendricks says. "Their accusers were now the accused."

One by one, all Nixon's top aides were discredited and disgraced, including John Mitchell, before Leon Wildes could subpoena him, and H. R. Haldeman, who had directly overseen the FBI's investigation of John. Finally on August 9, 1974, Nixon himself resigned in the nick of time to avoid impeachment. This was also the month when John's immigration case moved from INS jurisdiction to its last resort, the U.S. Court of Appeals. He testified that he had been marked for deportation because the Nixon government considered him a political threat, not because of a minor UK drug offense, and that he and Yoko had been almost a test bed for the dirty White House tricks exposed by Watergate. For the first time in their three-year uphill struggle, Wildes was conscious of sympathetic ears.

John had left the Pierre by now and was living with May in a small penthouse apartment on East Fifty-second Street, overlooking the East River. Among his neighbors in the block was Greta Garbo, the great screen siren of the prewar era, now the world's most celebrated recluse, next to Howard Hughes. John's apartment had a terrace from which, late one summer night, he swore he watched a UFO fly downriver and turn left over Brooklyn. He later described it in detail to a French journalist who interviewed him there, adding the corroborative testimony of his "girlfriend." "I hadn't been drinking—this is the God's honest truth. I only do that at weekends or when I see Harry Nilsson."

East Fifty-second Street was the nearest he would come to an alternative home in the whole Lost Weekend. Visitors included Paul and Linda McCartney and Mick Jagger, who was now living with his wife, Bianca, in Andy Warhol's house in Montauk, Long Island. In July, Julian arrived for a visit, his mother feeling confident enough now to let him stay with his father. Their new rapport continued to grow, the more so as Julian was showing signs of musical talent and had recently started guitar lessons. John showed him chords (shades of Julia!), gave him a drum machine, and, spurred by May, took trouble to make his stay enjoyable. But having an eleven-year-old in the small apartment was sometimes jarring to a man so unused to children. One morning Julian received the full lash of his tongue and fled in confusion for accidentally waking him too early after a heavy night.

Two months before Richard Nixon quit the White House came the end of another long-running war of nerves. In a transaction as furtively melodramatic as any in the Watergate saga, Phil Spector finally handed over the tapes of John's *Oldies and Mouldies* album sessions to a senior Capitol Records executive in exchange for $90,000. But John was in no mood to return to a project recalling the most lost of his months in L.A. The tapes as they stood, recorded amid drunken partying, celebrity intrusion, and gunfire, were nowhere near releasable standard. Besides, during his stay at the Pierre, he had begun writing material for a new album whose title, *Walls and Bridges*, suggested relief to be back in the river-girt citadel of Manhattan.

Made at the Record Plant Studios in July, it featured most of the same musicians he had worked with in L.A., but now under strict orders that there was to be no more drinking or carousing. Most of the tracks had an upbeat, brassy feel, strangely at odds with John's recurrent, often desperate admissions of longing for Yoko: "You don't know what you got until you lose it . . . Oh, baby give me one more chance" . . . "Bless you, wherever you are" . . . "I'm scared . . . I'm scarred." Every chord sequence seemed to awaken echoes of their previous work together; at one trompe l'oreille moment at the start of the third track, "Old Dirt Road," a distorted guitar produced an eerie semblance of Yoko's singing voice. She was there in spirit, almost deafeningly, in "Number 9 Dream," a hymn to the mystic numeral in John's life, suffused with the beatific happiness one can sometimes feel when asleep. He had, in fact, dreamed its falsetto chorus of "Ah bowakawa pousse pousse," though the "heat-whispered trees" in its first verse sprang from poetic senses wide awake. The voice calling "John" that sounded so Yoko was May, being a dutiful stand-in yet again.

"Steel and Glass," a track strongly reminiscent of "How Do You Sleep?" was taken to be a swipe at Allen Klein ("You leave your smell like an alley cat. . . ."). The only reminder of *Oldies and Mouldies*— and John's legal obligation to record a quota from Morris Levy's catalog—was a brief rendition of Lee Dorsey's "Ya-Ya," with no backing other than Julian on drums. "Nobody Loves You When You're Down and Out" was a wry reflection on his recent West Coast bender, containing another horrible moment of prophecy: "Everybody loves you when you're six foot in the ground."

A sax-driven party song, "Whatever Gets You Thru the Night," had backup vocals by Elton John, proving he could "do" John just as well as Harry Nilsson. In the fade-out, John called "Can you 'ear me, Mother?" which no American and only about one in ten thousand Britons would recognize as the catchphrase of an old music-hall star, Sandy Powell. When the track was picked for release as a single, Elton asked John to break a two-year abstinence from live performance by appearing onstage with him if it reached number one. John shook on the deal, but only because he thought such a simplistic rocker, sung in the unorthodox form of a two-man duet, could not be a hit "in a million years."

As a further mark of homage, Elton decided to cover "Lucy in the Sky with Diamonds"—a song till then regarded as unsingable by anyone but its author—and put it out as a British single, implicitly to keep John's memory alive back home. John went with May to the recording session, which was at Caribou Studios, nine thousand feet up in the Colorado Rocky Mountains. He loved Elton's reggae-influenced "Lucy" so much that he joined the studio band, credited as "the Reggae Guitars of Dr. Winston O'Boogie." As a memento of their partnership, Elton gave him an onyx pendant with a wall outlined in gold, a bridge in platinum, and WINSTON O'BOOGIE spelled out in diamonds. "I think he was a little fazed at being given jewellery by another man," Sharon Lawrence says. "And he didn't realise how extravagant Elton was. I remember him showing me the pendant and saying, 'It's diamante, isn't it?'"

Despite his apparent domestication by May, he continued to see other women, by no means all nameless one-night stands. "That fall of '74 there was one particular girl, who was an art director on a magazine," Bob Gruen remembers. "I was with John one night when he was in a phone booth calling her up and asking if he could come over and she was rightly telling him he was too drunk. I was nervous because he was making a lot of noise and I didn't want there to be any trouble with the police. He was ready not to be with May, he didn't want to live with her basically, but she was the one who ran his life, made all his arrangements. As he told me, 'I don't know how to get rid of her 'cause she's my phone-book.'"

He maintained constant contact with Yoko by telephone or surreptitious notes delivered via their mutual assistant, Jon Hendricks, and would regularly slip away to visit her at the Dakota, even though she continued to say he was "not ready" to come back permanently. "It used to be very nice," she remembers. "John would say all sorts of funny things about the girl he met the night before and how it didn't go well, I was telling him what happened to me because both of us had very bad times dating-wise, and we'd be laughing like crazy. I thought, 'This is great. We're just going to be great friends.'"

Now that they were on the same side of the continent once again, his jealousy and possessiveness receded; he had no objection to her seeing David Spinozza and even urged her to find several sexual partners as a precaution against cancer. "One day when he came here, he started that again, 'Have sex, have sex . . .'" Yoko remembers. "I told him I didn't know how to go about it. 'Just say do you wanna fuck,' John told me. He knew I could never do anything like that, but I realized he was saying he didn't want me to come on to another person romantically. He kept saying that women didn't know the difference between pure sex and romance, and that's why they weren't really emancipated. He said I could even go to Italy or somewhere and find a young gigolo, because many ladies do that.

"So finally I made a call to one person—a musician, because John had said, 'He'd be the type that you like.' But he sounded so high that I just hung up. Other people John suggested I didn't like because they were such heavy meat-eaters. John said, 'Oh, Yoko—if you're so particular, you're never going to find anybody.'"

The final months of the Lost Weekend found him working harder than at any time since he was a Beatle. Predictably, Morris Levy was not satisfied by having just one brief, botched-up track on *Walls and Bridges* and demanded that John give him the full pound of royalty-generating flesh specified by their legal agreement. There was thus no alternative but to round up Jim Keltner, Klaus Voormann, Jesse Ed Davis, and the others and begin the *Oldies and Mouldies* album again from scratch. To help keep the band sober and on track, rehearsals took place at a farm owned by Levy in upstate New York. Each day, John and his musicians would eat lunch around a big kitchen table while the Octopus entertained them with stories of other bands he had exploited or intimidated over the decades. "He told it so amusingly," Keltner says, "you just had to laugh."

While making *Walls and Bridges*, John had somehow found time to write and demo what would be the title track of Ringo's next album, *Goodnight Vienna*. In October, he returned to the Record Plant and began recording rock-'n'-roll standards like "Rip It Up," "Stand by Me," "Ready Teddy," "Slippin' and Slidin'," and "Peggy Sue" in a new spirit of concentration and respect. He did radio promotion for Ringo and further brushed up his public profile with disc-jockeying stints for KHJ-AM, Los Angeles, and WNEW-FM, New York (where one commercial he had to read out was for a nightclub ambiguously named the Joint in the Woods). On November 18, to his utter amazement, "Whatever Gets You Thru the Night," his single with Elton John, reached number one in the United States, closely followed on the album chart by *Walls and Bridges*.

He had promised to join Elton onstage if this should happen and, as Elton jovially made clear, there was to be no wriggling out of it. Two years ago, with Yoko and the Plastic Ono Band at his side, he could have walked into any arena with anyone. But the months adrift had sapped his never robust self-confidence, and the prospect of facing a new, young, glam-rock audience, never mind competing with such a mythic showman and extrovert, was terrifying.

Reluctantly, he agreed, or half-agreed, to keep his word at the final show of Elton's current U.S. tour, which was to be at Madison Square Garden on Thanksgiving night, November 28, 1974. In an attempt to prepare himself, he went to Boston a few days earlier to see Elton play the Garden, and almost gave up the idea there and then. Watching his co-duettist don the various guises of a cosmic pantomime dame, a Las Vegas chorus girl, and a camp Mad Hatter, all he could think was "Thank God it isn't me." And the audience reaction brought on weird déjà vu. "It was like Beatlemania," he would recall. "I was thinking 'What is this?' 'cos I hadn't heard it since the Beatles. I looked round and saw someone else playing the guitar."

On Thanksgiving Eve in New York, he joined Elton for a rehearsal that ended up lasting barely an hour and a half. Elton wanted him to sing "Imagine," but John didn't want to "come on like Dean Martin, doing my classic hits. I wanted to have some fun and play some rock 'n' roll, and I didn't want to do more than three because it was Elton's show after all." They agreed on "Whatever Gets You Thru the Night" and "Lucy," and, as a second choice from the Lennon-McCartney songbook, Elton suggested "I Saw Her Standing There," from the Beatles' very first album. This appealed to John for its antiquity and because its lead vocal always used to be sung by Paul.

There had been no official announcement of his appearance, but rumors were rife, the show was sold out, and Elton's right-hand man, Tony King, was besieged by illustrious claimants for the VIP front rows. One of the first calls King received was from Yoko: she requested seats for herself and David Spinozza, stipulating they should be near the stage, but out of John's direct sight line. And no one must let him know she intended to be there.

At the last moment, he almost chickened out, but old Beatle campaign reflexes triumphed, and he reported to the Garden's backstage area on schedule in a plain black suit, looking as if he were about to mount the scaffold. During the countdown to showtime, a messenger arrived with two boxes, one for him and one for Elton. Each contained a white gardenia from Yoko. She had taken care to choose identical blooms and express no favoritism in the accompanying cards, both of which read "Best of luck and all my love." Her instructions had been obeyed; John had no idea she was in the audience. "Thank goodness Yoko's not here," he said at one point. "Otherwise I know I'd never be able to go out there."

He was scheduled to appear about two thirds into the show, which meant hanging around for something like an hour and a half, listening to Elton's audience being ratcheted higher and higher. Stage fright struck in the usual place, and he had to rush to the men's room to throw up. In his agitation, he even forgot how to tune his guitar and had to ask Davey Johnstone from Elton's band to do it for him.

The audience was kept on tenterhooks until well into the second hour, when Elton suddenly sat back from his piano. "Seeing as it's Thanksgiving," he said casually, "we thought we'd make tonight a little bit of a joyous occasion by inviting someone up with us onto the stage." Waiting in the wings with Elton's lyricist, Bernie Taupin, John very nearly lost his nerve again. "He said, 'I'm not going on unless you go on with me,'" Taupin remembers. "So I just went forward a little way with him, then he sort of hugged me and I said, 'You're on your own.'"

As John walked onstage, the house lights went up and eighteen thousand people rose to their feet with a roar and thunderous stamping that shook even that applause-hardened edifice to its core. "The audience gave him a terrific reception," Yoko remembers. "But when he bowed, it was too quickly and too many times. And suddenly I thought, 'He looks so lonely up there.'"

To the audience, he seemed back in his element, lead-vocaling the surprise party hit that still had a sting in its tail (". . . don't need a gun to blow your mind . . ."), then, on reggae rhythm guitar, helping Elton put Lucy in the Ska with Diamonds. There was a whisper of Royal Variety Show mischief when he announced "a number [by] an old estranged fiancé of mine called Paul"—no one yet knowing the estranged fiancés were long reconciled. By the time the John-John partnership had done with "I Saw Her Standing There," Madison

Square Garden was beside itself. "Everyone around me was crying," remembers Margo Stevens, one of the large British contingent flown in especially for the occasion. "John was hugging Elton, and Elton seemed to be crying, too." It was a measure of Elton's generosity that he let the pandemonium go on and on, despite facing the uphill task of restarting his own set and continuing for another forty minutes. John would never make another stage appearance, but in this final one he never felt more loved.

Afterward Yoko came backstage and they sat for a long time, catching up and holding hands, while their respective escorts, May and David, hovered uneasily in the background. A passing photographer snapped them together, as lost in each other as two virgins on a first date.

28

BEAUTIFUL BOY

*This is Dr. Winston O'Boogie saying
goodnight from Record Plant East.*

t wasn't quite that straightforward. "Backstage at the Elton show
John was like he wanted to eat me up or something," Yoko remembers. "But I said, 'Oh, ple-ease don't start this again.' I really
didn't want to come back together so much because I thought
it would be the same thing all over again . . . the entourage . . .
people being so jealous, whispering to him . . . and the whole
world hating me. And also I lost my artistic credit. I couldn't make
anything without people attacking it. My career was killed and my
dignity as a person was totally gone.

"And do I want to go back to that because I love that guy? And
he's lost credit too, because people are saying he's crazy. I was thinking it's like a doomed love affair that could kill both of us. I thought
we could be friends, though that never happened with either of my
other ex-husbands. I thought, 'We're artists, we can just work together,' that's how naive I was."

John had already been begging for months to move back into

the Dakota, using every possible emotional lever. Yoko almost succumbed when he came over to the apartment from Fifty-second
Street and played "Bless You," the *Walls and Bridges* track most pointedly addressed to her. Almost but not quite. "It was such a beautiful
song. I cried, John cried and we hugged each other. I had to be so
strong-willed about it. I said 'Go,' he said 'Okay' and didn't try to
fight it."

Another pretext for a visit was that Yoko had managed to give up
smoking and he wanted to use the same method. Again she tried to
keep it friendly and businesslike, making him inhale Gitane after
Gitane until the ashtray overflowed with acrid butts and he was
almost nauseous. "We were in our bedroom and John said, 'So I
really burnt the bridge, right? You won't let me come back.' And it
was said in such a sad way that I said, 'Okay, you can come back.' I
was thinking to myself, 'What am I saying?' but I couldn't help it."

The reconciliation was made public when they appeared together
at the 1975 Grammy Awards ceremony, broadcast live from New
York. John presented one of the awards, bizarrely attired in a floppy
black beret, a velvet smock with ELVIS embroidered on it, a white
evening scarf, a dangling medallion inscribed DR. WINSTON O'BOOGIE,
and another white gardenia in his buttonhole. "Thank you, mother,
thank you . . ." he replied to the ovation from his music-industry
peers, including David Bowie, Paul Simon, Art Garfunkel, Andy
Williams, and Roberta Flack, as if that old music-hall comic Sandy
Powell had possessed him again. He himself did not figure in the
awards, though Paul McCartney and Wings won two (for Best Pop
Vocal Performance and Best Produced Non-Classical Recording),
and the Beatles received a special Hall of Fame citation. At the after-
awards party, Bob Gruen photographed him with Yoko in a state of
euphoria that made any official communiqué redundant.

During the Lost Weekend, he had kept a diary, faithfully recording every chaotic studio session, drunken binge, public humiliation,
and act of gratuitous vandalism. This he now showed to Yoko, then
burned in front of her as a symbol of his resolve to turn over a new
leaf. A further token was a formal renewal of their wedding vows in
a candlelit White Room at the Dakota, both of them dressed all in

white as they had been for the original quickie ceremony in Gibraltar, and surrounded by candles and banks of white carnations.

It was as if both had been born again. John came home with all the demons seemingly exorcized from his system—the drunkenness, the sexual ravenousness, the jealousy and possessiveness—everything but the insecurity and self-doubt that nothing and no one could change. Yoko, too, seemed different: less relentless in driving her own career forward, and more able, as John was, to enjoy the moment. Though they seemed to pick up where they had left off, there was now a deeper level of love—and liking—between them. "A lot of people when they separate get angry with each other," says Bob Gruen. "John and Yoko were never angry with each other, so when they reconciled they seemed better friends than before."

After Yoko's life-threatening miscarriages, they had given up hope of ever having a child together, despite being offered an unexpected ray of hope by their acupuncturist, Dr. Hong, in San Francisco three years earlier. "He told us, 'You're always together. If you separate for a while and then come together, you can have a baby,'" Yoko remembers. "We said, 'How dare you suggest that? We'll *never* separate. What are you talking about!' Then we did separate; when John came back we had great sex, and immediately I became pregnant."

At first, she was not sure she wanted to go through with it—or that John would—and was prepared to have an abortion. "I didn't want to trap him. I wanted him to be there because he wanted to be there. I said 'What do you want to do about it? It's up to you.' John said 'We're gonna have it, we're gonna have it. . . .' I wanted to make it up to him for all the suffering I had caused him because of the separation. He wanted the baby, so I was determined to have it."

Yoko was forty-two, an age then considered dangerously late for childbearing. With her history of miscarriages, the doctors advised that to be absolutely safe she ought to remain in bed throughout her pregnancy. From the moment he discovered her condition, John treated her with a tenderness and solicitude that would have astonished his first wife, Cynthia, waiting on her hand and foot, refusing to let her lift or carry the smallest weight. He accompanied her to all her medical consultations and prenatal classes—as yet by no means common practice for fathers-to-be—and made heroic efforts, yet again, to give up smoking. They decided on the natural childbirth method, without drugs or surgery, in which the fully sensate newborn is laid on its mother's abdomen for instant bonding to take place. John had no doubt that the baby would be a boy and, months too early, began scouting Manhattan babyware stores, wryly amused to discover one chic emporium called Lady Madonna, invoking the McCartney Beatles A-side of 1968. But after their previous heartbreaks, both Yoko and he were afraid to buy too much, for fear coming home from the hospital empty-handed again.

The Lost Weekend's musical legacy, his problematic rock-'n'-roll covers album, had appeared in February 1975. Even while trying to work his way back to Yoko, he had stayed focused on the finally reordered and rerecorded version, anxious to discharge his legal obligation to Morris Levy once and for all. To show that he and his band were not slipping back into old L.A. ways, he broke an iron rule and sent Levy several tracks in a rough mix. But, tired of waiting around for his royalty cut, the Octopus issued the unfinished tracks as an album on his own Adam VIII label, titling it *Roots: John Lennon Sings the Great Rock & Roll Hits*, jacketing it with a garish head shot from the *Let It Be* era and marketing it as a cheapo TV special offer. The result was a second round of litigation, with Levy suing John for defaulting on the judgment from their earlier court case and John countersuing for release of inferior product under his name without his authorization.

Bob Gruen attended the court hearing for John's action, taking a small camera in his pocket. When John was called to the witness stand, Gruen managed a couple of furtive shots without being seen. (Despite the strict illegality of this, the presiding judge later acquired a print and hung it proudly in his chambers.) "John had to explain why a rough-mix tape was not meant to be sold on the market, and he integrally described the difference between that and a final mix and how it was made," Gruen says. "He was incredibly clear and coherent and I remember thinking, if I was a musician this was the best description I could possibly have." Whereas Levy received damages of only $6,795 John was awarded more than $144,700 and succeeded in having the Adam VIII compilation withdrawn from sale.

Rush-released before too many TV viewers could send their money to Morris Levy, John's fully mixed album was entitled simply *Rock 'n' Roll*. Buyers who expected a straight nostalgia trip in the current mode were in for a surprise. Some of the tracks, like Buddy Holly's "Peggy Sue" and Gene Vincent's "Be-Bop-a-Lula," certainly were just as he used to play them with the Quarrymen and first-draft Beatles in Liverpool and Hamburg. Others, like Bobby Freeman's "Do You Wanna Dance?" and Larry Williams's "Bony Moronie," were slowed down almost beyond recognition; Chuck Berry's "Sweet Little Sixteen" seemed to have collided with the Coasters' "Little Egypt," while "You Can't Catch Me" sounded like the Beatles' *Come Together*—subtle payback for Levy's original complaint that John's lyric had plagiarized Berry's. The Ben E. King ballad "Stand by Me," destined for release as a single, had a faintly reggae feel, testifying to Elton John's influence, and an edge of passion—desperation even—missing from all the other safe old chestnuts.

The final track, Lloyd Price's "Just Because," wound up with a monologue in fruity faux-American tones: "Why, I must have been thirteen when that came out . . . or was it fourteen or twenty-two? I could have been twelve actually . . . This is Doctor Winston O'Boogie saying goodnight from Record Plant East, New York. We hope you had a swell time. Everyone here says hi. Good-bye." The cover was a black-and-white photograph of John taken during the Beatles' Hamburg days by their *exi* friend Jurgen Vollmer. In his leather jacket and Teddy Boy forelock, he leaned in a doorway while indistinct figures flashed by and a blur of red neon glowed overhead.

A major objective of the *Rock 'n' Roll* album was to reconnect with those many UK fans who, since 1971, had despaired of ever understanding him again. The promotional campaign included a long interview with BBC2's *Old Grey Whistle Test* program (for which he was partly recompensed in Chocolate Olivers, a luxurious British-made cookie as yet unavailable in New York). His interviewer, "Whispering" Bob Harris, asked if he planned a return to Britain once his immigration problems were sorted out. "Oh, you bet!" John replied.

"I've got family in England. I've got a child who has to keep coming over. Hello Julian! I've got my Auntie Mimi. Hello Mimi!" To maintain his profile back home, he even recorded a performance for a televised tribute to Lord Lew Grade, archetype of the hated "men in suits," whose ATV company had gobbled up Northern Songs in 1969.

The burning question for Whispering Bob and every other British interviewer, even after five years of new mega-achievers in the charts, was whether the Beatles might ever return. John's former fierce antipathy to the idea had by now softened to mere apathy. "If we got in the studio again and we thought we turned each other on again, then it would be worth it. . . . If we made a piece we thought was worthwhile, it goes out. But it's such pie in the sky, you know. I don't care either way. If someone wants to pull it together, I'll go along. I'm not in the mood to pull it together, that's for sure."

At this point he did not resemble a man contemplating retirement but, on the contrary, seemed to derive more pleasure and satisfaction from the music business than since his earliest Beatle days. In Los Angeles, he had chummed up with David Bowie, who now vied with Elton John as glam rock's premier attraction. Whereas Elton dealt in simple kitsch and pastiche, Bowie intrigued his public with elements of Brechtian theatre, classical mime, even antipop satire, through a comically hubristic alter ego named Ziggy Stardust. On the surface, his whey-faced, androgynous stage persona could not have been more different from the cheerily unpretentious super-icons of ten years earlier. Yet everything about even him—other than the question mark over his gender—was directly traceable back to the Beatles and, in particular, John.

Early in 1975, Bowie had come to New York to record an album called *Young Americans*, which was to include a cover version of "Across the Universe." John attended the session at Electric Lady Studios and, during a break, picked up a guitar and improvised a three-note riff around the single word "fame." The word and the riff gave Bowie his first number one single in America and helped launch the strutting, narcissistic disco style that would dominate record charts and pack dance clubs around the world for years to come. From rock-'n'-roll nostalgic, John found himself suddenly catapulted to the cutting edge.

Yoko had long since been granted third-preference visa status as an "alien of exceptional merit"—the final step to a green card. But even after the Immigration and Naturalization Service had been legally compelled to deal with John's application, it continued to prevaricate, suggesting that his solo musical career had less artistic merit than his Beatle one. He remained in the country on short extensions won by his lawyer, Leon Wildes, afraid even to take an internal flight in case the plane were diverted outside U.S. territory and he would not be allowed back in again. During the seemingly endless round of court appearances, he and Wildes once found themselves waiting in the same room as the INS lawyer. "I knew this guy, so I introduced John to him," Wildes remembers. "John took out a handkerchief, knelt down, rubbed his shoes with it, and said, 'Is there anything else I can do for you, Sir?'"

As Wildes had always hoped—and hoped ever more strongly as the country recovered its senses after the Nixon era—salvation came through the federal courts. Early in October, the Court of Appeals finally ruled on his main submission: that John's 1968 cannabis conviction in the United Kingdom had been unfair by American standards. The three-judge panel found in John's favor by two to one, and Judge Irving Kaufman remanded the case back to the immigration court. In legalese, the INS was recommended to use its "discretion"; in practice, it was told to cease all proceedings against John on the basis of an offense now proven to have been legally invalid.

Kaufman's twenty-four-page judgment said the court "did not take lightly Lennon's claim that he was the victim of a move to oust him on political grounds," and characterized the former "subversive" as something like a national hero. "If in our two hundred years of independence we have in some measure realized our ideals, it is in large part because we have always found a place for those committed to the spirit of liberty, and willing to help implement it. Lennon's four-year battle to remain in our country is testimony to his faith in the American dream." The verdict was leaked to Wildes a day ahead of its official publication, but John by then was hardly in a mood to savor the victory. Yoko had gone into labor, and he was with her at New York Hospital.

After all their plans for natural childbirth, the baby was born by cesarean section on October 9, John's thirty-fifth birthday. The delivery was difficult, and Yoko had to be given a blood transfusion while John waited in another room, racked by memories of previous miscarriages and badgered by insensitive hospital staff wanting to shake his hand or cadge an autograph. "Then I hear this crying. I'm paralysed, thinking, 'Maybe it's another one next door.' But it was ours. And I was jumping around and swearing at the top of my voice and kicking the wall with joy, shouting 'Fucking great!'"

It was a boy, weighing eight pounds ten ounces. "I just sat all night looking at him, saying, 'Wow! It's incredible,'" John would recall. "When [Yoko] woke up, I told her 'He's fine' and we cried." They could not give the baby his father's Christian name, since John's first son had been baptized John Julian; instead, they chose Sean, the Irish version of John, meaning "gift from God," and Taro, the traditional Japanese name for a firstborn.

The ordeal left Yoko desperately weak, and she was not thought ready to see Sean until he was three days old. However, John was with him virtually around the clock. Bob Gruen had a cousin on the maternity-ward staff, who later said he had never seen such an attentive new father. Concerns over mother and baby kept them in the hospital for much longer than normal. "When we finally left, John carried Sean through the long hallway of the hospital and got into the car," Yoko remembers. "He sat still, looking at the bundle in his arms and said 'Okay, Sean, we're going home.' And that was that."

His British family were notified of the great news, with an assurance that he'd bring the baby over to show them as soon as possible. All reacted with unreserved joy—except, alas, the one whose reaction mattered most to him. Aunt Mimi had never become reconciled to Yoko's nationality and the baby's Japanese middle name caused her dismay that it was not in her nature to hide. "Oh, John, don't *brand* him!" Mimi pleaded, cutting her nephew to the quick yet again.

John asked Elton John to be Sean's godfather, in recognition of the supportiveness and generosity that had helped bring about his reconciliation with Yoko. As she recalls, the invitation also had touch of Liverpool canniness. "John said that because Elton was gay, he wouldn't have any children of his own to leave his money to."

The only other Lennon album released in 1975 was *Shaved Fish*, a compilation of oldies, including "Cold Turkey," "Instant Karma," "Power to the People," "Happy Christmas (War Is Over)," "Give Peace a Chance," and "Imagine." In February 1976, John's contract with EMI/Capitol expired, and he made no move either to renew it or seek an alternative label.

"We decided—well, mainly John decided—that from here on, he was going to raise Sean and I was going to look after the business," says Yoko. "He had read somewhere that Paul had made $25 million. He said, 'We'll never have that kind of money; we haven't got any Daddy Eastman behind us, the way Paul has. I said, 'Okay, I'll try to make $25 million, but it's going to take me at least two years.' The deal was that we both stopped any kind of creative work. Neither of us was going to do any writing or recording and I wasn't going to do any art."

She says she was far from happy about leaving the parenting to John, in effect repeating what she had done with her daughter, Kyoko, and her ex-husband, Tony Cox. Had she been a more hands-on mother, she felt, Kyoko might not have disappeared from her life with such brutal finality. That thought was outweighed by the fear that if she formed too close a bond with the new baby, John's old obsessive jealousy and possessiveness would return. She wanted to ensure "Sean would be loved as a joyful addition to our family and not hated as a hindrance to our relationship as husband and wife. That's one of the reasons I agreed to take care of the business while John enjoyed his time with Sean."

The jokey farewell at the end of the *Rock 'n' Roll* album thus proved to have been for real, and gave John's career a pleasing symmetry. He was bowing out with the very same music—the very same song, "Be-Bop-a-Lula"—that he had played at Woolton fete that summer Saturday in 1957, when Paul McCartney walked into his life and the Beatles began.

Sean's birth seemed to dull, if never fully extinguish, the creative itch that had given him no peace since then: the unending cycle of next lyric, next chord sequence, next single, next album, next soaring hope and plummeting disappointment. He even canceled his subscription to *Billboard* magazine, indifferent now to who was in or out of the charts, what they had stolen from him, and what he might borrow from them. "He didn't want to know anything about what was happening in the business," Bob Gruen says. "If he ever had the radio on, it would be WPAT, the easy-listening station. He wasn't signed to anyone or contracted to anyone or trying to keep up with anyone or to surpass himself any more. He just dropped out."

Gone with the drugging and hell-raising were the adolescent selfishness, short attention span, and abhorrence of practicalities that the life of a rock star can legitimize forever. Though a nanny was employed for Sean, John always hovered nearby, ready to do anything needful, convinced that only he really knew how to do it properly. Even diaper changing, that grim horror of Julian's babyhood, was no problem this time around. Nature stepped in, closing his nostrils, making him breathe instinctively through his mouth, transforming what he expected to be disgust and resentment into tenderness and joy. Like many before him, he realized that the cure for a void in one's childhood is not to be looked after but to look after somebody else; that making a child's life secure makes one's own feel securer.

"The only part both of us found really hard was waking up in the middle of the night for feeds," Yoko remembers. "We couldn't handle it because neither of us was that way. So John said, 'Let's just drink Cognac to relax ourselves.' and that's what we did." He began playfully calling her "Mother," as if he were a northern workingman in hob-nailed boots and she a harridan in a hairnet, brewing tea on the kitchen range.

Getting Sean to sleep was his special responsibility. He would sit beside the cot and the dangling mobiles, stroking an acoustic guitar and softly singing some old Mersey folk air like "Liverpool Lou." When Bob Gruen called up one evening, John whispered down the line that he'd just got Sean off to bed. "I said, 'I was about to tell you about a rock-'n'-roll show, but it sounds like you're in a really nice place already,'" Gruen remembers. "People always say John gave up making music in this time, but really he didn't. He was singing lullabyes to his kid." When it was his turn to bottle-feed, he'd put on a rock-'n'-roll record and dance around with the baby in his arms, as he'd seen black nurses do on the maternity ward.

It wasn't just that he no longer went out drinking with his Lost Weekend cronies; rather than be tempted back into those bad old ways, he preferred not to see them at all. "There was a time when Keith Moon was in town—the third of the Musketeers with Harry Nilsson and John—and I had to let John know he was here," Gruen says. "The message I had to deliver was that Keith knew he was with the baby, and was all ready to come over and be quite polite and just have tea. John was like, 'I don't want to have tea with Keith Moon. If I see him at all, I want to get loaded and have a party!'"

Over the next two years, he was often to feel he had withdrawn only just in time from a world that could and, with increasing frequency did, cause "acute death." His old Black Power crony, Michael X, for instance, had come to a bad end in Trinidad, convicted of murder in 1972 and sentenced to hang. As a former colony, Trinidad still came under British law and acknowledged the Queen as sovereign. Via Jon Hendricks, John and Yoko organized a campaign to win clemency for Michael, which included a petition signed by the likes of Leonard Cohen and Angela Davis, two appeals to the Privy Council, the sovereign's legal advisory body, and a high-profile debate at Oxford University featuring the feminist Kate Millett. All in vain: under a death warrant personally signed by Elizabeth II, Michael was executed in Port of Spain's Royal Gaol in 1975.

The Lost Weekend never ended for Mal Evans, the former Beatles roadie, John's bodyguard-cum-nursemaid on so many wild West Coast nights. Still adrift in L.A., Mal had grown increasingly depressed and confused, and on January 4, 1976, he was shot dead at his girlfriend's apartment by police who later claimed he had waved an air rifle at them. Without consultation with his family back in Britain, he was cremated and his ashes were mailed to his widow, but got lost in the postal system and were never found. All that reached Lil Evans was a bill from his former landlord for cleaning the carpet stained with his blood.

On April 1, John's father, Freddie Lennon, died in Brighton General Hospital. Freddie's final years on the Sussex coast with his young wife, Pauline, had been happy and fulfilled. In 1973, their son, David, had been followed by a second boy, Robin. Pauline continued to be the breadwinner while Freddie looked after both children with the same surprising reserves of unselfishness and dedication John was to discover with Sean. After their last traumatic meeting at Tittenhurst Park in 1970, John had not contacted Freddie and Pauline, so was unaware that he now had a second half brother. In 1974, a British lawyer notified Freddie that he wanted to reestablish communication. But, terrified of inadvertently provoking him again, Freddie did not respond.

Seemingly unbridgeable though the gulf between them, Freddie never gave up hope of convincing John he had not walked out on him that day in 1946, thereby causing the wound that still bled into his music. This desire so far outweighed all fears of filial anger that in 1975 Freddie sat down to finish the autobiography he had been ordered to abort five years earlier. In a racy, readable style, touched by glimmers of his Bluecoat Boy education, he described his upbringing in the poor and humble but blade-straight Lennon clan John had barely known, his departure to sea, and all the wrong turns that came afterward. While never badmouthing John's mother—indeed, speaking of her with undiminished love and reverence—he set down the indisputable facts that Julia had been the one to stray and that he'd been ready to take her back and adopt her out-of-wedlock wartime baby, just as he'd later offered to forgive her affair with Bobby Dykins. Daddy, in short, was always more than willing to come home. Each chapter ended with a postscript addressed directly his son and remarking how, in early life at least, their situations had often been strangely similar.

CHAPTER 2

PS Dear John . . . Like yourself I too was fatherless, but of course the circumstances weren't quite as distressing as your own, which left you with a chip on your shoulder, and if I may say so, strangely enough gave you the impetus to rise above yourself to your present status.

CHAPTER 3

PS Dear John . . . The first time I heard your recording of 'Penny Lane', my thoughts immediately reverted to the Blue Coat Hospital, and of course Newcastle Road. I wondered whether some link from the past guided your pen, particularly when Mr Bioletti's barber's shop was mentioned, because he used to cut the hair of the boys in the Blue Coat.

CHAPTER 8

PS Dear John . . . Perhaps the reading of my light-hearted account of my marriage to your mother will bear comparison to the description in Hunter Davies's biography of your own first marriage. To think you took the plunge in the same Register Office twenty odd years later, following me across the road to the 'Big House' for a chicken dinner. But eventually we both found the right partner.

CHAPTER 20

PS Dear John . . . You will see that I preferred not to join the 'rat race', and I'm sure that had you not reached your present influential position in life through your talents, you too would reject the conventional 9 to 5 job in defiance of the establishment.

Even in the Beatle-mad Sixties, Freddie's life story had been of dubious commercial value; in the glam-rock mid-seventies, it did not even reach the first base of a literary agent. After a few crushing rejection letters, he gave up, put the manuscript in a drawer, and returned to being a prototype househusband. However, he made Pauline promise that if it had not been published when he died, she would make sure John received a copy.

Three months later, Freddie was diagnosed with terminal stomach cancer. By the time Pauline managed to get the news to John in New York, his father had already been admitted to Brighton General Hospital. John immediately put through a call to Freddie and also to the specialist who was treating him. Freddie by now was almost too weak to hold the receiver, but their brief conversation left him looking as if his "Little Pal" of that long-ago escape to Blackpool had miraculously returned. John gave him the telephone number at the Dakota, told him about his new grandson and promised a get-together once he was well again. Freddie mentioned his autobiography (as he also had to the surgeon treating him) and made John promise to read it; they chatted about music awhile, then signed off with a nonchalant Liverpudlian "See yer, la." Later that day, an enormous bouquet arrived at Freddie's bedside. "To Dad—Get well soon," read the accompanying card. "With much love from John, Yoko and Sean."

Freddie fell into a coma and died a few days afterward. As she had promised, Pauline sent a copy of the autobiography to New York, with the covering letter he had written months earlier:

Dear John

By the time you read this I will be dead, but I hope it will not be too late to fill the gaps in your knowledge of your old man which have caused you distress throughout your life.

. . . Since we last met on the occasion of your 30th birthday, I have been haunted by the image of you screaming for your Daddy and it is my sincere hope that when you have read this book you will no longer bear me any malice. Perhaps the revelations in my life story may bring you a clearer picture of how fate and circumstance control so much of our lives and therefore must be considered in our judgement of one another.

Until we meet again, some time, some place
Your Father
Freddie Lennon

But no reply came back from the Dakota. Pauline did not know whether the manuscript had reached John or been lost in the mail along with Big Mal's ashes.

On July 27, 1976, almost a year after his federal court victory, John applied formally for the green card that the Immigration and Naturalization Service had been left no grounds to deny him. Leon Wildes turned this pro forma immigration court hearing before Judge Ira Fieldsteel into a headline-grabbing parade of VIP charac-

ter witnesses. A letter read to the court from Episcopalian Bishop
Paul Moore called John "a gentleman of integrity"; Norman Mailer,
America's most celebrated writer, called him "a great artist." There
were tributes from the silent screen goddess Gloria Swanson, the
TV host Geraldo Rivera, and the musician John Cage, and others
from earlier hearings were recapped. Perhaps the pithiest came from
Thomas Hoving, director of the Metropolitan Museum, who as New
York Parks Commissioner had overseen the Beatles Shea Stadium
concert in 1965. "If he were a painting," Hoving said, "I'd hang him
in the Metropolitan Museum." Afterward, John faced the cameras
in the suit and tie he had become inured to, holding up the precious
permit, which actually was not green but blue. "It's been a long and
slow road, but I am not bitter," he said. Now I'm going home to crack
open a tea-bag and start looking at some travel catalogues."

Six months later, a statement from Apple announced that the tan-
gled legal dispute between the former Beatles and Allen Klein had finally been settled. Klein was to relinquish all managerial rights for a
one-time payment of just over $5 million, plus undisputed retention
of all previous commissions and expenses. Yoko had played a crucial
part in the two-year courtroom and boardroom marathon, and at its
conclusion even Klein was moved to praise her "tireless efforts and
Kissinger-like negotiating brilliance." John signed his portion of the
agreement at the Plaza Hotel, a fitting place for this final chapter in
Beatles history to end. Then, to show there were no hard feelings, he
and Yoko met Klein for dinner.

If one of the Beatles' former roadies had gone, the other was still
very much around in the capacity that had always been far more
than mere employee. Having weathered Klein's regime, Neil Aspinall now worked mainly with George Harrison, but his loyalty to
the other three, and their trust in him, remained as rock-solid as
ever. When the rift with Klein first became known, John called Neil
to the Dakota and, on George's and Ringo's behalf, asked him to
take over running Apple. The prospect was hardly alluring, with
Paul still suing the others, two different receivers now standing
guard over the company's finances, and the legal fight with Klein
gathering momentum. Neil was hung-over that day and, midway

through the conversation, had to excuse himself to go to "Albert," the guest bathroom, and throw up. "If I'd been asked to run Apple, I'd have thrown up as well," John remarked. Neil agreed, on condition that Paul, too, was happy with the idea; this assurance instantly given, he began work on the—to him—appropriate date of April Fools' Day, 1974.

He also received one of the apologies John was always scrupulous about giving, however long after the event. In 1969, when valuable executives as well as spongers at Apple seemed to be falling under the Klein axe, he had appealed to John to intervene, but been answered only by a telegram saying, "Don't bite the hand that feeds you." "After I took over Apple, John suddenly said one day, 'I'm sorry about the telegram,' " Neil remembered. "At first I had no idea what he was on about."

Apple might no longer trade from a Georgian house in London's Mayfair. But as time passed, and the Beatles' magic refused to dissipate, the company would grow far beyond anything they had ever imagined. So great was the volume of brilliant work they had left, and so ineradicable their effect on the pop psyche, they could be said never to have broken up at all—simply changed from a band into a brand.

John's used his new freedom to travel outside America by making a trip to Japan with Yoko and Sean that lasted almost the whole summer of 1977. In preparation, he took a six-week course of Japanese lessons at the Berlitz language school in Manhattan, clocking in conscientiously for eight hours each day and practicing vocabulary on Yoko every evening.

In Tokyo, she took him to see the Kudan house, ancestral home of her mother's Yasuda family, where she used to play in her little Western-style kilts and tam o'shanters. John insisted on throwing a party for her Ono relatives, which more than fifty people attended— all but a senior uncle who felt it more correct that they should come and visit him. A group photograph was taken with John in the center, rather like the ones at Quarry Bank High School he used to delight in subverting. But there now were no grimaces or horseplay. "He took a lot of trouble to look very dapper," Yoko says. He wore a dark suit, a tie, and a pink carnation. He wanted to show to my relatives that I married someone who was proper.'"

Sean was now an adorable two-year-old with enormous almond-shaped eyes and what could only be called a Beatle bob. Though he attended nursery school for some of the time, and a nanny was always on hand, John did many hours of footslogging with him around parks and Tokyo's Ueno Zoo, dealing with all the unpredictable mood swings and emergencies of the active toddler. Their reception was not unreservedly cordial, for many Japanese still regarded Yoko as a traitor both to her class and her sex. One taxi driver called her "a whore" and ordered them out of his vehicle.

After they had been away two months, their L.A. friend Elliot Mintz received a messenger-delivered first-class air ticket and an invitation—that is, a summons—to join them. The day before Mintz's departure, Elvis Presley was found dead of heart failure in the bathroom at Graceland, his Memphis mansion, aged only forty-two. Bloated by binge-eating and prescription drugs, handing out his sweat-soaked scarves to blue-rinsed matrons in Las Vegas, he had long been unrecognizable as the sublime young punk who had changed John's life twenty years earlier. John's reaction when Mintz telephoned with the news was, "Elvis died the day they put him in the Army." He asked Mintz to send two white gardenias to Graceland with a card saying, "love from John and Yoko." But already, every florist in the Memphis area had sold out.

Mintz joined the family party in Karuizawa, the small resort town seventy-five miles northwest of Tokyo where Yoko and her two siblings used to spend summer holidays, and where her mother, Isoko, still had a home. When Mintz arrived at their hotel, the Mampei, a note in his room informed him that John had taken a vow of silence. "When we met the next day, he spent about fifteen minutes explaining why he'd decided to take the vow of silence. Then he started asking me more questions about Elvis's death, so fortunately that was the end of it."

Kuruizawa was an almost foreigner-free resort where Yoko was occasionally recognized but John not at all, despite sometimes going around in a T-shirt lettered WORKING CLASS HERO. They spent several weeks there, following a healthy regimen of yoga, massage, meditation, and mineral baths, living mainly on fresh fish and homegrown vegetables, cleansing their systems of every impurity except the strong black coffee John could not do without. They did not use a limo but went around on bicycles, always led by Yoko with her long hair streaming behind her. In September, the party moved on to Kyoto, Japan's old imperial capital, to visit the most famous of its two thousand Buddhist temples and Shinto shrines and the palaces and gardens that mercifully had escaped wartime immolation. John was particularly impressed by a Japanese convent that, Yoko told him, had been one of the world's first shelters for battered women. "He took to Japanese culture quite naturally," Mintz remembers, "and seemed to derive a great deal of peace and reassurance from it."

Returning to Tokyo en route for home, they moved into the top-floor Presidential Suite at the grand luxe Hotel Okura. The suite had its own private elevator, opening into a lounge area so vast that John and Sean could play soccer in it. One evening when Mintz and John were there by themselves, the elevator doors opened and an elderly Japanese couple emerged, believing it to be some rooftop cocktail lounge. Not recognizing or even seeming to notice John, they settled themselves in chairs and waited to be offered drinks or food or for a cabaret to begin. With a wink at Mintz, John picked up a guitar and sang "Jealous Guy" softly to them. But they clearly had never heard the song, could not understand the English words, and expected better entertainment than this; in a few minutes, without acknowledging their serenader, they got up rather ill-temperedly and left.

During the time apart from John, Yoko had taken up Chinese astrology and numerology (initially, she admits, in hopes of finding a new sexual partner). Along with the subjects' astrological signs and the configuration of the planets, great importance is placed in the direction they are facing or moving at critical times. So powerful was this belief in Japan that travel agencies employ "direction masters" to work out their clients' most propitious routes. It now transpired that, although the signs were auspicious for Yoko to fly directly back from Tokyo to New York, the same did not apply to John and Mintz, and a more roundabout journey would have to be plotted for them. "We hung on at the Hotel Okura until John was starting to get stir-crazy while our direction master worked out our way back to the States," Mintz remembers. "At one point it even seemed like we'd have to go via South America."

Eventually their route was fixed as Tokyo–Hong Kong–Dubai–Frankfurt–New York. The twenty-six-hour flight was an arduous one, even in first-class, with four reserved seats between the two of them. On the journey, Mintz remembers, John was "melancholy, though not drunk," and talked at length about his childhood, his early sexual fantasies—and, of course, his mother—to the companion whose discretion was as absolute as a priest's in a confessional. The only stopover was in Frankfurt, where John, to his chagrin, was given a hotel room like a broom closet, while Mintz was allotted a comfortable suite—as he quipped, because the desk clerk mistook him for Paul McCartney. John did not see the humor, and insisted on trading places. All travel blues disappeared, however, when he arrived at JFK Airport and produced his green card, and the immigration officer said, "Welcome home, Mr. Lennon."

For Yoko, the joy of having Sean, and seeing John with him, was tempered by an ache that the family reunions in Japan aggravated afresh. She had not seen her daughter Kyoko since her ex-husband, Tony Cox, had disappeared with the girl after losing their last custody battle in Houston, Texas, four years earlier. The former adorable tot—facially a little like her new half brother—was now a teenager of fourteen. A crucial segment of her childhood had been taken from her mother, and legal guardian, yet notwithstanding John's wealth and instinted support, there seemed to be nothing that could be done. All appeals to Cox through the media to get back in touch had failed; all efforts by police and investigators to pick up his tracks after he left Houston had drawn a blank.

Cox's adventures during these years had once again been dictated by his involvement with alternative religions and gurus. Just before the 1973 custody hearing, he and his wife, Melinda, had undergone a religious conversion at a Dallas charismatic church. Kyoko also shared in the experience—mainly, she now says, because the church had generous facilities for children, and "I could be like a child for a change instead of always worrying about my parents. I *loved* going to Sunday School." After Cox's escape with her and Melinda, he approached members of other charismatic churches to hide them, but none would. Eventually, they found shelter with a cult named the Church of the Living Word, or the Walk, whose leader, John Robert Stevens, proclaimed himself "the returned Jesus." The Walk provided accommodation, subsistence, work for Cox and Melinda, and education for Kyoko at settlements in Iowa and Los Angeles. In return, Stevens made his disciples swear absolute obedience to him and forbade them any contact with their families or friends in the outside world.

Cox, Melinda, and Kyoko left the Walk in the mid-seventies, just before the malignity of cults and the megalomania of their leaders were revealed through events like the Jonestown Massacre. In late 1977, now living in Oregon and chronically hard up, Cox decided to yield to John and Yoko's pleas for contact. Fourteen-year-old Kyoko was not sure how she felt about the idea. Although she still missed her mother—and John—she had found a measure of security, thanks in large part to her stepmother, Melinda, and feared once again having to make "a Sophie's choice" between her parents. "Everything with my Dad always ended being messed-up," she remembers. "I couldn't bear the thought of things being messed-up again."

On November 10, Cox finally telephoned the Dakota from his Oregon hideaway as a prelude to a possible meeting. He kept a tape recorder running throughout the call, which was mostly taken up by John and himself, with interpolations from Kyoko in the background. Despite their long guerrilla war and John's chronic insecurity about Cox's influence over Yoko, the two men greet each other like blood brothers, agreeing how "fantastic" and "beautiful" it is to be in touch again, marveling that their old relationship could ever have broken down like this. At one point in their meandering chat, the subject of fathers comes up. Cox mentions that his has recently died of lung cancer, prompting John to talk about Freddie's death in Brighton nineteen months earlier. It transpires that Freddie's handwritten autobiography did reach him after all, and he has read and finally believed the explanation of why Daddy never came home. "It filled in a big hole in my life. I said, 'Oh, that's why he couldn't make it,' you know. Now I can understand a little bit."

Despite the warmth of this conversation, no meeting with Cox followed, and he made no further contact, fulfilling Kyoko's premonition that things would be messed up. She was not to see her mother again in John's lifetime.

A particular memory of the Japanese trip was to haunt Yoko in years to come. One day, leafing through a magazine, John happened on an old photograph of her maternal great-grandfather, Zenjiro Yasuda. Since the deal had always been that they talked only about his family, he knew nothing of the great Zenjiro, the Emperor's de facto banker, who enjoyed national fame at a pop-star level half a century before such things were dreamed of. Nor had Yoko herself ever put together the several ways in which Zenjiro's life paralleled John's—coming from the north of the country, being a musician and poet as well as a moneymaking phenomenon, having his portrait hung in homes and workplaces as an inspiration to others, always insisting on full partnership with his tiny but dynamic wife. Though Yoko did not learn this until much later, Zenjiro even had the same birthday as John. The only thing which, seemingly, marked him as from a different culture and more dangerous times was his fate at the hands of a young man professing to be his admirer.

John was fascinated by Zenjiro's photograph, which—especially since his conversion to Japanese clothes and manners—seemed to bear a more than passing likeness to himself. "That's me in a former life," he told Yoko.

"Don't say that," she replied. "He was assassinated."

29

HOMEBODY

I prefer it in mono.

According to legend, John spent the next three years as a virtual recluse walled up in the Gothic heights of the Dakota building, increasingly bereft of self-confidence or self-reliance and prone to weird fancies and delusions calculatedly fed to him by his wife. Like most legends, it has grains of truth, or half-truth. But overall, this vision of rock 'n' roll's answer to Howard Hughes is flatly contradicted by his real friends, as opposed to former employees with axes to grind.

"A recluse? Well, yes and no," Bob Gruen says. "The kind of recluse that can go to Bermuda or Long Island when he feels like it. Some people who stay at home are kinda pack-rats among their magazines. But John had a nice big expanse live in. He could take a half-a-block walk inside his home. There's a lot of places where the corner news stand is a shorter walk away than his kitchen was from his bedroom. It's true he sometimes didn't go out for days at a time, but that didn't mean he was cloistered like a hermit. If ever I called him up, he always asked me to stop by."

Elliot Mintz, his confidant and minder during the Lost Weekend, remained close to him and Yoko, and spent long hours with them at the Dakota. "There certainly were moments in those years when John wasn't exactly the life of the party," Mintz says. "He had his mood swings, as he always did, but for most of the time he was in good spirits. One certainly could never have called him a depressive. In general he seemed happy with the more modest, moderate way of life he'd chosen."

Much of the time he devoted to child care, determined to be there for Sean as his own father had not been for him—and as he had similarly neglected to be for his firstborn. Anyone who has looked after a child knows how totally it revolutionizes one's life and changes ones ideas of what is and is not important. Where once John had demanded novelty and diversion every other moment, his existence now became an unchanging cycle of mealtimes, bath-times, and bed-times—much like the routine his Aunt Mimi had once built around him—the days crowded, demanding, often joyful and triumphant, but with little or nothing to differentiate them once they had gone.

In other ways, he took care to make his regime the opposite of Mimi's. Remembering—still bitterly—how she used to raid his bed-room and throw away his drawings and writings, he treated every creative effort by Sean with the reverence due a Rembrandt. "Even if he makes a paint mark on a napkin, I keep it, I save it," visitors like Gruen and Mintz were told. "It's Sean. It's part of him." As the little boy learned to talk, he was initiated into John's world of comic voices and names, and recollections from the country named England they were going to visit together someday, though a certain epoch was never mentioned. One day while visiting a friend, Sean happened to see *Yellow Submarine* on TV. Afterward, he came running back into the apartment and shouted, "Daddy . . . were you a Beatle?"

At that time, the great fear on both John's and Yoko's minds was that Sean might be kidnapped. Despite the Dakota's stout defenses, it was not impregnable; now and then, an intruder managed to evade the copper-boxed sentry at the front gate, slip past the well-staffed internal reception desk, get into the right wood-paneled elevator, and reach the hallway outside apartment 72. However, late-seventies paparazzi were nowhere near as ruthless in hounding celebrities, and celebrities' children, as they would later become. No press pictures of Sean appeared until he was well into toddlerhood.

When it came time for the nanny to take over, John would retire into his and Yoko's bedroom overlooking the park and put on a bathrobe or Japanese kimono, content for "Mother" to wear the pants. In contrast with adjoining rooms, the décor here was simple, even spartan. The bed was a plain king-size mattress rigged between a pair of old wooden church pews. On the wall above the headboard pew hung a state-of-the-art "bodyless" electric guitar, a large number 9, and a dagger made from a Civil War–era kitchen knife intended, so he said, "to cut away the bad vibes . . . to cut away the past symbolically." Visitors were not allowed to come around to his side of the bed, a sacred area where he kept his writing and drawing materials, his Gitane packs and ashtray.

At the foot of the bed was a Sony giant-screen TV set that he'd seen in Japan and had specially imported long before they were available in New York. As always, this was left permanently on at low volume, the murmur of newscasts scarcely distinguishable from that of weather forecasts, game shows, movies, and soaps. With it was one of the new videotape players and a stock of tapes, mostly classic movies and comedy shows from England like *Monty Python's Flying Circus* and *Fawlty Towers*. (He often said he'd rather have been one of the Monty Python team than a Beatle.) The room was equipped with a five-button telephone console that never rang, only winked with soundless red lights as calls were directed elsewhere in the apartment. Half-watching, half-listening, reading, writing, doodling, he might have lost track of time altogether but for the changing treetops outside, from winter skeletons to frothy springtime pink and white, from summer's green to the blazing reds and russets of autumn.

Despite his pact with Yoko, and his duty to Sean, he had not cut himself off completely from music making, as he would one day claim. The apartment was full of expensive sound equipment, much of it not working properly, some not even unpacked from its cartons.

"John was always buying the latest high-tech stuff, but he never had the patience to follow the assembly manuals, and always had to call in a studio engineer to put it together for him," Elliott Mintz remembers. "Basically he didn't really like listening to stuff in stereo or quadraphonic, because they weren't what he'd grown up with. He used to wear a badge—as did Phil Spector—saying I PREFER IT IN MONO."

On the table beside his bed was a cheap cassette tape recorder on which he was always roughing out new songs, or revisiting old ones, with guitar or piano accompaniment, as well as extemporizing comedy routines or simply talking to himself in the thick northern accent of his childhood music-hall favorite Al Read. Dozens of Lennon compositions and performances were put on tape, some mere fragments, others fully formed, with all the power and charm of his greatest past. One told how he had been "saved by a TV preacher" after a black mood of depression that made him seriously contemplate jumping from his seventh-floor window. Another, entitled "Free As a Bird," might have been prompted by Central Park's grimy sparrows, possibly by memories of Liverpool's Liver Birds. Yet another was a loving recreation of Sam Cooke's "You Send Me."

In his retreat, he was not at all averse to being compared with Howard Hughes, particularly since the title of world's richest, most enigmatic recluse was currently up for grabs. Hughes had died in 1976, the cause of his resignation from the human race still unexplained, his fabulous wealth unable to save him from an end of awesome loneliness, squalor, and neglect. Elliot Mintz, who had studied his life extensively, lent John several books about him, and they often discussed the myriad Hughes phobias and obsessions—the terror of germs that made him wear Kleenex tissue boxes on his feet; his refusal to cut his hair or nails or to take any nourishment but sips of soup or ice cream; his fixation on a single film, Ice Station Zebra, which he would watch in his darkened, disinfected hotel suite on an endless loop.

But the analogy never really stood up. Whereas Hughes was terrified of human contact, John saw people and interacted with them every day. Whereas Hughes's mental processes were a mystery, John maintained a constant flow of correspondence with Aunt Mimi and his British family, and notes and memoranda to his staff. He also began to keep a journal again, in a series of leather-bound *New Yorker* desk diaries, recording his new quiet domestic life as scrupulously as he previously had his West Coast bachelor spree. Whereas Hughes lurked in eternal twilight, John was constantly out and about, both the city and the world. Though he failed to keep a promise to his cousin Liela to return to Britain in 1976, the green card continued to get plenty of exercise. In July 1978, he flew Yoko and Sean by private jet for a holiday on the Caribbean island of Grand Cayman. He made a second trip with them to Japan that August, and a third and—and final—one in the same month the following year.

Through his son, indeed, he was more connected to ordinary people and things than at any time since before the Beatles became famous. Several times a week, he took Sean swimming at the Y—the YMCA on West Sixty-sixth Street—preferring the cheery clamor of its pool to the many luxury hotel spas within easy reach. Rather than pay an instructor, he taught Sean to swim himself, making him totally confident in the water by the age of four. "John used to tell me, 'That's the one thing he'll always remember,'" Yoko says. "His Dad taught him to swim like a fish."

He was also often to be seen pushing Sean's buggy or arm in arm with Yoko in the meadows and dells of the great garden outside his door. After decades as a virtual no-go area, Central Park had been opened up by the new crazes for jogging, cycling, and skating, and John made full use of it. His thirty-eighth and thirty-ninth birthdays, and Sean's third and fourth, were celebrated by lavish parties at the parkside restaurant, Tavern on the Green, whose owner, Warner LeRoy, was his downstairs neighbor at the Dakota.

He became a familiar figure on nearby Columbus Avenue, where he would take Sean for pizza or breakfast at a coffee shop named La Fortuna. A favorite afternoon outing was to go down to Columbus Circle and along Central Park South to the Plaza Hotel, where shrieking crowds had besieged the newly arrived Beatles back in 1964, and have afternoon tea in its venerable Palm Court. Whenever he arrived, the string quartet would strike up "Yesterday," blissfully unaware that it was a Lennon-McCartney song in which he'd had no hand whatsoever. Occasionally someone would stop him and say, "Aren't you John Lennon?" "I get told that a lot," John would reply, or sometimes, "I wish I had his money."

Even during his longest homebound periods, the Dakota apartment never resembled any habitat of Howard Hughes. "There were always people around—assistants, psychics, tarot card readers, masseurs, maids, acupuncturists, odd-job people," Mintz says. "I believe there was one man whose sole job was keeping the brass doorknobs bright. Going from his bedroom to the kitchen for John was often like going through a subway station."

The kitchen was his other main comfort zone, a cavernous white inner space almost immune to noise from the street. His personal whims and fancies were everywhere, from the long, country-style table—like the one at Tittenhurst Park—to refrigerators with glass doors, so he could see what was inside without the trouble of opening them. On one wall was a painting of him, Yoko, and Sean, dressed in Superman costumes and soaring upward, hand in hand. Though he took no illegal drugs beyond the occasional "smoke" or magic mushroom, he remained as addicted to acrid French tobacco as ever. The kitchen was the haunt of three cats, Sasha, Misha, and Charo, respectively white, black, and brindled, who would all bound forward to greet John, rub themselves around his legs, and compete to curl on his knees. Calf's liver, bought for them from chic uptown butchers at $8 per pound, would often be cooking on the stove, its odor a Proustian memory of Aunt Mimi and Mendips.

Another surprising new pastime developed after both John and Yoko suffered a severe bout of gastric flu, then went on a liquids-only diet for forty days. "John's way of keeping on the diet was reading cookbooks and fantasizing about the recipes," Bob Gruen remembers. "He channeled all his craving for food into these amazing fantasies of dishes he'd never heard of, learning how to prepare them and what's good for you and what's not. Up to then, he'd always thought getting a bowl of cornflakes was cooking, and, being English, he could make a cup of tea. Yoko was a good cook but suddenly, after reading all these books, John got into it, too. I was at the apartment one night with my son, Chris, and he did a baked fish with steamed rice and vegetables that was really delicious."

Tormented by scents of warm bread during his diet, he even tried his hand at baking. When the first loaf came out of the oven, perfectly shaped, with an authentic golden-brown crust, he took a Polaroid snapshot of it, feeling he deserved as much applause as for any record ("I thought, 'Well, Jesus . . . don't I get a gold watch or knighted or nothing?'") For a time he prepared lunch every day, not only for Sean and Yoko but for their whole staff, feeding as many as ten or twelve around the long kitchen table. "The novelty of that wore off rather quickly," Mintz remembers. "He realized he was just turning himself into a galley-slave."

Finding himself such a good father to his second son inevitably made John want to be a better one to his first. The uncomfortable hiatus that had lasted since the final months of the Lost Weekend was broken in 1977, when Julian came from England to spend Christmas at the Dakota. A gangling fourteen-year-old in outsize glasses, he had gained little in resilience or self-confidence meanwhile, and arrived full of understandable forebodings. There continued to be little natural warmth between him and Yoko, for whom he was not only a potential rival for Sean but a reminder of her lost daughter. However, John was determined to establish a relationship that would not be broken again, and he seemed well on the way to succeeding. Central Park, that holiday season, lay under a thick fall of snow. Plunging downhill with him on a toboggan, Julian, too, seemed to have the perfect dad at last.

There was to be no corresponding thaw between John and Julian's mother. In June 1978, Cynthia Lennon published her autobiography, *A Twist of Lennon* (so titled because her third husband's surname was Twist). Written on a typewriter that Yoko had given Julian, the book was not recriminatory, ending with a quotation from the I Ching: "No blame." Even so, when John read an advance extract in the *News of the World*, he began legal moves to suppress it for "breach of marital confidence." The case reached the Appeal Court in London before being thrown out by Britain's most senior judge, Lord Denning. "It is as plain as it can be," said Denning, "that the relationship of these parties has ceased to be a private affair."

Despite his continued abstinence from *Billboard* magazine, John still kept abreast of what was happening in pop music. He admired the professionalism of the Bee Gees, would-be Beatles in the Sixties now riding the disco wave with their sound track to *Saturday Night Fever*. Among the newer British bands, he liked the Electric Light Orchestra, even if their symphonic-electronic style felt like "son of I Am the Walrus." He watched the continued transatlantic success of Bowie and Elton John without rancor, was amused by the way the Stones somehow still kept on rolling, surprised and scornful when Bob Dylan became a born-again Christian, and amazed that an apparently heterosexual band could have the nerve to call itself Queen. His main source of information was Bob Gruen, who photographed almost every major rock act that came through town and often urged him to come out and see some hot new attraction like Blondie or the New York Dolls. But putting Sean to bed always took precedence. "At one point I said, 'Am I bothering you by telling you about all this?'" Gruen remembers. "John said, 'No, I like to know what's going on. And some night, you never know, I may want to change my mind.'"

Still less inclined was he to socialize with any old cronies who might tempt him back to his former ways. Nor was it only overtly bad influences like Keith Moon and Harry Nilsson who found him permanently unavailable. In 1977, Mick Jagger moved into an apartment on the Upper West Side, within sight of the Dakota. Yet all his friendly overtures to John were ignored—an experience that even the hard-boiled head Stone found hurtful. "Does he ever call me?" Jagger complained. "Does he ever go out? No. Changes his number every 10 minutes. I've given up . . . just kowtowing to his bleedin' wife, probably."

In fact, he was sometimes almost tempted to join Jagger at the new disco club on West Fifty-fourth Street where all New York's *haute bohème* gathered. "He'd tell me he'd read in the papers about Mick and Bianca at Studio 54 and thought to himself, 'Shouldn't I be there, too?'" Elliot Mintz remembers. "It was the same when he read the bestseller lists in the *New York Times Book Review*, and was disappointed not to see his name. I'd say, 'But you haven't written a book.' 'That's not the point,' John would say."

Of all the books he read in this period, none had more effect than

David Niven's autobiography, *Bring On the Empty Horses*. "Niven had been friends with all the wild stars in Hollywood, and had been to all the crazy parties, but he'd come out sane at the end," Bob Gruen says. "After John read that book was when he started taking Polaroids of everyone who came to visit. He once told me, 'I'm gonna be David Niven. They're all gonna go on getting drunk, but I'm gonna stay home and write the book.' His plan was to live beyond the wild days and be the one to reminisce. He was gonna be the one that survived."

With the other ex-Beatles—"the in-laws," as Yoko drily called them—all issues were long since settled. He remained as fond as ever of Ringo, and felt intermittent concern that the simple, happy-go-lucky character who had so often kept him on the rails was now spectacularly plunging off them. After *Rotogravure* in 1976 (on which John broke retirement to play), Ringo had no more hit albums, lived mainly in a seafront condominium in Monte Carlo, and performed only on TV talk shows, frequently incoherent and always avoiding the subject of the Beatles, which did not leave very much else.

George, too, had failed to sustain his early solo success, following *All Things Must Pass* with a succession of uninspired albums (uninspired, that is, by Lennon and McCartney), alienating concert audiences by his humorlessness and tendency to preach, eventually diversifying into movies as backer of Monty Python's *Life of Brian* and cofounder of the HandMade Films production company. For some years, he felt resentment toward John for not supporting him on his 1974 American tour and for supposed dilatoriness in signing the Beatles severance contract. Even now that they were all right again, John felt George somehow regarded him as "the daddy who left home."

Between Paul and him, as he once told Elliot Mintz, "the wounds" had all healed. One might have expected a new mutual empathy now that John was leading the same domesticated existence he had once despised Paul for doing—a life of "pizza and fairy tales" no less. Instead, he put Paul and Linda in the same disruptive category as Jagger or Moon, resenting it hugely if they turned up at the Dakota while he was getting Sean off to sleep. Remote though the chance of

Lennon and McCartney ever working together again, it once almost happened. In 1976, the producer of the *Saturday Night Live* TV show, Lorne Michaels, humorously offered $3,000 if the Beatles would reform and do three songs. John and Paul happened to be watching the show at the Dakota, and considered taking a cab to the SNL studio for a surprise walk-on. But in the end, they couldn't be bothered.

One Christmastime, when Paul and Linda paid a visit to John and Yoko, Elliott Mintz was there also. The five went out for a meal to Woody Allen's favorite restaurant, Elaine's, on Second Avenue. As they didn't like anything on the menu, they asked if they could send out for pizza. That the legendarily fierce Elaine should have allowed this is testament to their combined magic. Later, back at the Dakota, says Mintz, "The conversation [between John and Paul] became less rhythmic, the words more sparse . . . it was obvious to me that the two of them had run out of things to say to each other."

While John reared their child, Yoko handled their finances, embarking on an ambitious program of investment and wealth creation, in case music alone should not be enough. That once dedicatedly anticommercial artist underwent a transformation into astute businesswoman, which, to anyone who knew her family background, was not so surprising. The long-suppressed genes of the Yasuda banking and trading dynasty had won through at last.

Her first step was acquiring additional space in the building where it had been so hard to gain a foothold. By 1979, five more units at the Dakota had been added to the Lennon domain: apartment 71, adjoining their original one and used purely for storage, a room on the eighth floor immediately above it, a second-floor studio, and a pair of large storerooms in the basement. The most important territorial gain was Studio One, two high-ceilinged ground-floor rooms just off the main vestibule that had formerly belonged to theatrical designer Jo Mielziner. One of these became the office of Lenono Music, the other a private sanctum for Yoko, emphasizing her detachment from the nursery world seven floors above. Here she worked a nine-to-five day at an enormous, gold-inlaid desk, under a trompe l'oeil ceiling of cloud-drifted blue sky.

Studio One's business was not always carried on by strictly conventional means. Yoko placed great reliance on her Japanese numerologist, Takashi Yoshikawa, and took few decisions, either business or personal, without first consulting him. Always central to her thinking was the necessity of traveling in certain directions at astrologically significant moments. During her separation from John, she had made the "ring around the world" that Yoshikawa counseled as a safeguard from evil, whose cycles were never-ending. When John returned home, he, too, wanted to make a ring around the world, even though, his directional coordinates differing from Yoko's, he would have to do it alone. Some time later, Neil Aspinall in London received a postcard from Hong Kong, addressed in a familiar scrawl. "What the hell's he doing there?" Neil said to his wife, Suzy, then turned to John's message. "What the hell's he doing there?" it read.

Yoko had always read tarot cards to foretell the future, sometimes with surprising accuracy. As a backup to Tashikawa's astrological, numerological, and directional counsels, therefore, she would regularly consult psychics. "I had five altogether," she says. "But never more than three at one time. We also had normal advice from lawyers and accountants, so it wasn't like I was listening to just one person—and in the end, I always made up my own mind." One psychic, a man named John Green, was on the permanent staff, living in the Lennons' Broome Street loft and receiving a stipend on a level with the lawyers and accountants. Renamed Charlie Swan—because there couldn't be two Johns around the Dakota—he spent several years in their employment, tasked with anything from predicting the outcome of their latest expansion scheme to staging the renewal of their wedding vows.

Through John Green they met a figure even more crucial to Yoko's business plan, also coincidentally with the surname Green. This was Sam Green, a Manhattan art dealer whose impressive circle of friends included the Rothschild family, Andy Warhol, and Greta Garbo. Sam Green had known Yoko in the early Sixties, and on her first visits to New York with John, made sure they were invited to Warhol's parties at the Factory. But he really won his spurs in 1977, when the Democratic Party returned to the White House in the person of a former peanut farmer named Jimmy Carter. With only three days notice, Green managed to get Yoko, John, and himself tickets to Carter's inaugural gala in Washington. Thereafter he outranked even the psychics as their "acquisitions guru."

The first major acquisition via Sam Green was a painting by the great French Impressionist Auguste Renoir. Titled *Jeunes filles au bord de la mer* (Young Girls at the Seaside), it had belonged to the French opera singer Lily Pons, who had recently died in Dallas, Texas. The problem was that most of John's money remained tied up with Apple in London and—for the kind of lifestyle he maintained—his U.S. dollar reserves were comparatively low. Green's solution was to have the Renoir shipped to London, where he paid for it in sterling, then brought it back to America. The idea was that after a decent interval, John and Yoko would sell it in dollars at a healthy profit. But they loved it so much that they couldn't bear to part with it.

Another investment strategy gave John his biggest dose of Liverpool déjà vu since exploring downtown New York. Just like his beloved Uncle George, he became a dairy farmer. America's milk producers at the time received generous tax breaks, and investigation showed that a cow of the premier Holstein-Friesian breed could appreciate in value almost as spectacularly as a French Impressionist. An expedition was mounted to Delaware County in upstate New York to inspect farms and herds currently for sale. Yoko preferred to stay in the limo with Sean, but, accompanied by Sam Green, John tramped over the fields, lost in memories of Uncle George in his milkman's peaked cap and brown overalls on the early-morning Woolton rounds with Daisy the cart horse. "He got really enthusiastic, talking about houses he'd like to build," Green remembers. "I got the feeling he wanted to live in the country more than anything." Subsequently Yoko bought four farms—"old McLennon's farms," John instantly dubbed them—and a herd of 122 Holstein cows and 10 bulls.

Sam Green's main advice was that they get into ancient Egyptian artifacts. The market for such things was still almost nonexistent, and remarkable treasures, two and three thousand years old, continually turned up in international salerooms or in the land of the pharaohs itself. Green viewed the exercise as a purely practical one, at a time when John happened to be facing heavy demands from the U.S. Internal Revenue Service. Hearing that a twelve-foot stone statue of Sekhmet, the lion-headed goddess, was available, he arranged to buy it for $300,000, but with an accompanying valuation of $1,000,000. The statue was then to be donated to a public park in Philadelphia, making its paper value tax-deductible.

Yoko's fascination with the relics as art, and her belief in their mystical and supernatural powers, turned what was to have been a cold-blooded investment into a personal passion. In 1978, Green learned of a gold sarcophagus that had lain in a Swiss bank vault for the past seventy years. Inside was the mummy of an unnamed young woman, evidently dating from Egypt's Greek period, as the inscription was in Greek, Egyptian, and Hittite. The only clue to her identity in any of the three tongues was that she had been "a princess who came out of the East to marry a man of great power"—a CV eerily similar to Yoko's. The sarcophagus was purchased, shipped to New York, and became the centerpiece of a dedicated Egyptian Room at the Dakota.

Inevitably, even the canny Yoko fell victim to the occasional scam. Early in 1979, she was told that a cache of extraordinary finds would shortly come on the market from a newly excavated site in Egypt. No such site really existed; her informant was planning to sell her some inferior items already long in circulation, dusted with a dramatic patina of desert sand. But, to the informant's dismay, she and John immediately set off for Cairo to view the alleged site, summoning Sam Green from London to meet up with them there. They checked into the Nile Hilton, unluckily just as it was about to be visited by America's new secretary of state, Cyrus Vance: for the first time ever, John had to give up his suite to someone more important.

As it chanced, a fellow hotel guest was Thomas Hoving, former director of New York's Metropolitan Museum, who had been a key character witness for John at his immigration trial. Hoving now found himself a witness to the frantic attempts to stop John and Yoko from heading off into the desert to view the nonexistent dig. "Yoko had been very nice after the immigration case, and sent me and my wife a huge bunch of flowers," he remembers. "But now she seemed very cold. I later learned that some guy back in New York was telling her I had an evil aura, and she had to get home right away."

"Then all the hotel phones went out of order," Sam Green recalls. "It was four days before Yoko could contact the numerologist to find out in which direction we should fly back to the States. John used the time to visit every genuine archaeological site and every museum I could get him into. He felt he'd been here in a previous life, and wanted to learn everything he possibly could."

Once Yoko had cared little about clothes; now her appetite for couture astonished even the famously spendthrift Elton John. "[She] has a refrigerated room just for keeping her fur coats," Elton reported after visiting the Dakota. "She's got rooms full of the clothes-racks like you see at Marks and Spencer. She makes me look ridiculous. I buy things in twos and threes, but she buys them in fifties." Special friend that he was, he could even publicly lampoon John's most famous lyric without chilling his welcome:

> Imagine six apartments
> It isn't hard to do.
> One is full of fur coats
> The other's full of shoes.

The same antimaterialist anthem cropped up one day when John was grumbling about the expense of his burgeoning empire to Neil Aspinall. "Imagine no possessions, John," Neil reminded him. "It's only a bloody song," he retorted.

The Dakota having been being thoroughly colonized, Yoko began looking for a base outside New York to which John and Sean could escape during the city's arctic winters and scorching summers. Initially, the most promising location seemed to be Palm Beach, Florida, with its year-round sunshine, gorgeous beaches, and inaccessibility to all but the megarich. During March 1979, they vacationed at a rambling oceanfront mansion named El Solano, which had once belonged to the Vanderbilt family and which Yoko would eventually buy. "It was a beautiful old Art Deco place," she says. "One room had a high ceiling like a ballroom. John used to love just sitting at the window and looking out at the ocean."

The large family group also included John's son Julian and Yoko's three young nieces, Reiko, Akiko, and Takako. Photographs of Julian during his visit show a boy clearly bewildered at being transplanted to Vanderbilt luxury from his mother's small house in Ruthin, northern Wales. Nor do Yoko's efforts to entertain him by demonstrating origami, Japanese paper folding, win his undivided attention. To celebrate his imminent sixteenth birthday, John chartered a yacht for a surprise party. Unfortunately, details of the event leaked out in advance and a group of young women began to circle the yacht in a speedboat with screams of "We love you, John!" forcing the jollifications to be cut short. This holiday would be the last time Julian ever saw his father.

As John's retirement had never been formally announced, there was intense puzzlement among the international media as month after month, then year after year passed with no new single or album from him, no madcap new ideas to mock, no new controversies to pump up, no new witticisms to relish. Interview requests continued to pour into Studio One, all of them given the same polite turndown on notepaper crested by a line drawing of the Dakota. Clearly some statement needed to be made, and eventually it was, via a paid insertion in the *New York Times*, the *Los Angeles Times*, and other major newspapers, headed "A Love Letter from John and Yoko to People Who Ask Us What, When and Why." This thanked people for their good vibes and for "respecting our quiet space" and said their silence was "a silence of love, not indifference."

That fall of 1979, in addition to his written journal, John sat down with his cassette recorder and announced "Tape one in the ongoing life story of John Winston Ono Lennon." The date was September 5, and he was waiting to accompany Yoko on an expedition to find a second home somewhere nearer to New York than Palm Beach. His initial intention seemed to be an exploration of childhood memories for the autobiography in David Niven mode he had mentioned to Bob Gruen. The tape begins with a description of 9 Newcastle Road, the terrace house near Penny Lane where he lived as a toddler with his parents and grandparents—its redbrick facade, its formal front parlor, the picture of a horse-drawn carriage on the wall, which ended up at his Aunt Nanny's home in Rock Ferry. He ponders about the first thing he can ever remember, decides it was "a nightmare," then suddenly complains, "This is boring. I can't be bothered doing it."

Instead, he turns to the musician who, more than any other except Paul McCartney, kept him on his creative mettle during the Sixties. A new Bob Dylan album, *Slow Train Coming*, has just been released, saturated with Dylan's new Christian consciousness. John finds its vocals "pathetic," its lyrics "just embarrassing," and mocks a particular track, "Gotta Serve Somebody," for evoking cafeterias rather than churches. But his main feeling is one of relief that such old rivals no longer have the power they once did to goad and unsettle him.

Thoughts pop up at random, literary as well as musical: a recent piece by Truman Capote in Andy Warhol's *Interview* magazine, a saying about George Bernard Shaw, worthy of *A Spaniard in the Works*, that "his brains went to his head." A snatch of bagpipe music recalls boyhood stays in Edinburgh ("one of my favorite dreams"), the annual military display under the castle ramparts, and his emotion during the closing recital by a lone piper. He remarks how the freedom he always felt in Scotland—and has felt in Japan, also—came largely from being an anonymous foreigner. The current house hunting with Yoko, he admits, is an attempt to re-create Scotland "within an hour from New York." But so far nothing has come close to the real place, which he intends to visit as soon as astrology and numerology permit. "In 1981, I'll take Sean there," he promises himself, "'cause that's a good year to go."

Thence to a memory that has lurked at the back of his mind for twenty-five years and been replayed to Yoko more times than she could count: "the time when I had my hand on my mother's tit in number 1 Blomfield Road." He recalls his fourteen-year-old self, lying beside Julia on her bed as she took a siesta in her black angora (or maybe cashmere) top and "dark green and yellow mottled skirt." He still feels the electric thrill of their accidental contact, still wonders if he should have tried to go further and whether Julia would have allowed it.

The Truman Capote article in *Interview* also receives further attention. Later published in Capote's essay collection *Music for Chameleons*, it features the gay author in nocturnal conversation with himself about his fatal addictions to drugs, alcohol, and sex. At one point there is a reminiscence of E. M. Forster, one of Britain's greatest twentieth-century novelists, who lived into his nineties but never became reconciled to homosexuality. Forster always hoped that when he reached old age, his sexual urges would vanish—but, instead, he told Capote, they seemed even more of a burden "I just thought 'shit!'" John comments. "'cause I was always waiting for them to lessen. But I suppose it's gonna go on for ever."

Soon after making the tape, he did find himself in possession of a second home "an hour from New York" but otherwise as unlike his idealized memories of Scotland as could be. Cannon Hill was an extensive property in Cold Spring Harbor, a chic summer resort on the north shore of Long Island. The rambling wooden house dated from the eighteenth-century whaling era and took its name from the antique cannon embedded beside the swimming pool. With it went a private beach and dock, looking out on a panorama of motorboats, sailboats, and skiffs, much like the scene Aunt Mimi saw from her bungalow in faraway Poole.

Yoko was often too immersed in business matters to leave New York, so John's most frequent companion on trips to Cold Spring Harbor with Sean would be his latest assistant, Fred Seaman. A journalism graduate from the City College of New York, discreet and cat-footed, Seaman bore an honored surname in the Lennons' inner circle: his father, Eugene, was a concert pianist, his uncle Norman was a classical music promoter who had staged some of Yoko's early performances, and his aunt Helen was Sean's nanny. His own employment was allegedly clinched by the fact that John's father had also been called Fred and had been a seaman—though the mariner in question was actually a steward, known then as Alf.

Anyone who stays in Cold Spring Harbor but doesn't go sailing is liable to feel exceedingly left out. Despite never having sailed in anything smaller than a Mersey ferry, John decided it would be nice for Sean, and enlisted the help of a boatyard named Coneys Marine in

nearby Huntington. The owner's young son, Tyler Coneys, recommended a fourteen-foot Javelin-class sailboat named *Isis* and offered
a course of personal tuition. Learning to sail after a certain age is
never easy, particularly for someone as physically indolent as John
had always been. But Tyler Coney remembers how determinedly he
set out to master practical skills, and how cheerfully he performed
drudging chores that he'd spent his whole life avoiding. One day, on
an outing with Sean and nanny Helen, Fred Seaman offered to steer
and demonstrated the fallacy of his surname by promptly capsizing
the boat. Fortunately, everyone was wearing life jackets, and Sean
was quite comfortable in the water, thanks to all those swimming
lessons at the Y. Even so, John made the whole crew swear not to
tell Yoko.

Before long, he was confident and competent enough to sail the
Isis without Tyler Coneys's guardianship. Weeks of salt air and
healthy exercise turned him lean and tanned, the picture of health in
all but the Gitane drooping from his lips. Out in "the great wet barnyard of Long Island Sound," as he found it called in F. Scott Fitzger-
ald's *The Great Gatsby*, no one noticed the modest little sailboat
bucking and tacking, or the anonymous, oilskin-clad figure with the
little boy beside him. Other celebrities lived along the shore, including Louis Comfort Tiffany, the stained-glass artist, and the singer
Billy Joel, whose hit ballad, "Just the Way You Are," was a favorite
of John's. Identifying Joel's all-glass mansion one day, he cupped his
hands to his mouth seadog-style and shouted, "Billy—I have all your
records!"

On October 9, he entered his fortieth year. The awful realization
dawned that time no longer stretched ahead in unlimited quantities,
that more of his life might be behind than ahead, that the weeks
were starting to fly by like days used to do, the months like weeks
used to, the years like months. He began to fret that Sean's childhood
was passing too quickly and that before he knew it, he'd no longer
be needed to supervise bath-time, sing lullabyes, or tie up a little life
jacket. "He used to say 'When we're 80, we'll be in rocking-chairs,
waiting for Sean's postcards,'" Yoko remembers. He even speculated
about what the two of them might do to fill the void in their lives

after Sean had gone away to college. One idea he often mentioned was to return to Britain and join the famous artists' colony in the Cornish village of St. Ives.

He remained completely faithful to Yoko—so far as she knew, or wanted to. "There was one time when he and another guy went off together to the ocean. Later on, John was showing me photographs of the two of them and I said, 'Wait a minute—someone else had to be there to take the photographs.' He just laughed and said, 'I can never get anything past you.' Then he told me there had been a young girl, she had long hair and she was so passionate about art, she reminded him of me when we first met. Later on, I believe a letter came in to the office, but I never asked him about it."

As middle age beckoned, he became increasingly nostalgic about his homeland, pining for British institutions and values he had once so angrily spurned. A strenuous outdoor weekend in Cold Spring Harbor would end with Sunday night back at the Dakota, watching *Masterpiece Theatre* on Channel 13, New York's Public Broadcasting System channel. The plays were classic BBC serials, introduced by the veteran broadcaster Alistair Cooke from a red leather buttonback armchair. With Yoko and the three cats, surrounded by the detritus of the *New York Times*'s mammoth Sunday edition, John would settle down to watch Robert Graves's *I, Claudius* or Daphne du Maurier's *Rebecca*.

Another ritual, unflaggingly maintained, was the regular letters and phone calls to Aunt Mimi. "He used to write me pages and pages, pouring out his thoughts, and they had little drawings and bits of his silliness all over them," Mimi remembered. "And always signed in the same way, 'Himself.'" On the phone, he still liked to tease her with the thicko Liverpool accent, which turned *th* into *d*, reciting the Scouser's litany "Dis, dem, dere" like some classical conjugation. Despite her financial dependence on him, aunt and nephew could still have furious rows. A dispute about the repainting of her bunga- low, for instance, ended with Mimi shouting "Damn you, Lennon!" and slamming the receiver down. As she was still fuming to herself, the telephone rang. "You're not still cross with me, Mimi, are you?" John's voice said anxiously.

During one call, he suddenly asked for the chinaware that was her pride and joy when they lived together at Mendips: the Royal Worcester and Coalport teapots, teacups, and dinner plates, kept on display in the mock-Tudor front hall, never sullied by the tiniest speck of dust. "I sent him parcel after parcel of stuff," she would remember. "He just seemed to want to have it all with him over there." He also wanted the elegant Victorian wall clock from the morning room, its dial inscribed "George Toogood, Woolton Tavern," on which his Uncle George (whose ancestors were Toogoods) had taught him to tell the time. Mimi even had to root out and pack up his once-hated uniform blazer from Quarry Bank High School, and his black-and-gold striped school tie. If ever obliged to wear a suit, he often set it off with the school tie half-unknotted and askew, as if baiting long-gone headmasters.

However he might pretend otherwise, it did occasionally get to him that Paul McCartney's Wings were among the biggest stadium attractions in the world, that Paul's "Mull of Kintyre" had sold more copies in the United Kingdom than the Beatles' "She Loves You," and that Paul's "Yesterday" was overtaking Bing Crosby's "White Christmas" as the world's most covered song. As usual, such insecurities struck coldest in the middle of the night. If Yoko were not already awake, he would rouse her, and they'd go into the huge white kitchen. "I would make tea, John would sit down, and the cats would all come to him. Whenever he was with a cat, sitting there and stroking its coat, he always looked just like Mimi."

As they sat there with the purring cats, the all-night Manhattan traffic a distant murmur, the picture of Mr., Mrs., and Baby Superman soaring up the wall, he would endlessly wonder just what magic facility it was that his old partner possessed and he did not. "He'd say, 'They always cover Paul's songs—they never cover mine,'" Yoko remembers. "I said to him, 'You're a good songwriter. It's not just June-with-spoon that you write. . . . Most musicians would be a bit nervous about covering your songs.'" His one crumb of comfort was that all those vexatious cover versions might never have existed but for him. "He always said he'd had two great partnerships," Yoko recalls. "One with Paul McCartney, the other with Yoko Ono, 'And I discovered both of them,' he used to say. That isn't bad going, is it?

Sometimes, Yoko recalls, she would awaken and find him crying, smitten by terror that she would die before he did—a logical thought because she was older. Once she heard him murmur in the darkness "Those bastards will throw you and Sean out on the street if I die and I don't know what to do . . ."

New York had become progressively less violent during the seventies, but it still could not be called a safe place to live. A week after John's thirty-ninth birthday, he and Yoko donated $1,000 to a fund for equipping the city's police with bulletproof vests. In November, he made his will, appointing Sam Green as Sean's guardian if Yoko should happen to have predeceased him. At year's end, the Beatles old record producer, George Martin, happened to be in New York, and had dinner with John at the Dakota. They had not seen each other since the miserable *Let It Be* sessions in 1969 nor had they communicated since John's belittlement of Martin in *Rolling Stone* magazine a year later. "Yoko quite tactfully kept out of the way for the whole evening, and we just reminisced about the good old times," Martin remembers. "I tackled him about the *Rolling Stone* interview. I said, 'What was all that shit about, John? Why?' He said, 'I was out of me head, wasn't I?' And that was as much of an apology as I got.

"He also said, 'You know, George, if I could, I would record everything the Beatles did all over again.' I blanched. 'Blimey, John, rather you than me. Everything?' He said, 'Everything.' I searched my mind for all the wonderful things we'd done, and said, 'What about "Strawberry Fields"?' He looked at me over his specs and said, '*Especially* "Strawberry Fields."' "

30

STARTING OVER

I am going to be forty and life begins
at forty, so they promise.

John celebrated New Year's 1980 quietly at home. In the spare apartment next to number 72, he had decorated a room as what he called an "old-fashioned gentlemen's club," with an ancient leather couch and 1930s kitsch bought from downtown flea markets. The centerpiece was a bubble-topped Wurlitzer jukebox that Yoko had given him on his thirty-eighth birthday, stocked with big old 78 rpm records by all his favorite balladeers, Bing Crosby, Frankie Laine, and Guy Mitchell.

This so-called Club Dakota boasted just one other charter member: Elliot Mintz. On New Year's Eve, John wrote Yoko a formal invitation to join them and had it delivered to her on a silver salver, accompanied by a white gardenia. She put on a black evening gown; he wore a secondhand tuxedo, set off by a white T-shirt and his Quarry Bank school tie. At midnight, they danced to "Auld Lang Syne" on the jukebox while Mintz took Polaroid snapshots, then the trio watched the fireworks burst like gunshots over Central Park.

The music business of 1980 was unrecognizable as the one John had left five years before. In Europe, it had been transformed by punk rock, a term first coined in New York during the early seventies but redefined by the mounting anger and nihilism of Britain's youth as the decade progressed. This punk rock was an uprising against the smug grandiosity of "supergroups" like Led Zeppelin, Yes, and Emerson, Lake & Palmer—a declaration of how it really felt to be a teenager amid endemic urban decay, inflation, and unemployment. Punk bands negated all the skill and musical ambition that had built up since *Sgt. Pepper's Lonely Hearts Club Band*, playing a version of early rock 'n' roll whose sole appeal was its ferocious volume and aggression.

They had names that made that long-ago controversy over "Beatles" seem laughable—the Sex Pistols, the Stranglers, the Vibrators, the Damned. They and their followers, both male and female, wore their hair greased into asymmetric spikes or planed into fluorescent red or orange Mohawks, assembled their wardrobes from bondage-fetishist catalogs and street-corner dumpsters, festooned themselves with murderous-looking chains and buckles, covered their generously exposed flesh with tattoos and pierced it with rings, studs, or outsize safety pins. Not since the Beatles' arrival in 1963 had such raw energy coursed through the British charts, nor such screams of anguished disgust arisen from older generations. The Sex Pistols' singer, Johnny Rotten, was said to have touched a new nadir by screaming abuse and even spitting at his audience, though customers of Hamburg's Kaiskerkeller Club might have recollected something similar from another Johnny as early as 1960.

The triumph of feminism meant that females could move into the male preserve of fronting bands, and deal in equally uncensored aggression, subversion, and sexual explicitness. With their unkempt coiffures, *Bride of Frankenstein* makeup, and glass-splintering vocal attack, punk chanteuses made Yoko's derided stage performances of the late Sixties look positively restrained. Back then, one of the kinder critical comments used to be that she "howled like a Banshee"; now the howlingest of the woman-led bands was named Siouxsie and the Banshees.

As punk in turn gave way to foppish "new romantics," robotic synthesizer wizards, white ska and reggae, and pioneer rappers, most of the great rock names of yesteryear cowered in their châteaux like French aristocrats during the Terror. But one enjoyed the same charmed afterlife as ever. In December 1979, the BBC announced a "Beatles Christmas" on the nation's TV screens, with showings of six of their films including the 1965 Shea Stadium concert and that erstwhile yuletide superflop, *Magical Mystery Tour.*

Newspapers full of new tattle about the Sex Pistols, the Specials, the Pretenders, or the Police still cleared headline space for yet another rumored Beatles reunion. Sid Bernstein, the promoter who had put them on at Carnegie Hall and Shea, took out regular full-page ads in the *New York Times*, offering more and yet more millions for what, even after all these years, would still be the hottest ticket on earth. Paul, George, and Ringo were reportedly not unamenable; the stumbling block was always said to be John. However, during the mid-seventies, an offer came in that even he could not refuse. "One guy wanted to pay something like $50 million for just one show," Neil Aspinall remembered. "Paul was ready to do it, even though he was busy with Wings at the time, and when I told John, he said, 'I'd stand on me head in the corner for that kind of money.' But the promoter wanted rights to an album and a film as well, so it all fell through."

When visions of dazzling wealth seemed unable to lure the ex-Beatles back together, appeals to their collective conscience took over. In September 1979, an international relief operation was launched for the refugees fleeing Communist-held Vietnam in armadas of leaky boats. Sid Bernstein put forward a plan for three Beatles concerts, in New York, Cairo, and Jerusalem, which would raise an estimated $500 million for the Vietnamese boat people and also be a significant peace gesture in the troubled Middle East. Despite his good relations with Bernstein—whom he frequently saw around Columbus Avenue—John felt unfairly pressured and accused the promoter of schmaltzily going down on one knee "like Al Jolson" to persuade him. He also pointed out, quite fairly, that every concert he and Yoko had given since the end of the Beatles had been for some good cause or other.

In December, the United Nations announced a relief program for victims of the genocidal Pol Pot regime in Cambodia, renamed Kampuchea. Paul McCartney out-Bangladeshed George Harrison by organizing four Concerts for Kampuchea at London's Hammersmith Odeon and a live album, featuring Wings, the Who, and Queen, along with punkish parvenus like the Pretenders, Elvis Costello, and the Clash. Once more, the media buzzed with expectation that the other ex-Beatles would join Paul onstage. But John would not pledge himself, even after a personal plea from the UN's Secretary-General Kurt Waldheim. The band had given the world their all for ten years, he said—and anyway if they tried performing together now after so long they would be "just four rusty old men." Rumors that he was secretly watching the shows from the wings sent ticket prices sky-high, though unfortunately into the pockets of scalpers rather than Kampucheans. When a toy robot wobbled across the stage during Wings' set, Paul took mild revenge for the Elton John Thanksgiving show by announcing, "It's not John Lennon."

The halo was soon to slip from the McCartney brow. On January 16, 1980, when he arrived in Japan to tour with Wings, customs officers at Tokyo's Haneda Airport discovered 219 grams (almost half a pound) of marijuana in Paul's luggage. He was arrested, handcuffed, and held in custody for nine days before intense diplomatic efforts secured his release. John, who had been labeled a drug criminal despite never knowing the touch of handcuffs or spending a single night behind bars, was amazed by this atypical lapse in caution— and obscurely offended that it should happen on what he regarded as home ground. Paul and Linda had even been bound for the Hotel Okura, thus, he felt, threatening to spoil the karma of the place for Yoko and him.

Nor was this the only intrusion by a fellow Beatle on territory he regarded as his. Despite all his intentions to become a David Niven memoirist, George stole a march on him in August 1979 by publishing an autobiography. Entitled *I Me Mine*, it came in a lavish limited edition of two thousand leather-bound, slipcased copies, signed by the author, illustrated by facsimiles of handwritten song lyrics (complete with coffee stains and cigarette burns) and priced at an astounding £148. John was hurt and angered by the book, feeling it had barely mentioned everything he had been to George, and done for George, since 1957. "By glaring omission, my influence on [George's] life is absolutely zilch and nil. . . . In his book which is purportedly this clarity of vision of each song he wrote, he remembers every two-bit sax player or guitarist he met in subsequent years . . . I was just left out as if I didn't exist." Actually, John receive eleven mentions, more than Paul, the Beatles, Eric Clapton, or even George's second wife, Olivia.

Yoko's forty-seventh birthday in February 1980 was celebrated by a trip back to the Palm Beach mansion El Solano, which by now had been added to their property portfolio. "When I woke up on my birthday morning, there was a gardenia beside my bed," she remembers. "Another one was lying near the door, another one was outside the room, there was a trail of them down the stairs and the whole hallway was full of gardenias. John had bought so many that the local florists had to get in supplies from outside the state. He did that for me because he knew gardenias were my favorite flower. And I felt so guilty because I'd gone back onto heroin and he didn't know."

In hindsight, she blames the combined pressures of being a conventional wife and mother, trying to build up John's fortune to the promised $25 million alongside Paul McCartney's, and, most of all, keeping their mutual vow to suspend all creative work. "If I even so much as sat down at the piano in my office, John would come in and say 'A-ah, you're doing it!' like he'd caught me out. To stop all that constant effort as an artist was impossible for me. I may have been quite good at doing business, but that wasn't me at all. I despised it."

One of the many fixers they employed happened to mention to Yoko one day that he could always get heroin if she ever needed it. "At the time, I was angry with him, like 'Why are you telling me this?' Then a few months later, I went to him and said, 'Okay, let's see it.'"

She never told John she had slipped back into the habit they had kicked together with such effort almost a decade earlier. "That meant I had to be very clever, but he's a smart guy and he knows all the signs." The only person from their shared circle whom she took into her confidence was their "acquisitions guru," Sam Green. By that time, according to Green, her habit had become "life-threatening." But she would not think of seeking professional help for fear that John and then the press would find out, and another wave of anti-Yoko stories be unleashed.

When she resolved to go cold turkey all over again, she sent John off to Cold Spring Harbor with Sean while she stayed in New York or sought sanctuary at Sam Green's home on Fire Island. "I told John I had really bad influenza and he and Sean mustn't come back or they'd catch it, too. When I went down to visit them, John still didn't realise what was going on . . . but he was so sweet to me. That's what he wrote the song 'Dear Yoko.'"

For much of this turbulent time for Yoko, as things turned out, John was not in the same home, the same town, or, finally, even the same country. As spring turned Central Park's trees into pink-and-white froth, the all-powerful numerologist, Takashi Yoshikawa—presciently but, alas, far, far too prematurely—detected clouds of evil beginning to form above his head and worked out the direction in which he needed to travel to escape them. At the end of May, he flew off alone on the prescribed course, ending up in Cape Town, South Africa.

But flying to Cape Town alone was just a prelude. As John's fortieth birthday loomed, he felt a desire, common to many men at that stage in life, for some great adventure outside all his previous experience. His voyages with the *Isis* on Long Island Sound had whetted his appetite for life afloat, and with his young sailing mentor, Tyler Coneys, he began discussing the possibility of a yacht trip into more challenging waters. He had no idea where he wanted to go, only that it must be in the direction his numerologist had prescribed to avoid the "clouds of evil"—southeast. From mainland America, the nearest southeasterly destination for sailing craft was the British island territory of Bermuda. Coneys undertook to organize the expedition in early June, to find a crew, and go along himself. When John reached Bermuda, Sean would fly out to join him, and they would spend several weeks there. Such a extended separation was not exactly inconvenient for Yoko at that moment, and she readily gave the plan her blessing.

Originally, her psychics were to have selected the yacht, but in the end Tyler Coneys's expertise took precedence. The chosen vessel was a forty-three-foot sloop, the *Megan Jaye*, based in Newport, Rhode Island, and skippered by a bearded salt named Hank Halsted. Astrology and numerology could not be denied, though, in the selection of John's sailing companions. Eventually, only four passed this unusual seagoing test: Tyler, his two cousins, Kevin and Ellen Coneys, and the skipper, "Cap'n Hank." The journey of seven hundred miles traversed busy cargo and tanker routes and unpredictable weather zones, including the notorious Bermuda Triangle, where ships and aircraft were wont to disappear without a trace. But the *Megan Jaye* was a modern, well-equipped vessel and her crew, though fewer than was usual on such a voyage, seemed more than capable of handling it.

On June 4, John bade Sean a tearful farewell and sailed out of Newport with his new group. The *Megan Jaye*'s equipment included a weather fax, which coughed out regular bulletins from larger craft with satellite forecasting systems. Each spoke confidently of an uneventful crossing, and, for a couple of days, this prediction seemed spot-on. The weather was idyllic, with unbroken brilliant sunshine, flat seas, and schools of dolphins curveting off the bows. John was particularly exhilarated to see a large bank of cloud dropping back behind the stern.

In the communal cabin, he found himself living in closer proximity to other people than he had since traveling around by van with the Beatles. He shared a watch with Tyler Coneys, and acted as ship's cook, providing a healthy diet dominated by vegetables and brown rice. Though he liked and got along with all three Coneyses, his closest rapport with Cap'n Hank, the shipmate nearest to him in age. Before becoming a charter skipper, Hank had lived through the psychedelic era, promoting rock concerts with acts like Big Brother and the Holding Company, at one stage even running a drug clinic. He treated John with a total lack of deference, mixed with profound respect for the musical talents so long inexplicably on hold. "You just affected 50 million people there to the positive, big boy," he said in one of their chats. "What are you going to do to follow that up?" The radio happened to be playing a lot of Wings tracks, like "Silly Love Songs" and "Coming Up." Tyler Coneys recalls how the sound of Paul's voice seemed to make "[John] think 'Jesus, what am I doing, sitting here? I should get up and do something because it's not that hard.'"

Then came one of those capricious weather changes for which the Bermuda Triangle is notorious. The first sign was the turning of the water from turquoise to gray, then blue-black. A flotilla of military ships appeared and circled the *Megan Jaye*, as if tut-tutting and shaking their heads. Then a storm broke, with 65 mph winds and twenty-foot-high waves—not the worst her experienced crew had ever known, but bad enough for a smallish yacht way out here, where one couldn't turn back or pull over to the side of the road. The most hardened sailors occasionally get seasick, and so it now was with all three Coneyses. As the *Megan Jaye* heaved and corkscrewed, Tyler, Kevin, and Ellen could take no further part in handling her, but only lie prostrate on their bunks. Cap'n Hank was unaffected, however—and so, amazingly, was John. A cleansing fast that he'd put himself through in the first days of the voyage undoubtedly helped. He said that having weathered heroin and cold turkey made any tempest seem small by comparison and that he'd "learned to control throwing up."

Cap'n Hank stayed at the wheel for forty-eight hours, then, dazed with fatigue, shouted to John in his usual unceremonious fashion, "I'm gonna need some help here, big boy." Though John had often steered the *Isis* off Cold Spring Harbor, this was like a Quarryman being told to back Jerry Lee Lewis. "Hey Hank . . ." he protested, "I've just got these little guitar-playing muscles here." But the skipper would brook no shirking: "That ain't the kind of strength I'm looking for . . . Just come back and drive this puppy and I'll tell you what to do."

John gingerly took over as helmsman, and Cap'n Hank barked out a few basic instructions ("You don't jibe . . . you don't let the wind get across the back of the boat") then gave him a course to follow. "He picked it up fast," his instructor would recall. "His intuition about this kind of stuff was remarkable."

Cap'n Hank remained watchfully close for a while, then decided it was safe to grab some desperately needed sleep. Left in charge of a forty-three-foot sloop, solely responsible for the safety of four people, John was at first almost paralyzed with panic. But gradually he connected with the boat and began to understand its responses, almost as if it had been some great silver-bodied guitar. His fear passed and he began to enjoy himself, roaring out every obscene sea chantey he had ever heard around Liverpool docks to the screaming audience of wind and waves. He also later remembered shouting "Freddie!" feeling a sudden kinship with the father who had sacrificed everything for the sea—and had returned from a watery Lost Weekend on a ship named *Monarch of Bermuda*. "When I came back on deck . . . this was a man who was just enraptured," Cap'n Hank would remember. "It was stimulus worthy of this stimulus-addict of a guy."

The storm changed John's status on the boat from celebrity passenger and paymaster to bona fide crew member, able to take on and handle anything the others did. He even helped Cap'n Hank carry out repairs to the mainsail after the *Megan Jaye* had drifted without sails for a whole day. (That would have been a sight for his Liverpool cousins, Mike and David, who remembered him being unable even to change a lightbulb.) He was unrecognizable as the landlubber who had come aboard in Newport—though to Cap'n Hank every surprising new capability seemed somehow natural. "I would venture to say that he discovered the tremendously strong man who had always been there."

As well as sustaining damage to fabric and fixtures, they had been blown a considerable way off course, and did not reach Hamilton, the Bermudan capital, until June 11. Before going ashore, John wrote an appreciative message in the logbook: "Dear Megan 'There's no place like nowhere' (TC 1980) + Thanks Hank love John Lennon." Underneath he sketched a sailboat, a shining sun, and his own smiling, bearded face,.

For a few days, he shared a small cottage with the three Coneyses (rented under the name of Yoko's psychic-in-chief, John Green). With his crewmates' departure and the arrival of Sean, plus a nanny and Fred Seaman, he rented a large stucco villa named Undercliff, on the outskirts of Hamilton. Here they enjoyed an idyllic seaside holiday lasting almost two months. John took Sean swimming every day; they paddled, built sandcastles, strolled round Hamilton's street market and Botanical Gardens, and had their portrait painted together as a gift for "Mother" by a young woman artist they met by chance on the beach. The tropical island abounded with reminders of England for John—and better even than that. One day, he was entranced to hear the wheeze of Scottish bagpipes float from a neighboring property. The piper turned out to be a man named John Sinclair, just like the White Panther martyr of yore. John dispatched a note of appreciation, accompanied by a bottle of Chivas Regal malt whiskey.

His adventure on the *Megan Jaye* proved the best possible remedy for the crisis in creativity that had all but drowned him. In Bermuda, he was suddenly seized with a desire to make another album. "I was so centred after the experience at sea, that I was tuned into the cosmos," he remembered. "And all these songs came . . . After five years of nothing. Not trying, but nothing coming anyway, no inspiration, no thought, no anything, then suddenly voom voom voom . . ." Like a long-dormant radio, his senses retuned to processing everything he saw and heard into words and chords. Bob Marley's "Hallelujah Time" on the radio, for instance, triggered the all-too-prophetic line: "We gotta keep living, living on borrowed time. . . ." He went into Hamilton, bought some cheap tape recorders and speakers, and began to lay down demos, usually working out on the terrace at night after Sean was in bed, with a background of cicadas and whistling tree frogs.

There were also some low-key crawls around Hamilton's pubs and discos with Fred Seaman and a couple of friendly local journalists, though nowadays John seldom drank more than one glass of wine—and even that knocked him out. On one such outing, he heard "Rock Lobster" by the B-52s, an American new wave band, which, like Blondie and Talking Heads, had eagerly picked up on British punk rock. The style of the two female vocalists, at once girlish and slightly camp, was just like Yoko's a decade earlier, when no one wanted to listen to her. "So I called her on the phone and I said, 'There's someone doing your act there,'" he remembered. "'They're ready for you this time, kid.'"

Some of the songs that took shape on Underhill's terrace were reworkings of rough ideas demoed at the Dakota, then put aside;

others sprang into his head virtually complete. Every one dealt with the life he had been leading these past five years and testified that, by and large, it had been a happy and fulfilled one. "Darling Boy," later retitled "Beautiful Boy," was a hymn of joy to Sean, affording a peep into his warm, safe nursery world ("The monster's gone, he's on the run and your daddy's here. . . .") and tempering impatience to see him come of age with a poignant self-reminder to appreciate every moment ("Life is what happens to you while you're busy making other plans"). "Watching the Wheels" was a self-portrait of one thankful to have escaped the Elvis trap, content to let the machinery of the business grind on without him, the painted horses named Paul or Mick continue their interminable circuits, while he devoted himself to important things like "watching shadows on the wall." "Woman" was seemingly addressed to Yoko, a delicate letter of appreciation "for showing me the meaning of success" and an apology for causing "sorrow and pain"—which in the end went out to every woman who had nurtured him, back to Julia, Mimi, and the aunts: "After all, I'm forever in your debt."

The old insecure, fearful John had not completely vanished. An edgy rock track called "I'm Losing You" revealed his awareness that something was going on with Yoko, and that the outcome could be disastrous. When she flew out for a visit, he spent days beforehand telling Sean that "Mommy's coming," the way mothers usually did with children when daddies interrupted work to spend time with them. Once at Underhill, however, she spent most of her time on the telephone, selling one of their pedigreed Holstein milk cows— and getting a record price of $250,000. After she returned home, John rang her repeatedly, but was unable to get through. "It drove me crackers," he remembered, "just long enough to write a song." Superstitious as ever, he changed the working title to "(Afraid I'm) Losing You," in case it became a self-fulfilling prophecy. At the Botanical Gardens one day, he spotted a clump of yellow freesias of the extra-large variety 'Double Fantasy,' growing under a cedar tree. There could have been no better description of his life with Yoko or title for the album he was now itching to make with her.

By the time he returned to New York on July 29, Yoko had already lined up a producer. They both agreed they wanted someone young and contemporary rather than a legend of yesteryear, and Jack Douglas seemed to fit the bill to perfection. He had been a studio engineer at the New York end of the *Imagine* album, then had gone on to produce hugely successful new acts like Aerosmith and Cheap Trick. When Douglas first heard the demos John had made in Bermuda, with their cicada and tree-frog chorus, he wondered whether he had a real role at all: "They were already so much fun to listen to."

Work began at the Hit Factory Studios, West Forty-eighth Street, on August 4. John turned up wearing a broad-brimmed black hat and carrying one of the briefcases from his large collection. His first act was to tape a large photograph of Sean above the mixing desk.

It was firmly impressed on Jack Douglas that *Double Fantasy* was as much Yoko's album as John's, and that the songs she had been simultaneously writing in New York were to alternate with his rather than go on a separate side, where they might be bypassed altogether. John called the project "a conversation between a man and a woman," and that was the effect, although they sang not a single duet and even recorded their respective tracks at different times of day. The anxious, doom-laden "I'm Losing You" segued into a part two by Yoko called "I'm Moving On," in which all its worst fears seemed about to be realized. "Beautiful Boy," John's elegy to Sean, was answered by her "Beautiful Boys," a tribute to the two of them. The fade-out of his "Dear Yoko" gently reproached her for her abstraction in Bermuda, while hopefully anticipating another holiday there together: "When you come over next time, don't sell a cow . . . spend some time. . . ."

The complement of top session musicians did not include any old crony of John's who might lead him astray again. Indeed, the studio atmosphere suggested a health spa more than a rock album. Yoko created a special "quiet room" for the two of them, softly lit, with palm trees and a white piano. Instead of cocaine and Cognac, the band were served tea and sushi ("dead fish," John called it); a plate of sunflower seeds and raisins stood beside every microphone, and shiatsu massages were available on request. Sean's picture stayed over the mixing desk, a constant reminder that sessions must end in time for John to get home and say good-evening to him. One night, when he could not leave the studio in time, he relayed a message to Sean: "I love you, sweet dreams, see you tomorrow." "He says, 'I love you, too,' Yoko called from the telephone. "I hope he does," John said, "because I'm the only daddy he's got."

Douglas wanted to give the album a contemporary edge and, to that end, enlisted Bun E. Carlos and Rick Nielson, drummer and guitarist of Cheap Trick (who by an odd coincidence were currently working at George Martin's AIR Studios in Montserrat) to play on "I'm Losing You." But, funky as their contribution was, it simply did not fit. The spirit of *Double Fantasy* was Matisse rather than Picasso, soothing and reassuring rather than challenging and unsettling like John-and-Yoko albums of old. "Beautiful Boy" ended with sounds of sea and children's voices that could as easily have came from Bournemouth as Bermuda. And where once John had screamed, "I don't believe in Beatles," he now reminisced freely about what he called "the B's" and was happy to use them as a shorthand when telling the musicians what he wanted. He described "Woman," for instance, as "an early Motown/Beatles circa 1964 ballad"—though in fact its honeyed "Oooo . . . well well" chorus was more like a Paul ballad or even a Wings one. Drummer Andy Newmark would later recall being told unceremoniously, "Andy, I want to get this in three takes, play like Ringo."

One track above all, John's "(Just Like) Starting Over," signified that, whatever Bermuda Triangle his marriage had passed through this summer, it was back on an even keel and sailing confidently forward once more. Beginning with three light pings on a Tibetan "wishing bell"—a conscious contrast with the ominous tolling that had preceded "Mother"—it was a relaxed ballad, for which he pre-scribed an "Elvis/Orbison feel." His tone was lighthearted, at one point even breaking into a little laugh (something, strangely enough, never heard in a John song before). But the message was in utter earnest: a plea to Yoko to heal their recent difficulties with some quality time alone together, including in bed; an insistence that "no one's to blame"; a declaration that "our life together is so precious" and "our love is still special." Those dark clouds, it seemed, had all rolled away.

The news that John Lennon was recording again sent a tremor throughout the transatlantic music industry. As Apple had long since ceased to be an active record company, it was assumed that a bidding war would break out among the major labels to secure *Double Fantasy* and his subsequent output. By that time, top artists who signed recording deals received huge advances against royalties that he never had, either as a Beatle or subsequently. Privately, he set a benchmark of $22.5 million, the figure recently agreed between Paul McCartney and Columbia. But the nonnegotiable proviso was that he and Yoko had to be signed together. Any record boss who balked at this—or even showed surprise—was automatically ruled out. That fate even befell the celebrated Ahmet Ertegun, cofounder of the Atlantic label, which had dominated black music throughout the seventies and might have been expected to head John's wish list. In desperation, Ertegun himself went to the Hit Factory to plead his case, but could not obtain an audience and was asked to leave.

In the end, the prize went to a brand-new, untried company, Geffen Records. Its owner, David Geffen had started the hugely successful Asylum label in the early seventies but, like John, had retired from the business midway through the decade, in his case after being misdiagnosed with cancer. Geffen made clear from the start that he would be signing two artists of equal merit; though unable to match the big labels in financial terms, he promised personal care and absolute commitment to them both. His trump card (apart from good astrological readings) was offering a contract before hearing a note of the album.

To celebrate John's fortieth and Sean's fifth birthday on October 9, Yoko hired five skywriting planes to inscribe HAPPY BIRTHDAY JOHN AND SEAN LOVE YOKO nine times in the sky over Manhattan. A group of well-wishers gathered outside the Dakota with birthday cards and tributes, hoping John would come out and receive them, but they were told he was asleep. Later, he and Yoko posed for an official birthday snapshot, and their assistant, Fred Seaman, announced that they would be touring the United States, Japan, and Europe "next Spring."

That summer saw the end of the famous rock concerts at Cen-

tral Park's ice-skating rink. Over the decade, major names like Fats
Domino, Jimi Hendrix, Otis Redding, the Who, and Bruce Spring-
steen had performed against the backdrop of trees and skyscrapers,
just a few hundred yards from the Dakota. Bob Gruen had photo-
graphed most of them, and so he did this last-ever bill, topped by the
Pretenders. Afterward, the band's vocalist, Chrissie Hynde, asked
Gruen to give her best wishes to John, who was still working at the
Hit Factory. "When I told John there'd would be no more concerts,
he said 'Good . . . thank goodness they're finally stopping . . . it keeps
Sean awake,'" Gruen remembers. "I was stunned to hear this from
John Lennon, Mister Rock 'n' Roll. That was a sign of how much
he'd grown up."

"(Just Like) Starting Over" was released as a single in the
United Kingdom on October 24 and in America three days
later. With it, John's life was thrown open wide to the media again.
There had been widespread rumors that his retirement had brought
terrible physical changes, which might prevent his ever reappearing
in public. Some reports said he had gone completely bald; others that
the septum of his nose had been destroyed by cocaine.

Yet here he was, the same old John, if a little thinner and more
lined of face, his hair still almost Beatlishly abundant, his accent unchanged despite the Americanisms that peppered it. Here were the
same articulateness, honesty, and irresistible wit, but all somehow
calmer and mellower, as if deep inside him a storm had finally blown
out. And—defying the heaped-up insults, defamations, and curses of
the past decade—here was Yoko, still with him at every moment.

The "new man" concept had yet to born, and the revelation of
his child care and bread baking generated as many column inches
as any nude record cover or Jesus analogy ever had. At the time, he
had never considered himself a pioneer, but was now widely so perceived, not at all to his displeasure. Thanks to his example, the word
househusband entered general usage on both sides of the Atlantic. "It's
the wave of the future," he said. "And I'm glad to have been in the
forefront of that, too."

But any idea that he and Yoko had turned into a staid, middle-aged couple, sipping Ovaltine and watching *Masterpiece Theatre*, was soon confounded. On November 23, they went to the Sperone Gallery in SoHo to shoot a video sequence for a music track yet to be decided. As the camera turned, they undressed, climbed onto a bed, kissed each other, then simulated having sex. It was the scenario everyone had expected at their bed-ins all those years ago, and not even the wildest punks and postpunks had yet dared stage one like it.

Double Fantasy was scheduled for release on November 24. The main prepublicity was to be a *Playboy* interview, a twenty-thousand-word slot at the front of the magazine, given to only a select few in the arts, literature, and politics. As ever, the conversation had to be with Yoko also. *Playboy*'s interviewer, David Sheff, having been pronounced astrologically sound, received even more time than *Rolling Stone*'s Jann Wenner, ten years before. The sessions took place in the Dakota apartment, in Yoko's office, at the Record Plant, and at John's favorite café, La Fortuna. Around his neck he wore the heart-shaped diamond necklace he had bought her after their bust-up over the Concert for Bangladesh in 1971. She had given it back to him—a symbol of reconciliation forever.

To *Playboy* he represented himself as a kind of rock-'n'-roll Rip van Winkle who had awoken from a long slumber, feeling more re-freshed and energized than ever in his life before. "The experience of being a full-time parent gave me the spirit again. I didn't realize it was happening. But then I stepped back for a moment and said, 'What has been going on? Here we are. I'm going to be forty, Sean's going to be five. Isn't it great? We survived.' . . . I am going to be forty and life begins at forty, so they promise. Oh, I believe it, too. Because I feel fine. It's like twenty-one . . . you know, hitting twenty-one. It's like, wow, what's going to happen next?"

During one interview session at the apartment, a loud scream came from the street below. "Another murder at Rue Dakota," John quipped.

In fact, it was not *Playboy* but *Newsweek* that carried the first in-terview with him about his retirement and revival. To make up for spoiling *Playboy*'s scoop, he sat down with David Sheff and went over dozens of songs in the Lennon-McCartney oeuvre, identifying which had been written by him, which by Paul, and where and how much they had collaborated. "This," he told Sheff, "will be the reference book."

"(Just Like) Starting Over" received massive airplay, was generally liked rather than loved, and soon appeared in the middle reaches of the singles charts. *Double Fantasy* inspired more equivocal feelings, particularly in Britain. People were not sure how they felt about this new house-trained Lennon, and Yoko's involvement still presented a problem to many. In the music press, now written for punks by punks, some reviews were downright savage. *Melody Maker* said the album "reeked with self indulgent sterility" and summed it up as "a godawful yawn." Along with its herald single, it would be number one all too soon.

John was still renting Underhill, and had meant to return to Bermuda—by plane this time—once the first wave of promotion was over. But the superfocused Hit Factory sessions had laid down twenty-two tracks, only fourteen of which could be used on *Double Fantasy*. Still on overdrive, he decided he wasn't yet ready for another vacation and instead went back with the same producer and musicians to begin a follow-up, to be called *Milk and Honey*. At the same time, he wanted to produce a solo album for Yoko, named after a recent *SoHo Weekly News* headline about her—*Yoko Only*.

He also began seriously thinking about the return to Britain he had been promising his family there since 1975. Just lately, his nostalgia for his homeland had increased to the point where he'd choke up if he so much as read the name Liverpool. His ban on seeing old cronies was relaxed only once—when a bit of unspoiled Liverpool in the person of Ringo Starr visited New York that autumn. They met at the Plaza for what was supposed to be an hour but ended up as five. By the time they parted, John had promised to play on Ringo's new album, *Can't Fight Lightning*, the following January.

His Aunt Mimi had no doubt that she would be seeing him again soon, after a separation of nine years. "He used to tell me that he would sit sometimes night after night, looking out of the window and facing in the direction of Liverpool," Mimi remembered. "He used to say he could see ships leaving New York. He would see their lights twinkling and he would wonder whether they were coming back to Liverpool. . . . John was wanting to come home on the *QE2* . . . he wanted to sail up the Mersey. He was very homesick towards the end."

Mimi was still just as unabashed by his fame and wealth, and as disapproving of his extravagance, even—especially—if she herself was the object. To mark the release of *Double Fantasy*, he sent her a matching pearl necklace and brooch. "You're daft," she told him next time they spoke on the phone. "Go on, Mimi, spoil yourself . . . just for a change," John laughed.

Making a triumphant homecoming to Liverpool on the *QE2* was no idle fantasy. One night at the Hit Factory, he received a surprise transatlantic call from an old Liverpool friend he had not seen in more than fifteen years. It was Joe Flannery, Brian Epstein's former love, who used to keep open house for the Beatles when they were earning a few pounds a night. John was delighted to hear from "Flo Jannery" and pumped him for news of the entertainment agency he now ran with Brian's younger brother, Clive. Flannery, too, heard of the plan to charter the *QE2*, and promised to find out whether the Mersey could handle such a big ship these days. To other people, John said that after his exploits on the *Megan Jaye*, he fancied sailing across the Atlantic.

The interviewers kept on coming, with John's greatest media champion oddly in the rearguard. It wasn't until December 3 that *Rolling Stone* writer Jonathan Cott visited the Dakota, accompanied by photographer Annie Leibovitz. For the formidably talented and persuasive Leibovitz, John and Yoko would parody the popular conception of their relationship, she lying on the floor fully clothed while he clung to her, naked and vulnerable, like a baby ape with its mother. A second shoot at the apartment was arranged for December 8.

To Jonathan Cott, John said he was essentially no different from the angry, self-flagellating refugee Beatle whose bile had filled two issues of the magazine ten years earlier. "I get truly affected by letters from Brazil or Poland or Austria—places I'm not conscious of all the time—just to know somebody is there, listening. One kid living up in Yorkshire wrote this heartfelt letter about being both Oriental and English and identifying with John and Yoko. The odd kid in the class. There are a lot of kids who identify with us. They don't need the history of rock 'n' roll. They identify with us as a couple, a biracial couple who stand for love, peace, feminism, and all the positive things of the world.

"You know . . . give peace a chance, not shoot people for peace. All we need is love. I believe it. It's damned hard but I absolutely believe it. We're not the first to say 'Imagine no countries' or 'Give peace a chance' but we're carrying that torch, like the Olympic torch, passing it from hand to hand, to each other, to each country, to each generation. That's our job. . . . I've never claimed divinity. I've never claimed purity of soul. I've never claimed to have the answer to life. I can only put out songs and answer questions as honestly as I can, but only as honestly as I can, no more, no less.

"I used to think that the world was doing it to me and that the world owed me something, and that either the conservatives or the socialists or the fascists or the communists or the Christians or the Jews were doing something to me, and when you're a teenybopper that's what you think. I'm 40 now. I don't think that any more, 'cause I found out it doesn't fucking work. The thing goes on anyway and all you're doing is jacking off and screaming about what your mommy or daddy or society did . . . I have found out personally . . . that I am responsible for it as well as them. I am part of them."

On December 6, he did a long interview with BBC Radio 1 deejay Andy Peebles, giving the same generous measure he had to *Playboy* and *Rolling Stone*. Peebles asked about his "sense of security," living in what was still a hazardous city by comparison with London. John replied that the great thing here was that people left you alone. "It took me two years to unwind. I can go right out this door now and go in a restaurant. You want to know how great that is? Or go to the movies. I mean, people come up for autographs and say 'Hi,' but they don't bug you, you know. It's just . . . 'Oh, hey, how you doin'?'" After the interview, Peebles said he hoped there would soon be another Lennon show in Britain. John asked if he really thought there'd be any interest.

For those who set store by such things, the great puzzle must be why the numerologist on permanent watch for dangers to John did not at this point send him away on a journey to the far side of the world, and why none of the psychics in Yoko's employ foresaw what was about to happen. Later, she would realize that in the weeks beforehand she had received two different warnings, both equally oblique and ambiguous. "This one female psychic told me, 'There's going to be a woman and I see that she's crying like crazy. I think she's your sister because she looks very much like you, with very long hair, and she's going to go through some terrible situation, and she has a young son, and she's holding him and she's going to be devastated about something. She's probably your sister, so you'd better be very nice to her and console her.' I said, 'I have a sister but she doesn't have long hair and she doesn't have a child.' But that was me she was talking about."

Another psychic, a male, went off on a surprising tangent when she went to him with a routine staff problem. John wanted to dismiss Fred Seaman, but Yoko hoped to find an excuse not to. "And the guy said, 'Something incredible is going to happen and your life is going to change, so don't do anything now, just leave it alone and wait.' That was enough for me to convince John not to let Fred go, and instead I sent him to the house in Bermuda to relax."

During that weekend of December 6–7, Bob Gruen dropped by the Record Plant, and was struck by how happy John seemed. "We sat on the floor for a couple of hours, just shooting the shit and talking . . . about how he was going to put a new band together and go back on the road . . . how he wanted me to go with him, and who we'd meet in London, and his favorite restaurants in Paris and favorite shops in Tokyo. He seemed to have such a positive vision and a sense of hope for the future. He was about to come back with the conclusions to all his screaming and his searching and his wandering and his therapies. He'd discovered he could be grounded with his family and sober, and still put out a message people could relate to. He seemed finally to understand what it was to be alive and to be a leader, in the sense that he could think and express what everyone else was feeling."

Day or night, there were generally a few people waiting outside the Dakota's West Seventy-second Street entrance, beside the Gothic arch and the copper sentry box. John called them "Dakota groupies," though these days they were likelier to be male than female. A few had shared the Sixties with him, but the majority tended to young men and woman who had grown up well after the Beatles' heyday but not found anything in their own pop heritage remotely as magical. John as a rule was friendly and patient, always pausing to sign autographs and chat, but from time to time a pushy or overdemanding individual would annoy him. This weekend, there had been such an addition to the group, a pudgy twenty-five-year-old named Mark David Chapman. John never knew his name—indeed, he would not be known as such until after becoming bracketed in the public's mind with Lee Harvey Oswald and John Wilkes Booth.

Chapman had been born in Fort Worth Texas, the son of an Air Force sergeant, and spent a rootless childhood in Texas, Indiana, and Virginia. An archetypal nerd, overweight and without distinction, he was mocked and bullied at each school he attended, and took to seeking refuge in an imaginary world of "little people" who gave him the affection and feeling of power he otherwise lacked. As a teenager, he got into drugs, experimented with LSD, and then became a devout Christian. But his main solace for the joylessness of his life was Beatles music.

To begin with, he seemed to have impulses John would have applauded; he worked on a YMCA program for the resettlement of Vietnamese boat people and spent time in Beirut during the midseventies Lebanese civil war. He received commendations for his work and once had his hand shaken by President Gerald Ford. Later, he migrated to Honolulu in Hawaii, where he began to have psychiatric problems and on one occasion attempted suicide. In 1979, in weird symbiosis with John, he married a Japanese American woman several years his senior.

The media reports of John's emergence from retirement and substantial new wealth turned Chapman's former fan-worship into ferocious hatred. He felt that, by acquiring large houses and pedigreed cattle, John had betrayed the ideals of the Beatles—and therefore betrayed him personally. As later with many a school and college

campus mass-assassin, "voices" in his head dictated that these grievances could be avenged only by blood. His parallel obsession was with
Holden Caulfield, anarchic narrator of J. D. Salinger's *The Catcher in
the Rye*. He came to believe that if he made an end to John, he would
be able to step into the book's pages, transfigured into Holden.

On Friday, December 5, Chapman flew from Honolulu to New
York, wearing a rucksack containing fourteen hours of Beatles music
on cassette. He checked into the Sixty-third Street YMCA (later
switching to the Sheraton Hotel) and bought a copy of *Double Fantasy* and the issue of *Playboy* containing John's interview. He hung
around outside the Dakota for most of the weekend, but did not see
John until Sunday. Breaking the Dakota groupies' convention of politeness and distance, he came overly near and began to take photographs. "John got angry and ran after him to try to take the camera,
though I shouted to him not to do it," Yoko remembers. "He didn't
get the camera, and when he came back he said, 'If anyone gets me,
it's going to be a fan.'"

On Monday, December 8, John had breakfast at La Fortuna on
Columbus Avenue, then had his hair cut in fifties Teddy Boy style for
Annie Leibovitz's second *Rolling Stone* shoot. Back at the Dakota, he
and Yoko gave another extended interview, this time to RKO Radio.
"We've been together longer than the Beatles, do you know that?" he
said at one point. "People always think in terms that John and Yoko
just got together and then the Beatles split. We've been together
longer than the Beatles!" He said *Double Fantasy* was for "the people
who grew up with me. I'm saying 'Here I am now, how are you?
How's your relationship going? Did you get through it all? Weren't
the Seventies a drag? Here we are, well let's try to make the Eighties
good because it's still up to us to make what we can of it.'"

Afterward, he posed for Leibovitz with his Teddy Boy cut, wearing a black leather blouson, blue jeans, and cowboy boots. Except for
the backdrop of skyscrapers and treetops behind him, he could have
been ready to go onstage at Hamburg's Kaiserkeller.

At about four p.m., he set off with Yoko for the Record Plant,
hitching a ride with the RKO team after the nonappearance of their
own limo. As John got into the car, Chapman appeared, held out his

copy of *Double Fantasy,* and was rewarded by a scribbled autograph. "Is that all you want?" John reportedly asked him. The moment was captured by an amateur photographer from New Jersey named Paul Goresh, who habitually staked out the Dakota (and had once conned his way inside posing as a video repair man). Chapman would later say that he had meant to deliver his retribution then, but John's niceness temporarily disarmed him.

John spent the next six hours working on a Yoko song, originally meant for *Double Fantasy*, called "Walking on Thin Ice." During the early evening, David Geffen dropped by to say that, despite its apparent mixed reception, the album was about to go gold. John also found time to telephone Aunt Mimi and talk further about his imminent homecoming. He was pleased with the night's work, and had cassettes of the track made to take away with him. When they stopped work, at around 10:30, Yoko suggested having dinner at the nearby Stage Deli, but John wanted to return to the Dakota first. "The last thing he had on his mind," she remembers, "was getting back and seeing Sean before he went to sleep." On his way out of the Record Plant, he paused to sign an autograph for the switchboard operator, Rabiah Vincent.

There seemed no safer direction to be heading than home.

The December night was exceptionally mild, and shadowy figures could be seen at the corner of West Seventy-second as usual. Instead of driving through the arch to the safety of the inner courtyard, the limo drew up at the curb. As John got out, Chapman came forward, still clutching his autographed copy of *Double Fantasy*. He softly called "Mr. Lennon," then produced a .38 handgun, dropped into the two-handed combat stance familiar from innumerable cop movies, and fired five shots. John kept walking, went up the stairs into the porters' vestibule, then collapsed on the floor, scattering the cassettes he had been carrying. A few seconds later, Yoko burst in, screaming, "John's been shot!" The young duty porter, Jay Hastings, rang the alarm that connected to the police, then knelt beside John with thoughts of trying to administer a tourniquet. This being clearly futile, Hastings gently removed John's glasses and covered him with his porter's jacket.

Two cruising police cars were at the scene within minutes. Unlike later specimens of his kind, Chapman had not taken his own life, but was leaning against the Dakota's brickwork, calmly reading *The Catcher in the Rye*, on whose flyleaf he had written "This is my statement." His gun and copy of *Double Fantasy* lay nearby. John was put into one of the squad cars and taken to Roosevelt Hospital on West Fifty-ninth Street, with Yoko following in the second car. He was rushed into the emergency room, but, at 11:07, was pronounced dead.

For days afterward, up in apartment 72, whenever the kitchen door opened, three cats came bounding forward to greet him.

SEAN REMEMBERS

It's a nice memory, just floating around in the
ocean with my dad and this capsized boat.

meet Sean Lennon in a small, cluttered apartment in the quiet
part of London's Chelsea known as "World's End." Though he
has become a songwriter-performer like his father—and a brilliant one, if in a totally different way—there is nothing grandiose
about his gigs. A few weeks earlier, I had watched him play at a
converted pub in downmarket Shepherds Bush before he moved
on to Russia and Eastern Europe. Sean and his manager stayed at an
anonymous tourist hotel in the suburbs while his three-piece backing band lived together in a tiny trailer parked outside the hall.

Now aged thirty-two, he is like his father circa 1969—the same
restless brown eyes behind circular glasses; the same nose; the same
dark, curly beard; even the same wreaths of cigarette smoke. Only in
his profile do you also see Yoko and the Japanese side of his ancestry.
He has John's vivid turn of phrase and chronic inability to resist a
pun ("My parents were transparent . . . trans-*parent* . . ."). The mel-
lifluous American-accented voice at times can sound almost British,

at times almost Liverpudlian, as if some indestructible part of John still remains at his core And, just as John once did for *Rolling Stone* or *Red Mole*, he sits back, puts his stockinged feet up, and lets everything out.

His time with his father lasted for only five years and ended at a point where, for most children, memory is barely functioning. He admits that, before my arrival, he has been trying to retrieve as much as possible from that unconnected, inevitably self-centered toddler's-eye-view. "I remember my Dad teaching me how to make a paper airplane, which I still know how to do in the way that he taught me—and flying paper airplanes. I remember we used to watch *The Muppets* together, and *Jekyll and Hyde*, but I wasn't allowed to watch any other television. And when we did watch those shows which were, I think, back-to-back once a week, he would turn off the TV during the commercials which was really frustrating to me because often we'd have missed a bit of the show when he turned it back on."

Yet even at that tender age, he glimpsed "the little child inside the man," to quote one of John's last pieces of self-analysis: "I remember that Alice, our black cat, had jumped out the window after a pigeon and died, and I remember that was the only time, I think, I ever saw my dad cry."

So many of the memories involve water: the warm, blue ocean of Bermuda; the chill, gray waves of Long Island Sound; or the chlorinated shallows at the YMCA. "I remember swimming, a lot, in Bermuda, in the ocean especially. That was on the famous trip when he did the whole boat thing and also wrote a bunch of songs for what turned into *Double Fantasy*. I remember some strange kind of house that he was writing songs in. I remember swimming a lot in the pool at Cold Spring Harbor and I remember that he really enjoyed watching me swim. He was proud of the fact that I was a good swimmer.

"I remember that at Cold Spring Harbor there was a green sailboat and I think in my mind that I named it *Flower* . . . I remember Fred Seaman accidentally flipping the boat over and us all being in the water, my dad swimming next to me, and I remember seeing my flip-flops that I'd got in Japan floating away. I was very upset because I loved those flip-flops, but he said, 'Don't worry, we'll get you another pair . . .' I said, 'Are there any fish in the water?' and he was like, 'Yes,' which really scared me. So I remember my dad protecting me in the water. It's actually a nice memory, just floating around in the ocean with my dad and this capsized boat."

As a rule, the only memorable childhoods are unhappy ones. Sean was idyllically happy with John, yet their hours, days, and months together linger in a thousand vivid impressions, often of simply doing nothing in particular together in the Dakota apartment's wide, white rooms, with Central Park's treetops like a variegated salad basket outside. "I remember that around the house he always wore a blue-and-white floral patterned *yukata*, which is like a casual kimono, and he always had a ponytail. He burned incense a lot as well, and I remember his glasses. I remember him playing guitar and hitting the strings myself and us singing together. He used to sing this song about 'Popeye the sailor man, lives on the Isle of Man'. . .

"I remember that he was always barefoot, he rarely wore shoes and if he did it was mostly flip-flops. And for some reason he was very interested in teaching me now to pick up pens and other things between my toes. He would do that all the time because he was double-jointed and a very, very flexible man. I remember him putting his leg over his head in the passenger seat of our Mercedes station wagon. I remember jumping on the bed a lot. Oh . . . I remember one time he accidentally let one of the heavy wooden doors at the Dakota slam on my finger. And he was very upset about that. My fingernail eventually fell off about two weeks later."

At times, John's presence is so close, one feels almost an intruder for listening. "He was a very thin man at that point, and I remember the look of his ankles and his legs, they were very sharply defined in my mind—his knees and his ankles and his legs. I don't remember his hands but I remember his face, his neck, his hair, his calves, and that bump on the right side of your ankle. I remember the feel of the stubble on his chin very clearly, and wondering about the scar I could see underneath it. I remember him telling me that he got that scar through a car accident with Kyoko, my sister. I don't think he told me the whole kidnapping story at that point, only that she was with her father, Tony. I found out about all that after my dad passed away. And I think he told me that he never drove again after the accident."

There were also rather strict lessons in table manners, an area where John had never previously distinguished himself. "I remember him teaching me how to cut and eat steak, which was a mystery to me at age four; how to stick the fork in and cut behind it, and that was how you got a piece in your mouth. I think it was that night when he got very upset with me, I think because of something I did very cheekily with the steak. He did wind up yelling at me very, very loudly to the point where he damaged my ear, and I had to go to the doctor. I remember when I was lying on the floor and hurting, and him holding me and saying, 'I'm so sorry . . .' He did have a temper, though; I don't think that's a secret."

Not surprisingly, the dearest memory is the sound of John's voice. "Every night when I was going to sleep, he'd come in the room and say, 'Good-night, Sean,' and he'd flick the light switch in the rhythm of his words, so that they'd wink in time. There was always something very comforting about that. I had a bunkbed even though I was the only child in the house, and a mobile of silver airplanes above my head. And I very much remember the shadows that were cast on the wall by the cars going along Central Park West, seven flights down. I remember watching those shadows move by, from left to right, and I remember thinking of the words 'watching shadows on the wall' from 'Watching the Wheels.' When he wrote and recorded that song, I remember thinking somehow that he'd been watching the same shadows I had."

Sean had been oblivious to everything late on the night of December 8, 1980, when John returned from the Record Plant at that particular moment just to snatch a good-night kiss from him. Initially he could make no sense of what greeted him the next morning—the grim-faced strangers coming and going through those formerly safe white rooms; his father's unexplained absence and the pandemonium below on West Seventy-second Street; the police barriers; the TV crews; the flowers; the moan of grief that would reverberate all around the world.

"I remember being in [my] bedroom and someone telling me my mom wants to talk to me, and sensing the very strange atmosphere in the house and there are all these crowds of people outside. My mom is sitting in bed under the blanket, and I swear I remember seeing a newspaper, and almost understanding something about the headline. I remember standing there and her telling me, 'Your dad's been shot and killed,' and I remember that the thing that felt most important to me was that I didn't want her to see me cry. I remember saying to her, 'Don't worry, Mom, you're still young. You'll find somebody else,' because at five years old I thought that sounded like a very mature thing to say."

The multitude in the street below, and in Central Park, chanting his father's peace anthems between tears, only added to Sean's fear and bewilderment. "In retrospect I find it very sweet that we were able to mourn with everybody, but at the time it was terrifying. So I remember walking away slowly out of the room, and it being so hard for me not to cry, and as soon as my mom couldn't see me, running down the hall and bursting into tears and slamming the door, throwing myself on the floor and crying and crying. I think for days I cried."

In the terrible days that followed, there were times when the five-year-old felt completely alone. "Afterwards, my mom seemed very tired, I'll put it that way. She stayed in bed a long time. I remember different people trying to comfort me. But my mom and dad didn't really maintain family relationships, they'd 'burned a lot of bridges,' as my mom would put it. So it's not like we had a lot of other people around who were like parental figures. My dad was gone: that was it. Everyone else was just an employee. And so I just remember not being able to be comforted by anyone."

Years were to pass before he pieced together who and what that ponytailed, flip-flopping tutor in table manners and singer of lullabyes had actually been. "Many of the impressions of my dad that I have are through the media. And I share those impressions with the rest of the world. I think that on some level when I was a kid I did feel jealous of the world for having known and spent more time with him than I got. But in a way the experience of someone that you can get through their work is really not comparable to the experience you can get from just sitting on someone's lap. That is more than songs and words and stuff can really explain. And that's reality—the way that the light hits someone's hair, the sound of their voice, the sound of their footsteps in the hallway."

As Sean grew older, he found the best way of coming close to John was through playing music. "I remembered him playing the piano, so I started playing, too. And when I did I always felt like I was communing with him, like a sacred prayer or something. Like somehow I was with him. Every time I'd make progress musically, I felt I was making progress in my relationship with him. And that was the case when I was a teenager: the better I got at playing guitar, the more I understood music. And now the more I understand songwriting, the more I feel I understand him, because he was a songwriter above all things."

Despite all the blandishments of the music industry, Sean refused to be turned into a John Lennon clone, as his half brother Julian briefly was in the mid-1980s. His main talent is as a lead guitarist where John usually stuck to rhythm; in his songs, thoughts and chords alike constantly spring off in unpredictable directions, more like early David Bowie than anything. His music resembles his father only in humanitarian spirit; for instance, his latest album, *Friendly Fire*, echoing the pernicious military doublespeak of Afghanistan and Iraq. "People sometimes think I'm trying to separate myself from John Lennon as a musician, but I'm not at all. The only reason I make music is because my dad was a musician and a songwriter. It's like I've inherited a craft, in the way an ironmonger's son might also become an ironmonger."

His mature assessment of his father's talent would delight John on many levels. "I think he had insecurities about everything: about grammar and writing, about knowing how to write and read music, about all the established ways of knowing things. And that was a handicap he turned to his advantage. He invented insecure song-writing—'I'm a loser and I'm not what I appear to be' or 'Help!'

"He said that Bob Dylan taught him to write in the first person about his real life, but Dylan never wrote a song that revealed his emotions like that. Dylan always observed other people's emotions; it's like he's a journalist—he's not saying it's good or bad—just articulating something that's in the air and jotting it down. That was an aspect of my dad's work but, to me, not the best one. 'Give Peace a Chance' is great, but that's not the one I want to go home and listen to; it's not as good as 'Hide Your Love Away' or 'Girl' or 'In My Life.' To me, those songs are on a whole other level. For a man to feel insecure and question himself the way my dad did in songs is a postmodern phenomenon. Artists like Mozart or Picasso never did; it's something that's only happened since the Second World War. And that's something he owns, that feeling of insecurity so many other songwriters since have tried to copy. He invented that."

The Beatles, Sean says, were an essential springboard for John, however irksome his life with them became. "I don't think my dad would have been commercial at all without Paul and the management and George Martin. I mean in the sense of making himself palatable to the masses, I don't think that was his area of expertise. I think he was very edgy and interesting, and 'edgy' and 'interesting' don't always cut it for the populace. I think the sugar around the Beatles with my dad as this core of intensity made them the ultimate package.

"When he turned his back on the Beatles and formed the Plastic Ono Band with my mom, that to me was like when Matisse turned his back on painting and decided that everything he wanted to say artistically from now on could be said by a few simple shapes cut out of paper. It was as if Elvis had left Vegas in the seventies and started to play with the punks. That *Plastic Ono Band* album, for me, is the greatest rock album any man ever made. That's why he's so much more for me than just a Sixties rock figure like a Jagger or a Clapton."

What are his favorite John Lennon songs? "[Those] have changed as I became more of a musician. The ones that I loved when I was a kid, loved, loved, LOVED, were 'Watching the Wheels.' And 'Woman.' Oh . . . 'Woman'! It just sort of shimmered, it felt like a dream. There's something so sweet and sparkly about that major chord change. And I remember knowing that he wrote it about my mom, and feeling just love, almost like a golden light, the love he had for my mom.

"That song broke my heart after he died; I couldn't listen to it for about ten years without getting upset because I was there when he recorded that, and I remember it coming into the universe. And I remember how when he died, *Double Fantasy* was all over the radio, you couldn't get away from it. Every time I heard his voice, it was like a knife in my heart, it hurt so much. And it took me a good ten years before hearing his voice wasn't an incredibly difficult thing."

And, he admits, it still is. "If I'm at a party and someone casually puts on *Sgt. Pepper*, it's hard for me. I can't just hang out, drink wine, smoke cigarettes, and listen to those songs. I'm not saying it's less intense for my mom. But she had him, she had a relationship with him. I think what hurts for me so much is that I didn't. And it really hurts to hear his voice and hear him sing. I have to feel very strong to deal with it.

"It's so beautiful—and it's my dad; it's that resonance of voice that I remember from my childhood, the first voice I ever heard. It's the first voice I ever heard speak English. It's the voice from which I learned to speak English."

To many, Sean's life might appear an enviable, effortless one, cushioned by the Lennon millions—the big houses and numerous servants; the private schools in New York and Switzerland; the doting love of a mother to whom he is everything; the reflected love of a whole planet. Yet there are signs that his chief inheritance from his father may be a horribly vulnerable heart. His romance with Elizabeth Jagger, daughter of Mick—which might have created the greatest dynastic union in pop—fizzled out when Elizabeth let it be known that she had yet to fall *properly* in love. Even more bruising was a relationship with the actress and model Bijou Phillips, whom he found to be cheating on him with his childhood friend and Dakota neighbor Max Leroy. Then Max was killed in a motorcycle accident before the two friends could reconcile. At one point in our conversation, Sean remarks that beautiful girls are doomed to a special kind of unhappiness, possibly his way of consoling himself for the unhappiness they cause him. One can almost hear an echo of John's most wounded song on *Rubber Soul*: "Aaah—*Gerl!*"

Sean admits he has little to do with the millions of people for whom his father has become a secular saint, who speak the name "John Lennon" in the same breath as "Albert Schweitzer" or "Nelson Mandela" and create monuments to him of every kind, from an airport in Liverpool to a "tower of light" in Iceland and a graffiti wall in Prague. "My mom doesn't really understand why I don't want to meet those who worship John Lennon, why I don't want to visit the John Lennon tribute concerts or go to the John Lennon Museum. It just hurts too much. I've sung 'This Boy' at a tribute concert because I love the song and I'm a professional musician, I can do any gig I'm asked to, but I didn't like doing it.

"It's not that I don't want to honor him, because I feel like my whole life is a living tribute to him. But to go to a museum or see a movie that depicts his life, it just hurts. Watching a show about him on Broadway for me was like going naked through the flames of Hell. Because those memories that I have of my childhood are so important to me. To see them co-opted to make a diorama in a museum or a Broadway show makes me feel like I'm being violated."

He accepts it is his duty to support Yoko in administering and protecting the Lennon legacy. "If I owe it to my mom to do it, I'll do it, because I love her the most. But on a spiritual level, it doesn't enrich my life to do interviews, to do tributes and museums and have my experience of my father turned into media. I don't read books about him, I don't need to see movies or shows about him. I don't need to prove to the world that he did all these things.

"And I don't think he'd be all that bothered that I've inherited his streak of rebelliousness. I have the music and I have the memories and that's what is precious to me. I have him in my heart."

ACKNOWLEDGMENTS

In September 2003, I suggested to John's widow, Yoko Ono, that I should become his biographer. I felt thoroughly qualified for the task: my book *Shout!* was regarded as the definitive work on the Beatles and I had known Yoko personally since 1981, when she invited me to the Dakota Building just five months after John's murder. Since then, surprisingly, there had been only two full-scale biographies of the man and his music, both published in the 1980s, neither doing him justice. Ray Coleman's *Lennon* was an honorable attempt but one that never quite brought John alive on the page, while Albert Goldman's malevolent, risibly ignorant *The Lives of John Lennon* could be totally discounted.

Yoko agreed to my suggestion, with the proviso that it should not be called an "authorized" biography. Over the next three years, in a series of interviews in New York and London, she spoke with remarkable honesty and passion about the life she and John had shared. She also made it possible for me to talk to others close to John, in particular their son Sean and her daughter, Kyoko. The only other condition was that she should read the manuscript for factual accuracy. I assumed she would approve of what I had written since it was in the same spirit as *Shout!*: candid about John's many flaws, but portraying him as both a massive influence on twentieth-century culture and an ultimately adorable human being. Part of my mission, too, was to correct some of the myths about Yoko herself, which after these years still make her a figure of hatred and ridicule for so many. I was amazed therefore when, in late 2007, she told me she was upset by the book and would not endorse it. Her reasons were various but the principal one was that I had been "mean to John." I hope that in time she may revise this judgment, for I do not think any other reader will share it.

As a journalist during the Sixties, I met John only twice: first in 1965, during what turned out to be the Beatles' last UK tour, and again in mid-1969, while he and Yoko were orchestrating their peace campaign from the Apple house in Savile Row. For his view of the world I have inevitably had to rely on quotes he gave to other people, collated from famously forthright sessions with magazines like *Rolling Stone* and *Playboy* and innumerable other sources, major and minor—for here was, perhaps, the only celebrity in history who never did a dull or dishonest interview. Otherwise, my aim was to reconstruct his life completely afresh, writing for a hypothetical reader who has never heard of him or listened to a note of his music, ignoring all preconceptions, including my own. Indeed, I would frequently find myself correcting inaccuracies and misjudgments which had been in every edition of *Shout!*

Biographers rely greatly on luck, and with this project my share was exceptional. Despite the widespread (and untrue) perception that I am "anti-Paul," Sir Paul McCartney agreed to answer questions of fact by e-mail, and did so promptly and in generous detail. Notwithstanding a conviction that he had nothing new left to say, the Beatles' nonpareil record producer Sir George Martin saw me at his AIR studios—situated fortuitously just a couple of streets from my London home—and said much that was fascinatingly new. The late Neil Aspinall, the Beatles' closest and most loyal associate, broke a forty-year rule not to talk to writers, granting me several interviews and also checking part of the manuscript. John's cousins Mike Cadwallader and Liela Harvey were both unstinting in their help, as was his stepmother, Pauline Stone, who showed me documents which cast somewhat different light on his much maligned father, Freddie. John's two closest friends from the New York years, Elliot Mintz and Bob Gruen, shared intimate memories and checked relevant portions of the text, I also received invaluable guidance from Leon Wildes, the lawyer who masterminded his fight against deportation from the United States.

Peter Trollope proved a brilliant researcher, tracking down lost links in John's life with an indefatigability worthy of Sherlock Holmes. For fact-checking and advice I am deeply indebted to Bill Harry, John's friend at art college, later founder-editor of *Mersey Beat* and author of the *John Lennon Encyclopedia*. Invaluable editorial help from my old *Sunday Times* colleague, Nick Mason, slimmed down the first draft from its original 360,000 words. Allan Kozinn of the *New York Times* provided CDs of John's lesser-known American radio interviews and took immense pains in weeding out errors from the manuscript—as did my fellow biographer Johnny Rogan during a six-hour session at London's Groucho Club. In Liverpool, many old friends made through *Shout!* were kind and hospitable all over again, notably Brian Epstein's old friend and adviser Joe Flannery, and former Quarrymen Colin Hanton and Len Garry. New ones also emerged, like Bill Heckle of Cavern City Tours, who gave me the run of his contacts book, and Colin Hall, the custodian of John's childhood home in Woolton, now run by the National Trust.

Although every care has been with fact-checking, a work of this size cannot hope to be 100 percent error-free. Few subjects generate experts like the Beatles and I am aware how many will be combing my text for the smallest slips. For these I apologize in advance and promise that as many as possible will be rectified in future editions.

Grateful acknowledgment is made to Sir Paul McCartney for the quotation from *Many Years from Now*, his authorized biography by Barry Miles (Secker & Warburg, 1997); to Pauline Stone for the unpublished writings and deposition of Freddie Lennon; to Michael Cadwallader for Mimi Smith's letters; and to Bill Harry for material from *Mersey Beat*.

Special thanks to Michael Sissons and Peter Matson for unfailing support and friendship; to Dan Halpern of Ecco, a rock throughout the long and often fraught composition process; to Trevor Dolby who commissioned the book for HarperCollins UK and Carole Tonkinson who took it over; to Carol MacArthur and Fiona Petheram at PFD, and Sam Edenborough and Nicki Kennedy at the Intercontinental Literary Agency for taking the book so enthusiastically to its non–English language publishers; to Tariq Mazid for ever reliable technical support; to Gordon Smith and Stephen Simou of Citroen Wells; and to François and Danièle Roux for giving me a summer sanctuary at La Colombe d'Or in St. Paul de Vence.

Grateful thanks also to: Helen Anderson, Les Anthony, David Ashton, Andrew Bailey, Tony Barrow, Dot Becker, Sid Bernstein, Cilla Black, Tony Bramwell, Peter Brown, James Burrows, Tony Calder, Ronnie Carroll, James Chads, Maureen Cleave, Tyler Coneys, John O'Connor, Wendy Cook, Ray Connolly, Celia Crighton, Rod Davis, Sheridon Davis, Jeff Dexter, Sonny Freeman Drane, John Dunbar, Ron Ellis, Royston Ellis, Horst Fascher, Yankel Feather, Colin Fellows, Michael Fishwick, Ray Foulk, June Furlong, Johnny Gentle, Olwen Gillespie, Harry Gooseman, Bob Green, Sam Green, Frances Greenhous, the late Eric Griffiths, John Gustafson, Rolf Harris, Jon Hendricks, Kevin Hewlett, Simon Hilton, Peter Hodgson, the late Nicholas Horsfield, Thomas Hoving, Peter Howard, Maurice Hyams, Patricia Inder, Arthur Janov, Vivian Janov, Tim and Joyce Jeal, Iris Keitel, Jim Keltner, Jonathan King, Astrid Kirchherr, Cosmo Landesman, Sharon Lawrence, Sam Leach, Caroline Lee, Spencer Leigh, Joyce Lennon, Richard Lester, Michael Lindsay-Hogg, Kenny Lynch, Barbara McKie, Laurie Mansfield, Gerry Marsden, Ann Mason, Albert Maysles, Barry Miles, Lee Montague, Colin Morris, Rod Murray, Paul du Noyer, Geoff Nugent, Andrew Oldham, Simon Osborne, William Pobjoy, Sir Cliff Richard, Dan Richter, Cynthia Riley, Charles Roberts, Craig Sams, Gregory Sams, Sandy Sams, Robert Sandall, Art Schreiber, Jackie de Shannon Tony Sheridan, Victor Spinetti, Peter Stockton, Ursula Stone, Peter Suchet, Jimmy Tarbuck, Joan Taylor, Klaus Voormann, Nigel Walley, Michael Ward, and Jane Wirgman.

Finally to my wife Sue, who suggested I should write this book, go all my love and gratitude.

PHILIP NORMAN
LONDON, 2008

INDEX